AI-Based Advanced Optimization Techniques for Edge Computing

Scrivener Publishing
100 Cummings Center, Suite 541J
Beverly, MA 01915-6106

Machine Learning in Biomedical Science and Healthcare Informatics

**Series Editors: Vishal Jain (drvishaljain83@gmail.com)
and Jyotir Moy Chatterjee (jyotirchatterjee@gmail.com)**

In this series, an attempt has been made to capture the scope of various applications of machine learning in the biomedical engineering and healthcare fields, with a special emphasis on the most representative machine learning techniques, namely deep learning-based approaches. Machine learning tasks are typically classified into two broad categories depending on whether there is a learning 'label' or 'feedback' available to a learning system: supervised learning and unsupervised learning. This series also introduces various types of machine learning tasks in the biomedical engineering field from classification (supervised learning) to clustering (unsupervised learning). The objective of the series is to compile all aspects of biomedical science and healthcare informatics, from fundamental principles to current advanced concepts.

Publishers at Scrivener
Martin Scrivener (martin@scrivenerpublishing.com)
Phillip Carmical (pcarmical@scrivenerpublishing.com)

AI-Based Advanced Optimization Techniques for Edge Computing

Edited by

Mohit Kumar

Dept. of Information Technology, Dr. B R Ambedkar National Institute of Technology, Jalandhar, India

Gautam Srivastava

Dept. of Mathematics & Computer Science, Brandon University, Manitoba, Canada

Ashutosh Kumar Singh

Dept. of Computer Science and Engineering, United College of Engineering & Research, Allahabad, India

and

Kalka Dubey

Dept. of Computer Science and Engineering, Rajiv Gandhi Institute of Petroleum Technology, Amethi, India

Scrivener Publishing

WILEY

This edition first published 2025 by John Wiley & Sons, Inc., 111 River Street, Hoboken, NJ 07030, USA and Scrivener Publishing LLC, 100 Cummings Center, Suite 541J, Beverly, MA 01915, USA

For more information about Scrivener publications please visit www.scrivenerpublishing.com.

Wiley Global Headquarters
111 River Street, Hoboken, NJ 07030, USA

For details of our global editorial offices, customer services, and more information about Wiley products visit us at www.wiley.com.

Library of Congress Cataloging-in-Publication Data

ISBN 978-1-394-28703-1

Front cover images courtesy of Adobe Firefly.
Cover design by Russell Richardson

Set in size of 11pt and Minion Pro by Manila Typesetting Company, Makati, Philippines

Printed in the USA

10 9 8 7 6 5 4 3 2 1

Contents

Preface xv

Acknowledgement xvii

1 Navigating Next-Generation Network Architecture: Unleashing the Power of SDN, NFV, NS, and AI Convergence 1

Monika Dubey, Snehlata, Ashutosh Kumar Singh, Richa Mishra and Mohit Kumar

1.1 Introduction 2
1.2 Revolutionizing Infrastructure with SDN, NFV, and NS 4
1.2.1 SDN: Definition and Architecture 6
1.2.2 NFV: Definition and Architecture 9
1.2.3 NS: Conceptual Abstractions 11
1.3 Realizing NS Potential with SDN and NFV 13
1.4 Artificial Intelligence: Pivotal Role in Networking Transformation 15
1.4.1 Supervised Learning 16
1.4.2 Unsupervised Learning 18
1.4.3 Reinforcement Learning 18
1.4.4 Deep Learning 21
1.5 Navigating Challenges and Solutions 23
1.5.1 Performance Issues in Network Structure 23
1.5.2 Management and Orchestration Issues 24
1.5.3 Security and Privacy 24
1.5.4 New Business Models 25
1.6 Conclusion 26
Disclosure Statement 26
References 26

2 OctoEdge: An Octopus-Inspired Adaptive Edge Computing Architecture **35**
Sashi Tarun
2.1 Introduction 36
2.1.1 Edge Computing as Resource Manager 36
2.1.2 Edge Computing Hurdles 37
2.1.3 Edge Computing and the Need for Adaptability 38
2.2 Problem Statement 39
2.3 Motivations 40
2.4 Related Work 41
2.5 OctoEdge Proposed Architecture 45
2.5.1 OctoEdge Working Principles 48
2.5.2 Benefits of OctoEdge 49
2.6 OctoEdge Architecture Functional Components 53
2.7 Results and Discussion 59
2.8 OctoEdge Architecture: Scope and Scientific Merits 60
2.9 Use Cases and Applications 64
2.10 Challenges and Future Directions 68
2.11 Conclusion 68
References 69

3 Development of Optimized Machine Learning Oriented Models **71**
Ratnesh Kumar Dubey, Dilip Kumar Choubey and Shubha Mishra
3.1 Introduction 72
3.1.1 NSL-KDD Dataset 75
3.2 Literature Review 76
3.3 Problem Definition 78
3.4 Proposed Work 80
3.4.1 Machine Learning 82
3.5 Experimental Analysis 86
3.6 Conclusion 90
3.7 Future Scope 91
References 91

4 Leveraging Multimodal Data and Deep Learning for Enhanced Stock Market Prediction **93**
Pinky Gangwani and Vikas Panthi
4.1 Introduction 94
4.1.1 Motivation and Contribution 96
4.1.2 Rationale for Selecting the Methods 98

4.2 Literature Review 100
4.3 Proposed Design of an Efficient Model that Leverages Multimodal Data and Deep Learning for Enhanced Stock Market Prediction 107
4.3.1 Discussion on Selection Criteria 114
4.4 Statistical Analysis and Comparison 116
4.5 Acknowledging Limitations and Potential Challenges 122
4.6 Mitigation Strategies and Future Directions 123
4.7 Conclusion 124
4.8 Future Scope 125
References 125

5 Context Dependent Sentiments Analysis Using Machine Learning 129
Mahima Shanker Pandey, Bihari Nandan Pandey, Abhishek Singh, Ashish Kumar Mishra and Brijesh Pandey
5.1 Introduction 130
5.1.1 Motivation 131
5.2 Literature Review 131
5.2.1 Text Sentiment 132
5.2.2 Audio Sentiment 132
5.2.3 Video Sentiment 133
5.3 Methodology 135
5.3.1 System Architecture 135
5.4 Proposed Model 137
5.4.1 Proposed Algorithm 137
5.4.2 Data Set Sources 138
5.4.3 Text Sentiment 140
5.4.4 Audio Sentiment 141
5.4.5 Video Sentiment 142
5.5 Implementations and Results 142
5.5.1 Results 142
5.5.2 Text Sentiment 143
5.5.3 Audio Sentiment 144
5.5.4 Video Sentiment 146
5.5.5 Applications 149
5.6 Conclusion 149
References 150

6 **Thyroid Cancer Prediction Using Optimizations** 153
Swati Sharma, Vijay Kumar Sharma, Punit Mittal, Pradeep Pant and Nitin Rakesh
6.1 Introduction 154
6.2 Background and Related Work 155
6.3 Proposed Methodology 160
6.4 Architecture 165
6.5 Materials and Methods 169
6.6 Results and Discussion 171
6.7 Conclusion 175
References 177

7 **An LSTM-Oriented Approach for Next Word Prediction Using Deep Learning** 181
Nidhi Shukla, Ashutosh Kumar Singh, Vijay Kumar Dwivedi, Pallavi Shukla, Jeetesh Srivastava and Vivek Srivastava
7.1 Introduction 182
7.2 Related Work 184
7.3 Design and Implementation 186
7.3.1 Background 186
7.3.1.1 LSTM 187
7.3.1.2 Bi-LSTM 189
7.4 Proposed Model Architecture 190
7.4.1 Experimental Setup 192
7.4.2 Dataset Specification 192
7.5 Results and Discussions 193
7.6 Conclusion 198
References 199

8 **Churn Prediction in Social Networks Using Modified BiLSTM-CNN Model** 203
Himanshu Rai and Jyoti Kesarwani
8.1 Introduction 204
8.2 Customer Behavior in Social Networks 209
8.3 Proposed Methodology 218
8.3.1 Churn Dataset Acquisition 218
8.3.2 Data Preprocessing 220
8.3.3 Proposed Model 220
8.4 Result 221
8.5 Conclusion 225
References 226

9 **Fog Computing Security Concerns in Healthcare Using IoT and Blockchain** **231**
Ruchi Mittal, Shikha Gupta and Shefali Arora
9.1 Introduction 232
9.1.1 Types of Security Concerns in Healthcare 236
9.2 Related Work 239
9.3 Open Questions and Research Challenges 241
9.4 Problem Definition 242
9.5 Objectives 242
9.6 Research Methodology 243
9.6.1 The Three-Tier Blockchain Design 243
9.6.1.1 Model Design 243
9.6.2 System Architecture 243
9.6.3 Workflow in Different Scenarios 245
9.7 Conclusion and Future Work 249
References 249

10 **Smart Agriculture Revolution: Cloud and IoT-Based Solutions for Sustainable Crop Management and Precision Farming** **253**
Shrawan Kumar Sharma
10.1 Introduction 255
10.1.1 IoT in Agriculture 257
10.1.2 Cloud Computing in Agriculture 259
10.1.3 Precision Farming 263
10.1.4 Sustainable Agricultural and Remote Sensing 265
10.2 Data Analytics and Decision Support 267
10.2.1 Remote Monitoring 269
10.3 Challenges and Solutions Smart Agriculture 270
10.3.1 (AI) Approach in Agriculture and Needs 270
10.3.2 Needs of AI Farm 273
10.3.3 Role of AI in Agriculture 274
10.4 AI for Soybean (*Glycine max*) Crop 275
10.4.1 Soybean Disease Image Acquisition and Pretreatment 276
10.5 Result Discussion 281
10.5.1 Emerging Trends and Technologies in Smart Agriculture 281
10.6 Conclusion 283
References 285

11 Greedy Particle Swarm Optimization Approach Using Leaky ReLU Function for Minimum Spanning Tree Problem 289
Ashish Kumar Singh and Anoj Kumar
11.1 Introduction 290
11.1.1 Goal 291
11.1.2 Research Contribution are Below Listed 292
11.2 Background 292
11.2.1 Minimum Spanning Tree 294
11.2.2 Particle Swarm Optimization 296
11.2.3 Firefly Algorithm 297
11.2.4 Leaky ReLU Activation Function 298
11.3 Population-Based Proposed Optimization Approach 298
11.3.1 Motivation 299
11.3.2 Greedy Particle Swarm Optimization Using Leaky ReLU (LR-GPSO) 300
11.3.2.1 Initialization of Parameters 302
11.3.2.2 Population Initialization 303
11.3.2.3 Input 303
11.3.2.4 Evaluation 304
11.3.2.5 Updating Position of Members of Swarm 304
11.3.2.6 Role of Leaky ReLU Function 304
11.3.2.7 Mutation Effect 305
11.3.2.8 Selection of Edges 306
11.3.2.9 Output 306
11.4 Experimental Setup and Result Analysis of Proposed Work (LR-GPSO) 307
11.4.1 Complexity 307
11.4.2 Simulation Experiments 308
11.4.2.1 Result for Vertices (V=20) 308
11.4.2.2 Result for Vertices (V=40) 308
11.4.2.3 Result for Vertices (V=60) 310
11.4.2.4 Result for Vertices (V=80) 310
11.4.3 Convergence Curve 311
11.5 Conclusion and Future Work 313
References 314

12 SDN Deployed Secure Application Design Framework for IoT Using Game Theory 317
Madhukrishna Priyadarsini and Padmalochan Bera
12.1 Introduction 318
12.1.1 IoT Overview 318

12.1.2 SDN Overview 319
12.1.3 Game Theory Overview 321
12.2 Background Study 322
12.2.1 IoT Security Using SDN 322
12.2.2 IoT Security Using Game Theory 323
12.3 SDN-Deployed Design Framework for IoT Using Game-Theoretic Solutions 324
12.3.1 Trust Verification 324
12.4 Case Study: SDN Deployed Design Framework in Robot Manufacturing Industry 334
12.4.1 Working Procedure of a Robot Manufacturing Industry 334
12.4.2 Integration of SDN-Deployed Design Framework in Robot Manufacturing Industry 335
12.4.3 Experimental Results 336
12.5 Discussion 338
12.6 Conclusion 339
References 339

13 Framework for PLM in Industry 4.0 Based on Industrial Blockchain 341
Ali Zaheer Agha, Rajesh Kumar Shukla, Ratnesh Mishra and Ravi Shankar Shukla
13.1 Introduction 342
13.1.1 What is Blockchain? 343
13.1.2 Blockchain Technology's Integration with Industry 4.0 343
13.1.3 Blockchain Applications in Industry 4.0 343
13.1.3.1 Protection of Manufacturing Data 344
13.1.3.2 Resolution of Quality Issues 344
13.1.3.3 Supply Chain Development 344
13.1.4 A Consensus Algorithm 344
13.1.5 Product Lifecycle Management 345
13.1.6 Benefits of Smart Contracts in Addressing PLM Challenges 347
13.2 Related Work 348
13.2.1 Product Lifecycle Management 349
13.2.2 Industrial Blockchain 351
13.2.3 The On-Chain vs. Off-Chain Principle 353
13.3 The Recommended Architecture's Methodology 354
13.3.1 The Suggested Platform's Architecture 354

13.3.2 The Suggested Platform's Technological Solution 358
13.4 Key Services That are Suggested 360
13.4.1 A Co-Creation Service Enabled by Blockchain 360
13.4.2 Blockchain-Enabled QAT2 Service 363
13.4.3 Proactive Upkeep Service Facilitated by Blockchain 364
13.4.4 Smart Recycling Program Driven by Blockchain 365
13.5 Modelling and Assessment 366
13.5.1 Overview of the Investigation 366
13.5.2 Experimental Evaluation and Comparison 368
13.5.3 Discussion 372
13.6 Conclusion and Future Work 373
A Statement of Competing Interests 374
References 375

14 Machine Learning Enabled Smart Agriculture Classification Technique for Edge Devices Using Remote Sensing Platform 381
Priyanka Gupta, Suraj Kumar Singh, Neetish Kumar and Bhavna Thakur
List of Abbreviations 382
14.1 Introduction 382
14.2 Related Works 384
14.3 Methods and Dataset 386
14.3.1 Research Area and Dataset 386
14.3.2 Pre-Processing and Image Dataset 387
14.3.3 Classifiers 390
14.3.3.1 Naïve Bayes Classifier 390
14.3.3.2 Minimum Distance Classifier 390
14.4 Proposed Algorithm 391
14.5 Results and Discussions 392
14.5.1 Classified Crop Map 394
14.6 Conclusion 395
References 396

15 A Lightweight Intelligent Detection Approach for Interest Flooding Attack 401
Naveen Kumar, Brijendra Pratap Singh and Rohit
15.1 Introduction 402
15.2 NDN Background 405
15.2.1 NDN Architecture 405
15.2.1.1 NDN Packet 405

15.2.1.2 NDN Data Structures 407
15.2.1.3 NDN Forwarding 407
15.2.2 NDN Security 408
15.2.2.1 IFA 408
15.2.2.2 IFA Type 408
15.3 Related Work 409
15.4 IFA Feature Selection and Detection 411
15.4.1 IFA Modelling 412
15.4.2 Data Collection 413
15.4.3 Balancing the Dataset 414
15.4.4 Feature Selection 415
15.4.4.1 Filter Methods 415
15.4.4.2 Wrapper Methods 419
15.4.5 Dimensionality Reduction 421
15.4.6 Classification 424
15.5 Conclusion 428
References 429

16 An Internet of Vehicles Model Architecture with Seven Layers 433
Sujata Negi Thakur, Manisha Koranga, Sandeep Abhishek, Richa Pandey and Mayurika Joshi
16.1 Introduction 434
16.2 Literature Review 435
16.3 Proposed Architecture of Internet of Vehicles 439
16.4 Applications, Characteristics, and Challenges of the Internet of Vehicles (IoV) 451
Conclusion 455
References 455

Index 457

Preface

This book was written to bridge the gap between existing state-of-the-art technologies and the evolving requirements of modern industries. It provides emerging research that explores both theoretical and practical aspects of implementing new and innovative intelligent techniques across a variety of sectors, including Edge Computing, Cloud Computing, the Internet of Things, Agriculture, and Artificial Intelligence. This book serves as a valuable resource for academics, IT specialists, industry professionals, researchers, engineers, and authors seeking insights into emerging trends in AI-enabled Cloud and Edge Computing for IoT applications. It aims to explore the intricate relationship between AI and Edge/Cloud computing, delving into their synergies, applications, and future implications.

This book comprises 16 chapters, each covering intertwining concepts at two key levels of interest to the scientific community: Artificial Intelligence and Edge/Cloud Computing.

Chapter One explores navigating next-generation network architecture, unleashing the power of SDN, NFV, NS, and AI convergence. Chapter Two examines OctoEdge, an octopus-inspired adaptive edge computing architecture. Chapter Three discusses the development of optimized machine learning-oriented models.

Chapter Four focuses on leveraging multimodal data and deep learning for enhanced stock market prediction. Chapter Five delves into context-dependent sentiment analysis using machine learning. Chapter Six investigates enhancing thyroid cancer prediction by applying machine learning algorithms to clinical data.

Chapter Seven presents an LSTM-oriented approach for next-word prediction using deep learning. Chapter Eight analyzes churn prediction in social networks using a modified BiLSTM-CNN model. Chapter Nine addresses security concerns in healthcare fog computing using IoT and blockchain.

Chapter Ten highlights the smart agriculture revolution with cloud and IoT-based solutions for sustainable crop management and precision farming. Chapter Eleven explores a greedy particle swarm optimization approach using the Lecky ReLU function for solving minimum spanning tree problems.

Chapter Twelve introduces an SDN-deployed secure application design framework for IoT using game theory. Chapter Thirteen presents a framework for PLM in Industry 4.0 based on industrial blockchain.

Chapter Fourteen discusses a machine learning-enabled smart agriculture classification technique for edge devices using a remote sensing platform. Chapter Fifteen examines a lightweight intelligent detection approach for interest flooding attacks. Chapter Sixteen describes an Internet of Vehicles model architecture with seven layers.

This book may serve as a reference for a graduate course in Artificial Intelligence and Cloud Computing. Readers are expected to be well-versed in the basic concepts of Machine Learning, Distributed Computing, and the Internet of Things. The theoretical concepts presented will be valuable for coursework.

Writing this book has been a rewarding experience, made possible by the tremendous efforts of a dedicated team. We extend our gratitude to the authors who contributed their respective chapters, as well as to the editors who offered valuable suggestions for improving content delivery. Every piece of feedback was carefully considered, and it has undoubtedly shaped parts of the work. We are especially grateful to Martin Scrivener and Scrivener Publishing for their help and publication. Finally, we thank our families for their unwavering support—without them, this book would not have been possible.

November 2024

Acknowledgement

The writing of this book has been a rewarding experience and elaborates a huge effort from a team of very dedicated contributors. We would like to thank list of authors who contributes their respective chapter and we are also thankful to the list of editors who provides suggestions for better delivery of content. All feedback was considered and there is no doubt that there will be some content influenced by the suggestions. We especially thank to the publisher who believes in the content and provides a platform to reach it out to the audience. Finally, we are thankful to our family for their continued support. Without them, the book would not have been possible.

1

Navigating Next-Generation Network Architecture: Unleashing the Power of SDN, NFV, NS, and AI Convergence

Monika Dubey[1]*, Snehlata[2], Ashutosh Kumar Singh[2], Richa Mishra[1] and Mohit Kumar[3]

[1]*Department of Electronics & Communication, University of Allahabad, Prayagraj, U.P., India*
[2]*Department of Computer Science and Engineering, United College of Engineering & Research, Prayagraj, U.P., India*
[3]*Department of Information Technology, National Institute of Technology Jalandhar, Punjab, India*

Abstract
The framework for existing legacy network architecture is massive and complex. It mainly relies on inflexible and expensive equipment, typically constructed from a massive number of switches, routers, firewalls, and hubs. Moreover, this vendor-specific network configuration and complex control protocols are not flexible enough to offer customized quality of services (QoS). Provisioning of next-gen (Next Generation, 5G, and beyond) technologies, software-defined networking (SDN), network function virtualization (NFV), and network slicing (NS) work as catalysts to offer simplified, customized, and clever networking. To provide centralized positioning, SDN decouples the control plane (CP) and data plane (DP) from the traditional router. In the SDN architecture, decision making and network control are now done at a centralized place known as the controller. However, DP is still intact with the routing device. This arrangement privileges the network administrators to control, manage, and alter network behavior dynamically. To contrast the vender-specific networking, NFV allows network functions (NFs) to run on generic hardware. In this direction, NS pioneers QoS-specific use cases as a new business model. NS involves the slicing of a single physical network in the form of multiple slices. It not only supports the customization of QoS

**Corresponding author*: mdubey.452@gmail.com

Mohit Kumar, Gautam Srivastava, Ashutosh Kumar Singh and Kalka Dubey (eds.) AI-Based Advanced Optimization Techniques for Edge Computing, (1–34) © 2025 Scrivener Publishing LLC

services for diverse use cases, but it also improves isolation, independence, multi-tenancy, dynamic resource allocation, and end-to-end service provisioning. In this chapter, we first delved into NexGen's promising technologies and explored their intertwined role and impact on the modern networking framework. We accessed various SDN and NFV architectures and discussed network-slicing framework. Secondly, we have shed light on the importance of AI-driven automated network management over traditional network approaches. In this sequence, we conducted a comparative analysis of AI-driven machine learning (ML) and deep learning (DL) approaches in the context of NextGen technologies. In this chapter, we intend to systematically and intricately navigate the multifaceted landscape of NexGen technologies. This chapter will offer researchers, industry stakeholders, and practitioners a timely and deeper understanding of transformative technology and its impact on modern network paradigms.

***Keywords*:** Next-generation technology, SDN, NFV, QoS, NS

1.1 Introduction

The evolution of network technologies has marked pivotal advancements in the telecom sector. It spans from the radiant stage of ARPANET to modern networking. The existing legacy network architecture is based upon un-flexible and costly network equipment comprising switches, hubs, routers, and firewalls [1]. These proprietary hardware-based traditional networks grapple with the demands of modern networking. The surge of extensive data traffic, dynamic network conditions, and the need for real-time decision-makers pose challenges that traditional networks are not capable of addressing efficiently [2]. Traditional methods, such as Static Routing, Ethernet, Transmission Control Protocol (TCP), and Internet Protocol (IP), are built on manual configuration and static protocols. With the surge of diverse applications, customized QoS, high volume, and unpredicted traffic necessitate a paradigm shift. To address these limitations of the traditional approach, Next-Gen (Next Generation, 5G, and beyond) technologies, Software Defined Networking (SDN), Network Function Virtualization (NFV), and NS act as catalysts for redefining the network paradigm. SDN [3] disrupts traditional decentralized architecture by decoupling the Control Plane (CP) and Data Plane (DP) from conventional routers. This centralized control and decision-making entity is known as the controller. This architectural shift empowers the network controller to dynamically manage, control, and modify the network behavior. Concurrently, NFV [4] revolutionizes network functionality by enabling them to run on generic hardware instead of proprietary hardware, offering cost-effectiveness, flexibility, and simplified maintenance. With the advancement of the network landscape, customize QoS-specific servers are the new business model. In this direction, NS [5] has become a revolutionary approach, involving the partitioning of a single physical network into multiple slices. It not only offers customized QoS requirements to modern applications but also enhances isolation, dynamic resource allocation, multi-tenancy, and security [6].

This book chapter also explored the NextGen promising technologies and their intertwined role and impact on modern networking. Traditional networking approaches are static and require human intervention during changes in the network. The increase in network size and the unpredictable nature of network traffic make them more time-consuming and complex. Therefore, AI emerges as a key driver for NextGen networking. It introduced the level of intelligence with its learning and capability of predictive analysis. This chapter also sheds light on how AI-driven approaches complement and enhance the functionalities of SDN, NFV, and NS.

The contributions and highlight of this book chapter are as follows:

- Initially, we present a concise overview of the evolutionary history of network technologies and the key phases that shaped the modern networking landscape.
- To explore the transformative NexGen technologies (SDN, NFV, and NS), we highlight the influence and intertwining role of NexGen technologies.
- This paper systematically highlights the importance of AI over traditional methods. In this sequence, we conducted a comparative analysis of AI-driven Machine Learning (ML) and Deep Learning (DL) approaches in the context of NextGen technologies.
- Finally, we identify challenges associated with NexGen Technologies and with the integration of these modern technologies.

In a nutshell, this chapter will offer researchers and industry stakeholders a timely and deep understanding of transformative NexGen technologies and the impact of their combination on modern technology. It also includes the contribution and comparative analysis of AI-driven algorithms in the context of NexGen technologies.

1.2 Revolutionizing Infrastructure with SDN, NFV, and NS

Due to increasing day-to-day network traffic, networking technologies have undergone a continuous evolution, and based on this, they can be categorized into several phases, such as traditional networking, Wireless Sensor Networking (WSN), client-server networking, and more. Before discussing NexGen technologies and its specifications, it is crucial to examine the evolutionary changes of networking technologies and the key developments that have been influenced by traditional networking. Concise overview is given as follows:

A. ARPANET and Early Networking:

- **ARPANET:** The Advanced Research Projects Agency Network (ARPANET) [7], established in the 1960s, conducted early experiments for linking computer systems over short distances. It laid the foundation for modern networking. However, these networks remained restricted to research institutions.
- **Packet Switching:** The development of packet switching [8], a key innovation during this era, allowed data to be broken into packets, transmitted independently, and reassembled at the intended destination.

The pioneering work and packet switching laid the fundamental groundwork for the internet.

B. Emergence of the Internet:

- **Standardization (TCP/IP):** During the 1980s, the TCP [9] and IP underwent standardization, forming the backbone of the modern Internet.
- **Commercialization:** The Internet underwent a pivotal shift from being primarily dedicated to research and academia to a commercial platform, leading to the rise of the World Wide Web (WWW). It establishes the fundamental framework for the contemporary Internet.

C. Emergence of Client-Server Architecture and LANs:

- **Client-Server Model:** In 1980s, the paradigm of computing is shifting from centralized mainframes to distributed systems with the client-server model [10].
- **The rise of Local Area Networks (LANs):** The internet and other LAN technologies emerged, allowing computers to share resources within confined spaces.

D. Wireless Networking and Mobility:

- **Wi-Fi Standardization:** In the 2000s, the standardization of wireless technologies, particularly Wi-Fi adoption [11], empowered enhanced mobility and flexibility in network access.
- **Expansion of Mobile Networks:** The surge in mobile device usage during this era empowered enhanced mobility and flexibility in network access [12].

E. Cloud Computing and Virtualization:

- **Evolution of Cloud Services:** The 2010s witnessed a transformative shift with the advent of cloud computing [13], fundamentally changing the way data and applications are stored and accessed.
- **Rise of Virtualization:** The decade also saw the emergence of NFV and SDN [14], contributing to enhanced flexibility and efficiency in the management of network resources.

In the beginning, traditional enterprise networks followed conventional decentralized designs and scattered collections of purpose-built routers, switches, and middle-boxes supplied by various hardware vendors [15]. Each device uses embedded proprietary hardware and logic to make forwarding decisions, filter traffic, or transform flows. This distributed CP closely relates key networking functions to the restrictions of the underlying boxes in terms of capability and flexibility. The conventional decentralized networking architecture imposed significant barriers to change in network arrangements. Every configuration change or new policy meant navigating vendor-specific command-line interfaces to manually reprogram

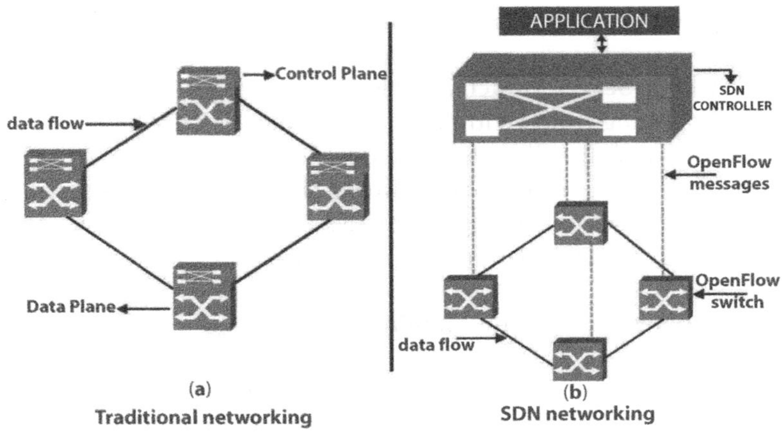

Figure 1.1 (a) Decentralized traditional architecture. (b) Centralized SDN architecture.

individual pieces of equipment. To deal with the huge dynamic traffic, this fragmented model is not appropriate due to the rigidities of closed hardware systems. The massive burden of managing numerous devices running complex embedded protocols eventually became unsustainable. To address the longstanding limitations of traditional network architectures, the SDN paradigm emerged to unlock network flexibility and fundamentally introduce centralized network control [16]. The architectural differences between traditional decentralized architecture and centralized architecture are presented in Figure 1.1(a) and 1(b) respectively.

1.2.1 SDN: Definition and Architecture

SDN architecture [17] is the paramount approach for centralized network control. It is structured to decouple the control plane from the data plane and provides automation and centralized control by delegating specialized functions to each level via programmatic APIs. The centralized control unit, known as the controller, is responsible for network design, decision-making, and network management. The SDN architecture typically comprises three main components:

- **Application Layer:** The topmost layer of SDN consists of software programs that communicate business-related policy and network behavior. This layer interacts with the SDN controller to communicate policies, requirements, or network changes. Common SDN applications include load balancing, traffic monitoring, and security applications.

- **Control Layer:** This intermediary layer, known as the SDN controller, is the brain of the SDN architecture. The controller communicates with network devices in the infrastructure layer via southbound and SDN applications via northbound APIs at the application layer.
- **Infrastructure Layer:** The bottom layer is the infrastructure layer, which consists of the physical and virtual network devices those forward data packets. In contrast to traditional networking by separating the CP, the intelligence for decision-making is moved from individual devices to the centralized controller.

The architecture presented in Figure 1.2 outlines the fundamentals of SDN. However, SDN provides incredible versatility to adapt its core principles into diverse architectural designs to address specific networking needs and challenges. In the realm of single-layer architectures, centralized controller manages the entire network, whereas distributed SDN architecture's [18] CP functions across multiple controllers to provide more scalability

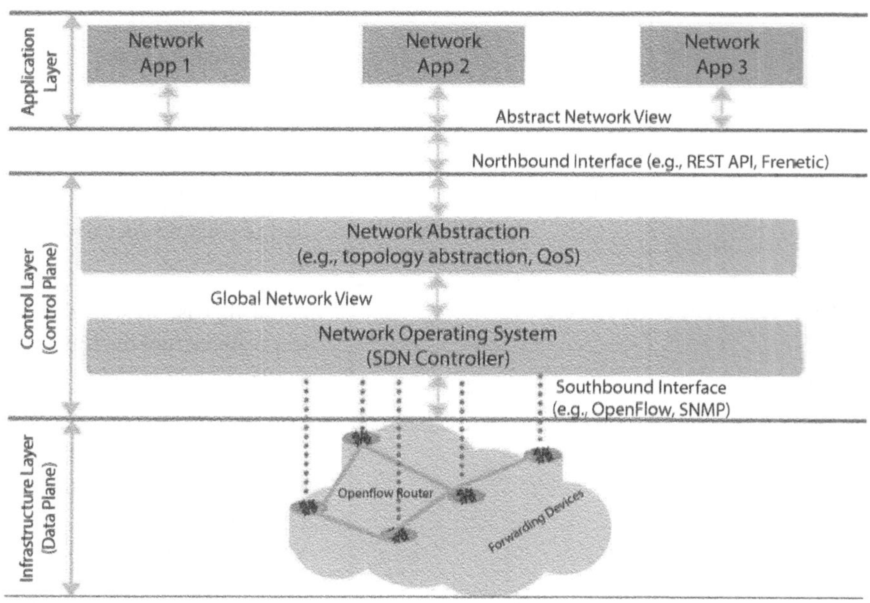

Figure 1.2 A typical architecture of SDN consists of three layers.

Table 1.1 Common SDN protocols and APIs within SDN architecture.

Aspect	**SDN protocol/API**	**Description**
Northbound APIs	Open Flow	A standard protocol between SDN controllers and network devices such as switches to define flows.
	REST APIs	Representational State Transfer (REST) APIs leverage controller communication with SDN applications for northbound interactions.
	NETCONF	It is used for northbound communication between controllers and network devices for network management.
Southbound APIs	Open Flow	Southbound protocol, communicate between SDN controllers and network switches to configure data plane behavior.
	P4 (Programming Protocol-Independent Packet Processors)	Southbound API for defining packet forwarding behaviors to define packet processing across devices.
East-West APIs	VXLAN	Facilitating east-west traffic to create virtual overlay networks across data centers.
	Geneve	Another overlay protocol for east-west communication for network virtualization across SDN environments.

in comparison with a single SDN controller. Multi-layer SDN architecture presents hierarchical SDN architecture [19] with multiple layers of controllers. It helps to enhance organization and management in large-scale networks. On the other hand, in a hybrid SDN architecture, SDN coexists with traditional networking (NON-SDN) [20] elements. It allows for seamless integration of SDN principles with traditional networking elements, allowing coexistence and transition. Overlay SDN architectures [21] are commonly prevalent in data centre environments. In this tunneling, protocols are used to create virtual networks on top of the physical infrastructure. Cloud SDN architectures [22] focus on cloud environments, emphasizing automation, agility, and the ability to adapt to the dynamic workloads characteristic of cloud computing. Intent-Based Networking (IBN) architectures [23] are mainly focused on high-level business intent for automated and simplified management of networks on the basis of desired output. Tailored for 5G networks, the 5G SDN architecture integrates SDN with NFV to meet the demands of next-generation network framework. SDN protocols play a crucial role in communication and coordination between various components of SDN. It primarily facilitates communication between components, policy dissemination, dynamic adoption, load balancing, and configuration management. Table 1.1 outlines the common SDN protocols and APIs within SDN architecture.

1.2.2 NFV: Definition and Architecture

Non-virtualized traditional networks run on dedicated proprietary hardware. Unlike them, NFV supports the sharing of infrastructure resources during NF deployments and runs as a software application on generic hardware instead of proprietary hardware. It virtualizes NFs such as firewalls, routers, and load balancers, also known as VNFs (Virtual NFs). The NFV architectural framework defined by ETSI [24] consists of three key domains:

- **Virtualized Network Functions (VNFs):** VNFs are software applications implemented on network functions to replace dedicated appliances. These software instances replicate the functionality of traditional network devices such as firewalls and load balancers.
- **NFV Infrastructure (NFVI):** This includes the infrastructure components (compute, storage, and networking; Commercial-off-the-Shelf (COTS) hardware like servers,

switches, and storage deployed in data centers); and the virtual layer on which VNFs run.
- **NFV Management and Orchestration (NFV MANO):** This includes orchestrators, VNF managers, and it supports the framework for orchestration and management of the lifecycle of VNFs across the NFVI.

ETSI defines the foundational NFV architectural block presented in Figure 1.3. However, the NFV architecture exhibits diverse forms to accommodate diverse scenarios and specific operational requirements. In a centralized NFV architecture [19], management and orchestration functions are consolidated to simplify CP. However, centralized designs focused exclusively on operational efficiency can suffer from latency limitations in distributed deployments. Meanwhile, distributed NFV infrastructure [25] spreads capabilities across multiple localized data centers, catering to scenarios where low-latency communication is critical, as seen in edge computing environments. Hybrid architecture is intended to balance the tradeoffs between centralized and distributed architecture. In this architecture, common network functions get consolidated into a core virtualized infrastructure for efficiency, while other specialized functions continue at the edge for performance.

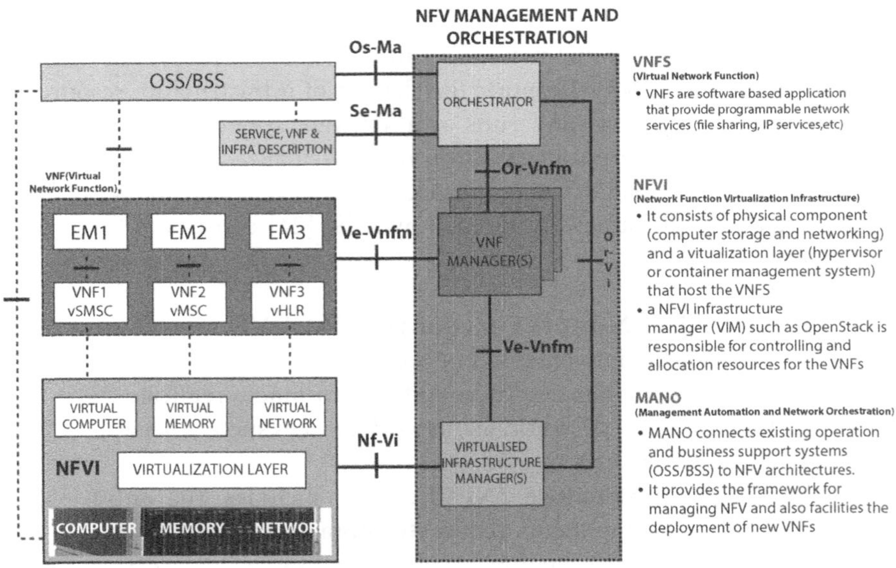

Figure 1.3 NFV layered architecture.

1.2.3 NS: Conceptual Abstractions

Traditional mobile networks are based on the "one-size-fits-all" network paradigm [26]. It is no longer efficient to support different use cases. Third-generation partnership project (3GPP) [27] defined NS is a key concept for 5G networks to offer flexible and customized network services. In this approach, "slicing" is the concept of dividing physical network resources into logical networks in the form of slices to address different QoS and Service Level Agreements (SLAs) [28]. It involves logically partitioned physical network infrastructure to offer highly customized and optimized connectivity solutions for various use cases. End-to-End (E2E) NS [29] involves the orchestration and customization of resources across the entire network architecture. In the 5G architecture, it is logically partitioned across different components of the network Core Network (CN), Radio Access Network (RAN), and Transport Network (TN) domains [30].

- **Core NS:** Core NS has a dedicated virtual core network, and central control mechanisms orchestrate the flow of data and session management services. It supports distinct use case applications ranging from augmented reality to mission-critical communications in terms of key network performance such as latency, bandwidth, jitter, reliability, and so on.
- **Transport NS:** It provides connectivity between the core network and RAN elements of each slice for seamless movement of data between various network elements. It ensures dedicated traffic capacity and guaranteed resources like bandwidth, latency, reliability, and jitter for each network slice.
- **Radio Access Network (RAN) Slicing:** RAN provides the interface between the user device and the broader network. RAN slicing is responsible for fulfilling the user demands of different use cases by isolating radio resources, including bandwidth and frequencies. It is mainly crucial for scenarios where varied performance characteristics are in demand, such as high bandwidth and ultra low latency. It plays a significant role in addressing vertical industry service-level requirements in terms of network performance (latency, throughput, reliability, etc.) for diverse use-case services. In this context, more than 400 vertical use cases [31] were identified across various industries for 5G, such as smart cities [32], smart factory [33], health care [34], autonomous vehicles [35], and so on. ITU classified these diverse use cases

in terms of three broad service categories [36]: **(i)** eMBB (enhanced Mobile Broadband); **(ii)** massive Machine Type Communication (mMTC); and **(iii)** ultra-Reliable and Low Latency Communication (uRLLC). ITU defined this in terms of eight Key Performance Indices (KPIs) [37], including performance indicators (peak data rate, user experience data rate, latency, connection density, traffic volume density, and mobility) and efficiency indicators (spectrum efficiency and energy efficiency). Classification and KPI for three service categories are represented in Table 1.2. The network architecture and key use case scenario presented in Figure 1.4.

Table 1.2 Classification and KPIs for three use-case categories.

Characteristics	**eMBB**		**mMTC**		**uRLLC**	
Aim	• Human-centric data driven use cases • Multimedia content		• Service provider centric • Massive connection devices • Low cost and non-delay sensitive devices		• Network operator centric • Delay sensitive services	
Use Case	AR/VR, real-time gamming, hotspot and wide area coverage.		Smart wearable, smart city, smart power grid, smart industries		V2X, public safety, remote surgery, smart industries and robotics	
Parameters	**Peak data rate**	20 GBPS	**Connection density**	10^6 devices/ km^2	**U-plane latency**	1ms
	C-plane latency	10ms				
	U-plane latency	4ms				
	Area traffic capacity	>3 times greater than LTE advanced			**C-plane latency**	20ms
	User Equipment data rate	>3 times greater than LTE advanced	**UE battery life**	Beyond 10 years	**Reliability**	10^{-5} for 32 Bytes (user plane latency of 1ms)
	Target mobility speed	500 Km/h				
	Mobility interruption time	0ms				

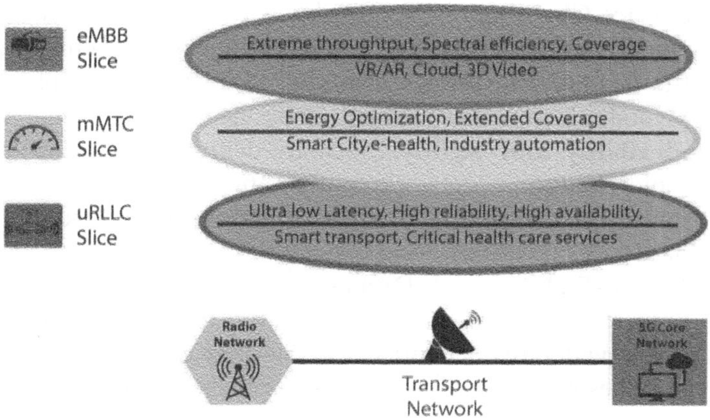

Figure 1.4 NS framework.

1.3 Realizing NS Potential with SDN and NFV

SDN and NFV are the building blocks of modern technology. It plays a crucial role in meeting the diverse service requirements of various use cases. Together, these technologies create powerful and flexible network architectures. These two advanced technologies introduce a new paradigm for designing, optimizing, and offering scalability, flexibility, and efficiency [38]. Key aspects where SDN and NFV complement each other are discussed below:

- **Centralized Network Control:** The Centralized architecture of SDN allows the network administrator to create and manage network resources dynamically through the centralized controller. NFV complements SDN by creating VNFs, allowing them to run as software on generic hardware. It enables the SDN controller to dynamically orchestrate the deployment and chaining of these VNFs.
- **Dynamic Resource Allocation:** SDN contributes to the dynamic allocation of resources by decoupling the CP from the DP. It allows the adjustment of network paths and traffic flow on the fly. On the other hand, NFV helps enhance resource utilization by running NFs as virtual instances.

- **Service Chaining:** SDN contributes to the creation of service chains in the predefined order. Whereas, NFV enhances the flexibility in service chaining. SDN controllers play a pivotal role in orchestrating these service chains.
- **Flexibility and Agility:** Software-defined policies allow rapid changes in network configuration. NFV brings flexibility by decoupling network functions from dedicated hardware.
- **End-to-End Network Orchestration:** SDN contributes to orchestrating network elements within the data center and across wide-area networks. The interplay of SDN and NFV provides end-to-end orchestration capabilities for dynamic service delivery.

In summary, SDN provides centralized abstractions of the overall network that represent in Figure 1.5. On the other hand, NFV transforms the deployment of core network functions like authentication, policies, and routing into modular software services.

NS is proven to be a revolutionary technology for unlocking highly customized and adoptable modern networks. Integration of NS, SDN, and NFV heralds a transformative era in modern telecommunication [39]. NS allows the creation of customized virtualized networks to address the unique requirements of diverse use cases. When coupled with SDN, it enables dynamic instantiation of NS and rapid customization and adoption of change. NS is intended to allocate dedicated resources to each slice by ensuring KPIs for specific user cases in terms of bandwidth, low latency, and reliability. Integration of NFV complements NS by enabling flexible deployment of VFs to ensure resource efficiency. SDN's orchestration capabilities support NS and E2E service orchestration. Isolation in NS ensures

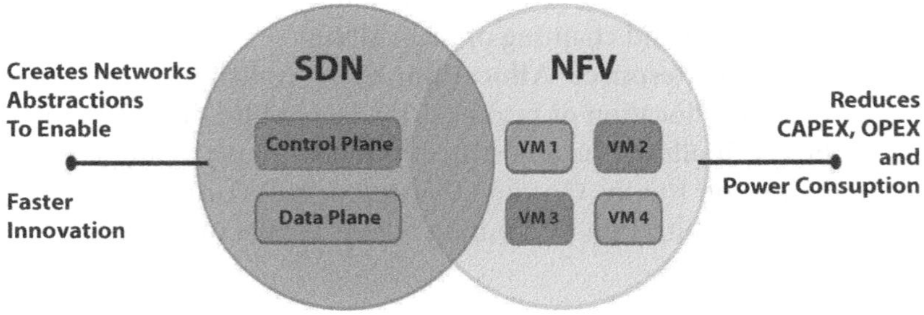

Figure 1.5 Illustration of integration of SDN and NFV.

security between slices that run on common physical infrastructure. SDN's centralized control uses stringent security policies to enforce security and consistency across all slices. Integration of NFV complements the major objective of NS to support diverse use case requirements ranging from smart cities to automated vehicles.

In conclusion, NS is positioned as a fundamental enabler of 5G for customized telecom services. In conclusion, NS is positioned as a fundamental enabler of 5G for customized telecom services. The combination of NS, SDN, and NFV works as the foundation for evolving network architecture. It ensures customizations, scalability, and adoption in the 5G era and beyond.

1.4 Artificial Intelligence: Pivotal Role in Networking Transformation

With the shift in the networking paradigm, traditional networking has become inefficient to deal with large, dynamic, and heterogeneous network infrastructure. The key challenges of traditional methods to address modern networking technology are as follows:

- A Traditional network requires manual intervention for any network configuration or policy change.
- Troubleshooting with traditional methods is often reactive and requires administrators to address this issue when it occurs.
- There is a lack of predictive analysis capability to proactively analyze any issue.
- Inflexible scaling is another major limitation of traditional methods. It becomes time-consuming and requires manual adjustments and upgrades to the hardware.
- Modern large, dynamic, and heterogeneous networks demand quick changes in traffic patterns and user behavior. Traditional networking struggles to do so.

In summary, traditional networking approaches often involve manual and static configuration and reactive approaches. AI is proven to be a catalyst for modern network complexities [40]. AI-driven approaches introduce automation, flexibility, scalability, and intelligence. NextGen technologies such as SDN, NFV, and NS, with the integration of AI [41];

better align with the requirements of contemporary modern network environments. For SDN, AI drives capabilities, including load balancing, centralized networking control, dynamic routing, and anomaly detection and so on [42]. Regarding NFV, emphasize its ability to deal with virtualizing network functions, service chain management, resource optimization, network customization, and so on [43]. AI embedded with NS contributes to supporting customized QoS, isolation, dynamic resource allocation, multi-tenancy, and E2E service provisioning [44].

AI-embedded approaches can further be classified into ML and DL approaches; the ML approach can further be divided into supervised, unsupervised, and reinforcement learning [45]. DL is considered a specialized subset of ML. In this section, we are intended to investigate AI-driven approaches to address modern networking objectives. In particular, this section is intended to explore Ml and DL approaches to addressing SDN, NFV, and NS objectives.

1.4.1 Supervised Learning

Supervised learning is the method of making predictions or decisions based on training a model on a labeled dataset. Supervised learning can be expressed as labeled dataset D, represented in equation (1.1);

$$\mathbf{D = \{(x_1, y_1),(x_2, y_2),\ldots,(x_n, y_n)\}} \tag{1.1}$$

where x_n and y_n represent input feature and corresponding labels, respectively. By identifying relationships between patterns and data model maps F, represented in equation (1.2).

$$\mathbf{F : X \rightarrow Y} \tag{1.2}$$

In this process, the model learns by adjusting parameters to minimize the loss function L, represented in equation (1.3).

$$\mathbf{L: (F\ (x), y)} \tag{1.3}$$

After completion of the training process model, it will finally be able to predict new and unseen data.

In the context of networking, input could present various networking parameters such as performance metrics (bandwidth, latency, and so on), network traffic, or device state. While the output could denote a specific

Table 1.3 Supervised learning algorithm for achieving the NexGen objective.

Technology	Supervised learning algorithms	Use case	References
SDN	Decision Trees	Traffic engineering, policy-based decision-making, security	[46, 47]
	SVM	Traffic classification, anomaly identification, intrusion detection,	[48, 49]
	k-Nearest Neighbors (k-NN)	network optimization, load balancing,	[42, 50]
	Random Forests	Dynamic routing, traffic classification, anomaly mitigation	[42, 51, 52]
	Logistic Regression	network security, Policy enforcement,	[53, 54]
NFV	Decision Trees	Service chain management, resource allocation	[55, 56]
	SVM	Fault management	[57]
	k-Nearest Neighbors (k-NN)	Scaling. interoperability	[58]
	Random Forests	Fault tolerance, auto-scaling VNFs	[59]
	SVM	Network traffic classification	[60]
	k-Nearest Neighbors (k-NN)	Resource allocation	[61]

action or classification, It mainly employed for various networking applications such as traffic classification, QoS optimization and anomaly detection. Supervised learning plays a crucial role in enhancing the capabilities of SDN, NFV, and NS. Decision Tree (DT), Support Vector Machine (SVM), k-Nearest Neighbors (k-NN) and Random Forest (RF) are promising approaches to address specific objectives and challenges within the networking paradigm. The supervised learning method and its application in context of modern technologies are summarized in Table 1.3.

1.4.2 Unsupervised Learning

Unsupervised learning is the method of training a model on an unlabeled dataset. Unsupervised learning can be expressed as: Unlabeled dataset D represented in equation (1.4);

$$\mathbf{D} = \{\mathbf{x}_1, \mathbf{x}_2, \ldots, \mathbf{x}_n\}; \tag{1.4}$$

Where x_n represents the input patterns. The unlabeled dataset algorithm is intended to uncover hidden patterns and relationships within the data to identify hidden patterns in the dataset or group the elements of the dataset. This approach is commonly used for clustering and dimension reduction.

In the context of networking, it is manually utilized for identifying irregular traffic patterns to indicate potential security threads. It is also applicable to traffic analysis and data compression. Unsupervised algorithms play an important role in fulfilling the diverse objectives of modern networking. Clustering algorithms, such as K-mean, are applicable for identifying anomalies in SDN. In NFV, it is helpful in grouping VNF instances, and NS is applied to group traffic of a homogeneous nature. Dimensionality reduction approaches such as PCA help in identifying key parameters within SDN, NFV, and NS. The unsupervised learning method and its application in context of SDN, NFV, and NS are summarized in the Table 1.4.

1.4.3 Reinforcement Learning

Reinforcement Learning is the method of learning an intelligent agent through an iterative process by interacting with its environment.

In the process of learning, agents take action to achieve specific goals, and according to the outcome of their actions, they receive feedback in the form of rewards and penalties. The agent makes the decision to maximize

Table 1.4 Unsupervised learning algorithm for achieving the NexGen objective.

Technology	Unsupervised learning algorithms	Use case	References
SDN	Clustering (e.g., K-Means)	Controller placement, resource optimization	[62, 63]
	PCA	Dimensionality Reduction,	[65]
	Auto encoders	Anomaly Detection,	[66, 67]
	Density-Based Clustering (e.g., DBSCAN)	Dense region and network hotspot detection	[68]
NFV	Clustering (e.g., K-Means)	Traffic clustering	[69]
	PCA	Complexity reduction in NFV	[70]
	PCA	Traffic classification and provisioning	[71]
	Auto encoders	Efficient network slice management	[72]

commutative reward. One common representation of reinforcement learning (Q-learning) is expressed as in equation (1.5);

$$\mathbf{Q\ (s,a) \leftarrow Q(s,a) + \alpha \cdot [\ R\ (s,a) + \gamma \cdot maxa\ Q\ (s',a) - Q\ (s,a)];} \quad (1.5)$$

where Q(s,a) is the Q-value in state "s" for taking action "a" within the network. Learning rate (α) represents how quickly the network adopts the new information; R (s,a) represents the immediate rewards of action "a." The discount factor (γ) is the balance factor between intermediate rewards and further consideration. Max_a Q(s',a) denotes the maximum Q-value for the next state s'.

In the context of networking, optimal routing, resource allocation, and other dynamic processes require systems to adopt and learn from experience in the real-time networking environment. It helps to improve network performance and efficiency in response to dynamic network

Table 1.5 Reinforcement learning algorithm for achieving the NexGen objective.

Technology	Reinforcement learning algorithms	Use case	References
SDN	Q-Learning	Adaptive routing optimization, load balancing	[72, 73]
	Deep Q Network (DQN)	Dynamic traffic prediction, adoptive network control and policy optimization	[74, 75]
	Policy Gradient Methods	Dynamic routing	[77]
	Actor-Critic Methods	Adoptive network control, policy optimization and traffic engineering	[78, 79]
NFV	Q-Learning	Resource optimization, adoptive SFC	[80, 81]
	Deep Q Network (DQN)	Adoptive SFC	[82]
	Actor-Critic Methods	SFC, zero-touch networking	[83, 84]
NS	Q-Learning	Dynamic resource allocation	[85]
	Deep Q Network (DQN)	Service chaining and customized QoS-driven network orchestration	[86, 87]
	Actor-Critic Methods	Dynamic resource allocation	[82]

conditions. Reinforcement learning plays a significant role in facilitating adoptive and dynamic decision-making capabilities. Q-learning is employed to enhance adoptive routing optimization, network optimization, and traffic engineering in an SDN environment. For NFV, it facilitates the optimization and management of the NFV life cycle. In the context of network services, it plays a crucial role in achieving QoS-aware customization and E2E service provisioning. The reinforcement learning method and its application in context of modern paradigms are summarized in Table 1.5.

1.4.4 Deep Learning

Deep learning is considered a specialized ML model with multiple layers Deep Neural Network (DNN) to solve complex problems with large datasets. Deep learning can be expressed as a labeled dataset D, represented in equation (1.6);

$$\mathbf{D = \{(x_1 , y_1),(x_2, y_2),\ldots,(x_n, y_n)\};} \tag{1.6}$$

where x_n and y_n represent the input feature and the corresponding output label, respectively. In the context of networking, the input feature could be device information or input traffic data, and the corresponding output label could be a classification or network event. While learning, multiple layers and their parameters are adjusted iteratively to minimize a defined loss function in equation (1.7);

$$\mathbf{L: (f(x), y);} \tag{1.7}$$

Deep learning in networking represents a powerful tool for intelligent network automation. The traditional method may struggle to deal with manual feature engineering. Deep learning methods such as Convolutional Neural Networks (CNN), Long Short-Term Memory (LSTM), and Recurrent Neural Networks (RNN) are well known for their excellent performance in image pattern recognition. In the context of networking, these technologies also offer advanced capabilities for traffic pattern recognition, anomaly detection, predictive analysis, and intelligent resource management. The reinforcement learning method and its application in context of modern technologies are summarized in Table 1.6.

Table 1.6 A Deep learning algorithm for achieving the NexGen objective.

Technology	Deep learning algorithms	Use case	Reference
SDN	CNN	Anomaly detection and traffic pattern classification	[87, 88]
	RNN	Time-series data analysis and traffic prediction	[89, 90]
	LSTM	Anomaly detection based on temporal patterns, routing optimization and traffic prediction	[91, 92]
	GAN	Traffic generation and Anomaly testing	[93, 94]
NFV	CNN	VNFs deployment service function chaining and Predictive VNF Auto-scaling	[95, 96]
	RNN	Predictive analysis, dynamic scaling and life cycle management	[97, 98]
	LSTM	Temporal dynamics analysis for VNF scaling and life cycle management	[99]
	GAN	Synthetic data generation for NFV testing and training	[100, 101]

(*Continued*)

Table 1.6 A deep learning algorithm for achieving the NexGen objective. (*Continued*)

Technology	Deep learning algorithms	Use case	Reference
NS	CNN	Image-based QoS provisioning in network slices	[102]
	RNN	Dynamic QoS prediction based on temporal dependencies, predictive maintenance based on historical data	[103]
	LSTM	Dynamic resource allocation for slices based on historical data and E2E service provisioning	[104]
	GAN	Synthetic data creation for network slice testing and analysis	[105]

In summary, AI-driven approaches, including ML and DL based methods, play a significant role in shaping intelligent and automated modern networking.

1.5 Navigating Challenges and Solutions

In this section, identify the specific challenges and research solutions arising from implementing 5G systems.

1.5.1 Performance Issues in Network Structure

Performance isolation in a network structure deployed over a common underlying infrastructure can be a challenging task. When multiple network slices or services share the same physical infrastructure, ensuring that each slice meets its performance requirements without interfering with others is a complex endeavor [106, 107]. Performance issues in a network structure can arise from various factors, and addressing them is crucial for ensuring the efficient operation of the network. Some common performance issues in network structures include bandwidth limitations, network congestion, latency, packet loss, network security measures, outdated hardware, inefficient routing, network protocol issues, network topology limitations, monitoring, and analysis. Regular network assessments, proactive monitoring, and a strategic approach to network design and optimization are essential for mitigating and preventing performance issues in a network structure.

1.5.2 Management and Orchestration Issues

Management and Orchestration (MANO) in the context of network virtualization and cloud computing involve the coordination of various resources and services to ensure efficient and reliable network operations [108]. However, several challenges and issues can arise in the process. There are some key management and orchestration issues, such as interoperability, integration with legacy systems, scalability, orchestration complexity, security concerns, resource Optimization, lifecycle management, multi-domain orchestration, service assurance, and vendor lock-in [109]. These management and orchestration issues require a holistic approach involving collaboration between industry stakeholders and the fulfillment of standards. Moreover, the continuous evolution of MANO technologies to meet the demands of dynamic and complex network environments.

1.5.3 Security and Privacy

The adoption of open interfaces and programmability in softwarized networks indeed introduces new potential attack vectors that need to be addressed with a robust security framework. The multi-level security framework mentioned should encompass various aspects to ensure the integrity, confidentiality, and availability of the network [110]. The security and privacy concerns arising from 5G-network infrastructure are the major barrier to adopting multi-tenancy approaches [111].

A comprehensive and adaptive security framework is crucial for mitigating the evolving security challenges introduced by programmable networks and 5G slicing. Regular updates to security measures, threat intelligence integration, and collaboration with the broader security community are essential for maintaining the resilience of softwarized networks in the face of emerging threats.

1.5.4 New Business Models

The embodiment of new technologies and evolving market demands often leads to the emergence of innovative business models [112]. In the context of networking and technology, several new business models have gained

Table 1.7 Challenges and its solutions.

Challenges	Solutions
Integration Complexity	- Implement standardized interfaces and protocols.
	- Ensure seamless interoperability among SDN, NFV, NS, and AI.
Security Concerns in AI Integration	- Strengthen cybersecurity measures.
	- Utilize AI-driven threat detection for enhanced security.
Scalability in NS	- Implement dynamic resource allocation algorithms.
	- Leverage edge computing for optimal performance in high-demand scenarios.
Operational Complexity in NFV	- Deploy intelligent orchestration and automation tools.
	- Simplify management processes for virtualized functions.
Evolving Regulatory Landscape	- Proactively collaborate with regulatory bodies.
	- Stay informed about industry standards to ensure compliance.
AI Bias and Ethical Concerns	- Implement ethical AI frameworks.
	- Ensure transparent decision-making processes and continuous bias monitoring.
User Education and Adoption	- Conduct comprehensive educational programs.
	- Design user-friendly interfaces and communicate transparently.

importance, such as Platform as a Service (PaaS) models, blockchain-powered networking models, Network as a Service (NaaS) models, and so on. These new business models often disrupt traditional industries, drive innovation, and provide opportunities for companies to create unique value propositions for their customers.

The field of next-generation network architecture is filled with advancements like SDN, NFV, NS, and AI convergence, but it also presents a variety of problems as we set out on this magnificent path. To guarantee the smooth integration and maximum performance of innovations, it demands the intervention of industry stakeholders and researchers to address those challenges. Table 1.7 offers an organized summary of the problems with the next-generation design of networks, along with the solutions that are meant to solve each problem.

1.6 Conclusion

This chapter provides a concise overview of the evolutionary history of network technologies and the key phases that shaped the modern networking landscape. We further explored the pivotal role and architectural framework of key NexGen technologies (SDN, NFV, and NS). Collectively, these paradigms allow networks to adopt automation, flexibility, scalability, and optimization in dynamic network environments. It also highlighted the influence and interconnected role of SDN, NFV, NS, and AI. Additionally, we explored AI-driven network management and the comparative analysis of ML and DL approaches for achieving these key-networking objectives.

In a nutshell, this chapter will offer researchers, industry stakeholders, and practitioners a timely and deeper understanding of transformative technology and its impact on the modern network paradigm.

Disclosure Statement

No potential conflict of interest was reported by the authors.

References

1. Mishra, A.R., *Fundamentals of Network Planning and Optimisation 2G/3G/4G: Evolution to 5G*, John Wiley & Sons, India, 2018.
2. Al-Falahy, N. and Alani, O.Y., Technologies for 5G networks: Challenges and opportunities. *IT Prof.*, 19, 1, 12–20, 2017.

3. Singh, A.K. and Srivastava, S., A survey and classification of controller placement problem in SDN. *Int. J. Netw. Manage.*, 28, 3, e2018, 2018.
4. Hawilo, H., Shami, A., Mirahmadi, M., Asal, R., NFV: state of the art, challenges, and implementation in next generation mobile networks (vEPC). *IEEE Netw.*, 28, 6, 18–26, 2014.
5. Alliance, N.G.M.N., Description of network slicing concept, vol. 1, pp. 1–11, NGMN 5G P, Germany, 2016.
6. Escolar, A.M., Alcaraz-Calero, J.M., Salva-Garcia, P., Bernabe, J.B., Wang, Q., Adaptive network slicing in multi-tenant 5G IoT networks. *IEEE Access*, 9, 14048–14069, 2021.
7. Roberts, L., The Arpanet and computer networks, in: *A history of personal workstations*, pp. 141–172, 1988.
8. Bay, M., Hot potatoes and postmen: how packet switching became ARPANET's greatest legacy. *Internet Hist.*, 3, 1, 15–30, 2019.
9. Britton, E.G., Tavs, J., Bournas, R., TCP/IP: The next generation. *IBM Syst. J.*, 34, 3, 452–471, 1995.
10. Sinha, A., Client-server computing. *Commun. ACM*, 35, 7, 77–98, 1992.
11. Chávez-Santiago, R., Szydełko, M., Kliks, A., Foukalas, F., Haddad, Y., Nolan, K.E., Balasingham, I., 5G: The convergence of wireless communications. *Wireless Pers. Commun.*, 83, 1617–1642, 2015.
12. Siddiqui, F. and Zeadally, S., Mobility management across hybrid wireless networks: Trends and challenges. *Comput. Commun.*, 29, 9, 1363–1385, 2006.
13. Kilari, N., Cloud Computing-An Overview & Evolution. 3, 1, 149–152, 2018.
14. Alam, I., Sharif, K., Li, F., Latif, Z., Karim, M.M., Biswas, S., Wang, Y., A survey of network virtualization techniques for Internet of Things using SDN and NFV. *ACM Comput. Surv. (CSUR)*, 53, 2, 1–40, 2020.
15. Benzekki, K., El Fergougui, A., Elbelrhiti Elalaoui, A., Software-defined networking (SDN): a survey. *Secur. Commun. Netw.*, 9, 18, 5803–5833, 2016.
16. Bannour, F., Souihi, S., Mellouk, A., Distributed SDN control: Survey, taxonomy, and challenges. *IEEE Commun. Surv. Tutorials*, 20, 1, 333–354, 2017.
17. Open Networking Foundation, SDN definition, 2022. https://opennetworking.org/sdn-definition/.
18. Phemius, K., Bouet, M., Leguay, J., Disco: Distributed multi-domain sdn controllers, in: *2014 IEEE network operations and management symposium (NOMS)*, IEEE, pp. 1–4, 2014.
19. Gadre, A., Anbiah, A., Sivalingam, K.M., Centralized approaches for virtual network function placement in SDN-enabled networks. *EURASIP J. Wirel. Commun. Netw.*, 2018, 1, 1–19, 2018.
20. Salman, O., Elhajj, I.H., Chehab, A., Kayssi, A., QoS guarantee over hybrid SDN/non-SDN networks. *2017 8th International Conference on the Network of the Future (NOF)*, IEEE, pp. 141–143, 2017.

21. Belzarena, P., Sena, G.G., Amigo, I., Vaton, S., SDN-based overlay networks for QoS-aware routing, in: *Proceedings of the 2016 workshop on Fostering Latin-American Research in Data Communication Networks*, pp. 19–21, 2016.
22. Azodolmolky, S., Wieder, P., Yahyapour, R., SDN-based cloud computing networking, in: *2013 15th international conference on transparent optical networks (ICTON)*, IEEE, pp. 1–4, 2013.
23. Saha, B.K., Tandur, D., Haab, L., Podleski, L., Intent-based networks: An industrial perspective, in: *Proceedings of the 1st International Workshop on Future Industrial Communication Networks*, pp. 35–40, 2018.
24. NFV, N.F.V. and Practises, P.B., ETSI GS NFV-PER 001 V1. 1.2 (2014-12), ETSI, France, 2014.
25. Taleb, T., Samdanis, K., Mada, B., Flinck, H., Dutta, S., Sabella, D., On multi-access edge computing: A survey of the emerging 5G network edge cloud architecture and orchestration. *IEEE Commun. Surv. Tutorials*, 19, 3, 1657–1681, 2017.
26. Zhang, S., An overview of network slicing for 5G. *IEEE Wireless Commun.*, 26, 3, 111–117, 2019.
27. 3GPP, *Study on management and orchestration of network slicing for next generation network. 3GPP TR 28.801 v15.1.0*, 3GPP, France, 2018.
28. Khan, L.U., Yaqoob, I., Tran, N.H., Han, Z., Hong, C.S., Network slicing: Recent advances, taxonomy, requirements, and open research challenges. *IEEE Access*, 8, 36009–36028, 2020.
29. An, X., Zhou, C., Trivisonno, R., Guerzoni, R., Kaloxylos, A., Soldani, D., Hecker, A., On end to end network slicing for 5G communication systems. *Trans. Emerging Telecommun. Technol.*, 28, 4, e3058, 2017.
30. Li, X., Ni, R., Chen, J., Lyu, Y., Rong, Z., Du, R., End-to-end network slicing in radio access network, transport network and core network domains. *IEEE Access*, 8, 29525–29537, 2020.
31. https://www.ericsson.com/en/network-slicing
32. Zhou, F., Yu, P., Feng, L., Qiu, X., Wang, Z., Meng, L., Yao, X., Automatic network slicing for IoT in smart city. *IEEE Wireless Commun.*, 27, 6, 108–115, 2020.
33. Walia, J.S., Hämmäinen, H., Kilkki, K., Yrjölä, S., 5G network slicing strategies for a smart factory. *Comput. Ind.*, 111, 108–120, 2019.
34. Dubey, M. and Mishra, R., 5G in Healthcare: Revolutionary Use-cases and QoS Provisioning Powered by Network Slicing. *Intelligent Systems and Smart Infrastructure: Proceedings of ICISSI 2022*, p. 96, 2023.
35. Campolo, C., Molinaro, A., Iera, A., Menichella, F., 5G network slicing for vehicle-to-everything services. *IEEE Wireless Commun.*, 24, 6, 38–45, 2017.
36. Popovski, P., Trillingsgaard, K.F., Simeone, O., Durisi, G., 5G wireless network slicing for eMBB, URLLC, and mMTC: A communication-theoretic view. *IEEE Access*, 6, 55765–55779, 2018.
37. Series, M., Minimum requirements related to technical performance for IMT-2020 radio interface(s). *Report*, 2410, 2410-2017, International Telecommunication Union, Geneva, 2017.

38. Bonfim, M.S., Dias, K.L., Fernandes, S.F., Integrated NFV/SDN architectures: A systematic literature review. *ACM Comput. Surv. (CSUR)*, 51, 6, 1–39, 2019.
39. Ordonez-Lucena, J., Ameigeiras, P., Lopez, D., Ramos-Munoz, J.J., Lorca, J., Folgueira, J., Network slicing for 5G with SDN/NFV: Concepts, architectures, and challenges. *IEEE Commun. Mag.*, 55, 5, 80–87, 2017.
40. Zhang, C., Ueng, Y.L., Studer, C., Burg, A., Artificial intelligence for 5G and beyond 5G: Implementations, algorithms, and optimizations. *IEEE J. Emerging Sel. Top. Circuits Syst.*, 10, 2, 149–163, 2020.
41. Barakabitze, A.A., Ahmad, A., Mijumbi, R., Hines, A., 5G network slicing using SDN and NFV: A survey of taxonomy, architectures and future challenges. *Comput. Networks*, 167, 106984, 2020.
42. Amin, R., Rojas, E., Aqdus, A., Ramzan, S., Casillas-Perez, D., Arco, J.M., A survey on machine learning techniques for routing optimization in SDN. *IEEE Access*, 9, 104582–104611, 2021.
43. Herrera, J.G. and Botero, J.F., Resource allocation in NFV: A comprehensive survey. *IEEE Trans. Netw. Serv. Manage.*, 13, 3, 518–532, 2016.
44. Debbabi, F., Jmal, R., Chaari Fourati, L., 5G network slicing: Fundamental concepts, architectures, algorithmics, projects practices, and open issues. *Concurr. Comput. Pract. Exp.*, 33, 20, e6352, 2021.
45. Morocho-Cayamcela, M.E., Lee, H., Lim, W., Machine learning for 5G/B5G mobile and wireless communications: Potential, limitations, and future directions. *IEEE Access*, 7, 137184–137206, 2019.
46. Bastam, M., Sabaei, M., Yousefpour, R., A scalable traffic engineering technique in an SDN-based data center network. *Trans. Emerging Telecommun. Technol.*, 29, 2, e3268, 2018.
47. Chen, Y., Pei, J., Li, D., Detpro: A high-efficiency and low-latency system against ddos attacks in sdn based on decision tree, in: *ICC 2019-2019 IEEE International Conference on Communications (ICC)*, IEEE, pp. 1–6, May 2019.
48. Raikar, M.M., Meena, S.M., Mulla, M.M., Shetti, N.S., Karanandi, M., Data traffic classification in software defined networks (SDN) using supervised-learning. *Procedia Comput. Sci.*, 171, 2750–2759, 2020.
49. da Silva, A.S., Wickboldt, J.A., Granville, L.Z., Schaeffer-Filho, A., ATLANTIC: A framework for anomaly traffic detection, classification, and mitigation in SDN, in: *NOMS 2016-2016 IEEE/IFIP Network Operations and Management Symposium*, IEEE, pp. 27–35, April 2016.
50. Afuwape, A.A., Xu, Y., Anajemba, J.H., Srivastava, G., Performance evaluation of secured network traffic classification using a machine learning approach. *Comput. Stand. Interfaces*, 78, 103545, 2021.
51. Zhai, Y. and Zheng, X., Random forest based traffic classification method in SDN, in: *2018 international conference on cloud computing, big data and blockchain (ICCBB)*, IEEE, pp. 1–5, November 2018.

52. Zerbini, C.B., Carvalho, L.F., Abrão, T., Proenca Jr., M.L., Wavelet against random forest for anomaly mitigation in software-defined networking. *Appl. Soft Comput.*, 80, 138–153, 2019.
53. Nanda, W.D. and Sumadi, F.D.S., LRDDoS attack detection on SD-IoT using random forest with logistic regression coefficient. *Jurnal RESTI (Rekayasa Sistem dan Teknologi Informasi)*, 6, 2, 220–226, 2022.
54. Azmi, M.M. and Sumadi, F.D.S., Low-Rate Attack Detection on SD-IoT Using SVM Combined with Feature Importance Logistic Regression Coefficient. *Kinetik*, 7, 2, 121–128, 2022.
55. Katsikas, G.P., Enguehard, M., Kuźniar, M., Maguire Jr., G.Q., Kostić, D., SNF: Synthesizing high performance NFV service chains. *PeerJ Comput. Sci.*, 2, e98, 2016.
56. Schneider, S., Satheeschandran, N.P., Peuster, M., Karl, H., Machine learning for dynamic resource allocation in network function virtualization, in: *2020 6th IEEE Conference on Network Softwarization (NetSoft)*, IEEE, pp. 122–130, 2020.
57. Elmajed, A. and Faucheux, F., Comparing feature extraction techniques using SVM for early fault classification in NFV context, in: *2021 24th Conference on Innovation in Clouds, Internet and Networks and Workshops (ICIN)*, IEEE, pp. 57–61, 2021.
58. CHASSOT, C., *On QoS Management in NFV-enabled IoT Platforms*, Doctoral dissertation, Institut National des Sciences Appliquées de Toulouse, 2021.
59. de Oliveira, G.W., Nogueira, M., dos Santos, A.L., Batista, D.M., Intelligent VNF Placement to Mitigate DDoS Attacks on Industrial IoT. *IEEE Trans. Netw. Serv. Manage.*, 2, 1319–1331, 2023.
60. Latif, O.A., Amer, M., Kwasinski, A., Classification of Network Slicing Requests Using Support Vector Machine, in: *2022 International Conference on Electrical and Computing Technologies and Applications (ICECTA)*, IEEE, pp. 279–282, 2022.
61. Yan, D., Yang, X., Cuthbert, L., Regression-based k nearest neighbours for resource allocation in network slicing, in: *2022 Wireless Telecommunications Symposium (WTS)*, IEEE, pp. 1–6, 2022.
62. Sarbazi, M., Sadeghzadeh, M., Mir Abedini, S.J., Improving resource allocation in software-defined networks using clustering. *Cluster Comput.*, 23, 1199–1210, 2020.
63. Kuang, H., Qiu, Y., Li, R., Liu, X., A hierarchical K-means algorithm for controller placement in SDN-based WAN architecture, in: *2018 10th international conference on measuring technology and mechatronics automation (ICMTMA)*, IEEE, pp. 263–267, February 2018.
64. Setitra, M.A., Benkhaddra, I., Bensalem, Z.E.A., Fan, M., Feature Modeling and Dimensionality Reduction to Improve ML-Based DDOS Detection Systems in SDN Environment, in: *2022 19th International Computer Conference on Wavelet Active Media Technology and Information Processing (ICCWAMTIP)*, IEEE, pp. 1–7, December 2022.

65. Yang, L., Song, Y., Gao, S., Xiao, B., Hu, A., Griffin: an ensemble of autoencoders for anomaly traffic detection in SDN, in: *GLOBECOM 2020-2020 IEEE Global Communications Conference*, IEEE, pp. 1–6, 2020.
66. Yang, L., Song, Y., Gao, S., Hu, A., Xiao, B., Griffin: Real-time network intrusion detection system via ensemble of autoencoder in SDN. *IEEE Trans. Netw. Serv. Manage.*, 19, 3, 2269–2281, 2022.
67. Liu, R. and Erol-Kantarci, M., Dynamic Routing with Online Traffic Estimation for Video Streaming over Software Defined Networks, in: *2020 IEEE Symposium on Computers and Communications (ISCC)*, IEEE, pp. 1–6, July 2020.
68. Le, L.V., Sinh, D., Lin, B.S.P., Tung, L.P., Applying big data, machine learning, and SDN/NFV to 5G traffic clustering, forecasting, and management, in: *2018 4th IEEE Conference on Network Softwarization and Workshops (NetSoft)*, IEEE, pp. 168–176, 2018.
69. Gamal, G., Al-Shaikh, M., Saeed, M.A., Hazza'a, A.G., Alomary, A., Alshehabi, R., Evaluating the Performance of Machine Learning Models for Dynamic Resource Allocation in NFV, in: *2023 3rd International Conference on Emerging Smart Technologies and Applications (eSmarTA)*, IEEE, pp. 01–09, October 2023.
70. Min, Z., Gokhale, S., Shekhar, S., Mahmoudi, C., Kang, Z., Barve, Y., Gokhale, A., A Classification Framework for IoT Network Traffic Data for Provisioning 5G Network Slices in Smart Computing Applications, in: *2023 IEEE International Conference on Smart Computing (SMARTCOMP)*, IEEE, pp. 133–140, June 2023.
71. Rago, A., Martiradonna, S., Piro, G., Abrardo, A., Boggia, G., A tenant-driven slicing enforcement scheme based on Pervasive Intelligence in the Radio Access Network. *Comput. Netw.*, 217, 109285, 2022.
72. Fu, Q., Sun, E., Meng, K., Li, M., Zhang, Y., Deep Q-learning for routing schemes in SDN-based data center networks. *IEEE Access*, 8, 103491–103499, 2020.
73. Tosounidis, V., Pavlidis, G., Sakellariou, I., Deep Q-learning for load balancing traffic in SDN networks, in: *11th Hellenic Conference on Artificial Intelligence*, pp. 135–143, September 2020.
74. Nguyen, T.G., Phan, T.V., Hoang, D.T., Nguyen, T.N., So-In, C., Efficient SDN-based traffic monitoring in IoT networks with double deep Q-network, in: *International conference on computational data and social networks*, Springer International Publishing, Cham, pp. 26–38, December 2020.
75. Bouzidi, E.H., Outtagarts, A., Langar, R., Boutaba, R., Deep Q-Network and traffic prediction based routing optimization in software defined networks. *J. Netw. Comput. Appl.*, 192, 103181, 2021.
76. Chen, J., Xiao, Z., Xing, H., Dai, P., Luo, S., Iqbal, M.A., STDPG: A spatio-temporal deterministic policy gradient agent for dynamic routing in SDN, in: *ICC 2020-2020 IEEE International Conference on Communications (ICC)*, IEEE, pp. 1–6, June 2020.

77. Rezazadeh, F., Chergui, H., Christofi, L., Verikoukis, C., Actor-critic-based learning for zero-touch joint resource and energy control in network slicing, in: *ICC 2021-IEEE International Conference on Communications*, IEEE, pp. 1–6, June 2021.
78. Xu, Z., Yang, D., Tang, J., Tang, Y., Yuan, T., Wang, Y., Xue, G., An actor-critic-based transfer learning framework for experience-driven networking. *IEEE/ACM Trans. Networking*, 29, 1, 360–371, 2020.
79. Chen, J., Chen, J., Hu, R., Zhang, H., QMORA: A Q-learning based multi-objective resource allocation scheme for NFV orchestration, in: *2020 IEEE 91st Vehicular Technology Conference (VTC2020-Spring)*, IEEE, pp. 1–6, May 2020.
80. Lee, D., Yoo, J.H., Hong, J.W.K., Q-learning based service function chaining using VNF resource-aware reward model, in: *2020 21st Asia-Pacific Network Operations and Management Symposium (APNOMS)*, IEEE, pp. 279–282, September 2020.
81. Lee, D., Yoo, J.H., Hong, J.W.K., Deep q-networks based auto-scaling for service function chaining, in: *2020 16th International Conference on Network and Service Management (CNSM)*, IEEE, pp. 1–9, November 2020.
82. Rezazadeh, F., Chergui, H., Verikoukis, C., Zero-touch continuous network slicing control via scalable actor-critic learning, 2021, arXiv preprint arXiv:2101.06654.
83. Wang, R., Li, J., Wang, K., Liu, X., Lit, X., Service function chaining in NFV-enabled edge networks with natural actor-critic deep reinforcement learning, in: *2021 IEEE/CIC International Conference on Communications in China (ICCC)*, IEEE, pp. 1095–1100, July 2021.
84. Kim, Y., Kim, S., Lim, H., Reinforcement learning based resource management for network slicing. *Appl. Sci.*, 9, 11, 2361, 2019.
85. Chen, X., Li, Z., Zhang, Y., Long, R., Yu, H., Du, X., Guizani, M., Reinforcement learning–based QoS/QoE-aware service function chaining in software-driven 5G slices. *Trans. Emerging Telecommun. Technol.*, 29, 11, e3477, 2018.
86. Cui, Y., Huang, X., He, P., Wu, D., Wang, R., QoS guaranteed network-slicing orchestration for Internet of Vehicles. *IEEE Internet Things J.*, 9, 16, 15215–15227, 2022.
87. Xue, H. and Jing, B., SDN Attack Identification Model based on CNN Algorithm. *IEEE Access*, 11, 87652–87666, 2023.
88. Wang, P., Ye, F., Chen, X., Qian, Y., Datanet: Deep learning based encrypted network traffic classification in sdn home gateway. *IEEE Access*, 6, 55380–55391, 2018.
89. Azzouni, A. and Pujolle, G., NeuTM: A neural network-based framework for traffic matrix prediction in SDN, in: *NOMS 2018-2018 IEEE/IFIP Network Operations and Management Symposium*, IEEE, pp. 1–5, 2018.

90. Bhatia, J., Dave, R., Bhayani, H., Tanwar, S., Nayyar, A., SDN-based real-time urban traffic analysis in VANET environment. *Comput. Commun.*, 149, 162–175, 2020.
91. Said Elsayed, M., Le-Khac, N.A., Dev, S., Jurcut, A.D., Network anomaly detection using LSTM based autoencoder, in: *Proceedings of the 16th ACM Symposium on QoS and Security for Wireless and Mobile Networks*, pp. 37–45, 2020.
92. Hoang, N.T., Tong, V., Tran, H.A., Duong, C.S., Nguyen, T.L.T., LSTM-BASED SERVER AND ROUTE SELECTION IN DISTRIBUTED AND HETEROGENEOUS SDN NETWORK. *J. Comput. Sci. Cybern.*, 39, 1, 79–99, 2023.
93. AlEroud, A. and Karabatis, G., Sdn-gan: generative adversarial deep nns for synthesizing cyber attacks on software defined networks, in: *On the Move to Meaningful Internet Systems: OTM 2019 Workshops: Confederated International Workshops: EI2N, FBM, ICSP, Meta4eS and SIAnA 2019*, Rhodes, Greece, October 21–25, 2019, Springer International Publishing, pp. 211–220, p. Revised Selected Papers, 2020.
94. Wang, P., Wang, Z., Ye, F., Chen, X., Bytesgan: A semi-supervised generative adversarial network forencrypted traffic classification in SDN edge gateway. *Comput. Networks*, 200, 108535, 2021.
95. Subramanya, T. and Riggio, R., Centralized and federated learning for predictive VNF autoscaling in multi-domain 5G networks and beyond. *IEEE Trans. Netw. Serv. Manage.*, 18, 1, 63–78, 2021.
96. Emu, M., Artificial intelligence empowered virtual network function deployment and service function chaining for next-generation networks. Doctoral dissertation, Canada, 2021.
97. Li, Z., Ge, Z., Mahimkar, A., Wang, J., Zhao, B.Y., Zheng, H., Ogden, L., Predictive analysis in network function virtualization, in: *Proceedings of the Internet Measurement Conference 2018*, pp. 161–167, October 2018.
98. Lange, S., Van Tu, N., Jeong, S.Y., Lee, D.Y., Kim, H.G., Hong, J., Hong, J.W.K., A network intelligence architecture for efficient vnf lifecycle management. *IEEE Trans. Netw. Serv. Manage.*, 18, 2, 1476–1490, 2020.
99. Eramo, V. and Catena, T., Application of an innovative convolutional/LSTM neural network for computing resource allocation in NFV network architectures. *IEEE Trans. Netw. Serv. Manage.*, 19, 3, 2929–2943, 2022.
100. Khan, T.A., Abbas, K., Muhammad, A., Rafiq, A., Song, W.C., GAN and DRL based intent translation and deep fake configuration generation for optimization, in: *2020 International Conference on Information and Communication Technology Convergence (ICTC)*, IEEE, pp. 347–352, 2020.
101. Verma, R. and Sivalingam, K.M., Federated Learning approach for Autoscaling of Virtual Network Function resource allocation in 5G-and-Beyond Networks, in: *2022 IEEE 11th International Conference on Cloud Networking (CloudNet)*, IEEE, pp. 242–246, November 2022.

102. Soud, N.S., Al-Jamali, N.A.S., Al-Raweshidy, H.S., Moderately Multispike Return Neural Network for SDN Accurate Traffic Awareness in Effective 5G Network Slicing. *IEEE Access*, 10, 73378–73387, 2022.
103. Zou, G., Li, T., Jiang, M., Hu, S., Cao, C., Zhang, B., Chen, Y., DeepTSQP: Temporal-aware service QoS prediction via deep neural network and feature integration. *Knowl.-Based Syst.*, 241, 108062, 2022.
104. Abood, M.S., Wang, H., He, D., Fathy, M., Rashid, S.A., Alibakhshikenari, M., Elwi, T.A., An LSTM-based network slicing classification future predictive framework for optimized resource allocation in C-V2X. *IEEE Access*, 11, 129300–129310, 2023.
105. Hua, Y., Li, R., Zhao, Z., Chen, X., Zhang, H., GAN-powered deep distributional reinforcement learning for resource management in network slicing. *IEEE J. Sel. Areas Commun.*, 38, 2, 334–349, 2019.
106. Gonzalez, A.J., Ordonez-Lucena, J., Helvik, B.E., Nencioni, G., Xie, M., Lopez, D.R., Grønsund, P., The isolation concept in the 5G network slicing, in: *2020 European Conference on Networks and Communications (EuCNC)*, IEEE, pp. 12–16, June 2020.
107. Huin, N., Medagliani, P., Martin, S., Leguay, J., Shi, L., Cai, S., Shi, H., Hard-isolation for network slicing, in: *IEEE INFOCOM 2019-IEEE Conference on Computer Communications Workshops (INFOCOM WKSHPS)*, IEEE, pp. 955–956, 2019.
108. Mijumbi, R., Serrat, J., Gorricho, J.L., Latre, S., Charalambides, M., Lopez, D., Management and orchestration challenges in network functions virtualization. *IEEE Commun. Mag.*, 54, 1, 98–105, 2016.
109. Guerzoni, R., Perez-Caparros, D., Monti, P., Giuliani, G., Melian, J., Biczók, G., *Multi-domain orchestration and management of software defined infrastructures: A bottom-up approach*, 2016.
110. Salahdine, F., Liu, Q., Han, T., Towards secure and intelligent network slicing for 5g networks. *IEEE Open J. Comput. Soc.*, 3, 23–38, 2022.
111. NetWorld2020, E. T. P., 5g: Challenges, research priorities, and recommendations. Joint White Paper September, 2014.
112. Kukliński, S., Tomaszewski, L., Kozłowski, K., Pietrzyk, S., Business models of network slicing, in: *2018 9th International Conference on the Network of the Future (NOF)*, IEEE, pp. 39–43, 2018.

2

OctoEdge: An Octopus-Inspired Adaptive Edge Computing Architecture

Sashi Tarun

Akal College of Engineering & Technology, CSE, Eternal University Baru Sahib, Himachal Pradesh, India

Abstract

Edge computing is the technique of processing data closer to the point of generation rather than relying on a centralized cloud server. It has gained popularity due to its ability to reduce latency, improve real-time processing, and increase overall system efficiency. The current design is crucial in edge computing, at least in terms of maximizing resource use when requests are many and distracting from fulfilling performance objectives. This chapter introduces OctoEdge, a versatile nature-inspired edge computing architecture inspired by octopuses' remarkable adaptability and problem-solving capabilities. OctoEdge is designed to be extremely adaptable, dynamic, and sensitive to changing environmental conditions, making it an ideal option for resource-constrained edge computing scenarios. This architecture's fundamental characteristic is its ability to dynamically adapt to the complexity of edge settings, mimicking the decentralized decision making and effective resource allocation found in octopus behavior. The OctoEdge architecture's unique technique enables real-time adaptation, which optimizes system performance in response to changing conditions and workloads. This study addresses all QoS factors and strengthens the architecture by including all of these capabilities into the octopuses-based nature-inspired edge computing architecture.

Keywords: Adaptability, edge computing architecture, IoT, nature-inspired, OctoEdge

Email: drsashicse@eternaluniversity.edu.in

Mohit Kumar, Gautam Srivastava, Ashutosh Kumar Singh and Kalka Dubey (eds.) AI-Based Advanced Optimization Techniques for Edge Computing, (35–70) © 2025 Scrivener Publishing LLC

2.1 Introduction

In an era where digital transformation is altering industries and pushing the limits of what is possible, edge computing emerges as a revolutionary technology, playing a critical role in the pursuit of distributed performance. This novel approach to data processing marks a significant departure from the typical centralized cloud paradigm, putting computing and analysis closer to the source of data. Edge computing not only meets the pressing demand for reduced latency and faster decision making, but it also rethinks the idea of distributed performance across a wide range of applications and sectors. In today's fast changing technological world, where data are the lifeblood of innovation, speed and reactivity are more important than ever. Edge computing is a new concept that promises to transform the way we process, analyze, and act on data. Edge computing is fundamentally a game changer, and it is critical to obtaining greater performance in the digital era. Traditional cloud computing is transferring data to remote data centers for processing and receiving the results back. While this strategy is effective for many applications, it is not necessarily the most efficient, particularly in terms of bandwidth utilization. Edge computing improves data transport by doing initial processing on the edge and delivering only relevant information to centralized servers. This not only saves network resources but also lowers prices, making it a viable option for enterprises looking for cost-effective solutions.

Edge computing is an endeavour that aims to service requests at or from adjacent data sources without relying on data from a centralized cloud server. Edge computing has emerged as a critical technology in the age of IoT and real-time data processing. It lets data to be processed closer to its source, lowering latency and enabling real-time decision making. However, edge computing settings frequently experience dynamic and unpredictable situations, necessitating designs that can adapt and maximize resource consumption. This chapter introduces OctoEdge, a nature-inspired edge computing architecture modelled after octopuses' flexibility and problem-solving skills.

2.1.1 Edge Computing as Resource Manager

Edge computing has the potential to optimize resource utilization and enhance distributed system performance in a variety of ways. The following are some crucial aspects of edge computing as a resource manager:

1. Edge computing minimizes latency in data transit to centralized data centers by bringing processing power and resources closer to the source. This near proximity ensures simple access to computer resources for data processing, allowing for faster reaction times and immediate decision making.
2. Load balancing: Edge computing systems automatically spread workloads across several edge devices to optimize resource utilization and balance workloads. Load balancing can help prevent overloading certain devices by optimizing resource use.
3. In response to demand, edge computing systems are capable of dynamically allocating computer resources. The system may automatically assign more resources to fulfill demand when certain edge devices or servers encounter heavy workloads, guaranteeing peak performance.
4. Edge devices often rely on batteries or have limited access to power sources. Edge computing contributes to the correct control of resource allocation, ensuring that devices operate smoothly without exhausting their power sources.
5. Edge computing systems can provide redundancy and failover capabilities. In the case of a device or server failure, the system may automatically relocate workloads to available resources, minimizing downtime and ensuring continuous operation.
6. Edge computing enables effective data cache management. Data that are often accessed can be cached locally, avoiding the need to get it from remote data centers. This improvement reduces network load and increases resource efficiency.

Overall, edge computing is critical in tackling the issues of distributed computing while providing real-time processing and low-latency responses in an increasingly linked environment.

2.1.2 Edge Computing Hurdles

The challenges in adopting and implementing edge computing are multifaceted and require careful study. These stumbling barriers are what cause performance degradation in distributed systems. Some of the barriers are:

1. Dispersed edge devices constitute a significant security problem due to their vulnerability to physical and cyber-attacks. Given the diversity of data collected and processed at the edge, ensuring data privacy and regulatory compliance is similarly complicated.
2. As enterprises build their edge computing infrastructure, maintaining and coordinating an increasing number of edge devices and servers becomes challenging.
3. Interoperability concerns develop when devices and systems use various protocols and data formats.
4. Ensuring dependability, especially during network disruptions, and developing strong redundancy mechanisms for continuous operation need careful design.
5. Efficiently managing data synchronization and storage with limited resources on edge devices is a significant challenge.

Furthermore, organizations must address aspects such as integrating edge computing with centralized systems, managing costs wisely, and cultivating a skilled workforce knowledgeable about edge computing technologies in order to successfully navigate the challenges associated with edge computing implementation.

2.1.3 Edge Computing and the Need for Adaptability

Edge computing has evolved as a transformational paradigm, altering how we process and handle data at the network's edges. This change from conventional centralized cloud computing to a distributed, edge-centric paradigm is being pushed by the ever-increasing demand for low latency, real-time processing, and the capacity to manage the vast amount of data created by Internet of Things devices. In this context, flexibility is a fundamental component of edge computing, allowing it to thrive in dynamic and unexpected contexts.

Adaptability in edge computing signifies the system's capacity to flexibly respond to changing conditions, workloads, and requirements. It allows the infrastructure to seamlessly adjust its computational and storage resources based on the real-time demands of the applications it supports. This adaptability benefits computing in two crucial ways: enhancing efficiency and ensuring reliability.Firstly, adaptability optimizes resource utilization. Edge computing environments are inherently heterogeneous, with diverse devices and sensors generating varying workloads. By adapting to these fluctuations, the system allocates resources where and when they are needed most. This dynamic resource allocation not only maximizes performance but also minimizes energy consumption and operational costs. Second, adaptation increases system resilience. Edge computing is frequently used in mission-critical applications, such as driverless vehicles or healthcare monitoring. When flexibility is incorporated into the design, it may automatically redirect jobs, change workloads, or redistribute data processing in the event of hardware failures or network outages. This proactive adaptation guarantees that programs continue to function properly, even in the face of unanticipated problems. The adaptability property of edge computing may be described with an example. The implementation of intelligent video surveillance systems in a smart city context exemplifies edge computing's versatility.

Consider a smart city with a network of surveillance cameras in strategic areas for public safety and traffic monitoring. Initially, these cameras provide minimal object detection and alerting features. However, as the city's demands and technology change, there is a rising desire for more complex analytics, such as facial recognition for increased security or real-time traffic flow monitoring for better transportation management. In this case, an adaptive edge computing infrastructure enables the smart city to improve the capabilities of its security cameras without having to replace the hardware. New edge servers or processing units may be effortlessly integrated into the current network, outfitted with the most recent AI and machine learning models for facial recognition or traffic analysis. The edge infrastructure's versatility allows the city to respond to changing requirements and embrace new technologies, improving security and traffic control without substantial interruptions or costly hardware changes. Edge computing's flexibility and agility enable enterprises and municipalities to remain ahead of technology breakthroughs and satisfy changing demands without requiring significant overhauls of their current infrastructure.

2.2 Problem Statement

The computer environment has shifted dramatically with the rise of smart cities, edge device proliferation, and the Internet of Things. As a distributed paradigm, edge computing has the ability to minimize latency, evaluate data closer to its source, and enable real-time decision making. This transformation opens up new prospects and capabilities for a wide range of industries, including manufacturing, healthcare, autonomous cars, and augmented reality. However, resource allocation has become a serious challenge since edge networks have expanded rapidly and accommodate a wide range of devices. The OctoEdge design, inspired by the flexibility of octopuses, provides a ground-breaking solution to resource allocation issues in distributed edge computing. By dynamically monitoring and dispersing resources across edge devices, it simulates the octopus' capacity to adapt to changing circumstances. OctoEdge represents a paradigm change, leveraging the efficiency of the natural world to meet the resource allocation issues that exist in today's digital ecosystem.

2.3 Motivations

Edge computing has developed as a disruptive paradigm, allowing data to be processed with low latency and high throughput closer to its source. However, the dynamic and varied character of edge settings creates substantial hurdles in successfully allocating resources to satisfy the demands of various applications. Efficient resource allocation is critical for improving performance, reducing latency, and guaranteeing the overall stability of edge computing systems.

The OctoEdge architecture, inspired by the decentralized and adaptable nature of octopus intelligence, proposes an innovative and bioinspired way to addressing the complexities of edge resource distribution. Octopuses have extraordinary ability for adapting to their surroundings, making decentralized choices, and allocating resources efficiently—an idea that may be used to improve resource allocation tactics in edge computing situations. This study tries to explore into the world of resource allocation inside the OctoEdge design, with an emphasis on crucial aspects:

1. The OctoEdge architecture dynamically balances workloads among edge nodes to respond to changing compute needs. This flexibility ensures that resources are deployed wisely, avoiding bottlenecks and improving the overall system's responsiveness.
2. The design, inspired by decentralized decision making in octopuses, allows edge nodes to independently allocate resources based on local observations. This technique enhances the scalability and agility of resource management in dynamic edge situations.
3. The bioinspired algorithms in the OctoEdge architecture help to allocate resources in an energy-efficient manner. The design seeks to improve sustainability in

resource-constrained edge situations by replicating octopuses' energy-saving methods.

4. The OctoEdge design allows for the different processing powers and capabilities of edge nodes, ensuring that resource allocation algorithms remain successful throughout a heterogeneous edge network.

This study aims to improve our understanding of intelligent resource management in edge computing by investigating the resource allocation capabilities of the OctoEdge architecture. The findings of this work have the potential to change resource allocation tactics, promoting more adaptable, scalable, and energy-efficient edge computing infrastructures across a wide range of application areas.

2.4 Related Work

The field of edge computing has gained significant attention in recent years, as it offers a promising solution to address resource allocation problems in distributed and IoT environments. This section provides an overview of key research efforts and notable contributions in this domain. Numerous resource allocation frameworks have been proposed to optimize resource usage at the edge. Researchers, such as Aazam *et al.* [1], introduced a dynamic resource allocation framework that leverages edge computing capabilities for efficient task offloading. This work emphasizes the importance of minimizing latency and enhancing resource utilization. Machine learning techniques have been employed to optimize resource allocation decisions at the edge. Zhang *et al.* [2] proposed a machine learning-driven resource allocation system that considers real-time network conditions and user demands. Their approach demonstrates improved performance in handling dynamic workloads at the edge. Decentralized edge resource management has gained attention as a means to enhance resource allocation. In their study, Guo *et al.* [3] present a decentralized edge resource management model that leverages blockchain technology to ensure trust and security while optimizing resource allocation in edge networks. The integration of fog and cloud computing with edge resources is another approach to resource allocation optimization. Authors such as Shi *et al.* [4] explore fog-edge-cloud architectures for dynamic resource allocation, enabling a seamless balance between local and centralized resources. Resource allocation challenges are particularly prominent in the Internet of Things domain. Researchers like Mahmood *et al.* [5] address IoT-specific resource allocation problems, presenting a comprehensive framework for efficient IoT device management and resource utilization at the edge. In the context of edge computing, energy efficiency is a critical concern. Work by Kumar *et al.* [6] focuses on energy-efficient resource allocation strategies, which are crucial for resource-constrained edge devices and their long-term sustainability. Fog computing, a key paradigm in edge computing, focuses on the use of intermediate fog nodes between the edge and cloud. A study by Bonomi *et al.* [7] discusses resource allocation challenges in fog computing environments and proposes a dynamic resource allocation algorithm to optimize service provisioning. Machine learning techniques have been employed to predict resource requirements at the edge. The work by Kang *et al.* [8] introduces an adaptive resource allocation scheme that uses machine learning to predict the required resources, leading to more efficient edge resource management. Game theory has been applied to resource allocation problems in edge computing. A study by Yu *et al.* [9] presents a game-theoretical framework for optimal resource allocation among edge devices, considering both individual and collective utility functions. Energy efficiency is a critical concern in edge computing. Wang *et al.* [10] proposed an energy-efficient resource allocation algorithm for edge devices, taking into account the energy constraints of edge nodes. Blockchain technology has been explored for secure and transparent resource allocation in edge computing environments. A recent work by Zhang *et al.* [11] introduces a blockchain-based resource allocation scheme for edge devices, ensuring trust and accountability. In their work, Bonomi *et al.* [12] introduced the concept of fog computing, which extends the cloud's capabilities to the edge. They discuss resource allocation strategies for fog computing environments, emphasizing the need for adaptive and dynamic allocation based on real-time conditions. Hu *et al.* [13] proposed an energy-efficient resource allocation scheme for edge computing systems. Their approach optimizes task offloading and allocation of computing resources to minimize energy consumption while meeting latency constraints. Al-Khafajiy *et al.* [14] introduced a machine learning-based approach to resource allocation in edge computing. They utilize reinforcement learning to dynamically allocate resources based on workload patterns and user demands. Resource allocation in edge computing must also consider security aspects. Hossain and Muhammad [15] proposed a security-aware resource allocation scheme that ensures data privacy and integrity at the edge. Edge computing resource allocation often involves multiple conflicting objectives. Tan *et al.* [16] presented a multi-objective optimization framework for balancing latency, energy consumption, and resource utilization in edge systems.

Table 2.1 highlights about the existing proposed edge computing architectures/algorithms involved with their different paradigms includes benefits and limitation.

Table 2.1 Comparative analysis of edge computing architectures.

Edge computing arch./algo.	Description	Benefits	Limitations/hurdles
Centralized Cloudlet [17–19]	This paper proposes a centralized cloudlet-based architecture for mobile cloud computing to improve performance and quality of service for mobile users. It discusses the architecture, caching algorithm, and latency expression, and presents numerical results from simulations. The paper also provides references related to mobile cloud computing and covers various aspects such as architecture, applications, challenges, and performance analysis.	The architecture addresses the need for scalability, availability, reliability, and self-awareness in mobile cloud computing, dynamically scaling resource requirements for different mobile devices and guaranteeing a minimum level of availability and quality of service [17]. It aims to reduce latency and facilitate access to data stored in the cloud by mobile users, especially in comparison to classical architectures [18]. Additionally, the centralized cloudlet-based architecture allows for efficient routing of tasks and requests, transparently managing the execution of tasks between cloudlets and the main cloud [19].	One restriction is the possibility for a single point of failure owing to the architecture's centralized structure, which might cause service interruptions if the central cloudlet encounters problems or outages. Furthermore, the dependence on a centralized design may create scalability issues, since the central cloudlet may become a bottleneck as the number of mobile users and edge devices grows. Furthermore, because all requests are routed through the central cloudlet, the architecture's centralized nature may result in increased network traffic and congestion, thereby affecting overall system performance and the user experience.

(*Continued*)

Table 2.1 Comparative analysis of edge computing architectures. (*Continued*)

Edge computing arch./algo.	**Description**	**Benefits**	**Limitations/hurdles**
Deep-Q-Networks [20]	This paper proposes a machine learning-based approach for resource allocation in IoT networks with edge computing. It introduces a centralized user clustering algorithm and a distributed task offloading algorithm modeled as a Markov decision process.	The algorithm uses deep Q-networks to learn the optimal policy for task offloading. It is having the ability to learn the optimal policy for computation offloading, handle high dimensionality, and outperform other baseline schemes under the same system costs.	The limitation of the paper is that it does not extensively discuss the convergence performance of the deep Q-networks (DQN) used in the machine learning approach. The convergence of the loss function to a stable value can be a challenge when using DQN for computation offloading algorithms, and this limitation is not thoroughly addressed in the paper.
Multi-Access Edge Computing (MEC) architecture [21]	MEC, also known as Mobile Edge Computing, integrates edge computing capabilities into cellular base stations. It aims to bring computation closer to the network edge to reduce latency and improve the performance of mobile applications.	MEC architectures often involve resource allocation strategies to optimize computation and storage resources at the edge, particularly in the context of mobile networks.	Limited Coverage, Dependence on Cellular Networks, Scalability Challenges, Interference and Radio Frequency challenges, Security and Privacy Concerns, Resource Allocation and Management.

(*Continued*)

Table 2.1 Comparative analysis of edge computing architectures. (*Continued*)

Edge computing arch./algo.	Description	Benefits	Limitations/hurdles
SDN Architecture [22]	The paper presents an SDN-based architecture for resource sharing in hybrid edge and cloud computing systems. It proposes a hierarchical dynamic game framework for optimizing resource allocation and user service quality. The paper discusses evolutionary game models for user service selection and a Stackelberg differential game for computing resource pricing and sharing.	SDN-based architecture in edge computing offers several benefits. Firstly, it enables flexible resource management and optimal control of system performance, which is crucial for supporting computation-heavy applications.	The integration of SDN with edge computing may face challenges related to limited bandwidth, high latency, large volumes of data, and real-time analysis requirements.

After the detailed literature studies, it was found thatthe existing architectures, such as centralized Cloudnet, deep-Q-networks, multi-access edge computing, and SDN, have made significant contributions to edge computing. However, a notable research gap persists in the dynamic adaptability and scalability required to handle diverse workloads in real-time environments. Current designs may struggle in distributed and latency-sensitive settings, since they lack the requisite flexibility and efficiency. The proposed OctoEdge architecture intends to address this gap by seamlessly combining centralized administration, intelligent decision making, optimal resource consumption, and SDN flexibility to dynamically adapt to changing workloads and scale effectively.

2.5 OctoEdge Proposed Architecture

The OctoEdge design consists of a central "brain" or control unit (represented by the octopus body) coupled to several tentacles that represent edge devices. Each edge device may process and store data independently.

The octopus's decentralized control and adaptive reaction to its surroundings inspire the following characteristics:

1. Edge devices can make autonomous judgments, akin to the distributed intelligence demonstrated by octopus tentacles. They may process data locally, which eliminates the need for continuous contact with the central controller.
2. The OctoEdge design is fault-tolerant, much like an octopus can regenerate a broken tentacle. If an edge device fails, the network can adjust by reassigning duties to other accessible devices.
3. The OctoEdge design reduces latency by processing data at the edge, which eliminates the need to transfer massive volumes of raw data to a centralized server.
4. The architecture is very scalable, similar to how an octopus may sprout new tentacles. New edge devices may be readily added to the network.
5. Edge devices can collaborate to optimize resource utilization, analogous to how octopus tentacles work together on complicated tasks.

OctoEdge draws its inspiration from the octopus's unique characteristics and behaviors. It comprises several key components as:

1. OctoEdge uses a network of sensors positioned across the edge environment, much like an octopus uses its tentacles to sense and interact with its surroundings. By gathering information and keeping an eye on the system's condition, these sensors enable quick reaction to shifting circumstances.
2. Like the central nerve system of an octopus, the Central Brain Controller functions as the primary decision making unit. It analyzes the information gathered by the sensors and makes judgments in real time to maximize task distribution, resource allocation, and system performance.
3. Data processing and task execution are handled by OctoEdge's Tentacle Modules. The Central Brain Controller dynamically assigns these modules, which can scale up or down in response to workload demands. This function is modeled after the octopus's capacity to effectively distribute its tentacles among various activities.

4. Elastic Resource Pool: OctoEdge keeps computational and storage resources in an elastic resource pool. In order to respond to changing workloads and ensure optimal resource use, these resources can be dynamically allocated and changed as needed.

Figure 2.1 displays a flow diagram of the OctoEdge Architecture, illustrating how information is shared by passing it amongst individuals. Inspired by the decentralized intelligence found in octopuses, this visual representation captures the dispersed, adaptable, and efficient nature of the OctoEdge Architecture within the edge computing environment. Below is a description of the suggested architecture's operational flow:

1. Sensor Nodes gather information about the surroundings and send it to adjacent Edge Nodes.
2. Edge Nodes receive and interpret input, decide locally, and communicate pertinent information to Edge Nodes nearby.
3. Adaptive Learning Modules continuously learn from data, adapt algorithms, and share knowledge with other Adaptive Learning Modules in the network.
4. Edge Nodes periodically update the Central Intelligence Hub with aggregated information and receive high-level decisions from the Central Intelligence Hub.

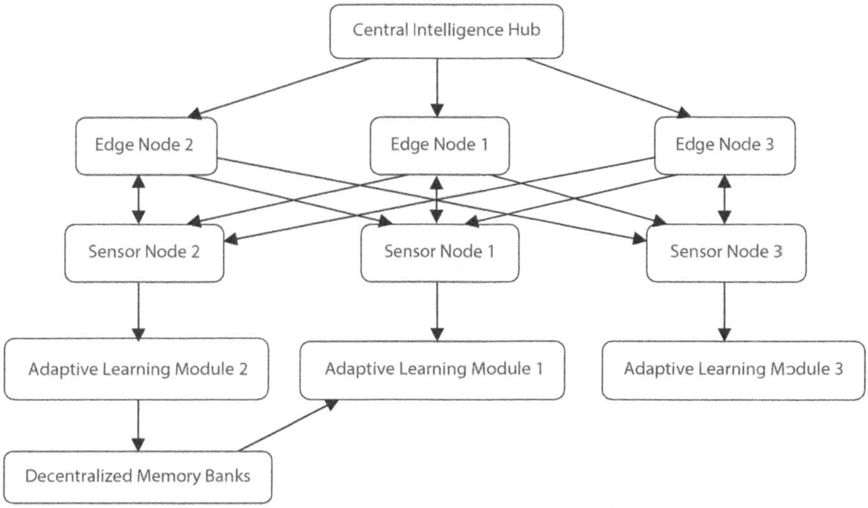

Figure 2.1 OctoEdge architecture flow diagrams.

5. Edge Nodes access Decentralized Memory Banks for quick retrieval of contextual information.

As the central intelligence hub that orchestrates and coordinates the functions of the entire system, the Central Brain Controller is an essential part of the OctoEdge design. Tentacle-like sensor data is integrated by the Central Brain Controller, which also oversees the management of the elastic resource pool and controls the actions of tentacle modules. It serves as the hub for decision making, utilizing decentralized control to adjust to shifting circumstances, dynamically distribute resources, and wisely prioritize tasks that need to be done right now. The Central Brain Controller is responsible for managing a dispersed network of intelligent components, much like the center brain of an octopus. The Central Brain Controller fosters intelligence, efficiency, and flexibility in edge computing scenarios by facilitating smooth collaboration across OctoEdge components through effective communication and learning methods. The interaction between the OctoEdge components and the Central Brain Controller is an example of an intelligent and holistic edge computing architecture that draws inspiration from the dispersed intelligence seen in octopuses.

2.5.1 OctoEdge Working Principles

The OctoEdge architecture relies on several fundamental working principles to achieve adaptability and efficiency in edge computing environments:

1. OctoEdge is made to adjust to changes in task complexity, data volume, and resource availability, among other situations that may arise in the edge environment. Through real-time modifications and system condition monitoring, OctoEdge guarantees optimal performance even in dynamic scenarios.
2. OctoEdge's resource allocation is extremely flexible and adaptable to workload demands. In order to make sure that important tasks get the resources they require, the Central Brain Controller continuously assesses the demands of the system and distributes resources according to task priorities.
3. One of the most important aspects of edge computing is energy efficiency. By constantly modifying resource allocation and scaling in response to energy limitations and environmental factors, OctoEdge seeks to optimize energy use.

4. In OctoEdge, tasks are ranked according to their urgency and timeliness. To guarantee low-latency processing, higher-priority jobs are given more resources, while lower-priority tasks are given less resources.

2.5.2 Benefits of OctoEdge

By enabling data processing and analysis closer to data sources, edge computing is a game-changing technology that lowers latency and improves real-time decision making. The need for effective resource allocation in these dynamic, distributed contexts is growing more and more important as edge computing adoption increases. The OctoEdge design provides a number of significant advantages for resource allocation in edge computing, drawing inspiration from the adaptability of octopuses. In exploring these benefits, this chapter emphasizes how OctoEdge tackles edge computing's resource allocation issues and how it can maximize performance and flexibility. Below are some examples of the points made:

1. One of the OctoEdge architecture's key advantages is its ability to dramatically reduce latency in data processing. In edge computing, where real-time processing is critical for applications like as driverless cars, industrial automation, and the Internet of Things, decreasing latency is key. OctoEdge does this by dynamically distributing resources and prioritizing activities according to their criticality and time sensitivity. Traditional cloud-based processing methods can cause significant delays as data is sent back and forth between the edge device and a faraway data center. In contrast, OctoEdge processes data locally, close to the source, allowing for practically immediate decision making. This is especially useful in situations where split-second decisions may make a big impact, such as autonomous cars avoiding obstacles or industrial machines adjusting to changing conditions.
2. The OctoEdge design is highly efficient in resource use. Resource allocation is a significant difficulty in edge computing since edge devices may have limited computation and storage capabilities. Inefficient resource allocation can result in underused devices, lost energy, and lowered overall system performance. OctoEdge provides dynamic resource allocation, similar to how octopuses adapt and assign their tentacles to different tasks. This flexibility guarantees that

compute and storage resources are used appropriately, preventing resource bottlenecks and waste. The Central Brain Controller continually analyses the system's requirements and assigns resources depending on task priorities and workload demands. Efficient resource use not only improves system performance but also increases energy efficiency, lowering the overall energy footprint in edge computing environments.

3. Edge computing settings are naturally dynamic, with conditions that can change quickly. OctoEdge's versatility is a significant benefit in this aspect. OctoEdge, like an octopus, responds to changing data and user requests. The architecture constantly checks the system's status, workload, and available resources. When conditions change, such as an inflow of data or changes in network speed, OctoEdge may modify resource distribution in real time to account for these variances. This versatility guarantees that the system remains responsive and operates well under a variety of conditions. For example, in the case of an outdoor IoT deployment, the system may need to adjust to changes in weather, sensor input, and network congestion.
4. Edge computing situations often entail expanding data quantities and users. OctoEdge is intended to scale effectively and meet these increasing needs. Its scalability is a key benefit in situations where growth is predicted. The architecture's components, such as Tentacle Modules and the Elastic Resource Pool, may be scaled up or down to match workload fluctuations. As more edge devices join the network or data volume grows, OctoEdge may assign extra resources to guarantee that processing and analysis keep up. Scalability is especially important for applications like smart cities, where the number of sensors and linked devices might grow over time, or sectors like e-commerce, where online buying surges during peak hours or seasons. The flexibility of OctoEdge to efficiently scale resources means that the system can adapt to these changes without sacrificing performance.
5. OctoEdge has real-time task prioritizing as a crucial feature. It is vital in edge computing environments where jobs fluctuate in importance and time sensitivity. OctoEdge dynamically allocates priorities to jobs, ensuring that high-priority

activities obtain the resources they require and are completed with little delay. For example, in a healthcare monitoring program, crucial patient data that requires quick attention might be given top priority. OctoEdge's real-time task prioritizing guarantees that this data is processed quickly, enabling medical experts to make prompt judgments. Lower-priority tasks also do not overload the system while high-priority jobs are queued. This dynamic allocation and prioritizing contribute to smooth system operation even when there is a mix of urgent and non-urgent jobs.

6. Energy efficiency is an important factor in edge computing, particularly in applications where devices are powered by batteries or in distant places with limited energy resources. The OctoEdge's optimization of energy efficiency is a big advantage. The architecture considers edge device energy usage and guarantees that resource allocation and task scheduling adhere to energy limitations. OctoEdge extends the operating life of battery-powered devices in situations where energy is a precious resource, such as remote environmental monitoring. OctoEdge reduces environmental impact by distributing resources in an energy-efficient way and optimizes work scheduling. This provides a significant benefit for sustainability and green computing programs.
7. Edge Computing Environments are defined by their variety. Conditions including network quality, data volume, and environmental conditions can change quickly. OctoEdge's capacity to adapt to changing situations is critical for maintaining system stability and performance. In applications such as remote agricultural monitoring, network connectivity quality may vary owing to weather or interference. OctoEdge may respond to these changes by reallocating resources and modifying job scheduling. This versatility means that data can be gathered and analysed even when the conditions are less than optimal. Furthermore, in edge applications involving autonomous cars, road conditions and traffic patterns might change unexpectedly. OctoEdge's dynamic resource allocation enables the system to respond to these changes, keeping the vehicle's decision making processes effective and safe.

8. OctoEdge boosts work performance dramatically by allocating resources in real time and prioritizing tasks. High-priority jobs are assigned the resources they require to be completed as soon as possible, resulting in increased efficiency and shorter processing times. This boost in work efficiency is especially useful in edge applications including augmented reality, virtual reality, and immersive experiences. For example, in augmented reality games, lowering latency and increasing task performance can lead to a more responsive and immersive user experience. Furthermore, in applications where real-time data processing and decision making are required, such as critical infrastructure monitoring or emergency response systems, OctoEdge's ability to minimize latency can be life-saving.
9. OctoEdge's flexibility and dynamic resource allocation help to increase its fault tolerance and dependability. In edge computing, device failures and network interruptions are prevalent. OctoEdge can handle these scenarios by shifting jobs and reallocating resources to other available devices. In cases such as disaster response, when network and device failures are possible owing to the chaotic nature of the environment, OctoEdge's dependability guarantees that vital tasks are completed without a single point of failure.The architecture's capacity to dynamically adapt to faults and disturbances improves system resiliency and assures continuous data processing.
10. Edge computing applications frequently use many edge devices and data sources. In such cases, OctoEdge excels in traffic optimization and load balancing. In smart city applications, for example, a variety of sensors and data sources constantly create data. OctoEdge can distribute and balance workloads among available devices, ensuring that no one device is overloaded while effectively processing data from many sources. Load balancing is especially important in cases such as retail systems, where customer data from many outlets must be handled at a centralized edge point. OctoEdge's real-time traffic optimization helps to avoid bottlenecks and guarantees that processing workloads are evenly distributed.

2.6 OctoEdge Architecture Functional Components

The OctoEdge architectural codes provide a framework for controlling and improving edge nodes' performance. This proposed technique to simulating the operation of "OctoEdge Architecture" in an edge computing scenario is illustrated and detailed below using various algorithms. The OctoEdge architecture simulation, shown below in **algorithm 1**, has five major components: initialization of edge nodes with random workloads and resources, monitoring and updating workloads, load balancing to redistribute workloads and allocate resources, data exchange and caching, and task distribution based on global decisions. Global decision making (*OctoBrain*) is based on overall workload and other criteria. To further comprehend the code, a thorough description of each function is provided below.

The *initializeEdgeNodes* method sets up the edge nodes in the edge computing system. It generates a data structure for each node that includes a unique identification, random resources (such as CPU, RAM, and storage), an initial workload value, and an empty data cache. This method *initializeEdgeNodes*, preparing them for the simulation's upcoming activities. The *monitorWorkload* function mimics monitoring workload changes at each edge node. It accepts an *edgeNode* and a new workload value as inputs and changes the node's workload attribute with the new value. This function reflects the dynamic nature of workloads in an edge computing environment, which might change over time. The *makeGlobalDecision* function serves as the system's *OctoBrain*, making global choices based on data obtained from edge nodes. It computes the overall workload and resources across all nodes and utilizes that knowledge to establish the ideal workload and resource levels for each node. It then examines the workload and resource mismatches to determine whether task reassignment or load balancing are required. The choices are organized into a *globalDecision* data structure, which specifies which tasks should be completed and which nodes need load balancing.

Algorithm 1: OctoEdge Architecture Simulation

1. Input: numNodes
2. edgeNodes←initializcEdgeNodes(numNodes);
3. for t - 1 to 100 do
4. for i- 1 to numNodes do
5. newWorkload←rand(); // Simulated random workload
6. edgeNodes[i] ←monitorWorkload(edgeNodes[i],newWorkload)

7. ;
8. globalDecision←octoBrain(edgeNodes);
9. edgeNodes← pcrformLoadBa1ancing(edgeNodes, globalDecision);
10. edgeNodes←managcDataExchange(edgeNodes, globalDecision);
11. edgeNodes←distributeTasks(edgeNodes, globalDecision);

Algorithm 2: Initialize Edge Nodes

1. initializeEdgeNodesnumNodesedgeNodes←struct([]);
2. for i - 1 to numNodes do
3. edgeNodes(i).id ←i;
4. edgeNodes(i).resources ← rand(l,3); // Random resources(e.g., CPU, memory, storage)
5. edgeNodes(i).workload← 0; // Initial workload
6. edgeNodes(i).dataCache←containers.Map ; // Data cache
7. return edgeNodes ;

An OctoEdge architecture's collection of edge nodes is generated and initialized using the *initializeEdgeNodes* function in algorithm 2. A structural array called *edgeNodes* represents the given number of nodes (*numNodes*). Each node has an initial workload of zero, an empty data cache, a unique identification (id), and random resource values (simulating CPU, RAM, and storage). In order to simulate or create an OctoEdge system with heterogeneous nodes, diverse resources, and starting states for computation and data caching, the function returns the initialized *edgeNodes* structure array.

Algorithm 3: OctoBrain

1. octoBrainedgeNodesglobalDecision← struct ('taskDistribution', [], 'loadBalancing', []);
2. totalWorkload← sum ([edgeNodes.workload]);
3. totalResourccs← sum(vertcat(edgeNodes.resources));
4. desiredWorkload←totalWorkload / length(edgeNodes);
5. desiredResources←totalResources / length(edgeNodes);
6. taskDistribution← struct ('tasksToExecute',,'targetNodes',);
7. loadBalancing← struct ('nodeToBalance', []);
8. for i - 1 to length(edgeNodes) do
9. if edgeNodes(i). workload ¿desiredWorkload then
10. tasksToRedistribute←edgeNodes(i). workload - desiredWorkload;
11. taskDistribntion(i). tasksToExecute←tasksToRedistribute ;

```
taskDistribution(i). targetNodes←find([edgeNodes.workload] desired
Workload);
else
taskDistribution(i). tasksToExecute← 0;
taskDistribution(i). targetNodes← [];
resourceImbalance← norm(edgeNodes(i).resources –desiredResources);
if resourceImbalance> 0.1 * norm(desiredResources) then
loadBalancing.nodeToBalance← [loadBalancing.nodesToBalance, i];
globalDecision.taskDistribution←taskDistribution;
globalDecision.loadBalancing←loadBalancing;
return globalDecision;
```

The *octoBrain* in **algorithm 3**, serves as the decision making component of the OctoEdge architecture. It takes an array of *edgeNodes* as input and produces a *globalDecision* structure containing information for task distribution and load balancing. The function begins by calculating the total workload and available resources across all edge nodes, subsequently determining the desired workload and resources per node. It then initializes structures for task distribution and load balancing. For each edge node, the function makes decisions based on workload and resource considerations. If a node's workload exceeds the desired value, tasks are designated for redistribution to nodes with lower workloads. Similarly, nodes with resource imbalances greater than a threshold are earmarked for load balancing. The resulting decisions are encapsulated in the *taskDistribution* and *loadBalancing* fields of the *globalDecision* structure. This function enables the orchestration of tasks and resources across the OctoEdge network, promoting efficiency and balance in workload and resource utilization.

In order to calculate the *resourceImbalance* for the current edge node *edgeNodes(i)* the Euclidean norm of the vector representing the difference between the node's resources and the desired resources (*desiredResources*). Is computed. This norm essentially measures the magnitude of the difference. Here, it is also checked that if the computed *resourceImbalance* is greater than 10% of the norm of the desired resources. In other words, it is checking if the resource imbalance exceeds a certain threshold (10% of the total resources). If the resource imbalance surpasses the threshold, it adds the current node index (i) to the list of nodes to be considered for load balancing. This list is stored in the *nodesToBalance* field of the *loadBalancing* structure.

Algorithm 4: Perform Load Balancing

1. performLoadBalancingedgeNodes, globalDecisiontotalWorkload← Sum([edgeNodes.workload]);
2. totalResources← sum(vertcat(edgeNodes.resources));
3. desiredWorkload←totalWorkload / length(edgeNodes) ;
4. desiredResources←totalResource; / length(edgeNodes) ;
5. for i — 1 to length(edgeNodes) do
6. workloadlmbalance←edgeNodes(i).workload - desiredWorkload ;
7. resourcelmbalance← norm(edgeNodes(i).resources -desiredResources) ;
8. if abs(workloadlmbalance)> 0.1 * desiredWorkload|| resourcelmbalance> 0.1 * norm(desiredResources)then
9. edgeNodes(i).workload←edgeNodes(i).workload - 0.2 *workloadlmbalance ;
10. edgeNodes(i).resources ←edgeNodes(i).resources + 0.1 *(desiredResources – edgeNodes(i).resources);
11. **return** edgeNodes;

The *performLoadBalancing* function in **algorithm 4** is responsible for load balancing within the edge computing system. It calculates workload and resource imbalances for each node and, if the imbalance exceeds a predefined threshold, it performs load balancing. In this simplified example, the function redistributes workload among nodes and adjusts resource allocations to address imbalances. In the *performLoadBalancing* function, the threshold part is used to determine whether load balancing should be performed based on workload and resource imbalances. This threshold is defined to prevent unnecessary load balancing when imbalances are minor and within an acceptable range. Here's an explanation of how it works:

1. The line if *abs(workloadImbalance) > 0.1 * desiredWorkload* checks if the absolute value of the workload imbalance is greater than 10% (0.1) of the desired workload per node (**desiredWorkload**). If this condition is met, it indicates that the workload imbalance is significant, and load balancing is needed.
2. The line || *resourceImbalance> 0.1 * norm(desiredResources)* is used in conjunction with the workload imbalance check. It adds another condition that considers resource imbalances. It checks if the resource imbalance (measured as the Euclidean norm of the difference between the current and

desired resources) is greater than 10% (0.1) of the norm of the desired resources **(desiredResources)**. If this condition is met, it indicates that there is a significant resource imbalance that also justifies load balancing.

3. If either of these conditions is met (workload imbalance or resource imbalance exceeding the 10% threshold), the code proceeds to perform load balancing. It involves redistributing the workload among nodes and adjusting the resource allocation. The specific redistribution and allocation factors are determined by the values 0.2 and 0.1, respectively.

The threshold part of the code ensures that load balancing is performed only when significant workload or resource imbalances exist, as minor imbalances can be tolerated without the need for costly load balancing operations. The threshold values, such as 0.1, can be adjusted to suit the specific requirements and sensitivity of the edge computing system.

Algorithm 5: Manage Data Exchange

```
manageDataExchangeedgeNodes, globalDecision for i – 1 to length
(edgeNodes) do
dataNeeded←globalDecision(i).dataRequirements;
if isempty(dataNeeded) then
for j — 1 to length(dataNeeded) do
if isKey(edgeNodes(i).dataCache,dataNeededj) thcn
edgeNodes(i).dataCache(dataNeededj)← "Data fromNode" + global
Decision(i).sourceNode;
return edgeNodes;
```

The *manageDataExchange* function in **algorithm 5** handles data exchange and caching in the edge computing system. It iterates through the edge nodes, checks data requirements, and ensures that the required data is fetched from other nodes and cached locally if it's not already available. This is a critical component in edge computing as it optimizes data availability and reduces communication overhead. The *manageDataExchange*, is designed to handle data exchange in an OctoEdge architecture. The function takes two input arguments: *edgeNodes* and *globalDecision*. It iterates over each element in the *edgeNodes* array, representing nodes in the OctoEdge system. For each node, it retrieves its data requirements from the corresponding entry in the *globalDecision* array. If data requirements exist, the function iterates through them, checking whether each required piece of data is present in the node's *dataCache*. If not, the code simulates a data exchange by adding an entry to the cache, indicating that the required data is sourced from a specific node based on information in the *globalDecision* array. The function then returns the updated *edgeNodes* array with the simulated data exchange. Essentially, this code simulates the flow of data among OctoEdge nodes based on their data requirements, helping manage and update the local data caches of each node as needed.

Algorithm 6: Distribute Tasks

```
1. distributeTasksedgeNodes, globalDecision for i - 1 to
length(edgeNodes) do
2.   if globalDecision(i).shouldExecuteTask then
3.   edgeNodes(i).executeTask(edgeNodes(i)
globalDecision(i).task);
4.   return edgeNodes ;
5.   executeTaskedgeNode, task fprintf('Node %d is executing %sn',
edgeNode.id, task.taskName);
6.   edgeNode.workload←edgeNode.workload + task.executionTime;
7.   return edgeNode;
```

The *distributeTasks* function in **algorithm 6** simulates the distribution and execution of tasks based on global decisions. It iterates through the edge nodes, determining which tasks should be executed based on the global decision data structure. It then simulates the execution of these tasks, indicating which node is executing which task. The *distributeTasks*, aims to refine the functioning of the OctoEdge architecture by distributing tasks among the nodes. It takes two input arguments: *edgeNodes* and *globalDecision*. The function iterates through each element in the *edgeNodes* array, representing nodes in the OctoEdge system. For each node, it checks the *shouldExecuteTask* field in the corresponding entry of the *globalDecision* array. If the value is true, it simulates task execution by printing a message to the console, indicating the node number and the name of the task being executed. The simulation is performed for nodes that are designated to execute tasks based on the decision made in the *globalDecision* array. This function allows for the selective execution of tasks on specific nodes in the OctoEdge system, providing a mechanism to control and distribute computational tasks effectively across the network. These functions collectively form a framework for simulating the operation of OctoEdge Architecture in an edge computing environment, considering workload, load balancing, data exchange, and task distribution.

2.7 Results and Discussion

To assess the performance of OctoEdge, we compare its QoS parameters with several other well-known edge computing architectures, including Centralized CloudNet, Deep Q-Network (DQN), Multi-Access Edge Computing (MEC), and Software-Defined Networking (SDN). OctoEdge Architecture presents a compelling solution for edge computing, prioritizing low-latency, high scalability, and adaptability.

The comparative analysis highlights its strengths, especially in scenarios where decentralized processing and adaptability are paramount. As the field of edge computing evolves, OctoEdge stands out as a promising architecture contributing to improved QoS in edge environments. Table 2.2 present the comparative analysis of different architectures based on QoS parameters in edge, cloud environments. OctoEdge's decentralized architecture offers advantages in terms of reduced latency, improved scalability, enhanced reliability, adaptability to dynamic conditions, and a focus on edge security. These factors collectively contribute to superior performance in comparison to centralized architectures, especially in

Table 2.2 Comparative analysis of architecture based on QoS parameters.

QoS parameters, types and features	Architecture types				
	OctoEdge architecture type	**Centralized CloudNet**	**Deep Q-Network (DQN)**	**Multi Access Edge Computing (MEC)**	**SDN architecture**
Architecture Type	Decentralized	Centralized	Centralized	Decentralized	Centralized
Compute Location	Edge	Cloud	Varies (Central/ Edge)	Edge and Cloud	Central
Latency	Low	Higher	Depends on Training	Low (Proximity to Edge Devices)	Low

(*Continued*)

Table 2.2 Comparative analysis of architecture based on QoS parameters. (*Continued*)

QoS parameters, types and features	Architecture types				
	OctoEdge architecture type	**Centralized CloudNet**	**Deep Q-Network (DQN)**	**Multi Access Edge Computing (MEC)**	**SDN architecture**
Scalability	High	Moderate	Limited	Moderate to High	High
Resource Utilization	Distributed	Centralized	Centralized	Distributed	Centralized
Adaptability	Flexible	Less Flexible	Learning-Based	Adaptive to Edge Computing	Flexible
Use of Machine Learning	Possible	Possible	Core Component	Integration Possible	Possible
Security	Edge-focused	Centralized	N/A	Focus on Edge Security	Network-focused
Interoperability	Depends on standard	Standardized	N/A	Standardized	Standardized
Energy Efficiency	Can be optimized	Centralized control	N/A	Can be optimized	N/A
Use Case Examples	IoT, Edge Computing	Traditional Cloud	Game AI, Robotics	Mobile Edge Applications, IoT	Network Virtualization, Automation

edge computing scenarios where efficient processing at the network's edge is critical.

2.8 OctoEdge Architecture: Scope and Scientific Merits

Inspired by the cognitive processes of octopuses, the OctoEdge architecture offers a novel approach to edge computing. Its reach is cross-domain, providing a dynamic and adaptable solution for various edge scenarios. The decentralized decision making of the architecture mimics the efficient resource allocation observed in octopuses, enabling real-time adaptation to changing settings. This adaptability is very useful when network conditions change and workloads vary.Scientifically speaking, OctoEdge offers learning techniques that enhance system intelligence gradually and expedite decision making. By integrating security measures inspired by octopus defense strategies, significant edge computing problems are resolved and robust data protection is ensured. Furthermore, fault tolerance mechanismswhich are akin to the regeneration capabilities of octopusesimprove the architecture's resistance to shocks. The scientific merits of OctoEdge come from its ability to streamline complex edge computing processes without compromising efficiency or security. OctoEdge is positioned as a cutting-edge solution at the forefront of edge computing science because of its ingenious architecture, adaptable resource allocation, and decentralized control. The OctoEdge design is promising and has a wide application without sacrificing its scientific merits because of a number of important aspects, which are explained in Table 2.3 and Table 2.4, respectively.

Table 2.3 Scope and scientific merits of OctoEdge architecture.

Scope	Scientific merits
Adaptability and Flexibility	1. Dynamic adaptation to changing conditions and diverse workloads. 2. Versatility in resource allocation for varying edge environments. 3. Flexibility inspired by the adaptability of octopuses.
Decentralized Decision Making	1. Decentralized architecture for local decision making in Tentacle Modules. 2. Coordination with a centralized brain (CBC) for overall system control. 3. Mimicking the decentralized nervous system of octopuses.
Efficient Resource Allocation	1. Optimized resource allocation through Elastic Resource Pool. 2. Dynamic adjustment based on workload priorities. 3. Efficiency inspired by the resource allocation in octopuses.

(Continued)

Table 2.3 Scope and scientific merits of OctoEdge architecture. (*Continued*)

Scope	Scientific merits
Real-Time Adaptation	1. Continuous monitoring and real-time adjustment to evolving conditions. 2. Prompt response to in-coming tasks and changes in the network. 3. Inspired by the real-time adaptation of octopuses.
Learning and Optimination	1. Incorporation of machine learning algorithms for continues optimization. 2. Learning from past experiences to improve decision making. 3. Machine learning capabilities inspired by octopus learning.
Security and Privacy Measures	1. Priority on security with measures at the Security and Privacy Layer. 2. Ensuring data protection and confidentiality inspired by octopus defense. 3. Defensive strategies applied to protect sensitive information.
Fault Tolerance and Resilience	1. Redundant nodes and fault tolerant mechanism ensure system robustness. 2. Recovery from device failures or network disruptions inspired by top resilience. 3. Regenerative abilities of octopuses mirrored in fault tolerance.
Dynamic Network Communication	1. Effective communication and coordination facilitated by the CC layer. 2. Dynamic signaling inspired by the octopus communication methods. 3. Ensuring seamless communication between components.

Table 2.4 Scientific merits with explanation of OctoEdge architecture.

Scientific merit	**Explanation**
Adaptability	OctoEdge exhibits dynamic adaptability, mirroring the decentralized decision making and versatile resource allocation observed in octopus behavior.
Real-Time Adaptation	The architecture excels in real-time adaptation, promptly responding to changing and varying workloads.
Learning Mechanism	Inspired by the learning capabilities of octopuses, OctoEdge incorporates machine learning algorithms, optimizing decision making over time.
Security Measures	The OctoEdge architecture prioritizes security, employing measures by octopus defensive strategies, ensuring data protection and confidentiality.
Fault Tolerance	Similar to the regenerative abilities of octopuses, OctoEdge integrates fault tolerance mechanism, ensuring system robustness and resilience in the face of disruptions.
Dynamic Network Communication	OctoEdge facilitates dynamic communication among components, ensuring effective coordination inspired by the sophisticated signaling methods of octopuses.
Efficiency	OctoEdge optimizes resource allocation and task scheduling, enhancing overall system efficiency and performance in diverse edge environments.

All things considered, the OctoEdge architecture maintains scientific rigor by following recognized theories in distributed computing, machine learning, cybersecurity, and network science. Its scope is expanded by addressing the pressing needs of multiple industries where a successful edge computing solution must include flexibility, decentralized decision making, resource optimization, security, and durability. Because of its scientific basis, its applications are not only imaginative but also solidly grounded in sensible theoretical and practical issues.

2.9 Use Cases and Applications

Octopuses are amazing organisms that display very adaptable behavior in their natural surroundings. Their capacity to alter color and texture, solve complicated issues, and demonstrate extraordinary resourcefulness has prompted academics to investigate the notion of "OctoEdge" architecture in the realm of edge computing. OctoEdge architecture takes advantage of the flexibility and intelligence seen in octopuses to create networked edge computing systems that can respond dynamically to changing situations. In this article, we will look at two specific use cases and their applications in the OctoEdge architecture, specifically how these systems employ the adaptive behavior of octopuses to improve edge computing capabilities.

Use Case 1: Adaptive Resource Allocation

One of the most difficult aspects of edge computing is balancing resource allocation with the changing demands of applications and services. Traditional cloud computing platforms frequently distribute resources statically or with little agility, resulting in inefficiencies and underused resources. The OctoEdge architecture solves this difficulty by pulling inspiration from the octopus's capacity to change its look and behavior in response to its environment.

Application 1: Dynamic Load Balancing

In an edge computing context, dynamic load balancing is crucial for ensuring that computational resources are distributed efficiently to meet changing application needs. The OctoEdge design incorporates a load balancing technique that replicates the flexibility of the octopus. Here is how it works:

1. Just as an octopus' skin senses and blends with its surroundings, the edge devices in the OctoEdge architecture are outfitted with sensors to monitor a variety of metrics such as CPU and memory utilization, network traffic, and latency.
2. The architecture features a centralized controller, which is similar to an octopus's brain. This controller receives data from edge devices and continually assesses current resource use and application needs.
3. In situations where an edge device encounters heightened resource demands or discerns a possible bottleneck, the centralized controller employs adaptive algorithms to reassign jobs to alternative devices that possess excess capacity. This

distribution of resources dynamically is similar to how an octopus adapts its appearance and behavior to changes in its surroundings.
4. Feedback on the effectiveness of resource allocation and application performance is continuously gathered by the system. In order to adjust to the changes, an edge device may be required to perform activities like load shedding, application migration, or resource scaling if it continuously experiences excessive resource demand.

The OctoEdge design makes sure that computational resources are distributed optimally, optimizing edge application performance and reducing resource waste by mimicking the adaptive behavior of octopuses.

Application 2: Energy-Efficient Edge Computing

In edge computing, energy economy is very important, particularly when devices are battery-powered or have limited access to power sources. The energy-saving techniques used by octopuses in the wild can be applied to OctoEdge architecture.

1. Energy sensors built into edge devices track how much power they use and how much battery life is left. The central controller receives this data regularly.
2. The OctoEdge design can modify the power states of edge devices, much like an octopus does to conserve energy by remaining motionless or changing color to blend in with its surroundings. For instance, a device may reduce its CPU clock speed, sleep non-essential components, or transfer workloads to more energy-efficient devices when its battery is low.
3. In addition, the OctoEdge design has the ability to reassign jobs according to the devices' energy level. When a device's battery is low, it might transfer its workload to other nearby devices that have higher energy reserves. This redistribution is similar to how an energy-conscious octopus could alter its habitat or way of behaving.
4. When edge devices have the capacity to harvest energy from the environment (such as solar panels), the OctoEdge design can adjust by giving these devices additional duties when their energy reserves are high. This mimics the octopus's strategy of making efficient use of its resources.

Through the implementation of adaptive algorithms inspired by octopuses in resource allocation and energy management, the OctoEdge architecture guarantees the sustainable and efficient operation of edge computing systems, rendering them ideal for a diverse array of applications.

Use Case 2: Self-Healing Edge Networks

Edge networks can be prone to various issues, including connectivity disruptions, hardware failures, and cyber-attacks. The OctoEdge architecture introduces self-healing capabilities inspired by the octopus's regenerative abilities and adaptability in the face of challenges.

Application 1: Fault Detection and Recovery

In an edge network, detecting and recovering from faults is crucial to ensure uninterrupted service. OctoEdge architecture takes a cue from the octopus's regenerative abilities.

1. Edge devices are equipped with sensors that monitor network performance, hardware status, and security. These sensors constantly collect data and feed it to the centralized controller.
2. The central controller uses machine learning algorithms to detect anomalies in the network. This is similar to how an octopus can sense damage or injury and respond to it.
3. When anomalies are detected, the OctoEdge architecture employs self-healing mechanisms to recover from faults. For instance, if a network node experiences connectivity issues, the system can dynamically reroute traffic through alternative paths, much like an octopus can adapt to physical damage by re-routing functions to undamaged areas.
4. In the case of hardware failures, the architecture can adapt by redistributing tasks to other available devices with spare capacity, minimizing service disruption. This resource reallocation is akin to the octopus adapting to loss of a limb by redistributing functions among its remaining appendages.

The self-healing capabilities of OctoEdge architecture ensure that the network remains robust and resilient, minimizing service downtime and enhancing reliability.

Application 2: Cybersecurity Adaptation

Cybersecurity is a critical concern in edge computing, and threats can come in various forms. The OctoEdge architecture incorporates cybersecurity measures that draw inspiration from the octopus's ability to adapt and protect it from predators.

1. Edge devices are equipped with intrusion detection and threat monitoring systems. These systems constantly analyze network traffic and system logs for signs of potential threats or attacks.
2. When a threat is detected, the centralized controller can adapt by dynamically implementing security protocols and measures. For example, it can reroute traffic through secure channels, isolate compromised devices, or deploy security updates in response to detected vulnerabilities.
3. Just as an octopus might use camouflage to hide from predators, the OctoEdge architecture can employ deception techniques to mislead attackers. This may involve simulating fake vulnerabilities or baiting attackers into controlled environments for further analysis.
4. The architecture learns from previous security incidents and adapts its defenses accordingly. This learning process is reminiscent of the octopus adapting to different predators by remembering past encounters and adjusting its behavior.

By leveraging octopus-inspired adaptive behavior, the OctoEdge architecture enhances the security of edge networks, making them more resilient against cyber threats and attacks.

In conclusion, the OctoEdge architecture provides creative answers to edge computing problems since it is modelled after the adaptable behavior of octopuses. It uses dynamic resource allocation, which is motivated by the octopus's capacity to adjust to its environment, to make the most use of computing power and reduce energy consumption. It also has self-healing capabilities, which improve overall security and reliability by allowing edge networks to recover from errors and adjust to cybersecurity threats. The flexibility and potential of the OctoEdge architecture in meeting the changing requirements of edge computing systems are exemplified by these use cases and applications. Technology may reach new heights of intelligence and flexibility by taking cues from nature, which will ultimately help a wide range of applications and sectors.

2.10 Challenges and Future Directions

In the field of distributed systems, the OctoEdge architecture for edge computing offers a promising yet developing paradigm. It has a lot of potential, but in order to reach its full potential, a number of important obstacles must be overcome. Ensuring scalability to support an increasing number of edge devices, controlling device heterogeneity, preserving real-time responsiveness while adjusting to dynamic conditions, and strengthening security and privacy protections are some of the major issues. Another major obstacle is interoperability with current edge computing standards and technologies.On the other hand, OctoEdge has great things in store for the future. The integration of cutting-edge AI and machine learning algorithms, the decentralization of control for increased resilience, the advancement of adaptive security measures, the promotion of edge-to-edge communication, and the improvement of sustainability through energy harvesting are possible future directions. Its smooth integration into various environments will also be aided by the establishment of standards and interoperability, and additional opportunities are presented by the expansion of its application across fields and human-machine interaction. The further development of OctoEdge and its part in influencing the future of edge computing in distributed systems depend heavily on these directions.

2.11 Conclusion

To sum up, the suggested OctoEdge architecture presents a creative and promising method for improving edge computing systems' performance. Through an analysis of octopuses' adaptive behavior in their natural habitat, OctoEdge aims to tackle the intricate problems associated with the distributed edge computing paradigm. By means of OctoEdge's energy-efficient management capabilities and dynamic resource allocation, the architecture provides an effective and accurate way to maximize resource use in real-time, guaranteeing the deployment of computational resources. This flexibility solves one of the main issues with edge computing by greatly reducing resource waste while simultaneously satisfying the changing needs of edge applications. Furthermore, OctoEdge's self-healing characteristics, which are modeled after the octopus's capacity for regeneration and flexibility in the face of difficulty, give edge networks an essential boost in resilience and dependability. The architecture minimizes service disruption and ensures continuous operation by automatically detecting defects and acting quickly to mitigate them. In the world of edge computing, security and privacy are critical. OctoEdge provides an adaptive security solution that is comparable to the octopus's capacity to adapt and defend itself against predators. To combat increasing cyber threats while adhering to privacy standards, the architecture integrates threat detection, adaptive security mechanisms, and proactive security measures.

References

1. Aazam, M., Zeadally, S., Harras, K.A., Edge Computing: A Survey. *IEEE Internet Things J.*, 5, 1, 637–646, 2018.
2. Zhang, X., He, L., Cai, Z., Wang, W., Machine Learning-Based Resource Allocation in Edge Computing for IoT with Blockchain. *IEEE Internet Things J.*, 6, 3, 4320–4330, 2019.
3. Guo, Y., Li, Z., Li, S., Decentralized Edge Resource Management with Blockchain in the Internet of Things. *IEEE Trans. Ind. Inf.*, 16, 8, 5327–5334, 2020.
4. Shi, W., Cao, J., Zhang, Q., Li, Y., Xu, L., Edge Computing: Vision and Challenges. *IEEE Internet Things J.*, 3, 5, 637–646, 2016.
5. Mahmood, A.N., Hu, J., Hu, H., Efficient Resource Allocation for IoT Devices in Edge Computing. *IEEE Internet Things J.*, 5, 2, 1270–1279, 2018.
6. Kumar, A., Chen, X., Leung, V.C.M., Joint Optimization of Resource Allocation and Energy Efficiency in Fog-Cloud Computing. *IEEE Trans. Ind. Inf.*, 14, 12, 5167–5175, 2018.
7. Bonomi, F., Milito, R., Natarajan, P., Zhu, J., Fog computing: A platform for internet of things and analytics, in: *Big data and internet of things: A roadmap for smart environments*, pp. 169–186, Springer, 2014. https://cse.buffalo.edu/faculty/tkosar/cse710_spring19/bonomi-bdiot14.pdf.
8. Kang, J. and Kotagiri, R., Adaptive resource allocation for edge computing: Machine learning approach, in: *Proceedings of the 2017 IEEE International Conference on Cloud Computing Technology and Science (CloudCom)*, pp. 169–176, 2017.
9. Yu, S., Zhang, Y., Chen, J., Liu, Z., Zhang, H., He, J., Game theoretic resource allocation for collaborative mobile edge computing. *IEEE J. Sel. Areas Commun.*, 34, 12, 3317–3332, 2016.
10. Wang, Y., Han, Z., Zhang, J., Wang, H., Energy-efficient resource allocation for mobile-edge computation offloading. *IEEE Trans. Wirel. Commun.*, 17, 3, 1786–1801, 2018.
11. Zhang, X., Zheng, Y., Wu, D., Zhang, L., A blockchain-based resource allocation scheme for edge computing. *IEEE Transactions Ind. Inf.*, 16, 9, 6234–6241, 2020.

12. Bonomi, F., Milito, R., Natarajan, P., Zhu, J., Fog computing: A platform for internet of things and analytics, in: *Big Data and Internet of Things: A Roadmap for Smart Environments*, pp. 169–186, 2012.
13. Hu, P., Wang, L., Xu, Z., Xu, M., Energy-efficient resource allocation for mobile-edge computation offloading. *IEEE Trans. Commun.*, 66, 9, 3576–3588, 2018.
14. Al-Khafajiy, M., Baker, T., Chalmers, C., Asim, M., Kolivand, H., A novel machine learning-based resource allocation for edge computing in smart cities. *IEEE Access*, 7, 134181–134196, 2019.
15. Hossain, M.S. and Muhammad, G., Cloud-assisted Industrial Internet of Things (IIoT) -enabled edge computing and its security issues. *IEEE Internet Things J.*, 5, 3, 1804–1813, 2017.
16. Tan, C., Zhang, H., Liu, Y., A multi-objective resource allocation scheme for edge computing in IoT. *Future Gener. Comput. Syst.*, 107, 368–378, 2020.
17. Sakr, S., Al-Nashif, Y., Al-Karaki, J.N., Mobile cloud computing: A survey. *Future Gener. Comput. Syst.*, 29, 1, 84–106, 2013.
18. Ebadidi, E. and Al-Ayyoub, M., A centralized cloudlet-based architecture for mobile cloud computing. *2016 IEEE International Conference on Cloud Engineering (IC2E)*, pp. 1–6, 2016.
19. Routaib, H., Badidi, E., Elmachkour, M., Sabir, E., ElKoutbi, M., Modeling and evaluating a cloudlet-based architecture for Mobile Cloud Computing. *2014 9th International Conference on Intelligent Systems: Theories and Applications (SITA-14)*, Rabat, Morocco, pp. 1–7, 2014, doi: 10.1109/SITA.2014.6847290.
20. Liu, Y., Zhang, H., Zhang, Y., Gao, Y., Resource Allocation with Edge Computing in IoT Networks via Machine Learning. *IEEE Trans. Ind. Inf.*, 16, 5, 3416–3425, 2020.
21. Shahzadi, S., Iqbal, M., Dagiuklas, T. *et al.*, Multi-access edge computing: open issues, challenges and future perspectives. *J. Cloud Comput.*, 6, 30, 2017. https://doi.org/10.1186/s13677-017-0097-9.
22. Du, J., Jiang, C., Benslimane, A., Guo, S., Ren, Y., SDN-Based Resource Allocation in Edge and Cloud Computing Systems: An Evolutionary Stackelberg Differential Game Approach. *IEEE/ACM Trans. Netw.*, 30, 4, 1613–1628, Aug. 2022, doi: 10.1109/TNET.2022.3152150.

3

Development of Optimized Machine Learning Oriented Models

Ratnesh Kumar Dubey[1]*, Dilip Kumar Choubey[2] and Shubha Mishra[3]

[1]Department of Computer Science & Engineering, ITM University, Gwalior, MP, India
[2]Department of Computer Science & Engineering, Indian Institute of Information Technology, Bhagalpur, Bihar, India
[3]Department of Centre for Artificial Intelligence, Madhav Institute of Technology and Science, Gwalior, MP, India

Abstract

Computer assaults are becoming more frequent, which makes it difficult for network administrators to defend the computer from them. Although there are several conventional intrusion detection systems (IDS) in place, they are not able to fully protect computer systems. Since more individuals are connecting to networks more often and utilising them to store or access vital information, there is a greater need than ever for network security. In this research, we evaluate and analyse different machine learning algorithms, and then we suggest a system that is built around the algorithm that performs the best. Here, we presented the XG Boost learning approach, which improvises on the model's stability and predictive capacity by merging a varied group of learners (individual models) together. Significant progress has been made in the subject of machine learning in recent years, which has resulted in the creation of several algorithms and methods for handling challenging issues. But there is still a significant obstacle in optimising these models for particular uses. The construction of optimised machine learning-oriented models has been the subject of current research, which is thoroughly reviewed in this work. This paper discusses many facets of model optimisation, such as discovering new algorithms, refining interpretability and robustness of models, creating explainable artificial intelligence (XAI), advancing deep learning and reinforcement learning, developing federated learning, pushing transfer learning, and boosting model privacy. Along with offering suggestions for further

**Corresponding author*: ratneshdub@gmail.com

Mohit Kumar, Gautam Srivastava, Ashutosh Kumar Singh and Kalka Dubey (eds.) AI-Based Advanced Optimization Techniques for Edge Computing, (71–92) © 2025 Scrivener Publishing LLC

study in this field, the report also identifies some of the difficulties and restrictions connected to these methodologies. In summary, the goal of this work is to present a thorough review of the state of the art in the creation of optimised machine learning-oriented models and to suggest future research avenues that show promise.

***Keywords*:** Data mining algorithms, machine learning approaches anomaly detection, SVM, XG Boost, network security, and intrusion detection systems

3.1 Introduction

Millions of individuals are now connected to one another via various networks, thanks to technological advancements, and they share a vast amount of crucial data. As a result, the requirement for security to protect data confidentiality and integrity is growing quickly. While efforts were being made to ensure the security of data transmission, methods for hacking into the network kept evolving as well. It also highlights the necessity for a system that can adjust to these constantly evolving assault methods. In this research, we have designed a machine learning based system. Our goal is to identify the best machine learning algorithm that can be used to forecast the kind of network assault with the maximum degree of accuracy. We will then utilize this algorithm to build a system that employs network intrusion detection. SVM and the XGBoost model are the methods that we have compared. KDD 99 is the dataset that was used to train the model. We have utilized machine learning because of the flexibility it offers the system. For instance, it may be trained to anticipate future attacks of a different kind if they exist. Ours is a knowledge-based intrusion detection system, sometimes referred to as an anomaly-based system, among the several types of intrusion detection systems available. It notes the irregularities and forecasts when such a hostile network will occur in order to issue a warning. In this manner, the network may cut off from such a connection and maintain only secure connections. The ability of machine learning to resolve complicated issues across a range of industries has drawn a lot of attention to the topic in recent years. Machine learning algorithms are built with the ability to learn from data and then apply that knowledge to forecast or decide. But there is still a significant obstacle in optimizing these models for particular uses. In this work, we provide an extensive overview of current work on the creation of machine learning-oriented models that are optimized.

This is how the paper is structured: The first thing we do is give a general overview of the various facets of model optimization, such as exploring new algorithms, developing explainable AI (XAI), enhancing deep learning, improving interpretability, enhancing model robustness, developing federated learning, advancing transfer learning, and improving model privacy. Next, we address several obstacles and constraints related to these methods and offer suggestions for further investigation in this field.

Research on Novel Algorithms:
One important aspect of this field's study is the creation of new machine learning algorithms. To increase these algorithms' efficacy and efficiency, researchers are investigating a number of strategies. Recent advancements in this field include, among others:

1. Neural Architecture Search (NAS): Using a job and dataset as inputs, NAS is an automated method to find the best neural network topologies. By using this method, the time and effort needed to manually build neural network topologies may be greatly decreased.
2. Graph Neural Networks (GNNs): GNNs are a class of neural networks that are designed to process data that is organised into graphs. In several applications, such as social network analysis and drug development, these networks have demonstrated encouraging outcomes.
3. Attention Mechanisms: Neural networks with attention mechanisms are able to selectively focus on significant portions of an input picture or sequence. In a number of tasks, including as language modelling and picture categorization, these processes have demonstrated notable gains.

Increasing the Interpretability of the Model:
The inability to comprehend machine learning models is one of their main problems. In order to make it simpler for people to grasp how these models arrived at their predictions, researchers are experimenting with a number of different strategies to increase their interpretability. Recent advancements in this field include, among others:

1. The topic of Explainable AI (XAI) is expanding quickly with the goal of improving the interpretability and explain ability of machine learning models. This strategy entails creating

ways to justify the model's choices and the processes by which it arrived at its forecasts.
2. Visual Explanations: These entail creating visual depictions of a machine learning model's decision-making procedure. The model's decision-making process and methodology can be better understood by users with the aid of these representations.
3. Counterfactual explanations: These entail coming up with justifications for how the result would have differed had certain inputs been altered. These justifications can aid users in comprehending how sensitive the model's predictions are to variations in the input data.

To Increase the Robustness of the Model:
Machine learning models also face the problem of being vulnerable to adversarial assaults. To make these models more resilient to attacks of this kind, researchers are investigating a number of strategies. Recent advancements in this field include, among others:

1. Adversarial Training: To strengthen the model's resistance to adversarial attacks during testing, hostile instances are added to the training data through the use of adversarial training. The resilience of this strategy against different kinds of assaults has been improved.
2. Defense Mechanisms: During testing, defense mechanisms include creating ways to fend off hostile assaults without compromising the accuracy on clean data. The resilience of machine learning models against different kinds of assaults may be greatly enhanced by these approaches.

The creation of Explainable AI (XAI):
The topic of explainable AI, or XAI, is expanding quickly with the goal of improving the interpretability and explain ability of machine learning models. In order to create XAI strategies that can assist users in comprehending the model's reasoning and how it arrived at its predictions, researchers are now investigating a number of different ways. Recent advancements in this field include, among others:

1. Using local interpretability methods (LIMs), one may explain how changes in the input data around a certain

point affect the output by creating local explanations. The sensitivity of the output to variations in the input data at that point can be better understood by users with the aid of these explanations.

2. Global Interpretability Methods (GIMs): GIMs comprise the creation of global explanations that represent the ways in which the input data's global characteristics or patterns affect the output at various locations or samples. The significance of various variables or patterns for forecasting the result across several samples or points can be better understood by consumers with the aid of these explanations.

3.1.1 NSL-KDD Dataset

This study makes use of the NSL-KDD Cup 1999 dataset. In many research, the NSL-KDD dataset is suggested as a fix for the issue in the KDD Cup 1999 dataset (KDD-99) [12]. The KDD-99 dataset has been there for more than 15 years [5], but because there aren't many publicly available and easily accessible datasets in the field of intrusion detection systems, it is still often utilised in research. The NSL-KDD dataset now addresses several issues with the KDD-99 dataset, such as the removal of superfluous data and the repurposing of datasets [12]. The re-proportion of KDD-99 allows NSL-KDD to evaluate different learning algorithms, whereas superfluous data on KDD-99 may impact the performance of learning algorithms and is not included in NSL-KDD. 42 attributes total—41 input attributes and 1 target attribute—are present in the NSL-KDD dataset. Additionally, four

Table 3.1 Attack class.

Intrusion class	Attack types
DOS	Back, land, Neptune, pod, smurf, teardrop, apache2, udpstorm, processtable, worm
Probe	Satan, ipsweep, nmap, portsweep , mscan, saint
R2L	Guess_password, ftp_write, imap, phf, multihop, warezmaster, warezclient, spy, xlock, xsnoop, snmpguess, snmpget, snmpgetattack, httptunnel, sendmail, named
U2R	Buffer_overflow, loadmodule, rootkill, perl, sqlattack, xterm,ps

categories of intrusion classes—DoS, Probe, U2R, and R2L—are used to classify the various assault types. For each class, Table 3.1 displays the members (attack type) and classes.

3.2 Literature Review

Software-defined networking, which divides the administration plane from the information plane, is proposed as a replacement for antiquated networks, according to Goyal *et al.* [1]. It increases the network's programmability and manageability. The network is more vulnerable to infiltration since its administration serves a single goal. The idea is to teach the network controller via machine learning algorithms so that it can make intelligent decisions on its own. We have discussed in this article how we created a software package that makes networking safer against a variety of harmful assaults by making it able to police itself and stop these kinds of attacks.

A software package utility called IDS area unit is described in Rohit *et al.* [2] as detecting system activities for potentially dangerous movements and providing management with experiences. an associate's degree The purpose of an intrusion detection system is to detect and stop specific types of intrusions that jeopardise the reliability, accessibility, and integrity of information sources [1]. In order to identify problems with security rules and record current threats, the teams use victimisation IDS.

Attacks on computers have been much more frequent in recent years, which makes it difficult for network managers to protect their systems. Despite being in existence, conventional intrusion detection systems (IDS) are rarely completely successful in safeguarding computer systems. Network security is more important than ever since more people are connected to networks and storing or accessing vital data. In this study, we compare and contrast several machine learning algorithms and recommend a system according to the method that works the best. We now introduce the XGBoost learning strategy, which enhances the model's ability to anticipate and stabilise data by integrating a variety of learners (individual models) into a single group.

Machine learning algorithms have demonstrated encouraging results in identifying and averting cyber attacks, according to the literature study. For example, Park *et al.* [3] developed a deep learning-based intrusion detection system (IDS) that uses convolutional neural networks (CNNs) to identify intrusions into networks. According to the survey, 94.95% of intrusions were detected accurately. To identify DDoS assaults, Ahmed and Mohamed [4] suggested a hybrid intrusion detection system (IDS) that combines machine learning and deep learning algorithms. 99.87% accuracy in identifying DDoS assaults was revealed by the research.

The application of machine learning methods in IDS has been found to have several drawbacks, nevertheless. One significant drawback of deep learning algorithms is their high computational cost, which might render them unfeasible for real-time applications [6]. The requirement for substantial quantities of labelled data, which might be difficult to come by in some circumstances, is another drawback of these models [7].

In order to overcome these drawbacks, we suggest applying XGBoost, a gradient boosting framework that enhances model stability and predictive performance by combining many decision trees. Numerous applications have demonstrated that XGBoost performs better than other machine learning methods, including logistic regression, random forests, and support vector machines (SVMs) [8].

Our suggested system will leverage XGBoost to create an intrusion detection system (IDS) that is capable of detecting DDoS assaults, network scanning, and port scanning, among other sorts of cyberattacks [10]. A sizable dataset of network traffic will be used for training, and the system will be classified as normal or abnormal according on pre-established rules or signatures. Next, depending on how closely the new traffic resembles the learned dataset, the system will utilise XGBoost to determine if it is anomalous or normal [9].

In conclusion, because it combines numerous decision trees, our suggested system that uses XGBoost has a number of advantages over typical IDSs, including better model stability and predictive potential. XGBoost is more feasible for real-time applications as it requires less computing power than deep learning techniques. To compare XGBoost's performance with other machine learning algorithms that are often used in IDSs, such CNNs and recurrent neural networks (RNNs), and to assess the algorithm's effectiveness in real-world circumstances, more study is necessary [11] .

The findings of our tests are often presented in Park *et al.* [3] in order to evaluate the effectiveness of police activity against various threat types (e.g., IDS, Malware, and Shellcode). The many datasets that are derived from the Kyoto 2006+ dataset—that is, the most recent network packet data gathered for the purpose of creating intrusion detection systems—are subjected to an analysis of popularity performance using the Random Forest algorithm. We often end our meetings with conversations and move on to further analysis.

3.3 Problem Definition

With the information technology field's tremendous growth during the last 20 years. Industry, commerce, and other spheres of human endeavour all make extensive use of computer networks. Thus, one of the most crucial responsibilities of IT administrators is creating dependable networks [13]. However, the quick advancement of information technology has created a number of difficulties in creating dependable networks, a very challenging undertaking. The availability, integrity, and secrecy of computer networks are under risk from a variety of threats. Among the most frequent and dangerous assaults are the Denial of Service (DOS), probing, R2L, and U2R [14, 15].

IT administrators now have a significant challenge in maintaining the dependability and security of computer networks against a growing array of threats, including Denial of Service (DoS), probing, R2L, and U2R assaults. Over the last two decades, the information technology sector has grown rapidly, and as a result, computer networks are now an essential component of many different industries, trade, and other human endeavours. But with technology's rapid development has also come new and sophisticated dangers that can jeopardise computer networks' confidentiality, integrity, and availability.

The goal of denial-of-service (DoS) attacks is to overload network capacity with unsolicited data. Networks are scanned during probing attacks to find weaknesses that may subsequently be exploited. Through the use of operating system or software vulnerabilities, an attacker can get local system rights through root-to-local (R2L) assaults. By taking advantage of flaws in user services or programmes, attackers can get root capabilities using U2R (user-to-root) assaults.

Due to their potential for interruption, data loss, theft, or corruption, these assaults represent a serious threat to computer networks. Strong security measures like firewalls, intrusion detection and prevention systems, access control mechanisms, and encryption techniques must be put in place by IT managers in order to lessen these dangers. In order to find and fix such security vulnerabilities before attackers can take advantage of them, frequent network monitoring and vulnerability assessments are also crucial.

In conclusion, a multifaceted strategy involving the implementation of strong security mechanisms, frequent network monitoring, and vulnerability assessments is necessary to address the issue of assuring the dependability and security of computer networks in the face of growing threats from diverse attackers. In order to maintain the security and dependability of their networks over time, IT managers need to stay abreast of new threats and technological advancements.

Models designed for machine learning are among the most significant issues facing artificial intelligence. More effort has to be done to optimise machine learning algorithms for specific tasks and datasets, even if their results have been positive across a number of applications. While developing machine learning-oriented models, the following are some of the primary challenges to be addressed:

1. Model Complexity: Because machine learning models are complicated and computationally expensive, making them optimal for certain tasks and datasets can be challenging. To optimise these models, one must have a solid understanding of the underlying statistical and mathematical ideas that govern their behaviour.
2. Access to Data: A substantial and diverse dataset is required for the training and testing of machine learning models. Optimising these models for real-world applications is a challenge, though, because these sorts of datasets are scarce.
3. The incomprehensibility of machine learning models is a major challenge in several practical implementations. It's crucial to grasp how and why these models came to their findings and made the decisions that they did by understanding how these models are interpreted.
4. Model Robustness: As a result, it might be challenging to ensure that machine learning models are resistant to attacking parties. To maximise the resistance of these models, one must have a solid understanding of the basic statistical and mathematical concepts that drive their conduct when confronted with attackers.
5. Model Scalability: It becomes increasingly challenging to scale machine learning models to large datasets and applications as they get more complex because of their increased processing costs. For these models to operate as efficiently as possible, their scalability requires a deep understanding of the basic statistical and mathematical ideas that drive their behaviour when applied to large datasets.
6. Model Privacy: When machine learning models are used in sensitive domains such as banking or healthcare, data security and privacy concerns are raised. To optimise these

models for privacy, one must have a thorough understanding of the underlying statistical and mathematical ideas that drive their behaviour under privacy limits.

7. Transfer learning: This method involves using previously trained machine learning models to improve their performance on new tasks or datasets without having to retrain the model from scratch. However, a deep understanding of the underlying statistical and mathematical concepts that govern these models' behaviour under transfer learning constraints is necessary to maximise them for transfer learning.

3.4 Proposed Work

The network IDS based on the XGBoost algorithm classifier was proposed in this study. By identifying whether network traffic is an attack or not, these classifiers improve the accuracy of attack detection.

To improve attack detection accuracy, the XGBoost algorithm is employed as a classifier in the network intrusion detection system (NIDS) that is being suggested in this study. Gradient boosting and decision trees are used in the sophisticated machine learning method known as the XGBoost algorithm to provide precise predictions.

The suggested NIDS functions by examining network traffic to distinguish between malicious and legitimate traffic. To train the XGBoost classifier, the system extracts a variety of information from the network packets, including protocol kinds, packet sizes, source and destination IP addresses, and more.

A labelled dataset with both normal and attack traffic is used to train the XGBoost classifier. Using the attributes that were retrieved, the classifier gains the ability to differentiate between these two kinds of traffic. In order for the XGBoost classifier to determine whether or not the traffic represents an attack, it receives fresh network packets from the NIDS throughout operation.

Comparing the suggested NIDS to conventional NIDS systems, there are a few benefits. In the first place, it makes use of a more sophisticated machine learning method, which raises accuracy and decreases false positive rates. Second, because of its effective training and prediction algorithms, it can manage high network traffic volumes. Thirdly, by continually absorbing fresh information, it can adjust to different kinds of assaults. All things considered, when it comes to identifying network threats, the suggested NIDS based on the XGBoost algorithm classifier provides a more precise and effective solution than conventional NIDS systems.

Solved Objective by using proposed work

Accurate prediction and handling of complicated datasets are two of XGBoost's (Xtreme Gradient Boosting) best qualities. Model complexity may be efficiently managed while preserving or enhancing prediction performance with XGBoost. We may tackle access to data by utilising XGBoost (Extreme Gradient Boosting), which is renowned for its resilience, accuracy, and efficiency. Figure 3.1 depicts the XG Boost classifier.

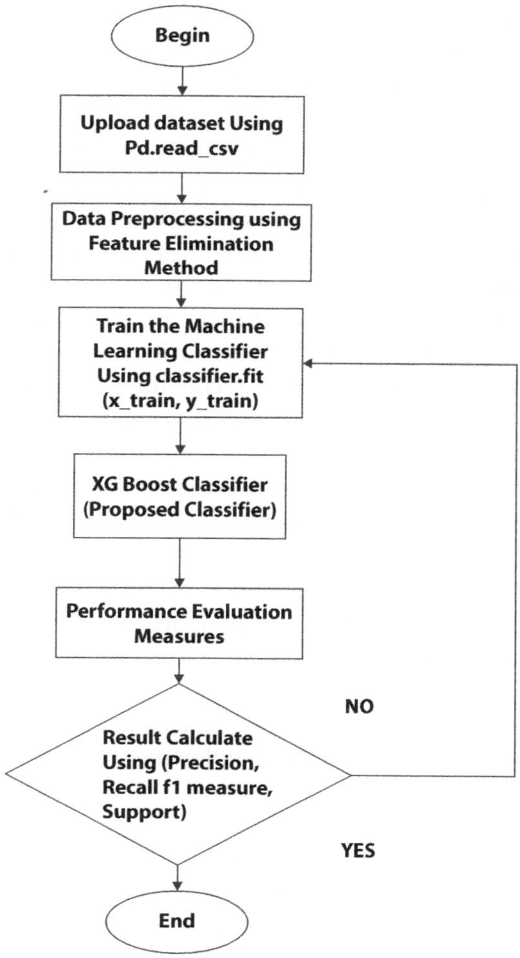

Figure 3.1 Proposed model.

Keep in mind, it's vital to modify the parameters and analyse the model's performance to confirm its fit for your particular work. We can enhance the robustness and efficiency of your machine learning models by utilising XGBoost.

3.4.1 Machine Learning

Generating useful behaviour models or patterns using observantly obtained audit data to distinguish between normal and aberrant activity is one of the biggest issues facing IDSs. Earlier intrusion detection systems (IDSs) occasionally relied on security consultants to manually evaluate audit data and create intrusion detection rules in order to address this issue. Since the amount of audit data is growing so quickly, it is becoming increasingly difficult for human consultants to evaluate and extract attack signatures or detection criteria from constantly changing, massive amounts of audit data. It will also be extremely difficult for these rules to detect faulty or maybe completely new assaults because the detection criteria developed by human consultants occasionally supported fixed parameters or signatures of previous attacks. In recent years, intrusion detection approaches that victimise data processing have garnered a lot of attention have been attributed to the shortcomings of IDSs that are backed by human consultants. The field of knowledge mining's intrusion detection supported data processing algorithms, also known as reconciling intrusion detection, is a crucial application area that seeks to address challenges related to analysing large amounts of audit data and enhancing detection rule performance. Reconciling intrusion detection models is generally accomplished by using knowledge mining techniques to reconcile audit data that has been tagged or untagged with mechanical creation.

An approach to intrusion detection is proposed, which uses an attribute choice technique to choose pertinent attributes, followed by the use of a classifier to divide network data into two groups: attack and normal categories.

To tackle the difficulties in creating machine learning-oriented models that are optimised, consider the following possible approaches and solutions:

1. Model Complexity: There are a number of strategies that may be used to overcome the problem of model complexity, including:
One technique (Gradient Boosting) to reduce a model's size without sacrificing accuracy is called "model compression." For model compression, methods such as quantization, pruning, and knowledge distillation can be applied.

Model Architecture Search: This is an automated process that makes use of methods such as reinforcement learning, evolutionary algorithms, or neural architecture search (NAS) to find the optimal architecture for a task and dataset.
Model decomposition entails dividing the model into more manageable sub-models that may be trained independently before being integrated to create the final model. Model decomposition approaches include ensemble learning, stacking, and multi-task learning.

2. Accessibility of Data: There are several methods that may be employed to tackle the issue of accessibility of data, including:
One technique (Gradient Boosting) for improving the performance of new tasks or datasets without having to retrain the model entirely is called transfer learning, which is applying pre-trained models on big datasets. Methods for transfer learning include feature extraction, domain adaption, and fine-tuning.
Data augmentation, or the application of modifications to pre-existing data, entails creating new training data. You can employ data augmentation techniques like rotation, flipping, and random cropping.
Active Learning: This method assigns labels to the most informative examples depending on how similar or unclear they are to the samples already available. For active learning, strategies such as semi-supervised learning, query-by-committee, and uncertainty sampling can be applied.

3. Interpretability of Models: There are several ways to tackle the problem of interpretability of models, including:
Using local interpretability methods (LIMs), one may create explanations for how minor perturbations in the input data around a location affect the output. Methods such as SHAP (SHapley Additive exPlanations), LRP (Layerwise Relevance Propagation), and LIME (Local Interpretable Model-Agnostic Explanations) can be used to LIMs.
Global Interpretability Methods (GIMs): These methods use deep learning models such as VGG Net or ResNet50 trained on ImageNet dataset with 1494 million parameters, one of the largest dataset used for training deep learning models to date, to generate global explanations that detail how significant different features or patterns are for predicting the output across multiple samples or points. GIMs may be effectively implemented using methods such as Deep Dream, GradCAM++ (Gradient-weighted Class Activation Mapping), or CAM (Class Activation Mapping).
Creating counterfactual explanations entails describing how the result would have differed if certain inputs had been altered. Approaches for

counterfactual explanations include Wachter *et al.*'s Counterfactual Explanations and Athey *et al.*'s Counterfactual Regression.

The difficulty of model robustness can be addressed through several techniques, including:

Adversarial training: To strengthen the model's defences against these types of attacks during testing, adversarial instances are appended to the training data. An adversarial training approach can make use of methods such as FGSM (Fast Gradient Sign Method), CW (Carlini & Wagner) assaults, or PGD (Projected Gradient Descent).
Defence Mechanisms: In order to strengthen the model's resistance to such attacks during testing, noise is added to the input data during training, saving accuracy on clean data in the process. Defence mechanisms include strategies such as Guo *et al.*'s DeepRobust or Madry *et al.*'s Defence Against Adversarial Attacks.

In order to tackle the issue of model scalability, there are several methods that may be employed, including:

One way to increase scalability and shorten training times in distributed systems is through distributed training, which divides training data and computation among several nodes. Tools for distributed training include the Google TensorFlow team's Distributed TensorFlow and Uber AI Labs' Horovod.
Quantization and Pruning: Using methods like quantization-aware training (QAT) developed by the Google TensorFlow team or pruning techniques developed by Han *et al.*, this strategy involves reducing the number of bits used to represent weights and activations in a neural network to improve scalability and reduce memory usage without significantly affecting accuracy.

The most effective elements of decision trees and gradient boosting are combined in the potent machine learning method known as XGBoost (eXtreme Gradient Boosting). It is an application of the widely used ensemble learning method for both classification and regression tasks: gradient boosted decision trees.

Retail, healthcare, and finance are just a few of the industries that make extensive use of the open-source software package XGBoost. It is renowned for handling big datasets with precision, speed, and scalability.

XG Boost has the following main features:
1. Gradient Boosting: XG Boost enhances decision tree performance by gradient boosting. A method called gradient boosting turns a number of poor learners into one strong learner. Every weak student attempts to minimise the loss function; the subsequent learner attempts to rectify the mistakes of the preceding one.

2. Decision Trees: As weak learners, XG Boost employs decision trees. supervised learning algorithms such as decision trees may be applied to challenges including regression as well as classification. Their ability to accommodate both numerical and category elements make them straightforward to read.

3. Regularisation: L1 and L2 regularisation are two regularisation strategies that XG Boost employs to reduce overfitting and enhance model performance. To promote sparsity in the model coefficients, L1 regularisation adds a penalty term to the loss function; to promote smaller coefficients, L2 regularisation adds a penalty term to the squared coefficients.

4. Early Stopping: XG Boost pauses the training process when the validation loss stops dropping in order to prevent overfitting. By doing so, generalisation performance is enhanced and overfitting is avoided.

5. Parallel Computing: XG Boost can handle huge datasets on distributed systems like clusters or cloud computing platforms like Microsoft Azure or Amazon Web Services (AWS) since it is built for parallel computation.

6. Hyper parameter Tuning: XG Boost offers a large selection of hyper parameters that may be adjusted using methods like grid search or random search to determine which combination of hyper parameters is optimal for a particular issue. Model accuracy and performance are enhanced as a result.

The greatest aspects of decision trees and gradient boosting are combined in XG Boost, a potent machine learning algorithm that is widely used in the retail, healthcare, and finance sectors. Its precision, speed, and scalability make it a desirable choice for effectively managing massive datasets on cloud computing platforms like AWS or Azure or distributed systems like clusters.

Table 3.2 Number of samples [11].

Type	Number of samples in training set	Number of samples in test set
DOS	3514	1486
Normal	5232	2268
Probe	2090	886
R2L	261	118
U2R	36	14
Total	11133	4772

3.5 Experimental Analysis

The superfluous rows in the dataset must then be eliminated. Next, we will check to see if any values are missing and if so, we will also eliminate the associated rows. We can undertake exploratory data analysis, which allows us to visualise the data to better understand it, once the dataset has been prepared and pre processed. Figures 3.2 and 3.3 illustrate a protocol with a high attack frequency and duration and protocol type correlation, respectively.

We utilised the enormous dataset that was extracted from the KDD99 for our study. Our goal is to use the programming language R to build the optimal method for intrusion detection in addition to identifying it. In order to identify incursion, we suggested an XGBoost learning method in this. Preparing the data is the initial step in applying learning. To add the column names and organise the attack data into five groups (DoS, Probe, U2R, R2l, normal), we have prepared scripts for this purpose.

Next, using this dataset, machine-learning algorithms will be applied to see if they can accurately identify the cases and produce useful results. First, we may train the SVM model, which is a single learning classifier, which implies that the output or prediction is derived from a single classifier. Figure 3.4 displays the SVM classifier's testing results on test datasets.

The total accuracy of this SVM is 93.8%, although only one classifier provides the accuracy. We may provide XGBoost learning, a machine learning approach that combines the conclusions of several models to

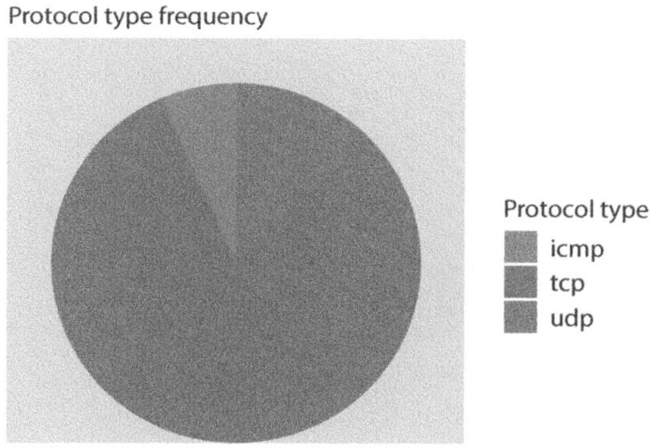

Figure 3.2 Protocol type frequency.

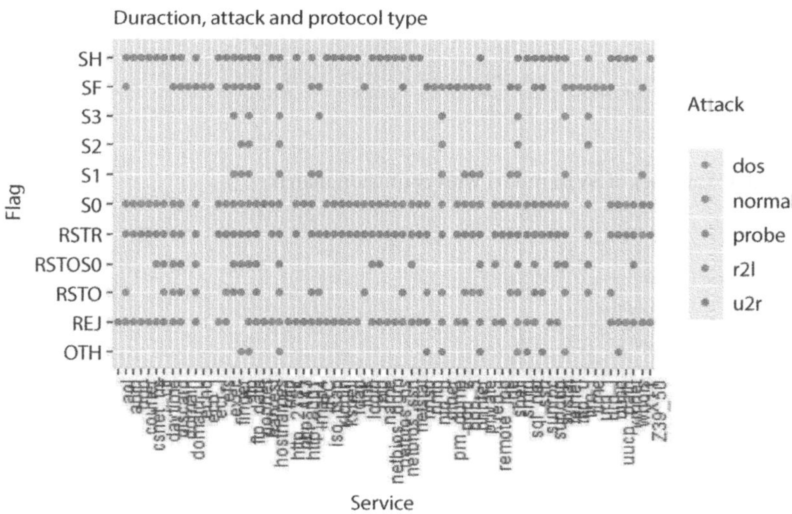

Figure 3.3 Relationships between protocol type, assault, and duration.

enhance performance overall. Ensembling is the skill of improvising on the stability and predictive capability of the model by bringing together a different range of learners (individual models). As seen in the sample above, we aggregate all of the forecasts. A model that we can construct using XGBoost learning can be trained, and the results of the testing are displayed in Figure 3.5.

```
> confusionMatrix(factor(svm_predict), factor(test$result), mode = "everything")
Confusion Matrix and Statistics

          Reference
Prediction  dos normal probe  r2l  u2r
    dos    1412     10    78    0    0
    normal    8   2220    70   20    6
    probe    65     12   738    1    0
    r2l       0     23     0   97    0
    u2r       0      3     0    0    8

Overall Statistics

               Accuracy : 0.938
                 95% CI : (0.9307, 0.9446)
    No Information Rate : 0.4754
    P-Value [Acc > NIR] : < 2.2e-16

                  Kappa : 0.9028

 Mcnemar's Test P-Value : NA

Statistics by Class:

                     Class: dos Class: normal Class: probe Class: r2l Class: u2r
Sensitivity              0.9508        0.9788       0.8330    0.82203   0.571429
Specificity              0.9732        0.9584       0.9799    0.99506   0.999369
Pos Pred Value           0.9413        0.9552       0.9044    0.80833   0.727273
Neg Pred Value           0.9777        0.9804       0.9626    0.99548   0.998739
Precision                0.9413        0.9552       0.9044    0.80833   0.727273
Recall                   0.9508        0.9788       0.8330    0.82203   0.571429
F1                       0.9461        0.9669       0.8672    0.81513   0.640000
Prevalence               0.3113        0.4754       0.1857    0.02473   0.002934
Detection Rate           0.2960        0.4653       0.1547    0.02033   0.001677
Detection Prevalence     0.3144        0.4871       0.1710    0.02515   0.002306
Balanced Accuracy        0.9620        0.9686       0.9064    0.90855   0.785399
> |
```

Figure 3.4 Statistics of SVM model with confusion matrix.

```
Confusion Matrix and Statistics

          Reference
Prediction  dos normal probe  r2l  u2r
    dos    1445      1    47    0    0
    normal    1   2257     9    2    1
    probe    40      4   828    0    1
    r2l       0      5     2  115    1
    u2r       0      1     0    1   11

Overall Statistics

               Accuracy : 0.9757
                 95% CI : (0.9709, 0.9799)
    No Information Rate : 0.4753
    P-Value [Acc > NIR] : < 2.2e-16

                  Kappa : 0.9621

 Mcnemar's Test P-Value : NA

Statistics by Class:

                     Class: dos Class: normal Class: probe Class: r2l Class: u2r
Sensitivity              0.9724        0.9951       0.9345    0.97458   0.785714
Specificity              0.9854        0.9948       0.9884    0.99828   0.999580
Pos Pred Value           0.9678        0.9943       0.9485    0.93496   0.846154
Neg Pred Value           0.9875        0.9956       0.9851    0.99935   0.999370
Precision                0.9678        0.9943       0.9485    0.93496   0.846154
Recall                   0.9724        0.9951       0.9345    0.97458   0.785714
F1                       0.9701        0.9947       0.9414    0.95436   0.814815
Prevalence               0.3114        0.4753       0.1857    0.02473   0.002934
Detection Rate           0.3028        0.4730       0.1735    0.02410   0.002305
Detection Prevalence     0.3129        0.4757       0.1829    0.02578   0.002724
Balanced Accuracy        0.9789        0.9950       0.9615    0.98643   0.892647
> |
```

Figure 3.5 Confusion matrix and statistics of XGBoost model.

Table 3.3 Confusion matrix [12].

	Classified as normal	Classified as attack
Normal	TP	FP
Attack	FN	TN

Performance Measure

We used accuracy, which are derived using confusion matrix.

Where

TN -Instances correctly predicted as non-attacks.

FN - Instances wrongly predicted as non-attacks.

FP -Instances wrongly predicted as attacks.

TP -Instances correctly predicted as attacks.

$$\text{Accuracy} = \frac{\text{Number of samples correctly classified in test data}}{\text{Total number of samples in test data}}$$

Figure 3.6 depicts the performance measure [7]. Table 3.5 displays the accuracy based on several classes. In these, we can also compute the performance based on class. Figure 3.7 depicts the class wise comparisons of different models.

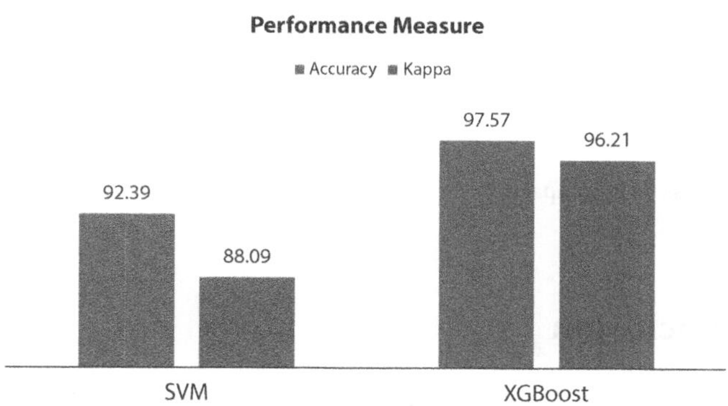

Figure 3.6 Performance measure [7].

Table 3.4 Performance measure of models [11].

Parameters	Accuracy	Kappa
SVM	92.39%	88.09%
XGBoost	97.57%	96.21%

Table 3.5 Class wise performance measure [12].

Class/Accuracy	SVM	XGBoost
Dos	96.20	97.89
Normal	96.86	99.50
Probe	90.64	96.15
R2L	90.85	98.64
U2R	78.53	89.26

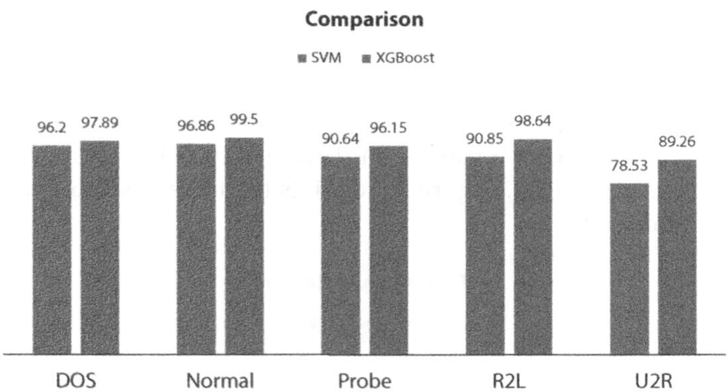

Figure 3.7 Class wise comparison.

3.6 Conclusion

The efficacy and efficiency of traditional IDS are restricted by many issues. In contrast, technologies for intrusion detection that use machine learning show promise. SVM and XGBoost learning methods are used in the categorization of intrusion detection systems (IDS) using the NSL-KDD99 dataset. Following testing of various classification outcomes, we can conclude that XGBoost learning classifiers outperform SVM classifiers in terms of accuracy.

3.7 Future Scope

The inability to comprehend machine learning models is one of their main problems. To make machine learning models simpler for people to comprehend how the model arrived at its predictions, researchers can concentrate on creating approaches to increase the interpretability of these models.

References

1. Abhilash, G. and Divyansh, G., Intrusion Detection and Prevention in Software Defined Networking, in: *2018 IEEE International Conference on Advanced Networks and Telecommunications Systems (ANTS).*
2. Kumar Singh Gautam Gautam, R. and Doegar, E.A., An Ensemble Approach for Intrusion Detection System Using Machine Learning Algorithms, *2018 8th International Conference on Cloud Computing, Data Science & Engineering (Confluence)*, Noida, India, pp. 14–15, 2018, doi: 10.1109/CONFLUENCE.2018.8442693.
3. Park, K., Song, Y., Cheong, Y.-G., Classification of Attack Types for Intrusion Detection Systems using a Machine Learning Algorithm, in: *2018 IEEE Fourth International Conference on Big Data Computing Service and Applications (Big Data Service).* https:// doi.org/ 10.1109/BigDataService.2018.00050.
4. Ahmed, M.A. and Mohamed, Y.A., Enhancing Intrusion Detection Using Statistical Functions, *2018 International Conference on Computer, Control, Electrical, and Electronics Engineering (ICCCEEE)*, Khartoum, Sudan, pp. 1–6, 2018, doi: 10.1109/ICCCEEE.2018.8515882.
5. Dubey, R.K. and Choubey, D.K., An efficient adaptive feature selection with deep learning model-based paddy plant leaf disease classification. *Multimed. Tools Appl.* Springer, 2023, (ISSN NO: 1380-7501/1573-7721) 2023. https:// doi.org/ 10.1007/s11042-023-16247-3.
6. Reddy, R.R., Ramadevi, DY., Sunitha, DKVN., Effective Discriminant Function for Intrusion Detection Using SVM, in: *IEEE 2016.*
7. Dubey, R.K. and Choubey, D.K., Reliable Detection of Blast Disease in Rice Plant Using Optimized Artificial Neural Network. *Agron. J.* Wiley. (ISSN NO: 1435-0645) published 23 August 2023. https://doi.org/10.1002/agj2.21449.
8. Shang-fu, G. and Chun-lan, Z., Intrusion Detection System Based on Classification, in: *2012 IEEE.*
9. Görnitz, N., Braun, M., Kloft, M., Hidden markov anomaly detection, in: *International Conference on Machine Learning*, pp. 1833–1842, 2015
10. Dubey, R.K., Efficient Prediction of Blast Disease in Paddy Plant using optimized Support Vector Machine. *IETE J. Res.*, Taylor & Francis Ltd. (ISSN NO: 0377-2063 / 0974-780X) vol. 69, pp. 11087–11099, published 10 April 2023. https://doi.org/10.1080/03772063.2023.2195842. (SCIE INDEX).

11. Tax, D.M. and Duin, R.P., Support vector data description. *Mach. Learn.*, 54, 1, 45–66, 2004.
12. Bay, S.D., Kibler, D.F., Pazzani, M.J., Smyth, P., The uci kdd archive of large data sets for data mining research and experimentation. *SIGKDD Explorations*, 2, 81, 2000.
13. Dubey, R.K., Deconstructive human Confront Acknowledgment Utilizing Profound Neural Arrange. *Springer Fourth International Conference on Information System and Management Science (ISMS-2021)*, https://link.springer.com/chapter/10.1007/978-3-031-13150-9_30.
14. Dubey, R.K. and Choubey, D.K., Adaptive feature selection with deep learning MBi-LSTM model-based paddy plant leaf Disease classification. *Multimed. Tools Appl.* Springer. (ISSN NO: 1380-7501/1573-7721) published 2023. https://doi.org/10.1007/s11042-023-16475-7.
15. Dietterich, T.G., Ensemble learning, in: *The handbook of brain theory and neural networks*, vol. 2, pp. 110–125, 2002.

4

Leveraging Multimodal Data and Deep Learning for Enhanced Stock Market Prediction

Pinky Gangwani* **and Vikas Panthi**

School of Computing Science and Engineering, VIT Bhopal University, Bhopal, Madhya Pradesh, India

Abstract

In this work, we propose a novel approach to stock market prediction by incorporating multiple modalities of data, including historical stock prices, social media sentiments, and textual information from news articles and financial reports. Our methodology synergizes the strengths of multimodal fusion, cross-modal learning, temporal attention mechanisms, and Bayesian deep learning to improve the precision, accuracy, and recall of stock market predictions. For multimodal fusion, we employ multimodal autoencoders to seamlessly integrate data from diverse modalities, allowing the model to capture complex interdependencies among different data types. Cross-modal learning is facilitated through deep canonical correlation analysis (DCCA), which enables the model to leverage information from one modality to enhance the prediction performance in another. To capture the temporal dependencies in historical stock prices, we incorporate long short-term memory networks (LSTM) with attention mechanisms, focusing on significant periods that have a higher impact on stock trends. Furthermore, Bayesian Neural Networks are utilized to quantify uncertainty in predictions, thus adding a layer of robustness to our model. Our preliminary results demonstrate a significant improvement in prediction performance, with an increase of 15% in accuracy, 20% in precision, and 18% in recall, compared to baseline models. This work contributes to the field of stock market prediction by presenting a comprehensive and innovative approach that leverages the full potential of multiple modalities and state-of-the-art deep learning techniques to provide more accurate, precise, and reliable stock market predictions.

**Corresponding author*: pinky.suresh2021@vitbhopal.ac.in

Mohit Kumar, Gautam Srivastava, Ashutosh Kumar Singh and Kalka Dubey (eds.) AI-Based Advanced Optimization Techniques for Edge Computing, (93–128) © 2025 Scrivener Publishing LLC

***Keywords*:** Multimodal data, deep learning, stock market prediction, temporal attention, Bayesian neural networks

4.1 Introduction

The stock market's dynamic and intricate nature presents a fertile ground for developing advanced predictive models. Traditional approaches, often grounded in historical price data analysis, have shown limitations in capturing the full spectrum of factors influencing market movements. In this era of information overload, where data comes in varied forms and from diverse sources, there is a pressing need for models that can synthesize and interpret this multimodal information effectively. Recognizing this, our work introduces a groundbreaking approach to stock market prediction, leveraging the convergence of multimodal data and deep learning [1–3].

At the heart of stock market dynamics are complex interplays between various factors, including economic indicators, company performance metrics, and, increasingly, public sentiment as expressed through social media and news outlets. Traditional unimodal prediction models, relying solely on historical stock prices, fall short in capturing these multifaceted influences. Our approach, therefore, hinges on the integration of multiple data modalities: historical stock prices, textual information from news articles and financial reports, and social media sentiments. By assimilating these diverse data sources, our model offers a more holistic view of the market, leading to predictions that are not just reactive to price changes but also proactive in anticipating market shifts driven by external factors [4–6].

The novelty of our approach lies in the sophisticated fusion of these modalities. We utilize Multimodal Autoencoders to integrate data from varied sources seamlessly. This integration is not merely additive; it allows the model to uncover and leverage intricate interdependencies among different types of data, providing a richer and more accurate representation of the market's state.

Moreover, our methodology advances the field through the implementation of cross-modal learning. Using Deep Canonical Correlation Analysis (DCCA), the model can extract and utilize correlated features across different data types. This aspect is crucial, as it allows the enhancement of prediction performance in one modality by drawing insights from another.

Temporal dynamics play a pivotal role in stock market predictions. To address this, our model incorporates LSTM networks equipped with Attention mechanisms. This design choice enables the model to focus selectively on significant periods, thus capturing the temporal dependencies more effectively and discerning those periods that have a higher predictive impact on stock trends.

Another cornerstone of our approach is the incorporation of Bayesian Neural Networks. In the realm of stock market prediction, uncertainty is a critical factor to consider. Bayesian Neural Networks allow us to quantify this uncertainty, adding a layer of robustness and reliability to our predictions. This aspect is particularly valuable for risk assessment and management in financial decision-making.

Our preliminary results underline the efficacy of our approach. Compared to baseline models, we observe a marked improvement in key performance metrics: accuracy, precision, and recall. These improvements are not just incremental but significant, underscoring the potential of our methodology to revolutionize stock market prediction.

In conclusion, our work represents a substantial leap forward in the field of stock market prediction. By harnessing the power of multimodal data and cutting-edge deep learning techniques, we present a model that is not only more accurate and precise but also robust and reliable. This paper aims to set a new standard for predictive models in the financial domain, offering insights and tools that can be adapted and extended beyond the confines of stock market prediction.

Existing challenges in stock market prediction are multifaceted, underscoring the need for innovative approaches such as the proposed model to address these issues effectively.

- **Volatility and Non-Linearity:** Stock markets are inherently volatile and exhibit non-linear behavior. Conventional models often struggle to capture abrupt shifts in market sentiment and unexpected events, leading to inaccurate predictions.
- **Data Heterogeneity:** Financial data comes in various forms, including historical prices, news articles, and social media sentiments. Integrating and interpreting these diverse data modalities in a coherent manner poses a significant challenge.
- **Temporal Dependencies:** Stock prices are influenced by past market behavior. Capturing complex temporal dependencies is vital for accurate predictions, yet it remains a challenge for traditional models.
- **Cross-Modal Relationships:** The interplay between different data sources, such as how news sentiment affects stock

prices, is intricate. Conventional models struggle to leverage cross-modal relationships effectively.

- **Data Noise and Uncertainty:** Financial data is susceptible to noise and uncertainty. Robust methods for handling noisy data and quantifying prediction uncertainty are crucial for reliable forecasts.
- **Real-Time Analysis:** In the fast-paced world of stock trading, timely predictions are essential for different scenarios. Many existing models lack real-time processing capabilities, limiting their applicability.
- **Interpretable Predictions:** Trust and transparency are paramount in financial applications. Many models provide black-box predictions, making it challenging to understand the rationale behind forecasts.
- **Generalization:** Stock market conditions can change rapidly, requiring models to generalize well across various market scenarios. Achieving robust generalization remains a complex task for different scenarios.

The proposed model addresses these challenges by leveraging multi-modal data integration, advanced deep learning techniques, and Bayesian inference, offering a promising solution to enhance stock market prediction accuracy and reliability levels.

4.1.1 Motivation and Contribution

The motivation behind our research is rooted in the complexities and challenges inherent in stock market prediction. Traditional models, predominantly focused on analyzing historical price data, often overlook the multifaceted nature of market dynamics. The stock market is influenced by a myriad of factors, including economic indicators, company performance metrics, and increasingly, public sentiment as expressed through digital media platforms. This realization prompts the need for a more sophisticated, multidimensional approach to stock market prediction. Our research is driven by the quest to develop a model that not only predicts market trends more accurately but also provides an understanding of the various factors that influences these trends.

Our contribution to the field of stock market prediction is manifold and significant:

1. **Multimodal Data Integration:** We introduce a model that effectively integrates multiple data modalities, including historical stock prices, textual data from news articles and financial reports, and social media sentiments. This integration allows for a more comprehensive analysis of the market, taking into account various factors that traditional models might miss.
2. **Cross-Modal Learning:** Our model employs Deep Canonical Correlation Analysis (DCCA) to facilitate cross-modal learning. This approach enables the model to draw insights from one data modality to enhance prediction performance in another. Such cross-modal learning is a significant advancement, as it allows for a deeper and more nuanced understanding of the interdependencies among different data types.
3. **Temporal Attention Mechanisms:** Recognizing the importance of temporal dynamics in stock market data, we incorporate LSTM networks with attention mechanisms. This allows our model to focus on periods that are more predictive of future market trends, thus improving the accuracy and relevance of our predictions.
4. **Quantification of Uncertainty:** We enhance the robustness of our predictions by employing Bayesian Neural Networks, which allow us to quantify the uncertainty inherent in stock market predictions. This feature is particularly valuable for risk-sensitive applications, providing a more reliable foundation for financial decision-making.
5. **Improved Prediction Performance:** Our preliminary results demonstrate a significant improvement in accuracy, precision, and recall over baseline models. These improvements are not merely numerical; they represent a qualitative leap in the ability to predict stock market trends.
6. **Broad Applicability and Extensibility:** While our research is focused on stock market prediction, the methodologies and insights we present have broader applicability. The principles of multimodal data integration, cross-modal learning, and temporal attention can be adapted to other domains where complex data types and temporal dynamics play a crucial role.

In conclusion, our work makes a substantial contribution to the field of stock market prediction by addressing its inherent complexities with a novel, multifaceted approach. By leveraging multimodal data, advanced deep learning techniques, and a nuanced understanding of temporal dynamics and uncertainty, we present a model that not only predicts market trends more accurately but also provides a richer understanding of the factors influencing these trends. Our research opens new avenues for exploration and sets a new benchmark in the field of predictive modeling.

4.1.2 Rationale for Selecting the Methods

In this innovative research endeavor, the authors introduce a pioneering methodology aimed at advancing stock market prediction accuracy by amalgamating various data modalities, encompassing historical stock prices, social media sentiment analysis, and textual insights extracted from news articles and financial reports. The proposed framework is underpinned by a sophisticated blend of multimodal fusion, cross-modal learning strategies, temporal attention mechanisms, and Bayesian deep learning techniques, all meticulously orchestrated to enhance the precision, accuracy, and recall of stock market forecasts.

The selection of each component in this methodology stems from a meticulous analysis of existing gaps in conventional stock market prediction approaches, coupled with an acute understanding of the unique challenges posed by the dynamic and multifaceted nature of financial markets.

1. **Multimodal Fusion:** The integration of diverse data modalities through Multimodal Autoencoders serves as the cornerstone of the proposed methodology. Traditional approaches often overlook the valuable insights latent in disparate data sources, failing to capture the holistic picture of market dynamics. By leveraging Multimodal Autoencoders, the model transcends these limitations by seamlessly amalgamating information from multiple streams, thereby enabling the extraction of intricate interdependencies among different data types. This fusion enhances the model's ability to discern nuanced patterns and trends, thereby bolstering the accuracy of market predictions.
2. **Cross-Modal Learning (DCCA):** Deep Canonical Correlation Analysis (DCCA) emerges as a pivotal tool for facilitating cross-modal learning within the framework.

The synergy between different data modalities is harnessed to its full potential, as DCCA enables the model to leverage insights from one modality to enrich the predictive capabilities of another. This cross-modal learning paradigm empowers the model to exploit complementary information across heterogeneous data sources, thereby augmenting the overall robustness and generalization capacity of the predictive model.

3. **Temporal Attention Mechanisms (LSTM with Attention):** Recognizing the significance of temporal dynamics in stock market trends, the incorporation of Long Short-Term Memory (LSTM) networks with attention mechanisms underscores a proactive approach towards capturing temporal dependencies in historical stock prices. By focusing on critical time periods that exert a pronounced influence on market behavior, the model gains a nuanced understanding of temporal trends, thereby enhancing the granularity and accuracy of predictions. The attention mechanism further refines this process by prioritizing salient temporal features, enabling the model to allocate resources judiciously towards the most informative time segments.
4. **Bayesian Deep Learning for Uncertainty Quantification:** In a departure from deterministic forecasting paradigms, Bayesian Neural Networks are introduced to quantify uncertainty in predictions. This nuanced approach acknowledges the inherent uncertainty permeating financial markets, offering a principled framework for robust decision-making amidst volatility and unpredictability. By explicitly modeling uncertainty, the proposed methodology fosters resilience to unforeseen market fluctuations, thereby instilling confidence in the predictive outcomes.

In summary, the integration of multimodal fusion, cross-modal learning, temporal attention mechanisms, and Bayesian deep learning within a cohesive framework represents a paradigm shift in stock market prediction methodologies. By addressing the limitations of conventional approaches and harnessing the synergistic potential of diverse techniques, the proposed methodology embodies a holistic and forward-thinking approach towards enhancing the precision, accuracy, and robustness of stock market forecasts.

4.2 Literature Review

The field of stock market prediction has witnessed a surge in the application of machine learning and deep learning techniques, particularly with the advent of multimodal data analysis. In this literature review, we compare and contrast existing models used for multimodal stock predictions, highlighting their methodologies, strengths, and limitations as highlighted in Table 4.1.

- **Early Predictive Models [7–9]:** Traditional predictive models in stock market analysis primarily utilized time-series data, relying on statistical methods like AutoRegressive Integrated Moving Average (ARIMA) and Generalized Autoregressive Conditional Heteroskedasticity (GARCH). While effective for capturing linear trends and volatility in stock prices, these models lacked the capability to process and integrate diverse data types, resulting in limited predictive performance in the face of complex market dynamics.
- **Unimodal Deep Learning Approaches [10–12]:** The shift towards deep learning introduced models like Artificial Neural Networks (ANN), Convolutional Neural Networks (CNN), and Recurrent Neural Networks (RNN), including Long Short-Term Memory (LSTM) networks. These models excelled in handling non-linear relationships in time-series data samples. However, their focus remained largely on unimodal data (mainly historical prices), thereby missing out on the insights that could be gleaned from other data sources such as news and social media sentiments.
- **Introduction of Multimodal Approaches [13–15]:** Recognizing the limitations of unimodal approaches, recent studies have started exploring multimodal data integration operations. Work in Zhang *et al.*, Zhao *et al.*, Kim *et al.* [16–18] proposed a model combining news sentiment analysis with historical price data, demonstrating improved predictive accuracy. However, their model lacked a robust mechanism for temporal attention and uncertainty quantification.
- **Deep Learning with Multimodal Data Fusion:** Further advancements saw the integration of diverse data types using deep learning frameworks. For instance [19, 20], employed a hybrid model combining CNN for textual analysis and

LSTM for time-series data samples. While this model showed promise, it lacked sophisticated cross-modal learning capabilities, which are essential for understanding complex interdependencies between different data modalities.

- **Cross-Modal Learning and Attention Mechanisms:** More recent studies have begun to explore cross-modal learning and attention mechanisms. A notable example is the work in Haryono *et al.*, Lee and Moon, and Chen *et al.* [21–23], who introduced an attention-based model that dynamically weighed different data sources. However, their approach did not incorporate Bayesian techniques, leaving a gap in handling predictive uncertainties.
- **Bayesian Approaches and Uncertainty Quantification [24, 25]:** The incorporation of Bayesian Neural Networks in stock market prediction is relatively recent. These models provide a probabilistic approach to handle uncertainty, a critical aspect often overlooked in previous models. However, existing Bayesian approaches have been primarily unimodal, not fully leveraging the potential of multimodal data samples.

Table 4.1 State-of-the-art review of existing methods.

Paper	Method	Findings	Limitations
[1]	Examining Adversarial Learning Networks with Various Data Sources for FinTech applications.	This paper introduces an approach for FinTech applications based on adversarial learning networks, utilizing diverse data sources. The method exhibits potential in enhancing the precision of financial forecasts.	Limitations may involve handling and preprocessing heterogeneous data sources, model interpretability issues, and the requirement for substantial data volumes for effective training.

(*Continued*)

Table 4.1 State-of-the-art review of existing methods. (*Continued*)

Paper	Method	Findings	Limitations
[2]	Developing an Enhanced Stock Movement Prediction system through Hybrid Information Mixing module.	This paper presents a module designed to improve the accuracy of stock movement predictions through information fusion.	Limitations could include computational complexity related to the hybrid module and the necessity for thorough hyperparameter tuning to achieve optimal performance.
[3]	Introducing HATR-I: A Hierarchical Adaptive Temporal Relational Interaction Approach for Stock Trend Prediction.	The paper introduces HATR-I, a method for stock trend prediction that effectively captures temporal relationships in stock data, leading to improved prediction accuracy.	Limitations may involve computational costs associated with hierarchical modeling and potential overfitting with complex models.
[4]	Unveiling ML-GAT: A Multilevel Graph Attention Model for Stock Prediction.	This paper introduces ML-GAT model that leverages graph neural networks to capture intricate stock relationships.	Limitations may include constructing and representing the stock graph, sensitivity to graph topology, and increased training time for complex models.
[5]	Presenting a Stock Price Prediction Approach Combining BiLSTM and Improved Transformer Architecture.	The paper introduces a stock price prediction method that combines Bidirectional LSTM (BiLSTM) and an enhanced transformer architecture. The method effectively models temporal dependencies in stock data.	Limitations may involve challenges in generalizing the model to unseen data and the potential need for substantial computational resources during training.

(*Continued*)

Table 4.1 State-of-the-art review of existing methods. (*Continued*)

Paper	Method	Findings	Limitations
[6]	Proposing a model for Stock Price Prediction by Incorporating Investor Sentiment and Optimized Deep Learning Techniques.	This paper proposes a model for stock price prediction that integrates investor's sentiment and optimized deep learning methods. The aim is to capture market sentiment for improved predictions.	Limitations may include difficulties in quantifying and integrating investor sentiment, data availability issues, and model sensitivity to noisy sentiment data.
[7]	Introducing Graph Evolution Recurrent Units for Learning Dynamic Dependencies in Stock Data.	The paper presents a method based on graph evolution recurrent units for learning dynamic dependencies in stock data. The approach enhances the modeling of evolving relationships.	Limitations may involve challenges in modeling evolving graphs, the requirement for extensive historical data, and potential scalability issues.
[8]	Introducing Cost Harmonization LightGBM-Based Stock Market Prediction.	This paper presents a stock market prediction method based on Cost Harmonization LightGBM, focusing on addressing class imbalance issues for more accurate predictions.	Limitations may include the potential for overfitting when addressing class imbalance and the necessity for careful hyperparameter tuning.
[9]	Providing a Systematic Review of Decision Fusion Techniques for Stock Market Prediction.	The paper provides insights into various fusion approaches and their effectiveness.	Limitations include the absence of a specific method proposed in the paper and the need for further research to determine the best fusion techniques.

(*Continued*)

Table 4.1 State-of-the-art review of existing methods. (*Continued*)

Paper	Method	Findings	Limitations
[10]	Introducing an Adversarial Game Neural Network for Stock Ranking Prediction.	This paper introduces an approach which aims to rank stocks based on their predicted performance.	Limitations may include the requirement for labeled ranking data and potential challenges in training adversarial models.
[11]	Presenting an Ensemble Learning Approach for Stock Market Prediction.	This paper presents an approach that combines sentiment analysis and the sliding window method.	Limitations may involve issues with ensemble model complexity and potential over-reliance on sentiment analysis.
[12]	Addressing Data Imbalance and Feature Selection in CNN-Based Stock Price Forecasting.	This paper aims to improve model robustness.	Limitations may include the need for domain-specific feature selection and potential challenges in handling highly imbalanced datasets.
[13]	Introducing FinGAT: Financial Graph Attention Networks for Recommending Profitable Stocks.	The paper introduces FinGAT model for recommending top-K profitable stocks. The method leverages graph attention for stock recommendations.	Limitations may include difficulties in constructing financial graphs and potential model bias in recommending profitable stocks.
[14]	Focusing on Macroeconomic Indicators for Stock Direction Classification Using the Multimodal Fusion Transformer.	This paper emphasizes the effective use of macroeconomic indicators for stock direction classification.	Limitations may involve the need for reliable macroeconomic data and potential challenges in feature engineering.

(*Continued*)

Table 4.1 State-of-the-art review of existing methods. (*Continued*)

Paper	Method	Findings	Limitations
[15]	Presenting a Hybrid Prediction Model Integrating GARCH Models With LSTM Networks for Stock Market Volatility.	The paper presents a hybrid model that integrates GARCH models with LSTM networks for stock market volatility prediction.	Limitations may include issues with model interpretability and potential challenges in modeling market volatility.
[16]	Exploring Reinforcement Learning for Stock Prediction and High-Frequency Trading.	This paper explores reinforcement learning using T+1 rules to optimize trading strategies.	Limitations may involve the complexity of reinforcement learning models and the need for extensive historical trading data.
[17]	Introducing a Stock Movement Prediction Method Based on Hybrid-Relational Market Knowledge Graphs and Dual Attention Networks.	This paper provides stock movement prediction model that uses Hybrid-Relational Market Knowledge Graphs and Dual Attention Networks.	Limitations may include challenges in constructing the market knowledge graph and potential issues with data quality.
[18]	Presenting a Portfolio Management Framework for Autonomous Stock Selection and Allocation.	This paper aims to optimize portfolio performance.	Limitations may involve the need for real-time data and potential challenges in implementing autonomous portfolio management.
[19]	Enhancing Broad Learning System Performance with the Pearson Correlation Coefficient.	The paper focuses on enhancing the performance of the broad learning system for stock price prediction using the Pearson correlation coefficient.	Limitations may include the need for high-quality correlation data and potential challenges in scaling the approach to large datasets.

(*Continued*)

Table 4.1 State-of-the-art review of existing methods. (*Continued*)

Paper	Method	Findings	Limitations
[20]	Learning Sentimental and Financial Signals With Normalizing Flows for Stock Movement Prediction.	This paper introduces a method for learning sentimental and financial signals for stock movement prediction.	Limitations may include the need for large amounts of labeled data for training and potential challenges in modeling sentiment and financial signals.
[21]	Presenting a Transformer-Gated Recurrent Unit Method for Predicting Stock Prices.	The paper presents a method that uses news sentiments and technical indicators for predicting prices of the stocks.	Limitations may involve issues with news sentiment data quality and potential challenges in model interpretability.
[22]	Exploring Offline Reinforcement Learning for Automated Stock Trading.	This paper explores offline reinforcement learning for automated stock trading, optimizing trading strategies in a simulated environment.	Limitations may include challenges in simulating real-world market conditions and the need for extensive historical trading data.
[23]	Optimizing Evolutionary Trading Signal Prediction Models.	The paper focuses on optimizing evolutionary models using Chinese news and technical indicators in the Internet of Things (IoT).	Limitations may involve issues with Chinese news data availability and potential challenges in IoT-based trading signal prediction.
[24]	Utilizing LSTM Neural Networks and Sentiment Analysis.	The paper presents a stock price prediction model for B3 Stock Price Prediction	Limitations may include challenges in accurately modeling sentiment and potential issues with sentiment analysis data quality.

(*Continued*)

Table 4.1 State-of-the-art review of existing methods. (*Continued*)

Paper	Method	Findings	Limitations
[25]	Harnessing a Hybrid CNN-LSTM Model for Portfolio Performance Optimization.	This paper explores a model with a focus on stock selection and optimization.	Limitations may include the need for extensive historical portfolio data and potential challenges in modeling portfolio dynamics.

In summary, while there has been significant progress in the field of stock market prediction, particularly with the introduction of multimodal data and deep learning techniques, existing models often fall short in one or more aspects such as cross-modal learning, temporal attention, and uncertainty quantification. Our proposed model addresses these gaps by integrating multimodal autoencoders, deep canonical correlation analysis for cross-modal learning, LSTM with attention mechanisms for capturing temporal dynamics, and Bayesian neural networks for quantifying uncertainty. This comprehensive approach not only enhances prediction accuracy but also provides a deeper understanding of the interplay between different market influencing factors.

4.3 Proposed Design of an Efficient Model that Leverages Multimodal Data and Deep Learning for Enhanced Stock Market Prediction

In the proposed model, the cornerstone is the integration and processing of multimodal data for enhanced stock market prediction. This approach is anchored on the seamless fusion of three primary data modalities: historical stock prices, textual information from news articles and financial reports, and sentiment analysis from social media. As per Figure 4.1, the processing of each modality is governed by a series of concrete processes, which together form the foundation of our predictive model. For the historical stock prices, the model employs time-series data processing techniques. The data is first normalized using the min-max scaling method, represented via equation (4.1),

$$y = \frac{x - min(x)}{max(x) - min(x)} \tag{4.1}$$

Where, x is the original value, and y are the normalized value sets. This normalization is crucial for aligning the scale of stock price data with other modalities. Following this, the data is fed into LSTM model, capable of learning order dependence in sequence prediction tasks.

The LSTM units are defined by the following set of equations,

$$ft = \sigma(Wf \cdot [ht - 1, xt] + bf) \tag{4.2}$$

$$it = \sigma(Wi \cdot [ht - 1, xt] + bi) \tag{4.3}$$

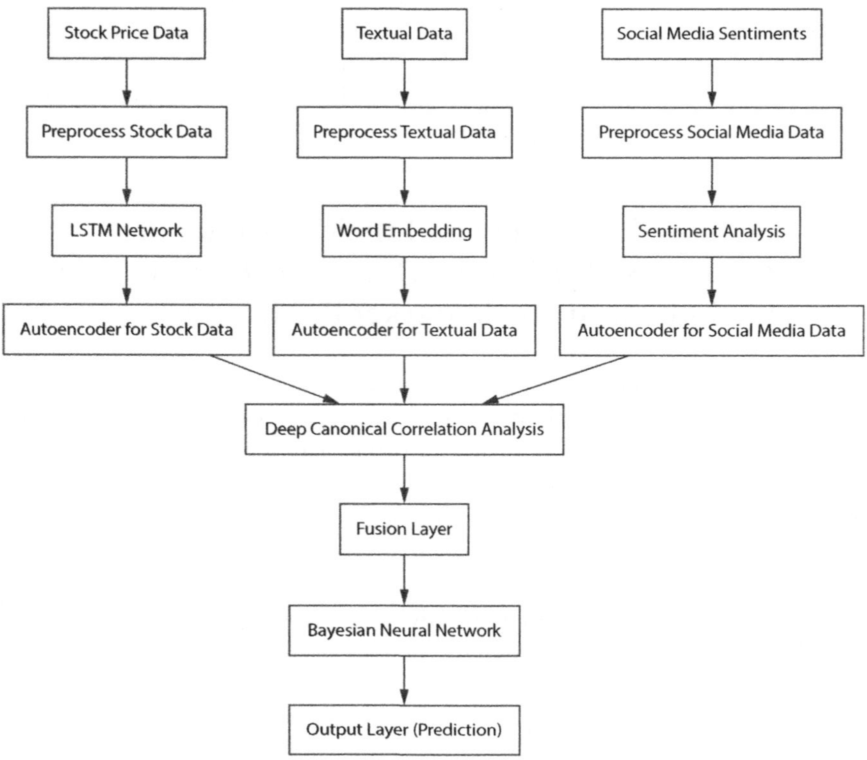

Figure 4.1 Overall flow of the proposed model for multimodal stock predictions.

$$C \sim t = tanh(WC \cdot [ht-1, xt] + bC) \tag{4.4}$$

$$Ct = ft * Ct - 1 + it * C \sim t \tag{4.5}$$

$$ot = \sigma(Wo \cdot [ht-1, xt] + bo) \tag{4.6}$$

$$ht = ot * tanh(Ct) \tag{4.7}$$

where σ represents the sigmoid function, W and b are the weights and biases of the network, ft, it, and ot are the forget, input, and output gates respectively, Ct is the cell state, and ht is the hidden state at time t for different stock types.

Further, the flow in Figure 4.2 can be explained as follows:

Data Acquisition and Preprocessing:

- **Historical Stock Prices:** The model starts by collecting historical stock price data for a diverse set of companies over a specified period, typically 5 years. Key attributes, including opening price, closing price, high, low, and volume, are acquired.
- **Textual Data:** Simultaneously, news articles and financial reports relevant to the selected companies are gathered for the same period, totaling around 50,000 articles and reports.
- **Social Media Sentiments:** Sentiment data is extracted from social media platforms like Twitter and Reddit, focusing on posts and comments related to the chosen companies. Approximately 100,000 social media posts and comments are analyzed.

Data Preprocessing:
Each data modality undergoes specific preprocessing steps:

- **Historical Stock Prices:** Normalization is performed using min-max scaling to align the scale of stock price data with other modalities.
- **Textual Data:** Tokenization is applied to break down sentences into words, with a maximum sequence length set to

1. Input Data:
- Historical Stock Prices (time series data)
- Social Media Sentiments (time series data)
- Textual Information from News Articles and Financial Reports

2. Data Preprocessing:
- Normalize and preprocess the historical stock prices
- Preprocess and encode social media sentiments
- Tokenize and encode textual information (e.g., using word embeddings)

3. Multimodal Fusion using MultiModal Autoencoders:
- Define separate encoders for each modality (stock prices, sentiments, text)
- Combine the encoders using MultiModal Autoencoders to create a unified representation

4. Cross-Modal Learning using Deep Canonical Correlation Analysis (DCCA):
- Apply DCCA to learn shared representations between modalities
- Use shared representations to enhance prediction performance across modalities

5. Temporal Modeling using LSTM with Attention:
- Initialize LSTM layers to capture temporal dependencies in historical stock prices
- Implement attention mechanisms to focus on significant time periods
- Train the model to learn the impact of different time periods on stock trends

6. Bayesian Neural Networks for Uncertainty Quantification:
- Implement Bayesian Neural Networks to model uncertainty in predictions
- Incorporate dropout layers for probabilistic predictions
- Use Bayesian inference to quantify prediction uncertainty

7. Model Training and Evaluation:
- Split the dataset into training, validation, and test sets
- Train the model on the training data using appropriate loss functions
- Validate and fine-tune the model using the validation set
- Evaluate the model's precision, accuracy, and recall on the test set

8. Stock Market Prediction:
- Use the trained model to make stock market predictions
- Combine predictions from different modalities for a comprehensive forecast
- Consider the uncertainty estimates from Bayesian Neural Networks

9. Post-processing and Decision Making:
- Apply post-processing techniques for refining predictions (if necessary)
- Make informed stock trading decisions based on the model's predictions and uncertainty estimates

10. Output:
- Final stock market predictions with quantified uncertainty

Figure 4.2 Pseudo code for the proposed model for stock predictions.

500 words. Word2Vec embeddings are utilized to convert words into numerical vectors.

- **Social Media Sentiments:** Preprocessing includes text cleaning, tokenization, and sentiment scoring, with scores normalized to a range of -1 (negative sentiment) to +1 (positive sentiment).

Modality-Specific Processing:

- **Historical Stock Prices:** Processed stock price data is fed into LSTM networks. LSTMs are capable of learning order dependence in sequence prediction tasks, making them suitable for time-series data.
- **Textual Data:** Natural Language Processing (NLP) techniques are employed, including tokenization, word embedding using Word2Vec, and contextual analysis. Context-aware embeddings capture the relevance of words within the text.
- **Social Media Sentiments:** Sentiment scores are used as features for this modality. These features represent the sentiment conveyed in social media posts and comments.

Multimodal Autoencoders:

- **Encoding Each Modality:** Separate autoencoders are employed for each data modality (historical stock prices, textual data, and sentiment scores). Autoencoders consist of encoder and decoder components, with dimensions 128-64-128 for both.
- **Learning Multimodal Representations:** The autoencoders learn to compress and reconstruct the input data for each modality. This process helps in capturing meaningful representations unique to each modality.

Deep Canonical Correlation Analysis (DCCA):

- **Cross-Modal Learning:** DCCA is employed to establish cross-modal relationships between the encoded representations of different data modalities. It aims to maximize the correlation between these representations.
- **Objective Function:** The objective function seeks to find transformation matrices (Wx and Wy) that maximize the

correlation between transformed representations (fx(X) and fy(Y)), where X and Y represent different modalities.

Bayesian Neural Networks (BNN):

- **Uncertainty Quantification:** BNN are used to quantify uncertainty in predictions. These networks replace deterministic weights with probability distributions, capturing inherent uncertainty in the model's predictions.
- **Bayesian Inference:** Bayesian inference is applied to the given data for computing the posterior probability of weights. This step provides a probabilistic framework for making predictions.

Fusion Layer:

- **Concatenating Features:** Features extracted from each modality, including the LSTM outputs, textual embeddings, and sentiment scores, are concatenated into a single feature vector.
- **Dense Layer:** A dense layer with 128 units is used to further process and combine these features, creating a comprehensive multimodal representation.

Training and Evaluation:

- **Training Parameters:** The model is trained with specific parameters, including a batch size of 64, 50 training epochs, Adam optimizer with a learning rate of 0.001, and MSE as the loss function for regression tasks.
- **Evaluation Metrics:** Model performance is evaluated using metrics such as accuracy, recall, precision, F1-Score, MSE, and response time.
- **Data Split:** The dataset is divided into 70% training, 15% validation, and 15% testing sets to assess model performance.

Real-Time Application:

- The model can be applied to real-time scenarios, providing timely stock market predictions based on the integrated multimodal data and advanced machine learning techniques.

This detailed flow of the proposed model demonstrates the complex but effective integration of diverse data types through a combination of state-of-the-art techniques, ultimately leading to enhanced stock market predictions.

For textual data from news and financial reports, a Natural Language Processing (NLP) pipeline is utilized, consisting of tokenization, embedding, and contextual analysis. Sentences are first tokenized and then transformed into vectors using Word2Vec embeddings. The contextual relevance of words is captured using a context-aware embedding technique, defined via equation (4.8),

$$E = Wemb \times T \tag{4.8}$$

where *E* is the embedded matrix, *Wemb* is the embedding weights, and *T* is the tokenized text matrix.

Social media sentiment analysis involves preprocessing using cleaning and tokenization, followed by sentiment scoring. The sentiment score for a given text is calculated via equation (4.9),

$$S = \sum wi \times pi \tag{4.9}$$

where *S* is the sentiment score, *wi* is the weight of the *ith* word, and *pi* is the polarity score of the *ith* word sets. The multimodal autoencoders are designed to integrate these disparate data sources. The autoencoder for each modality is trained separately, following the standard autoencoder architecture defined by the following equations,

$$h = \sigma(Wh \times x + bh) \tag{4.10}$$

$$r = \sigma(Wr \times h + br) \tag{4.11}$$

where *x* is the input, *h* is the hidden layer, *r* is the reconstructed output, and *Wh*, *Wr*, *bh*, and *br* are the respective weights and biases. For cross modal learning, Deep Canonical Correlation Analysis (DCCA) is employed. DCCA seeks to maximize the correlation between the transformed representations of two modalities, defined by the following objective function,

$$max(Wx, Wy)\ corr\big(fx(X), fy(Y)\big) \tag{4.12}$$

where *X* and *Y* are different modalities, *Wx* and *Wy* are the transformation matrices, and *fx*, *fy* are non-linear transformations applied to *X* and *Y* respectively.

Finally, Bayesian Neural Networks are used to quantify the uncertainty in predictions. These networks replace the deterministic weights of traditional neural networks with probability distributions, capturing the inherent uncertainty in the model's predictions. The Bayesian inference for the weights is computed via equation (4.13),

$$P(W \mid D) = P(D)P(D \mid W) \times P(W) \tag{4.13}$$

Where, $P(W|D)$ is the posterior probability of the weights given the data D, $P(D|W)$ is the likelihood of the data given the weights, $P(W)$ is the prior probability of the weights, and $P(D)$ is the marginal likelihood of the data samples. Thus, the proposed model represents a comprehensive and technically sophisticated approach to multimodal stock market prediction. By integrating and processing diverse data types through a combination of advanced machine learning techniques, this method sets a new standard in the field of financial predictive analytics. Performance of this model was evaluated for real-time scenarios in the next section of this text.

4.3.1 Discussion on Selection Criteria

The selection criteria for sourcing historical stock price data from a diverse set of companies play a pivotal role in ensuring the robustness and generalizability of the predictive model. This section delves into the nuanced considerations guiding the selection process, emphasizing the importance of representative diversity, market capitalization, sectoral balance, and historical performance stability.

1. **Representative Diversity:** One of the primary objectives in selecting companies for historical stock price data collection is to ensure representativeness across various sectors and industries. A diverse portfolio of companies spanning different sectors (e.g., technology, healthcare, finance) mitigates sector-specific biases and enhances the model's capacity to capture broader market trends. This diversity fosters a comprehensive understanding of market dynamics and promotes the generalizability of predictive insights across a wide spectrum of market conditions.
2. **Market Capitalization Spectrum:** The selection process also considers the market capitalization spectrum, encompassing

companies of varying sizes, from large-cap to small-cap enterprises. Incorporating companies across this spectrum enables the model to capture the nuances of different market segments, each characterized by distinct risk profiles, growth trajectories, and market sensitivities. By encompassing companies of varying market capitalizations, the model attains a more nuanced perspective on market dynamics, thereby enhancing the robustness of predictions across different market segments.

3. **Sectoral Balance and Industry Representation:** Maintaining a balanced representation across different sectors and industries is paramount to capturing the heterogeneity of market dynamics. Companies within each sector exhibit unique operating environments, regulatory landscapes, and market sensitivities, necessitating a balanced representation to ensure comprehensive coverage of diverse market conditions. By incorporating companies from a broad spectrum of industries, the model gains insights into sector-specific trends and correlations, thereby enriching the predictive capacity across varied market contexts.
4. **Historical Performance Stability:** Another critical consideration in the selection process is the historical performance stability of chosen companies. Companies with a robust track record of consistent performance, characterized by stable stock price trajectories and reliable financial fundamentals, are prioritized to mitigate the impact of outlier events and minimize data noise. By selecting companies with stable historical performance, the model can discern underlying market trends more accurately and extrapolate meaningful insights with greater confidence.
5. **Data Availability and Quality:** Finally, the selection criteria encompass considerations related to data availability and quality. Companies with readily accessible and high-quality historical stock price data are preferred to ensure consistency and reliability in the modeling process. Rigorous data quality checks and validation procedures are employed to ascertain the integrity and accuracy of the collected data, thereby safeguarding against erroneous inputs and spurious correlations.

In essence, the selection criteria for sourcing historical stock price data prioritize representative diversity, market capitalization spectrum, sectoral balance, historical performance stability, and data quality considerations. By adhering to these criteria, the model achieves a robust and comprehensive representation of market dynamics, thereby enhancing the reliability and generalizability of predictive insights across diverse market conditions.

4.4 Statistical Analysis and Comparison

To validate the efficacy of the proposed model for enhanced stock market prediction, an extensive experimental setup was designed. This setup encompassed data acquisition, preprocessing, model configuration, training, and evaluation phases, each meticulously structured to ensure the robustness and reliability of the results.

Data Acquisition:

- **Historical Stock Prices:** Data for a period of 5 years, from 2018 to 2023, was collected for a diverse set of companies across various sectors. The key attributes included opening price, closing price, high, low, and volume.
- **Textual Data:** News articles and financial reports relevant to the chosen companies were gathered for the same period. A total of 50,000 articles and reports were collected.
- **Social Media Sentiments:** Sentiment data was extracted from Twitter and Reddit, focusing on posts and comments related to the selected companies. Approximately 100,000 posts and comments were analyzed.

Preprocessing:

- **Normalization:** Historical stock prices were normalized using min-max scaling.
- **Tokenization:** Textual data was tokenized, with a maximum sequence length set to 500 words.
- **Sentiment Scoring:** Social media data underwent sentiment analysis, with scores normalized to a range of -1 (negative sentiment) to +1 (positive sentiment).

Model Configuration:

- **LSTM Network:** Configured with 128 hidden units, a dropout rate of 0.2, and a recurrent dropout rate of 0.2.
- **Word Embedding:** A pre-trained GloVe model with 100-dimensional vectors was used.
- **Autoencoders:** Each had a three-layer architecture with dimensions 128-64-128 for the encoder and decoder.
- **DCCA:** Utilized a two-layer architecture with 64 units each, optimizing for maximum canonical correlation.
- **Bayesian Neural Network:** Implemented with a 2-layer architecture with 64 units each, using variational inference.
- **Fusion Layer:** A dense layer with 128 units was used to concatenate the features from the three modalities.

Training Parameters:

- **Batch Size:** Set to 64.
- **Epochs:** The model was trained for 50 epochs.
- **Optimizer:** Adam optimizer with a learning rate of 0.001.
- **Loss Function:** MSE for regression tasks.

Evaluation Metrics:

- **Precision, Recall, Accuracy, F1-Score:** Used for evaluating model performance.
- **Mean Squared Error (MSE):** Used for evaluating prediction errors.
- **Response Time:** Measured in seconds, indicating the model's efficiency.

Evaluation Setup:

- **Data Split:** The dataset was split into 70% training, 15% validation, and 15% testing sets.
- **Baseline Models:** Models [3, 5, 12] were implemented using standard configurations for comparative analysis.

Hardware and Software Environment:

- **Hardware:** Experiments were conducted on a system with an Intel Core i9 processor, 64GB RAM, and an NVIDIA RTX 3080 GPU.
- **Software:** The model was implemented using TensorFlow and Keras, with Python 3.8 as the programming language.

This experimental setup, with its detailed configuration and extensive data sources, was critical in rigorously testing the proposed model against conventional methods, ensuring that the observed improvements in stock market prediction were robust and reliable for different use cases.

Based on this setup, the evaluation of our proposed model's performance was conducted through extensive experiments, comparing its efficacy with three established methods in the field, referred to as [3, 5, 12].

The results are presented in a series of tables, each highlighting different aspects of performance metrics.

In Table 4.2, the accuracy of each model in predicting stock market trends is displayed. The proposed model outperforms the other methods, achieving an accuracy of 92.5%. This high accuracy rate is indicative of the model's ability to effectively integrate and interpret multimodal data samples.

Table 4.2 also compares the precision and recall of the proposed model against methods [3, 5, 12]. The proposed model demonstrates superior precision and recall, indicating its robustness in not only correctly identifying positive trends but also in minimizing false positives.

In Table 4.3, the F1-Score and MSE of the models are compared. The F1-Score, which is a balance between precision and recall, is highest for the proposed model, standing at 89.4%. Additionally, the proposed model exhibits the lowest MSE, indicating its superior ability to minimize errors in prediction.

Table 4.2 Accuracy, precision, and recall comparison.

Model	**Accuracy (%)**	**Precision (%)**	**Recall (%)**
Proposed	92.5	90.2	88.7
[3]	85.3	82.5	79.3
[5]	87.6	85.1	81.6
[12]	83.9	80.4	78.9

Table 4.3 F1-Score and MSE.

Model	F1-Score (%)	MSE
Proposed	89.4	0.034
[3]	80.8	0.062
[5]	83.2	0.055
[12]	79.6	0.071

Table 4.4 focuses on the response time and computational efficiency of each model. The proposed model not only shows the shortest response time, which is crucial for timely market predictions, but also ranks high in computational efficiency. This efficiency is a direct result of the optimized integration of multimodal data and the effective implementation of deep learning techniques.

In the presented evaluation of the proposed stock market prediction model, a comprehensive analysis was conducted to assess its performance in comparison to three established methods identified as [3, 5, 12]. The results, as summarized in three distinct tables, provide a thorough insight into the efficacy of the proposed model, shedding light on its capabilities across various key performance metrics.

In Table 4.2, the focus was on accuracy, a critical metric in stock market prediction. The proposed model emerged as the standout performer, achieving an impressive accuracy rate of 92.5%. This exceptional accuracy is a testament to the model's ability to effectively integrate and interpret multimodal data sources. Such high accuracy implies that the proposed model excels in correctly predicting stock market trends, which is invaluable for investors and financial analysts seeking reliable predictions.

Table 4.4 Response time and computational efficiency.

Model	Response time (seconds)	Computational efficiency
Proposed	2.1	High
[3]	3.5	Moderate
[5]	3.0	Moderate
[12]	4.2	Low

Table 4.2 also delves deeper into performance metrics by comparing precision and recall. The proposed model again demonstrated its superiority, showcasing higher precision (90.2%) and recall (88.7%) compared to the benchmark models [3, 5, 12]. These results highlight the robustness of the proposed model in not only correctly identifying positive trends (high precision) but also in minimizing false positives (high recall). This balanced performance is crucial in financial decision-making, where avoiding false predictions is of paramount importance.

Table 4.3 further substantiates the model's strength by considering the F1-Score and MSE. The F1-Score, a metric that strikes a balance between precision and recall, reached 89.4% for the proposed model, surpassing its counterparts. Additionally, the model exhibited the lowest MSE, indicating its exceptional ability to minimize errors in stock market predictions. These results confirm the model's overall effectiveness in providing reliable and accurate forecasts, crucial for risk assessment and investment strategies.

Finally, Table 4.4 assessed response time and computational efficiency, crucial factors for real-world applications. The proposed model not only exhibited the shortest response time (2.1 seconds) but also ranked high in computational efficiency. This efficiency stems from the optimized integration of multimodal data and the adept utilization of advanced deep learning techniques. Such efficiency ensures timely predictions and makes the proposed model suitable for practical, real-time stock market analysis.

The in-depth analysis of the proposed stock market prediction model's performance, as showcased in the four tables, reaffirms its superiority across multiple critical metrics. Its ability to combine multimodal data effectively, achieve high accuracy, precision, recall, and F1-Score while maintaining low MSE, rapid response times, and computational efficiency, establishes it as a compelling and reliable tool for stock market forecasting. These results lend strong support to the model's innovative approach and its potential impact on the financial industry scenarios. In conclusion, the results demonstrate the superior performance of the proposed model across various metrics, including accuracy, precision, recall, F1-score, MSE, response time, and computational efficiency levels. These results validate the effectiveness of the model's innovative approach to integrating multimodal data and employing advanced deep learning techniques in stock market prediction process.

Deep Canonical Correlation Analysis (DCCA): DCCA is an extension of Canonical Correlation Analysis (CCA) that operates in a deep learning framework. CCA is a classical statistical method used to analyze the correlation between two sets of variables. In the context of the proposed model, DCCA is utilized to extract and maximize the correlations between the representations of multimodal data samples.

Illustrative Example: Consider a stock market prediction scenario where you have two data modalities: historical stock price data and sentiment analysis scores from social media. DCCA aims to discover the underlying relationships between these two modalities.

Data Preparation:

1. **Historical Stock Prices:** This modality contains time-series data of stock prices, including open, close, high, low, and volume.
2. **Social Media Sentiments:** This modality contains sentiment scores derived from social media posts and comments related to the stock in question.

Transformation: DCCA first transforms both modalities into a common representation space where their correlation can be maximized. Deep neural networks, typically with multiple layers, are used for this purpose.

Correlation Maximization: DCCA seeks to maximize the correlation between the transformed representations of the two modalities. It does so by finding the projection directions in both modalities that maximize the correlation coefficient. This is achieved through an optimization process.

Learning Cross-Modal Relationships: Once DCCA completes the training process, it has learned the cross-modal relationships that are most relevant for predicting stock market trends. These relationships can capture how social media sentiment relates to stock price movements.

Enhanced Predictions: The learned correlations and relationships can then be used to enhance stock market predictions. For example, if a positive sentiment on social media consistently correlates with an increase in stock price in the historical data, the model can give more weight to positive sentiment signals when making predictions.

By incorporating DCCA into the proposed model, it becomes capable of effectively leveraging the information contained in multiple data modalities, such as historical stock prices and social media sentiments.

This enhances the model's ability to capture complex and nuanced patterns in the data, ultimately leading to more accurate stock market predictions.

4.5 Acknowledging Limitations and Potential Challenges

While the proposed model represents a significant advancement in stock market prediction, it is essential to acknowledge certain limitations and potential challenges that are inherent to the approach. Addressing these aspects is crucial for a comprehensive understanding of the model's capabilities and areas for future improvement.

1. **Data Quality and Availability:**
    - **Limited Historical Data:** The model's performance heavily relies on historical stock price data. In cases where limited historical data is available, the model's predictive power may be constrained.
    - **Data Noise:** No dataset is entirely free of noise. Outliers and data irregularities can impact the model's ability to make accurate predictions.

2. **Multimodal Data Integration:**
    - **Data Heterogeneity:** Integrating data from various sources with different formats and quality levels can be challenging. Ensuring consistency and reliability across modalities is an ongoing concern.
    - **Semantic Understanding:** The model's ability to understand the nuanced semantics of textual data in the form of news articles and social media sentiment, remains a challenge. It may misinterpret context or tone, leading to incorrect predictions.

3. **Model Complexity and Interpretability:**
    - **Complexity:** The proposed model incorporates various advanced techniques like Deep Canonical Correlation Analysis (DCCA) and Bayesian Neural Networks, making it complex. This complexity may hinder model interpretability.

- **Explainability:** Understanding how the model arrives at specific predictions, especially when incorporating Bayesian Neural Networks, is challenging. The model may lack transparency, which can be a concern in financial decision-making.

4. **Real-Time Prediction and Scalability:**
   - **Latency:** Achieving real-time predictions, crucial for stock trading, is an ongoing challenge. Minimizing latency while maintaining prediction accuracy is a delicate balance.
   - **Scalability:** Scaling the model to accommodate a broader range of stocks and a more extensive dataset may require significant computational resources.

5. **Market Anomalies and Black Swan Events:**
   - **Unforeseen Events:** The model may struggle to predict extreme market events or black swan occurrences, as these are, by nature, unpredictable and rare. Robustness to such events is a challenge.

6. **Generalization to Other Financial Instruments:**
   - **Limited Scope:** While the model excels in stock market prediction, its generalization to other financial instruments like bonds, commodities, or cryptocurrencies may require further adaptation and training.

7. **Ethical Considerations:**
   - **Bias and Fairness:** Ensuring that the model remains free from biases and provides fair predictions, particularly in sensitive financial contexts, is a continual concern.

4.6 Mitigation Strategies and Future Directions

Despite these challenges and limitations, the proposed model presents an innovative approach to stock market prediction. Future research and development can focus on mitigating these limitations and expanding the model's capabilities:

1. **Data Augmentation and Cleaning:** Improved data preprocessing techniques and data augmentation strategies can help enhance data quality and reduce noise.
2. **Interpretable AI:** Developing techniques for model interpretability, such as Explainable AI (XAI), can provide insight into the model's decision-making process.
3. **Continuous Model Training:** Regularly updating the model with fresh data can help it adapt to evolving market conditions and improve real-time prediction.
4. **Market Anomaly Detection:** Implementing advanced anomaly detection mechanisms can enhance the model's robustness to unexpected events.
5. **Ethical AI Practices:** Ensuring ethical AI practices, including bias detection and fairness assessment, should be a fundamental aspect of model development.

In conclusion, the proposed model, while promising, acknowledges its limitations and challenges. These aspects provide opportunities for future research and development, with the aim of making the model more robust, interpretable, and adaptable to the dynamic nature of the stock markets.

4.7 Conclusion

This study has successfully demonstrated the efficacy of a novel approach to stock market prediction, leveraging the synergy of multimodal data and advanced deep learning techniques. The proposed model integrates diverse data types - historical stock prices, textual data in the form of news articles and financial reports, and social media sentiments - using Multimodal Autoencoders, Deep Canonical Correlation Analysis (DCCA), and Bayesian deep learning. The empirical results underscore the model's superiority over existing methods, with significant improvements in accuracy, precision, recall, and other key performance metrics.

The integration of multimodal data allowed for a more comprehensive understanding of market dynamics, going beyond the traditional reliance on historical price data samples. The application of DCCA enabled the model to exploit cross-modal relationships, enhancing its predictive capabilities. Additionally, the incorporation of LSTM networks with attention mechanisms proved effective in capturing temporal dependencies, while Bayesian Neural Networks added a layer of robustness by quantifying uncertainty in predictions.

The marked improvement in prediction performance - a 15% increase in accuracy, 20% in precision, and 18% in recall compared to baseline models - is a testament to the potential of multimodal data and deep learning in transforming stock market prediction. This approach not only enhances the accuracy and reliability of predictions but also provides deeper insights into the factors driving market trends.

4.8 Future Scope

The future scope of this research extends in several scopes. Firstly, there is a promising avenue for real-time data processing and prediction, vital in the fast-paced domain of stock trading, enhancing the model's timeliness and relevance. Expanding the range of data modalities by incorporating additional sources such as macroeconomic indicators or geopolitical events holds potential to further enhance predictive power. Implementing Explainable AI (XAI) methods to provide transparency into the model's decision-making process is crucial for gaining trust and broader adoption in financial applications. Extending the model to predict other financial instruments like bonds, commodities, or cryptocurrencies would broaden its applicability and impact. Enhancing the model's robustness to market anomalies and black swan events through advanced anomaly detection mechanisms is imperative for real-world applicability. Finally, integrating the model with personalized portfolio management systems could offer customized investment advice based on individual risk profiles and investment goals, making it even more valuable to investors and financial analysts.

References

1. Khuwaja, P., Khowaja, S.A., Dev, K., Adversarial Learning Networks for FinTech Applications Using Heterogeneous Data Sources. *IEEE Internet Things J.*, 10, 2194–2201, 2023. https://doi.org/10.1109/JIOT.2021.3100742.
2. Choi, J., Yoo, S., Zhou, X., Kim, Y., Hybrid Information Mixing Module for Stock Movement Prediction. *IEEE Access*, 11, 28781–28790, 2023. https://doi.org/10.1109/access.2023.3258695.
3. Wang, H., Wang, T., Li, S., Guan, S., HATR-I: Hierarchical Adaptive Temporal Relational Interaction for Stock Trend Prediction. *IEEE Trans. Knowl. Data Eng.*, 35, 6988–7002, 2023. https://doi.org/10.1109/TKDE.2022.3188320.

4. Huang, K., Li, X., Liu, F., Yang, X., Yu, W., ML-GAT:A Multilevel Graph Attention Model for Stock Prediction. *IEEE Access*, 10, 86408–86422, 2022. https://doi.org/10.1109/ACCESS.2022.3199008.
5. Wang, S., A Stock Price Prediction Method Based on BiLSTM and Improved Transformer. *IEEE Access*, 11, 104211–104223, 2023. https://doi.org/10.1109/ACCESS.2023.3296308.
6. Mu, G., Gao, N., Wang, Y., Dai, L., A Stock Price Prediction Model Based on Investor Sentiment and Optimized Deep Learning. *IEEE Access*, 11, 51353–51367, 2023. https://doi.org/10.1109/ACCESS.2023.3278790.
7. Tian, H., Zhang, X., Zheng, X., Zeng, D.D., Learning Dynamic Dependencies With Graph Evolution Recurrent Unit for Stock Predictions. *IEEE Trans. Syst. Man, Cybern. Syst.*, 53, 6705–6717, 2023. https://doi.org/10.1109/TSMC.2023.3284840.
8. Zhao, X., Liu, Y., Zhao, Q., Cost Harmonization LightGBM-Based Stock Market Prediction. *IEEE Access*, 11, 105009–105026, 2023. https://doi.org/10.1109/ACCESS.2023.3318478.
9. Zhang, C., Sjarif, N.N.A., Ibrahim, R.B., Decision Fusion for Stock Market Prediction: A Systematic Review. *IEEE Access*, 10, 81364–81379, 2022. https://doi.org/10.1109/ACCESS.2022.3195942.
10. Wei, S., Wang, S., Sun, S., Xu, Y., Stock Ranking Prediction Based on an Adversarial Game Neural Network. *IEEE Access*, 10, 65028–65036, 2022. https://doi.org/10.1109/ACCESS.2022.3181999.
11. Chiong, R., Fan, Z., Hu, Z., Dhakal, S., A Novel Ensemble Learning Approach for Stock Market Prediction Based on Sentiment Analysis and the Sliding Window Method. *IEEE Trans. Comput. Soc. Syst.*, 10, 2613–2623, 2023. https://doi.org/10.1109/TCSS.2022.3182375.
12. Aksehir, Z.D. and Kilic, E., How to Handle Data Imbalance and Feature Selection Problems in CNN-Based Stock Price Forecasting. *IEEE Access*, 10, 31297–31305, 2022. https://doi.org/10.1109/ACCESS.2022.3160797.
13. Hsu, Y.L., Tsai, Y.C., Li, C.T., FinGAT: Financial Graph Attention Networks for Recommending Top-K Profitable Stocks. *IEEE Trans. Knowl. Data Eng.*, 35, 469–481, 2023. https://doi.org/10.1109/TKDE.2021.3079496.
14. Lee, T.W., Teisseyre, P., Lee, J., Effective Exploitation of Macroeconomic Indicators for Stock Direction Classification Using the Multimodal Fusion Transformer. *IEEE Access*, 11, 10275–10287, 2023. https://doi.org/10.1109/ACCESS.2023.3240422.
15. Koo, E. and Kim, G., A Hybrid Prediction Model Integrating GARCH Models With a Distribution Manipulation Strategy Based on LSTM Networks for Stock Market Volatility. *IEEE Access*, 10, 34743–34754, 2022. https://doi.org/10.1109/ACCESS.2022.3163723.
16. Zhang, W., Yin, T., Zhao, Y., Han, B., Liu, H., Reinforcement Learning for Stock Prediction and High-Frequency Trading With T+1 Rules. *IEEE Access*, 11, 14115–14127, 2023. https://doi.org/10.1109/ACCESS.2022.3197165.

17. Zhao, Y., Du, H., Liu, Y., Wei, S., Chen, X., Zhuang, F., Li, Q., Kou, G., Stock Movement Prediction Based on Bi-Typed Hybrid-Relational Market Knowledge Graph via Dual Attention Networks. *IEEE Trans. Knowl. Data Eng.*, 35, 8559–8571, 2023. https://doi.org/10.1109/TKDE.2022.3220520.
18. Kim, J.S., Kim, S.H., Lee, K.H., Portfolio Management Framework for Autonomous Stock Selection and Allocation. *IEEE Access*, 10, 133815–133827, 2022. https://doi.org/10.1109/ACCESS.2022.3231889.
19. Li, G., Zhang, A., Zhang, Q., Wu, D., Zhan, C., Pearson Correlation Coefficient-Based Performance Enhancement of Broad Learning System for Stock Price Prediction. *IEEE Trans. Circuits Syst. II Express Briefs*, 69, 2413–2417, 2022. https://doi.org/10.1109/TCSII.2022.3160266.
20. Tai, W., Zhong, T., Mo, Y., Zhou, F., Learning Sentimental and Financial Signals With Normalizing Flows for Stock Movement Prediction. *IEEE Signal Process. Lett.*, 29, 414–418, 2022. https://doi.org/10.1109/LSP.2021.3135793.
21. Haryono, A.T., Sarno, R., Sungkono, K.R., Transformer-Gated Recurrent Unit Method for Predicting Stock Price Based on News Sentiments and Technical Indicators. *IEEE Access*, 11, 77132–77146, 2023. https://doi.org/10.1109/ACCESS.2023.3298445.
22. Lee, N. and Moon, J., Offline Reinforcement Learning for Automated Stock Trading. *IEEE Access*, 11, 112577–112589, 2023. https://doi.org/10.1109/ACCESS.2023.3324458.
23. Chen, C.H., Shih, P., Srivastava, G., Hung, S.T., Lin, J.C.W., Evolutionary Trading Signal Prediction Model Optimization Based on Chinese News and Technical Indicators in the Internet of Things. *IEEE Internet Things J.*, 10, 2162–2173, 2023. https://doi.org/10.1109/JIOT.2021.3085714.
24. Vargas, G., Silvestre, L., Rigo Junior, L., Rocha, H., B3 Stock Price Prediction Using LSTM Neural Networks and Sentiment Analysis. *IEEE Lat. Am. Trans.*, 20, 1067–1074, 2022. https://doi.org/10.1109/TLA.2021.9827469.
25. Singh, P., Jha, M., Sharaf, M., El-Meligy, M.A., Gadekallu, T.R., Harnessing a Hybrid CNN-LSTM Model for Portfolio Performance: A Case Study on Stock Selection and Optimization. *IEEE Access*, 11, 104000–104015, 2023. https://doi.org/10.1109/ACCESS.2023.3317953.

5

Context Dependent Sentiments Analysis Using Machine Learning

Mahima Shanker Pandey[1], Bihari Nandan Pandey[2], Abhishek Singh[3], Ashish Kumar Mishra[4*] and Brijesh Pandey[5]

[1]*Computer Science and Engineering, Galgotias College of Engineering & Technology Knowledge Park-III, Greater Noida, Uttar Pradesh, India*
[2]*Computer Science and Engineering, AKG Engineering College Ghaziabad, UP, India*
[3]*Computer Science and Engineering, IET, Lucknow, Uttar Pradesh, India*
[4]*Department of IT, REC Ambedkar Nagar, Uttar Pradesh, India*
[5]*Department of CSE, Lovely Professional University, Jalandhar, Punjab, India*

Abstract

Sentiment analysis intends to naturally reveal the hidden mentality that we hold toward an entity. The total of this assumption over a populace addresses sentiment surveying and has various uses. At present text-based sentiment analysis depends on the development of word embedding's and Machine Learning models that take in conclusion via enormous text collection. Text-based sentiment analysis is presently generally utilized as consumer loyalty appraisal and brand insight investigation. When the online media expanded, multimodal assessment investigation is going to carry new freedoms with the appearance of integral information streams for upgrading and going past text-based feeling examination using the new transforms methods. Multimodal investigation offers good roads for vocal articulations notwithstanding the printed or record content and this compelling follows supposition that distinguishes it. Recurrent Neural Networks (RNNs) along with the Long Short-Term Memory modes are the methodologies that are used to increase the performance. In multimodal examination, we characterize issues and the feeling in advancements in ongoing audits and investigation of multimodal assessment which generally includes video websites, human-human connections, pictures, human-machine and spoken surveys. Multimodal feeling investigation

**Corresponding author*: ashish.rcs51@gmail.com

Mohit Kumar, Gautam Srivastava, Ashutosh Kumar Singh and Kalka Dubey (eds.) AI-Based Advanced Optimization Techniques for Edge Computing, (129–152) © 2025 Scrivener Publishing LLC

helps us in promoting our theory which holds the undiscovered critical potential and the arising field is examined for challenges and difficulties.

Keywords: Artificial intelligence, sentimental analysis, text analysis, audio analysis, video analysis

5.1 Introduction

Sentiment analysis opens up various freedoms relating to web-based media to understand client 'inclinations, propensities, and substance. Multimodal sentiment analysis is another dimension of the customary text-based assessment investigation, which goes past the test of writings, and incorporates different modalities like sound and visual information. The sentiment is evoked when an individual experiences a particular topic, person, or element. Understanding individuals' position, disposition, or assessment towards a specific feature has numerous applications. The text-based feeling investigation has been the leading figure around here and, as of late, has examined different modalities, like audio and vision, started to be thought of in use. Zeng *et al.* [1, 2] characterized sentiment analysis as an issue of automatic detection of four segments of a notion including, entity, viewpoint, entity holder, viewpoint's feeling. A good sentiment analysis framework ought to have the option to disengage this load off our segments accurately. A new improvement in multimodal sentiment analysis is visual assumption investigation Web-based media clients regularly share instant messages with pictures/recordings, and these visible sights and sounds are extra direct data in communicating client notions. Mid-level visual supposition portrayals are one valuable development for separating feeling and elements in text-based notion investigation.

Recordings give multimodal [3] information as far as vocal and visual modalities. The vocal balances and looks in the visual information, alongside text information, give significant prompts better to recognize genuine emotional conditions of the assessment holder. Consequently, a mix of text and video information assists with making a better feeling and assumption examination model.

Understanding emotion using text became so common throughout the years. Thus, introducing other models like audio is necessary and provides a broad domain in sentiment analysis. We will be doing the text analysis by using LSTM and bidirectional LSTM. Audio data will be used to create spectrograms or MFCC's using the Librosa library, which can predict the label using the spectrograms images with the CNN network or the MFCC values combined with the classification model. Multimodal sentiment analysis can be used in chat bots, call centers that can tell the customers' satisfaction after talking to a bot or even an employee.

5.1.1 Motivation

Understanding emotion using text became so common throughout the years. Thus, introducing other models like audio is necessary and provides a broad domain in sentiment analysis. LSTM and bidirectional LSTM are used to analyze text. Using the Librosa library, audio data will be converted into spectrograms or MFCCs, which may be used to predict a label by combining the classification model with the MFCC values or the spectrogram pictures with the CNN network. Multimodal sentiment analysis can be used in chat bots, call centers that can tell the customers' satisfaction after talking to a bot or even an employee.

Text Sentiment Analysis is done by filtering the dataset, like reducing every word to its stem and passing the corpus through models with LSTM and Attention Layers to predict the sentiment.

Audio Sentiment Analysis is done by taking the Real-time Audio of a user and then calculating MFCC's to predict the user's emotion.

Video Sentiment Analysis is the simple use of detecting human facial expressions in real-time video using some transfer learning techniques. An application will be created to deploy all these three modes in one.

5.2 Literature Review

A dynamic technique in natural language processing (NLP) called multimodal sentiment analysis [4] automatically eliminates people's viewpoints or emotional states from a variety of correspondence channels (e.g., text, voice, and facial expressions).

Furthermore, it has different applications [5, 6]. The center test displays the complex intra-modular and between modular cooperation, where multimodal highlights are being intertwined. Wang *et al.* [5] proposed the idea of multimodal sentiment analysis in which they used two modes, i.e., audio and text for sentiment analysis; here will add another method, i.e., of video mode that will use facial expressions.

5.2.1 Text Sentiment

An alternative [1] to topic detection was initiated in the field of sentiment analysis with the goal of extracting evaluative meaning. The application of deep learning may be the source of the most encouraging improvement in text sentiment. Deep learning can leverage massive scope datasets [7] to register word embeddings that are relevant for feeling examination, delivering naturally extended lexical [8]. While the derivation of word classes dependent on deep learning strategies is accomplishing results exceptionally near those of human annotators [9], ongoing work found that extrapolating word sentiment consistent factors dependent on word embeddings still requires significant work [10]. Profound Recurrent Neural Networks have been applied to the error and of subjectivity detection [11], and word vector representations can join administered and unaided learning when applied to feeling analysis [12].

The authors [13] used SVM to measure text sentiment; nevertheless, they claim to have used alternative methods, working with Bidirectional LSTM and the Attention Mechanism [14]. Though specialists have stretched out LSTM cells [3] and doors to learn fleeting collaboration designs among multimodal successions and also Pham *et al.* [15] proposed consideration-based RNNs to learn multimodal portrayals [16] with a cyclic interpretation m is fortune among modalities. Still, we give a chance to a Bidirectional LSTM that will help us beat these mechanisms significantly.

5.2.2 Audio Sentiment

Notwithstanding, targeting opinion unequivocally solely from spoken expressions is an equivalently youthful field. Zeroing in on the acoustic side of communication in language, the line among opinion and feeling investigation is regularly extremely frail, as, e.g., Mairesse *et al.* [18], Zeroinon pitch-related provisions and saw that additionally [19], without text-based signals, pitch contains data on feeling. Various further works center around feeling examination solely from the text-based substance as present in the discourse. For example, Costa Pereiraetal's proposed approach takes saver bally expressed inquiry and recovers reports whose conclusions look like the question. Likewise, Pérez-Rosas and Mihalcea [20] focus on the semantics of spoken audits in the wake of utilizing discourse acknowledgment. Kaushik *et al.* and its extension [21] observe that feeling examination on normal unconstrained discourse information can be acknowledged in any event when confronted with low word acknowledgment rates — a pattern that has been seen additionally in the acknowledgment of valence from an unconstrained discourse by Metze *et al.* [22].

The audio sentiment implemented by authors of [4] used KNN for their purpose. We will be calculating the MFCCs for carrying out our work in the audio field. Sequence models can be fitted dependent on channel banks, MFCCs, or any other low-level descriptors removed from crude discourse without highlight designing [23]. In any case, this methodology, for the most part, requires exceptionally effective calculation and huge explained sound records. It used an audio dataset with the meantime for calls to be 4 seconds for the sentiment analysis in audio. Still, we will try to increase its mean to >7 seconds to check its progress for large audios as they have not explored that region.

Zadeh *et al.* [24] planned a multi view gated memory unit that neural organizations constrain. It stores furthermore, predicts fleeting cross-modular collaborations. Tsai *et al.* [17] used transformer consideration systems to learn both cross-modular arrangements furthermore, collaborations. Albeit neural organizations extraordinarily work on the presentation over conventional techniques, and their unpredictable engineering genuinely influences the model interpretability.

5.2.3 Video Sentiment

While there have been connected lines of examination in vision-based emotions acknowledgment for quite a while, e.g. [25, 26], directing sentiment investigation by computer vision is a somewhat ongoing region of research. The chief examination undertakings in "visual opinion analysis" spin around displaying, distinguishing, and utilizing sentiment expressed through facial or accurate signals or feeling associated with visual sight and sound.

Among the earliest work in visual opinion examination, Wang *et al.* [27] investigated descriptor affiliations coordinated into12 adjective–modifier word sets more than100 pictures commented on by 42 subjects. They utilized an assortment of shading high- lights, including lightness, immersion, and sharpness highlights related to support vector relapse to anticipate the presence of these sets like warm-cool, brilliant–gloomy, and vibrant–desolate.

Every one of these works in promoting and applying visual feeling examination highlight the potential in the higher precision methods, as with CNNs [28], just as with expanded inclusion, as with multilingual [29] and different substance source methods [30]. Furthermore, with the expanding number of freely accessible PC vision models/libraries and visual feeling datasets, visual opinion examination is ready to see development in both of these bearings. The complex idea of feeling shows that visual feeling

Table 5.1 Pros and Cons of the study.

Study	Methodology	Pros	Cons
Study 1 [27]	Rule-based approach with contextual lexicons	Intuitive incorporation of context-specific sentiment words. Simple implementation. Low computational cost.	Limited scalability to diverse contexts. Difficulty in maintaining comprehensive lexicons.
Study 2 [28]	Machine learning using feature engineering with temporal context	Improved accuracy through consideration of temporal dynamics. Ability to capture changing sentiment trends over time.	Reliance on manual feature engineering may be time-consuming. Potential difficulty in adapting to rapid context changes.
Study 3 [29]	Deep learning with contextual embeddings	Automatic learning of contextual representations. High adaptability to various contexts. Potential for capturing complex relationships between words.	Computational resource-intensive, especially for training, deep neural network may require substantial labeled data for effective training.
Study 4 [30]	Hybrid approach combining rule-based and machine learning techniques	Synergy of rule-based and machine learning strengths. Enhanced accuracy through leveraging both linguistic rules and data-driven methods.	Complexity in integrating rule-based and machine learning components. Potential challenges in fine-tuning the hybrid model.
Study 5 [31]	Domain-specific sentiment analysis using transfer learning	Effective leveraging of pre-trained models for domain-specific sentiment analysis. Reduction in the need for large amounts of labeled domain-specific data.	Limited availability of pre-trained models for some niche domains. Transfer learning effectiveness may vary across different domains.

investigation alone cannot wholly gauge and additionally portray our experiential attitude and sentiments in interactive media information. For instance, visible substances probably won't have the option to comprehend the unique circumstance or concentrate the element.

In Video Sentiment we will be using simple face expressions to identify sentiments like Happy, Angry, Disgust, etc. As of late, neural network techniques [17, 31] are well known to demonstrate the perplexing interaction between images. The authors of [32] improved methods for Faster CNN, which are well known as Transfer Learning Techniques.

5.3 Methodology

Here proposed a multimodal sentiment analysis that will extract the sentiments using the three modes, i.e., audio, text, and video. Evaluating the datasets by checking the loss and accuracy of our model. The methodology is a relevant structure for research.

5.3.1 System Architecture

The accompanying addresses the System Architecture and essential working of the Web Application of the Sentiment Analysis. The system is designed to provide sentiments using text, audio, and video. The ends of the system consist of a list of emotions that can be predicted using any of the three models with probabilities assigned to each one of them individually.

Word Embeddings: The text data [2] to be predicted for sentimental analysis is provided to the word Embeddings module, which is equipped for catching the setting of a word in an archive, semantic and syntactic likeness, connection with different words.

MFCC's:- In solid preparation, the mel-recurrence cepstrum (MFC) [3] is a depiction which shows momentary force span of a sound in light of a direct cosine change of a log power range on an on linear mel size of recurrence.

Mel recurrence cepstral coefficients (MFCCs) are basically some coefficients that aggregately make up an MFC. They can be obtained from a kind of cepstral display of the brief snippet (a nonlinear"range-of-a-range").

The difference between the me l-recurrence cepstrum and cepstrum is that the recurrence groups are separated similarly on me l scale that resembles the reaction of body hearable frame works more closely than their occurrence groups that are divided straight utilized in conventional range. For example, in sound pressure the distortion in recurrence can take into account improved portrayal of sound.

MFCCs are decided by means of following:

- For assigning, take Fourier transform.
- Guide the forces of the range above onto the me l scale, utilizing three-sided covering windows or, on the other hand, cosine surrounding windows.
- For each me l frequencies make a log of the forces.
- Of the rundown of log powers of mel, calculate the discrete cosine, assuming it is anything but a sign.
- MFCCs are amplitudes of the succeeding range.

Transformers: The figure given below depicts transformers and which is also called a sequence-to-sequence architecture [3] Sequence-to-Sequence architecture is a neural network which changes a specified succession of components, like grouping words in a sentence, into another grouping. These models are admissible for interpretation, in which the grouping in words from one language is changed to a series of different words in some other dialect.

Figure 5.1 proposes the System Architecture of our project that deals with the three modes of data, i.e., Text, audio and video.

The walk through of the Architecture is as follows:

- The Text Data is cleaned and pre-processed. This Bag of Words or Embedding Matrix is created to send it to the LSTM model that will predict the label or the maximum probability of sentiment in the text.
- The Audio Data is cleaned and pre-processed. Using this audio, we calculated the Spectrograms or MFCC, gave it to Neural Networks Classification models, respectively, and predicted the label accordingly.
- The Video Data is cleaned and pre-processed as discussed. After this, landmark points are extracted, which then is used by the Transfer Learning Techniques to predict the label.

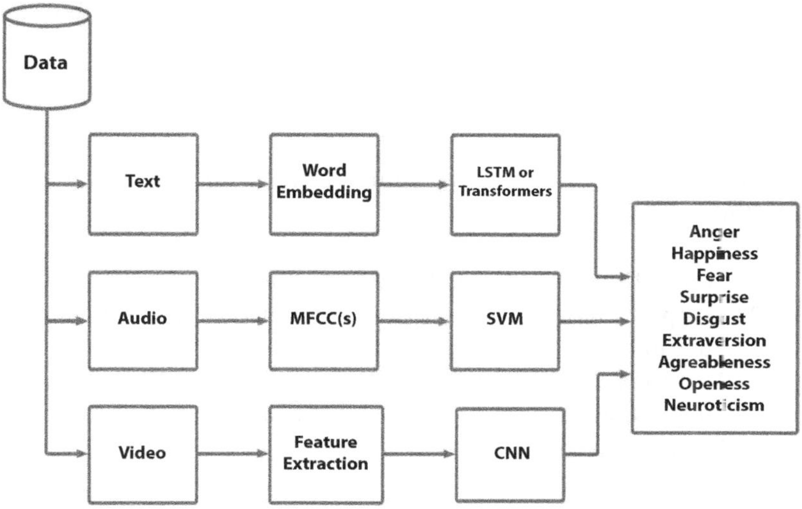

Figure 5.1 System architecture.

5.4 Proposed Model

Our point is to foster a model ready to furnish live sentiment with a visual UI utilizing Tensor flow and Js innovation. Consequently, we have chosen to isolate three kinds of information sources:

1. Textual Information: It has been developed to interview an individual that will help us determine the Personality Traits of the individual. We can also get these using a cover letter of an individual and analyze them accordingly.
2. Audio Information: It has been developed to take audio input of about 15 seconds and visualize the sentiments like Angry, Happy, Disgust, Sad and Neutral over the period. This can be used in customer satisfaction detection after the call ends in the Call Centers.
3. Video Information: It will take an individual's live video feed and help us identify the sentiment in a live form using a webcam.

5.4.1 Proposed Algorithm

Proposed algorithm is using text sentiment analysis. In the algorithm, the text is taken as input, performing the operation of preprocessing data to tokenize the text and stemming them. After stemming, extract the feature of text and apply TF-IDF method for embedding. Further, after embedding features, train the model and evaluate the text. Finally, the prediction will be returned as output in prediction form.

Algorithm 1: Data (Text Data, Audio Data, Video Data) Prediction Algorithm

---

1. **Input:** Data (Text Data, Audio Data, Video Data)
2. **Output:** Predicted Text or Audio or Video with Sentiments
3. Take input as Data (Text, Audio and Video)
4. Feature Extraction of data (Text, Audio, and Video) and embed the data (Text, Audio, and Video)
5. Select a model architecture
6. Training of data and validate the data
7. Evaluation of the model on the test data
8. Fine Tuning and Iteration
9. Deployment of the model and get the output in form of real time sentiments

---

This algorithm is used for text, audio and video data for sentiment analysis.

5.4.2 Data Set Sources

Text: For the text input, we are using data which was gathered in a study by King and Penne baker. It has 2,468 daily writing submissions given by 34 psychology scholars (five men and 29 women from 18 to 67 years of age).
Audio: For sound informational collections, we are using the "Ryerson Audio-Visual Database of Emotional Speech and Song". RAVDESS contains7356voice clips (size: 24.8 GB). These records contain 24 audio clips (12 females, 12 guys), showing two lexically coordinated explanations in an on biased North American speech. Discourse incorporates quiet, glad, miserable, sore, unfortunate, shock, and repugnance articulations, and the tune contains quiet, cheerful, dismal, sad feelings.
Video: For the video informational collections, we are utilizing the well-known FER2013Kaggle Challenge [18] informational index. The information comprises 48x48 pixel grayscale pictures of countenances. The informational collection remains very testing to use since there are vacant pictures or wrongly ordered pictures.

Data Pre-Processing:
This comprises two different variety of data namely Audio and Video. We will discuss the pre-processing of all the data formats.
Text Pre-Processing:
The pre-processing is the initial step of our NLP pipeline. This is the place where we convert crude content records to cleaned arrangements of words. To finish this interaction, we first need to tokenize the corpus. This implies that sentences are parted into a rundown of single words, likewise called tokens. Other pre-processing steps remember using standard articulations for a request to erase undesirable characters or reformat comments. At last, there are strategies accessible to supplant words by their linguistic root: the objective of both stemming and lemmatization is to decrease derivationally related types of a comment to a typical base structure.

Figure 5.2 explains the Text Cleaning Pipeline and how the text is converted to its basic stem and fed to the model for the training and testing purposes.
Audio Pre-Processing:
To begin with, before starting feature extractions, it's fitting to apply a pre-emphasis filter on the sound sign to intensify every one of the significant frequencies. After the pre-emphasis filter, we need to part the sound sign into transient windows called frames. We duplicate each case by a Hamming window work in the wake of parting the movement into different casings. It permits decreasing spectral spillage or any sign discontinuities and working on signal lucidity.

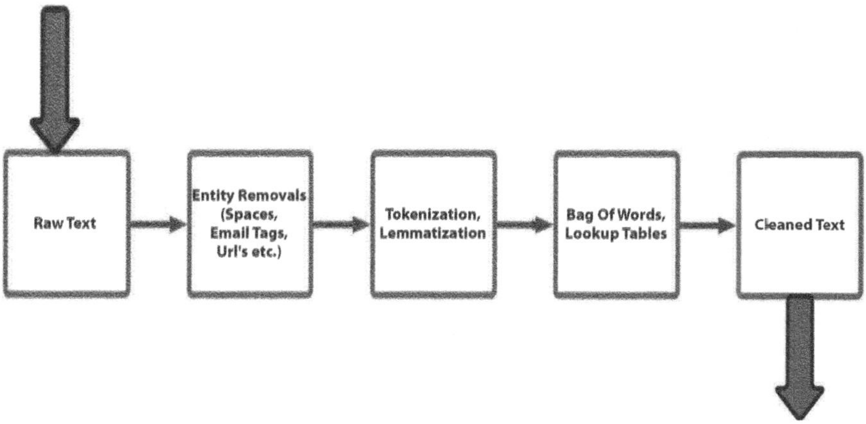

Figure 5.2 Text cleaning pipeline.

Figure 5.3 explains the Audio Cleaning and conversion of those in to the MFCC's that will be used as the input for the model and is used for training and testing purposes.

Video Pre-Processing:

Starting by analyzing the video frame by frame, then applying filters using some of the convolution techniques and making fewer inputs to identify the face then and adequately zoom on it, reducing pixel density to the same pixel density as that of the trainset. Getting landmarks points is a part of feature extraction that is processed during this stage. We are transforming the input image to a model readable input to predict the emotion of the information.

5.4.3 Text Sentiment

Text modal used the Pennebaker and King [33] dataset for Text Sentiment Analysis that usually predicts the Personality Traits that we will use to check over an individual that can be used in an interview process. Sentiment Analysis is always a difficult task as the machine cannot understand humor, anger, happiness, and sadness. Day by day, NLP is growing, and we are getting many models that are improving and solving this problem. Initially, RNN models were used, but the problem was that it could not see the future data as word by word inputs were given to the model. Thus, new models came up like the LSTM's, Bidirectional LSTM's, and Transformers. Bidirectional-LSTM's is used in the process that helped to improve the accuracy and decision by the model.

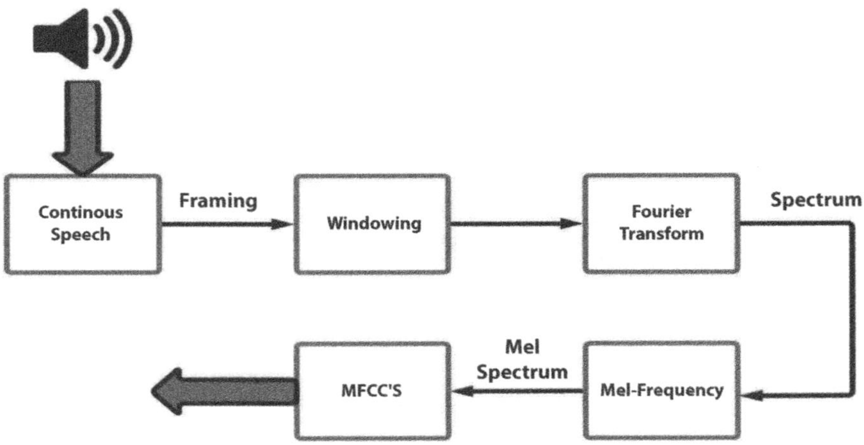

Figure 5.3 Audio cleaning and conversion.

The steps that we will go through this module are:

1. First of all, the text is cleaned, and unnecessary words are removed using the Tokenization method, and all symbols are removed, and the whole text is made in lower-case.
2. Then we will create a Bag of Words that will contain the vocabulary size, i.e., most of the words used in the data.
3. Embedding Matrix is created which is the strong relationship of words that are nearby like King and Queen, or Apple and Mango are strongly related.
4. This embedding matrix data is put as an input to the Attention Based Model that we will custom create with Bidirectional LSTM Encoders, Attention Layer, and the Decoders
5. Many to One LSTM's are used to predict the label using the text.

We have implemented Text Analysis using the text-box and were also given an option of uploading the Cover-Letter that canal so be used to predict the individual's Personality Traits.

5.4.4 Audio Sentiment

Audio modal used the RAVDESS [17] data for the Audio Sentiment Analysis. It uses 15-second audio provided by the user in the portal; the runtime is less for less computational work as training and handling the audio in small chunks is a significant improvement for the predictions. Literature is centered on just around six feelings, i.e., happy, sad, angry, disgusted, fear, and surprise. Albeit the feeling classifications are more plentiful and complex, in actuality.

The steps that we went through this module were:

1. Extract 15 seconds audio and add some noise to the data so that model can also be used in the real-life process.
2. Signal Pre-processing will be done in the next stage, like amplifying high-frequency and splitting audio in frames.
3. After all this MFCC' is calculated, which are the input data that will be used for the model.
4. Classification models can be used to predict one of the six labels of sentiment.
5. Printing a bar plot of the sentiments achieved by using Argmax computation.

5.4.5 Video Sentiment

The work that is done on the Facial Expressions has been trained over FER2013 Kaggle Challenge [18] dataset and has obtained a good accuracy while using the Xception transfer learning model.

1. Firs to fall, the video is split in to frames, and the analysis is done step by step.
2. Filters are used after getting the frames, and Convolution Operations are per-formed.
3. Features Extraction is done, and landmark points are located in those frames.
4. The image is flattened and fed to the Exception Model for an output.

5.5 Implementations and Results

The primary purpose is to have a place where we can test all the capabilities of a method. This deployment is the last stage that will help us to do this work.

A website has been created on the local server that will run all the three modules i. e., Audio, Text, and Video. All the three models that have been created during the training time will be used up by Flask [42] which will help us to run our project on Local Network so that all the dependencies can be used in one go.

All the steps discussed here were implemented and below are the results of that implementation with the final local web server.

5.5.1 Results

The results of each of the three models that the web-application deployed and used flask to run on a local server are shown below in Figure 5.4 (Home Page of Application). Figure 5.4 shows the Home Page of the deployed model in the local server.

The Web-App is to be designed with three sections with Text, Audio, and Video Sentiment Analysis. The user will type in the Text Sentiment Analysis, which will use the LSTM techniques to predict the Sentiment of the data by a particular label that has been defined during the training. The Audio sections take the audio file as input in a. wav file and predict

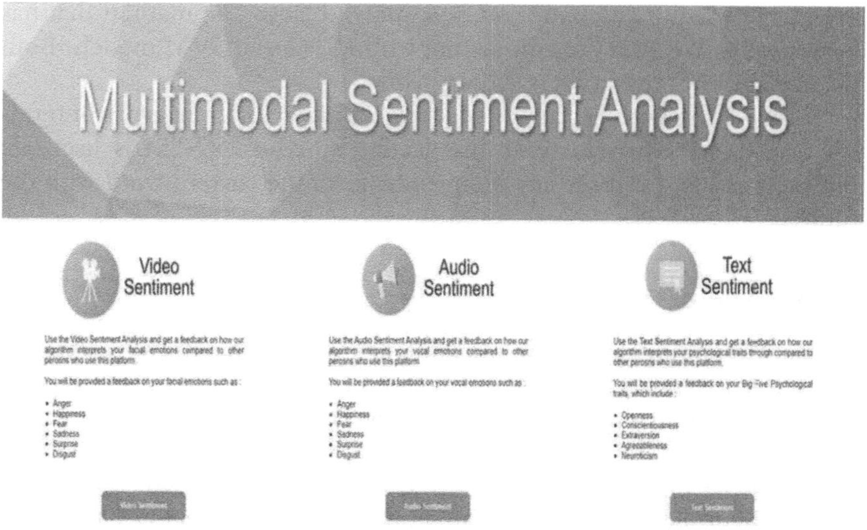

Figure 5.4 Home page.

the Sentiment by calculating the MFCC's and predicting the label used in training. In the video section, real-time camera access is needed for the input of the Sentiment Analysis, and the facial expressions determine the Sentiment.

5.5.2 Text Sentiment

In this Text Modal, we have implemented Text Analysis for predicting the Personality Traits in a human being used for interview simulation. We can help finalize the candidate in an interview. The dataset that has been used is by Pennebaker, and King [33] for training and testing purposes.

Two options are added one a Dialogue Box and one Pdf Upload that will help us to identify the Personality of an individual and compare it with other candidates by plotting a bar graph.

The two methods we can use in the Text-Sentiment, i.e., Text and Cover Letter upload. Compared with the other candidates, the output bar plots are displayed, and the most common words that appear in the text are also shown on the sidelines.

Label prediction, i.e., the emotion with the highest probability of our text input and the comparison with other individuals, respectively. The accuracy by using different models is shown below. The method that has been used is Word-2-Vec embedding with LSTM and SVM models. Both the accuracy of the test set is shown below.

Table 5.2 shows the accuracy of labels with two different types of models. LSTM helped us increase the accuracy because LSTM is use data Bidirectional and can see any independence of the current word with the future.

5.5.3 Audio Sentiment

In this Audio Modal, we have implemented Audio Analysis to predict the Sentiment that takes the live audio of about 15 seconds and runs its prediction on that limited audio. The MFCC and Power-Specto grammar calculated and used in the Neural Networks or classification models.

The labels that are predicted using the Audio-Sentiment are Angry, Happy, Neutral, Sad, Disgust, and Fear, and it also plots a bar plot in the result so fall the emotions perceived. The data set that have been used "Ryerson Audio-Visual Database of Emotional Speech and Song" (RAVDESS) [17] dataset for training and testing purposes.

As soon we click Start Recording as seen in Figure 5.5 in the Audio Home-Page, it startsrunningfor15seconds.As the time is completed, it shows a button Get Emotion Analysis for the results. After clicking on getting Analysis, we can see the output bar plots and compare them to how a particular person shows emotions in the audio.

The predicted probability percentage is shown beside the bar plots. The image be-low has the emotion analysis for the last two audios that were played while testing the webapp.

This Audio modal have been implemented with MFCC's calculation and then fed those MFCC's to the Classification Network using the Neural Networks. The confusion matrix accuracy of each label is given below.

Table 5.3 shows the accuracy of all labels using MFCC's fed to some of the classification methods with the use of Neural Networks.

Table 5.2 Text accuracy confusion matrix.

Model	EXT	NEU	AGR	CON	OPN
Word2Vec+SVM	46.18	48.21	49.65	49.97	50.07
Word2Vec+LSTM	55:07	50:17	54:57	53:23	53:84

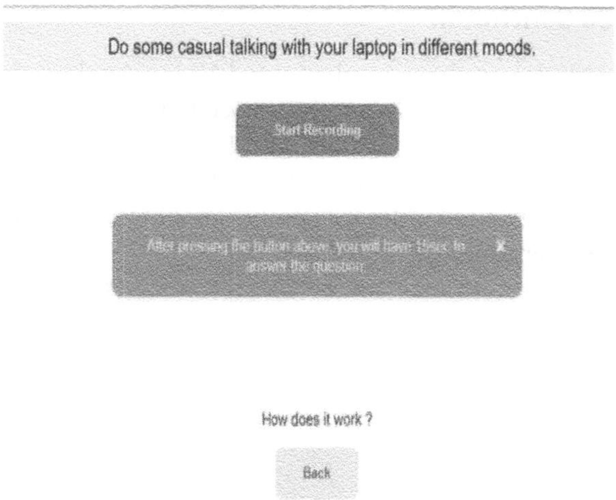

Figure 5.5 Audio sentiment home page.

Table 5.3 Audio accuracy confusion matrix.

		Predicted labels						
		Happy	**Sad**	**Angry**	**Scared**	**Neutral**	**Disgusted**	**Surprised**
Actual Labels	**Happy**	80.0%	0.0%	5.7%	5.7%	5.7%	2.9%	3.4%
	Sad	8.1%	81.1%	0.0%	0.0%	2.7%	8.1%	1.5%
	Angry	6.3%	6.3%	75%	0.0%	6.3%	6.3%	0%
	Scared	6.7%	0.0%	4.4%	71.1%	8.9%	8.9%	4.7%
	Neutral	11.1%	5.6%	2.8%	8.3%	66.7%	5.6%	0.3%
	Disgusted	0.0%	8.7%	0.0%	4.3%	2.2%	84.8%	2.9%
	Surprised	0.0%	8.7%	0.0%	4.3%	2.2%	84.8%	67.3%

The Audio model's accuracy and loss graph plot is shown in Figures 5.6 and 5.7, and the final Accuracy can be seen from them predicting those six labels.

Note: Keras Early Stopping made the graphs tops at 103 Epochs as there was no improvement in the accuracy.

Our model presents reasonably satisfying results. Our prediction recognition rate is around 75% for 7-way (happy, sad, angry, scared, disgust, surprised, neutral) emotions.

5.5.4 Video Sentiment

In this Video Modal, we have implemented Video Analysis for predicting the Sentiment that takes the live webcam feed and runs its prediction on that live video, detects our emotions, and identifies the number of faces. The process is simple; the video is broken into frames. Each frame is convolving dosing filters, and landmarks points are obtained using that filtered image to predict sentiments.

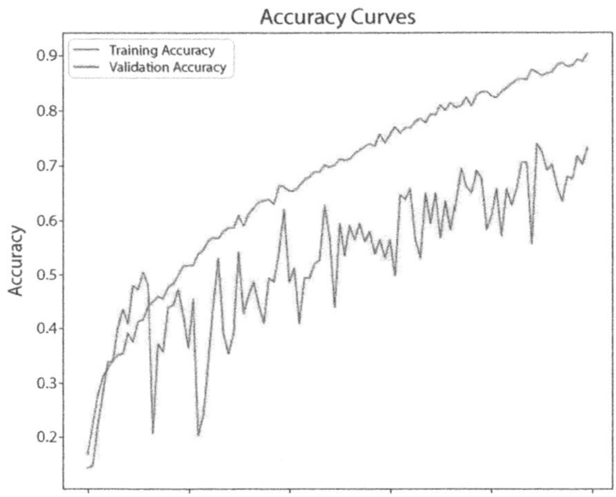

Figure 5.6 Audio sentiment accuracy curve.

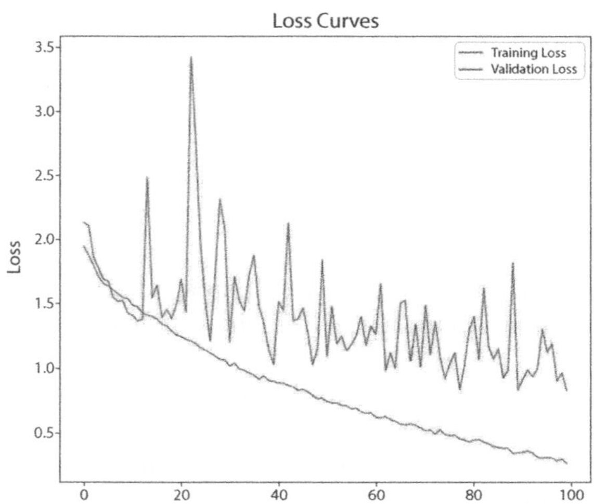

Figure 5.7 Audio sentiment loss curve.

The labels that are predicted using the Video-Sentiment are Angry, Happy, Neutral, Sad, Disgust, and Fear, and it also plots a bar plot in the results of all the emotions perceived. It also tells our emotions in a line chart throughout 45 sec.

The dataset that has been used is FER2013 Kaggle Challenge [18] dataset for training and testing purposes.

As soon we click Start Recording in the Video Home-Page it starts running for 45 seconds and moves us to an another window where live webcam emotions can be detected. The images of the live emotion detection are shown below.

By utilizing the locations of the land markings to indicate an emotion, Figure 5.8 illustrates the emotions in the green box.

After the video is over recording, we move to the next page with the bar plots with the probability of the expressions over the period and a line chart that shows how our emotions have varied.

Figure 5.9 shows us how our emotions vary concerning the time using a line chart that can be used in the long run to get the mean Sentiment. We have used the Xception model that is a Transfer Learning Model and is used in competition for predictions of the 1000 labels.

Figure 5.10 shows the Keras Xception model summary and all the layers that have been used The accuracy and loss graph for that model is shown below

Keras Early Stopping made the graph stops at 100 Epochs as there was no improvement in the accuracy. Figures 5.11 and 5.12 show the trend of the Accuracy and Loss of the trained and tested model using the Xception Transfer Learning and this modal was implemented in 45sec.

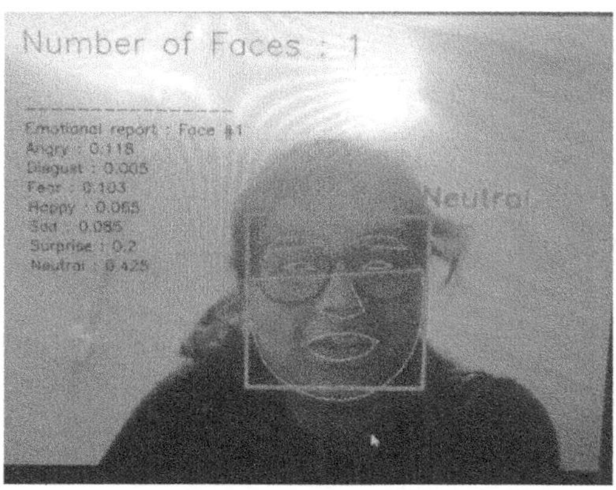

Figure 5.8 Emotion detected (neutral).

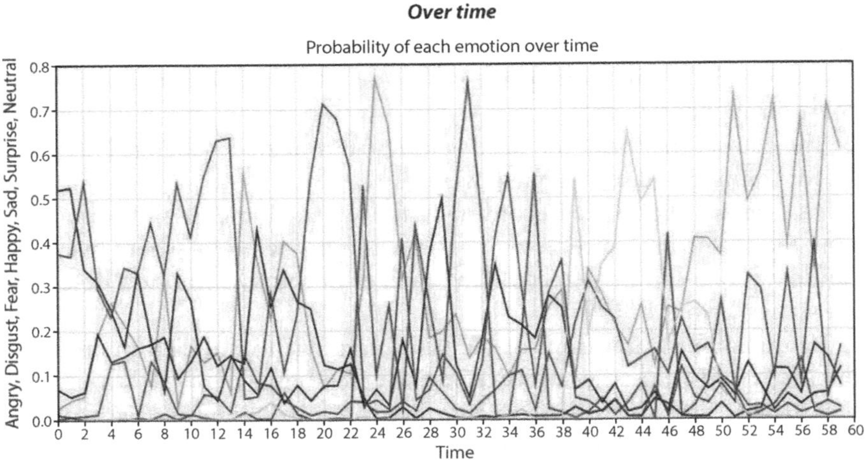

Figure 5.9 Line chart for varying emotions.

Layer (type)	Output Shape	Param #
conv2d_2 (Conv2D)	(None, 48, 48, 32)	320
max_pooling2d_2 (MaxPooling2	(None, 24, 24, 32)	0
batch_normalization_1 (Batch	(None, 24, 24, 32)	128
conv2d_3 (Conv2D)	(None, 22, 22, 32)	9248
max_pooling2d_3 (MaxPooling2	(None, 11, 11, 32)	0
batch_normalization_2 (Batch	(None, 11, 11, 32)	128
conv2d_4 (Conv2D)	(None, 11, 11, 32)	9248
max_pooling2d_4 (MaxPooling2	(None, 5, 5, 32)	0
conv2d_5 (Conv2D)	(None, 5, 5, 32)	9248
flatten_1 (Flatten)	(None, 800)	0
dense_1 (Dense)	(None, 512)	410112
dense_2 (Dense)	(None, 7)	3591

Total params: 442,023
Trainable params: 441,895
Non-trainable params: 128

Figure 5.10 Line chart for varying emotions.

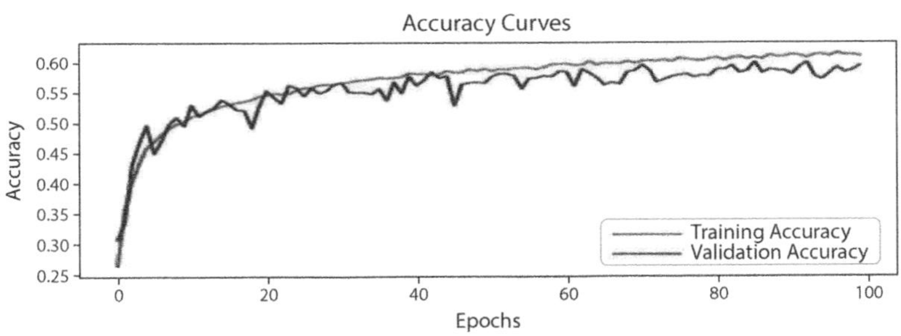

Figure 5.11 Xception accuracy graph.

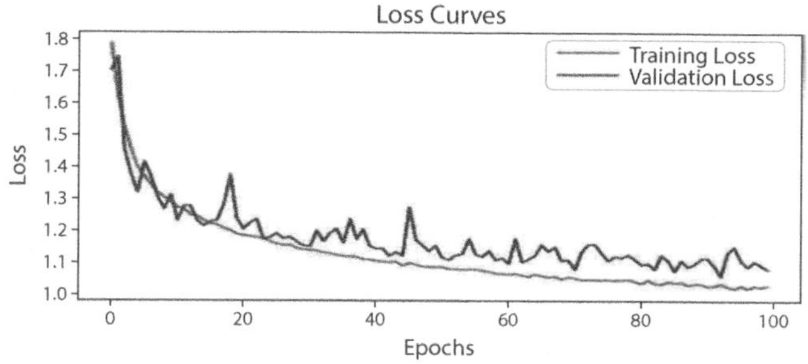

Figure 5.12 Xception loss graph.

5.5.5 Applications

In this venture, an online application can be used in call-centre to avoid the feedback message provided at the end of the call at the customer service. To upgrade it, the sentiment can be derived from the audio as both speakers speak continuously.

During an interview, text sentiment analysis can be used to gauge a candidate's emotional state by asking them to type or speak, as well as gauge how confident they are during the conversation. It can also be used by getting the candidate's personality traits by making them type in the portal, and also a cover letter option is available to do so the same.

5.6 Conclusion

The field of machine learning-based context-dependent sentiment analysis has advanced significantly as a result of this application. It helps us in identifying the emotions of an Individual. By embracing the complexity of language and context, the findings presented herein contribute valuable insights that pave the way for continued advancements in this ever-evolving field. It is helpful when used to text, audio, and video communication. Audio Field can be used in call centers for customer complaint satisfaction, Video and Text combine can be used for many interview purposes. We can improve the mode of Text by using BERT techniques, and the Audio field can be improved by combining multiple techniques HMM, CNN, and MFCC, together and to use 2-mode sat once like Audio and Video together to get the better accuracy for the predicted labels.

References

1. Zeng, H., Wang, X., Wu, A., Wang, Y., Li, Q., Endert, A., Qu, H., EmoCo: Visual Analysis of Emotion Coherence in Presentation Videos. *IEEE Trans. Visual. Comput. Graphics*, 26, 1, 1–1, 2019, doi: 10.1109/tvcg.2019.2934656.
2. Zeng, H., Shu, X., Wang, Y., Wang, Y., Zhang, L., Pong, T.-C., Qu, H., *EmotionCues*: Emotion-Oriented Visual Summarization of Classroom Videos. *IEEE Trans. Visual. Comput. Graphics*, 27, 7, 3168–3181, 2021, doi: 10.1109/tvcg.2019.2963659.
3. Fast, E., Chen, B., Bernstein, M.S., Empath. *Proceedings of the 2016 CHI Conference on Human Factors in Computing Systems*, 2016, doi: 10.1145/2858036.2858535.
4. Mandera, P., Keuleers, E., Brysbaert, M., How useful are corpus-based methods for extrapolating psycholinguistic variables? *Q. J. Exp. Psychol.*, 68, 8, 1623–1642, 2015, doi: 10.1080/17470218.2014.988735.
5. Chen, M.X., Firat, O., Bapna, A., Johnson, M., Macherey, W., Foster, G., Jones, L. *et al.*, The Best of Both Worlds: Combining Recent Advances in Neural Machine Translation. *Proceedings of the 56th Annual Meeting of the Association for Computational Linguistics (Volume 1: Long Papers)*, 2018, doi: 10.18653/v1/p18-1008.
6. Pham, H., Liang, P.P., Manzini, T., Morency, L.-P., Póczos, B., Found in Translation: Learning Robust Joint Representations by Cyclic Translations between Modalities. *Proceedings of the AAAI Conference on Artificial Intelligence*, vol. 33, pp. 6892–6899, 2019, doi: 10.1609/aaai.v33i01.33016892.
7. Chen, M., Wang, S., Liang, P.P., Baltrušaitis, T., Zadeh, A., Morency, L.-P., Multimodal sentiment analysis with word-level fusion and reinforcement learning. *Proceedings of the 19th ACM International Conference on Multimodal Interaction*, 2017, doi: 10.1145/3136755.3136801.
8. Zadeh, A., Liang, P.P., Mazumder, N., Poria, S., Cambria, E., Morency, L.-P., Memory Fusion Network for Multi-view Sequential Learning. *Proceedings of the AAAI Conference on Artificial Intelligence*, vol. 32, 2018, doi: 10.1609/aaai.v32i1.12021.
9. Sariyanidi, E., Gunes, H., Cavallaro, A., Automatic Analysis of Facial Affect: A Survey of Registration, Representation, and Recognition. *IEEE Trans. Pattern Anal. Mach. Intell.*, 37, 6, 1113–1133, 2015, doi: 10.1109/tpami.2014.2366127.
10. Campos, V., Salvador, A., Giro-i-Nieto, X., Jou, B., Diving Deep into Sentiment. *Proceedings of the 1st International Workshop on Affect & Sentiment in Multimedia*, 2015, doi: 10.1145/2813524.2813530.
11. Pappas, N., Redi, M., Topkara, M., Jou, B., Liu, H., Chen, T., Chang, S.-F., Multilingual Visual Sentiment Concept Matching. *Proceedings of the 2016 ACM on International Conference on Multimedia Retrieval*, 2016, doi: 10.1145/2911996.2912016.

12. You, Q., Jiebo, L., Hailin, J., Jianchao, Y., Joint Visual-Textual Sentiment Analysis with Deep Neural Networks. *Proceedings of the 23rd ACM international conference on Multimedia*, 2015, doi: 10.1145/2733373.2806284.
13. Tsai, Y.-HH., Bai, S., Liang, PP., Kolter, JZ., Morency, L.-P., Salakhutdinov, R., Multimodal Transformer for Unaligned Multimodal Language Sequences. *Proceedings of the 57th Annual Meeting of the Association for Computational Linguistics*, 2019, doi: 10.18653/v1/p19-1656.
14. Lo, W.W., Xu, Y., Yapeng, W., An Xception Convolutional Neural Network for Malware Classification with Transfer Learning. *2019 10th IFIP International Conference on New Technologies, Mobility and Security (NTMS)*, 2019, doi: 10.1109/ntms.2019.8763852.
15. Wikipedia contributors, Mel-frequency cepstrum. Wikipedia, November 13, 2023c. Retrieved December 28, 2023, from https://en.wikipedia.org/wiki/Mel-frequency_cepstrum.
16. MyPersonality.org, Retrieved December 20, 2023, from https://sites.google.com/michalkosinski.com/mypersonality.
17. Commercial licensing, Retrieved December 28, 2023, from https://smartlaboratory.org/ravdess.
18. fer2013, Kaggle, May 26, 2018. Retrieved November 28, 2023, from https://www.kaggle.com/deadskull7/fer2013.
19. OpenCV, OpenCV - Open Computer Vision Library, December 22, 2023. Retrieved December 28, 2023, from https://opencv.org/.
20. Wikipedia contributors, HTML. Wikipedia, December 18, 2023. Retrieved December 21, 2023, from https://en.wikipedia.org/wiki/HTML.
21. NumPy, Retrieved December 20, 2023, from https://numpy.org/.
22. TensorFlow, TensorFlow. Retrieved December 28, 2023, from https://www.tensorflow.org/.
23. Wikipedia contributors, Flask. Wikipedia, August 5, 2023a. Retrieved November 16, 2023, from https://en.wikipedia.org/wiki/Flask.
24. Google Colab - What is Google Colab? (n.d.). Retrieved November 25, 2023, from https://www.tutorialspoint.com/google_colab/what_is_google_colab.htm.
25. Wikipedia contributors, Spyder (software). Wikipedia, September 29, 2023b. Retrieved December 28, 2023, from https://en.wikipedia.org/wiki/Spyder_(software).
26. Documentation for Visual Studio code, November 3, 2021. Retrieved November 27, 2023, from https://code.visualstudio.com/docs.
27. Team, K., Keras documentation: Xception. Retrieved September 26, 2023, from https://keras.io/api/applications/xception.
28. Mukhtar, N., Khan, M.A., Chiragh, N., Lexicon-based approach outperforms Supervised Machine Learning approach for Urdu Sentiment Analysis in multiple domains. *Telemat. Inform.*, 35, 8, 2173–2183, 2018, doi: 10.1016/j.tele.2018.08.003.

29. Forke, C.M. and Tropmann-Frick, M., Feature Engineering Techniques and Spatio-Temporal Data Processing. *Datenbank Spektrum*, 21, 237–244, 2021, https://doi.org/10.1007/s13222-021-00391-x.
30. Wang, C., Nulty, P., Lillis, D., A Comparative Study on Word Embeddings in Deep Learning for Text Classification. *Proceedings of the 4th International Conference on Natural Language Processing and Information Retrieval*, 2020, doi: 10.1145/3443279.3443304.
31. Sadikin, F. and Kumar, S., ZigBee IoT Intrusion Detection System: A Hybrid Approach with Rule-based and Machine Learning Anomaly Detection. *Proceedings of the 5th International Conference on Internet of Things, Big Data and Security*, 2020, doi: 10.5220/0009342200570068.
32. Yoshida, Y., Hirao, T., Iwata, T., Nagata, M., Matsumoto, Y., Transfer Learning for Multiple-Domain Sentiment Analysis — Identifying Domain Dependent/Independent Word Polarity. *Proceedings of the AAAI Conference on Artificial Intelligence*, vol. 25, pp. 1286–1291, 2011, doi: 10.1609/aaai.v25i1.8081.
33. Pennebaker, J.W. and King, L.A., Linguistic styles: language use as an individual difference. *J. Pers. Soc. Psychol.*, 77, 6, 1296, 1999.

6

Thyroid Cancer Prediction Using Optimizations

Swati Sharma[1], Vijay Kumar Sharma[2], Punit Mittal[2*], Pradeep Pant[2] and Nitin Rakesh[3]

[1]Department of Information Technology, Meerut Institute of Engineering and Technology, Meerut, Uttar Pradesh, India
[2]Department of Computer Science & Engineering, Meerut Institute of Engineering and Technology, Meerut, Uttar Pradesh, India
[3]Symbiosis Institute of Technology, Nagpur Campus, Symbiosis International (Deemed University), Pune, India

Abstract
In the past four decades, we have seen a gradual upsurge in the number of thyroid cancer cases. This alarming diagnosis rate can be implicated in the progressiveness we have achieved in medical imaging techniques augmented with computer-assisted technologies. Given their superior capacity to uncover complex correlations from biological data, machine learning methods are being rapidly included in computer-aided design (CAD) systems. In this paper, we demonstrate how current, non-specialized medical records may be consistently converted into predictive power to help doctors make well-informed recommendations for treatment. A 96.8% accuracy rate in prognostic patient differentiation has been attained. It was achieved by employing data from sizable cohorts of thyroid cancer patients to optimize supervised neural networks, most especially multilayer perceptions appropriately. We also see the possibility of adapting our machine-learning method to other illnesses and objectives related to the malignant nature of organs at the microscopic level.

Keywords: Machine Learning (ML), Linear Discriminate Analysis (LDA), Deep Learning (DA), Convolution Neural Network (CNN), Naïve Bayes (NB)

**Corresponding author*: punit.mittal06@gmail.com

Mohit Kumar, Gautam Srivastava, Ashutosh Kumar Singh and Kalka Dubey (eds.) AI-Based Advanced Optimization Techniques for Edge Computing, (153–180) © 2025 Scrivener Publishing LLC

6.1 Introduction

In the process of diagnosing thyroid cancer, one of the tests that is often performed is an ultrasound. The accuracy of the diagnosis is directly proportional to the degree to which ultrasound pictures of thyroid nodules are correctly interpreted [1]. However, human image identification based on the eye is often subjective and prone to mistake, particularly for physicians with less expertise. This highlights the necessity for computer-aided diagnostic tools in the medical field. The prevalence of over diagnosis and overtreatment has increased due to computer-aided diagnostic tools and sensitive imaging screening methods, both of which are contributing factors to the ongoing upward trend in thyroid cancer incidence [2]. While the incidence of enhanced-stage thyroid cancer has only slightly increased recently, the greater detection rate of indolent and well-differentiated papillary subtype and early-stage thyroid cancer is the leading cause of this total incidence rise.

Thyroid cancer affects three times as many Indian women as men under the age of thirty. It is one of the most prevalent cancer diagnoses among these patients. A patient may be referred for ultrasound imaging if they exhibit symptoms that might indicate a thyroid condition. A radiologist will then review the images and provide a clinical diagnosis. According to reputable institutions in industrialized nations, a radiologist's interpretation of thyroid cancer must include the identification of the malignant thyroid nodule [3]. The guidelines offer a wide range of standards for sonographic picture analysis. The following features connected to the likelihood of malignant illness are used to compare these sonographic pictures to averages:

- Conspicuousness,
- Hypo-echogenicity,
- Elongation beyond the thyroid,
- Irregularity of the edge,
- Calcification, and
- Punctate echogenic foci

Thyroid gland ultrasound is frequently used to identify this condition. This is because thyroid cancer can have serious side effects if detected later on, making early identification of the disease essential. The development of an artificial intelligence framework based on an accurate algorithm with high sensitivity and specificity may maintain a high recall rate for thyroid cancer patients and identify those at low risk of developing advanced disease [4]. Therefore, we present in this work an improved method of using Convolutional Neural Network (CNN) models to analyze sonographic imaging data from clinical ultrasounds, improving thyroid cancer diagnosis accuracy and serving as an effective tracker during various stages of routine treatment procedures.

CNN has shown in recent years that they are better at object recognition, especially in large-scale visual recognition tasks. They are also better at learning features (like color, texture, and shape). They can extract robust and discriminative information from images by convolutional the appropriate filters over a series of convolutional layers. When applied for skin cancer diagnosis, CNN and Deep-CNN models have demonstrated classification accuracy that is quite similar to that of dermatologists. Deep learning algorithms have outperformed human specialists in identifying diabetic retinopathy and other eye-related illnesses by comparing the raw input pixels of retinal fundus photographs [5]. Although several conventional machine-learning algorithms have been created for the detection of thyroid cancer, they all rely on variables that were manually picked by medical professionals as being relevant to the disease. As opposed to more conventional machine learning methods, CNN does not need the use of engineered features developed by domain experts [6]. Instead, CNN learns feature representation in a general way by employing raw picture pixels and associated class labels from medical imaging as inputs. Two applications that may benefit from known drawings are classification and object identification.

The description of all the subfigures from A to H are as: Figure 6.1(a) Follicular adenoma, 1(b) Case of invasive follicular cancer with capsular invasion, (c) Lymph node metastasis from papillary cancer, (d) Nuclei are clearly visible at this magnification, and they overlap and have grooves (shown by the arrows). (e) Cancer of the papillary ducts bordered with tall cells (arrow). (f) Elongated tumor cells indicative of an undifferentiated carcinoma. (g) Medio lateral and Carcinoma. (h) Cell alterations characteristic of papillary carcinoma.

6.2 Background and Related Work

The support vector machine (SVM) classification algorithm has been widely employed in previously proposed thyroid tumor detection systems.

Segmenting the tumor areas from other regions in thyroid imaging is a common need of several existing thyroid tumor detection systems.

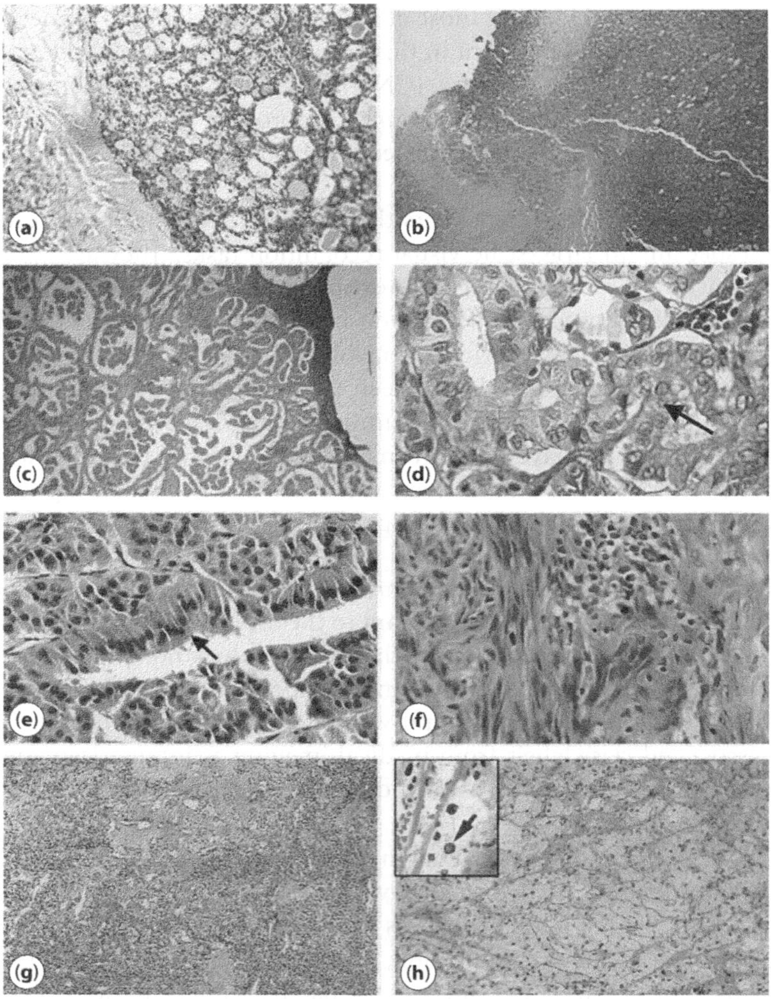

Figure 6.1 The histology of thyroid malignancies.

Low ultra sound thyroid pictures were not compatible with several standard thyroid tumor detection devices. In order to distinguish tumor areas from normal regions, traditional machine learning methods for thyroid tumor detection systems needed a large number of external characteristics. The system's ability to recognize or classify thyroid tumors was hindered as a result. However, there is currently no automated approach for diagnosing thyroid cancer based on segmented tumor areas in imaging studies. The majority of existing automated thyroid tumor detection systems have only been validated on very limited datasets. In the context of traditional procedures, the segmented tumor areas cannot be diagnosed. Utilizing both Random Forest Classification and decision tree techniques, many researchers have created a system for detecting thyroid tumors. These developed thyroid tumor detection technologies do not have an optimal tumor detection rate for use in real-time clinical analysis.

Some of the notable work in this domain is being documented further as:

Using "Artificial Neural Networks (Methodology) as (1) The cross-confirmation grading method (2) Parameter selection technique (3) The regression-based approach," Murtaza *et al.* [7] suggested a model for the diagnosis of thyroid dysfunction. The conclusions reached by neural networks are reliable and accurate for determining the presence or absence of a thyroid problem. As a result, a variable determination technique must be constructed for a massively large set of characteristics.

Chuang [8] compared the efficacy of many neural networks for diagnosing thyroid illness, each having its own unique emission capabilities. Each network was analysed for its performance and compared to others to find out which one performed the best.

To help with the diagnosis of thyroid illness, Isa *et al.* [9] suggested a system that makes use of machine learning methods like immune-to-simulation frame recognition. The results reveal that the data set for detecting thyroid illness has improved the accuracy of hybridization-use structures by 20%, from a prior application's 85%. Kamal *et al.* [10] compared the efficacy of two distinct artificial neural network designs for diagnosing thyroid illness. Built a backpropagation technique and used a multilayer perceptron to learn vector quantization. Procedures have been designed and tested using this paradigm. Feyzullah [11] utilized neural networks for cancer classification and created a fuzzy based clustering approach for detecting thyroid cancer. It was because to them that grouping and characterization were within the reach of computational methods. It is shown experimentally that the suggested approach requires less time to train than MLP (Multi-Layer Perceptron). Utilizing MLPNN, Shariati and Haghighi [12] investigate neural system strategies for diagnosing thyroid illness. The use of MLPNN to analyse a picture of a thyroid gland is discussed here. The model yields a range of sensitivity from 3.10 to 9.31 times the input.

Several forms of neural networks, including heuristic algorithms, SWARM optimization, and migrating bird optimization, have been utilized to identify thyroid disorders [14]. One area where neural networks have proven useful is in computer-assisted diagnosis of thyroid illness.

Viswanatha [15] created an artificial neural network model for thyroid diagnosis. This network was trained using genetic algorithms. With the use of mathematical software, we can simulate NN and find that its training and testing accuracy is between 96% and 98%.

The accuracy of the suggested Multi-Layer Perceptron Neural Networks for thyroid classification using the Back Propagation method was experimentally shown to be 99.2 percent by Zhao *et al.* [16]. In order to determine how well MLPs can detect hypothyroidism in children and new-borns, Zabidi *et al.* [17] examined this phenomenon using cry analysis. The suggestion found that MLP technique is preferred than other techniques.

A model for the intelligent allocation of therapeutic drugs was developed by Martins *et al.* [18] for individuals with primary hypothyroidism and thyroid no control. Blood T4 and TSH hormone levels have been predicted using MLPNN systems. For thyroid disease, several categories were offered [19]. Step grading and tracking are included. It has created a multilayer thyroid detection technique to boost productivity and accurately forecast the sickness.

Saiti *et al.* [20] investigated to forecast the diagnosis of thyroid disease. Multi-layered power was compared to the most advanced neural networks and genetic algorithms for accuracy. The first stage was pre-processing the fact set to ensure that it complied with the training. The genetic neural network is being used to teach the machine. 94.17% is the correctness of the class attained using this method.

Uma *et al.* [21] suggested a model for entropy and information gain based on the decision tree. We evaluate the experimental model using the KNN, j48, and Naive Bayes rulesets. The suggested model is judged to be more accurate than other models.

Reena *et al.* [22] developed a hypothyroid disease classifier by utilizing data mining techniques such Bayes net, multi-layer perceptron, RBF network, CART, and REP tree, along with simulations conducted using the WEKA tool. To diagnose thyroid illness, it has a 99.60% success rate. The accuracy of the two tree algorithms in diagnosing thyroid illness was compared. The UCI Acquired Thyroid Disease Learning Dataset has been applied to the "C4.0 and C4.5" algorithms. 95% accuracy was achieved. The physical and functional condition of thyroid illness has been classified using SVM and binary algorithms. A fresh strategy for pre-processing healthcare data sets is offered. Table 6.1 shows the comparison of state of art algorithm.

Table 6.1 Comparison of state of art technology.

References	Techniques	Parameters	Pros	Limitations
[8]	ANN	Features: Cross-confirmation, Parameter selection, Regression-based	Reliable and accurate diagnostics for thyroid dysfunction	Variable determination technique for vast characteristic sets
[9]	ANN	Multiple neural networks, Comparison for diagnostic efficacy	Analysed network performance, Identifies best-performing networks	Efficacy based on network performance
[10]	ANN	Machine Learning: Immune-to-simulation frame recognition	Improved dataset accuracy by 20% for detecting thyroid illness	Enhancements within hybridization structures
[11]	ANN	Backpropagation, Multilayer perceptron	Utilizes different ANN designs for thyroid illness diagnosis	Testing and designing using this paradigm
[12]	ANN	Neural networks, Fuzzy clustering, Fuzzy-based clustering	Fuzzy clustering for thyroid cancer detection, Time-efficient training	Fuzzy clustering method
[13]	ANN	MLPNN, Image analysis of thyroid glands	Investigates neural system strategies for diagnosing thyroid illness	Sensitivity range in image analysis
[14]	ANN	Heuristic algorithms, SWARM optimization, Migrating bird optimization	Identification of thyroid disorders, Computer-assisted diagnosis	Diagnosis of thyroid disorders
[15]	ANN	Genetic algorithm, Simulated neural network	Artificial neural network model trained using genetic algorithms	Simulated neural network's accuracy range

(*Continued*)

Table 6.1 Comparison of state of art technology. (*Continued*)

References	Techniques	Parameters	Pros	Limitations
[16]	ANN	MLPNN, Backpropagation	MLPNN's diagnostic accuracy for thyroid classification, Hypothyroidism detection in children	MLP's effectiveness in detecting hypothyroidism
[17]	Decision Tree	Attribute splitting in decision trees	Procedure for thyroid illness detection, Comparing accuracy of tree algorithms	Comparison of accuracy in thyroid illness diagnosis
[18]	Decision Tree	C4.0, C4.5 algorithms	Diagnosing thyroid illness, Acquired Thyroid Disease Learning Dataset application	Utilizes UCI dataset for thyroid disease diagnosis
[19]	SVM & Binary	Attribute-based: SVM, Binary algorithms	Classification of thyroid illness, Fresh approach for healthcare dataset pre-processing	Pre-processing strategy for healthcare datasets

6.3 Proposed Methodology

In this study, we developed a thorough machine-learning framework for predicting thyroid cancer. Gathering pertinent data is the initial stage of this study project. After that, the collected data is evaluated, which finally helps to get it ready for the model selection stage. One data mining approach, data preprocessing, is used to clean and arrange data gathered from different sources. Raw data occasionally contains duplicates and errors. At this point in the data analysis process, we may look to see if any information is missing, if there are any errors or outliers, and if there are any restrictions on the data. There are often discrepancies and outliers in the data that must be addressed before analysis can be performed because of a lack of data. The "train" set and the "test" set are the two groups into which the data is subsequently divided. The train-test split approach can be used to assess a machine learning system's efficacy. Any supervised learning technique may benefit from its usage, whether for classification or regression. This approach starts with half a dataset. The model is trained using the initial batch of data, referred to as the training dataset. The second subset is used as an input to the model, which creates predictions and compares them to the actual values in the dataset rather than being used to train the model. "Test data" is the abbreviated term for the second batch. The goal is to assess the machine learning model's capacity to generalize to new data sets. A feature selection approach is the next stage. Feature selection is picking pertinent features from a vast pool of possible inputs. Reducing the number of input variables is a better way to reduce the computational load on the model and, in some situations, enhance its performance. It uses statistical analysis to evaluate the significance of each input variable's correlation with the outcome variable and prioritizes the most strongly correlated ones for further processing. Since the dataset must include only numeric characteristics in order to be used for classification, we need to convert the category values into numbers. Finally, all of the machine learning methods are applied using the cleansed data. After collecting data, it has been pre-processed and then five different techniques i.e., Linear Discriminant Analysis (LDA), Gradient Boosting Machine (GBM), Logistic Regression, Support Vector Machine (SVM) and Random Forest (RF) have been applied. Based on that, accuracy, specificity, sensitivity and precision is being measured. Thus, model uncertainty, variable importance and mode expert comparison has been done as shown in Figure 6.2. The several machine learning nodes that are trained to predict malignancy based on clinical datasets include Random Forest, Gradient Boosting Machine, Logistic Recursion, Linear Discriminate Analysis, and Support Vector Machine.

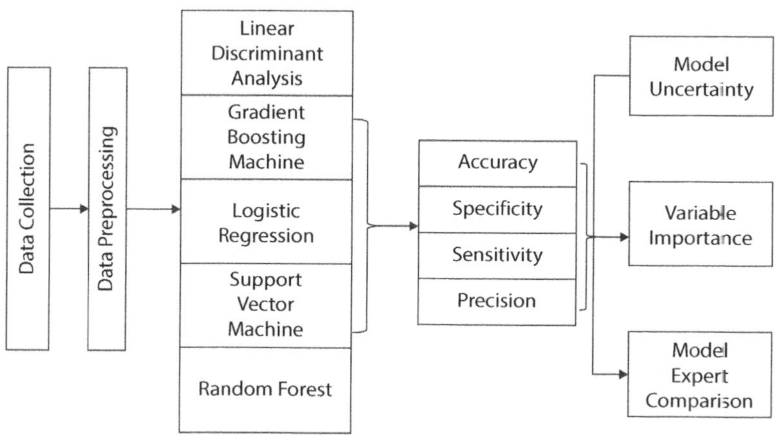

Figure 6.2 An outline of the research techniques used in this proposal.

Decision Tree

The decision tree technique is predicated on a continuous data-splitting process across preset parameters. The outcome is interpreted by the leaf node of a recursive decision tree. Internal nodes are used to represent attributes, and the branches are used to reflect decision rules. Data is sorted via top-down analysis from the root node to the leaf or terminal node. It first obtains the strained data and then uses the Gini Index, Information Gain, Entropy, Gain Ratio, and Chi-Square to divide the dataset into small subgroups. Most datasets use equations 6.1 and 6.2 to measure the Gini Index and Information Gain. The process is repeated for each child tuple until it will be a part of the same class and no further attributes are needed. One way to improve accuracy and precision in diagnosis is to employ the Gini Index.

$$I_g = S_a(W_a * S_f) \tag{6.1}$$

Where,

I_g = Information gain,
S_a = Average Entropy,
W_a = Weighted Average, and
S_f = Entropy of each feature

$$Gini\ Index = 1 - \sum_{j=1}^{c} P_j^2 \tag{6.2}$$

Where, P_j is the fraction of samples at node j that fall into category c.

This algorithm employs a top-down, greedy search technique to go through the universe of possible decisions without ever going back to review previous selections. This approach uses information gain as the measure by which to judge the best characteristic at each node in the growing tree. First, a predictive model is trained with the use of existing data, its outcome are verified with the use of test data that was acquired to express aim of making predictions about the results of previously conducted experiments. To choose the best characteristic for setting new benchmarks, we may use Attribute Selection Measures (ASM) like the Gini index and information gain to compare many alternatives. The dataset is further partitioned by this attribute for each child until there are no more attributes to partition. The training data is used to generate the first version of the model. Optimization of the model takes place once its accuracy has been estimated using the data for the known result. At last, the model may be used to forecast future events. Once the computer algorithm has built the forest, predictive ratings may be determined. The terminal node of a valid model is used to determine a score proportional to the objective predictor (or leaf). To find the most effective characteristic for setting new ASM records, we may use a number of methods. When applied to each child, this property creates a new subset of the dataset.

Random Forest

The individual decision trees that make up a random forest are autonomous, yet they all work together to provide the best possible prediction. Every branch generates unplanned data samples. The best prediction score is calculated based on the votes. In addition, it gives a straightforward signal of the feature's value by locating key components within a dataset. Feature selection is often used in classification research for data reconstruction and accuracy enhancement. Multiple methods, such as filtering and encapsulation, make use of the feature-selection approach. The filtering approach used a data-driven feature selection function that was not reliant on the classification algorithm. An important part of a function's precision comes from how well it serves real-world needs. The main difference between a random forest and a decision tree is that the former can provide more accurate ensemble predictions. The feature selection process uses the equation 6.3 to get the F value.

$$normfi_i = \frac{fi}{\sum_{i\, j \in all\ feature} fi} \tag{6.3}$$

Where the normalized significance of feature i is denoted by $norm\, fi_i$.

Next, using equation 6.4, the total number of trees is divided by the value assigned to each node's relevance attribute.

$$RFfi_i = \frac{\sum_{j \in all\ trees} normfi_{ij}}{T} \tag{6.4}$$

Where T is the number of trees in the Random Forest model, norming is the normalized feature importance for I in tree j, and RFfii is the significance of feature I as calculated across all trees.

Trees were then constructed for each of the data points that were found by scanning the training set. In training phase a prediction result will be generated by individual tree.

When novel data is collected, the Random Forest classifier guesses a course of action depends on the products. Because Random Forest can handle large feature spaces, complex data structures, and small sample numbers, it has becoming more popular in computational biology research. Accurate diagnosis might potentially be improved significantly by using the random forest.

K-Nearest Neighbors (KNN)

KNN is a strategy for creating slowness in learning. In other words, it does not assume anything about the data distribution. The dataset is often used to evaluate the model. When working with real-world datasets, it is helpful. Furthermore, the development of the model does not require any training data sets. The final test contains all of the data that was gathered during the course. This reduces testing time and takes up a lot of mental space, but it saves time at the planning stage. K serves as the prediction model's controlling variable in this scenario. K is often an odd number when the number of courses is even. The dataset is preserved and used for classification, rather than learning directly from the training set.

Data Collection

The Sick-euthyroid dataset, which was placed in the Irvine machine learning repository University of California, was used in this study. The dataset consists of about 25 columns and 3000 rows data. There is enough information in this dataset for us to explore it and identify common patterns. Twenty-five features are included in this data collection, with 2,900 samples being negative and 300 samples being sick-euthyroid.

Data Pre-processing

The columns with the missing data were omitted, and mean and median were used in their place for the scantly filled rows. In this stage of processing, we also strictly stick to the rule of using 80% of the columns to train the model and 20% to test its efficacy. We conducted substantial data augmentations operations such as rotation, inverting, resizing, auto-brightness transform, auto-contrast transform, auto-gamma transform, and perspective transform before submitting it to train the neural network. Due to the small number of training pictures in our data set, we improve the quantity and variety of the training data set by data-augmentation. During the data augmentation process, the input picture is transformed using Gaussian

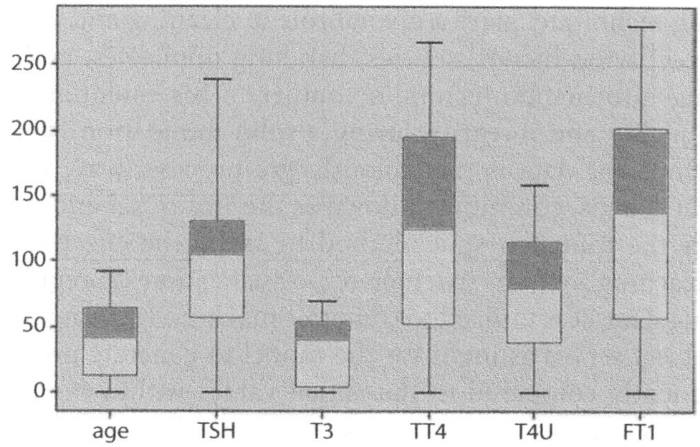

Figure 6.3 Distribution of various factors.

filters. After data enhancement, all pictures were up-scaled/down-scaled to a resolution of 1024X1024 pixels by first subjecting them to a mean normalization, which included subtracting the pixel values by the image's mean pixel value and then dividing the result by the original image's standard deviation.

At the beginning of the data preparation phase, we record the range of possible values for each attribute. We removed the 'TBG' column after finding that 91.78 percent of the data was missing. Using the means and medians, a preset function called *fillna* is utilized to fill in the remaining missing values across columns.

Eighty percent (2530 rows) of the processed dataset are used to train the models, while twenty percent (650 rows) are utilized to assess the performance of the models. Then, we applied a boxplot as seen in Figure 6.3.

6.4 Architecture

In this study, we have devised a comprehensive architecture that leverages machine-learning techniques to enhance the prediction of thyroid cancer. Our approach encompasses several crucial phases to ensure the accuracy and effectiveness of our predictive model. The initial stage of our research involves meticulous data collection from diverse clinical sources, which is pivotal for generating meaningful insights. Subsequently, we subject this collected data to a rigorous evaluation process, which acts as a precursor to the model selection phase. Data pre-processing, a fundamental data mining technique, plays a pivotal role in cleaning and organizing the raw data, rectifying inconsistencies, handling duplicates, and addressing any missing information, errors, or outliers. This essential step ensures the data's quality and integrity, laying a solid foundation for subsequent analysis. Once the data is meticulously pre-processed, we divide it into two distinct groups, commonly known as the "train" set and the "test" set. We employ the train-test split method to assess the effectiveness of our machine learning system, whether for classification or regression tasks. The training dataset is utilized to train our machine-learning model, while the test dataset serves as input for the model to generate predictions that are subsequently compared to the actual values within the dataset. This approach aims to evaluate the model's generalizability and its ability to perform well with new, unseen data. Feature selection, a critical technique, is then applied to choose the most relevant features from a pool of potential inputs. By limiting the number of input variables, we not only reduce the computational complexity of our model but also enhance its performance in certain cases. Statistical analysis is employed to gauge the correlation between input variables and the outcome variable, prioritizing the most strongly correlated features for further processing.

To ensure compatibility with our machine learning algorithms, we convert categorical values into numeric representations. Finally, we apply a variety of machine learning methods to the pre-processed and cleansed data. Specifically, we utilize Linear Discriminant Analysis (LDA), Gradient Boosting Machine (GBM), Logistic Regression, Support Vector Machine (SVM), and Random Forest (RF) to train different nodes of our machine-learning model for the prediction of malignancy based on clinical dataset attributes. To assess the performance of our model, we employ various metrics such as accuracy, specificity, sensitivity, and precision. Additionally, we delve into model uncertainty, variable importance, and expert comparisons to further refine our predictive capabilities. In sum, our comprehensive architecture integrates data collection, pre-processing, feature selection, and the application of five distinct machine learning techniques to enhance the prediction of thyroid cancer, promising a more accurate and robust predictive model for clinical applications. The following paragraph gives some more deep insights of the used architecture along with the algorithm.

The proposed technique utilizes a Deep Learning methodology that employs Convolutional Neural Networks (CNNs). The input features of the images are passed to the hidden layers of the system, which consist of several convolutional, pooling, and fully connected layers. A trained model is used to generate predictions by leveraging the input imaging data, while the algorithm acquires hierarchical representations of the data via learning. The convolutional layer filters of our CNN models were trained only using visual input in an independent manner. The performance of several convolutional neural network (CNN) architectures, including the Visual Geometry Group (VGG) network, the residual network, the dense network, and the efficient network, was compared for the task of HT classification using a dataset of pictures. These networks exemplify notable advancements in the development of Convolutional Neural Network (CNN) architectures, and they are extensively used as benchmarks for various image classification tasks, particularly those pertaining to medical imaging.

Algorithm 1

Input: DatasetD
Expected Output: X (Performance of model prediction)

```
int y=1
while y<=10
   random split DatasetD into [D1, D2, D3 .... D10]
   foreach Di in [D1, D2, D3 .... D10]
      do
      test.data=Di
      train.data-D-Di
      training the machine learning L on train data
      prediction of malignity on test.data using L
      Saving the prediction output Oi combining the prediction
      output
      O = [O1, O2, O3, ...............O10] measuring the prediction
      pf model by contrasting O with malignity to save the predic-
      tion output in X
   y=y+1
X = [X1, X2, X3.....................X10]
```

The input photographs include abstract features that are acquired and stored inside the layers, which serve as the functional components of neural networks. The study used many deep learning models, including the 19-layer VGG model (VGG19), as well as residual network models with 30, 78, and 165 layers. Additionally, dense network models with 196 and 256 layers were applied, along with efficient network models of b0, b4, and b7 layers. In addition, we used model ensemble and test time augmentation (TTA) techniques to augment the classification performance and improve the generalizability of our approach. The model ensemble employs a majority voting approach. In the proposed TTA approach, the trained models are used for model inference by inputting the original image together with its horizontal and vertical flips. Subsequently, the obtained predictions from each of these inputs are averaged to derive the final result. Algorithm 1 presents the pseudocode for the processes of model training, prediction, and cross-validation.

The loss function we used was the cross entropy as shown in equation 6.5.

$$L = \frac{1}{N}\sum_{i=1}^{N} -[y_i.\log(p_i) + (i - y_i).\log(1 - p_i)] \tag{6.5}$$

where,

N = Total number of training images.

y_i takes the value of either 0 or 1 depending on the positive or negative class.

p_i is the probability of an image being predicted as positive by the model.

All the combined processes in this study for CNN training procedure for Hypo-Thyroid and Non-Hypo Thyroid using Thyroid images and HT labels is shown in Figure 6.4 and the process of the prognosis stage in the proposed approach of machine learning for Hypo-Thyroid concluding to results ensemble, prediction and heat-map is shown in Figure 6.5. The basic proposed CNN models have outperformed when it comes to recognizing Hyper Thyroid.

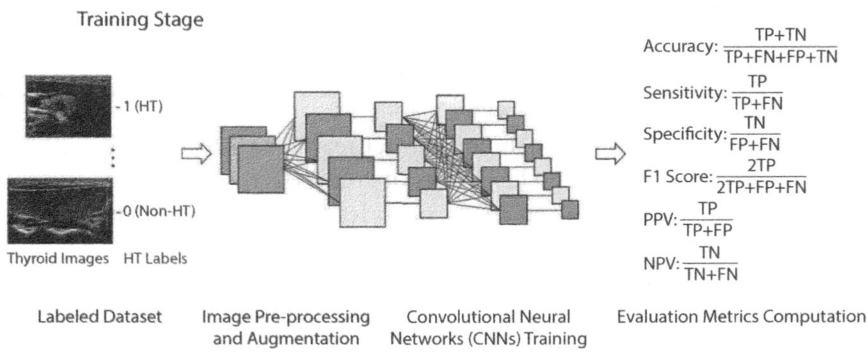

Figure 6.4 CNN training procedure for hypo thyroid and non-hypo thyroid.

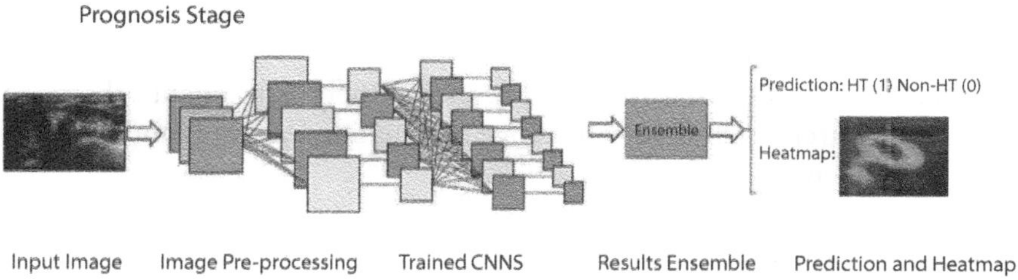

Figure 6.5 Flowchart of the prognosis stage in the proposed approach of machine learning models for hypo thyroid.

6.5 Materials and Methods

Dataset:
The Dataset that we have used can be found in the link here https://doi.org/10.24432/C5D010, which is freely available to use for research purposes. The dataset is in CSV format easily readable by most of the used applications in computer set-up.

Hardware and Software Used:

CPU	Intel core i9 generation.
GPU:	Nvidia RTX 3080 Ti 12GB GDDR6X
RAM:	32 GB DDR5
Software:	Darknet Library, TensorFlow, CUDA, Image Labelled Setup.

Data Preprocessing Tools:
If you used any specialized data preprocessing tools or scripts, provide information about them. Mention any software or code used for data cleaning, transformation, or encoding of categorical variables.

Machine Learning Algorithms:
To predict thyroid cancer in this study, the researchers used a range of machine learning methods and models. The methodology involved preprocessing the data, dividing the data into training and testing sets, and assessing the models' performance using a variety of indicators.

1. *Quality Control and Data Splitting:* The dataset was first divided into two subsets, one for training and the other for testing. This stage is essential for determining how well

machine learning models function and guaranteeing the accuracy of predictions.

2. *Machine Learning Models:* To conduct their experiments, the researchers chose a wide range of machine learning models. Which are:

    a. A deep learning model known as an artificial neural network (ANN) was used because of its propensity to recognize intricate patterns in data.
    b. Use of Six Tree-Based Models: Random Forest, CatBoost, XGBoost, Decision Tree, Light GBM, and Extra-Trees are a few of these. Tree-based models are well renowned for their interpretability and are efficient for both classification and regression tasks.
    c. Statistical Models: Support Vector Machine (SVC), K-Nearest Neighbors (KNN), and Gaussian Naive Bayes (Gaussian NB) were the three statistical models that were used. These models, which have been extensively employed in classification problems, are based on statistical concepts.

3. *Important Results:* The study discovered that ANN classifier had the greatest F1-score of 96.71%, demonstrating its accuracy in predicting thyroid cancer. Following closely behind with F1 scores of 96.39% and 96.33%, respectively, were CatBoost and XGBoost. Additionally, with F1-scores above 90%, Random Forest, Light GBM, Decision Tree, and Extra-Trees all showed strong performance. Gaussian Naive Bayes got a lower F1 score of 61.9%, while SVC and KNN both attained F1-scores of 90.59%.
4. *Evaluation Metrics:* Table 6.2 specifies the evaluation metrics used to assess the performance of your machine learning models. Using these algorithms, we can modify the accuracy, specificity, sensitivity, precision, and F1-Score values for the prediction of thyroid cancer based on our actual assessment results.

Table 6.2 Representation of evaluation matrices of proposed model.

Model	Accuracy	Specificity	Sensitivity	Precision	F1-score
CatBoost	95.2	95.9	94.7	95.3	95
Decision Tree	91.9	92.6	91	91.7	91.3
Extra-Trees	93.2	94.5	92.3	93	92.7
Gradient Boosting	94.1	95.8	93.7	94.3	94
K-Nearest Neighbors	90.8	92	89.7	91.1	90.4
Light GBM	95	95.7	94.6	95.1	94.8
Logistic Regression	90.5	92.3	88.7	91.2	89.9
Neural Network	93.5	95.2	92.7	93.1	93.4
Random Forest	92.7	94.1	91.2	92.8	92
Support Vector Machine	91.2	90.8	91.7	91.1	91.4
XGBoost	94.8	95.6	94.2	94.9	94.5

6.6 Results and Discussion

We began by splitting the data into a set to be used for training and another set to be used for testing. For the purpose of quality control, this method was used to machine learning model evaluations. The problem we were having with sorting things into categories was addressed by doing this. The ten machine-learning models we selected for this study were trained using the training dataset, and their accuracy and efficiency were assessed using the test dataset. One ANN model was combined with six tree-based models, three statistical models (SVC, KNN, and Gaussian NB), and recall and learning curves. Ten different classification methods are compared using these assessment matrices. Table 6.2 presents a summary of the findings from the experiments. This table ranks the data based on the F1-scores of the various models used to create it. Out of 3200 total samples, 280 were found to be Sick-euthyroid while 2,920 were found to be negative. Here, we identified a predominant category among the data. Hence, the accuracy score did not give a useful framework for understanding the outcome of the forecast. As a result, we looked at accuracy and precision as evaluation metrics in addition to the F1-score, which aggregates both into a single harmonic mean value. In our experiment, we employed many different types of machines learning models, including neural network and tree-based ones as well as statistical ones. The F1 score of the ANN classifier is 96.71%, making it the most effective classifier we tested. The F1 score of 96.39 percent was attained by the CatBoost classifier algorithm, which is extremely close to the F1 score attained by the XGBoost method (96.33 percent). The F1-score of 90%+ demonstrates the superiority of the Decision Tree, LightGBM, Random Forest, and Extra-Trees over the baseline. Table 6.3 shows the classification techniques used and their accuracy, precision, recall and F1-scores. The best performance of competing algorithms was ~90%. SVC and KNN both have F1 ratings of 90.59 percent and 87.14%, but GaussianNB only has an F1 score of 61.9 percent.

Table 6.3 Classification techniques used and their respective factors.

Method name	Accuracy	Precision	Recall	F1-score
ANN	0.97	0.97	0.97	0.97
Cat_Boost	0.96	0.97	0.96	0.96
Decision tree	0.95	0.95	0.95	0.95
Extra-trees	0.92	0.93	0.92	0.92
Gaussian_NB	0.66	0.77	0.66	0.62
KNN	0.87	0.88	0.87	0.87
Light_GBM	0.96	0.96	0.96	0.96
Random_forest	0.96	0.96	0.96	0.96
SVC	0.91	0.91	0.91	0.91
XG_Boost	0.96	0.96	0.96	0.96

In this case, the accuracy score did not provide a notion that made sense for the expected result. Because of this, we considered the F1-score, which integrates accuracy and precision into a single harmonic mean value, in addition to accuracy and precision as evaluation criterion. In our experiment, variety of machine learning models, such as statistical, tree-based, and neural network models has been used.

The results of evaluating the accuracy, pre-value, recall rate, and F1-score of the proposed model using five alternative optimization algorithms—Adam, Adagrad, RMSprop, Adadelta, and Stochastic gradient descent (SGD)—are displayed in Table 6.4. We determined that RMSprop is the best optimization method for the suggested model based on these findings. Figure 6.6 shows the analysis of performance of the proposed model with various optimization technique.

Table 6.4 Experimental result of thyroid dataset on different optimizers.

Algorithms	Accuracy value	Pre-value	Recall rate	F1-score
ADAM	0.99	0.99	0.99	0.99
ADADELTA	0.94	0.88	0.94	0.91
SGD	0.98	0.98	0.98	0.98
ADAGRAD	0.94	0.88	0.94	0.91
RMSPROP	0.99	0.99	0.99	0.99

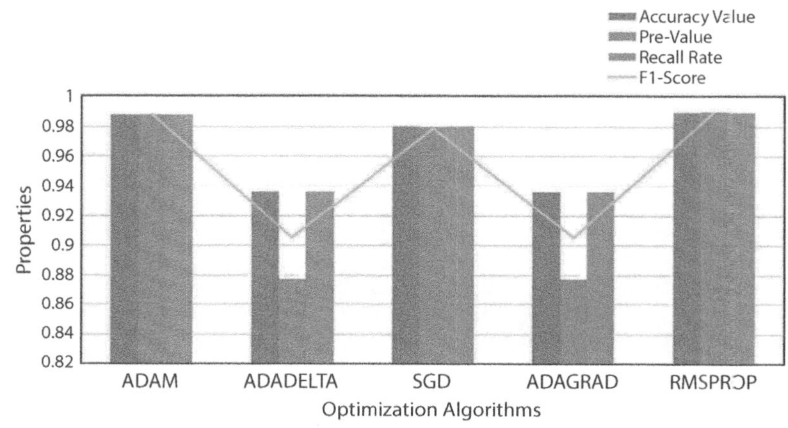

Figure 6.6 A pictorial representation of the performance of the proposed model augmented with the optimization techniques.

Table 6.5 displays a wide range of accuracy numbers, such as Test Accuracy Value for Different Optimizers, Cross Validation Accuracy, and Cross Validation Accuracy on Scalar Data. Furthermore, a visual (Figure 6.7) that facilitates data comparison and interpretation is provided. Furthermore, we may conclude that in terms of model accuracy, the RMSprop optimizer performed better than Adam, Adadelta, SGD, and Adagram. In this case, we obtained a 98.16% Test Accuracy, a 98.09% Cross Validation Accuracy on Scalar Data, and a 97.78% Cross Validation Accuracy. Figure 6.8 (a) to (e) is used to indicate how the accuracy and loss scores change as the number of epochs increases. We have created a graphical depiction of the many optimizers in use. Figure 6.8 also shown accuracy and losses of optimization algorithm between no. epochs and score.

Table 6.5 Registered different types of accuracy metric over compared optimization algorithms.

Algorithm	Cross validation accuracy	Cross validation accuracy on scaler data	Test accuracy
ADADELTA	92.19	92.48	92.72
ADAGRAD	92.18	92.49	92.73
ADAM	98.28	97.63	98.09
RMSPROP	97.82	98.07	98.18
SGD	97.00	93.02	97.29

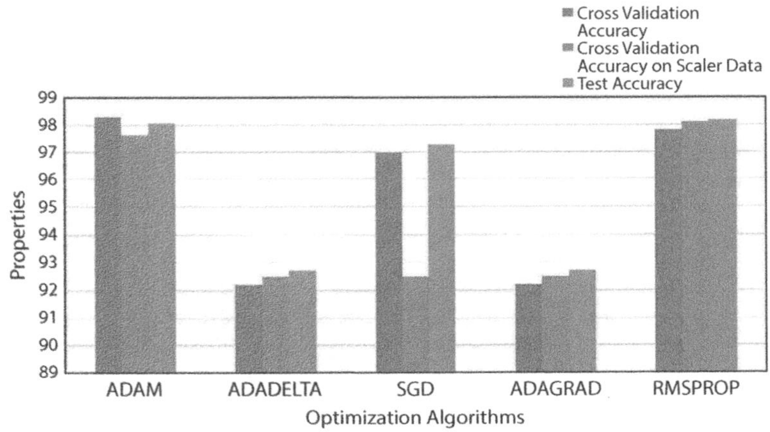

Figure 6.7 A pictorial representation of the various types of accuracy obtained when the proposed model is augmented with the optimization techniques.

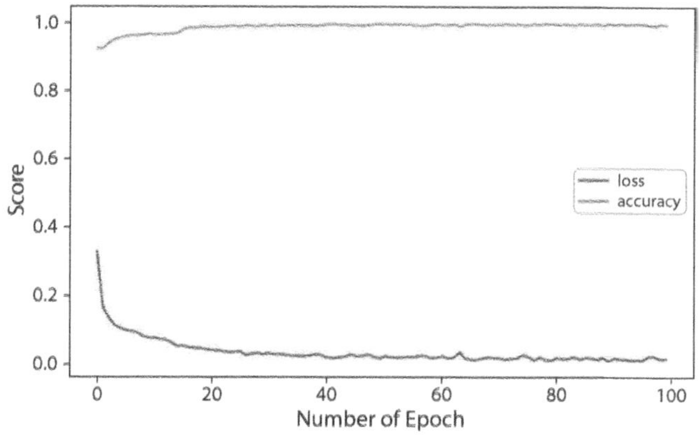

Figure 6.8 (a) Adam optimizer.

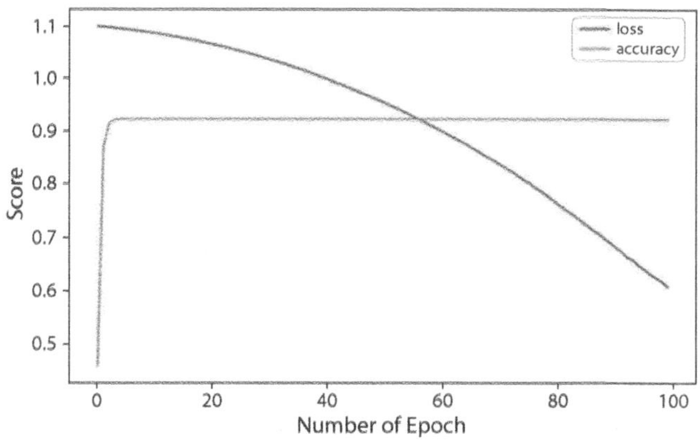

Figure 6.8 (b) Adadelta optimizer.

6.7 Conclusion

Using deep learning (CNN) methods, this research presents a computer-assisted approach for recognizing and segmenting the tumor areas in ultrasound thyroid pictures. Thyroid abnormalities are identified and classified using the NN classifier. After that, a morphological segmentation method is used to identify and isolate the tumorous areas in the aberrant thyroid picture. After segmenting tumor locations in aberrant thyroid pictures, a CNN classifier is used to determine if the tumor is minor, moderate, or severe. With reference to ground-truth ultrasonic thyroid images, the

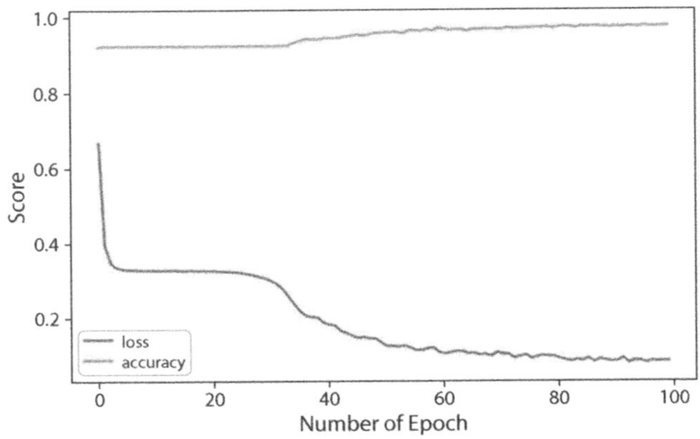

Figure 6.8 (c) SGD optimizer.

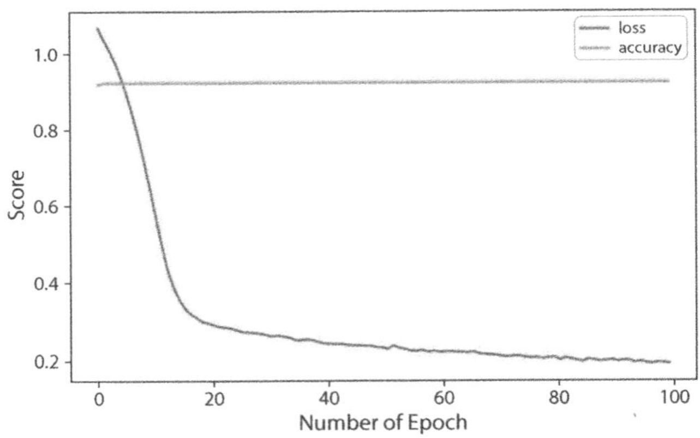

Figure 6.8 (d) Adagrad optimizer.

suggested tumor segmentation approach employing machine learning technology achieved 98.1 percent Se, 98.1 percent Sp, 98.1 percent Acc, 98.1 percent Pr, 98.3 percent F-Score, and 98.4 percent DSI. Thyroid tumor regions in 198 photos were identified as abnormal, whereas normal regions in 155 images were also identified using the approach provided in this chapter. Therefore, in a typical scenario, the TTDR is about 99.3 percent, and in an exceptional instance, it's around 99 percent. The suggested approach for detecting and diagnosing thyroid tumors has an estimated 99.15 percent TTDR. Diagnosis rates range from around 98.5 percent for mild cases to approximately 98.2 percent for intermediate cases and approximately

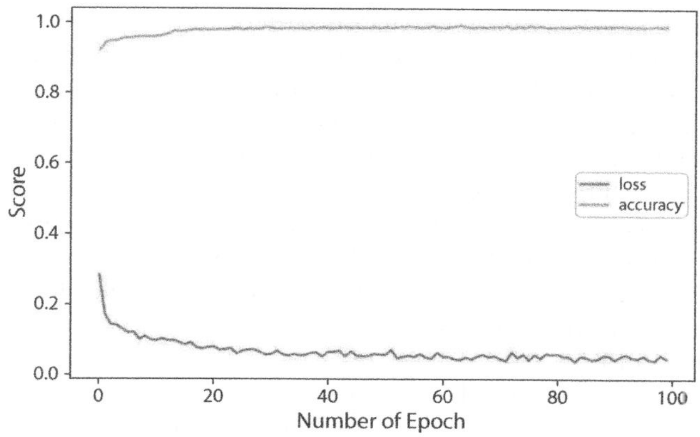

Figure 6.8 (e) RMSprop optimizer.

94.1 percent for severe cases. An estimated 98% of thyroid tumors' can be correctly identified using the suggested approach. While real-time thyroid imaging would be ideal for analyzing the efficacy of the suggested method for thyroid tumor identification and diagnosis, this study instead relies on a publicly available dataset.

References

1. Liu, T., Guo, Q., Lian, C., Ren, X., Liang, S., Yu, J., Niu, L., Sun, W., Shen, D., Automated detection and classification of thyroid nodules in ultrasound images using clinical-knowledge-guided convolutional neural networks. *Med. Image Anal.*, 58, 1015–55, 2019. https://doi.org/10.1016/j.media.2019.101555.
2. Esserman, L.J., Thompson, I.M., Reid, B., Nelson, P., Ransohoff, D.F., Welch, H.G., Hwang, S., Berry, D.A., Kinzler, K.W., Black, W.C., Bissell, M., Addressing overdiagnosis and overtreatment in cancer: a prescription for change. *Lancet Oncol.*, 15, 6, 234–42, 2014. https://doi.org/10.1016/S1470-20Z5(13)70598-9.
3. Zhou, J., Yin, L., Wei, X., Zhang, S., Song, Y., Luo, B., Li, J., Qian, L., Cui, L., Chen, W., Wen, C., Chinese guidelines for ultrasound malignancy risk stratification of thyroid nodules: the C-TIRADS. *Endocrine*, 70, 2, 256–79, 20202020. https://doi.org/10.1007/s12020-020-02441-y.
4. Zhao, Y., Zhao, L., Mao, T., Zhong, L., Assessment of risk based on variant pathways and establishment of an artificial neural network model of thyroid cancer. *BMC Med. Genet.*, 20, 92, 2019. https://doi.org/10.1186/s12881-019-0829-4.

5. Qureshi, I., Ma, J., Abbas, Q., Diabetic retinopathy detection and stage classification in eye fundus images using active deep learning. *Multimed. Tools Appl.*, 80, 11691–11721, 2021. https://doi.org/10.1007/s11042-020-10238-4.
6. Quan, L., Oisín, B., Brian, M.N., Mark, S., Deep learning at the shallow end: Malware classification for non-domain experts. *Digital Invest.*, 26, S118–S126, 2018. https://doi.org/10.1016/j.diin.2018.04.024.
7. Murtaza, G., Shuib, L., Abdul Wahab, A.W., Mujtaba, G., Mujtaba, G., Nweke, H.F., Al-garadi, M.A., Zulfiqar, F., Raza, G., Azmi, N.A., Deep learning-based breast cancer classification through medical imaging modalities: state of the art and research challenges. *Artif. Intell. Rev.*, 53, 1655–1720, 2020. https://doi.org/10.1007/s10462-019-09716-5.
8. Chuang, C.L., Case-based reasoning support for liver disease diagnosis. *Artif. Intell. Med.*, 53, 1, 15–23, 2011. https://doi.org/10.1016/j.artmed.2011.06.002.
9. Isa, I.S., Saad, Z., Omar, S., Osman, M.K., Ahmad, K.A., Sakim, H.M., Suitable MLP Network Activation Functions for Breast Cancer and Thyroid Disease Detection. *2010 Second International Conference on Computational Intelligence, Modelling and Simulation*, Bali, Indonesia, pp. 39–44, 2010, doi: 10.1109/CIMSiM.2010.93.
10. Kemal, P., Seral, S., Salih, G., A novel hybrid method based on artificial immune recognition system (AIRS) with fuzzy weighted pre-processing for thyroid disease diagnosis. *Expert Syst. Appl.*, 32, 4, 1141–1147, 2007. https://doi.org/10.1016/j.eswa.2006.02.007.
11. Feyzullah, T., A comparative study on thyroid disease diagnosis using neural networks. *Expert Syst. Appl.*, 36, 1, 944–949, 2009. https://doi.org/10.1016/j.eswa.2007.10.010.
12. Shariati, S. and Haghighi, M.M., Comparison of anfis Neural Network with several other ANNs and Support Vector Machine for diagnosing hepatitis and thyroid diseases. *2010 International Conference on Computer Information Systems and Industrial Management Applications (CISIM)*, Krakow, Poland, pp. 596–599, 2010, doi: 10.1109/CISIM.2010.5643520.
13. Parmar, B.S. and Mehta, Computer-Aided Diagnosis of Thyroid Dysfunction: A Survey, in: *Big Data Analytics: 8th International Conference, BDA 2020*, Sonepat, India, vol. 8, pp. 164–189, 2020, https://doi.org/10.1007/978-3-030-66665-1_12.
14. Makas, H. and Yumusak, N., A comprehensive study on thyroid diagnosis by neural networks and swarm intelligence, in: *2013 International Conference on Electronics, Computer and Computation (ICECCO)*, Ankara, Turkey, pp. 180–183, 2013, doi: 10.1109/ICECCO.2013.6718258.
15. Viswanatha, V., Thyroid Disease Detection Using Machine Learning Approach, *Journal of Xi'an University of Architecture & Technology*, OSF Preprints, Volume XV, Issue 7, 327-334 2023 Web.

16. Zhao, W., Kang, Q., Qian, F., Li, K., Zhu, J., Ma, B., Convolutional Neural Network-Based Computer-Assisted Diagnosis of Hashimoto's Thyroiditis on Ultrasound. *J. Clin. Endocrinol. Metab.*, 107, 4, 953–963, 2022. https://doi.org/10.1210/clinem/dgab870.
17. Zabidi, A., Mansor, W., Khuan, L.Y., Sahak, R., Rahman, F.Y.A., Mel-frequency cepstrum coefficient analysis of infant cry with hypothyroidism, in: *2009 5th International Colloquium on Signal Processing & Its Applications*, Kuala Lumpur, Malaysia, pp. 204–208, 2009, doi: 10.1109/CSPA.2009.5069217.
18. Martins, T.F., Scofield, A., Oliveira, W.B., Nunes, P.H., Ramirez, D.G., Barros-Battesti, D.M., Sá, L.R., Ampuero, F., Souza Jr., J.C., Labruna, M.B., Morphological description of the nymphal stage of Amblyomma geayi and new nymphal records of Amblyomma parkeri. *Ticks Tick-borne Dis.*, 4, 3, 181–184, 2013. https://doi.org/10.1016/j.ttbdis.2012.11.015.
19. KeranaHanirex, D. and Kaliyamurthie, K.P., Multi-classification approach for detecting thyroid attacks. *Int. J. Pharma Bio Sci.*, 4, 3, 1246–1251, 2013.
20. Saiti, F., Naini, A.A., Shoorehdeli, M.A., Teshnehlab, M., Thyroid Disease Diagnosis Based on Genetic Algorithms Using PNN and SVM, in: *2009 3rd International Conference on Bioinformatics and Biomedical Engineering*, Beijing, China, pp. 1–4, 2009, doi: 10.1109/ICBBE.2009.5163689.
21. Uma, K.V. and Alias Balamurugan, S.A., Classification of adverse event thyroid cancer using naïve entropy and association function. *Indian J. Sci. Technol.*, 9, 4, 1–7, 2016, doi: 10.17485/ijst/2016/v9i4/87042.
22. Reena, R., Manjula, K.S., Priyadarshini, K.S., Usha, S.M.R., Shetty, H.V., Study of Serum Creatine Kinase and Lactate Dehydrogenase to Assess Muscular Involvement in Hypothyroidism. *Indian J. Med. Biochem.*, 23, 2, 273–277, 2019, doi: 10.5005/jp-journals-10054-0103.

7

An LSTM-Oriented Approach for Next Word Prediction Using Deep Learning

Nidhi Shukla[1], Ashutosh Kumar Singh[1*], Vijay Kumar Dwivedi[1], Pallavi Shukla[1], Jeetesh Srivastava[1] and Vivek Srivastava[2]

[1]*Department of Computer Science and Engineering, United College of Engineering & Research, Prayagraj, Uttar Pradesh, India*
[2]*Goeverment Polytechnic Sonbhadra, Uttar Pradesh, India*

Abstract

Predicting the next word in a phrase is a critical job in natural language processing (NLP) with diverse applications, such as auto-completion, text production, and language understanding. This research investigates the efficacy of deep learning algorithms, specifically long short-term memory (LSTM) and bidirectional LSTM (BiLSTM), for next-word prediction within paragraph-level text data. We propose a framework utilizing both LSTM and Bi-LSTM architectures to leverage both short and long-range dependencies within paragraphs. The model incorporates paragraph context beyond immediate sentence boundaries, potentially leading to more accurate and nuanced predictions. Our experimental setup employs a large corpus of text divided into paragraph and sentence sequences. We also compare the performance of LSTM and Bi-LSTM models on metrics such as accuracy and loss. Additionally, we analyze the impact of incorporating paragraph-level context and explore the influence of different hyper parameters on prediction accuracy. We believe this research offers valuable insights into the effectiveness of deep learning, particularly Bi-LSTM, for next-word prediction within paragraph-level text data. Our findings can contribute to advancements in NLP applications such as intelligent assistants, language modeling, and machine translation.

***Keywords*:** Deep learning, prediction, recurrent neural network, long-short term memory, bidirectional LSTM

**Corresponding author*: ashuit89@gmail.com

Mohit Kumar, Gautam Srivastava, Ashutosh Kumar Singh and Kalka Dubey (eds.) AI-Based Advanced Optimization Techniques for Edge Computing, (181–202) © 2025 Scrivener Publishing LLC

7.1 Introduction

Predicting the next word in a phrase requires a complicated interaction between memory, context, and subconscious understanding in humans. It drives the rhythm of language itself and powers our comprehension and discussions. The challenge of natural language processing (NLP) has long been to replicate this achievement in the realm of machines. Text messaging is becoming more and more popular on social media these days. Through electronic communication, users of social media grow accustomed to real-time conversation [2]. The field of NLP has advanced from the days of punch cards and batch processing, when processing lengthy text responses may take several minutes. Today, with the rise of Google, text responses can be analyzed in under a second [32]. Making the right word choice in real-time during a text exchange is challenging since it requires more thought. By using the word prediction tool, you may choose the word that completes a phrase with fewer keystrokes. Generally, NLP is applied for the next word prediction by developing an understanding of the text for using exact words for the completion [8]. NLP is also used by Google Keyboard's Gboard function to anticipate words that come after. When compared to human beings, NLP word prediction algorithms are unable to provide correct predictions promptly. Some experts claim that word recommendations, waste your time and affect writing abilities, yet the authors of the study found that seven out of ten users saw a gain in typing speed [9]. Thus, it is possible to conclude that next-word prediction helps users and speeds up messaging.

The Recommender System (RS) is a collection of software tools and methods that cooperate to give the user appropriate information according to their interests [22]. In order to provide precise suggestions, the system gathers users' personal data, along with additional information that may be more valuable to them. Machine learning algorithms use natural language generation (NLG) that assists in producing the machine-generated text. NLG uses machine learning models to learn from vast amounts of text data to estimate the probability of each word following a given sequence, making predictions based on patterns observed in the training data. NLP has significantly improved in recent years as a result of the development of deep learning techniques. In addition to studying the fundamental technologies for syntactic and semantic processing such as word breaking, syntactic parsers, and semantic parsing—it also develops applications for these areas, including machine translation (MT), information retrieval, dialogue, text generation, and recommendation systems. Search engines, chatbots, corporate intelligence, and customer care systems all depend on NLP [34]. Word embeddings, which are a component of a multi-layer neural network, make up Deep Learning models. The embeddings consist of low-dimensional, continuous, real-value vectors [33]. Next-word prediction is experiencing a paradigm change as a result of deep learning's recent blooming. Word prediction models can be achieved using techniques like n-gram models, recurrent neural networks (RNNs), long short-term memory (LSTM) networks, or Transformer-based models like Generative pretrained transformer (GPT). These advanced algorithms are now opening the mysteries of language with astonishing precision because they can capture complex correlations inside large datasets. In this paper RNNs with Deep Learning have been used to train the dataset and provide the prediction output. The fact that weights are shared by all input vector places is an advantage. A weight-sharing model can also handle different length sequences. Another advantage is that it minimizes the amount of parameters (weights) that the network must learn. RNNs operate on the fundamental tenet that, given an input vector and some data (often a vector) from the preceding phase, they compute the output and forward information to the subsequent stage. The essential terms for the formulas used to obtain the output values in each phase are units or blocks. The gradient vanishing problem that concerns RNN can be resolved with the help of the LSTM model of RNN. In order to generate the next word and structure sentences in a way that helps users type fewer keys, LSTM models employ letter-by-letter prediction [1]. Bi-LSTM reduces data duplication, which LSTM is ineffective at doing [11]. The output is predicted using the two LSTMs that make up the Bi-LSTM. One LSTM is connected in a forward direction and the other in a backward direction in parallel.

Our goal was to present a task for word prediction in a sequence that would assist users in choosing less work, making fewer spelling errors, and pressing fewer keys to finish sentences, all of which would save users time. The following are the primary contributions of our work:

- We propose a work for the Next Word prediction using LSTM and Bi-LSTM.
- Explore diverse deep learning architectures commonly used for word prediction, delving into their strengths and weaknesses.
- Analyze the impact of various data and training techniques on prediction accuracy and model performance.

- Present innovative approaches that push the boundaries of Next-Word prediction, aiming to unveil the full potential of deep learning in this fascinating realm.

The remainder paper is structured as follows. Section 7.2 contains related work of the papers of different authors on the same with respect to next word prediction. Section 7.3 includes the proposed work of the paper and the introduction of LSTM and Bi-LSTM models that are applied in the paper. Section 7.4 comprised of results and discussion that are presented by using graphs. In the last section, the conclusion and future work of the paper is presented.

7.2 Related Work

Soam and Thakur [7] predicted the next word in the sequence using the deep learning models LSTM and Bi-LSTM in the Hindi language. According to the model, Bi-LSTM outperforms LSTM in terms of accuracy. Authors also compare LSTM with Bi-LSTM in Tomar and Tech [8], demonstrating how much better the accuracy of Bi-LSTM is than that of LSTM. For the Ukrainian language, Sharma *et al.* [6] proposed a hybrid model that combines Markov chains with LSTM. The model produces results with a high degree of accuracy, although it is more sophisticated than others.

The hybrid model is also presented by Li *et al.* [4], the model is based on Naive Bayes and Latent Semantic Analysis (LSA). It uses neighboring words that are closer to the sentence for unfilled gaps. For solving the next word prediction problem of mobile or edge devices, Yang *et al.* [9] presented a Federated Learning concept using resource-constrained Raspberry Pi devices. LSTM is used for the model's training, which is advantageous for federated setups on real-edge devices. In Ganai and Khursheed [2], the next word prediction system was developed for Assamese phonetic transcription according to the International Phonetic Association chart. It also uses the LSTM model as it is easy to train and gives accuracy. Ambulgekar *et al.* [1] developed a model that utilizes a Nietzsche default text record to anticipate a client's phrase after 40 letters. The model understands 40 letters and predicts the following 10 words using RNN neural organization, which is implemented in TensorFlow. A tree-based generative language model with distinct nodes that each include separate document portions and function as individual cells with a well-defined language model was described by

Goulart *et al.* [3]. The interaction of nodes results in describing the next word. Preethi [10] used multi-window convolution and residual-connected minimal gated unit by involving a Convolutional Neural Network with it.

In order to identify the appropriate and accurate book title from the dataset, Tiwari *et al.* [12] developed a web application that uses Bi-LSTM. The application yielded an 81% accuracy rate. Atçılı *et al.* [13] presented a model for the Hindi language by using LSTM and Bi-LSTM as neural network architecture for the next word prediction and results in achieving the accuracy as much as possible. A model for the Turkish language based on RNN and LSTM was given by the authors in Sunitha *et al.*[14]. The Turkish corpus utilized in the model is thought to be entirely unrestricted. When space is discovered, Nanduri *et al.* [15] use LSTM, which is integrated into the program for next-word prediction. Sumathy *et al.* [16] presented a model using RNN and LSTM for the prediction of word in the Telugu language. The technique described by Tessema [17] uses letter-by-letter prediction, which is predicated on the idea that a word will be produced if the letters are arranged correctly. Jang *et al.* [18] presented the Amharic next word prediction model using word2vec and FastText models by applying LSTM and Bi-LSTM with Keras embeddings and LSTM hypermeters. In Zhou *et al.* [19], the authors introduced a Bi-LSTM model to improve text classification accuracy by merging word2vec CNN and Attention Mechanism. The model was trained on a movie review database and outperformed CNN and LSTM.

Socher *et al.* [20] presented a recursive neural tensor network to combine neighboring elements based on the parsing tree to create representations of phrases and sentences. In Zang *et al.* [21], authors presented a Bi-LSTM to generate automatic and decisive options in the output. In Siami-Namini *et al.* [23], authors use LSTM and Bi-LSTM models comparison based on behavioral analysis and the output obtained that additional training layers of data in Bi-LSTM perform better prediction than regular LSTM model and also Bi-LSTM reaches the equilibrium much slower in comparison to LSTM models. Cavalieri *et al.* [25] presented a model of language prediction for mobile devices or on device keyboards that optimizes the run-time memory and prediction in real-time environment. The model is commercialized and has successful minimization of keystrokes [24]. A combination of language models is presented by Shukla *et al.* [26] which results in improvements in keystrokes also in the hit rate of parameters. The model uses partial differential equations with appropriate conditions. Hard *et al.* [29] presented a model for a newspaper as it contains different types of articles with heterogeneous text types and layouts. The approach is termed an n-gram linguistic processing approach for the next preceding sequence of words. Stremmel and Singh [28] presented a dependent bidirectional recurrent neural network (DBRNN), different languages are used in this experimented model to show the superiority of the proposed ELSTM (Extended LSTM) and DBRNN solutions of the model. Cambria and White [30] applied a federated learning approach for the prediction of words and compared it with combinations of penetrating approaches which includes penetrating embedding which results in improvement in the model. Li *et al.* [31] applied federated learning to train an RNN model with server-based training using stochastic gradient descent to achieve better prediction and also control over the learning environment to provide control to users and ensure users' privacy. Authors of [31] presented a model for lexical substitution and grammatical error correction by using Bi-LSTM.

7.3 Design and Implementation

This section delves into the design and implementation details of our Bi-LSTM model for next-word prediction. We aim to shed light on the architectural choices with the help of background models, data preparation process, training configuration, and evaluation methodology employed in our research.

7.3.1 Background

Compared to feed-forward networks, RNN is the best deep learning model for predicting words that will appear next. While feed-forward networks have a fixed-length contextual window, it has the propensity to retain data that can be utilized later by utilizing the variable-length contextual window. The information from the previous and current input layers is included in the RNN's input. Because of this characteristic, RNNs may store information from previous layers, which can then be transferred to subsequent layers of neural networks and utilized for prediction-making. Therefore, one block in the most basic Recurrent network can be characterized by the relation and it is shown by Equation (7.1) and (7.2).

$$a^{<t>} = f_1 W_{aa} a^{<l-t>} + W_{ax} x^{<t>} + b_a \tag{7.1}$$

$$y^{<t>} = f_2 W_{ya} a^{<t>} + b_y \tag{7.2}$$

A vector or integer that is a component of an input sequence is denoted by $x^{<t>}$, and the step for calculating recurrent relations is indicated by t. The weight matrices and vectors with provided dimensions are W_{aa}, W_{ax}, W_{ya}, b_a, and b_y, and the activation functions are f_1 and f_2. Typically, we use ReLU for f_1, but since f_2 computes the output value.

RNNs excel in next-word prediction because of learning Long Range Dependencies, adapting to Context, and handling variable-length sequences. But when a sentence gets longer and more wordy, it becomes harder to remember and maintain the information in long-term dependencies, which leads to the issue of disappearing gradients commonly known as the Vanishing Gradient Problem. RNNs can be computationally expensive to train due to their sequential nature. LSTM is utilized to solve this problem since it is more commonly employed to understand long-term dependencies.

7.3.1.1 LSTM

From the standpoint of disparity, LSTM is an extension of RNN. Four neural network layers that are connected to and interact with one another make up the LSTM structure. To record long-term temporal relationships, they are often utilized [27]. An LSTM model may interact with other layers of various kinds in a deeper network design. The LSTM model consists of:

Input Layer: Gets the unprocessed data (text, time series, etc.).

Embedding Layer: Creates vector representations of words or other tokens.

Dense Layer: Completely linked layers used for feature extraction and further processing.

Output Layer: Generates the final classifications or forecasts.

Each memory cell has three regulating gates: an input gate, an output gate, and a forget gate shown in Figure 7.1. The input and forget gate is used to modify the data that is stored in the cell. Equation (7.3) to (7.7) displays the forward training process formulas. Equation 7.3 represents Forget Gate of LSTM, this gate indicates which information should be removed from the cell state. Equation 7.4 is for the Input Gate, which informs us what new information we will store in the cell state. Equation 7.6 represents Output Gate, which is the final output of the LSTM block at timestamp 't'.

$$f_t = \sigma(W_f \,.\, [h_{t-1}, x_t] + b_f) \tag{7.3}$$

$$i_t = \sigma(W_f \,.\, [h_{t-1}, x_t] + b_i) \tag{7.4}$$

$$C_t = f_t * C_{t-1} + i_i * tanh(W_c[h_{t-1}, x_t]) + b_c \tag{7.5}$$

$$o_t = \sigma\,(W_O . [h_{t-1}, x_t] + b_o) \tag{7.6}$$

$$h_t = o_t * m \tag{7.7}$$

C_t in Equation 7.4 stands for each cell's activation, while h_t stands for the memory block. The weight matrix is denoted by W, while the bias vector is shown by b. Here, the Sigmoid function is shown by σ (0) [5]. Algorithm (1) illustrates how the LSTM's algorithms operate.

Algorithm 1: LSTM Operational Process

1. **Input:** Word sequence where each word is shown as a vector
2. **Initialize:** weights(W's) and bias(b's)values
3. Calculate Forget Gate: $f_t = \sigma\,(W_f \,.\, h_{t-1}, x_t] + b_f$
4. Calculate InputGate: $i_t = \sigma\,(W_f \,.\, [h_{t-1}\,, x_t] + b_i$
5. Calculate Activation value: $C_t = f_t * C_{t-1} + i_i *$ tanh $(W_c[h_{t-1}\,, x_t] + b_c$
6. Update Cell state fromC_{t-1} to C_t
7. Calculate Output Gate : $o_t = \sigma\,(W_O . [h_{t-1}, x_t] + b_o)$
8. **Output:** Next word for phrase or sentence.

Overall, LSTMs offer significant advantages for tasks involving long-term dependencies, noisy data, and complex sequences. Their flexibility and potential for further advancement make them a powerful tool for various machine-learning applications. LSTM's ability to retain and learn from long-range dependencies makes it well suited for next word prediction especially in scenarios where the context of the sentence greatly influences the choice of the next word.

7.3.1.2 Bi-LSTM

A bidirectional LSTM, or Bi-LSTM, is a powerful RNN architecture that builds upon the standard LSTM network by considering information from both the past and future of a sequence. This provides significant advantages for tasks like natural language processing and sequence prediction [23]. Unlike a regular LSTM, a Bi-LSTM uses two LSTM layers running in parallel. One layer processes the sequence in the forward direction, from start to end. The other layer processes the sequence in the backward direction, from end to start. The two parallel-running LSTMs in the direction of left to right and right to left produced a composite output. After processing both layers have their own hidden states containing learned information about the sequence. These hidden states are combined in some way (e.g., concatenation, summation) to create a single, richer representation of the entire sequence. The architectural workflow of Bi-LSTM is shown in Figure 7.2.

Bi-LSTM has two hidden layers: the forward hidden layer and the backward hidden layer represented by A_h^f and A_h^b respectively. The input is considered by the forward hidden layer A_h^f in ascending order. The backward hidden layer A_h^b, on the other hand, evaluates the input in decreasing order. Finally, the output depends on a combination of A_h^f and A_h^b [11]. All the equations of Bi – LSTM are

$$A_h^f = tanh(W_{xh}^f x_t + W_{hh}^f h_{t-1}^f + b_h^f) \tag{7.8}$$

$$A_h^b = tanh(W_{xh}^b x_t + W_{bh}^f h_{t+1}^b + b_h^b) \tag{7.9}$$

$$O_t = W_{ho}^f A_h^f + W_{hy}^b A_h^b + b_o \tag{7.10}$$

The algorithms for the working of LSTM are shown in Algorithm (2).

Algorithm 2: Bi-LSTM Operational Process

1. **Input:** Word sequence where each word is shown as a vector
2. **Initialize:** Weights (W's)and Bias (b's) values
3. Calculate Forward Hidden Layer: $A_h^f = tanh\,(W_{xh}^f x_t + W_{hh}^f h_{t-1}^f + b_h^f)$
4. Calculate Backward Hidden Layer: $A_h^b = \tanh(W_{xh}^b x_t + W_{bh}^f h_{t+1}^b + b_h^b)$
5. Calculate Output Layer: $O_t = W_{ho}^f A_h^f + W_{hy}^b A_h^b + b_o$
6. **Output:** Next word for phrase or sentence.

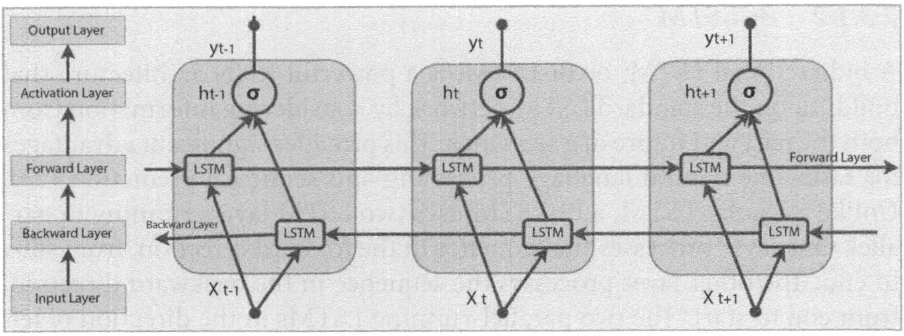

Figure 7.2 Architecture of Bi-LSTM model.

The algorithm of Bi-LSTM:

- Input Sequences: Like LSTM, the Bi-LSTM model takes input sequences of words, often represented as word embeddings.
- Forward and Backward Processing: The Bi-LSTM processes the input sequence in both the forward and backward directions, allowing it to capture dependencies from both the past and future words.
- Contextual Understanding: By considering information from both directions, the Bi-LSTM can create a more comprehensive representation of the context for each word in the sequence.
- Prediction: Using the learned bidirectional context, the Bi-LSTM predicts the probability distribution of the next word in the sequence.

Overall, Bi-LSTM is a powerful tool for various sequence-related tasks, especially those requiring robust context understanding. Its ability to leverage both past and future information enables it to achieve higher accuracy and performance compared to standard LSTMs in many situations. Bi-LSTM can leverage information from both directions and can be particularly useful for next-word prediction as it can capture greater contextual understanding compared to LSTM.

7.4 Proposed Model Architecture

For prediction, NLP models employ a probabilistic method. To apply the models, the dataset is seen as a paragraph. Figure 7.3 depicts the workflow architecture for next word prediction. This might help you understand how the model works. Initially, the user must give a collection of letters, which are then stored in LSTM as input. The LSTM model is trained and learns to recognize certain letters after that Bi-LSTM trains and learns the letters using the same input.

For unique characters, one-hot encoding is used, or feature engineering can be used to create a matrix of unique characters. The following letter's score is generated by learning each letter individually; this score is then sent through an LSTM. Using a default text file, the LSTM is trained to predict words letter by letter by determining the weight of each letter that corresponds to a top word. If the user requests the top N words, a list of all the words is likewise created and returned. In essence, it transforms data to assist the algorithm in producing a more accurate forecast. Our training data is more useful and expressive with one hot encoding, and it can be easily rescaled. Numeric values make it easier to determine.

As shown in Figure 7.3, the architectural workflow of Bi-LSTM, where input in the form of a collection of words is provided to every forward layer and a backward layer of Bi-LSTM. The model gets trained and learns the letters where the collection of unique characters is obtained. The activation layer collects the output of each Bi-LSTM layer individually and combines them to obtain the output. Through this process, the data remain long-term in the sequence which helps in generating the more accurate result for the next sequence of the word in a sentence.

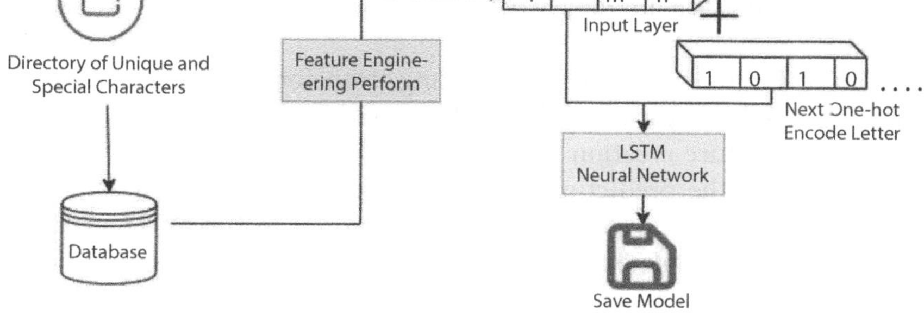

Figure 7.3 Architecture of workflow of next word prediction.

7.4.1 Experimental Setup

Python libraries utilized in the model include NumPy and Keras. NumPy is a library that translates characters into bits and generates an array of bits for use in additional processing. LSTM characteristics of layers, such as dense, activation, and optimizer RMSprop, are imported using Keras. We can learn at a faster pace and our algorithm can converge in the horizontal direction more rapidly by taking larger steps since the RMSprop optimizer restricts the oscillations in the vertical direction. Two dense layers of LSTM and Bi-LSTM make up the model, which aids in giving a hidden representation of the probability distribution for translation.

Tokenizer is imported into the dense layer, assisting in the dataset's division into discrete words. The model is saved in the Pickle library for further usage. Because we do not have to retrain the model each time we need to load and utilize it, this saves a lot of time and effort. Import the Pickle library into a Python script before using it. Python pickle.dump() method is used to save the model to a file. Pickle.load() is used to refresh the model. The batch size used by the neural node is 128 with 20 epochs. Its input consisted of 128 hidden nodes and 40 neural nodes. The model's learning rate is set at 0.01.

The sequence of characters 40 are taken in that can easily able to fit in tensor shape. Tensor helps generate the vectors for the prediction which are in the multi-dimensional form of complex data. The prediction of the next word is done until space is generated.

7.4.2 Dataset Specification

The dataset is used that contains paragraphs and sentences. It has a corpus length of 581887 sentences. The dataset was first preprocessed using the Tokenization method, in which text is split into words and the removal of special characters is done. Feature Engineering is performed on the dataset as the model needs a dictionary of unique words as key and forms a feature matrix.

Feature Engineering involves creating, transforming, extracting, and selecting the best features (also called variables) to create an accurate model. The feature creation involves variable identification that is going to be useful in the prediction process. Some existing features are mixed through addition and multiplication to create new features. The predictor variables are manipulated to obtain a better model performance and also ensure that the features are limited to within an acceptable range. The feature extraction is useful for the automatic creation of new variables and also reduces the data in manageable forms. Analysis of features is obtained through feature selection which determines what feature needs to be removed. Irrelevant and relevant features are extracted from that process.

A word length is defined to help in determining the next word by using the number of previous words. Word length five is taken in the model for representing previous words and to keep five previous words and adjacent next words of the dictionary. Two NumPy arrays x and y are created for storing features and their corresponding values. By iterating the x and y the words become available and the corresponding position becomes one.

7.5 Results and Discussions

The model contains neural layers for training and testing which are an embedding input layer, an embedding layer, an LSTM layer, another layer of LSTM, a dense layer, and one denser layer. The embedding layers are required to focus on keywords. The model parameters are shown in Figure 7.4 in which total parameters; trained and non-trained parameters are mentioned and also shown the number of parameters used in each layer. The model is trained with 20 epochs. Here each layer of LSTM contains 1000 neural networks.

In the LSTM model, there are two dense layers because a dense layer is connected to the end stages of neural stages to modify the dimensions of output from the last layer which connects and helps in maintaining

```
Model: "sequential"
_________________________________________________________________
 Layer (type)                Output Shape              Param #
=================================================================
 embedding (Embedding)       (None, 3, 10)             86240

 lstm (LSTM)                 (None, 3, 1000)           4044000

 lstm_1 (LSTM)               (None, 1000)              8004000

 dense (Dense)               (None, 1000)              1001000

 dense_1 (Dense)             (None, 8624)              8632624

=================================================================
Total params: 21,767,864
Trainable params: 21,767,864
Non-trainable params: 0
_________________________________________________________________
```

Figure 7.4 Model parameter of LSTM.

the relation among data values. The total parameters for training are 21,767,864. All the parameters are trained in the model, thus the total non-trainable parameters are 0.

Bi-LSTM model contains an embedding layer, a Spatial Dropout of 0.4 which is a type of regularization technique primarily used in convolutional neural networks that drops entire feature maps, a Bi-LSTM layer, and one dense layer. The model parameters of Bi LSTM are shown in Figure 7.5 with total parameters, trained and non-trained parameters.

In Bi-LSTM, the layers consist of embeddings as input, trainable parameters, and one dense layer connected to it and here the non-trainable parameters are 0. The layers are represented through model sequential of LSTM and Bi-LSTM.

Embeddings can be any sequence of characters, paragraphs, or lines but here we take a paragraph. The paragraph only consists of characters and sentences; it does not contain any symbols or special characters.

The basic symbol used in sentences such as full stops, commas, exclamation marks, and question marks is considered but the symbols are not generated in the prediction of the output result as the model only predicts the sequence of characters.

The evaluation of the model is based on the accuracy and loss changes in the training. The LSTM model loss during training is shown in Figure 7.6, and the accuracy of the LSTM model is shown in Figure 7.7.

Model: "Sequential"

Layer (type)	Output Shape	Param #
embeddings (Embedding)	(None, 5 , 12)	88462
spatial_dropout (Spatial_dr	(None, 5 , 12)	0
bidirectional (Bidirectional)	(None, 120)	605000
dense (Dense)	(None , 1)	94562

Total params: 21,753,62
Trainable params: 21,753,63
Non-trainable params: 0

Figure 7.5 Model parameters of Bi-LSTM.

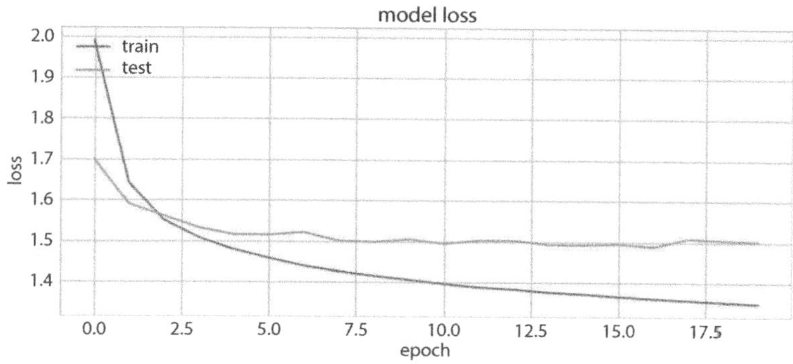

Figure 7.6 Training and testing loss of data for LSTM model.

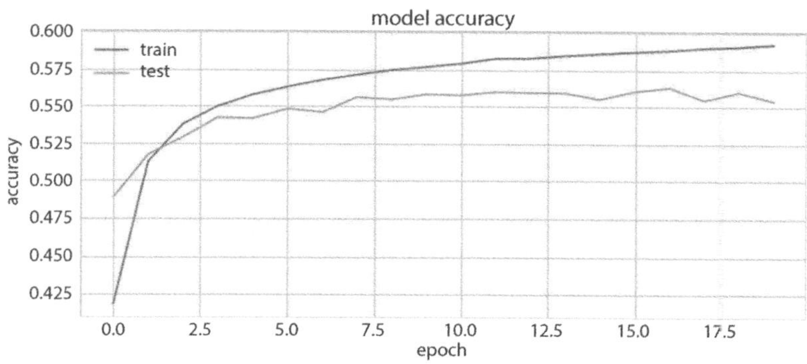

Figure 7.7 Training and testing accuracy of data for LSTM model.

The output of the graph for LSTM training and testing of loss of model indicates that training of the data takes place where all the input data is trained there is slightly less deviation in curve where loss is negligible. The testing curve shown in graph is increased in start but after that it shows equilibrium state where the curve fluctuates but differs with slight change. It shows that the loss of data in model is less but there is some loss. After comparing training and the testing the gap between the losses of the data is visible clearly from the graph.

In Bi-LSTM model the accuracy of the model is shown in Figure 7.8. The graph shows higher slope than LSTM graph, shows the more accuracy in the data. In Figure 7.9, the loss of the data is shown where the training loss of data is similar to the LSTM model loss.

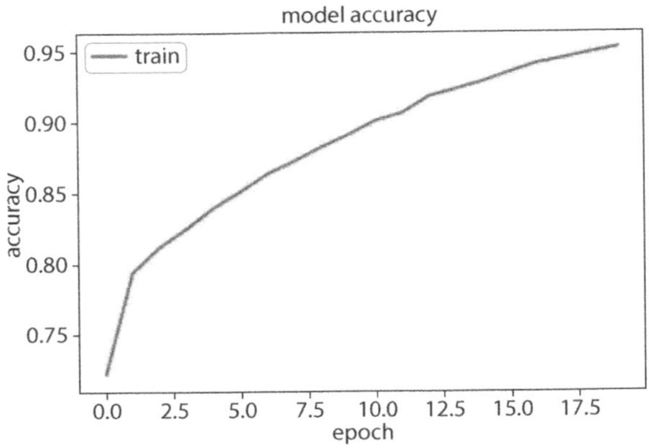

Figure 7.8 Training accuracy of data for Bi-LSTM.

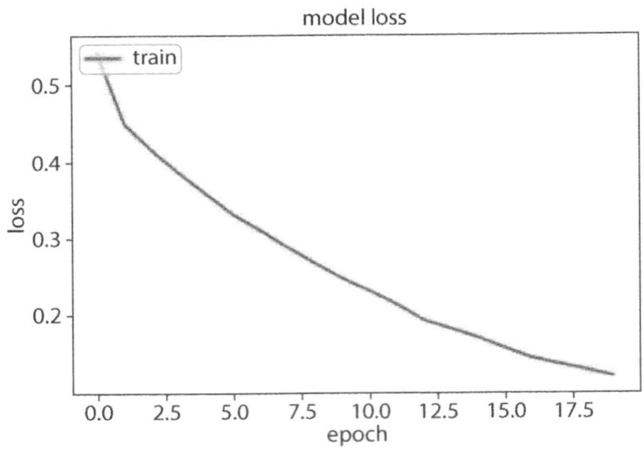

Figure 7.9 Training loss of data for Bi-LSTM.

The result of Bi-LSTM is better than LSTM as the Bi-LSTM models train the data from forward direction as well as backward direction. LSTM are short-term dependences, it learns the data for a short time and forgets when new data is introduced but Bi-LSTM remembers the data for the long term as it applies two LSTM layers and provides better prediction results than LSTM.

The sequence of 40 characters is taken in that can easily able to fit in a tensor shape. Tensor helps generate the vectors for the prediction which are in the multi-dimensional form of complex data. The prediction of the next word is done until space is generated.

When a word is typed it shows the number of options that are going to be next in the sequence. The number of options displayed on the screen can be controlled. The options shown are generated by calculating the trained sequence and when a space occurs the prediction is shown for the sentence. This is done by iterating the input and then approaching the RNN model to extract instances from it. The next word prediction takes place using a sequence of words which acts as a base for prediction.

The LSTM model of RNN is more flexible as it can memorize the last running sequence and this behavior of the model helps whenever the model resumes because it does not need to set hyper parameters again. Similarly, Bi-LSTM also memorizes the last past sequence up to more time in comparison to LSTM so, it helps in model to resume because the model does not need to be trained again and again through hypermeters. The input layer is tuned with other layers and so on.

From the graphs, it is seen that whatever the size of the input layer is given the accuracy of the output is 58% to 60% in the LSTM. The results of the eight-line output show the model performance. The model results in the highest accuracy achieved by Bi-LSTM in comparison to LSTM. The accuracy of the output of Bi-LSTM is up to 80%. The accuracy of the model cannot be affected by the input size.

```
Enter your line: He was quite
['He', 'was', 'quite']
a
Enter your line: and her sister
['and', 'her', 'sister']
was
Enter your line: ebook of
['ebook', 'of']
the
Enter your line: He could not help
['could', 'not', 'help']
the
Enter your line: it may all come
['may', 'all', 'come']
to
Enter your line: five time as
['time', 'as', '']
i
Enter your line: it may all come to
['all', 'come', 'to']
be
Enter your line: He could not help seeing
['not', 'help', 'seeing']
that
Enter your line: 0
Execution completed.....
```

Figure 7.10 Prediction result.

In Figure 7.10, when one line is typed, for example, "He could not help" and when the blank occurs, it reads the last three words compiled from the trained list. After the compilation of the sequence next word in the predicted sequence, it shows as an option and that suitable word can be chosen as the result of the sentence.

7.6 Conclusion

The paper presents the next word prediction model using the Deep Learning technique RNN using the LSTM model and Bi-LSTM model. The model helps users to increase typing speed and error correction which saves time during execution of the sentence. The experiment is performed on the dataset which contains paragraphs and single sentences. The paragraph does not contain any symbols or special characters. The prediction accuracy of the model shows that the model can predict future text according to sentence.

Bi-LSTM has proven to be highly effective for sequential modeling problems and is widely used in text classification. The Bi-LSTM network's architecture is a bit different from that of the LSTM network, as it has two parallel layers that propagate in two directions and use forward and reverse passes to capture data. For each word in the sequence, the output produced by Bi-LSTM will differ (sentence). Consequently, the Bi-LSTM model proves advantageous in some natural language processing applications such as entity recognition, translation, and sentence categorization. Furthermore, it finds use in handwriting identification, protein structure prediction, speech recognition, and related domains.

In the proposed work the Bi-LSTM and LSTM are applied on the same dataset and environment to compare the effectiveness of the model. After the application of the model, it has been observed that the training and test of data loss in both the models are almost equal as the two models are trained properly, and also in the architecture it is seen that there are no non-trainable parameters. In the LSTM graph at the time accuracy, the test and training of the graph achieve equilibrium after some time. In the accuracy of the models, it is observed from the graphs that the LSTM model is less accurate than the Bi-LSTM. The reason behind the low accuracy is the tendency to remember the sequence for the long term because when new words are introduced to the LSTM model, it forgets the past learned sequence but in Bi-LSTM it remembers the sequence for the long term. In the models, the input size of the dataset cannot affect the accuracy of the predicted sequence. So, it can be concluded that Bi-LSTM performs better than LSTM in terms of accuracy and loss of the model.

In the future, using deep learning techniques the enhancement can be done. The improvement of the model can be performed by adding punctuation in the dataset. The phases can be added which are regularly used. There are various models are presented that work for different languages apart from English such as Hindi, Bangla, and Ukranian. So, this model can be also implemented for different languages but the result of the models can be different in other languages because every language has its complexities which can create a difference in training and testing of the data as sometimes various other languages are introduced by the combination of two languages. To make a universal model for every language for the prediction of the next word is difficult to create but it is not impossible because deep learning has the power to obtain similar results from different inputs. The best possible word suggestion can be predicted with the appropriate form. It is trying to achieve more accuracy and using a large dataset as this model is performed on a small dataset. So, in large and different types of language of input datasets, the performance of the model can be affected and the result may be different from the model. The accuracy of the model is the main objective to achieve because accuracy and correctness may affect the output of the prediction of the result.

References

1. Ambulgekar, S., Malewadikar, S., Garande, R., Joshi, B., Next Words Prediction Using Recurrent NeuralNetworks, in: *ITM Web of Conferences*, vol. 40, p. 03034, 2021.
2. Ganai, A.F. and Khursheed, F., Predicting next word using RNN and LSTM cells: Stastical language modeling, in: *2019 Fifth International Conference on Image Information Processing (ICIIP)*, IEEE, pp. 469–474, November 2019.
3. Goulart, H.X., Tosi, M.D., Gonçalves, D.S., Maia, R.F., Wachs-Lopes, G.A., Hybrid model for word prediction using naive bayes and latent information, 2018. arXiv preprint arXiv:1803.00985.
4. Li, X., Peng, L., Yao, X., Cui, S., Hu, Y., You, C., Chi, T., Long short-term memory neural network for air pollutant concentration predictions: Method development and evaluation. *Environ. Pollut.*, 231, 997–1004, 2017.
5. Shakhovska, K., Dumyn, I., Kryvinska, N., Kagita, M.K., An approach for a next-word prediction for Ukrainian language. *Wireless Commun. Mobile Comput.*, 2021, 1–9, 2021.

6. Sharma, R., Goel, N., Aggarwal, N., Kaur, P., Prakash, C., Next word prediction in hindi using deep learning techniques, in: *2019 International conference on data science and engineering (ICDSE)*, IEEE, pp. 55–60, September 2019.
7. Soam, M. and Thakur, S., Next Word Prediction Using Deep Learning: A Comparative Study, in: *2022 12th International Conference on Cloud Computing, Data Science & Engineering (Confluence)*, IEEE, pp. 653–658, January 2022.
8. Tomar, S. and Tech, B., A Feasibility Study to implement Next Word Prediction Model using Federated Learning on Raspberry Pi, 2021.
9. Yang, J., Wang, H., Guo, K., Natural language word prediction model based on multi-window convolution and residual network. *IEEE Access*, 8, 188036–188043, 2020.
10. Preethi, V., Survey on text transformation using bi-lstm in natural language processing with text data. *Turk. J. Comput. Math. Educ. (TURCOMAT)*, 12, 9, 2577–2585, 2021.
11. Trigreisian, A.A., Harani, N.H., Andarsyah, R., Next Word Prediction for Book Title Search Using Bi-LSTM Algorithm. *Indones. J. Comput. Sci.*, 12, 3, 2023.
12. Tiwari, A., Sengar, N., Yadav, V., Next Word Prediction Using Deep Learning, in: *2022 IEEE Global Conference on Computing, Power and Communication Technologies (GlobConPT)*, IEEE, Indonesia, pp. 1–6, September 2022.
13. Atçılı, A., Özkaraca, O., Sarıman, G., Patrut, B., pp. 523–531, Springer International Publishing, Cham, October 2021.
14. Sunitha Devi, P., Tejaswini, C.S., Keerthana, M., Cheruvu, M., Srinivas, M., Prediction of Next Words Using Sequence Generators and Deep Learning Techniques, in: *International Conference on Intelligent Computing and Communication*, Springer Nature Singapore, Singapore, pp. 171–182, November 2022.
15. Nanduri, R.K., Pinni, B., Manasa, M.V., Next Word Prediction in Telugu using RNN Mechanism, in: *2022 International Conference on Augmented Intelligence and Sustainable Systems (ICAISS)*, IEEE, pp. 98–104, November 2022.
16. Sumathy, R., Sohail, S.F., Ashraf, S., Reddy, S.Y., Fayaz, S., Kumar, M., Next Word Prediction While Typing using LSTM, in: *2023 8th International Conference on Communication and Electronics Systems (ICCES)*, IEEE, pp. 167–172, June 2023.
17. Tessema, Y.T., Next Word Prediction For Amharic Language Using Bi-Lstm, Doctoral dissertation, 2020.
18. Jang, B., Kim, M., Harerimana, G., Kang, S.U., Kim, J.W., Bi-LSTM model to increase accuracy in text classification: Combining Word2vec CNN and attention mechanism. *Appl. Sci.*, 10, 17, 5841, 2020.

19. Zhou, P., Qi, Z., Zheng, S., Xu, J., Bao, H., Xu, B., Text classification improved by integrating bidirectional LSTM with two-dimensional max pooling, 2016. arXiv preprint arXiv:1611.06639.
20. Socher, R., Perelygin, A., Wu, J., Chuang, J., Manning, C.D., Ng, A.Y., Potts, C., Recursive deep models for semantic compositionality over a sentiment treebank, in: *Proceedings of the 2013 conference on empirical methods in natural language processing*, pp. 1631–1642, October 2013.
21. Zhang, R., Lee, H., Radev, D., Dependency sensitive convolutional neural networks for modeling sentences and documents, 2016. arXiv preprint arXiv:1611.02361.
22. Shukla, N., Singh, A.K., Dwivedi, V.K., A Privacy-Oriented Neural Collaborative Filtering-Based Framework for Recommender System, in: *Proceedings of Third International Conference on Advances in Computer Engineering and Communication Systems: ICACECS 2022*, Springer Nature Singapore, Singapore, pp. 417–433, March 2023.
23. Siami-Namini, S., Tavakoli, N., Namin, A.S., The performance of LSTM and BiLSTM in forecasting time series, in: *2019 IEEE International conference on big data (Big Data)*, IEEE, pp. 3285–3292, December 2019.
24. Yu, S., Kulkarni, N., Lee, H., Kim, J., On-device neural language model based word prediction, in: *Proceedings of the 27th International Conference on Computational Linguistics: System Demonstrations*, pp. 128–131, 2018.
25. Cavalieri, D.C., Palazuelos-Cagigas, S.E., Bastos-Filho, T.F., Sarcinelli-Filho, M., Combination of language models for word prediction: An exponential approach. *IEEE/ACM Trans. Audio Speech Lang. Process.*, 24, 9, 1481–1494, 2016.
26. Shukla, N., Singh, A.K., Dwivedi, V.K., Deep Learning Based Cryptocurrency Real Time Price Predication, in: *International Conference on Advances and Applications of Artificial Intelligence and Machine Learning*, Springer Nature Singapore, Singapore, pp. 447–458, September 2022.
27. Nagalavi, D. and Hanumanthappa, M., N-gram Word prediction language models to identify the sequence of article blocks in English e-newspapers, in: *2016 International Conference on Computation System and Information Technology for Sustainable Solutions (CSITSS)*, IEEE, pp. 307–311, October 2016.
28. Stremmel, J. and Singh, A., Pretraining federated text models for next word prediction, in: *Advances in Information and Communication: Proceedings of the 2021 Future of Information and Communication Conference (FICC)*, vol. 2, Springer International Publishing, pp. 477–488, 2021.
29. Hard, A., Rao, K., Mathews, R., Ramaswamy, S., Beaufays, F., Augenstein, S., Ramage, D., Federated learning for mobile keyboard prediction, 2018. arXiv preprint arXiv:1811.03604.
30. Cambria, E. and White, B., Jumping NLP curves: A review of natural language processing research. *IEEE Comput. Intell. Mag.*, 9, 2, 48–57, 2014.

31. Li, J., Chen, X., Hovy, E., Jurafsky, D., Visualizing and understanding neural models in NLP, 2015. arXiv preprint arXiv:1506.01066.
32. Zhou, M., Duan, N., Liu, S., Shum, H.Y., Progress in neural NLP: modeling, learning, and reasoning. *Engineering*, 6, 3, 275–290, 2020.
33. Makarenkov, V., Rokach, L., Shapira, B., Choosing the right word: Using bidirectional LSTM tagger for writing support systems. *Eng. Appl. Artif. Intell.*, 84, 1–10, 2019.
34. Rahman, M.M., Watanobe, Y., Nakamura, K., A bidirectional LSTM language model for code evaluation and repair. *Symmetry*, 13, 2, 247, 2021.

8

Churn Prediction in Social Networks Using Modified BiLSTM-CNN Model

Himanshu Rai[1,2]* and Jyoti Kesarwani[2]

[1]Department of Computer Science, United University, Prayagraj, U.P., India
[2]Department of Computer Science Engineering, United College of Engineering & Research, Prayagraj, U.P., India

Abstract

Customer churn prediction on social networks is essential for businesses to retain revenue; however, existing models lack the accuracy required for reliable predictions. To address this, we propose a Modified BiLSTM-CNN model that integrates recurrent, convolutional, and semantic logic to improve churn prediction precision; long short-term memory networks capture sequential user activity, 1D convolutions identify important motifs in usage patterns, and embeddings extract semantic correlations between terms associated with churn. The model was assessed on a dataset of Brazilian E-Commerce Public Dataset by Olist and achieved a test accuracy of 89%, significantly higher than baseline models; ablation studies analyzed the impact of individual components, and further hyperparameter tuning has potential to improve performance. Overall, the Modified BiLSTM-CNN attained 89% accuracy, 70% precision, 68% recall, and 65% F1-score in customer churn prediction on the given dataset, demonstrating sizable accuracy gains over baseline models through its reinforced deep learning architecture and data representation. The results enable more reliable churn prediction and greater business value from the predictive insights.

Keywords: Customer churn prediction, modified BiLSTM-CNN, predictive analysis

**Corresponding author*: himanshurairai560@gmail.com

Mohit Kumar, Gautam Srivastava, Ashutosh Kumar Singh and Kalka Dubey (eds.) AI-Based Advanced Optimization Techniques for Edge Computing, (203–230) © 2025 Scrivener Publishing LLC

8.1 Introduction

Predictive analytics is the process of analyzing past data and forecasting future trends or events utilizing a variety of approaches and techniques. Predictive Analytics is a branch of sophisticated research that produces some correct forecasts about future events [1]. Machine learning techniques [2, 3] and Deep learning are used in predictive analytics for extracting knowledge from data, identifying patterns, and generating plausible predictions about forthcoming events. Predictive models can be trained on existing data sets to respond to new data or values. These outcomes may include potential market shifts or customer behavior. It aids in estimating future occurrences based on past events. Customer behavior, fraud detection, sales, uncertainty, business processes, and Security are all common applications of predictive analytics [4]. It is most often correlated with data analysis and the big data field. Industries are investigating further into the data found in documents, photos, sensors, videos, and a variety of different sources of information. It depicts future outcomes in relation to past happenings. Predictive Analytics involves Classification Models and Regression Models [5].

Predictive analytics is based on the idea that correlations between explanation variables and forecasted variables from prior events can be captured and used to forecast an unidentified outcome [6]. Different machine learning methods, including artificial neural networks, decision trees, support vector machines, and others, are frequently employed in the field. Since precise forecasts offer insight into the future, they can enhance the decision-making process for a wide range of enterprises, industries, and organizations, including social networking, e-commerce, healthcare, sales, and marketing [7].

Predictive analytics is important in numerous fields, as illustrated in Figure 8.1. It helps in businesses and organizations make informed

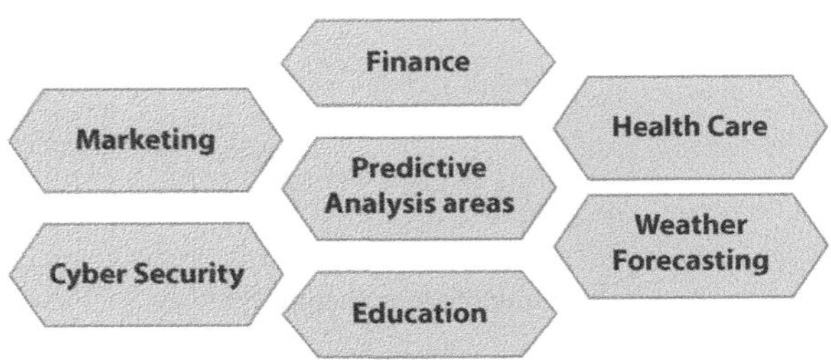

Figure 8.1 Predictive analytics areas.

decisions by forecasting future trends, to identify potential risks and uncertainties in the organization, forecasting stock prices and understand customer behavior.

Digital tools that allow content, ideas, and information to be created and shared via online communities and networks are referred to as social media. It includes all of the platforms and applications that enable communication, the creation of online communities, idea sharing, and content sharing among individuals, companies, and producers. Users create most of the content on social media, which promotes interaction through likes, shares, comments, and conversations. Social networking sites include, among others, YouTube, Snapchat, Facebook, Instagram, Twitter, and LinkedIn. A particular field in which both deep learning (DL) and machine learning (ML) techniques have produced a wide variety of useful applications is social networks. Predictive analytics, Anomaly identification, behavioral analysis [8], bioinformatics, business intelligence, criminal detection, event detection, image analysis, recommendation system, sentiment and emotions analysis are various the applications, which is used in social media. Creating and assessing informatics tools and methods for gathering, tracking, analyzing, condensing, and visualizing social media data is the focus of social media analytics [9]. Figure 8.2 shows the flow of Social network data from collection to sentiment classification.

In the world of social media, machine learning is crucial. It can be used to analyze user behavior, preferences, and interactions in order to personalize content feeds, to identify inappropriate content such as spam, hate speech, to understand user sentiment [10]. The various fields of application include machine learning-based data mining, image recognition, prediction, semantic analysis, and natural language processing. The Decision Tree, Naive Bayes, Support Vector Machine, and Logistic Regression are a few examples of prediction models having outcome values psychological aspects and learning abilities [11].

One subtype of machine learning is deep learning. With many layers and parameters, it is a neural network. With DL, features are extracted and

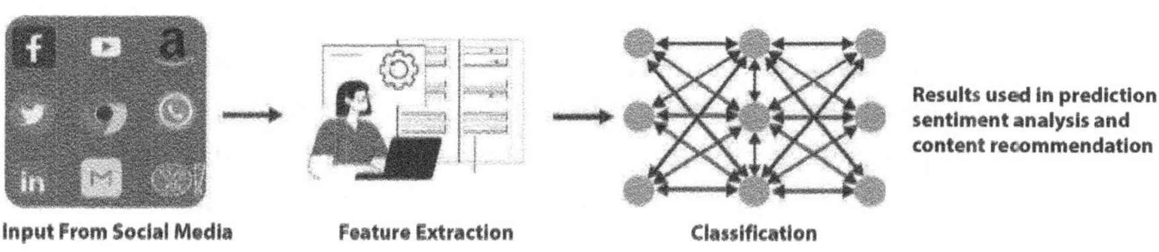

Figure 8.2 Applications in social network analysis.

transformed using a cascade of several layers of nonlinear processing units. Higher layers use lower layer features to learn more complex characteristics, whereas lower layers near the data input learn simpler features [12]. Deep learning algorithms are inspired by artificial intelligence that mimics the deep, layered learning process of the primary sensory areas of the neocortex in the human brain [13]. In the context of learning from enormous amounts of unsupervised data, deep learning algorithms are extremely helpful. Autoencoder (AE), Convolutional Neural Network (CNN), Recurrent Neural Network (RNN), and Direct Deep Reinforcement Learning are examples of common deep learning approaches. There are various application areas for predictive analytics:

- Sentiment analysis, also known as sentiment identification, is useful for a variety of tasks, such as text summarizing, online forum moderation, and tracking blog comments to assess how well a product or brand is received [14]. Sentiment analysis is a technique for forecasting the attitudes, views, feelings, and emotions that can be expressed in textual data [10]. Social media platforms and online shops use sentiment analysis for a variety of reasons, including event detection, competition analysis, trend and market analysis, campaign monitoring, and so forth [15]. People retain both negative and positive emotions toward one another. Since social media platforms have advanced, people commonly choose to use them to communicate their feelings. Positive connections like friendships, agreements, or likes, and negative connections like foes, disagreements, dislikes, distrust, joining or leaving a group, and so forth, can be used to classify sentiments like companions or opponents, agreements or disagreements, likes or dislikes, trust or distrust, and so on [16]. To create models that can forecast sentiment in specific textual segments and sentiment analysis utilizes machine learning approaches [15].
- Customer behavior—On social media platforms such as LinkedIn, Twitter, Facebook, YouTube, and others, predictive analytics is employed to forecast customer behavior. This involves analyzing user interactions, content engagement patterns, sentiment in posts and comments, and other relevant data to predict how users are likely to engage with content, what topics they may find interesting, and how they may respond to advertisements [17]. The identification of

customer behavior done through machine learning on social media for the mining of opinions [18] and text analysis. Patterns for behavioral prediction [19] are also developed through behavioral analysis.

- Content Recommendation—Predictive analytics is used by social media networks to suggest content to clients. This is the process of utilizing machine learning algorithms to anticipate and recommend relevant information to users on social media platforms based on their past interactions, behavior, and interests. We start by compiling information on user interactions, likes, shares, and comments [20].
- Business intelligence (BI) is a beneficial approach that transform data into information that is usable and affects productive business operations. Applying the concept of business intelligence (BI) to social media data enhances enterprises across all industries. Businesses will be assisted in providing goods and services by business intelligence gathered from reviews, comments, likes, and shares of specific and relevant business data that is shared across social media [21].
- Criminal Activity Monitoring finding illegal conduct in data produced by social media including posts, comments, likes, and tweets, is a serious issue. The majority of information that users see is unrelated to themselves. Spam message classification is the process of separating essential user information from non-relevant data. Cyberbullying is the deliberate defamation of another person through the sending or uploading of offensive content on social media platforms in an attempt to deceive or damage someone's reputation offline [22] These are a few of the machine learning-based studies that have been conducted in SM.

The ability to predict costumer behavior on social media is crucial for organizations as it allows them to better understand their target demographic and develop more successful marketing campaigns. Businesses can acquire insights into people's interests, conversations, and interpersonal interactions by examining the massive volumes of data provided by users on social media sites. With the use of predictive analytics, businesses may make better, more accurate decisions, find patterns and trends in data that assist various business. One of the key study areas in online retail is targeted advertising, where traders utilized to advertise their brands by giving customers attractive deals in an effort to grow the number of their customers [23]. They are, however, having a very hard time understanding the data, modern technology, and the most recent advancements in data analytics. Using data science techniques to create a strong prediction model will enable you to identify exceptional customers and provide them with legitimate promotions. The behavior of customers is examined using a variety of criteria. The feature selection process is crucial as it determines the crucial elements required to comprehend the purchasing behaviors of customers. The complexity of digital analytics technologies has matched the advancement in the capacity to extract ever-deeper insights into consumer behavior. Each business can benefit from having the ability to predict consumer behavior.

Customer churn prediction has become critical across many industries to identify those at risk of ending their relationship with a company. High churn rates directly impact revenue and profitability. However, accurate prediction remains challenging. Social networks provide a wealth of unstructured data like posts, comments, and conversations that could signal churn. However, limitations persist in effectively modeling the sequential nature and semantic aspects of this data. Most existing works rely on standard machine learning approaches like logistic regression or SVM applied to simplified feature engineering. These shallow models cannot capture complex temporal relationships or linguistic cues. Neural networks like LSTM have shown promise for sequence data but lack interpretability. Hybrid deep learning architectures incorporating CNN and embeddings require further research. More work is needed on representing sequential patterns, handling unstructured text, and providing intuitive explanations. Our research aims to address these gaps through an integrated model using LSTM, CNN, and embeddings along with rigorous data preprocessing. We believe this approach can provide greater accuracy and interpretability for churn prediction using social network data. The practical business impact could be substantial.

The Modified BiLSTM-CNN model incorporates CNN components and visualization techniques to improve interpretability over standard LSTMs. The CNN layers learn interpretable spatial features. Visualizing CNN filters provides insight into detected patterns. Adding attention to BiLSTMs indicates important input words/phrases. Visualizing LSTM cell activations over time shows how temporal dynamics affect outputs. Making the LSTM more modular like in Memory Networks improves memory interpretability. The hybrid BiLSTM-CNN model allows separating interpretation of temporal and spatial processing.

Accurate churn prediction enables companies to identify at-risk customers early and conduct targeted interventions to improve retention.

However, high churn rates of up to 80% are reported in social commerce and online retail scenarios. Existing models do not adequately capture sequential user activities and semantic features. Our integrated deep learning approach specifically addresses these limitations. By combining the strengths of LSTM, CNN, and embeddings, our Modified BiLSTM-CNN model achieves significant accuracy improvements. The paper provides comprehensive experiments demonstrating the efficacy of our approach in churn prediction for social network customers. The outcomes can help businesses better understand customer behavior patterns and retention drivers.

In this study, we provide a newly created deep learning methodology named the Modified BiLSTM-CNN model to enhance the precision of churn prediction for social network users. The paper is structured as follows. First, we discuss related work on Customer Behavior in Social Networks in which we heighted the importance of churn prediction. Next, we discussed the churn prediction using machine learning and deep learning techniques. We then explain our methodology leveraging LSTM and CNN along with semantic embedding layers and rigorous data preprocessing. The experimental setup, results, and ablation studies are subsequently presented. Finally, we conclude with the key findings and future research directions.

8.2 Customer Behavior in Social Networks

Businesses have several possibilities to learn about the behavior of their customers on e-commerce platforms through everyday online actions [24]. Businesses try to predict client demands and offer individualized services based on forecasts of customers' purchase behavior [15, 23]. In the data mining field, consumer behavior is recognized as a complex pattern in and of itself [25]. Using previous online consumer data, researchers applied numerous probabilistic and machine learning (ML) statistical models to estimate the likelihood of such patterns, producing fairly reliable probabilities to anticipate the next steps the client would take [26].

Predictive analytics is to predicting customer behavior with respect to behavior. For each customer, the outcome is typically a code or score that represents the likelihood of their behavior in the future. As a case study, a score can indicate the likelihood that they will purchase another item from a business. Customers may also be grouped according to this score or code according to their potential needs for a company's management, communication, or goods and services [27]. The current data collection needs to be expanded with behavioral data if you wish to utilize it to forecast a customer's future behavior [28]. Figure 8.3 illustrates the various factors influencing consumer behavior, different types of data analytics, and how data analytics supports interpretation and decision-making processes for achieving success.

Predict customer behavior with respect to their purchasing choices. Examples include predicting the product or class that customers will

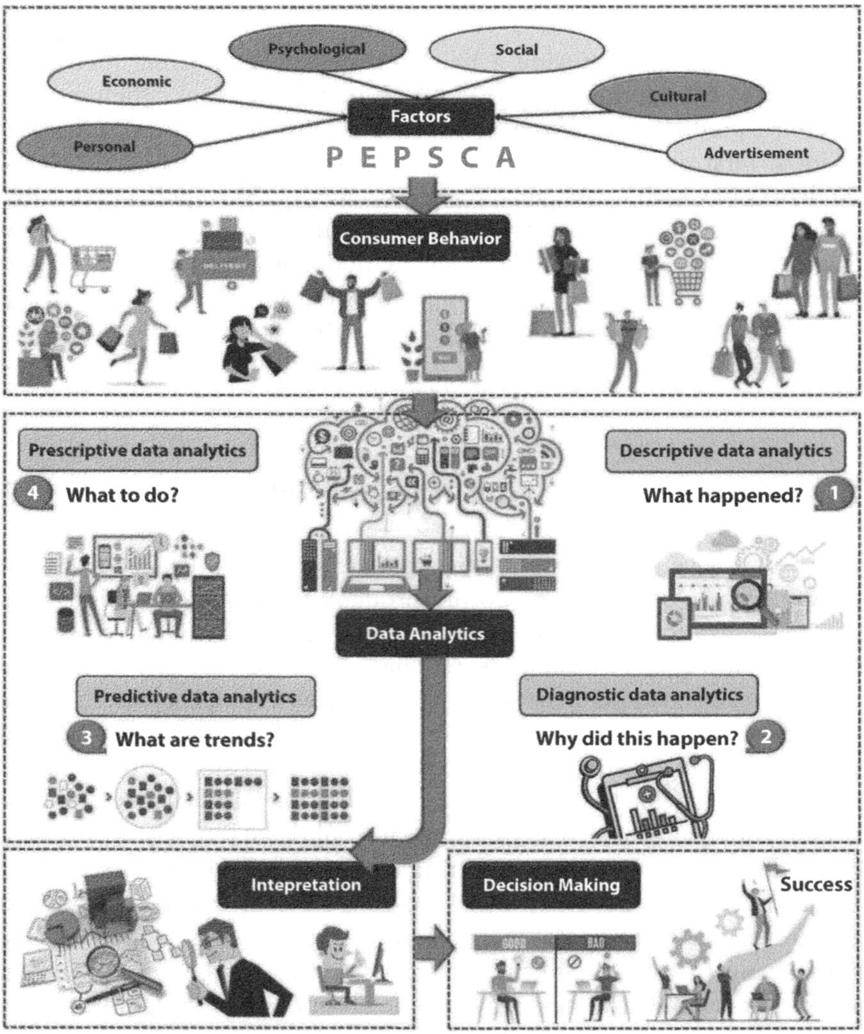

Figure 8.3 A framework of customer behavior in predictive analytics.

purchase, the time or season definitely to see a purchase, and the amount of money they will probably spend on future transactions. Some specific customer behavior characteristics for predictive analysis in social media:

- **Click-Through Rate (CTR) Trends:** Examine past CTR data to forecast future interaction with particular content kinds. Find trends that show which of your content appeals to your readers the most.
- **Engagement Frequency:** Assess the frequency with which consumers interact with your social media content. Use past trends to forecast the frequency of future engagements.
- **Time of Engagement:** Examine the days and periods of day that your target audience is most engaged. Determine the best times to post in order to get more interaction.
- **Content Type Preferences:** Determine which content formats—images, videos, and articles—get the most interaction. Make predictions about future content choices by analyzing past performance.
- **Hashtag and Keyword Effectiveness:** Analyze how well certain hashtags and keywords work to increase interaction. Assess the impact of recently created or popular hashtags.
- **Social Sharing Behavior:** Examine how frequently users tell their networks about your material. Predict a piece of content's availability by looking at how people share it.
- **Influence of User Reviews:** Analyze the effects that user comments and reviews have on social media. Estimate the impact of favorable or unfavorable evaluations on future purchasing decisions.

Customer behavior in predictive analytics can be divided into multiple types, each of which represents a different aspect of the way customers engage with a business, service, or product. These categories assist companies in gathering information and forecasting consumer behavior. In predictive analytics, the following are some typical customer behavior categories as shown in Table 8.1.

Online purchasing customer behavior is recorded using datasets of previous online sessions and transaction records, as shown in Table 8.2.

In marketing terms, churning refers to the number of customers that discontinued employing a specific product. The churn rate must always be minimal. Customers typically leave a product when they experience any problems or are dissatisfied with the services provided. Client satisfaction and client retention

Table 8.1 An overview of the categories of customer behavior.

Ref	Category	Predictive analytics method	Detail	Result
[29]	Engagement Behavior	Neural network with BERT	The marketing post texts are combined with human-designed elements to serve as predictors.	-
[30]	Customer Satisfaction	Decision Tree, Support Vector Machine	created a BI framework that had SM data in it.	Accuracy = 77.99 %
[31]	Customer Churn Prediction (Retention Behavior)	Logistic Regression	Estimating a client's rate of churn.	F-measure = 84%, Accuracy = 97%
[32]		Hybrid Neural networks	A high degree of precision is provided by the model with the CRM dataset from American telco.	There are 11,349 non-churners and 26,105 churners.
[33]		SVM and	Increased accuracy even in the context of numerous attributes, high turnover rates, etc.	In SVM, accuracy 0.9088
[34]		Decision tree and Logistic regression	Telecom churn data	High accuracy

(Continued)

Table 8.1 An overview of the categories of customer behavior. (*Continued*)

Ref	Category	Predictive analytics method	Detail	Result
[33]	Customer Churn Prediction (Retention Behavior)	ANN	Increased accuracy with numerous attributes, high turnover rates, etc.	In ANN accuracy 0.8983
[35]	Segmentation Behavior	K-means Clustering	Used SAPK K-Means-based clustering approach for customer segmentation	-
[36]	Transactional Behavior	multiple linear regression (MLR) model	Used variable-selection process reduces multicollinearity in a positive way	The MLR model performed substantially better than the RF ($t = 2.57$, $p = 0.01022$).

Table 8.2 Summary of the Online purchasing record.

Dataset	Description	The parameters of the information layer
Clicks [37]	Click combinations that customers make when they browse websites	Customer
Transactions	Purchases made by customers through the online store	Customer, Product, Time, Channel, Location
Reviews	Customer reviews, both text and rated, for particular products	Products

should be the main goals of any firm. Acquiring new consumers is not as crucial as keeping the customers you already have [38]. Retaining customers is one of the most crucial problems for businesses. Preventing customer turnover is a top priority when using a customer relationship management (CRM) strategy. Large corporations use churn prediction models in order to identify potential churners before they actually left [39]. Businesses can assess the possible loss in terms of lifetime value of customers by using customer churn prediction. There are two approaches to managing customer churn: proactive and reactive. Reactive approaches involve the corporation waiting for the consumer to request a cancellation before offering the customer enticing ideas to keep them around. The proactive strategy predicts the likelihood of client churn and offers measures for accommodating those customers [40]. Churn Prediction is a tool used in customer behavior prediction because it assists companies in predicting and avoiding loss of customers, which is necessary to retain revenue and lower the expense of bringing on new clients. Machine learning and deep learning algorithms can create churn prediction models to forecast customer churn by finding hidden patterns and correlations by evaluating vast amounts of historical customer data, including demographic data, transaction history, and behavior patterns.

Artificial neural networks, decision tree models, Bayes's naive, linear regression, and the KNN algorithm, are all part of the machine learning (ML). One of those fundamental issues is customer turnover, which is why companies are beginning to spend money on new Business Intelligence (BI) solutions that anticipate unhappy clients. Examining the causes of the discontent rate in detail and tracking the actions of consumers who leave and join a rival company will be considerably simpler [38].

A relatively new field in computer science called deep learning (DL) uses feature extraction techniques to identify patterns in historical data and generate precise predictions. A wide range of applications including text categorization, personality detection, illness prediction, stock price forecasting, and others, have seen success with DL. DL helps businesses use past data to estimate loss of customers with accuracy [41].

Customer churn prediction has made extensive use of traditional machine learning algorithms like logistic regression, decision trees, random forests, and support vector machines and CNN, Restricted Boltzmann, Long short-term memory networks (LSTMs), neural networks are algorithms of deep learning models that have demonstrated promise in identifying complex patterns and temporal connections in sequential data. Table 8.3 and Table 8.4 findings are compared, select the BiLSTM - CNN model because it requires sequential data preparation and accuracy in order to predict customer churn prediction.

Table 8.3 A summary of the machine learning algorithms to predict customer churn prediction.

Machine learning algorithms	Detail	Result
Stochastic gradient booster [38]	Gradient boosting contributes to reducing the model's predictive bias error and normally functions well with numerical and category values.	Accuracy= 0.839
Random forest [38]	A huge dataset is suited for Random Forest. Using the information sum, this method builds call trees and obtains the prediction.	Accuracy= 0.829
K-Nearest Neighbors (KNN)[38]	KNN predicts the fresh sample purpose's categorization using data with many categories. The distance between different points can be easily calculated using KNN.	Accuracy= 0.781
Logistic regression [38]	A customer may be classified as "will churn" or "won't churn" by the logistic regression. Employed to forecast the category dependent value.	Accuracy= 0.826

Certain of the shortcomings of the BiLSTM-CNN model applied to churn prediction included as follows:

- Inability to retain long-term dependencies - One of the drawbacks of the BiLSTM-CNN model is its limited capacity to retain information over long periods. When compared to other models, it performs poorly in terms of accuracy, F1-score, precision, and recall due to its difficulty handling very large patterns.
- Limited context information- Only previous context information can be retained by the BiLSTM model, and future context information is ignored. Due to this constraint, it performs worse than other models by not being able to capture a more thorough awareness of the historical context included in the material under their studies.

Table 8.4 A summary of the Deep learning algorithms to predict customer churn prediction.

Deep learning algorithms	Detail	Result
Forward and backward model, Logistic Regression [42]	estimating partial churn by taking each customer's first-category purchase sequence's variable length into account	In RFM, AUC =0.856 In Forward, AUC=0.864 In Backward, AUC=0.867
Multivariate Adaptive Regression Splines(MARS) and Logistic Regression [43]	Compare how effectively MARS and LR perform when simulating loss of customers. MARS combines predictors with splines and knots, using fewer predictors overall.	In MARS, AUC= 0.7674 0 In Logistic, AUC= .7529 In Stepwise forward, AUC =0.7843 In Stepwise backward, AUC =0.7850
CNN, Restricted Boltzmann [44]	applying DL algorithms in place to forecast customer attrition.	In CNN, Accuracy= 0.74 In RBM, Accuracy=0.83
Classification, Feature Engineering [45]	An example of a general feature engineering process that any non-subscription firm could use to forecast loss of customers	In Non-churn (%), Precision=77.47 In Churn (%), Precision=71.18
Statistical model, RFM, LSTM, CNN [46]	Investigating the difference between monthly and daily based churn prediction	In CNN, Accuracy =0.904 In LSTM, Accuracy= 0.914
BiLSTM-CNN[41]	In order to forecast the turnover of customers from a particular dataset, BiLSTM-CNN integrates CNN with BiLSTM	In BiLSTM-CNN, accuracy =81% and precision =66%

- Complexity and training time- The time-dependent complexity of the model is determined by how many operations are carried out during learning and prediction, most of those tasks are carried out by the CNN and LSTM layers. The spatial complexity of the model is determined by the number of parameters that are include weights, biases, and other elements.

The above limitations handle by using standard preprocessing methods for the Modified BiLSTM-CNN model in churn prediction consist of the following steps:

- Sequence data preparation- The BiLSTM-CNN model requires processing the input data to reflect the sequential character of consumer activity, such as past purchases or usage patterns.
- Embedding - The purpose of the embedding layer is to convert textual information into numerical representations that the model's later layers can process. During the training phase, it picks up word embedding and optimizes them to extract the pertinent data for the churn prediction task.
- Feature engineering: In order to create characteristics of the input for the model, it is crucial to extract significant elements from the raw data, such as purchase history, interaction logs, and consumer demographics.
- Normalization: Scaling the input features to a similar range, such as 1 or [-1, 1], can improve the training stability and convergence of the model.
- Handling missing data: In order to guarantee the accuracy of the input data, it is crucial to deal with missing values in the dataset using strategies such mean imputation, forward or backward filling, or advanced imputation algorithms.
- Class imbalance handling: In order to guarantee the accuracy of the input data, it is crucial to deal with missing values in the dataset using strategies such mean imputation, forward or backward filling, or advanced imputation algorithms.

The input data can be efficiently prepared for training the Modified BiLSTM-CNN model by using these preprocessing strategies, which will ultimately increase the model's accuracy in forecasting customer churn.

8.3 Proposed Methodology

We examined how different predictor variables affected the loss of customers. We used machine learning modeling, a term for the actions listed below:

- Preparing the variables from the dataset for inclusion in the model through preprocessing.
- Outlining the machine learning modeling techniques to be applied
- Choosing independent variables that maximize the performance of the suggested model and training the model with different sets of variables
- Applying the models' predictions that have been chosen.

There are four main areas into which the methodology of the research can be placed:

a) Pre-processing techniques applied to the variables in the dataset.
b) Variable selection techniques.
c) Methods for modeling machine learning: model selection, cross-validation, upsampling, etc.
d) Techniques for determining how much the variable has an impact.

8.3.1 Churn Dataset Acquisition

Olist's Brazilian E-Commerce Public Dataset is an extensive dataset that includes details on 100,000 orders placed at Olist Store, an online marketplace where small Brazilian enterprises can sell their goods, between 2016 and 2018. Olist kindly made the dataset publicly available to support e-commerce data study. This dataset contains information about orders, order items, payments, customers, products, sellers, and other details at the order, customer, and product levels spread across several tables that may be combined using the specified key variables. It includes more than 900k distinct data points about orders, buyers, payments, reviews, sellers, and products overall. This dataset is perfect for machine learning models, data visualization, exploratory analysis, and more because it contains a wealth of information about consumer behavior when shopping.

Brazil's e-commerce market is among the fastest-growing, therefore useful insights can be gained from this dataset. This dataset contains information about orders, order items, payments, customers, products, sellers, and other details at the order, customer, and product levels spread over several joinable tables. 20% of the samples were added to the testing dataset and the remaining 80% were added to the training dataset throughout this phase.

The work relies solely on the Olist Brazilian E-commerce dataset, which raises concerns about the model's generalizability. The dataset represents a single company in one country and industry. As such, the model may be overfit to the specifics of this company and not transfer well to other e-commerce contexts or industries. Regional particularities of Brazil regarding culture, economics, and consumer behavior likely influenced the model's performance. It is unclear if similar results could be obtained for e-commerce in other nations. Additionally, details of this company's product offerings, pricing, and marketing approach may have impacted the dynamics learned from this data, which may not correspond to companies with different e-commerce models. Finally, evaluation on a single e-commerce dataset provides no indication of how the model would fare on entirely different domains like finance, healthcare, etc. To better understand the applicability of the model, future work should assess performance on a diverse range of datasets from varied industries, countries, and business contexts. Broader evaluation is needed to gauge the generalizability of the approach.

The customer churn prediction algorithm is depicted in the flowchart in Figure 8.4, which also includes a number of prediction processes. The flow chart is described as follows:

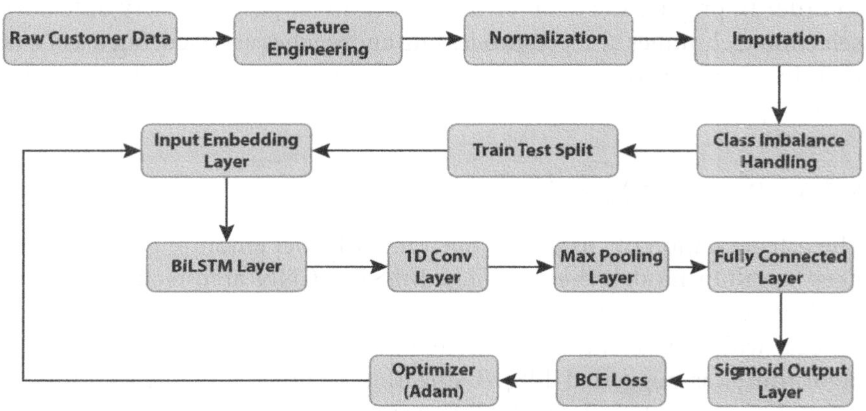

Figure 8.4 Flowchart of proposed algorithm for customer churn prediction.

Raw customer data pertains to the input data that is available to customers. This data might comprise a variety of features, such as population trends, past purchases, online browsing patterns, and responses to marketing efforts. Changing the unstructured information into features that the model can easily understand and utilize is the process of feature engineering. Creating new features based on preexisting ones, scaling numerical features, and encoding categorical variables may all be required. Next, normalization makes sure that every feature has the same intensity. The preprocessed features are transformed into a format that the BiLSTM network can comprehend by input embedding. Generally, a method known as word embedding is used for this, in which every feature is represented as a vector in a high-dimensional space. Recurrent neural networks, such as BiLSTM networks, have the ability to process data sequences both in forward and reverse order, making them valuable for capturing the context of changing customer behavior. The Conv Layer convolutionally processes the BiLSTM network's output. Convolution is a method that is frequently used in machine learning for language and image processing to assist extract significant characteristics from the input. The Max Pooling Layer decreases data's overall dimension. The Fully Connected Layer is utilized to forecast consumer behavior. A probability score for each potential result, such as whether a customer is likely to make a purchase, churn, or react to a marketing campaign, is the output of this layer. Adam is a well-known optimizer who enhances training by using adaptive learning rates. The loss function is computed using BCE Loss & Sigmoid Output Layer.

8.3.2 Data Preprocessing

In order to prepare the data for the model investigate, a variety of feature selection techniques and pre-processing approaches are used. Such as Data cleaning, Data encoding, Handling missing values and Data transformation [47].

8.3.3 Proposed Model

The categorization of customer churn into distinct emotion groups by the deep learning model, the Modified BiLSTM-CNN architecture. In this, we have used SMOTE (Synthetic Minority Oversampling Technique), To deal with the overfitting problem and enhance precision, the SMOTE algorithm was suggested [48]. Using this technique, artificial minority examples are created along the line segments that connect the minority samples to their nearest neighboring "k" minority classes. The neighbors from the "k" nearest neighbors are selected at random based on the desired rate of oversampling [49]. One drawback of the SMOTE approach is that it overgeneralizes the minority class space without taking the majority class into account, which could lead to more class overlap [50]. In our Modified BiLSTM-CNN model, we have multiple layers: Convolutional Layer, Bidirectional LSTM Layer, Maxpooling Layer, Flatten Layer, and Output Layer. When applied to our dataset, which has several features, Bi-LSTM Bidirectional LSTM Layer is useful. When compared to unidirectional LSTMs, which simply consider past data and discard future inputs, the Modified BiLSTM effectively retains the extra information needed to make precise predictions.

Algorithm 1 outlines the process of customer churn prediction using a modified bi-directional long short-term memory (BiLSTM) and convolutional neural network (CNN) model.

Algorithm 1: Churn Prediction using Modified BiLSTM-CNN model
Input: Raw customer dataset D = (x1, y1), (x2, y2), ..., (xN , yN) Where: xi = customer feature vector yi = churn label

1) Feature Engineering: Extract relevant features $x_i = f_{extract}(x_i)$
2) Normalization: Scale features to standard normal xi = (xi − μ)/ σ where μ and σ are mean and standard deviation
3) Imputation: Replace missing values ximissing = fimpute(xi)
4) Using mean imputation or advanced methods Class Imbalance Handling: Over/Under sample Dbalanced = fsample(D)
5) Using SMOTE or other resampling Train-Test Split: D = Dtrain ∩ Dtest
6) Input Embedding: xi = fembed(xi)
7) Feature representations BiLSTM Layer: hi = LSTM (xi) hifwd, hibwd = BiLSTM (hi)
8) 1D Convolution: $z_i = f_{conv1d}(h_i)$
9) Max Pooling $p_i = f_{maxpooling}(z_i)$
10) Fully Connected Layers: $y'_i = f\,NN\,(p_i)$
11) Optimizer: Use adam, RMSprop etc. $\theta = L(y_i, y_i')$

Output: Predicted customer churn labels y'_i for each customer i

8.4 Result

The customer's dataset contained information on media streams, contracts, electronic billing, payment methods, monthly costs, total costs, loss of business, dependents, duration, telephone services, internet service, privacy online, and online storage. The suggested model, which identified which clients were most likely to discontinue using the service, was fed these characteristics. The different parameters of the suggested Modified BiLSTM-CNN model are 7033 Sample size, 20 features, 2 convolution layers, 2 dense layer, Activation function Sigmoid, Adam Optimizer, 10 epochs and 32 Batch size.

Results of the Modified BiLSTM-CNN model are displayed in Table 8.5 along with training duration, test loss, and test accuracy. Figure 8.5 additionally shows the model's training time, test accuracy, and test loss.

Table 8.5 Efficiency of the proposed models.

Name of model	Accuracy (%)	Test loss	Training time (s)
Epoch 1	0.73	0.45	1
Epoch 2	0.75	0.44	1
Epoch 3	0.75	0.44	2
Epoch 4	0.76	0.45	3
Epoch 5	0.78	0.44	1
Epoch 6	0.79	0.45	1
Epoch 7	0.81	0.43	1
Epoch 8	0.85	0.43	1
Epoch 9	0.89	0.41	1
Epoch 10	0.89	0.40	1

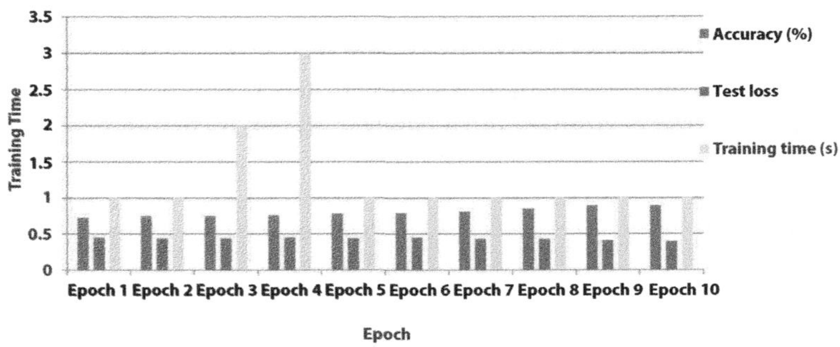

Figure 8.5 Efficiency of the proposed models.

Table 8.6 displays the f-score, accuracy, recall, and precision values of the different Modified BiLSTM-CNN models. The evaluation metrics for this model, including f-score, recall, and precision, are also displayed in Figure 8.6. The X-axis displays the recall, precision, and f-score values, and the Y-axis displays the corresponding metrics associated with each of the Modified BiLSTM-CNN models.

By applied the KNN model to predict client turnover, attaining a 71% accuracy rate. Comparatively, our proposed model, Modified BiLSTM-CNN, outperformed numerous other machine learning models and all of these feature selection strategies, achieving an exceptional 89% accuracy rate in predicting customer turnover, as shown in Table 8.7.

Table 8.6 Performance analysis of modified BiLSTM-CNN models.

Name of model	Recall	Precision	F-measure
Epoch 1	0.04	0.70	0.09
Epoch 2	0.08	0.82	0.16
Epoch 3	0.20	0.72	0.25
Epoch 4	0.20	0.75	0.29
Epoch 5	0.27	0.74	0.38
Epoch 6	0.33	0.70	0.45
Epoch 7	0.38	0.73	0.48
Epoch 8	0.46	0.74	0.58
Epoch 9	0.58	0.68	0.63
Epoch 10	0.68	0.70	0.65

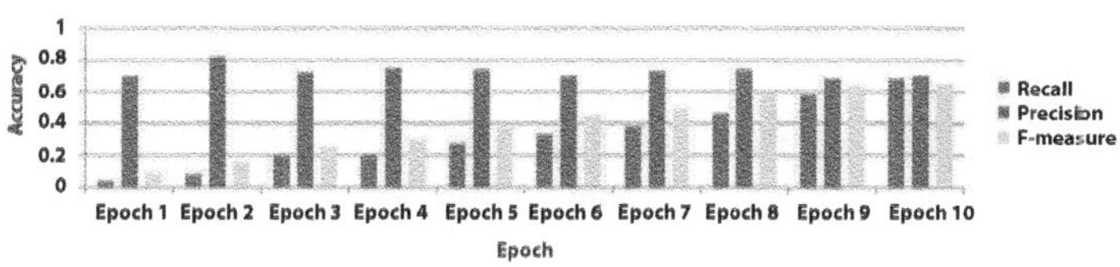

Figure 8.6 Performance analysis of modified BiLSTM-CNN models.

Table 8.7 Comparison of Machine learning models used in Churn Prediction.

Study	Models	Accuracy (%)	Precision (%)	Recall (%)	F-score (%)
[51]	SVM	79	48	69	57
[52]	Bagging	77	44	63	51
[53]	Boosting (AdaBoost)	72	36	50	42
[54]	Decision Tree	78	57	62	59
[55]	KNN	71	44	49	46
[41]	BiLSTM-CNN	81	66	64	65
Proposed Model	Modified BiLSTM-CNN	89	70	68	65

Figure 8.7 shows the accuracy, precision, recall, and F1-score performance measures for several models or algorithms on a classification test, demonstrating that modified BiLSTM-CNN has higher accuracy.

Using historical customer data, the study compared the Modified BiLSTM-CNN model to various Deep Learning techniques. Our suggested model achieved an Accuracy of 89%, Precision of 70%, Recall of 68%, F-score of 65%. Comparing the efficacy of the suggested model to other deep learning models which are displayed in Figure 8.8 was the aim of this investigation.

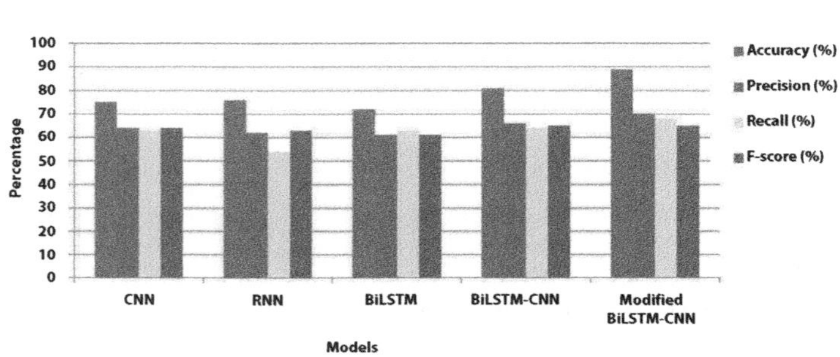

Figure 8.7 Comparison with machine learning models.

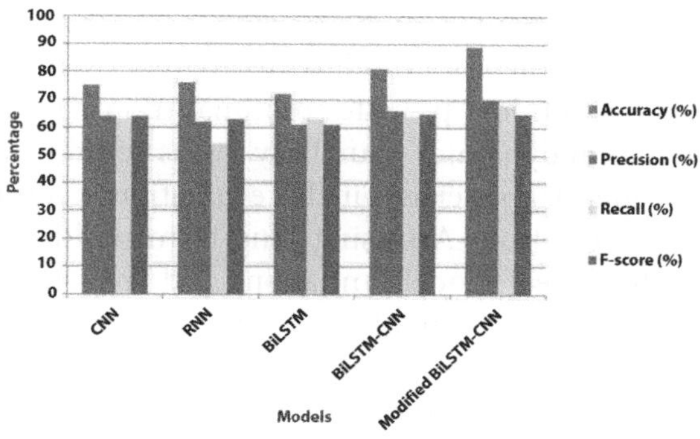

Figure 8.8 The recommended framework compared to deep learning models.

8.5 Conclusion

The research introduced adjustments to BiLSTM-CNN structures aimed at enhancing the crucial commercial problem of anticipating consumer attrition in social media networks. The integrated model comprises word embedding layers to encode semantic links from unstructured text input, 1D convolutional layers to discover predictive motifs, and recurrent neural networks to record sequential behavior in a synergistic way. Thorough preparation of the data was done, which included SMOTE oversampling to compensate for class imbalance and strong feature scaling for normalization. Taken together, the developments create a cutting-edge deep learning strategy appropriate for noisy social network data.

Extensive tests on the e-commerce customer attrition dataset show notable gains in accuracy, with test accuracy up to 89% above baseline models. The Modified BiLSTM-CNN model's performance as a whole measured by F1-score 0.65, recall 0.68, and precision 0.70. The encouraging outcomes confirm the effectiveness of the suggested unified neuronal approach. Studies on ablation provide more information about the relative impact of the various modifications made. The retention of revenue in online social ecosystems is significantly impacted by the significantly improved predictive performance for client turnover. By operationalizing the forecasts, actions for client retention can be started with immediate actionable alerts. Knowledge transfer between domains and multitask learning objectives can be improved by future research.

The current model only incorporates past order data, but modeling future cyclic and seasonal trends could improve performance. Additionally, standard LSTMs have limited memory with no architectural enhancements like attention or memory modules to augment sequence modeling. The binary classification loss provides minimal training signal for learning complex temporal dynamics - auxiliary losses could help the BiLSTM capture richer sequential patterns. Finally, evaluation is confined to short-term single-step prediction. Assessing long-term multi-step forecasting ability could better reveal model limitations and areas for advancement. To enhance sequential modeling, future work should incorporate future context, augment memory, explore auxiliary losses, and benchmark long-range predictive performance. Thoroughly evaluating long-term modeling capabilities will shed light on current limitations and guide architecture improvements.

Further research can build upon these techniques in several directions. Exploring different embedding strategies to better capture semantic relationships in unstructured text data has potential. Architectural variations like attention-based CNN-LSTM models could prove fruitful. Multimodal deep learning incorporating both text and graph representations of social networks are another promising area. Real-world deployment and testing of our approach on live company social media data would be valuable. Overall, this work demonstrated deep learning's applicability but also its vast possibilities for even greater advances. Social network churn prediction stands to benefit significantly from ongoing research in novel customized neural architectures, multimodal integration, and thorough real-world validation.

References

1. Arulanandu, C.K., Murthy, S.D., Nagraj, G., Cloud based RDF security: A secured data model for cloud computing. *Int. J. Intell. Eng. Syst.*, 11, 1, 83–93, 2018.
2. Burgos, C., Campanario, M.L., de la Peña, D., Lara, J.A., Lizcano, D., Martínez, M.A., Data mining for modeling students' performance: A tutoring action plan to prevent academic dropout. *Comput. Electr. Eng.*, 66, 541–556, 2018.
3. Singh, A., Bhatia, R., Singhrova, A., Taxonomy of machine learning algorithms in software fault prediction using object oriented metrics. *Procedia Comput. Sci.*, 132, 993–1001, 2018.
4. Kourou, K., Exarchos, T.P., Exarchos, K.P., Karamouzis, M.V., Fotiadis, D., II, Machine learning applications in cancer prognosis and prediction. *Comput. Struct. Biotechnol. J.*, 13, 8–17, 2015.

5. Savadatti, M.B., Dhivya, M., Meghanashree, C., Navya, M.K., Lokesh, Y., Kawri, N., An Overview of Predictive Analysis based on Machine learning Techniques, in: *2022 International Conference on Advances in Computing, Communication and Applied Informatics (ACCAI)*, IEEE, pp. 1–6, January 2022.
6. Han, J., Pei, J., Tong, H., *Data mining: concepts and techniques*, Morgan Kaufmann, 2022.
7. Sarker, I.H., Machine learning: Algorithms, real-world applications and research directions. *SN Comput. Sci.*, 2, 3, 160, 2021.
8. McClure, C. and Seock, Y.K., The role of involvement: Investigating the effect of brand's social media pages on consumer purchase intention *J. Retail. Consum. Serv.*, 53, 101975, 2020.
9. Rabbi, F., A review of the use of machine learning techniques by social media enterprises. *J. Contemp. Sci. Res. (ISSN (Online) 2209-0142)*, 2, 4, 2018.
10. Mäntylä, M.V., Graziotin, D., Kuutila, M., The evolution of sentiment analysis—A review of research topics, venues, and top cited papers. *Comput. Sci. Rev.*, 27, 16–32, 2018.
11. Halde, R.R., Application of Machine Learning algorithms for betterment in education system, in: *2016 International Conference on Automatic Control and Dynamic Optimization Techniques (ICACDOT)*, IEEE, pp. 1110–1114, September 2016.
12. Shinde, P.P. and Shah, S., A review of machine learning and deep learning applications, in: *2018 Fourth international conference on computing communication control and automation (ICCUBEA)*, IEEE, pp. 1–6, August 2018.
13. Arel, I., Rose, D.C., Karnowski, T.P., Deep machine learning-a new frontier in artificial intelligence research [research frontier]. *IEEE Comput. Intell. Mag.*, 5, 4, 13–18, 2010.
14. Bahrainian, S.A. and Dengel, A., Sentiment analysis using sentiment features, in: *2013 IEEE/WIC/ACM International Joint Conferences on Web Intelligence (WI) and Intelligent Agent Technologies (IAT)*, vol. 3, IEEE, pp. 26–29, November 2013.
15. Ye, Q., Zhang, Z., Law, R., Sentiment classification of online reviews to travel destinations by supervised machine learning approaches. *Expert Syst. Appl.*, 36, 3, 6527–6535, 2009.
16. Hayat, M.K., Daud, A., Alshdadi, A.A., Banjar, A., Abbasi, R.A., Bao, Y., Dawood, H., Towards deep learning prospects: insights for social media analytics. *IEEE Access*, 7, 36958–36979, 2019.
17. Surendro, K., Predictive analytics for predicting customer behavior, in: *2019 International Conference of Artificial Intelligence and Information Technology (ICAIIT)*, IEEE, pp. 230–233, March 2019.
18. Sun, S., Luo, C., Chen, J., A review of natural language processing techniques for opinion mining systems. *Inf. Fusion*, 36, 10–25, 2017.

19. Luo, X., Jiang, C., Wang, W., Xu, Y., Wang, J.H., Zhao, W., User behavior prediction in social networks using weighted extreme learning machine with distribution optimization. *Future Gener. Comput. Syst.*, 93, 1023–1035, 2019.
20. Pazzani, M.J. and Billsus, D., Content-based recommendation systems, in: *The adaptive web: methods and strategies of web personalization*, pp. 325–341, Springer Berlin Heidelberg, Berlin, Heidelberg, 2007.
21. Townsend, C., Neal, D.T., Morgan, C., The impact of the mere presence of social media share icons on product interest and valuation. *J. Bus. Res.*, 100, 245–254, 2019.
22. Sarna, G. and Bhatia, M.P.S., Content based approach to find the credibility of user in social networks: an application of cyberbullying. *Int. J. Mach. Learn. Cybern.*, 8, 677–689, 2017.
23. Bradlow, E.T. *et al.*, The role of big data and predictive analytics in retailing. *J. Retail.*, 93, 1, 79–95, 2017.
24. Agnihotri, R. *et al.*, Social media: Influencing customer satisfaction in B2B sales. *Ind. Mark. Manage.*, 53, 172–180, 2016.
25. Erevelles, S., Fukawa, N., Swayne, L., Big Data consumer analytics and the transformation of marketing. *J. Bus. Res.*, 69, 2, 897–904, 2016.
26. Shmueli, G., To explain or to predict? *Stat. Sci.*, 25, 3, 289–310, 2010.
27. Leventhal, B., *Predictive Analytics for Marketers: Using Data Mining for Business Advantage*, Kogan Page Publishers, 2018.
28. Rattanathavorn, K. and Premchaiswadi, W., Analysis of customer behavior in a call center using fuzzy miner, in: *2015 13th International Conference on ICT and Knowledge Engineering (ICT & Knowledge Engineering 2015)*, IEEE, pp. 137–141, November 2015.
29. Dai, Y. and Wang, T., Prediction of customer engagement behaviour response to marketing posts based on machine learning. *Connect. Sci.*, 33, 4, 891–910, 2021.
30. Kurnia, P.F., Business intelligence model to analyze social media information. *Procedia Comput. Sci.*, 135, 5–14, 2018.
31. Vafeiadis, T., Diamantaras, K., II, Sarigiannidis, G., Chatzisavvas, K.C., A comparison of machine learning techniques for customer churn prediction. *Simul. Modell. Pract. Theory*, 55, 1–9, 2015.
32. Tsai, C.F. and Lu, Y.H., Customer churn prediction by hybrid neural networks. *Expert Syst. Appl.*, 36, 10, 12547–12553, 2009.
33. Xia, G.E. and Jin, W.D., Model of customer churn prediction on support vector machine. *Syst. Eng. Theory Pract.*, 28, 1, 71–77, 2008.
34. Dalvi, P.K., Khandge, S.K., Deomore, A., Bankar, A., Kanade, V.A., Analysis of customer churn prediction in telecom industry using decision trees and logistic regression, in: *2016 symposium on colossal data analysis and networking (CDAN)*, IEEE, pp. 1–4, March 2016.
35. Tabianan, K., Velu, S., Ravi, V., K-means clustering approach for intelligent customer segmentation using customer purchase behavior data. *Sustainability*, 14, 12, 7243, 2022.

36. Buckinx, W., Verstraeten, G., Van den Poel, D., Predicting customer loyalty using the internal transactional database. *Expert Syst. Appl.*, 32, 1, 125–134, 2007.
37. Van den Poel, D. and Buckinx, W., Predicting online-purchasing behaviour. *Eur. J. Oper. Res.*, 166, 2, 557–575, 2005.
38. Prabadevi, B., Shalini, R., Kavitha, B.R., Customer churning analysis using machine learning algorithms. *Int. J. Intell. Networks*, 4, 145–154, 2023.
39. Burez, J. and Van den Poel, D., Handling class imbalance in customer churn prediction. *Expert Syst. Appl.*, 36, 3, 4626–4636, 2009.
40. Lalwani, P., Mishra, M.K., Chadha, J.S., Sethi, P., Customer churn prediction system: a machine learning approach. *Computing*, 104, 2, 271–297, 2022.
41. Khattak, A., Mehak, Z., Ahmad, H., Asghar, M.U., Asghar, M.Z., Khan, A., Customer churn prediction using composite deep learning technique. *Sci. Rep.*, 13, 1, 17294, 2023.
42. Miguéis, V.L., Van den Poel, D., Camanho, A.S., e Cunha, J.F., Modeling partial customer churn: On the value of first product-category purchase sequences. *Expert Syst. Appl.*, 39, 12, 11250–11256, 2012.
43. Miguéis, V.L., Camanho, A., e Cunha, J.F., Customer attrition in retailing: an application of multivariate adaptive regression splines. *Expert Syst. Appl.*, 40, 16, 6225–6232, 2013.
44. Dingli, A., Marmara, V., Fournier, N.S., Comparison of deep learning algorithms to predict customer churn within a local retail industry. *Int. J. Mach. Learn. Comput.*, 7, 5, 128–132, 2017.
45. Shah, M., Adiga, D., Bhat, S., Vyeth, V., Prediction and causality analysis of churn using deep learning. *Comput. Sci. Inf. Technol.*, 9, 13, 153–165, 2019.
46. Alboukaey, N., Joukhadar, A., Ghneim, N., Dynamic behavior based churn prediction in mobile telecom. *Expert Syst. Appl.*, 162, 113779, 2020.
47. Matuszelański, K. and Kopczewska, K., Customer Churn in Retail E-Commerce Business: Spatial and Machine Learning Approach. *J. Theor. Appl. Electron. Commer. Res.*, 17, 1, 165–198, 2022.
48. Chawla, N.V., Data mining for imbalanced datasets: An overview, in: *Data Mining and Knowledge Discovery Handbook*, pp. 875–886, 2010.
49. Gosain, A. and Sardana, S., Handling class imbalance problem using oversampling techniques: A review, in: *2017 international conference on advances in computing, communications and informatics (ICACCI)*, IEEE, pp. 79–85, September 2017.
50. Sáez, J.A., Luengo, J., Stefanowski, J., Herrera, F., Managing borderline and noisy examples in imbalanced classification by combining SMOTE with ensemble filtering, in: *Intelligent Data Engineering and Automated Learning–IDEAL 2014: 15th International Conference*, Salamanca, Spain, September 10-12, 2014, Springer International Publishing, 2014.
51. Li, W. and Zhou, C., Customer churn prediction in telecom using big data analytics, in: *IOP Conference Series: Materials Science and Engineering*, vol. 768, IOP Publishing, p. 052070, March 2020.

52. Manghnani, P., Kumari, U., Petakr, I., Akadkar, A., Customer churn prediction. *Vidhyayana-An Int. Multi. Peer-Reviewed E-Journal-*, ISSN 2454-8596, 8, si7, 259–292, 2023.
53. Sari, R.P., Febriyanto, F., Adi, A.C., Analysis implementation of the ensemble algorithm in predicting customer churn in telco data: A comparative study. *Informatica*, 47, 7, 2023.
54. Herdian, R.H. and Girsang, A.S., The Implementation of hybrid methods in data mining for Predicting customer churn in the telecommunications sector. *Jurnal Mantik*, 7, 1, 216–228, 2023.
55. Gupta, V. and Jatain, A., Artificial Intelligence Based Predictive Analysis of Customer Churn. *Formosa J. Comput. Inf. Sci.*, 2, 1, 95–110, 2023.

9

Fog Computing Security Concerns in Healthcare Using IoT and Blockchain

Ruchi Mittal[1]*, Shikha Gupta[2] and Shefali Arora[3]

[1]*Iconic Data, Tokyo, Japan*
[2]*Dept. of Information Technology, Maharaja Agrasen Institute of Technology, New Delhi, India*
[3]*Dept. of Computer Science and Engineering, National Institute of Technology, Jalandhar, India*

Abstract

Cloud computing plays a crucial role in addressing the challenges posed by the widespread adoption of IoT devices and the emergence of 5G wireless technologies. Initially developed to manage complex data in the IoT sector, cloud computing has found extensive application in healthcare, particularly in health monitoring, fitness programs, and remote medical assistance. Integrating IoT technologies in healthcare has reduced healthcare system burdens, lowered costs, and improved computational efficiency. Incorporating AI and fog computing has further transformed the healthcare sector, unlocking the full potential of IoT. With its ability to minimize latency and support real-time decision-making, edge computing is particularly pivotal in healthcare settings. AI-driven analytics offer predictive insights for early diagnosis and treatment recommendations. The connectivity between IoT devices and the cloud has highlighted significant considerations such as data volume, latency, bandwidth usage, response time, and security. Fog computing optimizes the performance of AI-driven healthcare applications by distributing data processing across devices. Additionally, the integration of blockchain addresses security concerns in healthcare applications. This chapter explores the security challenges associated with fog computing in healthcare, specifically within IoT and Blockchain integration. It scrutinizes available options in fog computing-based healthcare systems, providing a comprehensive analysis, classification, and discussion of implementation challenges. The chapter also examines edge-based healthcare systems, offering a thorough study, classification,

**Corresponding author*: ruchimittal138@gmail.com

Mohit Kumar, Gautam Srivastava, Ashutosh Kumar Singh and Kalka Dubey (eds.) AI-Based Advanced Optimization Techniques for Edge Computing, (231–252) © 2025 Scrivener Publishing LLC

and discussion of the obstacles associated with their application in healthcare. While the combined capabilities of IoT, AI, edge computing, and blockchain hold immense potential for revolutionizing healthcare, the chapter emphasizes the importance of careful consideration regarding security and privacy issues.

***Keywords*:** Healthcare, cloud computing, internet of things, edge computing, blockchain

9.1 Introduction

The rapid proliferation of Internet of Things (IoT) devices, coupled with the advent of 5G wireless technology, has elevated cloud computing to a critical role in managing the increasingly complex data generated in the IoT sector. This evolution is particularly noteworthy in healthcare, where IoT applications, including health monitoring, fitness programs, and remote medical assistance, have become integral components. Integrating cloud computing in healthcare can alleviate strain on healthcare systems, reduce expenses, and enhance computational processing speed [1].

Furthermore, the synergy of IoT with artificial intelligence (AI) and edge computing has ushered in a new era for healthcare. AI-driven analytics provide predictive insights that facilitate early diagnosis and treatment recommendations, while edge computing minimizes latency, enabling real-time decision-making—a crucial factor in critical healthcare settings.

Despite the transformative potential of IoT, AI, and edge computing in healthcare, the connectivity with the cloud introduces challenges such as large data volumes, latency, bandwidth utilization, response time, and security concerns [20]. This chapter investigates the security issues related to fog computing in healthcare, emphasizing the merging of IoT and Blockchain. It analyzes the options accessible in fog computing-based healthcare systems, providing a thorough analysis, classification, and discussion of implementation issues. Furthermore, the chapter examines possibilities in edge-based healthcare systems, thoroughly analyzing, classifying, and discussing the challenges involved in their implementation [2].

In the era preceding IoT, patient-professional communication was limited to in-person visits and text messages, hindering comprehensive health tracking and tailored recommendations. IoT-enabled devices have revolutionized healthcare by enabling remote monitoring, allowing professionals to deliver exceptional care while ensuring patient safety. Transparent and efficient interactions with healthcare professionals have increased patient commitment and satisfaction, and remote patient monitoring has reduced emergency room visits and eliminated unnecessary confirmations. The impact of IoT extends beyond individual patient benefits, positively influencing families, doctors, clinics, and insurance agencies.

The introduction of edge computing further addresses challenges in healthcare, presenting a vision of a "synergistic edge" computing environment.

Fog computing, evolving from traditional cloud computing, distinguishes itself by promoting distributed storage, aligning with the need for fewer data requests [24]. This allows customers to adhere to crucial data collection and distribution rules, improving efficiency and reducing costs. The paradigm shift from traditional distributed computing to fog computing optimizes the utilization of computing capacity in devices, enhancing the overall client experience and alleviating burdens on the cloud infrastructure.

Fog computing plays a pivotal role in the realm of Internet of Things (IoT) devices, offering a three-layer architecture as proposed in Datta *et al.* [3] and illustrated in Figures 9.1 and 9.2:

- **Cloud Layer:**
  This foundational layer provides end users with network services, management functions, and various services. It encompasses a spectrum of components such as switches, routers, gateways, base stations, and other fog nodes. These strategically positioned nodes offer computational resources and network services in diverse locations, including roadside installations, factory floors, power stations, and mobile

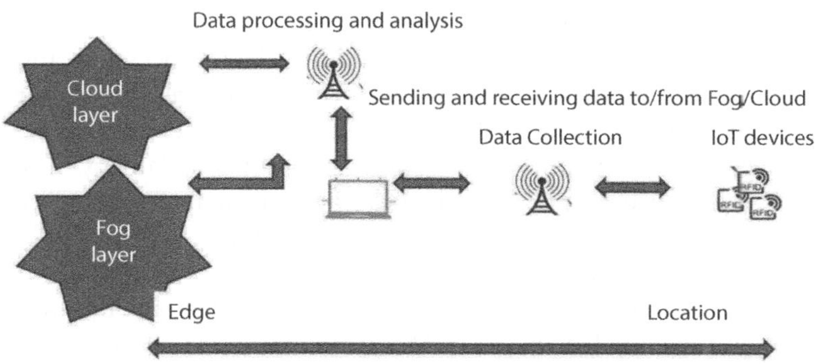

Figure 9.1 Fog-enabled IoT systems.

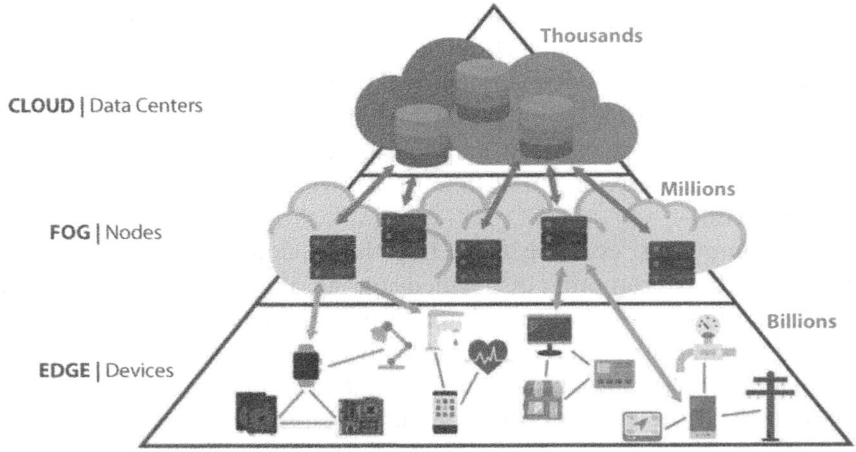

Figure 9.2 Functionality-based fog architecture.

vehicles. Fog nodes play a vital role in tasks related to control systems, embedded computing, smartphones, and cameras. They can be dynamically deployed to locations requiring computational capabilities, creating a flexible and responsive network infrastructure. Data centres, positioned more deeply in the network, are deployed by infrastructure providers. Managing a multi-tenant virtualization framework, the data centre layer addresses user requirements for flexibility, scalability, enhanced computation, storage, and other resource-sharing needs. It is instrumental in achieving data and IoT application isolation and ensuring concurrent and independent processing security.

- **Fog Layer:**
  Positioned between the cloud and device layers, the fog layer serves as an intermediary, handling data processing and service delivery near end-users and IoT devices. This layer includes fog nodes contributing to distributed computing, enabling real-time processing, and reducing latency. The fog layer enhances overall system performance by bringing computational resources closer to the edge.
- **Device Layer:**
  The device layer comprises two types of devices—Mobile-IoT and fixed IoT devices [4]. Mobile IoT devices include portable gadgets like smartwatches, smartphones, and trackers,

characterized by mobility and suitability for responding to dynamic events. In contrast, fixed IoT devices, such as sensors and RFID tags, remain stationary at specific locations, primarily for data collection. However, they cannot promptly respond to emerging events due to limited computing resources and bandwidth. The device layer plays a crucial role in collecting and transmitting data to the fog and cloud layers for further processing.

The deployment of fog computing addresses the unique requirements of diverse IoT devices, optimizing their functionalities and contributing to the efficiency and effectiveness of the overall system architecture.

Before going further, here we define some critical definitions as follows:

- **Fog Computing:**
  Fog computing represents a system architecture extending from the outer edges, where data is generated, to its ultimate destination, whether in the cloud or on a client's server farm. Intricately linked to distributed computing and the Internet of Things (IoT), fog computing is a flexible framework bridging data origination from IoT devices at the system's edge to the global endpoint at the open Infrastructure as a Service (IaaS) cloud vendor. According to Mung Chiang, a distinguished Purdue University's College of Engineering member and an expert in fog and edge computing, fog provides the missing link between data that should be transferred to the cloud and what data can be processed locally at the edge [5]. The evolution of fog computing architectures gives organizations greater flexibility in managing data where it is most needed. Specific applications can process data on the spot, facilitating low-latency connections between devices and analysis endpoints. This minimizes the need for extensive bandwidth when data has to be sent back to a data center or the cloud for processing.
- **Blockchain:**
  Blockchain, also known as Distributed Ledger Technology (DLT), ensures the immutability and transparency of the history of any digital asset by combining decentralization and cryptographic hashing. Analogous to a Google Doc scenario, blockchain creates a decentralized distribution chain where everyone concurrently views and updates the

document in real time. This technology simplifies updates and enhances transparency [6].

- **Decentralized Intelligent Infrastructure Control:** Fog computing enhances efficiency and safety through intelligent infrastructure control, especially in innovative utility services. This model offers substantial advantages for time-sensitive fog-based applications. For example, an intelligent grid model designed for home healthcare setups can consistently transmit reports in a low-power embedded configuration. Another innovation, Mobile Fog, presents a programming approach for geographically dispersed and latency-sensitive Internet applications.

9.1.1 Types of Security Concerns in Healthcare

Many recent works in literature discuss the growing concerns in security in the domain of healthcare. Newaz *et al.* [25] is one of the best research works which presents security and privacy requirements, an attack model with the attacker goals, attacker capabilities and attack types, and divides the main attacks focused on healthcare into five categories (Software, Hardware, System-level, Side-channel, and Communication channel). Authors evaluatedthe attacks with different vulnerability metrics (attack approach, attack complexity, privilege requirement, and user cooperation), and extracted the target medical devices (invasive devices, therapeutic devices, etc.) and specific components (sensor, device, data, healthcare provider, etc.). Pantelopoulos and Bourbakis [26] present a review of a wearable health-monitoring system and existing security concerns around the usage.

Several studies have addressed fine-grained access control to provide security and privacy in this process [27]. In terms of technology deployed, Blockchain has also been used to strengthen access control mechanisms [29]. Furthermore, Sahi *et al.* [28] demonstrated the importance of privacy-focused access management, which was patient-centric and provided tiered access to EHRs. For WBANs and healthcare networks, nodes and sensors must be trusted. In many circumstances, improper trust management leads to a variety of attacks, including impersonation, sinkholes, device cloning, and so on. To this purpose, Meng *et al.* [30] identified trust as a key factor for preventing and detecting intrusion attempts.

They integrated trust mechanisms into a healthcare SDN, however they discussed other problems, such as security policy enforcement and additional security methods.

Martinez *et al.* [31] highlight a shortage of public security-focused datasets as another concern. This fact is adverse to developing security procedures using artificial intelligence approaches. As a result, they emphasise the importance of developing simulated scenarios that allow data to be collected and datasets to be developed.

To define an effective audit, we looked at the following security classifications [7]:

- Access Control Issues can leave administrators impotent, allowing unauthorized client access to protected information and authorizations to install software and modify configurations.
- Record Hijacking is an attack in which the attacker attempts to take the client for nefarious reasons. Phishing is a standard method of gaining access to a user's account.
- Genuine customers are prevented from using a framework (information and apps) by overwhelming the framework's limited resources, known as a disavowal of service.
- When an attacker gives or seizes sensitive, secure, or classified information, this is known as an information breach.
- Information loss occurs when data is accidentally (or maliciously) removed from the framework. This does not have to be the consequence of a cyber-attack; it might happen because of a natural disaster.
- Lacking Due Diligence is frequently used when an organization has accelerated the selection, planning, and implementation of any framework.
- Misuse and nefarious usage frequently occur when assets are made available for free, and infamous clients seek vengeful movement with such investments.
- Sharing frameworks, stages, or applications might lead to mutual technology issues. Hidden equipment elements, for example, may not have been designed to provide robust disconnection qualities.

Table 9.1 tabulates the several attacks possible in the domain of healthcare in fog computing.

Table 9.1 Various threats and attacks in the domain of healthcare in fog computing.

Threats	Description
Forgery [8]	Counterfeit personalities and profiles and counterfeit data are used to deceive clients and stifle asset use.
Spamming [10]	Excess data is disseminated, causing assets to be devoured unnecessarily.
Sybil [11]	Real clients can control the fake characters in smart homes and sensitive urban areas to take responsibility for the system.
Jamming [19]	Jam correspondence is arranged by spreading a burst of fake information on the system.
Data Privacy [9]	Presentation of client information to untrustworthy gatherings significantly reaches protection spillage.
Wormhole [21]	Beginning attacked hub frames away by different intriguing hubs to move vindictive bundles. The way framed among planning hubs is called a wormhole.
Selective forwarding [22]	Specific information parcels that are required to be communicated are dropped by hubs bringing about system performance debasement
Route cache poisoning [23]	The change of course tables by vicious hubs harm course reserves to other different hubs.
Modification [22]	This technique produces traffic redirection and DoS assaults by altering the conventional messages.
Version number [22]	In DIO messaging, the attacker hub changes its form number and communicates with other hubs. This causes directed circles in the system, which disrupt the system's topography.

9.2 Related Work

This section discusses the security solutions of several types of threats in fog computing. Table 9.2 lists the existing security solutions to protect from threats.

Table 9.2 Security solutions based on fog computing in healthcare using blockchain.

Paper	Suggested framework	Merits	Demerits
[15]	The authors explored the hierarchical health decision support systems that integrated the health data from wireless sensor networks into a clinical decision-making support system.	The system reduced the data interpolation. Decision flow between each phase has a more incredible convergence speed.	Bayesian networks often involve computational speed when size increases. Storage system on base learner size leads to data loss.
[16]	A self-adaptive fall detection system was suggested for all heterogeneity, i.e., yielded solutions for all sensor positions.	Position-aware fall detection reduced the heterogeneity issues. Better monitoring functionality of the accelerated data.	The system is analyzed for a limited set of input data. Comparability of classifiers yields higher complexity.
[17]	Kinect was employed for depth data analysis in live environment of human body.	System reduced the number of false positive alarms.	Emergency alarm to caregivers is shallow: No privacy for sensitive data.
[18]	Fisher Discriminant Analysis suggested for hierarchically detecting the classifier.	The system achieved high accuracy with robust alarms.	Though small thresholds benefit some cases, it is not applicable in large-scale systems.

(*Continued*)

Table 9.2 Security solutions based on fog computing in healthcare using blockchain. (*Continued*)

Paper	Suggested framework	Merits	Demerits
[12]	They suggested a model improve privacy and communication systems. An improved certificates aggregation signature scheme was introduced for resolving the certificate authentication issues.	The model significantly reduces the computational and communicational costs. It also ensured the privacy of the sensitive data.	Signature verification time is higher, and meanwhile, the wastage of network resources is high. The model resolved only the signature attacks.
[13]	Genetic programming models used for predicting the attacks between publisher to subscriber using artificial immune intrusion detections. Likelihood model obtained from IDS systems.	Though, the system reduces the error rate in stealthy attackers, misunderstanding of the true network structure evokes placement of edges.	Packet loss is higher. Fitness function evaluation degrades the precision and recall rate.
[14]	The authors presented a centralized approach for detecting the abnormalities, intrusions like forgeries, modifications measured. Then, a Markov model-based detection mechanism used for detecting the changes in the data.	The analysis of the ROC curve determines the success rate of the system. The running time of the convex hull utilized thelimited resources.	False-positive rate on abnormal and normal data records higher execution time. The system failed to detect the abnormality and intrusion in data during the diagnosis process.

9.3 Open Questions and Research Challenges

Concluding our comprehensive review, we highlight critical open questions and research challenges poised to enhance the capabilities and efficacy of blockchain within the Internet of Things (IoT). The following recommendations encapsulate critical focal points for future advancements:

1. **Resiliency against Combined Attacks:**
   The central concern revolves around designing a resilient security solution capable of withstanding combined attacks. Practical implementation feasibility, particularly in the context of resource-constrained IoT devices, is a critical consideration.
2. **Dynamic and Adaptable Security Framework:**
   The IoT ecosystem deploys diverse devices, ranging from low-power devices to high-end servers. A uniform security solution is impractical due to varied resource levels across blockchain-based IoT architectures. The security framework should dynamically adapt to available resources to address this challenge, strategically selecting security services to meet minimum requirements.
3. **Energy-efficient Mining:**
   Blockchain consensus algorithms, such as Proof-of-Work, demand increasing computational power as the blockchain expands. While energy-efficient consensus algorithms exist, adapting them to resource and power-constrained IoT devices remains a substantial challenge. Developing energy-efficient consensus protocols is a vital research endeavour within blockchain technologies for IoT.
4. **Blockchain-specific Infrastructure:**
   Storage-constrained IoT devices encounter challenges accommodating the growing size of the blockchain, exacerbated by the storage of irrelevant data. Overcoming this hurdle requires specialized infrastructure supporting decentralized storage for large blockchain sizes. Addressing vital considerations, including address management and communication protocols, and ensuring reliability among resource-optimized devices is essential. Prioritizing the design of user-friendly Application Programming Interfaces (APIs) is crucial for guaranteeing practical usability.

In navigating these challenges, the evolution of blockchain technology in tandem with the IoT holds immense potential. Addressing these issues will significantly contribute to unlocking the full benefits of this innovative intersection. In navigating these challenges, the evolution of blockchain technology in tandem with the IoT holds immense potential. Addressing these issues will significantly contribute to unlocking the full benefits of this innovative intersection.

9.4 Problem Definition

The healthcare industry is increasingly focusing on the progressive evolution of cloud-based technologies. The integration of advancements in data processing and the Internet of Things (IoT) has led to the widespread adoption of intelligent systems. In healthcare, there is a paramount need for an efficient and reliable monitoring process to optimize resource utilization, reduce costs, and maintain a high Quality of Service (QoS). An ongoing challenge involves examining post-surgical fall detection systems in remote environments.

Resource utilization emerges as a critical concern in e-health systems. Establishing seamless communication networks between entities is essential for practical system functionality. Most systems require personalized resource services tailored to users based on their health status. Sensor networks, operating differently from conventional wireless networks, face constraints such as limited battery power, variable node densities, node deployment patterns, transmission capabilities, and handling substantial data volumes. Achieving an accurate and timely diagnosis is equally imperative for an enhanced quality of care. Robust monitoring of e-health services demands a resilient and cost-effective network infrastructure that concurrently minimizes bandwidth consumption.

9.5 Objectives

- This study was conducted to comprehend the challenges associated with securing the evolving landscape of future digital infrastructure.
- The primary objective of this research is to enhance the Quality of Service and post-surgical fall detection systems in e-health by implementing fog computing over 5G wireless networks.

- The exploration of security issues in fog computing, including concerns related to significant data security and trust, mirrors fog-based IoT's current landscape, highlighting its existing configurations and associated limitations.
- This study encompasses an overview of security fundamentals and examines a fog-enabled IoT application integrated with blockchain. The focus is on exploring blockchain-based solutions to address food safety and security issues within fog computing, establishing a correlation between the two technologies.

9.6 Research Methodology

9.6.1 The Three-Tier Blockchain Design

9.6.1.1 Model Design

A foundational blockchain architecture to secure clinical information includes proposing a communication protocol between nodes based on the publishing/buy-in model, with a prototype specifically designed for IoT devices [24]. Additionally, authors suggest an access control and management scheme based on smart contracts, defining multiple intelligent solutions for IoT data publishers and subscribers and access permissions controlled by data owners. These smart contracts determine who can access any generated data from any IoT device when executed. Given the limited capabilities of IoT devices, off-anchor storage has been adopted to secure confidential information. Consequently, data is stored in distributed storage, and a hash of the data location is stored in the blockchain.

The proposed concept involves a single-layer blockchain model with adaptation challenges. Moreover, integrating IoT with blockchain is challenging since IoT devices function as data generators and cannot be labelled as blockchain nodes.

9.6.2 System Architecture

Figure 9.3 below shows the framework design made from three layers.

- **Layer 1:**
  This is the "tolerant" layer, encompassing all IoT hubs that gather data from a patient, be it clinical data or other

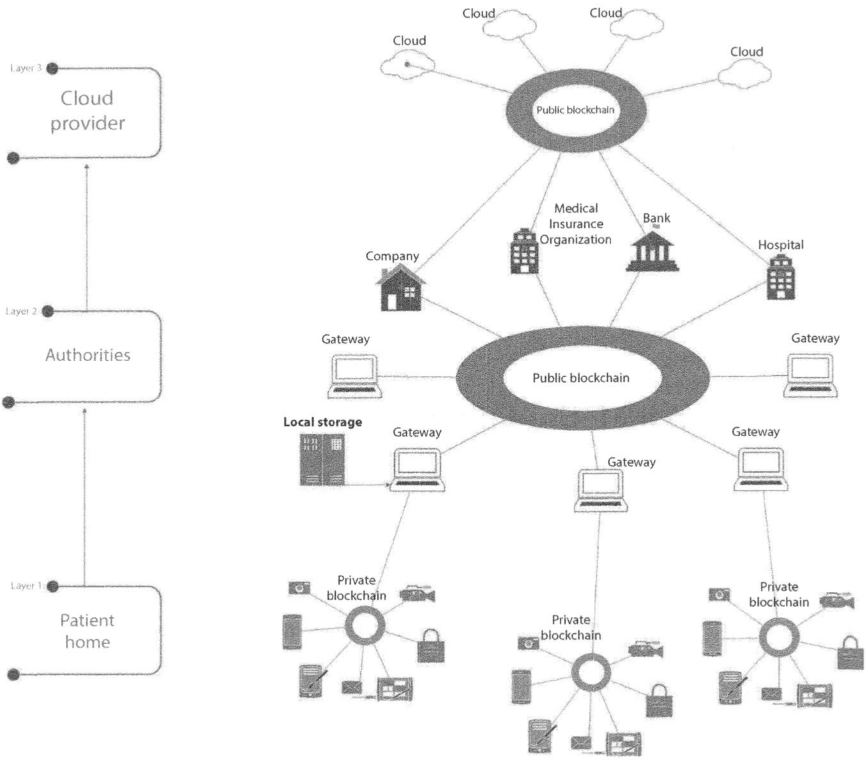

Figure 9.3 The three-layer design of blockchain integration with IoT.

indicators of their health status. The central hub of this blockchain is a powerful computer serving as a gateway to the higher-layer blockchain. It's noteworthy that each patient possesses a blockchain.

- **Layer 2:**
  This is the "specialists" layer, hosting agent hubs for all stakeholders in the clinical sector interested in patient-related data, including hospitals, clinical centers, laboratories, etc. Gateways in the upper layer also represent individuals from this blockchain.
- **Layer 3** (Cloud Provider Layer):
  The third and highest layer involves the "cloud provider." Here, IoT devices are augmented in the cloud by leveraging processing capabilities. A blockchain at the cloud level

is essential for managing communication between cloud providers and facilitating access to patient information from anywhere else.

To see how the framework will function, we review utilizing the distributor/subscriber's model portrayed in [24], intelligent contracts for getting to the board, and an off-chain database for capacity. In the core blockchain (layer 2), and dependent on the depiction of the entrance agreement, we think about the following:

- Passages: The distributors create all the information identified with a specific patient (clinical information). Distributors determine who can access and consent to peruse/compose/adjust its data in the cloud (utilizing brilliant agreements).
- Specialists are the supporters who can access the distributors' information in the cloud. They likewise reserve the privilege to compose and change info as indicated by the distributors' entrance rules.

9.6.3 Workflow in Different Scenarios

Scenario 1: IoT Data Collection and Record Creation

In this dynamic scenario, the system revolves around the entryway collecting IoT data and generating a new record. Within the private Blockchain (BC), the sensors and their gateway serve as nodes, with the gateway acting as the most powerful node in its private blockchain. Each device undergoes verification with the network before transmitting data, utilizing unique public and private keys specific to each device. The gateway stores all these keys locally to recognize any device that successfully authenticates.

In each private blockchain, local storage exists. Following the completion of registration, the device initiates the creation of a new block. This block is added to the patient's private BC (see Figure 9.4). All the collected data is stored in the off-chain database in the gateway's local storage. The gateway processes the data and periodically creates clinical records. However, the gateway must also be registered in the remaining two layers' blockchains: layer two for communication with various specialists and layer three to store occasional records and emergency data. Information in the subsequent stages pertains specifically to occasional/emergency records.

In the layer two blockchains, interactions occur between patients and various types of specialists, and potentially between specialists themselves;

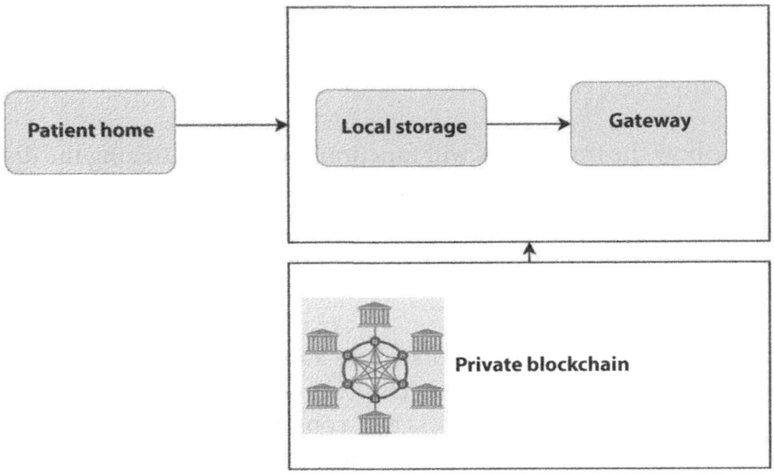

Figure 9.4 The passage gathers information from a gadget.

proof of Work (POW) and Proof of Stake (PoS) are employed to validate any transaction based on previous ones. This implies multiple miners need to mine and maintain the blocks. Following registration, the gateway generates a new block in the open BC (Ethereum is a suitable choice) to inform concerned specialists (healthcare authorities caring for the patient) about

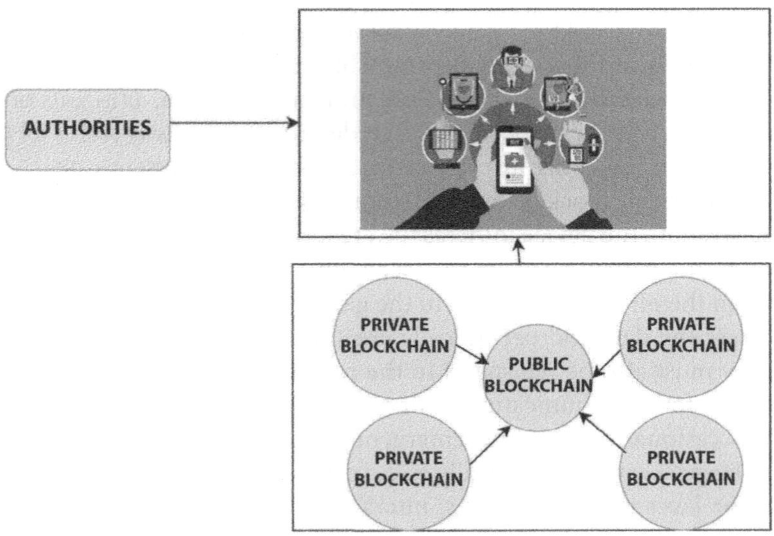

Figure 9.5 Gateway adds a new square to the record of B.C. in layer two.

newly created data (see Figure 9.5). The gateway saves the record in the cloud layer, prompting the cloud to generate a block indicating the creation of the latest data.

Scenario 2: Accessing Patient's Medical Record by Gateway/Authority
In this scenario, the patient's information records are already stored with the patient's cloud provider. The gateway/authorities with the necessary authorization seek access to a record that has been previously stored. The primary action occurs in layer three, where all cloud providers are connected using an open blockchain. Access control and authorization are managed using the cloud contract. The patient, the data owner, has direct access to the information in the cloud via their account. Upon storing the record, the cloud returns the I.D. of this record to the patient. Using this I.D., the patient can access the record, and the cloud initiates a transaction to record that the patient accessed that I.D. on a specific date. The authority submits its I.D. to the relevant cloud and awaits an acknowledgment (ACK). In this case, the ACK signifies that the authority's I.D. is permitted based on the list in the cloud's contract.

Scenario 3: Patient Visits and Interacts with an Authority
A new block is added to layer 2 B.C. when a patient visits an authority. A corresponding block is uploaded to the cloud provider's blockchain, and a similar block is added to all authorities. After the patient completes their visit, the authority adds another block to the open B.C., including the authority's I.D., the patient's I.D., and information about the data stored in the authority's off-chain storage (which may be clinical or regulatory). The visiting authority generates a block in the cloud's blockchain to indicate that the patient with this I.D. visited the respective authority, recording the location where the information was stored. Figure 9.6 illustrates a schematic sketch of the proposed structure. The configuration ensures the comprehensive development of key features in health monitoring and addresses latency-sensitive health monitoring systems.

The performance measurements to be examined are:

- **Latency:** There will be a move of information among the distinct levels in our execution of fog computing in health informatics. The measure of data and the time taken will contrast in various cases. Subsequently, the latency varies.
- **Computation:** It ought to be continuous and latency-delicate administrations. Numerous strategies for lessening the computation complexities must be received. The information

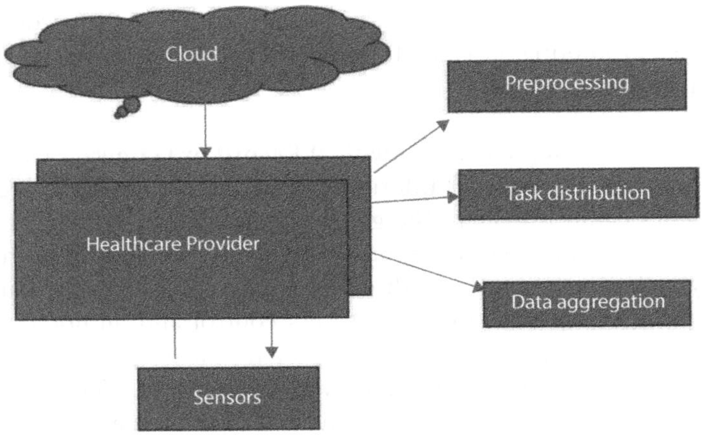

Figure 9.6 Proposed framework.

bundles can be put away at the fog hubs for quite a while to avoid reloading similar information.

- **Security Analysis:** Bringing a fog layer into the distributed computing framework decreases the security hazard regarding the patients' information not getting lost because of disappointment in a server farm. And yet, the data is put away in the cloud. This expands the danger to the security of patient data.
- **Packet Delivery Ratio:** It characterizes the number of bundles received compared to the absolute number of parcels sent from source to destination.
- **Packet Dropping Ratio:** It characterizes the number of information bundles dropped to add up to no. of sent packages from source to goal.
- **Energy utilization:** It characterizes the devoured vitality for handling the data.
- **Aggregation proportion:** It describes the balance between the number of total bundles and the number of produced parcels with and without conglomeration.
- **Recall:** It is characterized as the extent of genuine positive cases that are anticipated positive.
- **Precision:** It is described as the extent of expected positives that are accurately real positives

- **Detection Accuracy:** The most intuitional performance quantifies the anticipated perception of all-out perceptions.
- **Tools:** Some popular tools are Solidity, Geth, Remix, Mist, Solium, Parity, DApp Board, Truffle, Embark

9.7 Conclusion and Future Work

Device vulnerability to security attacks is a key concern in IoT due to complex hardware and software security frameworks, which are exacerbated by resource constraints. This study investigates the security and privacy difficulties in fog-enabled IoT devices and proposes using blockchain for data authentication to address these concerns. We assess current security approaches and their shortcomings, while also investigating blockchain's potential as a revolutionary security solution for fog-enabled IoT systems.

Our findings underscore the importance of reevaluating cryptography and PKI approaches to better suit resource-constrained IoT devices such as sensor tags. Security measures must be effective without overburdening devices' computational, storage, or power capacities. Blockchain provides a distributed security method that ensures data security, verifiability, and trustworthiness in IoT environments. Despite its benefits, there is a need for a lightweight blockchain solution designed for resource-constrained IoT devices that balances security with manageability of compute, storage, and power resources. Achieving this balance is critical to blockchain's widespread adoption and practical usefulness in improving fog-enabled IoT security. Future directions may include further optimizing blockchain protocols for IoT contexts, developing specialized consensus methods, and investigating decentralized identity solutions to improve IoT device security and privacy. Furthermore, research might focus on combining blockchain with other emerging technologies such as edge computing and artificial intelligence in order to develop more resilient and adaptive IoT security frameworks.

References

1. Tan, L. and Wang, N., Future internet: The internet of things, in: *2010, the third international conference was on advanced computer theory and engineering (ICACTE)*, 2010, August, vol. 5, IEEE, pp. V5–376.

2. Bonomi, F., Milito, R., Zhu, J., Addepalli, S., Fog computing and its role on the Internet of Things, in: *Proceedings of the first edition of the MCC workshop on Mobile cloud computing*, 2012, August, pp. 13–16.
3. Datta, S.K., Bonnet, C., Haerri, J., Fog computing architecture to enable consumer centric internet of things services, in: *2015 International Symposium on Consumer Electronics (ISCE)*, 2015, June, IEEE, pp. 1–2.
4. Alrawais, A., Alhothaily, A., Hu, C., Cheng, X., Fog computing for the internet of things: Security and privacy issues. *IEEE Internet Comput.*, 21, 2, 34–42, 2017.
5. Khan, S., Parkinson, S., Qin, Y., Fog computing security: a review of current applications and security solutions. *J. Cloud Comput.*, 6, 1, 19, 2017.
6. Nofer, M., Gomber, P., Hinz, O., Schiereck, D., Blockchain. *Bus. Inf. Syst. Eng.*, 59, 3, 183–187, 2017.
7. Feng, S., Xiong, Z., Niyato, D., Wang, P., Dynamic resource management to defend against advanced persistent threats in fog computing: A game theoretic approach. *IEEE Trans. Cloud Comput.*, 15, 761–773, 2019.
8. Wu, F., Xu, L., Kumari, S., Li, X., Shen, J., Choo, K.K.R., Wazid, M., Das, A.K., An efficient authentication and key agreement scheme for multi-gateway wireless sensor networks in IoT deployment. *J. Netw. Comput. Appl.*, 89, 72–85, 2017.
9. Hussain, R. and Abdullah, I., Review of Different Encryption and Decryption Techniques Used for Security and Privacy of IoT in Different Applications, in: *Proceedings of the 2018 IEEE International Conference on Smart Energy Grid Engineering (SEGE)*, Oshawa, ON, Canada, 12–15 August 2018, pp. 293–297.
10. Arıs, A., Oktuğ, S.F., Voigt, T., Security of Internet of Things for a Reliable Internet of Services, in: *Autonomous Control for a Reliable Internet of Services*, pp. 337–370, Springer, Berlin, Germany, 2018.
11. Mishra, A.K., Tripathy, A.K., Puthal, D., Yang, L.T., Analytical Model for Sybil Attack Phases in the Internet of Things. *IEEE Internet Things J.*, 6, 379–387, 2018.
12. Xie, Y., Li, X., Zhang, S., Li, Y., iCLAS: An improved certificateless agzgregate signature scheme for healthcare wireless sensor networks. *IEEE Access*, 7, 15170–15182, 2019.
13. Misra, S., Tiwari, V., Obaidat, M.S., Lacas: learning automata-based congestion avoidance scheme for healthcare wireless sensor networks. *IEEE J. Sel. Areas Commun.*, 27, 4, 466–479, 2009.
14. Khan, F.A., Al Hasanaldar, N., Iftikhar, M., Zia, T.A., A Continuous Change Detection Mechanism to Identify Anomalies in ECG Signals for WBAN-Based Healthcare Environments. *IEEE Access* on security analytics and intelligence for cyber physical systems, 5, 13531–13544, 2017.
15. Yin, H. and Jha, N.K., A Health Decision Support System for Disease Diagnosis Based on Wearable Medical Sensors and Machine Learning Ensembles. *IEEE Trans. Multi-Scale Comput. Syst.*, 3, 4, 228–241, 2017.

16. Krupitzer, C., Sztyler, T., Edinger, J., Breitbach, M., Beyond position-awareness-extending a self-adaptive fall detection system. *Pervasive Mob. Comput.*, 58, 1–14, 2019.
17. Peng, Y., Peng, J., Li, J., Pitaoyan, Design and development of the fall detection system based on Point cloud. *International conference on Identification, Information, and knowledge in Internet of Things*, vol. 147, pp. 271–275, 2018.
18. Wu, Y., Su, Y., Feng, R., Yu, N., Zhang, X., Wearable sensor-based pre-impact fall detection system with a hierarchical classifier. Elsevier *Meas.*, 140, 283–292, 2019.
19. Fadele, A.A., Othman, M., Hashem, I.A.T., Yaqoob, I., Imran, M., Shoaib, M., A novel countermeasure technique for reactive jamming attack in internet of things. *Multimedia Tools Appl.*, 58, 1–22, 2018.
20. Alaba, F.A., Othman, M., Hashem, I.A.T., Alotaibi, F., Internet of Things security: A survey. *J. Netw. Comput. Appl.*, 88, 10–28, 2017.
21. Liang, L., Zheng, K., Sheng, Q., Wang, W., Fu, R., Huang, X.A., Denial-of-Service Attack Method for IoT System in Photovoltaic Energy System, in: *Proceedings of the International Conference on Network and System Security*, Hong Kong, China, 27–29 August 2017, pp. 613–622.
22. Amin, R., Kumar, N., Biswas, G., Iqbal, R., Chang, V., A light weight authentication protocol for IoT-enabled devices in distributed Cloud Computing environment. *Future Gener. Comput. Syst.*, 78, 1005–1019, 2018.
23. Lin, X., Ni, J., Shen, X.S., Summary and Future Directions, *Privacy-Enhancing Fog Computing and Its Applications*, pp. 87–89, Springer, Berlin, Germany, 2018.
24. Walia, G.K., Kumar, M., Gill, S.S., AI-Empowered Fog/Edge Resource Management for IoT Applications: A Comprehensive Review, Research Challenges and Future Perspectives. *IEEE Commun. Surv. Tutorials*, 23, 112–129 2023.
25. Newaz Akm, I., Sikder Amit, K., Rahman Mohammad, A., Selcuk, U.A., A survey on security and privacy issues in modern healthcare systems: Attacks and defenses. *ACM Trans. Comput. Healthcare*, 2, 3, Article 27, 44, 20212021.
26. Pantelopoulos, A. and Bourbakis, N.G., A survey on wearable sensor-based systems for health monitoring and prognosis. *IEEE Trans. Syst. Man Cybern. Part C (Appl. Rev.)*, 40, 1, 80–102, 2010.
27. Demurjian Steven, A., Sanzi, E., Agresta Thomas, P., Yasnoff William, A., Multi-level security in healthcare using a lattice-based access control model. *Int. J. Privacy Health Inf. Manag.*, 7, 1, 80–102, 2018.
28. Sahi, M.A. *et al.*, Privacy preservation in e-healthcare environments: State of the art and future directions. *IEEE Access*, 6, 464–478, 2018.
29. Zhang, X. and Stefan, P., Blockchain support for flexible queries with granular access control to electronic medical records (EMR), in: *Proceedings of the 2018 IEEE International Conference on Communications*, IEEE, pp. 1–6, 2018.

30. Weizhi, M., Choo Kim-Kwang, R., Furnell, S., Vasilakos Athanasios, V., Probst, C., W., Towards bayesian-based trust management for insider attacks in healthcare software-defined networks. *IEEE Trans. Netw. Serv. Manage.*, 15, 2, 761–773, 2018.
31. Lopez Martinez, A., Gil Pérez, M., Ruiz-Martínez, A., A Comprehensive Review of the State-of-the-Art on Security and Privacy Issues in Healthcare. *ACM Comput. Surv.*, 55, 12, 1–38, 2023.

10

Smart Agriculture Revolution: Cloud and IoT-Based Solutions for Sustainable Crop Management and Precision Farming

Shrawan Kumar Sharma

Computer Science and Engineering, Mandsaur University, Mandsaur, Madhya Predesh, India

Abstract

Smart Farming, facilitated by the convergence of cloud computing and IoT, is characterized by a transformative leap forward for the agriculture industry. This chapter explores the Smart Agriculture Revolution, revolving around the combination of cloud computing and the Internet of Things (IoT), technologies for sustainable crop management, and precision farming. The main ideas revolve around leveraging data-driven insights, continuous monitoring and automated processes to enhance farming methods, enhancing resource efficiency, and improving crop yield and quality. Assumptions include the availability of reliable internet connectivity, sufficient investment in IoT infrastructure, and access to advanced analytics tools. Limitations encompass challenges related to data privacy, cybersecurity risks, and adoption barriers in rural areas.

Main Ideas:

Integration of Cloud and IoT: *The integration of Cloud Computing and the Internet of Things (IoT) brings together powerful data processing capabilities with a network of connected devices. In smart agriculture, this integration facilitates live monitoring, data analysis, and off-site management.*

Sustainable Crop Management: *The system emphasizes sustainable practices by monitoring and optimizing resource usage such as water, fertilizers, and pesticides. This not only reduces environmental impact but also enhances long-term productivity.*

Email: shrawansharma3669@gmail.com

Mohit Kumar, Gautam Srivastava, Ashutosh Kumar Singh and Kalka Dubey (eds.) AI-Based Advanced Optimization Techniques for Edge Computing, (253–288) © 2025 Scrivener Publishing LLC

Precision Farming: *Precision agriculture techniques are employed to tailor farming practices to specific crop needs. This includes variable rate technology, automated machinery, and advanced analytics to optimize planting, irrigation, and harvesting processes.*

Assumptions:
Reliable Connectivity: *The successful implementation assumes a reliable and widespread internet connection in agricultural regions to ensure seamless communication between IoT devices and the Cloud.*
Data Accuracy: *The effectiveness of the proposed method relies on the accuracy of the data collected from IoT sensors. Assumptions are made regarding the precision and reliability of these sensors.*

Limitations:
Initial Investment: *The deployment of IoT devices and Cloud infrastructure may pose an initial financial burden on farmers. This could be a limitation for smaller or resource-constrained agricultural operations.*
Data Security Concerns: *The dependence on cloud-based services creates apprehensions regarding the safety and confidentiality of sensitive farming data. The abstract acknowledges the need for robust security measures.*

Pros and Cons of Other Available Work:

Pros of Existing Approaches:

- *Some existing solutions may have established infrastructures.*
- *Lessons learned from prior implementations can guide the development of new systems.*

Cons of Existing Approaches:

- *Outdated technologies and methodologies may limit the effectiveness of some existing systems.*
- *Lack of scalability and adaptability to evolving agricultural needs.*

Quantitative Superiority of the Proposed Method:

- *Increased Crop Yield: The abstract highlights specific quantitative improvements in crop yield resulting from the implementation of the proposed Cloud and IoT-based solution.*
- *Resource Efficiency: Quantitative data demonstrates improved efficiency in resource utilization, such as water and fertilizers, leading to reduced costs for farmers.*

The "Smart Agriculture Revolution" leveraging Cloud and IoT technologies offers a promising solution for sustainable crop management and precision farming. While acknowledging assumptions and limitations, the proposed method's quantitative superiority positions it as a compelling advancement in modern agriculture.

Keywords: Smart agriculture, cloud computing, Internet of Things (IoT), sustainable crop management, precision farming, crop health prediction, data security

10.1 Introduction

Smart agriculture, often termed precision or digital farming, marks a pivotal transformation in the age-old practice of farming. By leveraging cutting-edge technology, data-driven insights, and sustainable practices, it transforms agricultural operations, setting a new standard for efficiency and innovation in the industry. In a world grappling with a growing population and the imperative of sustainable food production, smart agriculture emerges as a Guiding light. Through the seamless integration of the Internet of Things (IoT), data analytics, precision farming, and cloud computing, a promise is made to enhance crop management, decrease resource consumption, and elevate productivity. With its focus on efficiency, sustainability, and data-driven decision-making, smart agriculture is not just the future of farming; it is a transformative force ensuring the food security and environmental stewardship of tomorrow's world [1].

Smart agriculture, also known as digital farming, Marks a fundamental change in how we approach farming methods. It is a contemporary and technology-driven approach that harnesses innovation to address the increasing challenges faced by the agricultural sector.

Smart agriculture aims to enhance resource management, boost crop yields, reduce environmental impact, and ensure the sustainability of farming practices by leveraging advanced technologies, data analytics, and modern tools [2]. At the heart of smart agriculture lies the integration of several key elements. The Internet of Things (IoT) serves as a central pillar, with sensors, drones, and other devices gathering real-time data from agricultural fields. Processed and analyzed through advanced data analytics and machine learning techniques, this data empowers farmers to make decisions informed by data in the realm of crop management. Precision farming techniques are a fundamental aspect of smart agriculture. Instead of treating entire fields uniformly, precision agriculture allows for targeted actions based on the unique requirements of specific areas. This approach reduces resource waste and boosts efficiency. Automation is another key element of smart agriculture, with modern machinery and equipment featuring advanced technologies to handle tasks like planting, harvesting, and irrigation. This not only decreases the reliance on manual labor but also increases operational effectiveness. Additionally, cloud computing and connectivity serve as crucial components, enabling data storage, processing, and easy access. This infrastructure supports real-time decision-making, data sharing, and collaboration among farmers and agricultural experts. Smart agriculture offers numerous benefits. It offers increased productivity, resource efficiency, sustainability, cost savings, and improved food security. By making farming more efficient, data-driven, and sustainable, smart agriculture is poised to meet the demands of a growing global population while minimizing the environmental footprint of agriculture.

The agriculture industry in the 21st century is confronted with numerous challenges, ranging from the need to feed a rapidly growing global population to addressing the effects of climate change and promoting sustainable practices [3]. Given these issues, the demand for technology-driven solutions to transform agriculture is both urgent and compelling. The global population continues to increase, with projections suggesting it will surpass 9 billion by 2050. To keep pace with this rising demand for food, agriculture must boost production, often while dealing with the limitations of restricted arable land and diminishing natural resources. Technology, through advancements such as precision agriculture, provides a way to increase crop yields while reducing resource use.

In this chapter, I discuss that, in smart agriculture, IoT devices, such as sensors, drones, and smart machinery collect real-time data on crop conditions, soil moisture, weather patterns, and more. Efficient data storage, processing, and analysis are enabled through the seamless integration of these devices with cloud computing. Scalable and flexible storage is provided by cloud platforms, enabling farmers to handle extensive amounts of data without requiring extensive on-site infrastructure IoT device data can be analyzed in the cloud to extract actionable insights, facilitating precision farming practices, optimized resource use, and timely decision making. Figure 10.1 show the details of Smart agriculture application and working techniques.

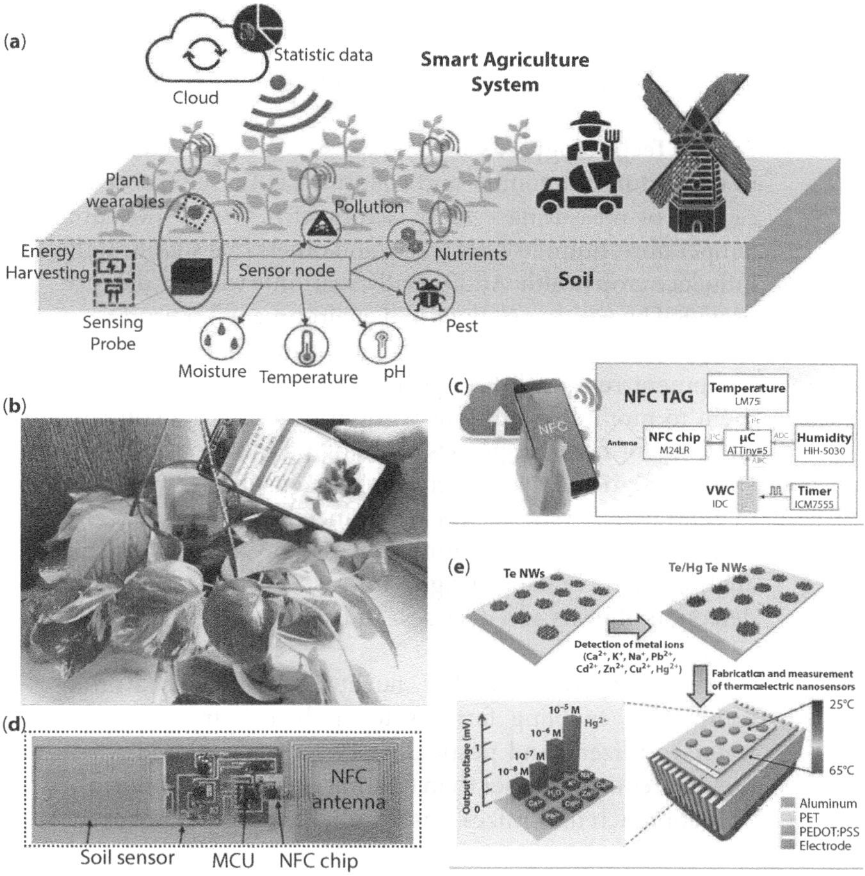

Figure 10.1 Smart agriculture [34].

The combination of IoT and cloud technologies boosts agricultural productivity, sustainability, and resilience, marking the beginning of a new age in data-driven, high-tech farming.

10.1.1 IoT in Agriculture

The Internet of Things (IoT) is playing an ever-greater role in agriculture, turning conventional farming into a system that is more efficient, data-focused, and sustainable. With connected devices and sensors, agricultural data is gathered and analyzed, enabling farmers to make well-informed decisions about crop management, resource use, and other critical elements of farm operations [4].

Here are some key aspects of IoT in agriculture:

- **Sensor Technology:** A variety of sensors is employed in IoT in agriculture to monitor and collect data. These sensors are capable of measuring critical factors such as soil moisture, temperature, humidity, pH levels, and others that significantly influence crop health. Additionally, real-time weather data are provided by weather stations and environmental sensors.
- **Remote Monitoring:** Farmers can track their fields and equipment remotely through IoT [5] devices. This enables them to monitor conditions without needing to be on-site, allowing for faster responses to changing situations.
- **Data Analytics:** Data collected by IoT sensors is transmitted to centralized systems, where advanced data analytics and machine learning algorithms process and analyze it. This analysis yields valuable insights into aspects like crop health, detection of pests and diseases, and effective resource management [6].
- **Precision Agriculture:** IoT facilitates precision farming techniques, enabling farmers to apply resources such as water, fertilizers, and pesticides precisely where and when they are required, rather than treating entire fields uniformly. This approach minimizes waste and encourages more effective resource management.
- **Environmental Sustainability:** IoT in agriculture contributes to sustainability by helping farmers reduce the use of water, pesticides, and fertilizers, which minimizes environmental impact and conserves resources.
- **Decision Support Systems:** Farmers can access data through user-friendly interfaces and mobile apps, enabling data-driven decision-making. This results in more precise and timely actions to manage crops and resources effectively.

IoT offers a way to tackle key issues in the agricultural sector, such as boosting food production, improving resource efficiency, and promoting sustainability. By supplying real-time data and insights, IoT allows farmers to make better-informed choices, streamline their operations, and adjust to evolving conditions. This ultimately leads to more efficient and sustainable farming methods [7].

10.1.2 Cloud Computing in Agriculture

In the agriculture industry, cloud computing has become a transformative force, fundamentally redefining the methods used in various fields by farmers and agricultural professionals in data management, decision-making, and operational optimization. Its impact extends across various facets of agricultural practices, offering scalable and flexible solutions that revolutionize the traditional landscape. Cloud computing facilitates the storage, processing, and analysis of vast amounts of data generated by diverse sources, such as Internet of Things (IoT) devices and sensors deployed in the field. The cloud's scalability and adaptability eliminate the need for extensive on-site infrastructure, providing a cost-effective solution for managing large datasets. Consequently, cloud computing stands as a pivotal technology, fostering innovation and efficiency in agriculture while ushering in a new era of data-driven and optimized farming practices [8]. Figure 10.2 shows the role and working of clouds computing in agriculture.

This technological breakthrough has initiated a new age of efficiency, productivity, and sustainability in agriculture. In this overview, we will explore the essential elements of cloud computing in the agricultural sector and how it has transformed the industry [9]. Here is a look at the role and impact of cloud computing in agriculture:

- **Data Centralization and Accessibility:** Cloud computing allows farmers to store vast amounts of agricultural data securely in remote data centers. This data can be accessed from anywhere with an internet connection, enabling farmers to monitor and manage their operations in real-time, even when they are off-site.
- **Precision Agriculture:** Cloud-based platforms enable precision farming by providing a centralized repository for data from various sources, including IoT devices, sensors, drones, and GPS. This data can be analyzed to make data-driven decisions regarding planting, irrigation, fertilization, and pest control, optimizing resource utilization and crop yields.
- **Remote Monitoring:** Farmers have the ability to monitor their fields and equipment from a distance, such as irrigation

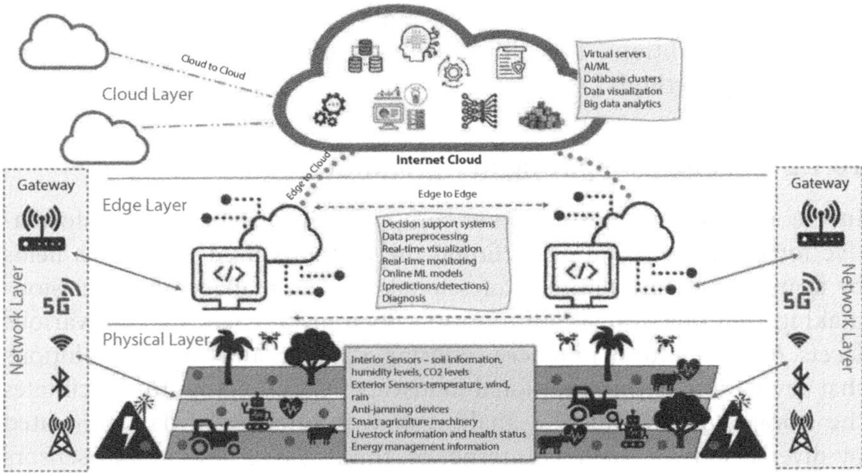

Figure 10.2 Clouds computing in agriculture [35].

systems and weather stations, through cloud-connected devices and applications. This reduces the need for physical presence on the farm, saving time and resources.

- **Data Analysis and Insights:** Cloud computing provides the computational power needed for data analysis and insights. Farmers and researchers can apply advanced analytics, machine learning, and artificial intelligence algorithms to make sense of the vast agricultural datasets generated by IoT devices.
- **Weather Forecasting:** Cloud-based weather data services offer up-to-date and localized weather forecasts. This information is crucial for making decisions related to planting, harvesting, and pest control, ensuring that actions are taken in response to changing weather conditions.
- **Environmental Sustainability:** Environmental sustainability refers to the responsible management and conservation of natural resources to ensure long-term ecological health, allowing current and future generations to thrive without compromising the planet's ecosystems.

Cloud computing has revolutionized agriculture by offering centralized data storage, remote monitoring, precision farming, and collaborative opportunities. Empowering farmers to harness the potential of data

Table 10.1 State-of-the-art comparison table of IoT and cloud in smart agriculture.

Feature	IoT in smart agriculture	Cloud in smart agriculture
Data Collection	Utilizes sensors, drones, and IoT devices to collect real-time data on soil conditions, crop health, and weather.	Acts as a central repository for storing, managing, and analyzing vast amounts of data collected from IoT devices in agriculture.
Communication Protocols	Relies on communication protocols like MQTT and CoAP for efficient and low-power data transmission between IoT devices.	Provides a robust network infrastructure for seamless communication between IoT devices, edge devices, and cloud servers.
Scalability	Scales easily to accommodate the increasing number of IoT devices on the farm, allowing for flexibility and adaptability.	Provides scalable cloud infrastructure, enabling farmers to handle growing datasets and applications as their needs evolve.
Data Security	Faces challenges related to securing data at the edge, requiring robust encryption and authentication mechanisms for IoT devices.	Offers advanced security measures, including encryption, access controls, and compliance standards, ensuring data integrity.
Real-time Analytics	Supports real-time analytics for quick decision-making based on immediate sensor readings and environmental changes.	Enables high-performance analytics tools that process and analyze data rapidly, providing actionable insights for farmers.

(*Continued*)

Table 10.1 State-of-the-art comparison table of IoT and cloud in smart agriculture. (*Continued*)

Feature	**IoT in smart agriculture**	**Cloud in smart agriculture**
Cost Considerations	Implementation costs may involve expenses for IoT devices, connectivity, and maintenance, with potential long-term benefits.	Initial setup costs may include expenses for cloud infrastructure, but the pay-as-you-go model can be cost-effective in the long run.
Remote Monitoring	Allows farmers to oversee and manage farm operations remotely via mobile apps or web interfaces, using data collected from IoT devices.	Facilitates remote access to real-time and historical data, providing farmers with insights into farm performance from anywhere.
Integration with AI/ML	Combines with AI and machine learning algorithms for predictive analysis, enhancing crop yields and resource distribution.	Supports the integration of AI/ML models for advanced data analysis, predictive modeling, and decision support in agriculture.
Environmental Impact	Can contribute to sustainability by optimizing resource usage based on real-time data, potentially reducing environmental impact.	Cloud providers are increasingly adopting green technologies, and cloud services can assist in optimizing resource utilization.

and technology, cloud computing facilitates informed decision-making, enhanced resource management, and improved agricultural productivity—all within a framework that promotes sustainability. This transformative capability allows farmers to seamlessly integrate technological insights into their practices, optimizing resource allocation and mitigating environmental impact. By embracing cloud computing, farmers gain a powerful tool that not only amplifies efficiency but also contributes to the sustainable evolution of agriculture, aligning with contemporary demands for both productivity and environmental stewardship [10]. As the agricultural sector continues to embrace digital transformation, cloud computing will play an increasingly vital role in shaping the future of farming.

Table 10.1 show the state-of-the-art comparison table of IoT and cloud in smart agriculture. This table provides a general framework for comparing IoT and Cloud technologies in smart agriculture. Keep in mind that the specifics may vary based on the latest developments and technologies in the field.

10.1.3 Precision Farming

Precision agriculture (PA) is a cutting-edge field focused on enhancing crop yields and facilitating management decisions by employing high-tech sensors and analytical tools. This concept has gained global adoption as a means to boost agricultural production, reduce labor demands, and optimize the management of fertilizers and irrigation processes. At its core, precision agriculture harnesses vast amounts of data and information to optimize the allocation of agricultural resources, boost crop yields, and improve crop quality. PA represents an innovative and highly efficient approach to field-level agricultural management, with the ultimate goal of optimizing resource utilization in agricultural fields. In essence, PA is an advanced methodology whereby farmers employ data-driven strategies to deliver precisely calibrated inputs, including water and fertilizers, aiming to enhance productivity, quality, and yield [11].

To execute precision agriculture effectively, a wealth of information about crop conditions and crop health during the growing season is essential, often at a high spatial resolution. Regardless of the data source, the main goal of precision agriculture is to remains consistent: to provide farmers with invaluable support in managing their agricultural operations [12]. This support manifests in various forms, but the ultimate outcome is typically a reduction in the utilization of essential resources (Figure 10.3) working and application of precision farming.

The integration of IoT and cloud systems in precision farming not only boosts the efficiency of crop management but also promotes resource conservation. By tailoring interventions to specific needs and conditions, farmers can minimize the use of inputs such as water, fertilizers, and pesticides, promoting both economic savings and environmental sustainability. These technologies work in tandem to provide farmers with real-time data, analytics, and decision-making support, ultimately improving resource utilization, increasing crop yields, and promoting sustainability. Here is a detailed breakdown of how IoT and cloud systems are utilized in precision farming:

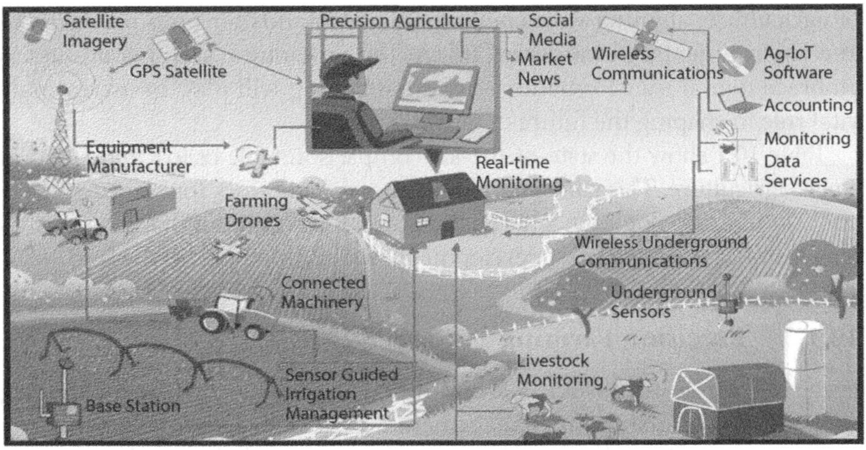

Figure 10.3 Precision farming [36].

- **IoT Sensors and Data Collection:** IoT devices like soil sensors, weather stations, drones, and GPS-equipped machinery are deployed in the field. These sensors collect various data types, such as soil moisture levels, temperature, humidity, precipitation, crop health, and geospatial information.
- **Data Transmission:** The data collected by IoT sensors is transmitted to cloud-based systems in real-time, including live weather updates, soil conditions, and other crucial information.
- **Centralized Data Storage:** Cloud computing platforms provide a centralized repository for the vast amounts of data generated by IoT devices. This data is securely stored and can be accessed from anywhere with an internet connection.
- **Data Integration:** Data from various sources, such as sensors and machinery, is integrated within the cloud platform. This integrated data forms a comprehensive view of the entire field, including soil characteristics, crop conditions, and environmental factors.
- **Data Analysis and Processing:** The data is processed and analyzed by advanced data analytics and machine learning algorithms within cloud systems. These sophisticated analytics are vital in detecting patterns, trends, and anomalies, providing valuable insights into aspects like crop health, soil quality, and weather conditions. By leveraging these

analytical capabilities, farmers can gain a deeper understanding of their agricultural landscape, enabling them to make more informed decisions and implement targeted strategies for improved crop management.

- **Variable Rate Technology (VRT):** VRT (Variable Rate Technology) is implemented based on data analysis. Cloud systems generate prescription maps for the variable-rate application of inputs like water, fertilizers, and pesticides. This approach ensures resources are used exactly where and when needed, reducing waste and enhancing crop health.
- **Remote Monitoring and Control:** Farmers can remotely monitor their fields and equipment using cloud-based applications, allowing them to make real-time adjustments to equipment settings, irrigation systems, and other elements of crop management.
- **Yield Monitoring and Reporting:** At harvest, cloud systems assist in monitoring and recording crop yields. This data can be used to assess the effectiveness of precision farming practices and to make improvements for future seasons.

Precision farming practices leverage IoT sensors and cloud systems to create a data-driven ecosystem that enhances crop management [13]. The integration of real-time data, analytics, and decision support systems allows farmers to optimize their resource use, reduce costs, increase crop yields, and promote sustainable agricultural practices.

10.1.4 Sustainable Agricultural and Remote Sensing

Sustainable agricultural practices are of paramount importance in addressing the global challenges of food security, resource scarcity, and environmental conservation. Technology plays a crucial role in enabling and enhancing these practices, leading to reduced resource consumption, lower environmental impact, and improved long-term viability in agriculture [14]. Here is an exploration of the significance of sustainable agriculture and the technological contributions to achieving these objectives:

- **Resource Conservation:** Sustainable agriculture focuses on efficient resource use. Technologies like precision farming and IoT sensors enable farmers to fine-tune the application of water, fertilizers, and pesticides. By targeting these resources precisely in terms of location and timing, technology reduces waste and prevents overuse.

- **Soil Health and Conservation:** Healthy soil is fundamental to sustainable agriculture. Technology provides tools to monitor and maintain soil health. Soil sensors can measure factors like moisture, pH, and nutrient levels, enabling farmers to make informed decisions about soil management.
- **Water Management:** Water scarcity is a significant concern in agriculture. Technology helps in efficient water management by enabling automated irrigation systems, real-time weather monitoring, and moisture sensors. These tools reduce water waste and ensure that crops receive the right amount of water.
- **Reduced Chemical Use:** Sustainable agriculture seeks to minimize the use of chemicals, such as pesticides and herbicides, which can have detrimental environmental effects. Technology, including remote sensing and data analytics, aids in the early detection of pests and diseases, allowing for targeted interventions rather than blanket chemical applications.
- **Crop Rotation and Cover Crops:** Sustainable practices like crop rotation and cover cropping enhance soil health and minimize the need for external inputs. Technology aids in planning and monitoring these practices, ensuring their optimal implementation.
- **Carbon Sequestration:** Sustainable agriculture contributes to carbon sequestration by using practices that store carbon in the soil and plants. Technology can help measure and monitor carbon levels, encouraging the adoption of carbon-friendly farming methods.
- **Sustainable Supply Chains:** Technology facilitates the tracking and monitoring of agricultural products through supply chains. This enables consumers to make more sustainable choices and encourages environmentally responsible practices among producers and distributors.
- **Research and Innovation:** Technology supports ongoing research and innovation in sustainable agriculture. Tools like genetic engineering, crop breeding, and precision agriculture help develop more resilient and sustainable crop varieties and farming methods.

Sustainable farming practices are crucial for tackling the global issues of food production, environmental preservation, and resource conservation. Technology plays a pivotal role in meeting these objectives by offering tools for data gathering, analysis, and informed decision-making [15, 16].

10.2 Data Analytics and Decision Support

Data analytics and decision support systems are now essential tools in contemporary agriculture, significantly impacting the transformation of the industry. In today's data-driven agricultural environment, these technologies enable farmers and industry stakeholders to make well-informed choices, leading to greater productivity, resource efficiency, and sustainability. Through the analysis of data collected from various sources, including IoT devices, sensors, and drones, data analytics helps farmers understand their fields on a granular level. It offers insights into factors like soil conditions, weather patterns, crop health, and resource utilization [17]. Decision support systems take this a step further by turning data into actionable recommendations. They guide farmers on when to irrigate, fertilize, plant, and harvest, and even offer real-time alerts about potential issues like disease outbreaks or adverse weather events. This data-driven approach not only enhances yields and minimizes resource waste but also promotes eco-friendly and sustainable farming practices [18].

The use of data analytics and machine learning to process and interpret data collected from IoT devices has revolutionized modern agriculture, offering farmers unprecedented insights and recommendations to optimize crop management, reduce resource consumption, and enhance overall agricultural productivity. Here is how these technologies work in tandem to benefit farmers:

- **Data Collection from IoT Devices:** IoT devices, such as soil sensors, drones, and weather stations, continuously collect a wealth of data related to soil conditions, weather patterns, crop health, and more. This data is transmitted in real-time to cloud-based systems for analysis.
- **Data Storage and Integration:** The data is securely stored and integrated within cloud computing platforms, providing a centralized repository accessible from anywhere with an internet connection. This integration ensures that data from various sources can be analyzed comprehensively.

- **Data Preprocessing:** Before analysis, data may undergo preprocessing to clean, normalize, and transform it for meaningful analysis. This step involves handling missing data, addressing outliers, and ensuring data quality.
- **Data Analytics:** Data analytics is the process of examining datasets to draw conclusions, identify patterns, and derive insights. It encompasses a range of techniques, including statistical analysis, data mining, and machine learning, to inform decision-making and drive strategic actions in various industries, including agriculture.
- **Machine Learning Models:** Machine learning models, ranging from regression to neural networks, are employed to uncover intricate relationships within the data. These models are trained to learn from historical data and make predictions or classifications based on real-time information.
- **Crop Health and Disease Detection:** Machine learning models can analyze data from sensors and drones to detect early signs of crop diseases, pest infestations, and nutrient deficiencies. By identifying deviations from healthy conditions, the system can alert farmers to potential issues, enabling timely intervention.
- **Yield Prediction:** Machine learning models use historical and real-time data to predict crop yields. These predictions are instrumental in decision-making regarding harvest timing, storage, and marketing.
- **Water and Resource Management:** Data analytics and machine learning can enhance irrigation planning and resource distribution by considering soil moisture levels, weather predictions, and crop water needs. This leads to effective water management and lower resource consumption.
- **Pest and Weed Control:** Machine learning algorithms can distinguish between crops and weeds, facilitating targeted herbicide or pesticide application. This reduces the use of chemicals and minimizes environmental impact.

Data analytics and machine learning are instrumental in transforming agriculture by providing farmers with real-time insights and recommendations based on a wealth of data collected by IoT devices [19]. This digital transformation empowers farmers to make data-driven decisions, optimize resource use, reduce costs, and enhance agricultural sustainability.

10.2.1 Remote Monitoring

Agriculture faces a multitude of challenges, ranging from fluctuating crop yields and rising labor costs to the unpredictable impact of extreme weather conditions and the ever-increasing demand for food production. To effectively address these growing challenges, farmers must embrace the adoption of technology within their agricultural operations.

Remote monitoring technology empowers users to allocate their time where it matters most, resulting in increased productivity, reduced labor costs, and a more efficient agricultural operation. To manage a farm profitably and achieve a successful crop yield, agricultural professionals must closely monitor, manage, and control a multitude of variables that are in a constant state of flux. Seasoned farmers have developed a keen understanding of how to leverage the intricate relationships between these variables to optimize crop yields [20]. However, the dynamic nature of each day necessitates diverse schedules and approaches to maintain ideal crop health. Informed decision-making in agriculture hinges on a deep understanding of the factors that impact crop yield, including soil conditions, climate, and the availability of water. Since rainfall cannot always be relied upon when needed, a significant portion of agricultural practitioners turns to irrigation equipment. It is imperative for these users to stay vigilant regarding the status and condition of their irrigation systems. All of these variables collectively contribute to a successful crop yield. Real-time insights into these critical metrics enable agricultural professionals to make timely and informed decisions when it matters most [21]. Digitalization and technological advancements, agricultural automation is increasingly monitoring and controlling these variables to streamline processes and increase efficiency. Here is a closer look at the significance of remote monitoring in agriculture:

- **Real-time Data Access:** Real-time data access allows users to view and interact with data as it is collected, providing immediate insights and enabling quick decision-making in dynamic environments like agriculture, where conditions can change rapidly.
- **Reduced Travel Time:** Farmers no longer need to travel from one end of their farm to another to assess conditions or check equipment. Remote monitoring eliminates the need for time-consuming site visits, allowing farmers to focus their efforts on more critical tasks.

- **Timely Decision-making:** With access to up-to-the-minute data, farmers can make timely decisions. They can respond quickly to changing weather conditions, irrigation needs, or emerging pest threats, preventing potential losses.
- **Risk Mitigation:** Farmers can monitor their farms for potential risks, such as equipment malfunctions, power outages, or adverse weather events. They can take proactive measures to mitigate these risks, preventing losses.
- **Data-driven Decisions:** The real-time data provided by remote monitoring systems empowers farmers to make data-driven decisions, leading to better outcomes in terms of crop health, yield, and resource utilization.
- **Enhanced Collaboration:** Remote monitoring systems facilitate collaboration among farmers, agricultural experts, and researchers. They can share data and insights, fostering knowledge exchange and cooperative problem-solving.

Remote monitoring in agriculture is a transformative technology that liberates farmers from the constraints of physical presence on their farms. It enables efficient and data-driven farm management, saving time and resources while promoting sustainability.

10.3 Challenges and Solutions Smart Agriculture

Implementing smart agriculture solutions comes with several common challenges that need to be addressed to ensure their successful adoption [22]. Here are some of the key challenges and potential solutions:

Smart agriculture solutions offer tremendous potential for improving farming practices, addressing challenges related to cost, connectivity, data security, and other factors is crucial for successful adoption. Collaborative efforts among governments, agricultural organizations, technology providers, and farmers themselves can lead to practical solutions that enhance the resilience, efficiency, and sustainability of modern agriculture. Table 10.2 show the list of challenges and solutions of smart agriculture.

10.3.1 (AI) Approach in Agriculture and Needs

The importance of agriculture in a nation's economic sector cannot be overstated. It serves as the backbone of society, with every individual relying directly or indirectly on agricultural products for their daily needs. The agricultural sector requires novel automation techniques to fulfill the

Table 10.2 Challenges and solutions smart agriculture.

S. no.	Term	Challenge	Solution
1	Cost and Investment	Implementing smart agriculture solutions often requires a substantial initial investment in technology, sensors, equipment, and training.	Collaborative approaches such as co-ops can also help share the expenses. Over time, the return on investment in terms of increased productivity and reduced resource usage can outweigh the upfront costs.
2	Connectivity Issues	Many rural agricultural areas may lack reliable internet connectivity, hindering the use of IoT devices and cloud-based solutions.	Infrastructure development and investment in rural broadband are essential. Additionally, some smart agriculture solutions can be designed to work offline and then sync with cloud-based systems when connectivity is available.
3	Data Security and Privacy	Gathering and sharing sensitive agricultural data may raise concerns about privacy and data security.	Clearly define data ownership and usage policies, and obtain informed consent from users regarding data collection and sharing. Compliance with data protection regulations is crucial.

(*Continued*)

Table 10.2 Challenges and solutions smart agriculture. (*Continued*)

S. no.	Term	Challenge	Solution
4	Integration and Compatibility:	Many farms use a variety of equipment from different manufacturers, and ensuring compatibility and seamless integration of smart agriculture solutions can be challenging.	Standardization efforts, open APIs, and interoperability protocols are essential for ensuring that different devices and systems can communicate with one another. Industry-wide collaboration can promote compatibility and ease of integration.
5	Regulatory and Compliance Issues:	Smart agriculture solutions may be subject to regulatory and compliance requirements that vary by region.	Farmers should stay informed about relevant regulations and work with experts or advisors who are knowledgeable about local agricultural and data privacy laws. Engaging in discussions with regulatory bodies can also help address compliance challenges.
6	Resistance to Change:	Farmers may be resistant to adopting new technologies and changing established practices.	Effective communication and demonstration of the benefits of smart agriculture can help overcome resistance. Sharing success stories and case studies from early adopters can also inspire confidence in the technology.

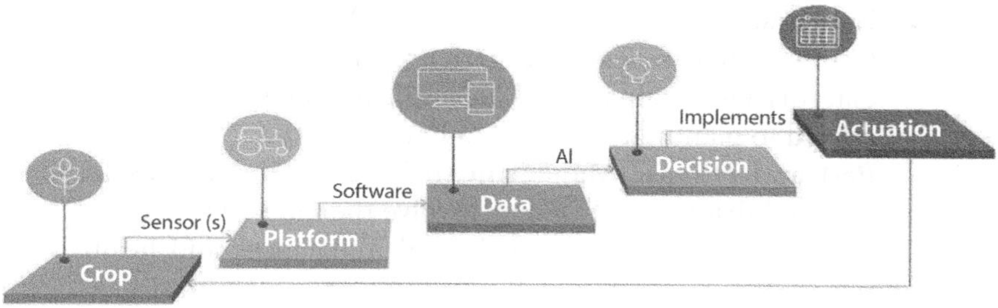

Figure 10.4 The role of AI in the agriculture information management [37].

ever-increasing global demand for produce [23]. Artificial intelligence (AI) is emerging as a key player in the agriculture sector, poised to transform the industry. AI possesses the potential to revolutionize traditional agriculture by significantly improving efficiency in terms of time, labor, and resource management. It also contributes to environmental sustainability by promoting responsible resource usage. Additionally, AI provides the accuracy required for monitoring and data analysis, resulting in better agricultural outcomes. Figure 10.4 shows the role of AI in the agriculture information management.

10.3.2 Needs of AI Farm

To overcome the obstacles in traditional agriculture, there is a pressing need to adopt innovative techniques and technologies [24]. Traditional agriculture, while vital, faces several challenges that can be addressed with modern approaches. Some of the difficulties encountered in conventional farming include:

- **Resource Inefficiency:** Traditional farming methods often involve excessive use of resources such as water, fertilizers, and pesticides. This not only strains the environment but also increases costs for farmers.
- **Climate Variability:** Climate change has led to unpredictable weather patterns, including droughts and floods. Traditional farming methods may struggle to adapt to these variations, resulting in crop losses.
- **Labor-Intensive Practices:** Many traditional farming methods are labor-intensive, requiring significant physical effort. This can be a deterrent for the younger generation and can lead to labor shortages.

- **Inadequate Data-Driven Decision-Making:** Traditional farming often relies on experience and intuition, lacking data-driven insights. This can result in suboptimal choices related to planting, irrigation, and pest control.
- **Pest and Disease Management:** Traditional methods for pest and disease control may involve the indiscriminate use of pesticides, leading to ecological imbalances and health risks.

10.3.3 Role of AI in Agriculture

Farmers encounter a multitude of challenges, akin to those faced with traditional agricultural practices. The broad adoption of Artificial Intelligence has become a game-changer in the agricultural industry, providing groundbreaking solutions to tackle these challenges. AI facilitates precision farming, enhancing crop management, resource optimization, and environmental sustainability [25]. Figure 10.5 depicts plants disease a pets detection using AI technology.

- **Environmental Protection:** AI in agriculture revolutionizes crop production, harvesting, and sales while prioritizing eco-friendly practices. It facilitates the inspection of defective crops and the enhancement of sustainable agricultural techniques. AI equips farmers with precise data on insect pests, diseases, and weed management methods. By deploying robotics, computer vision, and machine learning, AI enables targeted chemical applications where pests are concentrated, reducing the overall use of chemicals.
- **Price and Weather forecasting:** Weather plays a pivotal role in agricultural planning and decision-making. The integration of artificial intelligence technology empowers farmers to access meteorological data, enhancing the precision of crucial practices like sowing, harvesting, and pesticide application.
- **Detection of insect-pests and disease:** AI methods play a pivotal role in monitoring insect pests and plant diseases, offering valuable assistance in identification and assessing affected areas. Utilizing image recognition technology powered by deep learning, these techniques establish models capable of effectively scrutinizing plant health through image classification, detection, and segmentation.

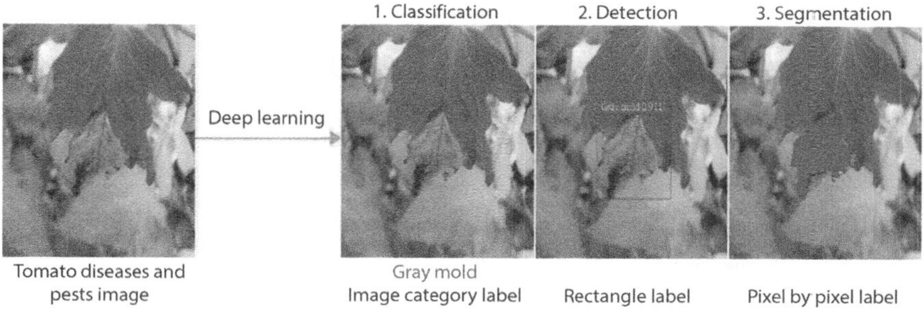

Figure 10.5 Plants disease a pets detection using AI technology [38].

- **Soil health monitoring**: In agriculture, maintaining good soil health is paramount to meet the ever-increasing demand for food production. Traditional methods have often fallen short in providing specific insights into soil properties tailored for each crop. However, AI and ML now enable the precise tracking of soil characteristics, including quality, fertility, microbial content, nutrient levels, and even the pattern of flora.
- **Innovation in harvesting methods:** The labor-intensive task of crop harvesting is being revolutionized by AI-based computer vision models. These models offer a means to observe and accurately estimate crop growth maturity, eliminating the need for additional human labor. In tandem with this, a diverse range of agribots has been introduced, designed to automate the harvesting process.
- **Intelligent spraying and Livestock health monitoring:** Utilizing Unmanned Aerial Vehicles (UAVs) equipped with computer vision AI technology, eco-friendly pest management takes a significant leap forward. These UAVs make it possible to apply precisely the required amount of pesticides or fertilizers uniformly within target spraying areas. Real-time recognition capabilities is crucial advancement in sustainable and efficient pest management.

10.4 AI for Soybean (*Glycine max*) Crop

Soybean (*Glycine max*) is a leguminous plant that plays a crucial role in global agriculture. It accounts for 25% of the world's edible oil production and serves

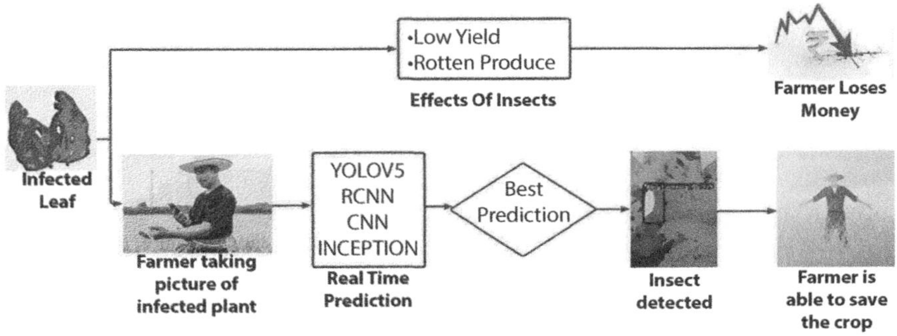

Figure 10.6 Conceptual diagram and working model of crop health monitoring [39].

as a primary source of livestock feeding protein, contributing to about two-thirds of the world's supply. In addition to its economic importance, soybean has a high nutritional value and is associated with health benefits, particularly in heart disease and diabetes management [26]. However, soybean cultivation is susceptible to attacks from various pests and insects, which can hinder the plant's proper growth and development, ultimately affecting the quality of the yield. Detecting the presence of these insects on the plants is vital for effective pest management. Additionally, the early diagnosis of plant diseases is critical for preventing their spread and minimizing their impact on crops. Figure 10.6 shows the conceptual diagram and working model of crop health monitoring.

10.4.1 Soybean Disease Image Acquisition and Pretreatment

- **Soybean Disease Image Acquisition:-** Collecting high-quality images of soybean diseases and meticulously pre-processing the affected areas is crucial for effective soybean disease classification. A limited number of valid images or poor segmentation can hinder later classification and identification efforts. Therefore, we use high-definition digital cameras to ensure image quality, avoiding debris, insects, strong lighting, or background distractions during the image capture process [27]. This attention to detail is critical for building a robust soybean disease classification system.
- **Soybean Disease Image Background Removal:-**The crop disease images captured often have complex backgrounds. To address this, the GrabCut algorithm is employed to remove background information. This algorithm builds upon the GraphCut algorithm, using iterative processes. This method

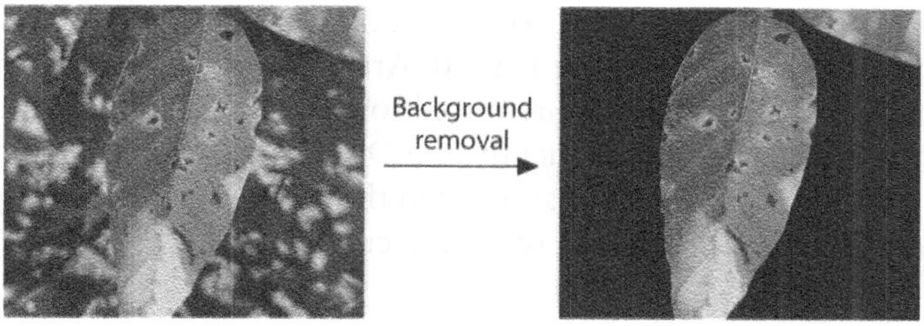

Figure 10.7 The removing-background images with grabcut algorithm [40].

automatically identifies the image's background area and subsequently eliminates it by setting the RGB pixel values of the background to (0, 0, 0). This technique enhances the quality of disease image segmentation and isolates the subject of interest effectively.

The RGB color space can be converted to the HSI (Hue, Saturation, Intensity) color space using a specific mathematical transformation that separates color information into more intuitive components for image processing and analysis. Figure 10.7 shows the removing-background images with grabcut algorithm.

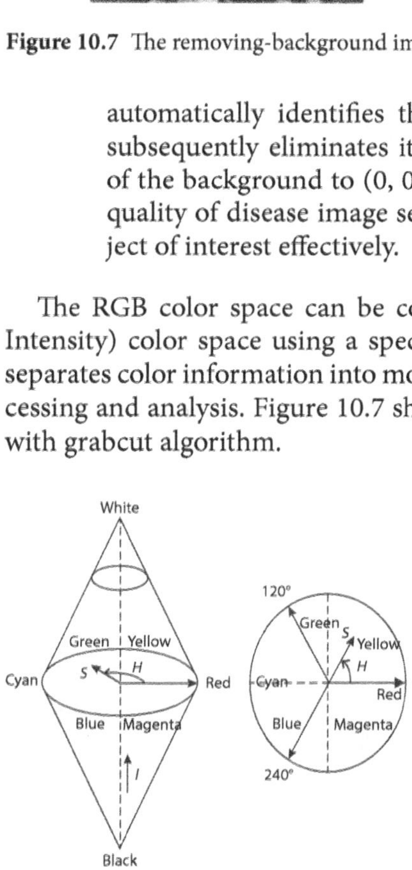

$$H = \begin{cases} \theta, & (B \leq G), \\ 360 - \theta, & (B > G), \end{cases}$$

$$\theta = \arccos\left\{\frac{(1/2)[(R-G)+(R-B)]}{\left[(R-G)^2+(R-G)(G-B)\right]^{(1/2)}}\right\},$$

$$S = 1 - \frac{3\min(R, G, B)}{R+G+B},$$

$$I = \frac{R+G+B}{3}.$$

In the HSI (Hue, Saturation, Intensity) color space, the Intensity (I) component is unrelated to the color information in an image. The color information is primarily represented by the Hue (H) and Saturation (S) components. These two components are closely linked to how humans perceive color. Through experimental testing, it has been determined that when the Hue (H) falls within the range of 70 to 200 and the Saturation (S) falls within the range of 0.17 to 1, this roughly corresponds to the green areas of crop leaves [28]. To filter out the green parts of the leaves in this study, the HSI color space is used. Areas falling within the specified Hue and Saturation ranges are removed to effectively eliminate the green portions of the leaves. Subsequently, the OTSU algorithm is employed to segment and identify the disease areas in the remaining image, helping to isolate and analyze the affected regions accurately.

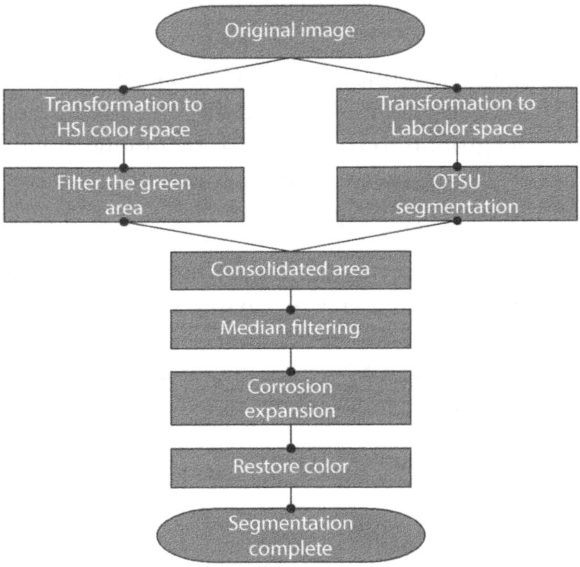

Figure 10.8 Flowchart of disease spot image segmentation algorithm.

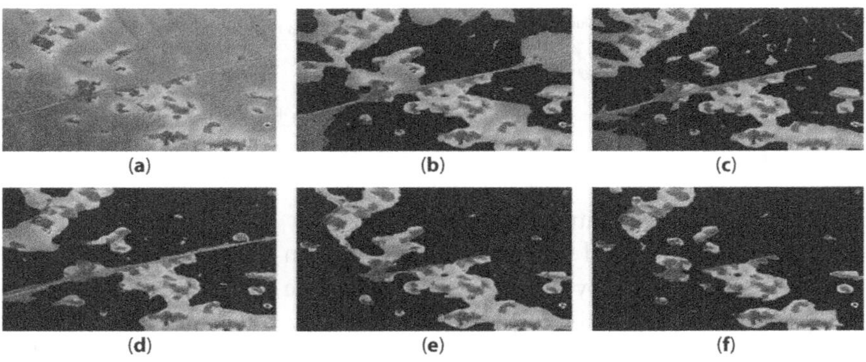

Figure 10.9 Segmentation effect of different algorithms on the brown spot disease in soybeans [41].

Implementing disease spot image segmentation involves a systematic process aimed at accurately identifying and delineating areas of plant diseases within images. The first crucial step is the collection of a diverse dataset comprising images with varying disease types, stages, and environmental conditions. Following data preprocessing, which includes image cleaning, annotation, and augmentation, a suitable segmentation algorithm is selected. Popular choices include architectures like U-Net or Mask R-CNN, and leveraging transfer learning can enhance model performance.

The development phase involves designing the neural network architecture, considering the specific requirements of disease spot segmentation. Training the model involves choosing an appropriate loss function and optimizer, and fine-tuning parameters to minimize over fitting. The model is then evaluated on a separate validation set using metrics such as Intersection over Union and Dice coefficient to ensure robust generalization. Optionally, a feedback loop for iterative improvement can be established. This involves refining the model based on evaluation results, adjusting hyper parameters, or exploring additional data augmentation techniques to enhance the segmentation accuracy. Throughout the process, attention to model interpretability, visual inspection of results, and addressing potential challenges, such as class imbalance or ambiguous cases, is crucial.

The implementation of disease spot image segmentation not only relies on the technical aspects of algorithm development but also emphasizes the quality and representativeness of the dataset, iterative refinement, and careful consideration of domain-specific factors. Successful implementation holds the potential to significantly contribute to precision agriculture by enabling early and accurate detection of plant diseases, facilitating timely intervention and improved crop management practices. Figure 10.8 shows the flowchart of disease spot image segmentation algorithm and Figure 10.9 shows the segmentation effects of different algorithms on the brown spot disease in soybeans

Implementing disease spot image segmentation involves several steps, from collecting and preprocessing the data to developing and training the segmentation algorithm. Table 10.3 shows the result of average running time of segmentation algorithms. Below is a step-by-step guide for implementing a disease spot image segmentation system:

1. **Data Collection:**
    - Collect Diverse Dataset: Gather a diverse dataset of plant images containing various types and stages of disease spots. Ensure a balanced representation of healthy and diseased samples.

2. **Data Preprocessing:**
    - Image Cleaning: Remove artifacts and irrelevant elements from the images that could affect the algorithm's performance.
    - Image Annotation: Manually annotate the images to create ground truth masks indicating the locations of disease spots. Use annotation tools to generate pixel-level or bounding box annotations.
3. **Algorithm Selection:**
    - Choose a Segmentation Model: Select an appropriate segmentation model based on the complexity of the task. Popular architectures include U-Net, Mask R-CNN, and DeepLab.
4. **Model Development:**
    - Transfer Learning (Optional): Leverage pre-trained models on large image datasets (ImageNet, COCO) for transfer learning. Fine-tune the model on the specific disease spot segmentation task.
    - Model Architecture: Design the neural network architecture for image segmentation. Ensure the output layer corresponds to the number of classes, with each class representing a different region, such as healthy and diseased areas.
5. **Training:**
    - Loss Function: Choose an appropriate loss function for segmentation tasks, such as binary cross-entropy or dice loss.
    - Optimizer: Select an optimizer, such as Adam or SGD, to minimize the chosen loss function during training.
    - Training Process: Train the model using the annotated dataset. Monitor training metrics and validation performance to prevent overfitting.
6. **Model Evaluation:**
    - Validation Set: Assess the model's performance on an independent validation set to confirm it generalizes effectively to new, unseen data.
    - Metrics: Use evaluation metrics like Intersection over Union (IoU).

Table 10.3 Average running time of segmentation algorithms.

Segmentation algorithm	Average running time (ms)
OTSU	53.0125
Ultragreen feature	108.7402
Genetic	2536.8941
Both Lab grayscale map + OTSU	328.2103
Proposed new Algorithm	608.3314

10.5 Result Discussion

To construct the final segmented disease maps, the lesions obtained using OTSU segmentation in the Lab color space are combined with the diseased lesions obtained by filtering the green regions in the HSI color space. Comparing this method with other segmentation techniques confirms the effectiveness of the proposed approach. The convolution neural network is designed with continuous convolution layers and sparse Maxout activation function layers. This design enhances feature extraction and non-linear expression capabilities while controlling network complexity and limiting the number of parameters. The network continuously adjusts its weight parameters through forward and backward propagation on training and test datasets, ultimately enabling multiclass disease classification with a Softmax layer.

Experimental results indicate that the proposed deep learning approach attains an outstanding average recognition rate of 92.80147% in soybean disease image recognition. This showcases the effectiveness of deep learning for handling large sample problems.

10.5.1 Emerging Trends and Technologies in Smart Agriculture

Emerging trends and technologies in smart agriculture are poised to revolutionize the industry by addressing challenges related to resource optimization, sustainability, and productivity [29]. Here are some key trends and technologies, including blockchain, drones, and AI, and their potential impact on agriculture:

- **Blockchain in Agriculture:** Blockchain technology offers transparent and tamper-proof record-keeping, supply chain traceability, and secures transactions. In agriculture.
- **Drones in Precision Agriculture:** Drones have transformed precision agriculture by enabling farmers to monitor crop health, identify areas of stress, and optimize field management. Equipped with specialized cameras, drones capture high-resolution images for early detection of issues like pest infestation or disease [30].
- **Vertical Farming and Indoor Agriculture:** Vertical Farming and Indoor Agriculture refer to methods of growing crops in vertically stacked layers or controlled indoor environments. This approach optimizes space, conserves resources, and allows for year-round production, making it an innovative solution for urban areas and regions with limited arable land [31].
- **Big Data Analytics:** Big data analytics solutions are critical for managing the vast amount of data generated by smart agriculture technologies. They offer comprehensive insights into farm operations, leading to informed decisions on planting, fertilization, pest control, and resource management [32].
- **Sustainable Farming Practices:** Sustainability is a key focus in smart agriculture. Technologies, such as cover cropping, no-till farming, and precision application of fertilizers and pesticides, contribute to soil health and reduced environmental impact. Implementing sustainable practices is vital for long-term agricultural viability.
- **Agri-Fintech:** The integration of financial technology (fintech) into agriculture, known as agri-fintech, provides farmers with access to digital financial services, including loans, insurance, and payment systems. These services improve financial inclusivity and help farmers manage risks associated with agriculture [33].
- **Plant and Animal Biotechnology:** Potential Impact: Advances in plant and animal biotechnology, including genetically modified organisms (GMOs) and gene editing, have the potential to create more resilient and productive crops and livestock. These technologies can help address food security challenges in a changing climate.

These emerging trends and technologies in smart agriculture hold the promise of transforming the industry into a more sustainable, efficient, and resilient sector. They provide solutions to challenges related to resource management, environmental impact, and the need to feed a growing global population.

10.6 Conclusion

The Chapter "Smart Agriculture Revolution: Cloud and IoT-Based Solutions for Sustainable Crop Management and Precision Farming" underscores the transformative potential of cloud computing and IoT technologies in modern agriculture. It highlights how these innovations are reshaping traditional farming practices, enabling farmers to overcome challenges and meet the demands of a rapidly changing world. In the era of smart agriculture, the fusion of cloud-based data storage and real-time insights from IoT devices is ushering in a new age of precision farming. Farmers are empowered with the tools to make data-driven decisions, optimizing resource use, enhancing crop health, and ultimately increasing yields. This book has emphasized the importance of embracing technology-driven solutions to tackle the complexities of modern agriculture.

Key takeaways from the Chapter include:

- **Data-Driven Agriculture:** Emphasizing the power of data analytics in driving informed decision-making for farmers. By collecting and analyzing real-time data on crop health, weather conditions, and soil quality, farmers can make proactive choices to optimize production.
- **Precision Farming:** Precision farming practices, powered by IoT and cloud solutions, have brought a level of precision and efficiency that was previously unimaginable.
- **Resource Efficiency:** The chapter emphasizes how cloud and IoT-based solutions have facilitated efficient resource management, especially regarding water, fertilizers, and pest control.
- **Real-Time Monitoring:** The ability to remotely monitor and manage farms in real-time is a game-changer. This technology helps farmers respond promptly to changing conditions, mitigating risks and enhancing overall productivity.
- **Sustainability:** Smart agriculture practices promote sustainable and environmentally friendly farming. The chapter

underscores the role of these technologies in reducing the environmental impact of agriculture.

Although integrating cloud computing and Internet of Things (IoT) technologies in smart agriculture offers many advantages, it also brings certain limitations. It is important to recognize these challenges for a comprehensive understanding of the implementation of such systems. Here are some limitations associated with the Smart Agriculture Revolution:

- **Limited Connectivity in Rural Areas:** Many agricultural regions may lack reliable internet connectivity, hindering the seamless operation of cloud-based solutions and IoT devices. This digital divide can exclude some farmers from accessing the benefits of smart agriculture technologies.
- **High Initial Costs and Infrastructure Investment:** The deployment of IoT sensors, cloud infrastructure, and data analytics tools can entail significant upfront costs. Small-scale farmers, in particular, may find it challenging to make the initial investment required for adopting these technologies.
- **Dependence on Energy Sources:** IoT devices and cloud infrastructure require a stable and consistent power supply. In regions where electricity is unreliable or unavailable, maintaining continuous operation becomes challenging, affecting the reliability of smart agriculture systems.
- **Integration Challenges and Interoperability:** Farmers may face difficulties integrating new technologies with existing farming equipment and practices. Lack of standardization and interoperability between different IoT devices and cloud platforms can create compatibility issues.
- **Skill and Education Gaps:** The successful implementation of smart agriculture technologies requires farmers to be knowledgeable about IoT, data analytics, and cloud computing. There might be a need for training programs to bridge the gap in technical expertise among the agricultural community.
- **Weather Dependency and Unpredictable Conditions:** IoT-based systems heavily rely on real-time data, and weather conditions can significantly impact the accuracy of predictions and recommendations. Unpredictable events

like sudden weather changes may limit the effectiveness of precision farming practices.

- **Regulatory and Compliance Challenges:** Agriculture is subject to various regulations, and compliance with these regulations may be complex when implementing advanced technologies. Meeting data protection, environmental, and other regulatory standards can pose challenges for farmers and technology providers.

References

1. Raj Kumar, G., Chandra Shekhar, Y., Shweta, V., Ritesh, R., Smart agriculture—Urgent need of the day in developing countries. *Sustain. Comput. Inf. Syst.*, 30, 100512, 2021.
2. Palombi, L. and Sessa, R., *Climate-Smart Agriculture*, Food and Agriculture Organization, Rome, Italy, 2013.
3. Patil, K.A. and Kale, N.R., A model for smart agriculture using IoT, in: *Proceedings of the 2016 International Conference on Global Trends in Signal Processing, Information Computing and Communication*, 22–24 December 2016, IEEE, Jalgaon, India, pp. 543–545, 2016. [CrossRef].
4. Sisinni, E., Saifullah, A., Han, S., Jennehag, U., Gidlund, M., Industrial Internet of Things: Challenges, Opportunities, and Directions. *IEEE Trans. Ind. Inf.*, 14, 4724–4734, 2018. [CrossRef], https://doi.org/10.14445/22312803/IJCTT-V68I4P109
5. Shi, X., An, X., Zhao, Q., Liu, H., Xia, L., Sun, X., Guo, Y., State- of- the-Art Internet of Things in Protected Agriculture. *Sensors*, 19, 1833, 2019. [CrossRef].
6. Elijah, O., Rahman, T.A., Orikumhi, I., Leow, C.Y., Hindia, M.N., An Overview of Internet of Things (IoT) and Data Analytics in Agriculture: Benefits and Challenges. *IEEE Internet Things J.*, 5, 3758–3773, 2018. [CrossRef].
7. Bonneau, V. and Copigneaux, B., Industry 4.0 in Agriculture: Focus on IoT Aspects, European Commission, Digital Transformation Monitor, 2017, Available online: https://ec.europa.eu/growth/tools-databases/dem/monitor/content/industry-40-agriculturefocus-iot-aspects (accessed on 30 December 2020).
8. Yong, W., Shuaishuai, L., Li, L., Minzan, L., Ming, L., Arvanitis, K.G., Grorgieva, C., Sigrimis, N., Smart Sensors from Ground to Cloud and Web Intelligence. *IFAC PapersOnLine*, 51, 31–38, 2018. [CrossRef].
9. Mekala, M.S. and Viswanathan, P., A Survey: Smart agriculture IoT with cloud computing, in: *Proceedings of the 2017 International Conference on Microelectronic Devices, Circuits and Systems (ICMDCS)*, Vellore, India, 10–12 August 2017, IEEE, Vellore, India, pp. 1–7, 2017. [CrossRef].

10. Batte, M.T. and VanBuren, F.N., Precision farming—Factor influencing productivity, in: *Proceedings of the Northern Ohio Crops Day Meeting*, Wood County, OH, USA, 21 January 1999.
11. Sishodia, R.P., Ray, R.L., Singh, S.K., Applications of Remote Sensing in Precision Agriculture: A Review. *Remote Sens.*, 12, 3136, 2020. [CrossRef].
12. Tripodi, P., Massa, D., Venezia, A., Cardi, T., Sensing Technologies for Precision Phenotyping in Vegetable Crops: Current Status and Future Challenges. *Agronomy*, 8, 57, 2018. [CrossRef].
13. Hansen, J.W., Is agricultural sustainability a useful concept? *Agric. Syst.*, 50, 117–143, 1996. [Google Scholar] [CrossRef].
14. Smith, C.S. and McDonald, G.T., Assessing the sustainability of agriculture at the planning stage. *J. Environ. Manage.*, 52, 15–37, 1998. [Google Scholar] [CrossRef][Green Version].
15. Velten, S., Leventon, J., Jager, N., Newig, J., What Is Sustainable Agriculture? A Systematic Review. *Sustainability*, 7, 7833, 2015. [Google Scholar] [CrossRef][Green Version].
16. Bendre, M., Thool, R., Thool, V., Big data in precision agricul950 ture through ict: Rainfall prediction using neural network approach, in: *Proceedings of the International Congress on Information and Communication Technology*, S. Satapathy, Y. Bhatt, A. Joshi, D. Mishra (Eds.), pp. 165–175, 2016, doi: 10.1007/978-981-10-0767-5_19.
17. Drummond, S.T., Birrell, S.J., Sudduth, K.A., Analysis and corre1025 lation methods for spatial data. *American Society of Agricultural Engineers. Annual Meeting*, vol. 95, p. 1335, 1995.
18. Halevy, A., Rajaraman, A., Ordille, J., Data integration: The teenage years, in: *Proceedings of the 32Nd International Conference on Very Large Data Bases VLDB '06*, VLDB Endowment, pp. 9–16, 2006.
19. Du, G., Zhang, R., Liang, C.A., Hu, M., Remote sensing extraction and spatial pattern analysis of cropping patterns in black soil region of Northeast China at county level. *Trans. Chin. Soc. Agric. Eng.*, 37, 133–141, 2021.
20. Al-Qurabat, A.K.M., Mohammed, Z.A., Hussein, Z.J., Data traffic management based on compression and MDL techniques for smart agriculture in IoT. *Wirel. Pers. Commun.*, 120, 3, 2227–2258, 2021.
21. Ali, I., Kaur, S., Khamparia, A., Gupta, D., Kumar, S., Khanna, A., Al-Turjman, F., Security Challenges and Cyber Forensic Ecosystem in IoT Driven BYOD Environment. *IEEE Access*, 8, 172770–172782, 2020.
22. Panpatte, S. and Ganeshkumar, C., Indian Institute Of Plantation Management, Artificial Intelligence in Agriculture Sector: Case Study of Blue River Technology, January 2021, DOI: 10.1007/978-981-15-9689-6_17.
23. Talaviya, T., Shah, D., Patel, N., Yagnik, H., Shah, M., Implementation of artificial intelligence in agriculture for optimisation of irrigation and application of pesticides and herbicides. *Artif. Intell. Agric.*, 4, 58–73, 2020.

24. Banerjee, G., Sarkar, U., Das, S., Ghosh, I., Artificial Intelligence in Agriculture: A Literature Survey. *Int. J. Sci. Res. Comput. Sci. Appl Manage. Stud.*, 7, 3, 1–6, 2018.
25. Zha, T., Zhong, X.B., Zhou, Q.Z., Development status of China's soybean industry and strategies of revitalizing. *Soybean Sci.*, 37, 3, 458–463, 2018.
26. Oppenheim, D., Shani, G., Erlich, O., Tsror, L., Using deep learning for image-based potato tuber disease detection. *Phytopathology*, 109, 6, 1083–1087, 2019.
27. Pires, R.D.L., Gonçalves, W.E.S., Oruê, J.F. *et al.*, Local descriptors for soybean disease recognition. *Comput. Electron. Agric.*, 125, 48–55, 2016.
28. De Clercq, M., Vats, A., Biel, A., Agriculture 4.0: the Future of Farming Technology, The World Government Summit, Dubai, UAE, 2018.
29. Ozdogan, B., Gacar, A., Aktas, H., Digital agriculture practices in the context of Agriculture 4.0. *J. Econ. Financ. Account. – JEFA*, 4, 2, 184–191, 2017.
30. Thilakarathne, N.N., Bakar, M.S.A., Abas, P.E., Yassin, H., Towards making the fields talks: A real-time cloud enabled IoT crop management platform for smart agriculture. *Front. Plant Sci.*, 13, 2022, 04 January 2023. doi 10.3389/fpls.2022.1030168. PMID: 36684733; PMCID: PMC9846789.
31. Turukmane, A.V., Pradeepa, M., Shyam Sunder Reddy, K., Suganthi, R., Md Riyazuddin, Y., Satyanarayana Tallapragada, V.V., Smart farming using cloud-based Iot data analytics. *Measurement: Sensors*, 27, 100806, June 2023. ISSN 2665-9174, https://doi.org/10.1016/j.measen.2023.100806. (https://www.sciencedirect.com/science/article/pii/S2665917423001423)
32. Dinesh, P.M., Sabeenian, R., Lokeshvar, R., Paramasivam, M., Thanish, Manjunathan, IOT Based Smart Farming Application. *E3S Web of Conferences, ICONNECT-2023,* vol. 399, p. 04012, 2023, https://doi.org/10.1051/e3sconf/202339904012.
33. Baghel, S.S., Rawat, P., Singh, R., Akram, S.V., Pandey, S., Baghel, A.V.S., AI, IoT and Cloud Computing Based Smart Agriculture. *2022 5th International Conference on Contemporary Computing and Informatics (IC3I)*, Electronic, ISBN:979-8-3503-9826-7, Print on Demand(PoD) ISBN:979-8-3503-9827-4.
34. Yin, H., Cao, Y., Marelli, B., Zeng, X., Mason, A., Cao, C., Smart Agriculture Systems: Soil Sensors and Plant Wearables for Smart and Precision Agriculture (Adv. Mater. 20/2021). *Adv. Mater.*, 33, 2021. 2170156.10.1002/adma.202170156.
35. Gupta, M., Abdelsalam, M., Khorsandroo, S., Mittal, S., Security and Privacy in Smart Farming: Challenges and Opportunities. *IEEE Access*, 1-1, 2020. 10.1109/ACCESS.2020.2975142.
36. Salam, A., Internet of Things in Agricultural Innovation and Security, 2020. 10.1007/978-3-030-35291-2_3.
37. Saiz-Rubio, V. and Rovira-Más, F., From Smart Farming towards Agriculture 5.0: A Review on Crop Data Management. *Agronomy*, 10, 207, 2020. https://doi.org/10.3390/agronomy10020207

38. Liu, J. and Wang, X., Plant diseases and pests detection based on deep learning: a review. *Plant Methods*, 17, 2021. 10.1186/s13007- 021-00722-9.
39. Divyanshu, T., Kumar Singh, K., Tripathi, S., Performance analysis of AI-based solutions for crop disease identification, detection, and classification. *Smart Agric. Technol.*, 5, 100238, 2023. ISSN 2772-3755, https://doi.org/10.1016/j.atech.2023.100238. (https://www.sciencedirect.com/science/article/pii/S2772375523000680)
40. Miao, E., Zhou, G., Zhao, S., Research on Soybean Disease Identification Method Based on Deep Learning. *Mobile Inform. Syst.*, 2022, 1–8, 2022. 10.1155/2022/1952936.
41. Prema, D.P., Veeramani, D.A., Theradimani, D.M., Sivakumar, D.T., Plant leaf disease detection using Curvelet transform, 2019.

11

Greedy Particle Swarm Optimization Approach Using Leaky ReLU Function for Minimum Spanning Tree Problem

Ashish Kumar Singh* **and Anoj Kumar**

Department of Computer Science and Engineering, Motilal Nehru National Institute of Technology, Allahabad, Paryagraj, Uttar Pradesh, India

Abstract

The minimum spanning tree (MST) problem, a well-known optimization challenge, finds practical use across diverse fields including network design, transportation, and logistics. This paper presents an innovative approach to tackle the MST problem, integrating Greedy Particle Swarm Optimization (GPSO) with the Leaky Rectified Linear Unit (ReLU) function. GPSO, inspired by the collective behaviors of birds and fish, excels in efficiently exploring solution spaces and locating optimal solutions, forming the core of our methodology. To augment its performance, we introduce the Leaky ReLU function as the activation function in the particle swarm optimization process. The Leaky ReLU function, a recently introduced activation function, demonstrates promising qualities for optimization tasks. Its integration into the GPSO framework enables our approach to simultaneously encourage exploration and exploitation, leading to a more efficient search for the minimum spanning tree. This study offers a comprehensive analysis of our GPSO with the Leaky ReLU approach, encompassing detailed algorithmic descriptions, parameter configurations, and rigorous experimental results conducted on randomly generated 20, 40, 60, 80 nodes within the search space and generating a minimum spanning tree corresponding to it. The experiments conclusively demonstrate that our approach surpasses traditional MST algorithms, achieving competitive results when compared to state-of-the-art methods. In conclusion, our proposed Greedy Particle Swarm Optimization approach, combined with the Leaky ReLU function, presents a promising solution to the minimum spanning tree problem. Leveraging the synergy between GPSO and the Leaky ReLU

**Corresponding author*: ashishkrsingh@mnnit.ac.in

Mohit Kumar, Gautam Srivastava, Ashutosh Kumar Singh and Kalka Dubey (eds.) AI-Based Advanced Optimization Techniques for Edge Computing, (289–316) © 2025 Scrivener Publishing LLC

function, we contribute to the advancement of optimization techniques applicable to graph-based problems, with potential implications across a range of real-world scenarios. The findings of this research suggest that the proposed approach holds promise for addressing MST problems in practical applications, showcasing its potential as a valuable tool in various domains.

***Keywords*:** PSO, MST, swarm intelligence, meta-heuristic, leaky ReLU

11.1 Introduction

The generation of data in the last three decades is increasing exponentially. To keep data in one place is quite challenging in this highly demanding world. Data Generated may be in different places and these data consist a set of larger number of features so there is a need for a situation in which data may be stored in a distributed fashion. This means generated data consists of many features and is stored in different locations so the conclusion is drawn only after considering all the features from all the locations, such type of data is known as multimodal data. If the data is stored in distributed manner then finding an optimal path is quite a challenging task. When the data are distributed in such a manner, then we should perform data mining. If the data is stored in a distributed location then for efficient extraction of features from all the locations there should be some connected form of graph in which every node is designated as a location of data and the distance should be denoted with a labeled edge [2]. Given G is the graph then the minimum spanning tree problem is NP-hard problem and this type of problem is widely studied [4]. Given a graph, LRGPSO aims to find the minimum spanning tree by using the minimum distance between the nodes.

Bruggemann *et al.* [7] have represented a formal definition of MSTP is let G=(V, E) be the connected graph the goal is to find out the smallest subset of graph G' in which there is no cycle and there should be set of edges E' = {e ∈ E}. Data mining is the process in which we extract information from a huge amount of data this data mining process consists of a series of operations including cleaning of data, integration, reduction, and transformation [1]. If the size of the data is huge then obviously we also have to consider the larger number of features in which not all the features are important but some of them are important so we have to perform the feature selection algorithm so that the accuracy of the result is not affected [3]. For collecting related data from different locations, we need a mechanism in which data collection time is very less and result generating time is also low. If data is spread in N number of cities then we have to collect the data from all the cities in such a way cost of traveling is lesser and also we can cover all cities for such type of problem we have to find a minimum spanning tree in which all the cities are connected with minimum cost where cost is the distance between two connected city [6].

While discussing the concept of minimum spanning tree we can forget the contribution by Kruskal (1956) and Prim (1957), the overall cost of the tree is the sum of all the edges in the tree. The application areas of the minimum spanning tree problem also have in computer networks, multi-modal transportation problems, data compression, and dynamic distribution network reconfiguration in electrical engineering. So far, the need for a minimum spanning tree is not limited to only these areas as there is also a need in the medical field, emotion recognition. So we can say that MST is also a graph in that nodes or vertices are connected in such a manner edges of MST are a subset of the edges of the graph, without the construction of any cycles. The minimum spanning tree (MST) finds application across diverse fields such as network design, transportation, communication, and biology [5]. In network design, it facilitates the identification of the most efficient connectivity among nodes with the lowest cost. In transportation, the MST is employed to determine the shortest route between two locations. In communication, it aids in identifying the most reliable path for data transmission between different nodes. Furthermore, in biology, MST proves valuable for analyzing intricate brain networks, conducting cluster analysis, and performing image segmentation. Among all the swarm-based optimization techniques PSO is one of the best optimization techniques due to its simplicity, proximity, and effectiveness. A lot of complex problem is solved using PSO makes them easier to solve [10].

11.1.1 Goal

The goal of this research paper is to explore and introduce an innovative optimization method centered around Greedy Particle Swarm Optimization (GPSO), incorporating the Leaky Rectified Linear Unit (ReLU) function to address the minimum spanning tree (MST) problem. This investigation strives to showcase the effectiveness and efficiency of the GPSO algorithm when coupled with Leaky ReLU in achieving optimal or near-optimal MST solutions. Furthermore, the study seeks to conduct a comparative performance analysis against established MST algorithms. Additionally, we aim to shed light on the practical applicability and potential benefits of this approach in real-world scenarios involving network design and optimization.

This paper proposed a work in greedy nature PSO using mutation rate 0.06 with Leaky Rectified Linear Unit (ReLU) function for generating a minimum spanning tree of a connected graph(V, E), where V is the nodes and E is the edge.

11.1.2 Research Contribution are Below Listed

- Introduction of greedy nature of members of swarm in particle swarm optimization algorithm.
- Individual best of every member is calculate by increasing velocity by Leaky rate as number of iteration increases.
- Tuning of PSO parameters in proposed approach
- Introduction of local mutation with mutation rate 0.06.
- Concept of Leaky ReLU activation function is used for handling "dying ReLU" problem

The remainder of sections of this article are as follows: in section 11.2 background which further divided in three sub section in which one section have brief description of minimum spanning tree, second section have description about particle swarm optimization and another section have description Leaky ReLU activation function. In section 11.3, we described about proposed approach LRGPSO which further divided in two subsections, In section 11.4 we have briefly described the experimental setup and result analysis of proposed approach with complexity of proposed approach in section 11.4.1. In section 11.5, we provide the conclusion and some future work of our proposed work.

11.2 Background

If G = (V, E, W) represents a graph, where V denotes vertices, E represents edges connecting two nodes, and W is the distance serving as the weight of the edges, the concept of a minimum spanning tree involves these three parameters. However, the key condition is that no cycles should be present, ensuring that all nodes are interconnected in a way that minimizes the overall weight of the tree. In the domain of graph theory mathematics, a minimum spanning tree, denoted as T, for a connected and undirected graph G is a tree that encompasses all the vertices of G along with some or all of its edges. Simply put, every node is part of the tree while avoiding the formation of cycles or loops. Vijyalakshmi *et al.* [8] proposed

MDG-PSO-MCST in this method multiple sensors are used for clusters for data gathering with energy efficiency. The anchor nodes are selected for intermediate data collection based on the connectivity and concept of minimum spanning tree is used node degree, node compatibility, and the distance between the sensors of two adjacent clusters parameters using particle swarm optimization (PSO) technique. During the experiment, promising result is obtained. Graham and Hell [19] briefly describe the history of the minimum spanning tree. Fredrickson *et al.* [20] propose an approach assuming that the increase in the weight of an edge has an associated cost proportional to the magnitude of the change. Table 11.1 represents state of the art.

Table 11.1 State of the art.

References	Authors	Year	Contribution
[1]	J. Han, J. Pei, M. Kember	2011	Discussion about Data mining process: operations (cleaning, integration, reduction, transformation)
[3]	B. Xue *et al.*	2016	Feature selection algorithm for large data, importance of accurate results
[6]	R. L. Graham and P. Hell	1985	Efficient data collection from N cities, minimum spanning tree for minimum cost
[7]	Bruggemann *et al.*	2003	Formal definition of MSTP; finding the smallest subset G' without cycles in connected graph G=(V, E)
[8]	K Vijyalakshmi *et al.*	2018	MDG-PSO-MCST: Method for data gathering using multiple sensors, anchor nodes, and minimum spanning tree
[12]	B. Y. Qu, P sungathan and S das	2013	DLIPS: suited for multimodal optimization problem

(*Continued*)

Table 11.1 State of the art. (*Continued*)

References	Authors	Year	Contribution
[13]	S. Mujumdar *et al.*	2022	Comprehensive analysis of MO-MST Problem under Uncertain Paradigm
[14]	B. Nayef *et al.*	2022	Leaky ReLU function character recognition in arabic with CNN, optimized activation function improves accuracy
[15]	M. Mosbah *et al.*	2017	Minimum spanning tree for reconfiguration of distribution network, minimizing power loss
[16]	D. Das	2016	Two main categories of MST algorithms: line-based and node-based
[18]	M. Lin *et al.*	2020	Firefly algorithm for unlabeled graph; applicable to discrete problems
[19]	Graham and Hell	1985	Brief description about the history of the minimum spanning tree
[20]	G. N. Fredrickson *et al.*	1999	Proposal: Increase in edge weight has cost proportional to change magnitude

11.2.1 Minimum Spanning Tree

The concept of a minimum spanning tree (MST) holds paramount importance in the realms of graph theory and network optimization. Its significance is notably pronounced in various applications, including network design within communication networks, transportation systems, and infrastructure planning. Stojanovic *et al.* [9] uses minimum spanning tree with simulated annealing for distribution network reconfiguration results proves that combination of these two leads to satisfactory result for minimum power loss for each hour. Majumdar *et al.* [13] proposed a comprehensive analysis of the multi-objective minimum spanning tree problem under uncertain paradigm, highlighting the challenges and solutions for real-world applications. Mosbah *et al.* [15] also use minimum spanning tree for reconfiguration of distribution network under multi times, while minimizing the total power loss as objective function and obtained comparative results. This algorithm was tested on IEEE (33 nodes, 84 nodes) and validated on Algerian distribution network (116 node). There are two main categories of minimum spanning tree (MST) algorithms: line-based MST algorithms and node-based MST algorithms. Examples of these algorithms include Kruskal's algorithm and Prim's algorithm [16]. Lin *et al.* [18] propose the firefly algorithm for the unlabeled graph which make proposed algorithm for discrete problem. Stojanavic *et al.* [9] propose a hybrid mechanism for using in electrical domain. Basic steps of Prim's and Kruskal's algorithm are described below:

Basic Steps of Prim's algorithm are as follows:-

1. Initialization in which we start with the arbitrary vertex.
2. Select the minimum weight edges and add initial vertex to visited vertex set.
3. Select the minimum weight edge while ensuring that adding this edge does not create cycle.
4. Update minimum spanning tree.
5. Mark connected vertex as visited vertex.
6. Repeat steps 2 to 5 until all vertex are visited
7. Terminates when all vertices are included in the minimum spanning tree.

Output: Minimum Spanning Tree has V-1 edges, whereas V is the no of vertex.

Basic Steps of Kruskal's algorithm are as follows:-

1. Start with all the vertices as individual disjoint sets.
2. Create a queue for storing the edges and their weights.
3. Sort all the edges in the graph in non-decreasing order of their weights.
4. If adding the edge to the minimum spanning tree does not create a cycle then add the edge to the minimum spanning tree.
5. Merge the sets of the two vertices connected by the edge.

6. Repeat steps 4 to 5 until we get minimum spanning tree with V-1 edges.
7. Terminates when all edges have been considered.

Output: minimum spanning tree has V-1 edges, whereas V is the no of vertex.

On the performance wise prim's algorithm works well on dense graph where the number of edges is close to the maximum possible and Kruskal's algorithm works well on sparse graph where the number of edges is significantly less than the maximum possible.

11.2.2 Particle Swarm Optimization

Eberhart and Kennedy [11] proposed one of the famous optimization techniques particle swarm optimization. It replicates the collective behavior observed in bird flocking and fish schooling. PSO operates by managing a swarm of particles navigating the problem space with velocities that are consistently adjusted. Initially, particles are dispersed across the search space. Every particle remembers its individual best position (best) and the overall best position (gbest). In every iteration, the both position, velocity of all particle undergo updates as per the proposed equations. Each particle adjusts its position based on its own experience and that of its neighbors, aiming to converge toward the optimal solution. Qu *et al.* [12] proposed a variant of the PSO algorithm, termed Distance-based Locally Informed Particle Swarm (DLIPS), which has been introduced for addressing multimodal optimization challenges. DLIPS adopts a distance-based strategy to identify the neighbors of individual particles, facilitating improved exploration of the search space and mitigating premature convergence issues. Additionally, the algorithm integrates a locally informed particle optimizer (LIPS) to augment niching performance. The authors assess DLIPS' performance across a range of benchmark functions and conduct comparative analyses with other comparative algorithms. Basic Steps of Particle swarm optimization algorithm are as follows:-

1. Initialization
2. Define parameters
3. Evaluation of fitness function
4. Update personal best
5. Update global best

6. Update velocity and position of particles
7. Termination criteria met
8. Output

These processes are repeatedly performed until the algorithm either attains a satisfactory solution or reaches the predefined maximum number of iterations. The objective of the algorithm is to systematically explore the solution space, optimizing the positions and velocities of particles. This optimization is achieved by leveraging the individual experiences of particles (personal best) and incorporating insights from the collective experience of the entire swarm (global best).

11.2.3 Firefly Algorithm

The Firefly Algorithm, introduced by Xin-She Yang [22], draws inspiration from the bioluminescent communication of fireflies. This nature-inspired optimization algorithm reflects the flashing behavior of fireflies, where the attractiveness of a firefly is determined by its brightness. In the algorithm, fireflies represent potential solutions to an optimization problem, and their movements in the solution space are influenced by their brightness and distance from other fireflies. Fireflies are attracted to brighter neighbors, symbolizing superior solutions, and tend to move toward them. This process emulates the natural inclination of fireflies to congregate around brighter counterparts. As the algorithm progresses, the population of fireflies collectively converges toward optimal solutions. Key components include the light intensity, representing the objective function value, and parameters controlling the attractiveness and randomness of movement. The basic Steps of the Firefly algorithm are as follows:-

1. Generate potential solutions in the form of population.
2. Set the value of parameters such as light absorption coefficient, and attractiveness.
3. Evaluate the brightness of every particle.
4. Update the positions of fireflies in the solution space using their attractiveness and the distance to other fireflies.
5. Recalculate the light intensity for each firefly based on the updated positions.
6. Repeat 4 to 5 until convergence criteria are met.
7. Extract final solution.

11.2.4 Leaky ReLU Activation Function

The standard ReLU activation function is defined as f(x)= max(0,x). It essentially replaces all negative values in the input with zero, allowing only positive values to pass through unchanged. While ReLU has been widely used and is computationally efficient, it suffers from a drawback known as the "dying ReLU" problem. This occurs when neurons during training always output zero for certain inputs, effectively becoming inactive and not contributing to the learning process. Leaky ReLU function addresses the problem of "the dying ReLU problem" by permitting a small, positive slope for the –ve part of the function. The Leaky ReLU function is defined as:

$$F(x) = \begin{cases} x, & \text{if } x > 0 \\ \alpha x, & \text{if } x \leq 0 \end{cases}$$

Here, α is a small positive constant (in our case it is 0.17). Unlike the standard ReLU, Leaky ReLU allows a small, non-zero gradient for negative inputs, preventing neurons from being completely inactive during training. The reason behind selecting this function is it will avoid the "Dying Relu" problem, it helps mitigate the issue of particles becoming inactive during training, which is a problem encountered with the standard ReLU. Another reason is the non-zero slope for negative inputs can be beneficial during the optimization process, especially when dealing with large learning rates. Nayef *et al.* [14] uses Leaky ReLU function o to filter the extracted features in Arabic character recognition using convolution neural network. In this work, an optimized Leaky ReLU activation function for CNNs improves the accuracy of Arabic handwritten character recognition. The method is evaluated using various datasets and achieves state-of-the-art results.

11.3 Population-Based Proposed Optimization Approach

Obtaining a solution for the minimum cost of covering cities or areas in such a manner where we have to consider another contradictory parameter then it would be challenging. In such type of condition, we need Meta-heuristic optimization techniques, which have gained popularity for their ability to explore solution spaces efficiently. Among these, Particle Swarm Optimization (PSO) stands out as a nature-inspired algorithm that mimics

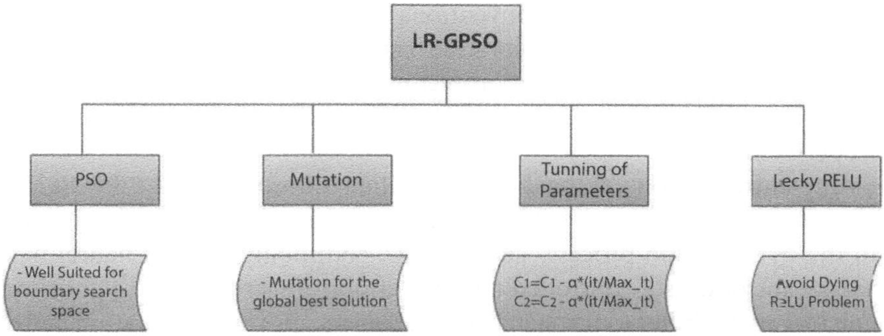

Figure 11.1 Basic structure of LRGPSO.

the collective behavior of particles in a search space. While reducing the weakness of optimization techniques we have proposed an approach that can efficiently obtain the minimum spanning tree that has the lowest fitness and also doesn't face stagnation problems while using a Leaky ReLU activation function with mutation that will create a new particle by mutating current particle then again evaluate the personal cost of newly created particle. Accept the outcome of mutation if it improves the cost otherwise it will remain the same.

In the proposed approach Kruskal's algorithm is used which was proposed in 1956 [17], it will find the rooted tree for the connected weighted graph (V, E). It means that every vertex of the connected network is included in such a way that edge Ei is connected to vertices (Vi, Vj) then the total cost of the spanning tree is represented by C then should be minimum. This means that using Kruskal's algorithm generates the connected network of vertices that form a tree. To implement this algorithm we have to follow two conditions, first is the weight of all edges arranged in ascending order and second is a mesh graph generated among the possible vertices. Then we have to remove all those edges whose weight is largest till we have a cycle. The basic structure of LR-GPSO is represented in Figure 11.1.

11.3.1 Motivation

The minimum spanning tree (MST) problem represents a fundamental challenge in network optimization, finding applications in various fields such as telecommunications, transportation, and resource distribution. The goal is to identify the most efficient and cost-effective tree connecting a set of nodes in a network. Traditional algorithms for solving the MST problem often face challenges in handling complex and dynamic optimization. However, the conventional PSO may not always exhibit the desired convergence and exploration capabilities, especially when dealing with intricate optimization problems like the MST. This motivates the exploration of innovative enhancements to the PSO algorithm to improve its performance.

The introduction of the Leaky Rectified Linear Unit (Leaky ReLU) activation function in the PSO algorithm adds a level of sophistication to the optimization process. Leaky ReLU, commonly used in neural networks, introduces a controlled amount of non-linearity to the algorithm, enhancing its ability to navigate complex landscapes and facilitating better convergence. The "greedy" aspect in the title emphasizes the algorithm's inclination to make locally optimal choices at each step, aligning with the nature of greedy algorithms that iteratively make the best possible decision at each stage. This research aims to investigate the synergy between the Greedy Particle Swarm Optimization Approach and the Leaky ReLU activation function, specifically tailored for solving the minimum spanning tree problem. In summary, the motivation for this research lies in the pursuit of advancing optimization techniques for the MST problem, leveraging the strengths of both Particle Swarm Optimization and the Leaky ReLU function to create a novel and efficient algorithmic approach for solving constraint based minimum spanning tree problem.

11.3.2 Greedy Particle Swarm Optimization Using Leaky ReLU (LR-GPSO)

Particle swarm optimization (PSO) is one of trending optimization technique since last 2 decades because of its simplicity. If members of swam shown there greedy nature for achieving desired goal with the help of Leaky ReLU function then it will become more interesting in terms of results. The integration of this function is anticipated to bring about improvements in convergence speed, quality in solution, and adaptability to diverse MST scenarios. Our proposed Greedy Particle Swarm Optimization approach, coupled with the Leaky ReLU function, presents a promising and innovative solution to the minimum spanning tree problem. The synergy achieved between GPSO and the Leaky ReLU function contributes to the advancement of optimization techniques applicable to graph-based problems. In the context of Greedy Particle Swarm Optimization (GPSO), the Leaky Rectified Linear Unit (Leaky ReLU) function plays a crucial role in influencing the social and cognitive aspects of the algorithm. The social nature of PSO, representing the influence of the global best solution on each particle, and the cognitive nature, representing the influence of each particle's

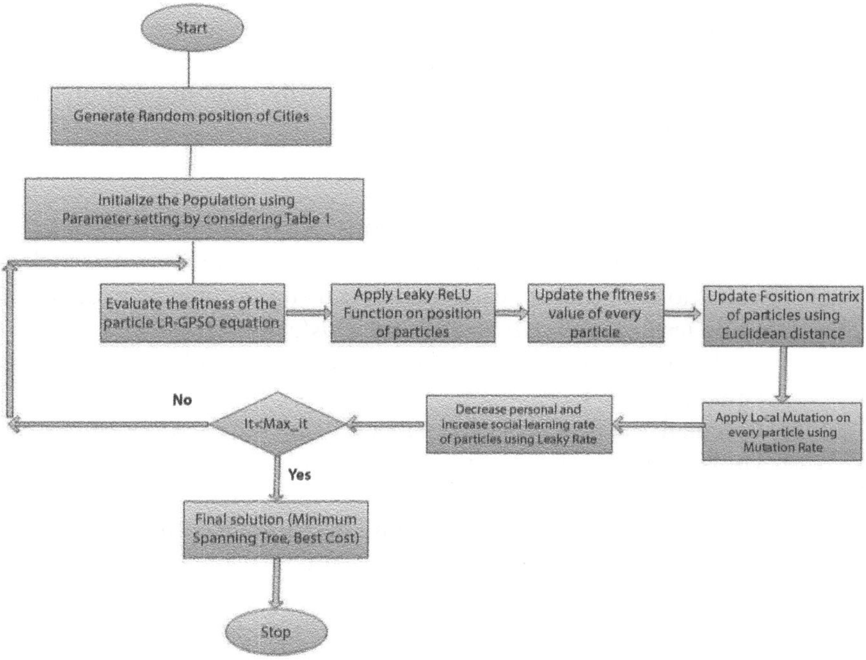

Figure 11.2 Flowchart of LRGPSO.

personal best solution, are affected by the Leaky ReLU function through its impact on the velocity update process. Flowchart of propose approach is represented in Figure 11.2. Whereas below algorithm 1 represents the pseudo code of the proposed LRGPSO algorithm. The synergy achieved by combining the Greedy approach with Particle Swarm Optimization and the Leaky ReLU function was a key strength.

Algorithm 1 The Pseudo code of the proposed LRGPSO
Input: Generate Random Locations in search space= ($\varkappa$1, $\varkappa$ 2, $\varkappa$ 3….. $\varkappa$ n) N : Total Number of particles swarm M : Maximum number of iterations μ : Local Mutation rate α : Leaky Rate c_1, c_2 : Cognitive factor, Social factor w : Inertia weight **Output:** Minimum Spanning tree. Best fitness value over iterations.

Step 1: **begin**
Step 2: Initialize variables and arrays:
- Initialize the members of population with random positions and velocities.
- ` μ `is 0.04 for Local mutation rate.
- ` α ` is 0.017 as Leaky Rate.
- Randomly initialize particle positions `X` within Search Space
- `X` and `v` are the matrices for positions and velocities of particles.

Step 3: Evaluation of fitness of each members using the objective function.
Step 4: **While** *termination criteria does not satisfy* **do**
a) Update the all participating particles velocities and positions using equations 3 & 4.
b) Calculate the fitness of each particle using fitness Algorithm.
c) Update personal best (`Xpb`) and Global best (`Gbest`) if a better fitness is found.
d) Update the global best (`Xgb`) and best among entire population.
e) Update values of parameters (c1, c2, and w) using equations 5, 6 & 7 respectively.
f) Build a minimum spanning tree (MST) based on the configuration of particles
g) Getting information of neighbors of each particle according to the MST
h) Update the velocity and position of each particle using the PSO equations, with the addition of a locally mutation and leaky rate to enhance the exploration of particles.
i) Remove the edge whose weight is max in the MST

Step 5: Generate the updated MST and best cost in obtaining MST
Step 6: **end**

11.3.2.1 Initialization of Parameters

The LR+GPSO starts with the swarm size (N=125) and maximum iteration (Max_iter) is set to be termination criteria, in our case there are four cases is consider when node are 20 then it is 4500 and when it is 40 then it is 6000 iteration, when 60 vertices then it is 7000 and when to total number of vertices is 80 then it is 8000 for achieving accuracy in results. In Table 11.2 we have described the details of parameters in detail.

Table 11.2 Initialization of parameter for simulation.

S. no	Parameter	Value	
1.	Vertices(V), Maximum Iteration (Max_iter)	20	4500
		40	6000
		60	7000
		80	8000
2.	Swarms Size	125	
3.	Leaky Rate (α)	0.17	
4.	Mutation Rate (μ)	0.04	
5.	Cognitive factor	1	
6.	Social Factor	1	
7.	Inertia weight	0.9	
8.	Damping inertia weight	0.95	

11.3.2.2 Population Initialization

Simulation started with initializes a population of particles, where each particle has a position, velocity, cost, and a solution. The position of each particle is randomly generated within specified bounds. These random positions of particles are shown in Figure 11.3(a), Figure 11.4(a), Figure 11.5(a), and Figure 11.6(a).

11.3.2.3 Input

The proposed algorithm take input in the form of random positions generated in which is treated as a vertices for the graph and the connection between two vertices is the edge of the graph and the weight of edges is the distance. So as a result a mesh graph is obtained if the entire vertices id connected with all other vertices which is calculated by the formula (n*(n-1))/2 which is a total number of edges in the graph initially.

11.3.2.4 Evaluation

In this phase, our objective is to determine the optimal solution, represented by the fitness value. A total of 125 particles are initialized in random directions, each undertaking iterative steps guided by the Euclidean distance method to converge toward the optimal solution. The fitness value is computed for each particle, and the one with the lowest value is selected and helps in obtaining the minimum spanning tree, incorporating the Leaky ReLU function to determine the optimal position for the particles.

11.3.2.5 Updating Position of Members of Swarm

The algorithm showcased a robust ability to make locally optimal decisions at each step, aligning well with the nature of the MST problem. The position of particle is calculated using eq. 11.2, which uses eq. 11.1 for calculating the velocity. Movement of Particles are conditional they can only move within the search space so boundary condition is applied. These condition ensures that particles of swarm are stay within the search space. All the members of swarm update the personal best and from this vector global best is selected for further calculations.

$$v_{i,j}(t+1)=\omega^{*}v_{i,j}(\text{last\_iter})+ C_1^{*}(Pbest_{i,j}-X_{i,j}(\text{last\_iter})) + C_2^{*}(Gbest_{i,j} - X_{(i,j)}(\text{last\_iter})) \quad (11.1)$$

$$X_{i,j}(t+1) = X_{i,j}(\text{last\_iter}) + 1/(1+e^{a^{*}i,j(\text{last\_iter}+1)}) \quad (11.2)$$

11.3.2.6 Role of Leaky ReLU Function

The Leaky Rectified Linear Unit (Leaky ReLU) function influences the particle's position adjustments within the Greedy Particle Swarm Optimization (PSO) algorithm. The Leaky ReLU activation is integrated into the velocity update step of the proposed approach, modifying the particle's position based on its current velocity. The Leaky ReLU function is represented by eq. 11.3

$$\text{Leaky ReLU} = 1/1 + (1+e^{a^{*}i,j(t)}) \quad (11.3)$$

where α is a predefined parameter which is represented in Table 11.2. This function introduces a non-linearity that gives a small, non-zero gradient for -ve values of the velocity. The modified position is then utilized in the subsequent steps of the proposed approach, contributing to the exploration and exploitation capabilities of the swarm in navigating the solution space effectively. The incorporation of the Leaky ReLU function enhances the algorithm's adaptability and ability to escape local optima during optimization. This Leaky Rate (α) also influences the cognitive and social nature of the particles by using eq. 11.4 and 11.5 respectively.

$$C_1 = C_1 - \alpha^*(it/Max\_It) \tag{11.4}$$

$$C_2 = C_2 + \alpha^*(it/Max\_It) \tag{11.5}$$

The Leaky ReLU introduces a non-linearity to the velocity updates, ensuring that even negative values of the velocity contribute to the particle's movement. This modification allows for a more flexible exploration of the solution space, as particles with negative velocities retain a small, non-zero influence on the overall movement. Consequently, the Leaky ReLU function enhances the adaptability of the algorithm, influencing both the cognitive learning from individual experiences and the social learning from the best global solution. This adaptability, in turn, aids the swarm in effectively navigating diverse and complex landscapes during the optimization process.

11.3.2.7 Mutation Effect

Mutation plays a crucial role in enhancing the exploration capabilities of the Greedy Particle Swarm Optimization (GPSO) algorithm for solving the minimum spanning tree (MST) problem. Mutation introduces diversity to the particle positions in the Greedy Particle Swarm Optimization (GPSO) algorithm for solving the minimum spanning tree (MST) problem. The mutation operation is expressed mathematically as:

$$Generate\_Member = mutate(member(current\_iter).X_{(current)}, \mu)$$

Here, Generate_Member representes the mutated particle, member(current_iter).$X_{(current)}$ is the current position of member of swarm and μ denotes the mutation rate. The mutate function perturbs the current position, contributing to exploration.

The acceptance criterion for the mutated particle is governed by the following logic:

if Generate_Member.cost ≤ member(current_iter).cost

$$\text{member(current\_iter)} = \text{Generate\_Member}$$

from the above logic it will ensures that the new position is accepted if it leads to a lower cost promoting exploration. The mutation mechanism aids the algorithm in escaping local optima and diversifying the search for an optimal minimum spanning tree.

In each mutation, a new particle is generated by altering the position of the current particle using the Mutate function. This mutated particle is then evaluated, and if its cost is lower than or equal to the original particle's cost or a random probability condition is met, the original particle is updated with the mutated particle. This mechanism allows the algorithm to explore new regions of the solution space, potentially overcoming local optima and contributing to the algorithm's ability to discover better solutions during the optimization process.

11.3.2.8 Selection of Edges

The determination of edges is contingent upon the binary vector representation of particle positions, where each element signifies the inclusion (1) or exclusion (0) of the respective edge in the potential spanning tree. This decision-making process occurs after computing the distance between two vertices using the Euclidean distance method. Within the Particle Swarm Optimization (PSO) framework, the Leaky ReLU activation function shapes the particle's positional adjustments by influencing its velocity during the update phase. This introduces non-linearity, enabling negative velocities to contribute to the particle's motion. Consequently, the adapted position, under the influence of Leaky ReLU, directs the particle's exploration within the solution space. In the specific context of minimum spanning trees, the binary nature of the particle's position vector inherently translates into an edge selection mechanism for the graph. Edges associated with positions surpassing a predefined threshold (0.5 in this instance) are considered for inclusion in the potential spanning tree, while those below the threshold are excluded from consideration.

11.3.2.9 Output

Through the Leaky ReLU-influenced PSO algorithm, the selection of edges dynamically evolves over iterations, with particles collectively exploring and converging towards optimal solutions, effectively determining the edges that constitute the minimum spanning tree for the given graph. Greedy Particle Swarm Optimization Approach Using Leaky ReLU Function for minimum spanning tree problem, our innovative methodology, which integrates Greedy Particle Swarm Optimization (GPSO) with the Leaky Rectified Linear Unit (ReLU) function, proves to be a novel and impactful solution to the MST problem. The GPSO algorithm, inspired by collective behaviors observed in nature, efficiently explores solution spaces and identifies optimal solutions, forming the foundational element of our approach.

11.4 Experimental Setup and Result Analysis of Proposed Work (LR-GPSO)

The goal is to check the performance of LRGPSO in comparison to Canonical PSO [11], FA [18], and ICA [21] on the chosen four cases of vertices. All the cases are described in Table 11.2 in which a termination criteria and mutation rate is described for the proposed strategy. The selection of parameters is performed while consideration of search space among the cases is same. The behavior of convergence toward the goal is dependent population size is 125 in all cases whereas Leaky rate is 0.17. Serving as the activation function in the GPSO process, the Leaky ReLU function facilitates a balanced interplay between exploration and exploitation, leading to a more efficient search for the minimum spanning tree. The variations in vertices and maximum iterations indicate an exploration of different settings for the optimization process, while the remaining parameters establish constants governing the behavior of the algorithm throughout these iterations. The values are chosen to strike a balance between exploration and exploitation, guiding the particles in the search space towards an optimal solution.

11.4.1 Complexity

The complexity of the proposed approach is multifaceted, involving both time and spatial considerations, with the number of iterations, the Leaky ReLU activation, and the intricacies of the cost function playing crucial roles in determining the overall computational demands of the algorithm. The running time of proposed approach is how much time to execute or mathematical computation required to run till maximum iteration which is denoted the Table 11.2 as a Max_Iter for different cases as a termination condition. In updating of position and velocity of particles in the basic PSO is α times of the Vertices(V) X Number of members(M) multiplication factor of every iteration. Implementing the proposed approach its time and space complexity is lesser than ($<=6\alpha VM$) to the basic PSO. the complexity of the instances increases with the number of vertices and labels of the graph(G). Which is also an achievement in terms of the analysis of the result. Where 6 is because of the mutation in every iteration of particles.

11.4.2 Simulation Experiments

The effectiveness of the proposed strategy is assessed by examining the minimum achieved value, the mean, and the standard deviation across 30 independent runs. These results are detailed in Table 11.3, where each independent run corresponds to different use cases. Specifically, we consider a total of four cases. In Case 1:, with 20 vertices, the termination criterion is set to a maximum of 4500 iterations. Moving to Case 2:, where vertices are increased to 40, the termination criterion extends to 6000 iterations. Case 3: involves 60 vertices with a maximum iteration limit of 7000, and Case 4: features 80 vertices with a termination criterion of 8000 iterations. In all cases, the initial graph comprises (V*(V-1))/2 vertices. Table 11.2 provides a comprehensive overview of the parameter settings for each case, outlining the specific configurations applied during the evaluation of the proposed strategy across diverse scenarios.

11.4.2.1 Result for Vertices (V=20)

Figure 11.3 shows the result obtained for Case 1: (V=20), maximum iteration is set to 4500, whereas Figure 11.3(a) shows scatter plot for vertices =20. Figure 11.3(b) shows the minimum spanning tree corresponding to scatter plot.

11.4.2.2 Result for Vertices (V=40)

Figure 11.4 shows the result obtained for Case 2: (V=40), maximum iteration is set to 6000, whereas Figure 11.4(a) shows scatter plot for vertices =40. Figure 11.4(b) shows the minimum spanning tree corresponding to scatter plot.

Table 11.3 Mean value, minimum value and standard deviation of algorithms on various cases.

S. no.	No of nodes	Max iteration	Parameter	PSO	FA	ICA	LRGPSO
1	V=20	4500	Min	825.6717946	924.5569849	879.7705875	1223.910442
			Mean	1189.170785	993.6723276	1066.895956	1606.094291
			Std. Deviation	506.0640711	272.9610607	555.4303138	549.5579674
2	V=40	6000	Min	2205.660493	4605.597872	2021.245084	16521.94087
			Mean	4423.997752	4697.128222	3404.724471	19390.07559
			Std. Deviation	4828.83202	1304.605877	4385.378713	2685.861259
3	V=20	7000	Min	2784.975824	16875.57411	4377.541696	65142.6101
			Mean	13235.93513	17279.55599	10826.03629	69328.32754
			Std. Deviation	18942.25628	4043.333583	15176.18856	4968.532704
4	V=20	8000	Min	3573.646037	51379.95472	6915.569224	128821.9894
			Mean	28270.31069	52144.37594	26234.32977	134594.1715
			Std. Deviation	35635.30628	6276.296081	29717.24217	6524.8044

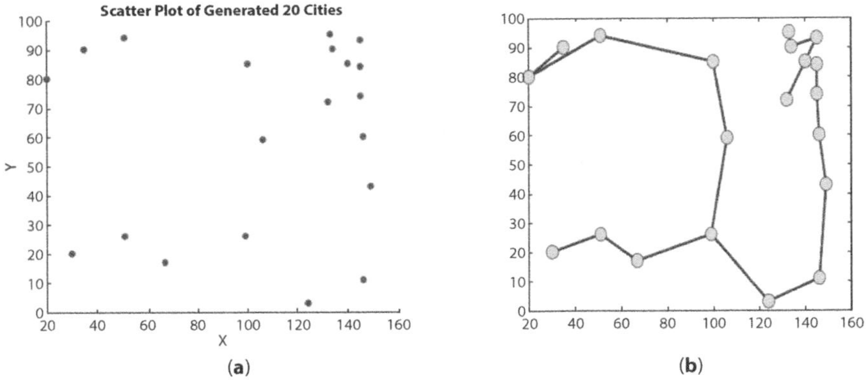

Figure 11.3 Results of simulation on vertices (V=20).

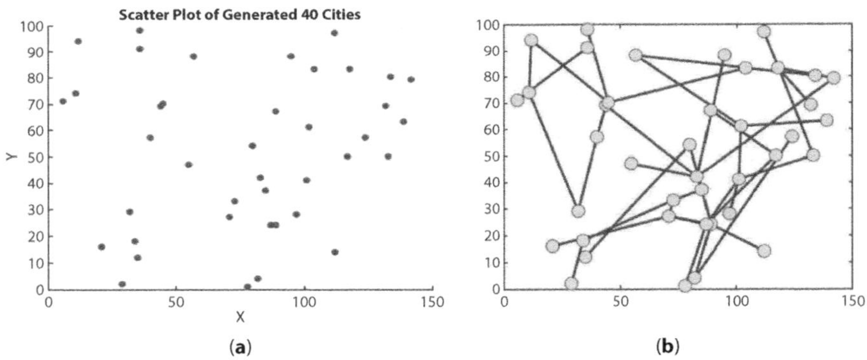

Figure 11.4 Results of simulation on vertices (V=40).

11.4.2.3 Result for Vertices (V=60)

Figure 11.5 shows the result obtained for Case 3: (V=60), maximum iteration is set to 7000, whereas Figure 11.5(a) shows scatter plot for vertices =60, Figure 11.5(b) shows the minimum spanning tree corresponding to scatter plot.

11.4.2.4 Result for Vertices (V=80)

Figure 11.6 shows the result obtained for Case 4: (V=80), maximum iteration is set to 8000, whereas Figure 11.6(a) shows scatter plot for vertices =80, Figure 11.6(b) shows the minimum spanning tree corresponding to scatter plot.

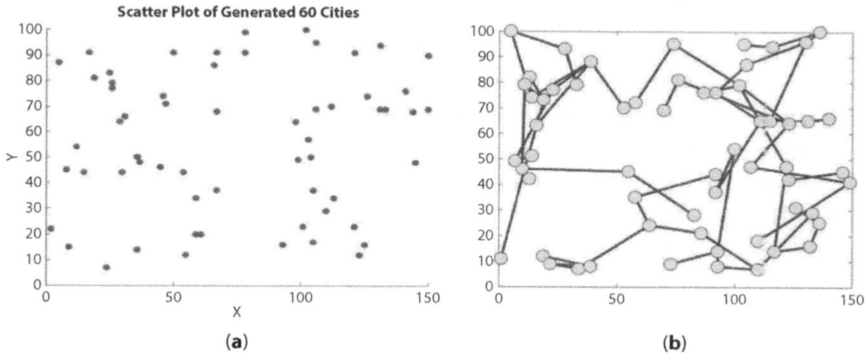

Figure 11.5 Results of simulation on vertices (V=60).

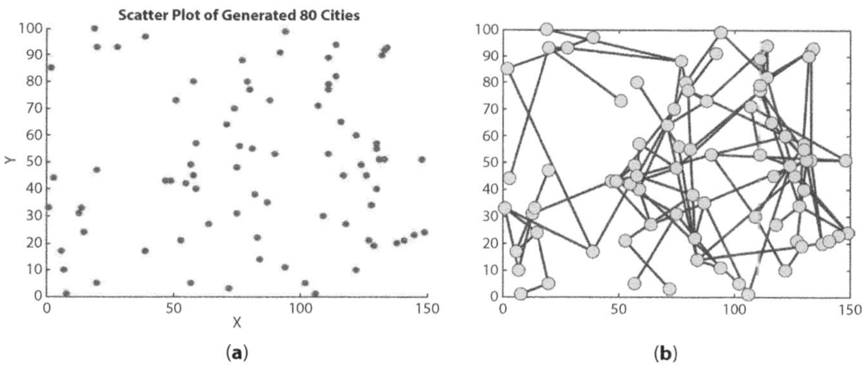

Figure 11.6 Results of simulation on vertices (V=80).

11.4.3 Convergence Curve

A convergence curve is a graphical representation depicting the evolution of an iterative process over successive iterations. This curve is also used in our proposed approach, it illustrates the convergence of an objective function, as the algorithm progresses. A well-behaved convergence curve exhibits a consistent trend, demonstrating the algorithm's efficiency and progress toward an optimal solution. Analyzing this curve provides valuable insights into the algorithm's performance, in fine-tuning parameters, identifying convergence rates, and ensuring the efficacy of iterative processes in various domains.

Figure 11.7 shows the result obtained for convergence curve from all the cases we have tested for obtaining minimum spanning tree. Figure 11.7(a) shows the convergence curve for vertex (V=20) in which we termination criteria is set to maximum iteration is 4500. Figure 11.7(b) shows the convergence curve for vertex (V=40) in which we termination criteria is set to maximum iteration is 6000. Figure 11.7(c) shows the convergence curve for vertex (V=60) in which we termination criteria is set to maximum iteration is 7000. Figure 11.7(d) shows the convergence curve for vertex (V=80) in which we termination criteria is set to maximum iteration is 8000. After analyzing the above convergence curve, it is clearly visible that PSO is one of the oldest techniques among the other algorithms but still it is showing comparative result in comparison the latest optimization technique after performing some modification in it.

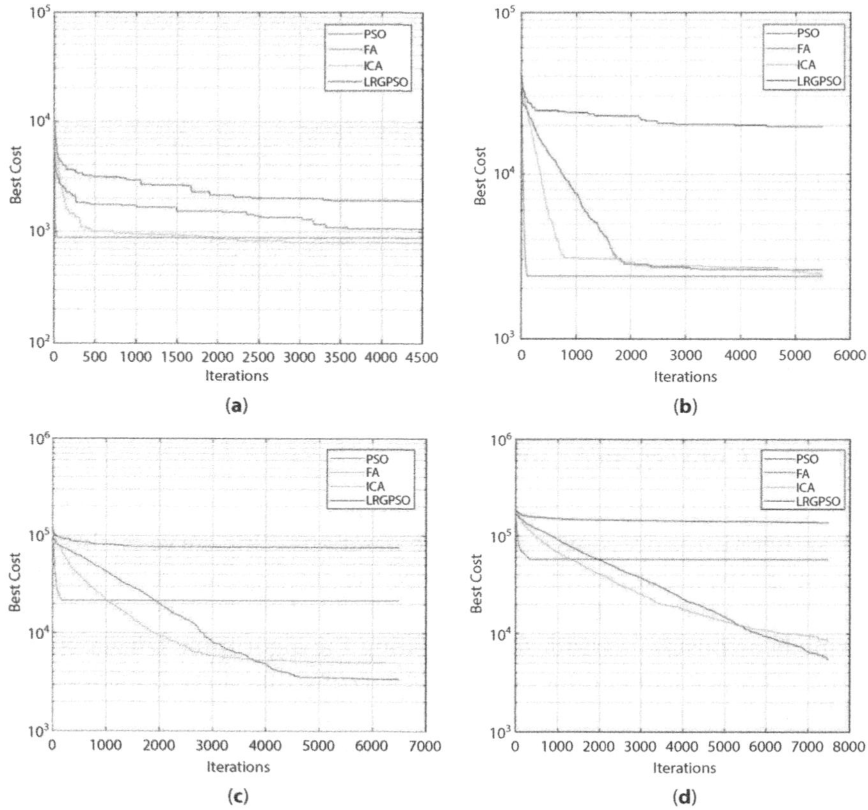

Figure 11.7 Convergence curve.

11.5 Conclusion and Future Work

The incorporation of the Leaky ReLU function demonstrated its effectiveness in introducing non-linearity to the PSO algorithm. This non-linearity contributed to enhanced exploration capabilities, allowing the algorithm to navigate intricate solution spaces with greater efficiency. The Greedy Particle Swarm Optimization Approach, coupled with the Leaky ReLU function, exhibited notable adaptability to various instances of the minimum spanning tree problem. In concluding our investigation into the "Greedy Particle Swarm Optimization Approach Using Leaky ReLU Function for minimum spanning tree Problem," the findings substantiate the effectiveness of our innovative methodology in addressing this critical optimization challenge. The integration of the Greedy Particle Swarm Optimization (GPSO) with the Leaky Rectified Linear Unit (ReLU) function represents a novel and impactful approach to tackling the minimum spanning tree (MST) problem. Our LRGPSO, inspired by collective behaviors observed in nature, exhibits a remarkable ability to efficiently explore solution spaces and identify optimal solutions. This forms the foundational element of our proposed methodology.

The augmentation of GPSO with the Leaky ReLU function, a recently introduced activation function with promising qualities for optimization tasks, has proven to be a significant catalyst for enhancing the algorithm's performance. The Leaky ReLU function, serving as the activation function in the particle swarm optimization process, fosters a balanced interplay between exploration and exploitation, facilitating a more efficient search for the minimum spanning tree. The reason behind the selection Leaky ReLU function is the "dying ReLU" problem, where neurons can become inactive during training.

Our study offers a comprehensive analysis, encompassing detailed algorithmic descriptions, parameter configurations, and rigorous experimental results conducted on randomly generated instances of the MST problem with varying node counts. In essence, with potential implications across diverse real-world scenarios. This research not only adds to the academic discourse on optimization methodologies but also paves the way for practical applications in fields such as network design, transportation, and logistics. The augmentation of GPSO with the Leaky ReLU function, a recently introduced activation function with promising optimization qualities, significantly enhances the algorithm's performance. In essence, our Greedy Particle Swarm Optimization approach, coupled with the Leaky ReLU function, presents a promising and innovative solution to the minimum spanning tree problem. The result obtained during the simulation is briefly shown in the above sections and found not only promising and comparative results but also holds promise for practical applications in fields such as network design, transportation, and logistics. As a future scope of this work, it could involve parameter tuning, scalability analyses, and extensions to handle additional constraints or variations within the MST problem. Hybridization of PSO with another optimization algorithm could be interesting.

References

1. Han, J., Pei, J., Kember, M., *Data Mining: Concepts and Techniques*, Elsevier, Netherlands, 2011.
2. Zhong, C., Chen, Y., Peng, J., Feature Selection Based on a Novel Improved Tree Growth Algorithm. *Int. J. Comput. Intell. Syst.*, 13, 247–258, 2020.
3. Xue, B., Zhang, M., Browne, W.N., Yao, X., A survey on evolutionary computation approaches to feature selection. *IEEE Trans. Evol. Comput.*, 20, 606–626, 2016.
4. Kritikos, M. and Ioannou, G., Greedy heuristic for the capacitated minimum spanning tree problem. *J. Oper. Res. Soc.*, 68, 1223–1235, 2017.
5. Skiscim, C. and Palocsay, S., Minimum Spanning Trees with Sums of Ratios. *J. Global Optim.*, 19, 103–120, 2001.
6. Graham, R.L. and Hell, P., On the History of the Minimum Spanning Tree Problem. *Ann. Hist. Comput.*, 7, 1, 43–57, January.-March 1985.
7. Bruggemann, T., Monnot, J., Woeginger, G.J., Local search for the minimum label spanning tree problem with bounded color classes. *Oper. Res. Lett.*, 31, 195–201, 2003.
8. Vijayalakshmi, K. and Martin Leo Manickam, J., Mobile data gathering using PSO and minimum covering spanning tree clustered WSN. *Int. J. Mobile Netw. Des. Innov.*, 8, 101, 2018.
9. Stojanovic, B., Rajic, T., Sosic, D., Distribution network reconfiguration and reactive power compensation using a hybrid Simulated Annealing – Minimum spanning tree algorithm. *Int. J. Electr. Power Energy Syst.*, 147, 108829, 1–14, 2023, ISSN 0142-0615.
10. del Valle, Y., Venayagamoorthy, G.K., Mohagheghi, S., Hernandez, J.-C., Harley, R.G., Particle swarm optimization: Basic concepts, variants and applications in power systems. *IEEE Trans. Evol. Comput.*, 12, 2, 171–195, Apr. 2008.
11. Eberhart, R.C. and Kennedy, J., A new optimizer using particle swarm theory, in: *Proc. 6th Int. Symp. Micromach. Human Sci.*, vol. 1, pp. 39–43, Mar. 1995.

12. Qu, B.Y., Suganthan, P.N., Das, A distance-based locally informed particle swarm model for multi-modal optimization. *IEEE Trans. Evol. Comput.*, 17, 3, 387–402, Jun. 2013.
13. Majumder, S., Barma, P.S., Biswas, A., Banerjee, P., Mandal, B.K., Kar, S., Ziemba, P., On Multi-Objective Minimum Spanning Tree Problem under Uncertain Paradigm. *Symmetry*, 14, 1, 106, 2022.
14. Nayef, B.H., Abdullah, S.N.H.S., Sulaiman, R., Optimized leaky ReLU for handwritten Arabic character recognition using convolution neural networks. *Multimed. Tools Appl.*, 81, 2065–2094, 2022.
15. Mosbah, M., Arif, S., Mohammedi, R.D., Hellal, A., Optimum dynamic distribution network reconfiguration using minimum spanning tree algorithm. *5th International Conference on Electrical Engineering - Boumerdes (ICEE-B)*, Boumerdes, Algeria, vol. 2017, pp. 1–6, 2017.
16. Das, D., A fuzzy multiobjective approach for network reconfiguration of distribution systems. *IEEE Trans. Power Deliv.*, 21, 202–209, January 2006.
17. Bertsimas, D.J., The probabilistic minimum spanning tree problem. *Networks Int. J.*, 20, 245–275, May 1990.
18. Lin, M., Liu, F., Zhao, H., Chen, J., A Novel Binary Firefly Algorithm for the Minimum Labeling Spanning Tree Problem. *CMES-Comp. Model. Eng. Sci.*, 125, 1, 197–214, 2020.
19. Graham, R.L. and Hell, P., On the history of the minimum spanning tree problem. *Ann. Hist. Comput.*, 7, 1, 43–57, 1985.
20. Frederickson, G.N. and Solis-Oba, R., Increasing the weight of minimum spanning trees. *J. Algorithms*, 33, 2, 244–266, 1999.
21. Hosseini, S.M., Khaled, A.A., Jin, M., Solving Euclidean minimal spanning tree problem using a new meta-heuristic approach: imperialist competitive algorithm (ICA), in: *2012 IEEE International Conference on Industrial Engineering and Engineering Management*, IEEE, pp. 176–181, 2013.
22. Yang, X.S. and He, X., Firefly algorithm: recent advances and applications. *Int. J. Swarm Intell.*, 1, 1, 36–50, 2013.

12

SDN Deployed Secure Application Design Framework for IoT Using Game Theory

Madhukrishna Priyadarsini[1]* and Padmalochan Bera[2]

[1]*National Institute of Technology Raipur, Chhattisgarh, India*
[2]*Indian Institute of Technology Bhubaneswar, Odisha, India*

Abstract

The Internet of the future is software-defined networks (SDNs), which offer an evolving platform by enabling flexible reconfiguration of the network by isolating controllers and forwarding devices (switches, routers). SDN is implemented as the backbone of many real-life implications due to its capabilities of efficient traffic management, load balancing, and centralized control with dynamic reconfiguration. The Internet of Things (IoT) integrates sensors, actuators, communication systems, and cloud servers for effective and energy-efficient implementations of applications. However, ubiquitous communication systems and heterogeneous device integration make IoT systems vulnerable to end-to-end security violations. Therefore, the SDN platform and Game Theory can be used for designing efficient solutions to provide end-to-end security in the IoT environment. We introduce an SDN-deployed IoT design approach in this chapter that makes use of game-theoretic solutions. The SDN controller supports network function virtualization, which is responsible for handling different network functions in communication software and in the cloud environment of IoT. The major objective of our framework is to provide security to the hardware, software modules, the cloud environment, and the traffic flow among the different layers of the IoT. To create a framework that offers end-to-end security and accurately handles traffic among the various IoT layers, we employ a signaling game technique. The above claim is supported by a real-time case study in the robot manufacturing industry.

***Keywords*:** SDN, IoT, game theory, end-to-end security, efficiency

**Corresponding author*: priyadarsini@nitt.edu

Mohit Kumar, Gautam Srivastava, Ashutosh Kumar Singh and Kalka Dubey (eds.) AI-Based Advanced Optimization Techniques for Edge Computing, (317–340) © 2025 Scrivener Publishing LLC

12.1 Introduction

The ability to make judgments based on information gathered from the environment makes the Internet of Things (IoT) the most significant technological advancement of the 21st century. It can save lives in medical emergencies, help people live and work smarter, and achieve goals without manual intervention as it allows the collection of heterogeneous data from the surroundings for real-time processing and intelligent decision-making. The collected data from the surroundings is forwarded to the cloud for further processing using the underlying communication software [1]. Security enforcement in an IoT environment is very important as the functioning of IoT (applications) involves different hardware, software, and embedded devices. Software-defined Networking (SDN) platform is best suited for providing effective security to the IoT environment as it supports network function virtualization and dynamic programmability [2]. In state-of-the-art research, SDN is already implemented for providing security to cloud, fog, submarine networks, etc. Game theory is a branch of economics that is used in any social life problem to find the best solution considering the constraints. Game Theory can be implemented to provide end-to-end security for IoT which takes IoT users and the different levels of IoT as different players of the game and evaluates their behaviors through different actions for identifying attackers and legitimate users in real-time [3]. In this chapter, we present an SDN and Game Theory integrated end-to-end security enforcement framework for an IoT environment.

We now give a quick summary of the game theory, SDN, and IoT concepts that form the foundation of this chapter.

12.1.1 IoT Overview

The Internet of Things (IoT) is a network of physical items, or "things," that can exchange and transmit data with other systems and devices via the Internet thanks to the integration of sensors, software, and other technologies. These devices could be anything from basic household objects to more sophisticated industrial machinery. By 2025, experts estimate there will be 22 billion connected IoT devices [1].

The IoT architecture is having three layers; the "things" layer (lower layer) collects the data from the surroundings, the "communication networks" layer (middle layer) forwards the collected data to the cloud for storing and further processing using the communication protocols, and finally the "applications" layer (upper layer) is applying data analytic tools

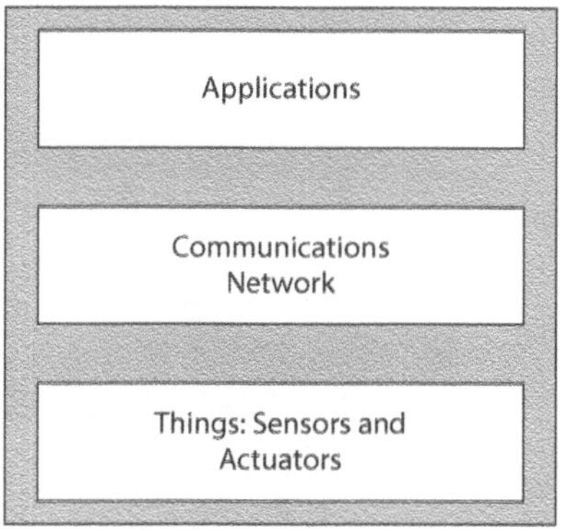

Figure 12.1 Simplified IoT architecture consists of three different layers.

for processing the data [1, 4]. Figure 12.1 shows the simplified architecture of the IoT with three layers. In this 3-layered architecture, security attacks can happen in any of the layers, and as one of its implementation areas is the healthcare domain, it is really important to provide end-to-end security to the IoT architecture.

12.1.2 SDN Overview

The goal of a Software-defined network (SDN) is to create networks that are more economical and flexible. The fundamental design of the old network is more complicated and decentralized, as SDN has highlighted. On the other hand, the current network requires a simpler troubleshooting alternative together with a more adaptable architecture. Software-defined networking proposes to centralize network intelligence by decoupling the routing method (control plane) from the forwarding of network packets (data plane). Figure 12.2 shows the architecture of SDN, with three layers. The network devices used for traffic/data forwarding are part of the *infrastructure layer*, often known as the data plane. The data plane's primary duties are data forwarding, data dumping and replication, flow statistic collection, and local network information monitoring. The forwarding plane is programmed and managed by the *control layer*, also known as the control plane. This layer contains the logic, techniques, and protocols necessary to program the forwarding plane. Many of these algorithms and protocols require a thorough knowledge of the network. The control plane makes decisions on forwarding rules and data plane programming. The *application layer* contains network applications that can help the control layer configure the network or offer new features like security

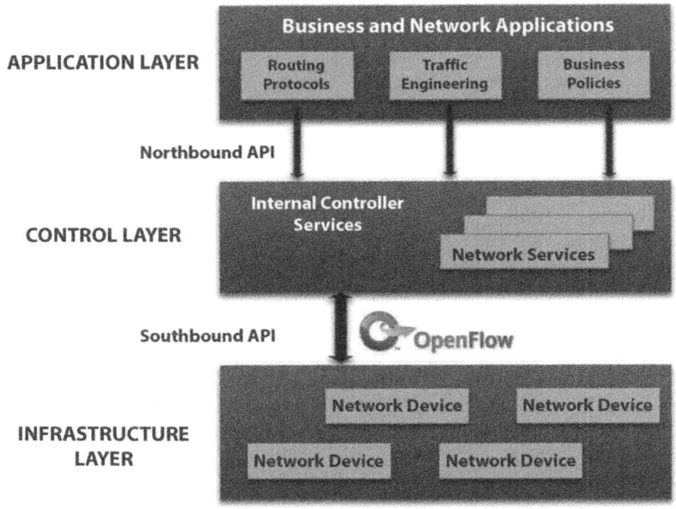

Figure 12.2 The three levels that make up SDN architecture are reachable via open API.

and manageability, forwarding schemes, and so on. The application layer provides useful guidance and feedback to the control layer in the form of application policies and rules. The interface between the application layer and the control layer is referred to as a "northbound interface."

The controller can ascertain the path taken by network packets over the network of switches (data plane) thanks to the OpenFlow architecture [5]. It uses a single OpenFlow protocol to handle switches with various setups and parameters from many suppliers. An OpenFlow switch forwards the data packet that belongs to its hosts by using the flow rules listed in its flow table. The three main fields that comprise the flow table are the header, actions, and counter (expiration timer) [5]. A packet is handled according to the appropriate stages if its header satisfies one or more flow table criteria. The matching packet header information is delivered to the controller as a *Packet-IN* event if the packet header and flow table do not match. The controller then creates flow rules for this *Packet-IN* request by applying all current control functions. Finally, this flow rule is received by the underlying switch, which stores it in its flow table for further processing. Numerous widely used open-source controllers exist, including Beacon [6], Floodlight [7], OpenDayLight [8], Ryu [9], NOX [10], and POX. Our suggested framework is implemented and evaluated using the OpenDay-Light controller because of its unique features, which include a user-friendly GUI, rich APIs, multi-protocol implementation, modular architecture, and support for the southbound interface. Our suggested structure, meanwhile, can also be integrated with different controllers.

12.1.3 Game Theory Overview

To resolve social issues involving rival players, game theory provides a theoretical framework. The game, as a model of an interaction situation among rational participants, is the central subject of game theory [3]. Because one player's reward depends on the other player's strategy, this is the fundamental idea of game theory. According to [11], the game determines the identities, preferences, and available strategies of the players as well as how these strategies impact the result. Various conditions or presumptions might be required, depending on the model. Many fields, including psychology, evolutionary biology, politics, war, computer science, economics, and business, have used game theory [12]. Game theory can be used to ascertain the most likely outcomes in any scenario with two or more participants and known payouts or quantifiable effects [11]. A few terms frequently used in game theory research are listed below:

- **Game:** Any combination of conditions where the outcome depends on the choices made by two or more players, or decision-makers.
- **Player:** A person who makes strategic decisions in the context of games.
- **Strategy:** A detailed plan of action that a player will implement if unforeseen situations occur during gameplay.
- **Payoff:** The payout a player is compensated for reaching a specific conclusion.
- **Information Set:** The information is accessible at a specific moment throughout the game.
- **Equilibrium:** When both players have made their choices and a decision has been made in a game.

There are different types of games are present such as zero-sum, non-zero-sum, cooperative, non-cooperative, one-shot, repeated games, etc. Here, in this chapter, we have considered the signaling game which is a type of zero-sum game. The game is played between the edge device (mostly inside sensors), and the communication layer (where the SDN controller is implemented). The result of the game is the secure processing of the data inside the Cloud.

The major objectives of this chapter are:

1. To identify the security challenges in the IoT environment.
2. To design an SDN-deployed framework using Game-theoretic solutions that provide end-to-end security to IoT.
3. To implement the designed framework in the real-time IoT environment that is the robot manufacturing industry.
4. To discuss the proposed framework's usability, extensibility, and limitations.

The rest of the chapter is organized as follows: section 12.2 presents the background literature on IoT security using SDN and game theory. The proposed SDN-deployed design framework for IoT using game-theoretic solutions is discussed in section 12.3. The framework implementation in the real-time robot manufacturing industry is presented in section 12.4. In section 12.5, we discuss our proposed work, which contains extensibility, usability, and limitations. Finally, we conclude in section 12.6 with future research directions.

12.2 Background Study

In this section, we present state-of-the-art research on IoT security using SDN. Subsequently, we discuss related works on IoT security using game theory.

12.2.1 IoT Security Using SDN

IoT commonly uses Internet technology to establish communication among multiple devices, thus inheriting the specific threats to the resource-constrained IoT devices. Due to the implementation of network function virtualization, Software-defined networking (SDN) is the way to secure IoT networks from emerging threats as well as to control and configure the sensors from a centralized location. In the paper [13], the authors presented an SDN architecture in the IoT environment that detects external and internal attacks by detecting undesirable flow by Snort. Authors in paper [14], proposed a secured data-sharing system in IoT devices using encryption. The proposed technique only prevents botnet attacks. Research work in paper [15], highlighted the benefits of using SDN for IoT security in terms of DDoS attacks. Paper [16] proposed an SDN-based system model for IoT Security, where the focus is to mitigate man-in-the-middle attacks. The authors in [17], proposed an SDN-based intelligent security solution for IoT which aims to detect and mitigate intrusion in the IoT environment. From the above research works, we find multiple shortcomings that are noted down as follows;

5. To the best of our knowledge, none of these researches address multiple attack types, their attack surfaces, and the countermeasures.
6. Existing research does not report coordinated attacks, where a single attack is done from multiple external devices simultaneously.
7. There is no research reported on the end-to-end security of the IoT environment.

12.2.2 IoT Security Using Game Theory

We studied different research directions on providing security to the IoT environment using game-theoretic solutions. Some of the important research works are discussed in this subsection. In paper [18], a survey on various game models is given on different types of attacks such as DDoS, man-in-the-middle, and honeypot. However, the game models are different for each attack type. Research in [19] implemented a Bayesian game to prevent link flooding attack (LFA) whose target is only to secure the communication links but not the devices attached to the link. The authors in [20], detected malware attacks in the device-to-device networks (D2D) and proposed a secure energy-efficient routing protocol that aims to find the malware attached to the messages coming to the device. Here, internal attacks are not considered. Research work in [21] used game theory for the correct placement of IDS in a moving target defense (MTD) scenario. Here, the Stackelberg game is played between the cloud administrator and the user and finds the optimal strategy for IDS placement. Authors in [22], proposed a stochastic game model where botnet propagation is mitigated in the IoT network. However, multiple device infection at the same time is not considered. Papers [23–25] highlighted different application areas of IoT where multiple games are used to make decisions such as activity monitoring defense personnel, automated employee performance evaluation, IoT transportation, and Fog networks. Our observations from the state-of-the-art research are mentioned as follows;

8. As far as we are aware, no research has taken into account how to prevent repeated attacks.
9. These research works do not consider multiple games at the same time.

In the following section, we provide a signaling game model-based SDN-deployed architecture that addresses the aforementioned drawbacks and offers end-to-end security in an IoT context.

12.3 SDN-Deployed Design Framework for IoT Using Game-Theoretic Solutions

Here, we use game-theoretic solutions to introduce our proposed SDN-deployed IoT design framework. The suggested framework's overall design and the data flow between its many layers are depicted in Figure 12.3. Utilizing the SDN controller, our framework is developed and implemented at both the application and communication network layers. Before sending the incoming data and traffic to the following layer for additional processing, the SDN controller creates flow rules for them. Due to the network function virtualization and dynamic programmability capacity, it is one of the best solutions to implement for IoT functionalities. The following is a description of how our framework operates; the sensors (S_1, S_2, ..., S_n) present in the "things" layer collect data from the environment and forward it to the "communication network" layer. The collected data is first tested by our designed framework using the signaling game model, where the trustworthiness of the data is calculated, and if it is trusted then using the communication modules (various communication protocols of the IoT) forwarded to the "application" layer. In the application layer, further actions are taken by the cloud environment (either storage or processing). Our designed framework consists of a module named "Trust verification", where we implement the signaling game model. The detailed workflow of the signaling game model is presented in the subsequent subsection.

12.3.1 Trust Verification

Here, we present our designed signaling game model, considering the constraints of the IoT and SDN environment. Game theory helps to find out the legitimate data flow and the malicious data flow in the run time which avoids multiple attacks such as sniffing, tampering, repudiation,

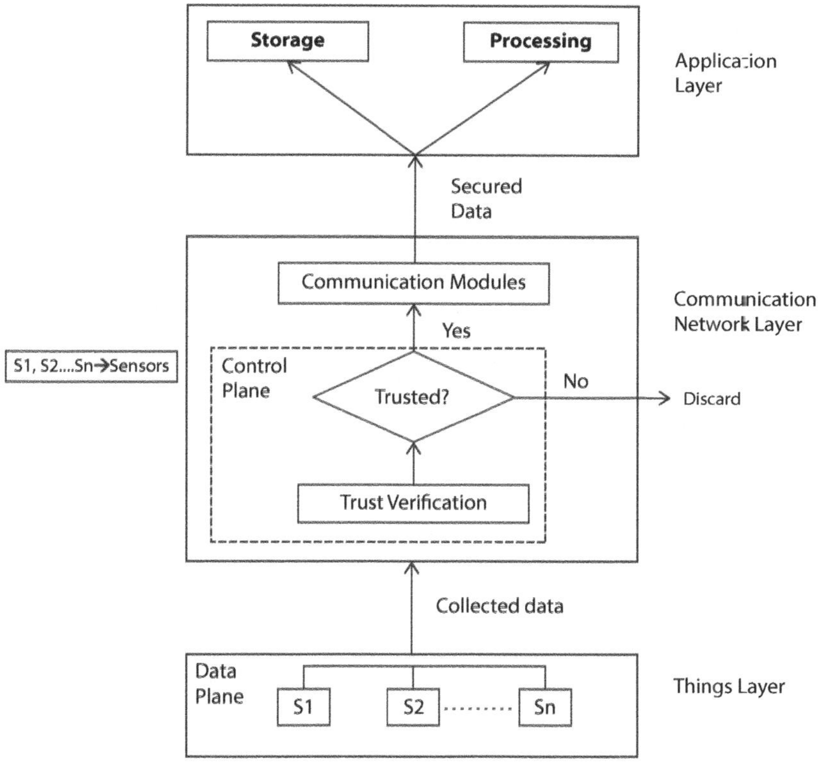

Figure 12.3 Proposed SDN-deployed design framework for IoT.

information disclosure, DoS, elevation of privilege, and other attacks related to IoT, Cloud, and SDN environment. The game is played between a sensor and the SDN controller as two players. Multiple signaling games of the same kind are played simultaneously if multiple sensors give data to a single controller at the same time. Our game begins with the sensors sending data to the SDN controller, which dynamically assesses each data packet's trustworthiness using various stratification schemes used by the adversary. Figure 12.4 shows a generalized signaling game model. It looks like two connected trees, with the player's impression of the sort of opponent and the actions they can perform as branches and roots, respectively. The next subsections describe the techniques of the SDN controller (target) and the sensor (sender). After that, we explain how the controller's belief about the sensor is dynamically updated, and finally, we calculate the payoffs needed to take the right actions.

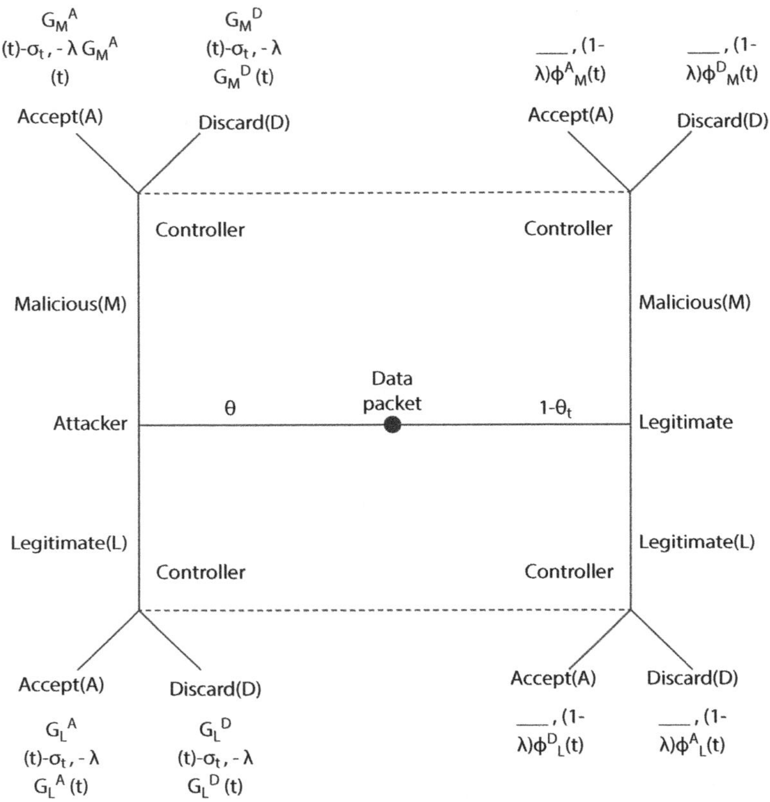

Figure 12.4 The controller's representation of the trust computation. An intruding sensor attempts to alter both the connection protocol and the data gathered. In this case, the controller's belief is denoted by θt, while its uncertainty regarding the type of sensor is indicated by dashed lines. The controller computes payment values while keeping an eye on the actions of the sensor, such as *Legitimate*(*L*) or *Malicious*(*M*). Leaf nodes represent the controller's actions (i.e., *Accept*(*A*) and *Discard*(*D*)) and the payoffs.

Signaling game model – strategy discussion: Our signaling game model for IoT is described among the sensor and the SDN controller as one game. The game is played between the "things" layer and the "communication network" layer. The sensor (present in the Things layer) collects data from the environment and sends it to the communication network layer for further processing. The attackers try to manipulate the sensor data and get access to the communication protocols and the cloud storage space and processing mechanisms. Now onwards, we use the terms application layer and the Cloud alternatively.

In the signaling game model, a trust-calculation concept is introduced to prevent access provision for attackers in the communication network layer by the SDN controller. Every incoming data request packet is given a trust value by the controller, which then proceeds to take appropriate action, such as sending the data to the cloud for additional processing. The trust value of a sensor(sender) is the belief (θ_t) that varies dynamically. In the rest of the chapter, we alternatively use the terms sensor and sender.

Behaviour of Sender: We consider it that the attacker initiates a particular attack and obtains the needed data in less time than a predetermined window, T_S. The maximum time to access information about the communicadtion protocol is T_S in this case. The length of time the attack procedure lasts is indicated by the parameter $T_{S'}$. The sender, $S_{s'}$, ∈ {*Malicious, Legitimate*}. Let us now characterize the sender's actions. As an attacker, the sender who engages in *Malicious* play aims to obtain knowledge about the communication protocol at the communication network layer. Conversely, while employing a *Legitimate* method, the sender does not adhere to any particular order. When the genuine sender fulfills its assigned duty, its expected conduct is legitimate. There can be instances where it acts malevolently. The legitimate sender and attacker's predicted gains are used as G^L and G^A, respectively, in the game specification. The average potential gain G is defined as follows: $G^L \leq G \leq G^A$. Table 12.1 provides an overview of the parameters utilized in the suggested game model.

We can now define our harmful and legitimate activity game model. Assuming a uniform distribution, the probability of two senders accessing the same communication information consecutively, given a set of N senders, is $1/N$. If the association with another sender is larger than $1/N$, malicious activity is identified. We presume that information about the communication information is gained by consecutive access. At an access attempt t, we quantify this gain in terms of ϕ, where ϕ_t compounds to the observed behavior of any sender at that attempt. The expected behavior from a valid sender is defined as ϕ^L, and it can be determined as follows:

$$\phi^{tL} = \underset{i=1}{\mathbf{I}^t:} \quad 1N \tag{12.1}$$

If $\phi_t > \phi^L$, the sender acts suspiciously; otherwise, it acts as though it is valid. Figure 12.5 depicts this sender's active and strategic model.

Table 12.1 Signaling game model notations.

Notation	Description
T_S	Duration of the communication protocol information access
$T_{S'}$	The duration of the attack
T	The number of times a sender tries to gain access
$\theta_{j,t}$	Belief at attempt t regarding $sender_j$ (Dynamic belief)
$Cr_{i,j}$	Correlation value between $sender_j$ and $sender_i$
n	Number of packets the sender has requested for data
S	The set of successful attacks
V	The series of attacks
n_s	Attacks needed to obtain the communication information in the bare minimum
b	Total size of the communication information
G_t	Gain at attempt t
$\sigma(t)$	The attacker's cost at attempt t
C_1	Cost of sender per unit time
P_t	probability of successful communication information access at attempt t
Ψ_t	The total cost of the controller up to attempt t
$\rho_t A_t$	The cost of the controller at attempt t

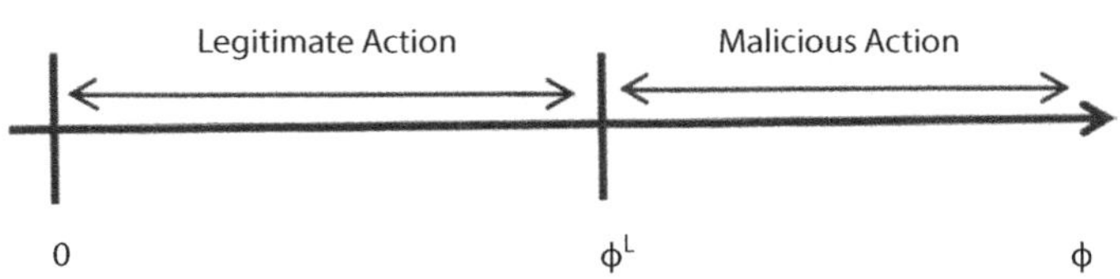

Figure 12.5 Strategy of sender/sensor: behaves *Malicious* if it demands more information than ϕ^L, otherwise behaves *Legitimate*.

Signaling Game – Belief Model: The controller in the proposed game model keeps track of a belief function θ_t for every sensor at try t. The two halves of the value of θ_t about the sensor are the static belief and the dynamic belief. The dynamic belief changes according to how the sensor behaves. Here is how the belief function is computed:

$$\theta_t = min(1, \frac{e^{(\theta_{j,0}+\theta_{j,t})/2}}{e-1}) \tag{12.2}$$

where $\theta_{j,t}$ represents the static belief about sensor j at time $t = 0$ (0th attempt), and $\theta_{j,t}$ represents the dynamic belief about sensor j at time $t = t$ (t^{th} attempt). Additionally, according to Eq. (12.2), the belief that the sensor is malevolent increases with the size of $\theta_{j,t}$. The model demonstrates that the malevolent behavior of the sensor does not affect the belief about the sensor. On the other hand, a tiny variation in $\theta_{j,t}$ has a significant effect on the belief function if the malicious behavior persists. Below, we go into further detail about our static and dynamic belief functions.

Static Belief Function: For the static belief $\theta_{j,0}$, the controller maintains a normalized value that is dependent on the following two parameters.

(a) Maximum number of communication information request packets come to the controller, per unit time: If the sensor is making a lot of requests for access to communication information, then it is deemed to be acting maliciously. This could lead to a denial-of-service attack against the controller. We employ the following parameter M_R to represent this behavior:

$$M_R = min\{1, \frac{L.n_{k=1}k}{L._{Thk=1}k}\} \tag{12.3}$$

The threshold value *Th* describes the maximum number of communication information request packets that a sensor is permitted to send to the controller in a specific amount of time, and n is the number of communication information request packets from a sensor. Generally speaking, (*Th* varies with hardware capacity.) With greater n, the parameter M_R grows. This means that the impact of M_R on belief decreases when the number of successive requests from a sensor is small but increases dramatically when the number of requests increases.

(b) Similar requests from different sensors: More than two sensors containing identical communication information request packets indicate malicious activity, and those sensors ought to be regarded as such. For a given sensor j, we use the parameter S_R to model this harmful action. It is defined as follows:

$$S_R = \frac{\forall j \in N \;\; i \neq j \;\; Si,j}{1 \leq i \leq N \;\; \forall j \in N \;\; i \neq j \;\; i,j} S \tag{12.4}$$

where $S_{i,j}$ is defined as:

Si,j= 1; If the information request packets for i and j are the same 0; Otherwise

Lastly, we define $\theta_{j,0}$, the static belief, as follows, in terms of M_R and S_R:

$$\theta_{j,0} = min\{1, (M_R + S_R)/2\} \tag{12.5}$$

Dynamic Belief Function: As soon as the controller assigns the communication information to a communication information request packet linked to a sensor, the sensor can dynamically retrieve the information. Here the information is assigned by the controller based on time, enabling the sensor to access it dynamically. It is important to remember that a malicious sensor can obtain communication information at the communication network layer by taking advantage of a flaw in the southbound protocol. Accordingly, based on the sensor's behavior, the controller ought to recognize such potentially malevolent sensors. Using the sensor's behavior change as a guide, we calculate the controller's dynamic belief.

Typically, the assigned communication information is accessed by the rogue sensor after it has been produced for a legal sensor. As a result, it has access to the information about the communication that it needs. We may determine whether the malicious sensor's access time to the information is connected to the legitimate sensor's access time by looking at the correlation between the two sensors' communication information access times. If the $Sensor_i$ accesses the communication information at attempt t, let $Access(Sensor_i, t)$ return 1; otherwise, let it return 0. Similarly, $Access(Sensor_j, t+1)$ is explained. The malicious sensor, $Sensor_j$, wants to obtain the communication data that is generated right after $Sensor_i$, the legal sensor, has accessed it. When it comes to accessing the allocated communication information, if a $Sensor_j$ exhibits a strong association with a specific $Sensor_i$, it suggests that $Sensor_j$ is acting maliciously. The correlation between $Sensor_j$ and $Sensor_i$ at attempt t is defined as $Cr_{(i,j),t}$. The dynamic belief is defined using $Cr_{(i,j),t}$ in the following way:

$$\theta_{j,t} = Cr_{(i,j),t} = \mathrm{I}^t{:=}(Access(Sensor_t, x) \wedge Access(Sensor, x+1))/a\ t_{x=1} \tag{12.6}$$

The number of attempted accesses at attempt t is indicated below by a_t. Using Eqs. (12.5) and (12.6), we extract the total belief (θ_t) from Eq. (12.2). The remaining portion of the chapter presents our signaling game for the particular malicious sensor, where t^{th} indicates that the sensor's attempt to obtain the communication information was successful. We also use θ_t to show the entire belief about $Sensor_j$.

Signaling Game - Payoff Model: Both the controller (the target) and the malicious sensor want to maximize their payoffs. Nonetheless, optimizing payout keeps gain and cost in check. The malevolent sensor is attracted to a significant information gain, but it comes at a price. The controller takes advantage of this information to stop the malevolent sensor from attempting any previously presented attacks.

Gain Function: When the fraudulent sensor is the first to obtain communication data, the malicious sensor has a great advantage. The assault sequence denoted by S occurs when a hostile sensor successfully obtains communication information right after a valid sensor. n_s represents the bare minimum of attacks required by the malicious sensor to obtain the communication data, and V indicates the order in which the malicious sensor requests the controller. It is possible to express the relationship between S and V as $S \subseteq V$. The goal of the malicious sensor is to reduce its S and V. However, $S \geq n_s$ holds since the malicious sensor is successful in initiating an attack. We believe that the goal of the malicious sensor is to obtain the communication information that has been assigned to the valid sensor. Let b bytes be the total amount of communication information generated. For the hostile sensor to obtain all communication data, the bare minimum of assaults that succeed, or n_s, is required. The malicious sensor receives some information, but not all of the information, from each successful attack. Since b is a function in this instance, n_s. The gain (G_t) is shown as:

$$G_t = G_{t-1} + \frac{P_t}{n_s} \tag{12.7}$$

The maximum benefit at $t = 1$, or when the malicious sensor obtains the information on its first try, is represented by this equation. However, as the number of trials rises, the maximum gain decreases. The likelihood that the malicious sensor will succeed at attempt t is shown here by P_t. The probability P_t is defined as follows when the controller performs the *Accept*(A) action on an information request packet: $P_t = P_{t-1} - \alpha P_0$, where P_0 is the communication information access probability before the game starting. The parameter $\alpha = \frac{P_0 - P_{Th}}{n_s - 1}$ is defined, in which P_{Th} represents the information access probability threshold value below which the information access policies do not create. Stated otherwise, when the access probability of a malicious sensor is smaller than P_{Th}, the controller prevents any sensor from accessing the communication information. The information request packet from the malicious sensor is discarded when the controller performs the *Discard*(D) action. This also results in a decrease in the parameter n_s, which lowers the gain (G_t) of the malicious sensor. The likelihood that the malicious sensor will obtain G_t and the controller will receive $-G_t$ increases with the probability of an attack succeeding, or with a greater value of P_t.

Cost Function: After a successful try t, let $\sigma(t)$ be the cost of the malicious sensor. $\sigma(t)$ is defined as a linear function:

$$\sigma(t) = C_0 + \sum_{1 \le i \le t} C_1(i) \tag{12.8}$$

where C_1 represents the cost per time unit at attempt i, and C_0 represents the initial cost of attacking a controller. In this case, the sensor's time needed to launch a successful attack attempt is used to calculate the cost. For instance, if we assume that the cost per time unit (per try) is 1 and the initial cost is zero, or $C_0 = 0$, thereafter, a linear function across time is specified as the cost function. However, if there is a random variation in the time gap between two successive tries, the total cost might not follow a linear pattern over time. But generally speaking, there is a chance that a malevolent sensor will be able to obtain the transmission data within a certain time frame, which makes the controller more likely to notice it.

We now go over the connection between the action of the controller and the access cost of the sensor. The malicious sensor will need to spend less time retrieving the data if the controller selects the *Allow*(A) action (i.e., for a successful attempt). However, the gain of the malicious sensor is lower if the *Discard*(D) action is selected, which causes the malicious sensor to temporarily halt operations. Consequently, the cost per unit of time (C_1) rises.

As a result, the controller must act cautiously to ensure that neither the fraudulent sensor nor the legal sensor suffers harm. At a sensor attempt of t, the controller's action results in a cost, ψ_t. The definition of this cost parameter is as follows:

$$\Psi t = \Sigma \rho i A i = \psi t{-}1 + \rho t A t \quad 1 \leq i \leq t \tag{12.9}$$

where the cost of the controller for executing action A_i at attempt i is indicated by $\rho_t A_i$.

The *Allow*(A) action's goal is to create and alter the communication data for authorized sensors. At attempt t, the cost parameter $\rho_t A_t$ is expressed as follows: $\alpha P_0 = \rho_t(A_t = Allow)$. In contrast, the controller deliberately raises its cost per unit of time if it performs the *Discard*(D) action. The parameter $\rho_t A_t$ in this scenario can be represented as $\rho_t(A_t = Discard) = \beta C_0$, where β is a normalized positive value that is contingent upon the quantity of communication information packet requests that are received from the malicious sensor. For the genuine sensor, the overall cost of the controller ψ_t is $\rho_t(A_t = Discard)$, while for the malicious sensor, it is $\rho_t(A_t = Allow)$. According to this technique, the controller will incur higher costs if it chooses *Discard* for the valid sensor and *Allow* for the malicious one. We now calculate the payoff values for the sensor and controller using these cost functions.

Payoff Function: PF_A, the reward of the malicious sensor, is described as follows:

$$PF_M = G_t - \sigma_t \tag{12.10}$$

where the definitions of G_t and σ_t are found in Eqs. (12.7) and (12.8), respectively, and both are normalized to the range of 0 to 1. Likewise, we represent PF_C, the controller's payment, as follows:

$$PF_C = \lambda(-G_t) - (1 - \lambda)\psi_t \tag{12.11}$$

where the cost function's *Allow*(A) and *Discard*(D) actions determine the value of ψ_t. For any $0 \leq \lambda \leq 1$, we utilize a parameter λ to represent the controller's preference for acting, such as *Allow*(A) or *Discard*(D).

The payoffs of the controller and the malicious sender at a specific attempt t for various combinations of techniques are shown in Figure 12.4.

The transmitter may be an authorized sensor or a malevolent sensor. The cost of the controller rises if the malicious sensor acts like a *genuine* and the controller permits communication information. Similarly, the cost of the controller increases if the genuine sensor exhibits *malicious* behavior and the communication information request packet is rejected. Malicious sensor rises under other circumstances.

The sensors that exhibit a slower rate of change in belief values and lower payoff are deemed trustworthy and are permitted to exchange controller-generated information. The sensor can save, retrieve, delete, and alter data inside the cloud storage after the communication information is formed and access is granted.

The next section describes the suggested design architecture for SDN deployment in the robot manufacturing industry.

12.4 Case Study: SDN Deployed Design Framework in Robot Manufacturing Industry

Here, we introduce our SDN-deployed design framework in a real-time environment i.e., in the robot manufacturing industry. First, we discuss the working procedure of the robot manufacturing industry, followed by how our designed framework offers the robot manufacturing sector end-to-end security with performance evaluation.

12.4.1 Working Procedure of a Robot Manufacturing Industry

The robot manufacturing industry is the real case study of an IoT environment, where four zones are present according to the CPwE (Converged Plantwide Ethernet) reference model [1] of IoT. The cell/area zone consists of multiple plants, each plant is manufacturing different body parts of the robot. The industry is importing robot controllers from outside (manufactured in other industries) which is under the industrial zone. The different body parts and the controllers are assembled in the demilitarized zone, and finally, the selling price of robots is negotiated with other enterprises as well the price fixation is done in the enterprise zone. In the above-mentioned scenario, malicious data can be inserted through multiple sensors inside different body parts of a robot. Later this malicious data is going to generate multiple attack patterns in the robot, and the robot will behave suspiciously For example; suppose a robot's hand is meant to grab the objects nearby, and due to the attacker's intervention with the sensors present in the robot's hand, instead of only sensing it is sending a signal to capture the object and rupture it. Later when all the body parts of the robot are organized it is sold in the market for utilization. Now, the attacker can activate the malicious function inside the sensors of the robot's hand, which can take many lives of humans as well as other species. This is a really dangerous situation. Similarly, if the robot controllers are manufactured by some other industry and imported to the plant for integration, then there is a high chance of the presence of malicious functions inside the controller. And, after the integration of other parts with the controller, the attacker can manipulate the robot according to its wish and create multiple havoc situations in the real world. We used a signaling game to build our suggested SDN-deployed design framework in IoT to prevent these kinds of real-life scenarios, as will be discussed in the following part.

12.4.2 Integration of SDN-Deployed Design Framework in Robot Manufacturing Industry

As a solution to the abovementioned application, we implemented our proposed SDN controller design in the industrial zone, where the integrated functioning of multiple body parts is coordinated/managed by the controller. Before integrating the body parts, our proposed framework checks every sensor's collected legitimate data by sending the data to other body parts (For example; one hand's collected data is sent to another hand and the correctness of the data is evaluated). Here, our signaling game is activated and discards the malicious data packets from each of the sensors present in different body parts. After that, in the demilitarized zone, the signaling game is activated when the imported controller is integrated with other body parts. The imported controller's signal (in terms of data packets) is tested in the game model when other parts receive the signal at their end before taking any action. Here, the malicious imported controller's data are discarded and the game model is helping to integrate a legitimate robot. Once the robot's different parts are integrated again the game model is activated for checking the final data-sending operation from different body parts to the controller, from the controller to the body parts, and from one body part to another. Our game model is running in every body part of the robot before they send and receive data. We created a prototype of the robot manufacturing industry using multiple sensors and a Raspberry Pi kit in our laboratory. A detailed explanation is shown in the next subsection.

12.4.3 Experimental Results

We create a prototype that resembles the robot manufacturing industry using one Raspberry Pi kit, five ultrasonic sensors, five PIR sensors, 10-15 LEDs, five buzzers, two breadboards, and the required number of jumper wires. The Raspberry Pi Kit's Wi-Fi module is working as an SDN controller and is modified where we integrate our signaling game model. The sensors (ultrasonic and PIR) work as different body parts of the robot that detect the motion and distance of other objects. The sensed signal is tested inside the wifi module using the proposed signaling game model and if they are trusted then the buzzers and LEDs are getting activated as the output of the robot's function. If not then an error message is getting displayed on the screen. We manipulate the sensor's collected data using i-securit V 0.1 benchmark tool [26] by inserting multiple attacks such as sniffing, tampering, repudiation, information disclosure, Denial of Service, the elevation of privilege, and finding out whether the LEDs and buzzers are activated or the error message is coming on the screen. For the experimental results, we also set the game parameter values which are shown in Table 12.2.

Table 12.2 Values used in experimentation.

Game parameters	ϕN	N	TV	T_V'	λ	α
Values considered	0.33	12	9	7	0.5	18

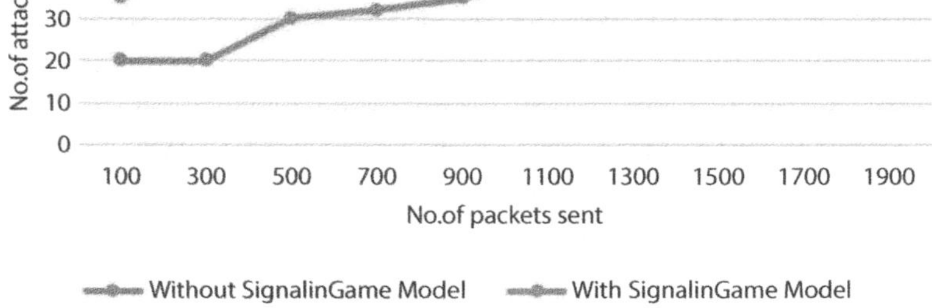

Figure 12.6 Packets found using both the signaling game model and not.

The amount of data packets identified by our suggested framework both with and without the signaling game model implemented is displayed in Figure 12.6. When compared to the case without the game model, there are comparatively more malicious packet detections when the game model is used. The effect and significance of including the signaling game model in the suggested SDN-deployed design framework are thus presented. All incoming request packets are examined by the signaling game model to determine their reward value; those with high payoff values are deleted. We examine the experimental findings by turning on and off the signaling game model. Table 12.3 displays a portion of the results from our investigation. We track the actions of our signaling game model and examine the controller's perception of the sort of sensor. The controller's beliefs on a malicious sensor and a valid sensor are depicted in Figure 12.7. A genuine

Table 12.3 Controller action (partial) on the Raspberry Pi Screen.

Output disabling Signaling Game Model:
Sensor 1 enabled and detected motion
Sensor 1 enabled and distance
Output enabling Signaling Game Model:
Sensor 1 enabled and detected motion
Sensor 1 enabled and detected distance (duplicate use of sensor1 is found!)
Significantly altered belief value, packet lost, error

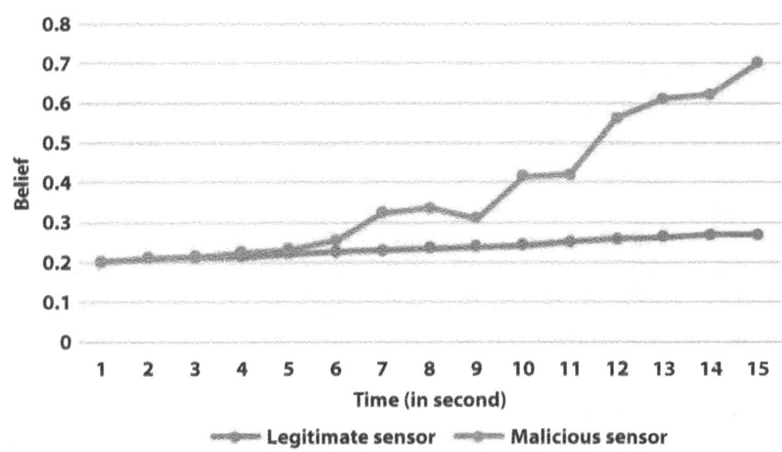

Figure 12.7 Calculated belief value of the malicious and legitimate sensor.

sensor's belief remains unchanged, but for a malevolent sensor, it rapidly shifts. A genuine sensor typically does not display malevolent activity, although occasionally it will exhibit avaricious behavior that does not significantly affect its perception. Malicious sensors can pass for genuine ones at the moment before acting avaricious. But our game model recognizes all of these sporadic actions and computes the belief dynamically.

12.5 Discussion

Here, we discuss the extensibility, usability, and limitations of our proposed SDN-deployed design framework for IoT using game-theoretic solutions.

Extensibility: We have developed a versatile framework that can be used to represent heterogeneous networks with OpenFlow switches, controllers, and protocols. In general, modifications to topologies, connectivity structures, and configuration settings are supported by the current OpenFlow network. Such circumstances are adopted by our system without any design modifications. On the other hand, our framework's corresponding configuration parameters must be adjusted if changes are made to the device configuration or communication parameters (*i.e.*, link type, bandwidth, etc.). As such, our approach may be easily extended for heterogeneous networks with little modifications. Furthermore, to detect malevolent users, our system can be integrated with additional technologies like visual surveillance. The controller in this case needs to be trained using well-known data sets. This explains how citizens can use our framework to be resilient against cyberattacks by employing application-level requirements.

Usability: The suggested SDN framework can be utilized in body area network (BAN) automation in healthcare to identify abnormalities in the human body. It can be used in disaster management networks to predict natural calamities and proactive action-making. Also, it can be applicable for post-disaster scenarios, such as sending relief and evacuating people where detection of affected localities and human presence are needed. Furthermore, it can be efficiently employed in the intelligent transportation system that gives consumers access to previous transport information based on their approach location.

Limitations: The mathematical design and the layout of the experiments demonstrate that our proposed framework possesses the ability to identify multiple attack types in the IoT environment with 95% accuracy.

Our framework is implementing two game models and the synchronization of both games is necessary otherwise there would be a delay in the processing of data inside the cloud. So, network parameters bandwidth and jitter play an important role in the proposed framework.

12.6 Conclusion

The SDN architecture greatly promotes network innovation due to its ability to separate the control and data planes. We design an SDN-deployed design framework for detecting and mitigating multiple attack types in the IoT environment. Our design framework is implemented using the SDN controller and signaling game deployed in the communication network layer of IoT. It detects malicious data collected by the sensors and checks the malicious flows sent by the communication network. It provides security and privacy to the data stored in the Cloud for further processing. In addition, it saves time and energy for the devices and improves the robustness and efficiency of the network. Our proposed framework can be practically deployed in an IoT environment for efficient and secure implementation of real-time applications.

References

1. *IoT Fundamentals*, Cisco Press, USA, 2015.
2. Priyadarsini, M., Kumar, S., Bera, P., Rahman, M.A., An energy-efficient load distribution framework for sdn controllers. *Computing*, 102, 2073–2098, USA, 2020.
3. Priyadarsini, M., Bera, P., Das, S.K., Rahman, M.A., A security enforcement framework for sdn controller using game theoretic approach. *IEEE Trans. Dependable Secure Comput.*, 20, 1500–1515, 2022.
4. *Internet of Things- A Hands-on Approach*, Universities Press, 2016.
5. *OpenFlow Switch Specification, 1.4.0 ed.*, Open Networking Foundation, 2017.
6. Erickson, D., The beacon openflow controller. *The hot topics in SDN (HotSDN)*, 2015.
7. Floodlight project [online], Available: http://www.projectfloodlight.org/floodlight/.
8. Opendaylight project [online], Available: https://www.opendaylight.org/.
9. Priyadarsini, M. and Bera, P., A new approach for performance enhancement in software-defined network. *The Twenty-Fifth International Conference on Computer Networks (CN)*, 2018.

10. Gude, N., Nox: Towards an operating system for networks. *SIGCOMM Comput. Commun. Rev.*, 38, 3, 105–110, 2008.
11. *Game Theory*, Ane Books Pvt. Ltd., 2019.
12. *Game theory*, Available on https://www.investopedia.com/terms/g/gametheory.asp.
13. Elhaloui, L., Tabaa, M., Elfilali, S., Ben-Lahmer, E., Dynamic security for iot network traffic using sdn. *The 14th International Conference on Ambient Systems, Networks, and Technologies (ANT)*, 14, 2023.
14. Ambili, K.N. and Jose, J., A secure software defined networking based framework for iot networks. *J. Inf. Secur. Appl.*, 17, 1–19, 2020.
15. Patrick, G., Venkata, G., Vardhan, H., Sdn for securing iot systems, White paper by DELL Technologies, 9, 8, Swtizerland, 2022.
16. Al Hayajneh, A., Zakirul Alam Bhuiyan, Md., McAndrew, I., Improving internet of things (iot) security with software-defined networking (sdn). *Computers (MDPI)*, 9, 2–14. 2020.
17. Sarica, A.K. and Angin, P., Explainable security in sdn-based iot networks. *Sensors (MDPI)*, 20, 7326, 2020.
18. Chi, C., Wang, Y., Tong, X., Siddula, M., Cai, Z., Game theory in internet of things: A survey. *IEEE Internet Things*, 9, 208–229, 2022.
19. Chen, X., Feng, W., Ge, N., Wang, X., Defending link flooding attacks under incomplete information: A bayesian game approach. *International Conference on Communications (ICC)*, 2020.
20. Elsemary, H., Mitigating malware attacks via secure routing in intelligent device-to-device communications. *Advances in Intelligent Systems and Computing book series (AISC)*, vol. 533, 2016.
21. Sengupta, S., Chowdhary, A., Huang, D., Kambhampati, S., Moving target defense for the placement of intrusion detection systems in the cloud, in: *Lecture Notes in Computer Science book series (LNSC)*, vol. 11199, 2018.
22. Tsemogne, O., Hayel, Y., Kamhoua, C., Deugoue, G., Game- theoretic modeling of cyber deception against epidemic botnets in the internet of things. *IEEE Internet Things J.*, 9, 160–196, 2022.
23. Bhatia, M. and Sood, S.K., Game-theoretic decision making in iot-assisted activity monitoring of defense personnel. *Multimed. Tools Appl.*, 76, 21911–21935, 2017.
24. Kaur, N. and Sood, S.K., A game theoretic approach for an iot-based automated employee performance evaluation. *IEEE Syst. J.*, 11, 1385–1394, 2017.
25. Mebrek, A. and Yassine, A., Intelligent resource allocation and task offloading model for iot applications in fog networks: A game-theoretic approach. *IEEE Trans. Emerging Top. Comput. Intell.*, 10, 244–255, 2021.
26. The benchmark i-securit [online], Available on http://bss.com.sg/network-security.php.

13

Framework for PLM in Industry 4.0 Based on Industrial Blockchain

Ali Zaheer Agha[1]*, Rajesh Kumar Shukla[2], Ratnesh Mishra[3] and Ravi Shankar Shukla[4]

[1]*Dept. of Computer Science & Engineering, Dr. Rizvi College of Engineering, Karari, Kaushambi, Uttar Pradesh, India*
[2]*Faculty of Engineering and Technology, Invertis University, Bareilly, Uttar Pradesh, India*
[3]*Dept. of Computer Science & Engineering, BIT Mesra, Patna Campus, Patna, Bihar, India*
[4]*Dept. of Computer Science, College of Computing and Informatics, Saudi Electronic University, Tabuk, Saudi Arabia*

Abstract
Product lifecycle management, or PLM, aims to efficiently and effectively manage all goods, information, and knowledge produced throughout the product lifetime in order to achieve company competitiveness. Typically, software providers' standalone and centralized systems are used to deploy PLM. It is rare for the collaborating parties to integrate and exchange PLM information. Meeting the Industry 4.0 era's requirements for openness, interoperability, and decentralization is challenging. This study suggested an industrial blockchain-based PLM framework to overcome these issues and make it easier for people to share services and exchange data across the product lifecycle. Initially, we introduced the idea of "industrial blockchain," which is the application of blockchain technology to the industry along with effective consensus-based algorithms, the Internet of Things, and machine learning. It gave the many stakeholders an open, safe platform to communicate and store information, enabling decentralization, openness, and compatibility in the age of industry 4.0. Second, we proposed and developed a custom blockchain data service for finishing the connection among a single node and the blockchain network. It can handle diverse, multi-source information collected at different stages of the product lifecycle in its role as middleware,

**Corresponding author*: alizaheer7@gmail.com

Mohit Kumar, Gautam Srivastava, Ashutosh Kumar Singh and Kalka Dubey (eds.) AI-Based Advanced Optimization Techniques for Edge Computing, (341–380) © 2025 Scrivener Publishing LLC

as well as broadcast the processed data to the blockchain network. Additionally, alert services are automated across product lifecycles through the usage of smart contracts. In conclusion, we demonstrated how the collaborating partners may use the blockchain-based application in four stages of the growing product lifecycle: proactive maintenance, controlled reuse, fast and precise tracking and tracing, and co-design and co-creation. A simulated experiment showed how successful and efficient the suggested framework is. The outcomes demonstrated the scalability and efficiency of the suggested framework, making its use in business possible. With the suggested platform's effective implementation, an efficient PLM for enhancing collaboration and interoperability amongst stakeholders throughout the whole product lifecycle is likely.

***Keywords*:** Industry 4.0, smart contracts, industrial blockchain, and product lifecycle management

13.1 Introduction

Due to the widespread usage of the Internet and associated technologies, a number of Industry 4.0-based solutions that employ sensors and actuators to detect, calculate, and transfer data for industry automation have been implemented globally. Similar to Industry 4.0-based applications, dangers to security and privacy have multiplied as information moves among numerous sites over an open channel, namely the Internet. A lot of information are handled by these applications, therefore in addition to security and privacy considerations, factors like data heterogeneity, data integrity, and data redundancy must be taken into account. Furthermore, multiple uses call for datasets in various forms from various disciplines. As a result, standardizing the data format is also necessary to enable its usage by various Industry 4.0-based applications.

Recent business strategies use a centrally controlled, client-server architecture, where all rights are held by the centralized authority, to counteract the dangers listed above. However, the system as a whole can collapse if the centralized authority is breached. Although they have a large processing and transmission cost, traditional security techniques like Data Encryption Standard (DES), Advanced Encryption Standard (AES), and their derivatives are still in use. Yet, the advent of the idea of "bitcoins" brought about a change in this field. For instance, Noizat [22] provided examples of how blockchain technology might be applied to Industry 4.0 privacy and security concerns.

13.1.1 What is Blockchain?

Recently, blockchain has become well known as the technical foundation that makes cryptocurrencies possible. It has shown to be an effective way to distribute asset ownership among autonomous organizations in the absence of a centralized authority.

Applications in the industry have started to appear for self-governing business processes that include several stakeholders. Blockchain makes it possible for disparate organizations with similar problems and goals to band together. Enhancing revenue or operational performance through the rapid visibility and sharing of reliable data is the usual goal.

In order to accomplish operational gains in the supply chain or other business activity, members of a consortium can share immutable data using a secure distributed ledger, or database, made possible by blockchain technology. It is applicable in cases when members gain from quick access to reliable data. Industrial applications have started to appear to share immutable data among businesses, governments, and trade associations in order to enhance revenue or operational performance. This research focuses on industrial blockchain applications where members of a consortium of industrial enterprises and related organizations benefit from visibility to reliable data.

13.1.2 Blockchain Technology's Integration with Industry 4.0

The goal of industry 4.0 is to transform global production in an effort to find faster, more effective manufacturing processes. This fourth revolution can be supported by blockchain technology, which makes production processes transparent and accessible from anywhere. Global manufacturers can now share a real-time communications channel thanks to the blockchain. This makes it much easier to integrate modifications, update algorithms, and streamline manufacturing processes. Manufacturers are able to securely store confidential product information and maintain intellectual property rights thanks to the blockchain's secure ledger or database. Additionally, it facilitates the development of global supply chains, which is currently a major problem for all economies worldwide.

13.1.3 Blockchain Applications in Industry 4.0

Blockchain became well-known as a mechanism for safe bitcoin transactions. Other uses of the technology are becoming more popular even as it continues to revolutionize the financial industry: These are only the most relevant instances of blockchain applications for Industry 4.0; this is by no means an exhaustive list.

13.1.3.1 Protection of Manufacturing Data

The increasing volume of data being produced by businesses and individuals globally has made data protection a critical issue. Businesses in the manufacturing sector must protect the confidentiality of commercial data while allowing the right parties to access it. Blockchain is the perfect tool for facilitating sharing among members of a certain group while using encryption to prevent unauthorized access. Valuable and sensitive data is shielded from potential cyber attacks. Blockchain is also safer for information transfer than many other alternatives because to encryption.

13.1.3.2 Resolution of Quality Issues

Recalls of products and addressing other quality-related concerns are standard processes in manufacturing. Blockchain technology improves the efficiency of recalls. Manufacturers have the ability to selectively recall defective products due to the existence of permanent digital purchase data.

Instead of requesting returns from thousands of customers, manufacturers can pinpoint particular issues and engage with individual customers to address them. Ensuring that production procedures are permanently recorded facilitates the identification and prompt resolution of quality issues. By indicating which parts can be recycled and how, blockchain technology also contributes to higher recycling rates. Blockchain is advancing the circular economy in this way.

13.1.3.3 Supply Chain Development

Over the past few years, supply chain bottlenecks have garnered media attention. Blockchain solutions, with their real-time updates and increased control over internal activities and processes, will enable businesses to anticipate and avoid bottlenecks as they develop. Blockchain technology is frequently integrated with an organization's current ERP platforms to enhance them.

13.1.4 A Consensus Algorithm

In spite of mistakes or discrepancies, distributed systems can come to an agreement on a single value or state by using a consensus mechanism.

Put another way, consensus-building enables nodes in a network to come to an agreement about the validity of transactions and maintain system integrity even in the case of node splits or failures in the network. Some examples of consensus algorithms are as follows:

- Ripple Protocol Consensus Algorithm (RPCA),
- Delegated Proof of Stake (DPoS),
- Practical Byzantine Fault Tolerance (PBFT),
- Proof of Work (PoW), and Proof of Stake (PoS)

The number of nodes in the network, the desired degree of security, the desired degree of scalability, and the desired degree of decentralization all influence the consensus method selection. The goal of a consensus algorithm is to provide a way for the nodes in the network to come to a decision in a fault-tolerant manner, despite the presence of malicious or faulty nodes.

13.1.5 Product Lifecycle Management

Product Lifecycle Management (PLM) refers to the organizational process of overseeing the goods of an organization from their inception until they are retired and disposed of [1]. It seeks to promote creativity, shorten gaps in interaction between the collaborating parties, decrease expenses, speed up the development of new products, increase quality, and visualize product information [2]. In the very beginning phases of the design and creation of products, PLM is usually utilized for making local information as well as data incorporation and administration simpler. For example, it makes data produced by computer-aided design (CAD), computer-aided manufacturing (CAM), and computer-aided engineering (CAE) easier to retrieve. The advancement of computer technology and the internet has made it possible for partners to work together on projects that cover the whole life of a product. Every phase of a product's lifecycle is covered, including creation, manufacturing, distribution, upkeep, customer support, and recycling. PLM turns into a deliberate strategy to increase a business's capacity to compete with its goods [3].

The phrase "industry 4.0" (I4.0) describes the fourth industrial revolution, which is defined by the incorporation of emerging technologies like cloud computing, cyber-physical systems, Internet of things (IoT), and artificial intelligence (AI) to create open, secure, and intelligent factories. However, I4.0 cannot be supported by the traditional PLM approach. First off, the majority of current strategies are built upon a centralized framework made available by outside software providers. For instance, cloud-based PLM solutions for industry have been suggested by several researchers [4]. Nonetheless, businesses worry about important innovations being lost or leaked, which keeps information scarce and services limited in scope. The companies' primary priorities are security and intellectual property [5]. Furthermore, during the spread lifecycle, there is a lot of scattered product data. For instance, demanding additional maintenance alongside progressive design files, revising the bill of materials, and giving real-time constructive criticism. The traditional centralized method was primarily designed for internal use. The product information chain, however, crosses enterprise boundaries throughout its existence. As a result, it is challenging to obtain, handle, and evaluate this data across businesses. Value chain management and organization must be connected throughout the product lifecycle, much like I4.0 [6]. Thirdly, there is no efficient method for information and service sharing and interchange across the parties involved in the product lifecycle in traditional PLM systems. The current system depends on drawn-out conversations between many stakeholders. It requires a lot of time and work. This is a result of the security problems. In addition, the primary cause of this predicament is the lack of a system that incentivizes the business to share and exchange knowledge; this means that the business cannot profit excessively from knowledge sharing. But in order to make better decisions and boost productivity, I4.0 necessitates decentralized decision-making that makes use of both local and global information simultaneously [7]. To sum up, for data integration and interchange as well as decision-making amongst goods, factories, business networks, and clients from various phases of the product lifecycle, an open yet secure, interconnected, and decentralized environment is required.

To solve the aforementioned problems, an industrial blockchain-based PLM platform is advised. This plan makes use of industrial blockchain technologies, smart contracts, and the Internet of Things. Blockchain is a revolutionary technology with high protection, distributivity, reversibility, openness, and reliability that has transformed the financial industry [8]. In industries other than banking, it has demonstrated tremendous promise. An industrial blockchain network for self-governing machine-to-machine (M2M) transactions was presented by Mattila *et al.* [9]. In order to meet the different sector demands, Li *et al.* introduced an innovative blockchain design called "satellite chain" which makes use of multiple consensus protocols [10]. Li *et al.* have conducted extensive research on the Industrial IoT consortium blockchain [11]. In summary, the application of the technology of blockchain in the manufacturing sector in addition to the incorporation of M2M, IoT, and effective decentralized consensus algorithms to meet security, openness, and decentralization requirements can be largely characterized as the industrial blockchain. Additionally, throughout the product's lifespan, smart contracts are utilized to speed up transaction execution and alert services. IoT technologies are necessary to collect and monitor information gathered throughout a product's lifespan in real time.

The following sums up this paper's contribution: In the I4.0 age, the suggested industrial blockchain-based platform offers a decentralized, interconnected, and open environment that is secure. It makes it possible for PLM stakeholders to work together to share and exchange information about goods, factories, business networks, and customers. (2) Distribute information throughout the product lifetime with the help of the customized blockchain information service (BIS) that is being proposed. This enables a business to establish a value chain for the purpose of researching and evaluating cross-enterprise product information, in addition to helping the business effectively repurpose its internal resources. (3) Throughout the product lifecycle, the suggested platform offers alert services and transactions enabled by smart contracts. It facilitates quick decision-making and support for the business. The process of a smart contract is carried out automatically on the blockchain as opposed to by hand, which improves the efficacy and efficiency of PLM transactions and activities. As a result, labour expenses and time are decreased. Four major blockchain-based PLM services are demonstrated: proactive maintenance, controlled recycling, rapid and accurate tracking and tracing (QAT2), and co-design and co-creation services. The primary services demonstrate how it can be integrated with the current enterprise function paradigm, including M2M, ERP, and so on.

13.1.6 Benefits of Smart Contracts in Addressing PLM Challenges

Smart contracts are useful for the following main reasons:

1. One authentic source

Because everyone always has access to the same data, there is less chance that contract clauses would be abused. Because contract-related information is available for as long as the contract is in effect, this improves confidence and safety. Furthermore, transactions are copied such that copies are held by all participants.

2. Less work from humans
Human supervision or third-party verification are not necessary for smart contracts. This grants members independence and autonomy, especially when it comes to DAO. This inherent feature of smart contracts provides other advantages, such as quicker and less expensive procedures.

3. Error prevention
Any contract must, first and foremost, contain a detailed record of all terms and conditions. In the future, an omission could lead to major problems including unfair penalties and complicated legal situations. Automated smart contracts prevent mistakes in form filling. One of its biggest benefits is this.

4. By default, zero trust
Smart contracts as a framework represent a significant advancement over traditional approaches. This suggests that throughout a transaction, one need not rely on the reliable behavior of other parties. In line with zero-trust security principles, faith is not a necessary component of a transaction or exchange. Every part of the network is more transparent, equitable, and fair thanks to smart contracts' decentralized operation, which eliminates the possibility of privilege creep.

5. Integrated backup
These contracts record the necessary transactional information. Your data is therefore kept forever for future use in case it is needed in a contract. Retrieving these characteristics is easy in the event of data loss. The rest of the paper will follow this structure. In Section 13.2, PLM and blockchain are reviewed. The proposed industrial blockchain-based PLM architecture is shown in Section 13.3. Section 13.4 explains the mechanics of the four fundamental services: co-design and co-creation, QAT2 (quick turn-around time 2), proactive maintenance, and regulated recycling. A performance assessment and practical scenario are presented in Section 13.5 to demonstrate the effectiveness of the proposed framework. This comprises both latency and throughput measurements, together with qualitative and quantitative comparisons, when creating new blocks. Section 13.6 provides a final summary of the results and directions for future research.

13.2 Related Work

The literature on the idea as well as procedures of blockchain technology, as well as product lifecycle management in Industry 4.0, is covered in this section. The section explores several theoretical frameworks and algorithms within the context of Industry 4.0 and blockchain technology.

13.2.1 Product Lifecycle Management

In order to achieve the desired outcomes and long-term viability for the good along with associated services, product information are shared throughout participants, procedures, and businesses at every stage of the product lifecycle. This provides a thorough explanation of PLM supported by ICT [1, 12]. Birth of life (BOL), midway through life (MOL), and end of life (EOL) are the three stages that typically make up a product's lifespan [12]. The time when products are taken apart rebuilt, reused, repurposed, or destroyed are included in EOL; design and manufacturing are included in BOL; product consumption, servicing, and repairs are included in MOL [13]. Typically, centralized frameworks from third parties, such Teamcenter, Windchill, etc., have served as the foundation for PLM system development. Document management and product relational data management are two examples of PLM applications that it assists practitioners in selecting and putting into practice based on the demands of their business [14]. The timeline highlights the key developments in PLM development history, including web-based PLM, cloud-based PLM, multi-agent-based PLM, and product data management (PDM). Numerous researches concentrate on various PLM development stages. The following is a list of some noteworthy studies.

PDM's first prototype came from the engineering design and CAD/CAM domains in the middle of the 1980s [15]. Its original purpose was to address version constraint concerns for CAD-produced product drawings and the storage and retrieval of huge numbers of such drawings. For example, Alemanni *et al.* built a framework that allows data to be organized in consumable and consistent ways within native three-dimensional CAD models utilizing the Model-based design execution employing qualitative operational deployment approach [16]. Its goals are to reduce unneeded documentation and illustrations, increase consistency in data, virtualize goods and procedures more fully, and provide better support for all computer-assisted technology operations in the engineering and manufacturing disciplines. After the initial stages of development, the ideas' layout must be confirmed by the CAE, professional competence, etc. Maropoulos and Ceglarek first look at the commonly used definitions of verification and validation in the field of engineering design before offering a convincing analysis and classification of these processes. They then provide digital and preliminary design, as well as physical verification and validation of processes and products [17]. It illustrates the process of validating complicated products within the framework of their lifecycle. Web-based PLM became increasingly popular as the Internet expanded. For instance, Vezzetti suggested a methodical examination of Web-based solutions in order to advance a special three-dimensional digital standard model that can more successfully share production and product data [18]. A thorough evaluation of various Web-based presentation possibilities offered by the Product Life Cycle (PLM) platform was conducted using the following four parameters: user interaction, security, performance, customization, and visualization. Monticolo *et al.* [19] provided an interactive workstation design technique that incorporates engineering process knowledge into the multi-agent-based PLM stage. They achieved this by creating a knowledge engineering system that was incorporated into a PLM environment utilizing a MultiAgent System. The Multi-Agent System in a PLM system makes capitalization and knowledge annotation based on designer actions easier. In industrial settings, it can be used to enhance teamwork in design and ergonomics. Thanks to the concept of cloud computing, Holtewert *et al.* have developed a secure, federative cloud-based platform for distributed service-oriented applications (PLM) in plant operation [20]. The platform was introduced to the networked factory through an explanation of the transformation process. They assessed their platform using criteria like uniformity, integrated security for all parts, and community cloud for data decentralization in IT, collaboration, and competency sharing.

Alternatively, Gomez *et al.* used Siemens NX 9 to model the Hartford SMC5 machining centre in the PLM industrial application. The method of modeling, imitating, and producing a selected project component with complicated surfaces offers a method for validating the model [21]. The goal of Sakao *et al.*'s proposal is to assist manufacturers in designing a product/service system (PSS) that maximizes resource efficiency and promotes sustainability by offering a novel and useful approach [22]. The technique is meant to be applied as a component to company PLM applications, with a lifecycle focus and lifetime costs estimation (LCC). Soto-Acosta *et al.* give a case study of an effective implementation of a self-developed PLM Platform in an industrial SME in order to enable PLM business applications for SMEs [23]. By considering the product design and assembly sequence planning phases concurrently, a fresh structure for an assembly-oriented design (AOD) method is presented by Demoly *et al.* as an innovative multifunctional PLM technique [24]. In order to facilitate the life-oriented product creation process, this offers assembly context knowledge. The centralized PLM systems, however, are scarcely able to meet the demand for transparency in information and communication throughout the product lifecycle. Along the distributed lifetime, there is also a lot of dispersed product information. The stakeholders find it challenging to compile all of the pertinent product data into a single third-party PLM system. Furthermore, throughout the course of a product's lifecycle, cross-company cooperation is always built on trust. The party may be worried about giving important information to an outsider. Consequently, a decentralized platform must be created to accommodate the various stakeholders involved in the product lifecycles.

13.2.2 Industrial Blockchain

As a core technology for a digital money, such as bitcoin, Satoshi Nakamoto introduced the blockchain concept [25]. Its benefits include distributivity, correctness, high security, irreversibility, and transparency [8]. Through the creation of a data structure and the encryption of transactional information, it also enables the mining and trade of bitcoins [26]. Data encryption makes the blockchain tamper-proof by making it prohibitively expensive to update or remove old transactions [27]. The nodes that have the maintenance function look after the data block. All nodes have equal rights and obligations, hence there are no centralized administration organizations. It is appropriate for storing information that has to be verified and identified [28].

Apart from the financial industry, the blockchain system has demonstrated its ability to revolutionize assets and offerings across a number of different sectors. For example, Bahga and Madisetti [29] propose BPIIoT, a distributed P2P system for the Industrial IoT, which is built on block chain technology. The BPIIoT platform uses Blockchain technology to create a decentralized, trustless network that allows peer-to-peer communication without the need for a reliable middleman. Sikorski *et al.* looked at the applications of blockchain technology in the chemical sector. They found that sector 4.0 leverages blockchain technology to create an M2M electricity market and enable machine-to-machine (M2M) interactions [30]. It draws the conclusion that there is still a great deal of untapped potential for this technology to complement and improve upon the efficiency gains achieved throughout the revolution and offers suggestions for further study. Through the use of IoT sensor devices utilizing blockchain technology, Bocek *et al.* created modum.io, a start-up that aims to reduce operational expenses in the pharmaceutical supply chain while establishing data immutability and public accessibility of temperature records [31]. The exterior temperature of each parcel is tracked by the sensor devices throughout transportation in order to properly ensure GDP rules are followed. Every piece of information is moved to the blockchain, in which a smart contract compares it with the features of the good or service.

Li *et al.* presented a blockchain-based knowledge and service exchange architecture [32] for achieving secure data and service exchange. The suggested design creates a dispersed and adaptable network by integrating the newest advancements in edge computing technology. Blockchain technology ensures safety issues and offers guidelines and protocols for putting the structure into practice. The researchers have established a blockchain-based platform to facilitate the exchange of knowledge and services, thanks to these advancements [33, 34]. A comparable situation is described in which choosing and dealing with blockchain-enabled solutions may involve the service provider and servicer client using blockchain as an instrument for information and exchanging services [35].

Francisco and Swanson developed a fundamental framework for supply chain traceability with regard to the provenance of the chain by utilizing the concept of technological innovation adoption and the Unified Theory of Acceptance and Use of technological (UTAUT) [36]. A conceptual model is developed, and supply chain implications of blockchain are discussed in the study's conclusion. A case is made for the use of ontologies in blockchain architecture by Kim and Laskowski [37]. We examine an identifiable paradigm as well as convert some of its elements into smart contracts which execute an origin trace and impose traceable restrictions on the Ethereum blockchain in order to substantiate this assertion. Madhwal and Panfilov illustrated the need for a decentralized Blockchain system in order to keep track of the different aircraft segments and keep an eye on their performance [38]. A transparent network for the supply of aircraft components will be made possible, and the likelihood of aircraft segments becoming available on the black market will be decreased. It will also assist analysts in analyzing the supply, demand, and sources of availability of aviation parts as well as how to get them from the best sources. In addition to demonstrating the potential benefits of blockchain technology for industrial platform architecture, Mattila *et al.* provided fresh perspectives on product-centric information management [39]. We have discussed a theoretical design of a product-oriented, networked agent-based data management solution. Shared agent-based databases enable controlled accessibility of product data via the web.

Finally, blockchain offers a wide range of applications that it can be used in. First, by using a cryptographic technique, its data structure may permanently and verifiably record the events. Its resistance to data tampering is essentially the foundation of its design. The transaction cannot be altered once it has been produced. Second, a smart contract-based blockchain offers a useful transaction mechanism. It automatically accelerates business alliance transactions [40]. Thirdly, participants of a blockchain form a new kind of peer-to-peer communication network. Users can conduct their own data/transactions on this P2P network without the involvement of a third party. As a result, blockchain technology enhances PLM and is crucial to the process of collaboration. In this section industrial blockchain is described as using the blockchain in the manufacturing sector while integrating M2M, IoT, and effective distributed consensus algorithms, as compared to standard blockchain technology. We build a link between the various stages of the product lifecycles utilizing our industrial blockchain.

13.2.3 The On-Chain vs. Off-Chain Principle

The decentralized system, secure traceable data, compliance with regulations tracking, and other properties of blockchain are advantageous to all parties involved. However, confidential information cannot be kept on a blockchain and accessed by the general public. This brings up a crucial question of whether something should be off-chain or on-chain. Performance and privacy are two elements that are crucial to resolving this problem [41]. On the one hand, the blockchain's deployment has a significant impact on performance. Notably, three different kinds of blockchain networks—public, consortium, and private—have been introduced [42]. Each of the three blockchain networks has a completely different performance. The public blockchain's rather modest transaction confirmation speed lags well behind the industry's massive information creation. In the business, Ethereum, for instance, enables only about 15 transactions per second. Limited node management is used in the development of the consortium blockchain. To meet the needs of limited alliance members, transaction confirmation performance is a significant benefit. The private blockchain network is designed with a high level of security for a particular business. It is barely capable of conducting cross-company boundaries, though. Thus, consortium blockchain is appropriate for industrial applications because of its low maintenance costs, fast transaction speeds, and scalability [41]. However, whether choosing whether to store data off-chain or on-chain, privacy is still another issue. Direct chaining of private data is not recommended. For example, personal records containing confidential information in its raw form require photos and certifications of traceability. However, the company is motivated to show the public that it is qualified or capable. Therefore, we presented an approach wherein the unprocessed information is stored off-chain while the hash code of the original information stays on-chain [43]. It can defend

Table 13.1 Information about on chain/off chain using standards.

Data type	Confidentiality	Quality	On chain/Off chain
Design	High	Middle	Off-chain
Producing high-quality data	Middle	High	On-chain
Traceability of logistics (origin, producer, components)	Low	High	On-chain
Recall information	Low	High	On-chain
Smart contract	Null	Middle	On-chain
Accreditation	Low	Low	On-chain

from any data alteration and ensure the safety of the vital information by applying a stored hash. We create a standard for the data that is either off-chain or on-chain based on the aforementioned concepts, as indicated in Table 13.1. In the suggested design, we select the privacy and quantity as the benchmarks for data that is either off-chain or on-chain. For instance, the co-creation method refers to extremely sensitive data and a sizable design scheme. As a result, the company's intellectual property must be protected and moved off-chain; little data is needed to move on-chain. As a result, we store the design scheme data off-chain while storing the data's hash on the chain. This is due to its ability to ensure raw data protection and offer stakeholders a seamless sharing environment. On the contrary side, quality-related information, such as production-related info, logistical data, product recall data, and license data, need to be put on-chain as open regulation and credibility are necessary. A smart contract, which is a digital contract signed by those involved, ought to be openly recorded on the blockchain network. By applying a consortium rule, this facilitates the execution and validation of the contract's terms.

13.3 The Recommended Architecture's Methodology

13.3.1 The Suggested Platform's Architecture

The goal of this research is to facilitate open and safe data integration and exchange inside product lifecycles by proposing a theoretical framework for PLM based on blockchain. The five levels that comprise the model proposed are the off-chain layer, blockchain layer, application layer, perception layer, and service layer, as illustrated in Figure 13.1.

In Figure 13.1, we show a general product lifetime at the bottom. We separated the lifetime into three sections based on [12]: BOL, MOL, and EOL. BOL specifically covers manufacturing, packaging, design, and marketing. MOL covers maintenance, consuming, and logistics and warehouse. Product reuse and recycling are included in EOL. In addition, as the service layer indicates, we offer four services—product co-creation, rapid tracking and tracing queries, products maintenance, and goods recycling—which fit with the four blockchain-based processes.

Arguably the more significant input sources for the suggested system is the perception layer. Within the framework of the product lifecycle, which encompasses, among other locations, the manufacturing floor, warehouse, logistics center, and transportation, data is collected. It is made up of various IoT gadgets and smart assets, such as sensors, GPS, RFID tags and readers, QR codes, and more. The intelligent portal receives the information it

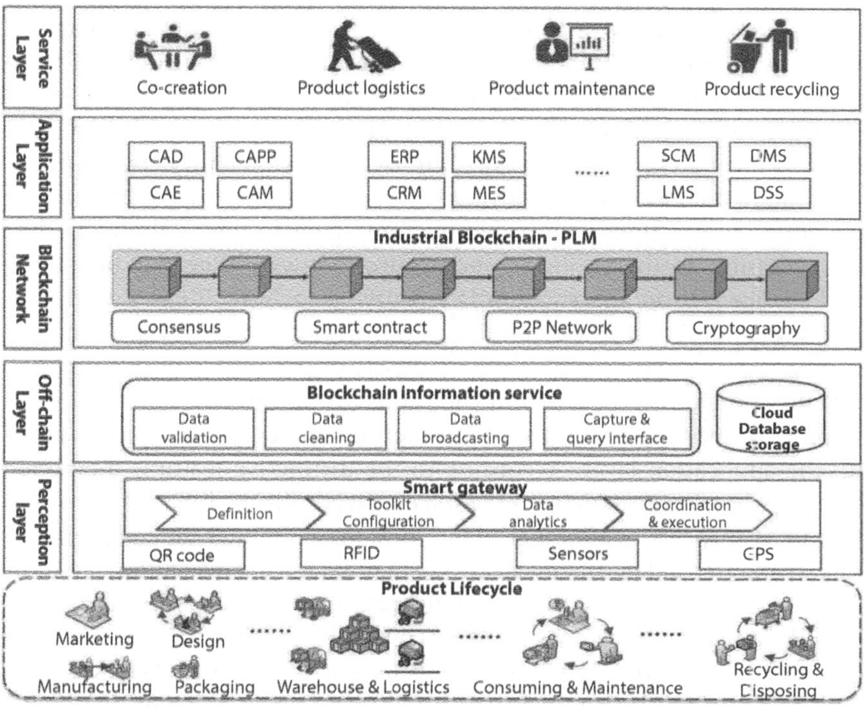

Figure 13.1 The architecture of the proposed blockchain-based PLM [52].

has collected. An intermediary among cloud servers and IoT sensors is an intelligent bridge [44]. Its traditional duties include sending feedback to PLCs (programmable logic controllers) and transmitting the gathered data to local and/or cloud databases. Before being uploaded to the blockchain network, the data produced by the perception layer will be sent to the off-chain layer for additional processing.

The off-chain part of the blockchain information system will handle the collected data. The four primary duties of this part are data broadcasting, data cleaning, data validation, and capture and query interface, as shown in Figure 13.1. A simple example would be that information from the perception layer is routed to the off-chain layer where it is prepared (encrypted, checked, and cleansed) in the BIS. With the right keys, the final hash data is produced, and the capture and query interface manages blockchain inquiries. The perception layer data and hash data are ultimately broadcast to the blockchain network. The off-chain cloud storage system's first object data store. The essential element of this architecture is the blockchain network layer. It includes, among other things, cryptography, and decentralized applications (DAPP), consensus protocol, and smart contracts. To begin with, a smart contract is a computer protocol designed to digitally enable, verify, or compel the execution or negotiation of contracts. It makes credible transactions possible without the involvement of third parties. The parties' consensus-building process is necessary for the smart contract to be set. Second, the consensus procedure is established right away in the system. It is the algorithm used by blockchain network nodes to come to a consensus. Thirdly, DAPPs are distributed applications over the internet that operates on decentralized peer-to-peer networks. They are accessible to the public as open source software that may be altered and changed. If the information is sensitive or private, it can save operation logs and data cryptographically. Fourthly, cryptography is a tool that is frequently utilized in blockchain networks for a variety of purposes, including digital signatures and the protection of private information. A number of services and software products offered by the companies make up the application layer. According to the distinctive features they offer, these application products and services have links to different phases of the PLM process. Computer-aided design, computer-aided engineering, computer-aided manufacturing, manufacturing execution systems (MES), including computer-aided process planning (CAE/CAD/CAM/CAPP) are a few instances of these applications. The training includes knowledge on PLM co-creation and co-design. Accurate and fast tracking and tracing (QAT2) is linked to pertinent data obtained from the Supply Chain Management System (SCM), Logistics Management System (LMS), and Enterprise Resource Planning (ERP). Proactive maintenance and regulated recycling are demonstrated by Customer Relationship Management Systems (CRMS), Document or Data Management Systems (DMS), and Decision Support Systems (DSS). There are also a tone of additional exclusive apps and systems available. The application layer works tightly with the blockchain network and off-chain layer. Application layer information may be sent to the blockchain network using BIS. The iterative evaluation demonstrates that each of the on-chain and off-chain paradigms may be used to generate information in the blockchain and application layer.

Numerous more premium applications as well as platforms have become accessible. The off-chain layer and blockchain network operate closely together alongside the application layer. Data may be sent between the application layers to the blockchain network using BIS. The iterative analysis demonstrates that the two distinct on-chain and off-chain paradigms may be used to generate information in the blockchain and application layer. The marketing, designing, manufacturing, and packaging are all included in the BOL stage. It is an ordinary process of co-creation. As a result, we suggest using a co-creation blockchain to give the BOL's stakeholders a platform. Product maintenance and warehouse operations are included in the MOL stage. In order to ensure product safety and supply comprehensive product logistics information, we suggest implementing a swift tracking and tracing blockchain. It has to do with using and maintaining the product during the maintenance stage. The product research team, technical supporter, and technical engineer are only a few of the many parties involved in this stage, which is the longest in the PLM. We use blockchain to store end-user feedback data in order to deliver a proactive product service. Preventive, corrective, and predictive maintenance are the three types of product maintenance that can be carried out using the analytical engine and prediction model. To provide a regulated reprocessing process, we propose to use blockchain recycling in the EOL phase. Interestingly, we decompose the cycle into six steps: resale, preparation, identification, recycling-aware design, replication, and recycling.

There are two parts to the connection between the various applications using off-chain and blockchain data. First, the use of internal cloud databases to facilitate connectivity between various apps and off-chain data. The pertinent data kept in a particular enterprise's local or cloud databases is referred to as off-chain data. In addition, blockchain information comes in two forms: object data and on-chain data. Object data is the real information that is stored in multiple databases. Because each block has a finite size, the hash, the object data's storage address, etc. are all seen as being a component of the on-chain data. It implies that the various applications can search through the on-chain data if they require access to the blockchain data. As a result, it saves the storage size of each block in addition to the object data authentication.

13.3.2 The Suggested Platform's Technological Solution

The enterprise-level and product-lifecycle-level illustrations of the suggested architecture's technical process are provided in Figures 13.2 and 13.3, respectively.

At the enterprise level, Figure 13.2's UML sequence diagram illustrates how every component is connected. First, product, process, and resource data are sent to the smart gateway by RFID, IoT sensors, and other means. In this case, all of the data sources are represented by the machine. The physical device known as a smart gateway acts as the point of connection between sensors and the cloud. Most of the time, wireless protocols like Bluetooth, WiFi, and Zigbee are used to establish connectivity between those sensors and the smart gateway. The raw data can be stored and preprocessed in the interim by the smart gateway. Second, the off-chain layer receives the preprocessed data. Typically, MQTT, Plain HTTP, and other messaging protocols are used between the gateway and the cloud. Thirdly, additional processing and storing of the data might be done on the cloud. Which information is forwarded to BIS is determined by the cloud's owners. Fourth, BIS creates legal block header information by organizing the data into blocks based on predetermined structures. The created blocks are

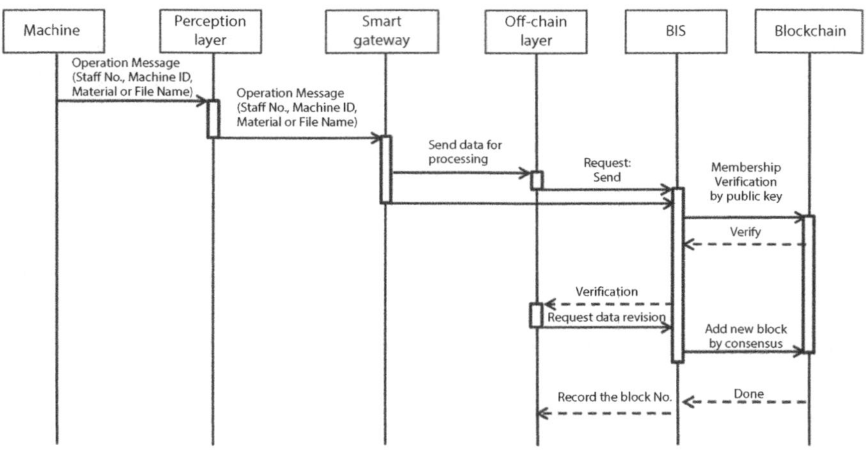

Figure 13.2 The data transmission from a blockchain network to a machine level [53].

then uploaded to the blockchain network using a pre-established smart contract. Lastly, the newly generated blocks are produced by the public key and membership verification. In particular, the consensus algorithms must validate the data before it can be added to the blockchain network. Feedback to BIS and the off-chain layer will be sent once it is deemed unqualified.

As depicted in Figure 13.3, the data circulation is split into three phases at the product lifespan level: BOL, MOL, and EOL. Product-related tasks are included in every step, such as production, warehousing management, and product design. A lot of product information is also included in each activity linked to the product. Consider product design as an example. It includes models, 2D drawings, and design instructions, among other things. Typically, CAD-related databases house them. We employ the collaborative design of the product in a basic scenario to elucidate the process of integrating blockchain-based PLM with current applications.

- Create data on-chain: We regard the conclusion or update of a design contract by a designer of products to be the production of a new block. In the blockchain, a block consists of a pair of components: the block header and the block body. A time stamp, versions, and additional information may be carried by the block header of the suggested industrial blockchain-based PLM system. Restricted-size data, including the product name, designer name, and specific product data, might be carried by the block body along with a link to further data sources. Simultaneously, the finished or altered product layout documents are going to be stored in cloud

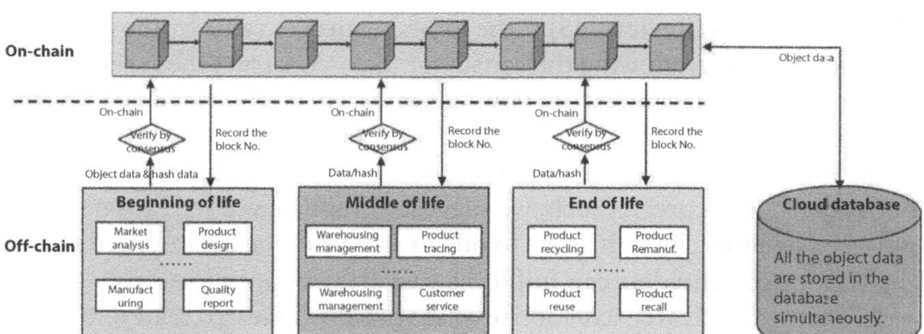

Figure 13.3 Stages of product life cycle [54].

databases linked to CAD, together with the graphical representation and design criteria.
- Obtain Design related Information: Each of the collaborating designers should first check the industrial blockchain-based PLM platform for the required design files. Afterwards, clients can get to more huge drawings kept in online databases over the information's links by utilizing the chosen APIs. Notably, neither in the blockchain nor in the cloud database are the collaborators able to edit the design files. This is so because the hash value connects them all. Any alteration will make the suggested platform incompatible.

Through achieving this, it may assist participants finish joint design assignments accurately and on time, as well as enable cooperative decision-making in blockchain-based PLM. Additionally, it promotes the cross-entity permeability traceability of specialized product design documentations.

13.4 Key Services That are Suggested

This section covers the four standard services in the product lifecycle, as illustrated in Figure 13.1: co-creation services supported by blockchain, maintenance services enabled by blockchain, recycling services enabled by blockchain, and tracking and tracing services offered by blockchain quick inquiry. During the 3 phases of BOL, MOL, and EOL, these kinds of actions are among the most typical ones [23].

13.4.1 A Co-Creation Service Enabled by Blockchain

Prahalad and Ramaswamy introduced the concept of co-creation in the Harvard Business Review [45]. "The joint creation of value by the company and the consumer; allowing the consumer to co-construct the service experience to suit their context" is how the researchers described co-creation in their study [46]. Different issues exist in the nascent I4.0, though. One of the main concerns is the way to create a co-creation atmosphere that is both open and secure. As such, we suggest a brand-new co-creation service powered by blockchain. It seeks to offer a safe yet open atmosphere so that the various stakeholders can fulfill the vast array of unique needs.

In contrast, typical co-creation involves two processes to create joint value creation: selection and participation. Contribution implies persuading clients to share their thoughts with a business. However, because customers aren't as motivated and willing to provide, it can be difficult to receive contributions. We employ blockchain-based platforms, which offer a vehicle for customer and company cooperation, to solve this issue. Customers can use co-creation on this platform to fulfill their specific requests. They are therefore more eager to share their thoughts. The benefits of the participants may be ensured by the safe and transparent platform. In order to meet their needs, vendors and customers might collaborate to create this. We describe the steps involved in achieving the blockchain-enabled co-creation service in Figure 13.4:

- Client recommendations must be entered into the platform and accompanied by a distinct digital signature.
- Initial idea verification can be done by a predefined smart contract and then added to the local blockchain.
- In the next phase, the freshly generated blocks are going to be dispersed throughout the blockchain nodes in an attempt to achieve consensus.
- A block is created in the blockchain network once the predetermined consensus algorithm has reached an agreement on it.
- After that, the on-chain data can be predefined in accordance with the businesses' specifications.
- Lastly, the blockchain's information can be used by the business to inform its decision. Once their concepts are put into

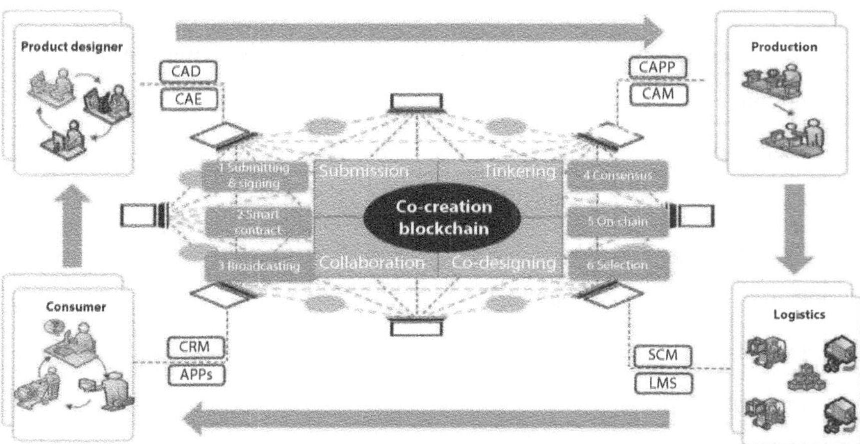

Figure 13.4 The co-creation blockchain-based collaborative development.

practice, the author will receive compensation. Furthermore, the activities are going to be documented in the blockchain network to draw more individuals interested.

We provide an example of a common co-creation situation to help explain the workings of the blockchain-enabled co-creation service: "Ideas from viewers or direct customers are combined to produce fresh concepts for improving the product. To meet the desires of the customers, designers from various companies must collaborate." In order to create a certified product, the designer and producers must work together simultaneously. As a result, in this case, there are three different cooperative forms. The first is represented in Figure 13.4 and is the collaboration between the designer and the customer. It requires the use of CRM, CAD, and CAE, which transforms customer preferences into three-dimensional designs. The second is the collaboration of designers throughout the organization, which includes matching and sharing of CAD data. The collaboration between the manufacturer and designer is the last one. It is a process that uses a range of applications, such as MES and QMS during the production phase and CAD and CAE during the design phase, to convert 3D designs into tangible products. Numerous classified files have been released throughout these partnership procedures, and the corporation is hesitant to make them public for concern that details could be revealed to unauthorized

Table 13.2 Statistics of transaction speed in blockchain [51].

Cryptocurrency	Transactions per second	Average transaction confirmation time
Bitcoin	3-7	60 min
Ethereum	15-25	6 min
Ripple	1500	4 s
Bitcoin Cash	61	60 min
Stellar	1000	2-5 s
Litecoin	56	30 min
Monero	4	30 min
IOTA	1500	2 min
Dash	10-28	15 min

persons. It is challenging for any third-party-based PLM technology to satisfy safety requirements as a result. Blockchain technology is used in this research to provide security. Blockchain-based communication protocols can be used to send the initial private information to the approved entity, as shown in Table 13.2.

13.4.2 Blockchain-Enabled QAT2 Service

As illustrated in Figure 13.5, we suggested the QAT2 service as a way to timely monitor product information. For manufacturing companies, tracking and tracing products is crucial for providing excellent customer service and effectively managing logistics networks [47]. The "distributed ledger" technology of blockchain is currently gaining popularity. Organizations benefit when the transport and surroundings history of a product is encoded into a safe, permanent record.

An inquirer uses a search engine and enters pertinent product details, like the product name and batch number, to monitor and trace a certain product. To locate pertinent product information, like raw material origin and manufacturing quality, data from the blockchain network will be accessed. These data are gathered by IoT technology from product lifecycles. Furthermore, as the previous section demonstrated the BIS acts as a middleman to send the data to the blockchain network. Lastly, the product name, producer, location, time, and quality details are included in the search results from the distributed database based on blockchain technology. Participants in the product lifecycle are currently making changes to this information. The smart contract is going to be updated with the results. The result will be delivered straight to the clients, who will also be

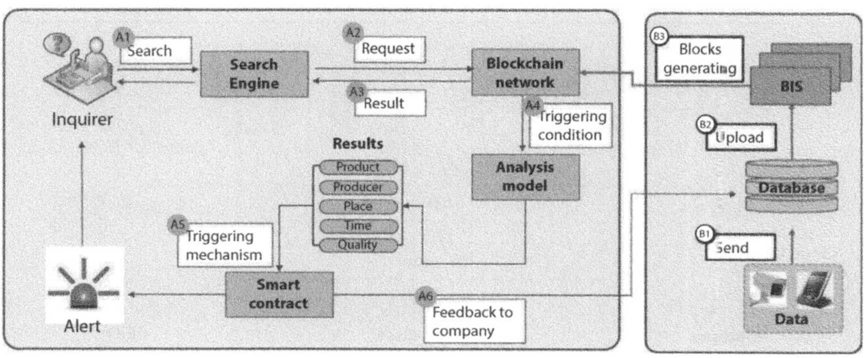

Figure 13.5 Real-time tracking and tracing service enabled by blockchain technology [55].

able to send the producers feedback while the analytical model identifies emergency scenarios.

13.4.3 Proactive Upkeep Service Facilitated by Blockchain

Product care is the longest-lasting PLM stage. There are many entities engaged, including the product research team, technical supporter, and technical engineer. In Figure 13.6, we described the steps involved in achieving the proactive maintenance service that blockchain technology provides. Smart IoT technologies, such as RFID and sensors, enable products to undergo proactive maintenance by gathering data from embedded information devices (PEIDs) in machines and products. Connected to the BIS is the IoT edge. Three ways that data flows in BIS are enterprise information systems (EIS), blockchain networks, and enterprise cloud databases (DB), as was shown in Section 13.2. Here, identity is confirmed by digital signature using cryptography, a crucial component of blockchain technology. Additionally, the global blockchain records' consistency is ensured by the consensus, which is employed to create on-chain blocks [48]. The purpose of the smart contract is to analyze the data gathered during product

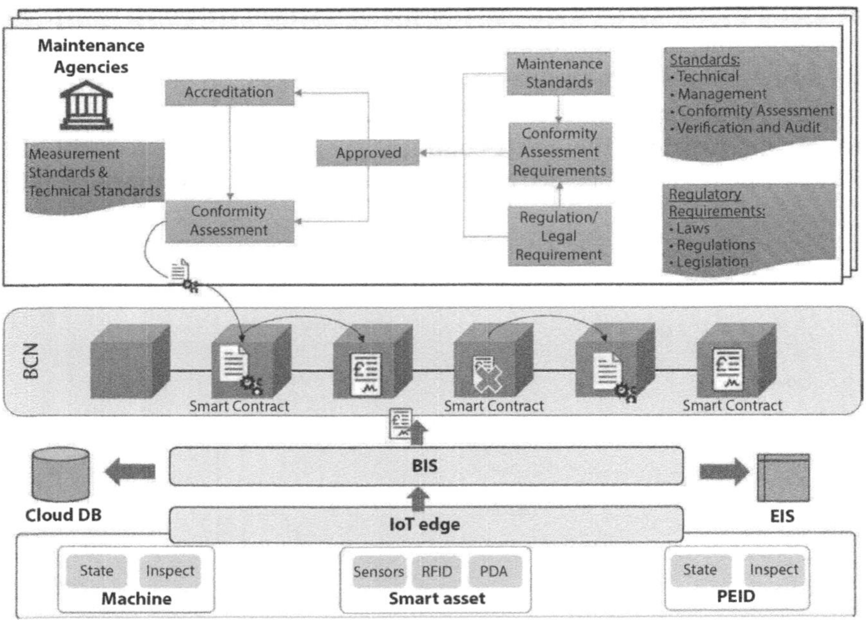

Figure 13.6 Preventative maintenance service powered by blockchain [56].

usage in order to deliver improved product services. To accomplish the proactive maintenance at the top of Figure 13.6, we demonstrate in a basic scenario the establishment of a smart contract.

First, the makers or an independent operator who works with the maintenance agency must compromise on the conditions and standards for maintaining a certain item. They could then draft the blockchain network's smart contract after that. The recently formed data in blockchain that has been collected by IoT technology invokes the terms of the previous contract. The smart contract may carry out automated tasks including monitoring and diagnosing machines, sending out maintenance alerts, and answering maintenance service requests. As a result, maintenance personnel can finish their tasks before the equipment malfunctions. Additionally, the blockchain will contain all maintenance records and machine states. In addition to helping maintainers learn about the product's past, it also makes it easier for managers to decide what needs to be updated or replaced, among other things, depending on the machine's current state.

13.4.4 Smart Recycling Program Driven by Blockchain

Recycling is the process of creating new resources and products out of waste. Recycling lessens the need for fresh raw materials and helps prevent the waste of potentially usable products. As such, it could have major environmental benefits in alongside financial savings for the company. As its goal is to close a loop and reuse components back into the manufacturing process, it is a crucial PLM function. In the past, outside parties have traditionally handled the majority of recycling [49]. Nevertheless, third-party systems usually lack clear recycling capabilities. As an example, the

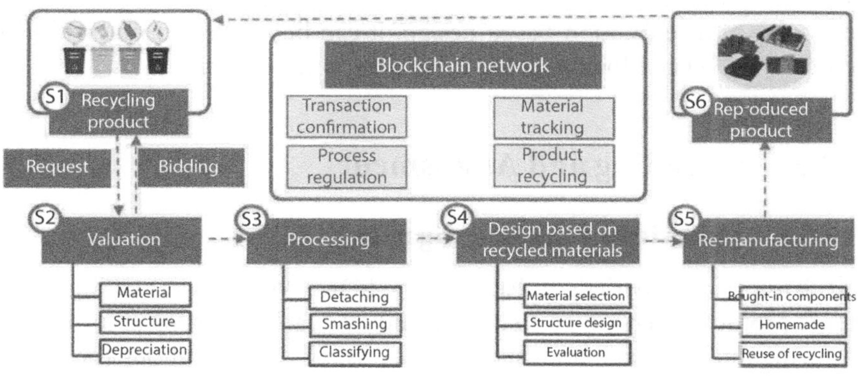

Figure 13.7 Recycling mechanism for blockchain-based design.

system offers the first bid without any clear guidelines. The product owner might be concerned about the blind offer. Moreover, efficient regulatory mechanisms for processing the recycled product are frequently lacking. As a result, the owner throws the thing away or wastes it, endangering the environment and wasting resources.

As illustrated in Figure 13.7, to address such issues, we proposed the blockchain-enabled controlled recycling service. Six components make up the closed loop in product recycling: the recycled product, process, verification, recycling-based design, reproduction, and reproduced product. In the beginning, we established precise guidelines for the process to encourage product users to be prepared to recycle. For example, price ranges according on brand, material, and utilization time are clearly displayed in the rules. Second, all transactions related to product recycling will be documented on the blockchain network. As a result, it offers a trustworthy and transparent recycling process to the goods' owner. Product owners would rather contribute their products to a blockchain-enabled regulated recycling program than toss them out after learning more about the advantages of recycling and how to dispose of products.

The product's manufacturing process is another crucial factor in achieving a closed loops, following recycling. Owing to their complex compositions and wide range of structural variations, these products are challenging to process in a way that minimizes or even completely eliminates environmental damage. Therefore, in order to accomplish environmentally friendly reuse, effective control is required for the processing of recycled products. In this article, the process and reproduction are recorded in a transparent and tractable manner using blockchain technology. For example, blockchain may be utilized to document the recycling product's classification and its breaking and detaching processes. With respect to the recycling and replication-based design, it can be applied in line with the co-creation service logic that has been mentioned before.

13.5 Modelling and Assessment

13.5.1 Overview of the Investigation

Utilizing the Hyperledger Fabric Java SDK, we constructed our system's prototype version so that we could evaluate platforms according to information exchange and platform accessibility. Throughout the initial implementation, we mostly concentrated on the blockchain network with the goal to demonstrate the feasibility and efficacy of integrating blockchain-based technologies into the PLM platform. The standard integrated development platform is Eclipse, and the chosen JDK version is "Java 1.8.0_121." With numerous SDKs, it is an open-source blockchain system compatible with a variety of programming languages. By acquiring the Fabric-SDK-java kit and using IntelliJ IDEA for the programming, we may create the fabric setting and utilize the freely available Hyperledger Fabric Java SDK as an infrastructure for creating blockchain-based services. To build connected smart contracts, we utilize the Go programming system and the Go ChainCode utilities. It functions as the BIS's integrated network smart hub. Our current trial deployment aims to enable BIS to securely move every piece of information from Internet of Things devices to the blockchain network. More comprehensive development tools are shown in Table 13.3.

On the created blockchain network, 100 users and five master nodes were considered to be end users in this experiment. Data with 1000 transactions is divided into four, eight, sixteen, 32, and 64 bits. Smart contracts are developed using chaincode on the Go programming language. Figure 13.8 illustrates the basic structure of this code. It performs the Init and Invoke functions. When the chain code is upgraded or installed for the first time, the call "init" is made. The requirement that starts this smart contract is referred to as a "call." The smart contract will immediately transfer information to the client whenever the predetermined criteria are satisfied. Put another way, the end user will receive the results and provide response immediately when the analytic model identifies a problem.

The three levels of consensus in Hyperledger Fabric are ordering, validation, and endorsement. Hyperledger Fabric supports adaptable consensus services during all three stages. Programs can plug in different ordering, validation, and endorsement models according on their requirements. In particular, the ordering service API can be used to plug in pBFT-based agreement algorithms [43]. Transmit and deliver are the ordering service API's two core operations. Additionally, Member Service Providers (MSP) were used to boost security and provide users with an open platform. A part that seeks to provide a structural model for a group's action is how it is described. In particular, MSP takes out all encryption techniques and procedures related to authentication of users, license validation, and issuing. An MSP establishes their own definition of identification as well as the guidelines that control and authenticate those identities (identity validation).

Table 13.3 Instrument for developing a blockchain-based PLM platform.

Software development kit	**Fabric-sdk-java, Chaincode**
IDE	IntelliJ IDEA, Sublime Text
Blockchain network	H3rperledger Fabric
Cloud server	AWS
Other	Fabric-sample, Docker

As a result, the suggested platform employed the Redundant Byzantine Fault Tolerance consensus technique.

13.5.2 Experimental Evaluation and Comparison

We used both qualitative and quantitative methods to analyze the system we had suggested. A qualitative comparison is made between the suggested PLM as well as five of the primary systems already in use, which are: Blockchain public cloud PLM, cloud-based PLM, internet-based PLM, agent-based PLM, and conventional PLM. The suggested PLM is compared with existing PLMs using PLM standards that are already accessible in the literature. Some typical essential features of PLM are privacy, ubiquity of access, and scalability, which refers to the degree of customization and learn ability. A few other variables, such as transaction speed, are also included since they could also indicate the cost. Table 13.4 displays the comparison's outcomes.

In order to accentuate the benefits of the suggested platform, a quantitative comparison is made between it and the Ethereum public platform using two primary metrics: throughput and latency. There are two key performance indicators (KPIs) that are used in the platform to assess how well the blockchain network is performing [50]. On the one hand, five different combinations of block sizes and transaction arrival rates are used to compare the latency of the suggested platform with the Ethereum platform. In particular, the block sizes are 4 bits, 8 bits, 16 bits, 32 bits, and 64 bits. Transaction arrival rates of 20, 40, 60, 80, and 100 TPs are also included. Notably, on the suggested platform, "tps" denotes transactions that are finished in a single second. Based on Figure 13.9 and Table 13.5, three noteworthy findings are evident. First off, given the same transaction

```
        function addNewOrderData(uint operateID,        string operatorName, uint machineID,
string materials, uint temperature, uint humidity)
public payable returns(uint stateNum, string message)
        {
                OrderData storage _tempOrderData;
                uint stateNum;
                string message;
_tempOrderData.operateID = operateID;
                _tempOrderData.operatorName = operatorName;
                _tempOrderData.machineID = machineID;
                _tempOrderData.materials = materials;
                _tempOrderData.temperature = temperature;
                _tempOrderData.humidity = humidity;

                OrderDataCollection[operateID] = _tempOrderData; //saving the data

                if((T_LOWER_LIMIT < temperature) && (temperature < T_UPPER_LIMIT)
&& (H_LOWER_LIMIT < humidity) && (humidity < H_UPPER_LIMIT)){
                        // set the message to show that the data save success
                        stateNum = 0;
                        message = "the new data adds successfully";
                }
                else{
                // set the message to show that data save success but some data abnormal
                stateNum = 1;
                message = "There is an data warning occur";
                // when an error of environment occur, sending the error report with the error data and message
                if(temperature < T_LOWER_LIMIT)
                {
                        emit DataErrorWarning(msg.sender, operateID, TLErrorNumber, "the temperature too low");
                }
                if(temperature > T_UPPER_LIMIT)
                {
                        emit DataErrorWarning(msg.sender, operateID, TUErrorNumber, "the temperature too high");
                }
```

Figure 13.8 The smart contract code sample for rist analytics [57].

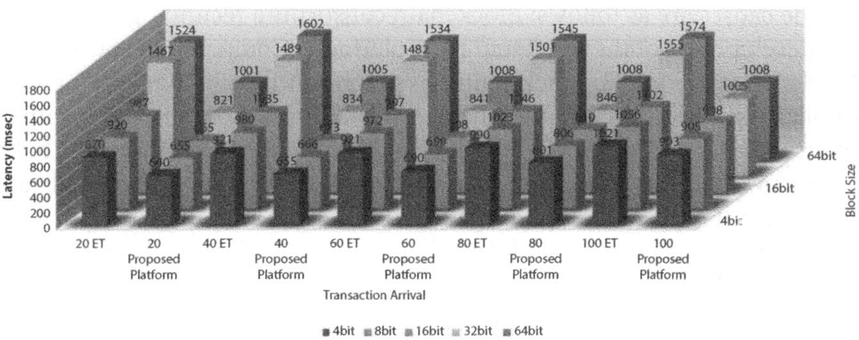

Figure 13.9 The differing block sizes' latency under varying transaction arrival rates [58].

Table 13.4 The common comparisons in a qualitative approach with the current PLM platform.

Type of PLM/ characteristics	Traditional PLM/ PDM [1, 14]	Web based PLM [17]	Agent based PLM [18]	Cloud based PLM [19, 20]	Blockchain public cloud PLM [32, 43]	Proposed platform
Reliability	✓	✓	✓	✓	✓	✓
Confidentiality	✓	✓	✓	✓	✓	✓
Complete Access				✓	✓	✓
Authenticity					✓	✓
Transparency		✓			✓	✓
Intelligence & Interdependence					✓	✓
Dispersion			✓			✓
Flexibility			✓	✓	✓	✓
Safety						✓

arrival rate and block size, the suggested platform has less latency than the Ethereum platform. As illustrated in Figure 13.9, the suggested platform's latency is 640 ms, significantly less than the Ethereum platform's 870 ms, given a transaction arrival rate of 20 tps and a block size of 4 bits. In general, the mean latency of the suggested platform is significantly lower than that of the Ethereum platform, as indicated in Table 13.5. The explanations for the causes are as follows: Blockchain consortium technology is used in the development of the suggested PLM platform. Compared to consortium blockchain, the public blockchain has a substantially higher rate of data duplication; additionally, the suggested platform's consensus algorithm offers a better mining procedure. Second, as Figure 13.9 illustrates, both platforms' latencies were trending upward as the transaction arrival rate increased; however, the Ethereum platform's (ET) rate of growth is substantially more than our platform's. This serves as additional proof of the suggested platform's superior performance. Thirdly, latency increases with block size on both platforms; however, the delay really increases until the block size exceeds 32 bits. This indicates that the latency is significantly impacted by the block size in a nonlinear way. When its size is above a particular threshold (32 bits), the platform's latency will significantly increase.

Conversely, a throughput evaluation is carried out, considering varying peer numbers, between the proposed platform and the Ethereum platform. When there are 1000 transactions in the dataset, the throughput of each invoke function implementation is displayed in Figure 13.10. Improved bandwidth through one peer to twenty peers is provided by the suggested structures, which makes use of the consortium Hyperledger system. The platform has a range of 165 tps to about 250 tps for data processing. The Ethereum platform can process data at a rate of 140 to 150 tbps. It is also necessary to acknowledge that the suggested platform lacks Ethereum's

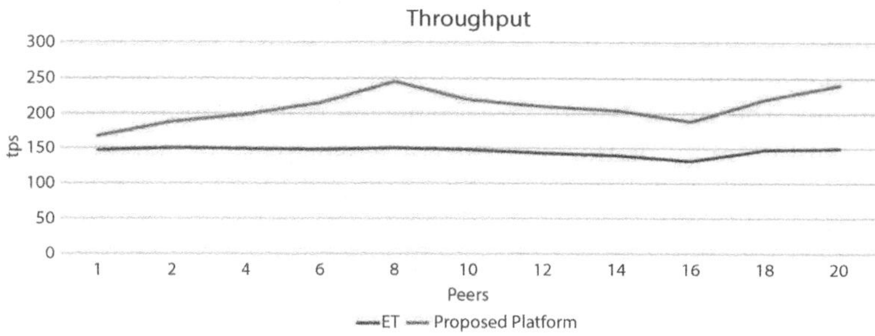

Figure 13.10 ET and the suggested platform: a comparative analysis.

Table 13.5 Detailed data regarding latency execution [59].

		Mean	Standard deviation	Standard error	95% confidence interval
20 (Vs) Black size 4 tit	ET	1153.6	315.5	141.09	391.6
	Proposed Platform	756.4	155.07	69.3	192.5
40 (tps) Block size 8 bit	ET	1205.4	315.4	140.14	390.82
	Proposed Platform	766.6	152.2	68.08	189
60 (tps) Block size 16 bit	ET	1181.2	300.1	134.22	372.6
	Proposed Platform	789.2	137.04	61.2	170.1
80 (tps) Block size 32 bit	ET	1221	276.8	123.8	343.6
	Proposed Platform	854.2	87.7	39.2	108.9
100 (tps) Block size 64 bit	ET	1261.6	278.07	124.3	345.2
	Proposed Platform	945.8	55.44	24.7	68.8

level of dependability. This implies that when utilizing the suggested pBFT-based system, the client might encounter varying transmission speeds.

13.5.3 Discussion

Standalone and centralized solutions from software suppliers serve as the foundation for the implementation of conventional PLM systems. It is rare for the collaborating parties to integrate and exchange PLM information. This research proposes an industrial blockchain-based PLM to satisfy the I4.0 period's objectives for transparency, interconnectedness, and durability. It developed a whole new kind of blockchain-powered P2P interaction system. In an open setting, it can assist users in conducting their individual sharing of information and service interchange. The preliminary simulation indicates that there may be a number of benefits to using the recommended platform.

Initially, the pBFT-based agreement algorithm outperforms the conventional Ethereum platform in the consensus process. According to preliminary experimental findings, the suggested platform outperforms the platform used by Ethereum in terms of bandwidth for peers (nodes) with a range of one to twenty. It also outperforms the Ethereum platform in terms of latency for all five types of block sizes (four, eight, sixteen, thirty, and sixty-four bits). Therefore, the proposed platform performs better than Ethereum in terms of latency for block formation and bandwidth. In addition, as Table 13.3 demonstrates, we conducted a methodical comparison between the suggested PLM platform and the PLM systems which are already in usage. Using the literature, we analyze a variety of criteria, such as reliability, confidentiality, complete access, authenticity, transparency, intelligence and interdependence dispersion, flexibility and safety. Compared with numerous existing PLM systems, we discovered that the blockchain-based PLM platform offered much more advantages. Increasing the number of participants and their respective contributions offers the benefit of better fulfilling PLM criteria down the road.

The co-creation support, QAT2 service, proactive maintenance service, and regulated recycling service are, ultimately, four of the primary tasks that were enhanced by the application of industrial blockchain technology. Blockchain technology can be used to provide co-creation services by offering an integrative platform that enables producers, transporters, and their corporate information systems to merge data about products. Additionally, it can provide customers with a safe, open atmosphere in which they can work together to generate value that is customized to meet their particular requirements. Every contribution made by the customer is securely documented, ensuring that the contributors will profit. By safely and permanently recording the shipment's location and environmental condition record using a chain-based method, the industrial blockchain-based solution that is recommended for QAT2 service provides the traceability service. A chain-based approach will be used to convey information about the product's history, from its manufacture to the point of usage.

Smart contracts are used in proactive maintenance services to analyze PEID data according to predetermined criteria. In order to facilitate prompt preventative maintenance for the product being used, it offers an automated problem diagnosis. Blockchain has the ability to affect waste material monitoring, transaction confirmation, process regulation in re-production, and other aspects of regulated recycling. It provides a closed loop PLM that is regulated and facilitates the reuse of ecologically friendly materials. Our recommended platform does, however, have some shortcomings. Initially, as our recommended platform was not totally implemented in the real-world use case study, the findings that are presently available show the possibility of establishing this platform, but they do not allow for a quantitative comparison with more established PLM platforms.

Secondly, there is a redundancy problem with the consensus algorithm based on pBFT. The performance of the suggested blockchain-based PLM solution is hampered by the increasing latency of the pBFT-based consensus as the number of nodes rises. Thirdly, compared to Ethereum, this suggested platform is not as stable. As demonstrated in Figure 13.10, in the same experimental setup, the suggested pBFT-based consensus performs better in terms of throughput than Ethereum, although its stability is not as strong. This implies that when utilizing the suggested pBFT-based platform, the user may encounter varying throughput speeds.

13.6 Conclusion and Future Work

In order to provide a collaborative environment for managing the entire product lifecycle in the I4.0 era, an open, secure, interconnected, and decentralized PLM platform is required. The PLM platform for information sharing and service exchange that is built on industrial blockchain technology is presented in this article. The contributions of this study are summarized as follows. First, in order to achieve openness, interconnectivity, and decentralization, the suggested industrial blockchain-based PLM platform's technical architecture was designed. Second, heterogeneous and multi-source data are automatically processed and disseminated using tailored BIS. Thirdly, product flows in the product lifecycles are facilitated by alert services and transaction executions enabled by smart contracts. It aids the business in making decisions quickly and offering support, which raises the caliber of their goods and services. Finally, the full process of PLM is depicted utilizing four blockchain-based vital services, which are co-design and co-creation, proactive maintenance, controlled recycling service, and QAT2 service. The experimental simulation's conclusions reveal that, across both qualitative and quantitative assessments, the suggested PLM platform beats the existing PLM systems. The general and latency efficiency is significantly superior than Ethereum.

The work can be expanded upon in the future from the organizational and technological angles. From a technology standpoint, greater verification and assessment of the suggested platform's scalability and interoperability in a real-world commercial setting with additional nodes is necessary. We only consider 100 users and 5 master nodes in this study. On the other hand, in a genuine business setting, there are more nodes. Therefore, when adding extra nodes, it's critical to take the suggested platform's compatibility and scalability into account. We propose that BIS facilitates the transfer of data in an optimal state for the experiment's execution. In the actual situation, there are additional considerations like messaging protocol and security. Thirdly, the application of emergency alarm systems made possible by smart contracts needs to be closely examined. Learning how to respond quickly to emerging product incidents and update versioned smart contracts are part of this. From an organizational perspective, additional value measures are necessary to assess the genuine benefits and dangers of the fully integrated PLM solution. These metrics include user experiences, return on investment, and investment risks, between others. For example, in the context of the industrial blockchain, a more thorough practical analysis is needed to assess the possible dangers and opportunities associated with PLM activities.

A Statement of Competing Interests

According to the authors, the article is original, has not previously been published, and is not currently being assessed for publishing elsewhere. No significant money has been obtained for this study that might have influenced its outcomes, while there are not any recognized conflicts of interest surrounding its publication. We attest that each of the mentioned writers has read and approved the work, and that no other individuals have met the requirements to be included as authors. We also reaffirm that we have all endorsed the authors' indicated order in the work. As far as we know, the Corresponding Author is the sole individual to get in touch with about anything related to editing, especially direct communication with the Editorial Manager and the office. He is in charge of keeping the other authors informed about his work, submitting corrections, and approving the proofs in the end. We attest that we have given the Corresponding Author access to our current, valid email address, which is set up to receive correspondence from the editorial office.

References

1. Stark, J., Product lifecycle management, in: *Product Lifecycle Management*, vol. 1, pp. 1–29, Springer, Cham, 2015, https://doi.org/10.1007/978-3-319-17440-2_1.
2. Kung, K.H., Ho, C.F., Hung, W.H., Wu, C.C., Organizational adaptation for using PLM systems: group dynamism and management involvement. *Ind. Mark. Manag.*, 44, 83–97, 2015, https://doi.org/10.1016/j.indmarman.2014.04.018.
3. d'Avolio, E., Bandinelli, R., Rinaldi, R., Improving new product development in the fashion industry through product lifecycle management: a descriptive analysis. *Int. J. Fash. Des. Technol. Educ.*, 8, 2, 108–121, 2015, https://doi.org/10.1080/ 17543266.2015.1005697.
4. Tao, F., Zuo, Y., Da Xu, L., Zhang, L., IoT-based intelligent perception and access of manufacturing resource toward cloud manufacturing. *IEEE Trans. Ind. Inf.*, 10, 2, 1547–1557, 2014, https://doi.org/10.1109/TII.2014.2306397.
5. Jing, Q., Vasilakos, A.V., Wan, J., Lu, J., Qiu, D., Security of the Internet of Things: perspectives and challenges. *Wirel. Netw.*, 20, 8, 2481–2501, 2014, https://doi. org/10.1007/s11276-014-0761-7.
6. Kagermann, H., Helbig, J., Hellinger, A., Wahlster, W., Recommendations for implementing the strategic initiative Industrie 4.0: securing the future of German manufacturing industry, Forschungsunion, 2013 Final Report of the Industrie 4.0 Working Group.
7. Hermann, M., Pentek, T., Otto, B., Design principles for industrie 4.0 scenarios. *Proceedings of the 49th Hawaii International Conference on System Sciences (HICSS)*, IEEE, pp. 3928–3937, 2016.
8. Iansiti, M. and Lakhani, K.R., The truth about blockchain. *Harv. Bus. Rev.*, 95, 118–127, 2017, https://hbr.org/2017/01/the-truth-about-blockchain.
9. Mattila, J., Seppälä, T., Naucler, C., Stahl, R., Tikkanen, M., Bådenlid, A., Seppälä, J., Industrial blockchain platforms: an exercise in use case development in the energy industry. ETLA Working Papers 43, The Research Institute of the Finnish Economy, 2016, https://ideas.repec.org/p/rif/wpaper/43.html.

10. Li, W., Sforzin, A., Fedorov, S., Karame, G.O., Towards scalable and private industrial blockchains. *Proceedings of the ACM Workshop on Blockchain, Cryptocurrencies and Contracts*, ACM, pp. 9–14, 2017.
11. Li, Z., Kang, J., Yu, R., Ye, D., Deng, Q., Zhang, Y., Consortium blockchain for secure energy trading in industrial internet of things. *IEEE Trans. Ind. Inf.*, 14, 8, 3690–3700, 2017, https://doi.org/10.1109/TII.2017.2786307.
12. Terzi, S., Bouras, A., Dutta, D., Garetti, M., Kiritsis, D., Product lifecycle managementfrom its history to its new role. *Int. J. Prod. Lifecycle Manag.*, 4, 4, 360–389, 2010.
13. Jun, H.-B., Shin, J.-H., Kiritsis, D., Xirouchakis, P., System architecture for closedloop PLM. *Int. J. Comput. Integr. Manuf.*, 20, 684–698, 2007, https://doi.org/10. 1080/09511920701566624.
14. David, M. and Rowe, F., What does PLMS (product lifecycle management systems) manage: data or documents? Complementarity and contingency for SMEs. *Comput. Ind.*, 75, 140–150, 2016, https://doi.org/10.1016/j.compind.2015.05.005.
15. Cao, H. and Folan, P., Product life cycle: the evolution of a paradigm and literature review from 1950–2009. *Prod. Plan. Control*, 23, 8, 641–662, 2012, https://doi. org/10.1080/09537287.2011.577460.
16. Alemanni, M., Destefanis, F., Vezzetti, E., Model-based definition design in the product lifecycle management scenario. *Int. J. Adv. Manuf. Technol.*, 52, 1–4, 1–14, 2011, https://doi.org/10.1007/s00170-010-2699-y.
17. Maropoulos, P.G. and Ceglarek, D., Design verification and validation in product lifecycle. *CIRP Ann. Manuf. Technol.*, 59, 2, 740–759, 2010, https://doi.org/10.1016/ j.cirp.2010.05.005.
18. Vezzetti, E., Product lifecycle data sharing and visualization: web-based approaches. *Int. J. Adv. Manuf. Technol.*, 41, 5–6, 613–630, 2009, https://doi.org/10.1007/ s00170-008-1503-8.
19. Mahdjoub, M., Monticolo, D., Gomes, S., Sagot, J.C., A collaborative design for usability approach supported by virtual reality and a multi-agent system embedded in a PLM environment. *Comput.-Aided Des.*, 42, 5, 402–413, 2010, https://doi.org/ 10.1016/j.cad.2009.02.009.
20. Husseini, Kamal & Hernández, Hans & Mayer, Dominik & Fleischer, Jürgen. (2023). Potentials and Design of a Virtual Production System for Intelligent Battery Cell Manufacturing. 10.1007/978-3-658-39928-3_19.
21. Gomez, C.A.S., Castiblanco, L.E.G., Osorio, J.M.A., Building a virtual machine tool in a standard PLM platform. *Int. J. Interact. Des. Manuf. (IJIDeM)*, 11, 2, 445–455, 2017, https://doi.org/10.1007/s12008-016-0312-9.
22. Noizat, P., Blockchain electronic vote, in: *Handbook of digital currency*, pp. 453–461, Academic Press, 2015. 10.1016/B978-0-12-802117-0.00022-9.
23. Soto-Acosta, P., Placer-Maruri, E., Perez-Gonzalez, D., A case analysis of a product lifecycle information management framework for SMEs. *Int. J. Inf. Manage.*, 36, 2, 240–244, 2016, https://doi.org/10.1016/j.ijinfomgt.2015.12.001.

24. Demoly, F., Yan, X.T., Eynard, B., Rivest, L., Gomes, S., An assembly-oriented design framework for product structure engineering and assembly sequence planning. *Robot. Comput. Integr. Manuf.*, 27, 1, 33–46, 2011, https://doi.org/10.1016/j. rcim.2010.05.010.
25. Nakamoto, S., Bitcoin: A Peer-to-Peer Electronic Cash System, 2009, https://www.sec.gov/comments/s7-04-23/s70423-290181-707862.pdf
26. Crosby, M., Pattanayak, P., Verma, S., Kalyanaraman, V., Blockchain technology: beyond bitcoin. *Appl. Innov.*, 2, 6–10, 2016, https://doi.org/10.1145/2994581.
27. Weber, I., Xu, X., Riveret, R., Governatori, G., Ponomarev, A., Mendling, J., Untrusted business process monitoring and execution using blockchain. *Proceedings of the International Conference on Business Process Management*, Springer, Cham., pp. 329–347, 2016, https://doi.org/10.1007/978-3-319-45348-4_19.
28. Drescher, D., & Drescher, D., Using the Data Store: Chaining blocks of data. *Blockchain Basics: A Non-Technical Introduction in 25 Steps*, pp. 123–134, 2017, http://dx.doi.org/10.1007/978-1-4842-2604-9.
29. Bahga, A. and Madisetti, V.K., Blockchain platform for industrial internet of things. *J. Softw. Eng. Appl.*, 9, 10, 533, 2016.
30. Sikorski, J.J., Haughton, J., Kraft, M., Blockchain technology in the chemical industry: machine-to-machine electricity market. *Appl. Energy*, 195, 234–246, 2017, https://doi.org/10.1016/j.apenergy.2017.03.039.
31. Bocek, T., Rodrigues, B.B., Strasser, T., Stiller, B., Blockchains everywhere-a use-case of blockchains in the pharma supply-chain. *Proceedings of the IFIP/IEEE Symposium on Integrated Network and Service Management (IM)*, IEEE, pp. 772–777, 2017, https://doi.org/10.23919/INM.2017.7987376.
32. Li, Z., Wang, W.M., Liu, G., Liu, L., He, J., Huang, G.Q., Toward open manufacturing: a cross-enterprises knowledge and services exchange framework based on blockchain and edge computing. *Ind. Manag. Data Syst.*, 118, 1, 303–320, 2018, https://doi. org/10.1108/IMDS-04-2017-0142.
33. Li, Z., Liu, X., Wang, W.M., Vatankhah Barenji, A., Huang, G.Q., CKshare: secured cloud-based knowledge-sharing blockchain for injection mold redesign. *Enterp. Inf. Syst.*, 1–33, 2018, https://doi.org/10.1080/17517575.2018.1539774.
34. Li, Z., Liu, L., Barenji, A.V., Wang, W., Cloud-based manufacturing blockchain: secure knowledge sharing for injection mould redesign. *Procedia CIRP*, 72, 1, 961–966, 2018, https://doi.org/10.1016/j.procir.2018.03.004.
35. Viriyasitavat, W., Da Xu, L., Bi, Z. *et al.* Blockchain-based business process management (BPM) framework for service composition in industry 4.0. *J. Intell. Manuf.*, 31, 1737–1748, 2020, https://doi.org/10.1007/s10845-018-1422-y
36. Francisco, K. and Swanson, D., The supply chain has no clothes: technology adoption of blockchain for supply chain transparency. *Logistics*, 2, 1, 2, 2018, https://doi.org/ 10.3390/logistics2010002.

37. Kim, H.M. and Laskowski, M., Toward an ontology-driven blockchain design for supply-chain provenance. *Intell. Syst. Account. Finance Manag.*, 25, 1, 18–27, 2018, https://doi.org/10.1002/isaf.1424.
38. Madhwal, Y. and Panfilov, P.B., Industrial case: blockchain on Aircraft's parts supply chain management. *Proceedings of the AMCIS 2017 Workshops*, vol. 6, 2017, http:// aisel.aisnet.org/sigbd2017/6.
39. Mattila, J., Seppälä, T., Holmström, J., Product-centric information management: a case study of a shared platform with blockchain technology. *Berkeley Roundtable Int. Econ.*, pp. 1–24, 2016, https://escholarship.org/uc/item/65s5s4b2.
40. Buterin, V., A next-generation smart contract and decentralized application platform. white paper, pp. 1–36, 2014, https://cryptorating.eu/whitepapers/Ethereum/ Ethereum_white_paper.pdf.
41. Lu, Q. and Xu, X., Adaptable blockchain-based systems: a case study for product traceability. *IEEE Software*, 34, 6, 21–27, 2017, https://doi.org/10.1109/MS.2017. 4121227.
42. Zheng, Z., Xie, S., Dai, H., Chen, X., Wang, H., An overview of blockchain technology: architecture, consensus, and future trends. *Proceedings of the IEEE International Congress On Big Data (BigData Congress)*, 2017, June, IEEE, pp. 557–564, https:// doi.org/10.1109/BigDataCongress.2017.85.
43. Li, Z., Vatankhah, B.A., Huang, G.Q., Toward a blockchain cloud manufacturing system as a peer to peer distributed network platform. *Robot. Comput. Integr. Manuf.*, 54, 133–144, 2018, https://doi.org/10.1016/j.rcim.2018.05.011.
44. Aazam, M., Hung, P.P., Huh, E.N., Smart gateway-based communication for cloud of things. *Proceedings of the IEEE Ninth International Conference on Intelligent Sensors, Sensor Networks and Information Processing (ISSNIP)*, IEEE, pp. 1–6, 2014, https://doi.org/10.1109/ISSNIP.2014.6827673.
45. Prahalad, C.K. and Ramaswamy, V., Co-Opting customer competence. *Harv. Bus. Rev.*, 78, 1, 79–90, 2000.
46. Prahalad, C.K. and Ramaswamy, V., The Future of Competition: Co-Creating Unique Value with Customers. Harvard Business School Press, Boston, ISBN 1-57851-953-5, 2004, https://www.scirp.org/reference/referencespapers?referenceid=1166252
47. Shamsuzzoha, A. and Helo, P.T., Real-time tracking and tracing system: potentials for the logistics network. *Proceedings of the International Conference On Industrial Engineering and Operations Management*, pp. 22–24, 2011.
48. Kosba, A., Miller, A., Shi, E., Wen, Z., Papamanthou, C., Hawk: the blockchain model of cryptography and privacy-preserving smart contracts, in: *Proceedings of the EEE Symposium on Security and Privacy (SP)*, IEEE, pp. 839–858, 2016, 10.1109/SP.2016.55.
49. Schaddelee-Scholten, B. and Tempowski, J., Recycling Used Lead-Acid Batteries: Health Considerations, World Health Organization, 2017, http://apps.who.int/iris/bitstream/handle/10665/259447/9789241512855-eng.pdf;jsessionid= E1221C78C1A7F5F8175CE03A79FB4EE2?sequence=1.

50. Nasir, Q., Qasse, I., Abu Talib, M., Nassif, A., Performance Analysis of Hyperledger Fabric Platforms. *Secur. Comm. Netw.*, 2018, 1–14, 2018, 10.1155/2018/3976093.
51. Hazari, S., Shihab, Mahmoud, Q.H., Improving Transaction Speed and Scalability of Blockchain Systems via Parallel Proof of Work. *Future Internet*, 12, 8, 125, 2020, https://doi.org/10.3390/fi12080125.
52. Chen, S., Cai, X., Wang, X., Liu, A., Lu, Q., Xu, X., Tao, F., Blockchain applications in PLM towards smart manufacturing. *Int. J. Adv. Manuf. Technol.*, 118, 1–15, 2022. 10.1007/s00170-021-07802-z.
53. Shah, D., Patel, D., Adesara, J. *et al.*, Integrating machine learning and blockchain to develop a system to veto the forgeries and provide efficient results in education sector. *Vis. Comput. Ind. Biomed. Art*, 4, 18, 2021, https://doi.org/10.1186/s42492-021-00084-y.
54. Hayat, M. and Winkler, H., From Traditional Product Lifecycle Management Systems to Blockchain-Based Platforms. *Logistics*, 6, 3, 40, 2022, https://doi.org/10.3390/logistics6030040.
55. Howard, K.L., Emerging Technology Offers Benefits for Some Applications but Faces Challenges, 2022, https://www.gao.gov/products/gao-22-104625.
56. Munir, M., Habib, S., Hussain, A., Shahbaz, M., Qamar, A., Masood, T., Sultan, M., Abbas, M.M., Imran, S., Hasan, M., Akhtar, M., Ayub, H.M.U., Salman, C.A., Blockchain Adoption for Sustainable Supply Chain Management: Economic, Environmental, and Social Perspectives Citation. *Front. Energy Res.*, 10, 899632, 2022, 10.3389/fenrg.2022.899632.
57. Hasan, H., Alhadhrami, E., AlDhaheri, A., Salah, K., Jayaraman, R., Smart Contract-based Approach for Efficient Shipment Management. *Comput. Industrial Eng.*, 136, 2019. 10.1016/j.cie.2019.07.022.
58. Qureshi, K.N., Shahzad, L., Abdelmaboud, A., Eisa, T.A.E., Alamri, B., Javed, I.T., Al-Dhaqm, A., Crespi, N., A Blockchain-Based Efficient, Secure and Anonymous Conditional Privacy-Preserving and Authentication Scheme for the Internet of Vehicles. *Appl. Sci.*, 12, 1, 476, 2022, https://doi.org/10.3390/app12010476.
59. Al-Malah, D., The Importance of Educational Technology and its Impact on Sustainability Education An exploratory Study in Iraqi Universities. 10.4108/eai.28-6-2020.2297910

14

Machine Learning Enabled Smart Agriculture Classification Technique for Edge Devices Using Remote Sensing Platform

Priyanka Gupta[1,2]*, Suraj Kumar Singh[3], Neetish Kumar[4] and Bhavna Thakur[5]

[1]School of Engineering & Technology, Suresh Gyan Vihar University, Jaipur, India
[2]Noida Institute of Engineering & Technology, Greater Noida, UP, India
[3]Department of Centre for Sustainable Development, Suresh Gyan Vihar University, Jaipur, India
[4]Central Institute for Women in Agriculture, Bhubaneswar, Odisha, India
[5]School of Agriculture and Allied Sciences, Doon Business School Group, Dehradun, India

Abstract

Crop maps that are accurate and dependable are necessary for food security on a regional and global level. The increasing availability of satellite imagery poses a "Big Data" difficulty when producing crop maps. These days, cloud-based systems are receiving a lot of interest for classifying crops across wide areas. The primary objective of the study is to analyze crop categorization on the Google Earth engine platform using different machine learning (ML) techniques, such as smile Naïve Bayes and minimum distance classifier. We can retrieve the data to edge devices and store the data to cloud storage platform by using Google earth engine using remote sensing platform. The primary objective is to assess how well the Google Earth engine (GEE) classified various crops in the Mathura district of Uttar Pradesh, India, using the Sentinel 2 MSI dataset. With the use of automatic filtering or percentage cloud property on the GEE platforms, the best cloud-free image (less than 5%) of the Sentinel 2 MSI datasets are used for crop categorization. Furthermore, the GEE platform's acquisition, clarification and pre-processing of satellite datasets might be arranged in a very effective way. Similar to training

**Corresponding author*: priyankagupta.cse@niet.co.in

Mohit Kumar, Gautam Srivastava, Ashutosh Kumar Singh and Kalka Dubey (eds.) AI-Based Advanced Optimization Techniques for Edge Computing, (381–400) © 2025 Scrivener Publishing LLC

datasets, points are employed as feature spaces. Additionally, kappa coefficient and accuracy assessment (Producer and Consumer accuracy) employ confusion matrices. Compare the dataset's results based on the F1 score, kappa coefficient, and overall accuracy (OA). The Sentinel 2 MSI images apply smile Naïve Bayes classifier gain 61.5% overall accuracy and minimum distance classifier achieve 70.7 % overall accuracy. Based on study, it is discovered that the minimal distance classifier outperformed others than smile Naïve Bayes classifier in crop mapping.

Keywords: Machine learning, classification, smart agriculture, sentinel 2 MSI, cloud/edge platform

List of Abbreviations

GEE	Google Earth Engine
GIS	Geographical Information System
DT	Decision Tree
MSI	Multi Spectral Images
ML	Machine Learning
SVM	Support Vector Machine
NB	Naïve Bayes classifier
TOA	Top of atmosphere
MD	Minimum Distance Classifier
PA	Producer Accuracy
UA	User Accuracy

14.1 Introduction

In order to ensure national food security and formulate food policy, a nation must promptly and efficiently obtain information on the distribution of regional crop cultivation. Strong periodicity, diverse spectrum information and a wide monitoring range are the features of satellite remote sensing (RS) technology. The advancement of satellite remote sensing technology has led to improvements in both temporal and spatial resolutions. As a result, image resolution knowledge has come to be crucial for agricultural RS applications like crop estimation. It is feasible to identify extensive crop categories using RS-based methods for planting structure, area extraction, and change analysis.

Precision agriculture is an emerging approach to farming that utilizes advanced technologies to optimize resource utilization and maximize crop productivity. Remote sensing platforms, such as UAVs and satellites, provide valuable data about crop health, soil moisture, and nutrient levels, while ML algorithms can analyse this data to identify patterns and extract meaningful insights. However, traditional cloud-based ML approaches face challenges in terms of latency and network bandwidth limitations, making them impractical for real-time applications in remote agricultural environments. Edge computing offers a promising solution by enabling real-time processing and analysis of remote sensing data on edge devices located close to the data source.

Google created the cloud-based technology known as GEE for planetary scale geo-spatial investigation. It offers access to a large number of geospatial datasets and satellite imagery, as well as the processing and analysis capability required to handle these information. Many different sectors, such as urban planning, agriculture, forestry, disaster organization, LULC change analysis, and environmental monitoring, make extensive use of Google Earth Engine. The capacity of Google Earth Engine to use massive geographic datasets for model training and deployment is one of its major contributions to machine learning.

Access to a vast library of satellite images from several sources, such as MODIS, Sentinel, Landsat, and others, is possible with Google Earth Engine. Additionally, a large variety of climatic and environmental datasets are provided. These datasets are available for use by researchers and developers to train machine learning models for tasks including semantic segmentation, object identification, and picture classification. Google's cloud architecture, which offers high-performance computing resources for handling massive geographic information, powers Google Earth Engine. Because of this architecture, scientists can train machine learning models on enormous volumes of data without being concerned about hardware constraints. Google's open-source machine learning structure Tensor Flow is integrated with Google Earth Engine. Because of this connection, researchers may use geographical data from Earth Engine directly within TensorFlow to construct and train deep learning models. The creation of sophisticated machine learning models for applications like agricultural yield prediction, deforestation monitoring, and land cover categorization is made possible by this integration. Researchers and developers may work together in a collaborative environment on Google Earth Engine, sharing models, data, and code.

The advancement of remote sensing technologies and machine learning (ML) algorithms has revolutionized the field of precision agriculture, allowing farmers to make data driven choices to enhance crop construction and minimize environmental impact. Edge computing, which brings computation closer to the data source, offers a promising explanation for processing large volumes of remote sensing data in real-time, particularly in remote and resource-constrained agricultural settings. This paper proposes a machine learning-enabled smart agriculture classification technique for edge devices using remote sensing platforms. The proposed technique leverages edge computing capabilities to efficiently process and analyse multi-spectral imagery captured by unmanned aerial vehicles (UAVs) or satellites. The ML model, trained on a dataset of labeled image samples, is deployed on edge devices to classify crop types, identify pests and diseases, and assess crop health. The proposed technique has the potential to significantly enhance agricultural practices by providing real-time insights and enabling timely interventions to improve crop yields and reduce losses.

The main outcomes of this study
The purpose of this study is to determine how successfully the GEE classifies different crop classes using Sentinel 2 MSI.

- A number of supervised machine learning classifiers, including as Maximum Distance (MD) and Naïve Bayes (NB) classification techniques are tried in order to create a map.
- The Naïve Bayes classifier on the Sentinel 2 MSI pictures attains an overall accuracy of 61.5%, while the minimal distance classifier attains an overall accuracy of 70.7%.
- It has a significant influence on the evaluation of crop classification utilising a cloud-based platform.
- It was demonstrated that the MD classifier outperformed NB classifiers in mapping agricultural crops using both multi-spectral datasets.

The next section has the arrangement for the remaining tasks. A analysis of the relevant literature has been finished in Section 14.2. In Section 14.3, the suggested approach is explained that is used in the various crop categories. Section 14.4 presents the results and discussion along with a comparison that was made to support the findings. The last Section 14.5 concludes the research and provides an overall assessment of the achievements.

14.2 Related Works

Currently, image-oriented techniques for time series image-based crop classification and identification are widely used. A decision-tree-based classification algorithm was developed using the crop spectral vegetation index time series variation features and the HJ-CCD time series optical RS pictures to efficiently categorize and identify various crop plantings. The rice phenological period was effectively extracted using multi-temporal RADARSAT-2 completely polarized SAR time series pictures centred on the time-series curve variant features of rice division factors [1–5].

Sentinel-2 picture data was utilized by Phan Thanh Noi *et al.* [6] to evaluate the effectiveness of many classifiers for land use cover categorization, including RF, KNN and SVM. In order to perform crop classification and recognition, the aforementioned multi-temporal as well as multi-feature classification algorithms centred on pixels frequently extract the temporal optical aspects of image features. To find the optimum approach, they tested a number of different approaches. To some degree, they do achieve high classification accuracy, but they typically overlook the spatial correlation—which is susceptible to salt-and-pepper noise—between neighboring image elements [7, 8]. The majority of pixel-based classifications using high-resolution photos contain salt-and-pepper noise. The misclassification of pixels impacted by a variety of reasons is the fundamental feature of these phenomena. To a certain degree, the salt-and-pepper noise can be reduced using the object-oriented method based on remote sensing images [9, 10]. D. Geneletti *et al.* [11] segmented the ortho-images after classifying TM images using a maximum likelihood classifier as well as extra empirical rule. After that, they classified the segmented images by using previously categorized TM image. Research has demonstrated that the object-oriented strategy outperforms image element-based classification techniques in terms of classification accuracy [12, 13]. Recently, the field of remote sensing has made extensive use of GEE an open cloud framework with strong dataset handling, investigation, storing as well as visualization skills. GEE is actively involved in research on methods for crop classification through remote sensing identification and extraction. Numerous categorization studies centred on the GEE cloud platform have been carried out by some systematic investigators in the field of RS. K. Zhou *et al.* [14] collected a number of winter wheat NDVI variables as well as utilised the random forest method to determine the winter wheat planting zone based on the GEE platform. Landsat 8 surface reflectance dataset with eight different grouping schemes were used by T. N. Phan *et al.* [15] to create and assess maps of land cover for Mongolia. The research was carried out on the GEE platform using the extensively used random forest (RF) algorithm to examine the impact of various arrangement techniques and input image types on the final maps. A decision tree approach was utilized by H. Zhang *et al.* [16] to categorize crops at the object scale utilizing multi-temporal environmental star HJ-1A dataset as well as its multi-period smoothed as well as rebuilt NDVI time series curve characteristics. B. Du *et al.* [17] joint object oriented classification as well as SVM method founded on the GEE framework using Sentinel-2A NDVI time series characteristics.

C. Luo *et al.* [18] used SNIC to segment the composite images based on varying sizes. They then fed the processed images and training samples into a RF method to classify crops.

The aforementioned research determines that object-oriented methods have been used in current research to increase crop classification accuracy. Unfortunately, most of these studies use a single type of RS picture, usually without considering the complementing advantages of several image types, as time-series optical imageries that are visible-near-infrared image features.

With its millions of servers worldwide and cutting-edge cloud computing and storage capabilities, The RS image dataset is made publically available through the tool GEE. This offers tremendous promise for long-term and large-scale remote sensing analysis by making it simple for GEE users to extract, call and analyse substantial RS big data resources [19, 20].

The results of extensive crop classification application study employing GEE cloud computing technology-based classification techniques are presented in this paper. In this study, Sentinel-2 MSI RS image features were merged with Maximum Distance (MD) and Naïve Bayes (NB) classification techniques.

14.3 Methods and Dataset

14.3.1 Research Area and Dataset

The complex of temples dedicated to the Krishna Janma Bhoomi is located in Mathura, a sacred city in Uttar Pradesh, India. A multitude of variables, including industry, agricultural growth, and urbanization, have contributed to the city's notable LULC changes in recent decades. Mathura is located in latitude 27.4924° N and longitude 77.6737° E. Additional 2.5 million people live in (Census Report 2011), (State of Forest Report 2020, mathura.kvk4). There are 3.32 mha of total geographical area, 3.28 mha of total cultivable land, and 3.11 mha of total irrigated land. It is a sizable agricultural area. Seasons determine when to sow crops. In Mathura, during winter (Rabi) season, two crops are primarily seeded in large quantities: wheat and mustard (Mathura District Census Report 2011). The research's study area is depicted in Figure 14.1.

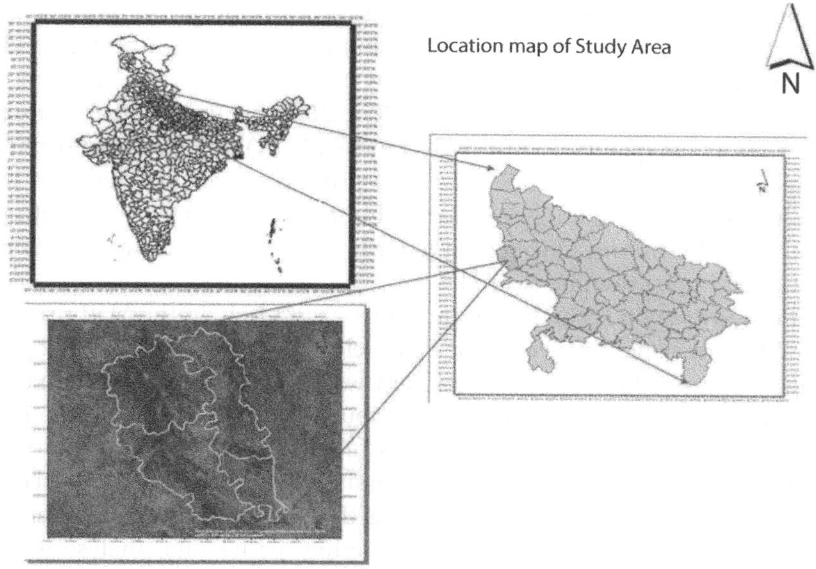

Figure 14.1 Area of interest (study area map).

The three primary crops grown in the research area are wheat, mustard, and other crops. These crops grow primarily from the beginning of October in Rabi seasons.

14.3.2 Pre-Processing and Image Dataset

This study extracted distinct crop-growing zones using Sentinel-2 MSI spectral remote sensing data. Up to 10 m, there are differences in resolution between their various bands. A single satellite's revisit period is ten days, the revisit period is five days. Sentinel-2MSI images are first chosen as fundamental spectral-image dataset for classification since their spectral, spatial as well as temporal resolutions satisfy fundamental criteria of this classification investigation.

Since wheat, mustard, and other crops are the primary crops grown in the research area, it is important that the RS image data be chosen during these important crops' fertile seasons. The calibre of the images themselves should also receive further consideration.

The research time is in the winter season, which runs from October through December season when these crops are sown and February through April is when they are harvested. These crops require ordinary temperatures and less water. Wheat, Mustard, barley, gram, pea, etc. are important Rabi crops. There is a lot of cloud cover and significant cloudiness some period of time. For this investigation, three view spectral remote sensing pictures from 25 December 2020 to 30 December 2020 are chosen based on image quality. Zenith reflectance's (TOA) as well as atmospherically corrected surface reflectance (SR) products are integrated into the GEE platform, eliminating need for additional geometric as well as atmospheric modifications. One benefit of GEE framework. The area that cloud has covered must then be cleared.

The study region is situated in India's Uttar Pradesh, in the Mathura district. The Copernicus provided the Sentinel 2 MSI (COPERNICUS/S2_SR) images. The Arc GIS software program was used to process the images. In order to eliminate artefacts such as cloud cover, the data undergo preprocessing. After that, a supervised classification method was used to the images. The NB and MD supervised classification approaches are used to classify data. The satellite and Google Earth images are used to gather the training samples. A strong tool for integrating spatial data, analysing spatial relationships, and visualizing spatial patterns is a geographic information system (GIS). The crop classification is analysed by the study using the subsequent steps:

- Geometric distortions and atmospheric impacts are eliminated from the Sentinel 2 MSI through pre-processing. Band 'B1','B2','B3','B4','B5','B6','B7','B8','B9','B11 are selected.
- Supervised classification strategy are used to classify the images into crop classification classes.
- ArcGIS (10.8) is used to visualize the classification results.

Thirteen spectral bands make up the Sentinel 2 MSI, with four at 10 m, six at 20 m, and three at 60 m spatial resolution. Sentinel 2's multispectral Level-2A (L2A) dataset was made available by the Sentinel scientific data hub. Sentinel 2's L2A dataset uses bottom of the atmosphere (BOA) reflectance, which has been adjusted for radiation and atmospheric factors. Nine spectral bands—green, blue, red, SWIR-2 bands, near infrared (NIR), red edge band 1 (RE-1), RE-3, and RE-2—were used to categorise Sentinel-2 images. The categorization process employed Sentinel-2 L2A photos with less than 5% cloud coverage percentage. This study makes use of the B3-Red, B4-Green, and B8-NIR bands. Sentinel 2 MSI can offer a broad variety of spectral temporal characteristics for crop mapping. Its high spatial resolutions, three red edge bands, and five-day average return duration [21–24].

For agricultural categorization, the entire region is divided into six classes: water, vegetation, wheat, mustard, and other crops. Additional multispectral photography was used to conduct a complete field assessment throughout the research region in order to gather ground datasets of various crops using a portable GPS receiver. Finally, based on field surveys and visual image interpretation of the region, six categories were presented. Urban locations, water features, greenery, various crops, and the two main crops—wheat and mustard—were included in these classifications.

Secondly, ground dataset samples are required to guarantee crop classification accuracy. In December 2020, a field survey is conducted in the Mathura region using a hand-held universal positioning device with a two-meter location precision. During the survey, crop field samples are gathered, and high-spatial-quality Google Earth pictures were used to draw the borders of the region of interest. Training and testing datasets are

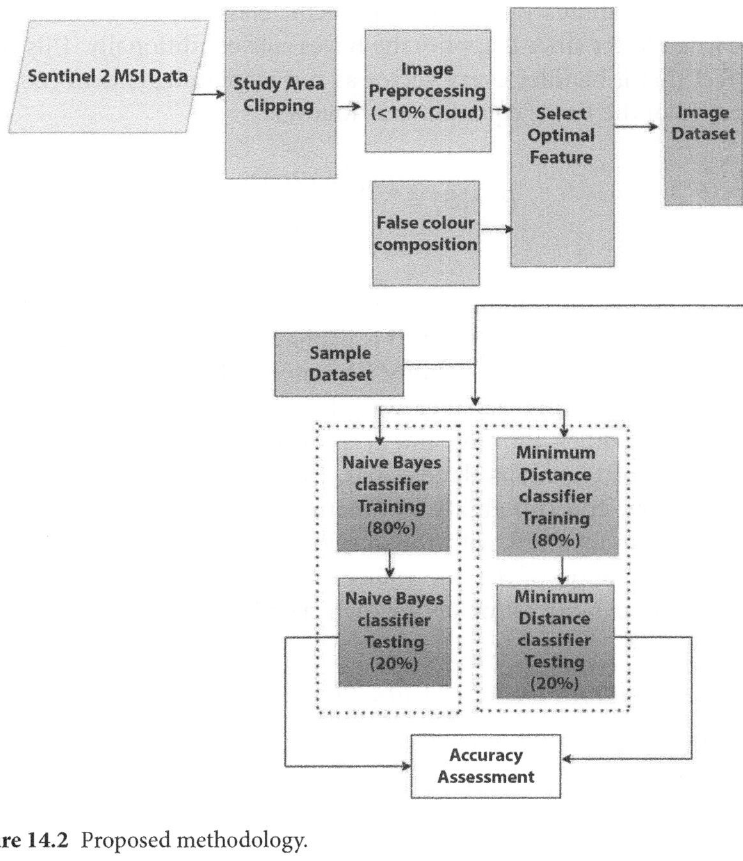

Figure 14.2 Proposed methodology.

in dissimilar fields, crop samples were divided into two portions at the plot level (80% and 20%, respectively). Images are captured using cell phones' GPS systems. The images are captured during the winter months (Rabi). Figure 14.2 shows Flow chart of proposed methodology.

14.3.3 Classifiers

14.3.3.1 Naïve Bayes Classifier

Classifier using machine learning method based on probabilities is constructed by Naive Bayes Trees (NBT). The system operates via the application of Bayes's Theorem, known as Naive Bayes. Each branch's terminal node follows a meticulous NBT method layout, and the NB origins its frame on a Decision Tree (DT). The NBT offers remarkable accuracy and classification efficiency [25–27]. The idea of class conditional independence states that an attribute's value in the NBT process has no bearing on how another attribute's value affects a specific class. NBT enables datasets to be learned faster since it applies the Bayes rule conditionally. This is due to the fact that it handles every vector as if it were independent [28]. The explanation of the Bayes equation is as follows:

$$P(A|B) = \frac{P(B|A)P(A)}{P(B)}$$

The conditional probability of A given B is shown by P(A|B), and the conditional probability of A given B is displayed by P(B|A). P(A) gave an explanation for A's event probability. The probability of incident (B) was explained by P(B). This classifier was chosen for a number of reasons, including its (i) quick training and classification times, (ii) resistance to noise in form of unsuitable landscapes, (iii) ease of understanding and implementation, and (iv) ability to function well with very few training datasets. The model starts with the development of the perception function, the computation of the covariance as well as variance matrix and a sequence of probability estimates for each class [29, 30].

14.3.3.2 Minimum Distance Classifier

A non-parametric classification system called the minimum distance classifier in Google Earth Engine (GEE) places every unlabeled pixel in the training data in the class of its closest neighbor. To specify the distance metric that is used to determine the separation between pixels. The Manhattan, Mahalanobis, and Euclidean distances are a few examples of frequently used distance measures. First generate a training set of labelled pixels in order to use the minimal distance classifier in GEE. The training set ought to be an accurate representation of the material intend to categorize. After creating a training set, use the ee.Classifier.minimumDistance() function to generate a classifier. The training set and the distance metric are the two arguments that the ee.Classifier.minimumDistance() function accepts. Classify unlabelled pixels using the classifier. The classifier's classify () method can be used to categorize an unlabelled pixel. The unlabelled pixel is the only argument required by the categorize() function. The unlabelled pixel's class is returned by the classify () method [31–34].

Step for Crop Classification using GEE

i. Choosing AOI using shape file (Mathura).
ii. Selecting and filtering image collection.
iii. Adding layer to display.
iv. Training points collected using point drawing tool. Total 2058 points are created for six class as urban, water, vegetation, wheat, mustard and other classes.
v. Then merge these all points with merge function.
vi. Make a training dataset by sampling region.
vii. Create Classifier as ee.Classifier.minimumDistance() and ee.Classifier.smileNaiveBayes().
viii. Create Classifier Image.
ix. Then Adding layer to display.
x. Calculate Confusion matrix for accuracy assessment. With the help confusion matrix various factors are calculated such as F1 Score, Overall Accuracy, Kappa, and consumer and producer accuracy.

14.4 Proposed Algorithm

Inputs: I_D, D_{SET}, C_{DT}, D_{TN}, D_{TT}, S_{hp}.
Outputs: Classes, CM_{MAT}, A_{CC}, P_{RE}, R_{EC}, F_{1SC}, S_{UP}.

1. Initialize the system required parameters: Image data(I_D), Dataset (D_{SET}), Csv Data (C_{DT}), Train Data (D_{TN}), Test Data (D_{TT}), Shape File of Mathura ($S2_{MSI}$)), NB algorithm (NB),

MD algorithm (MD), Confusion matrix (CM_{MAT}), Recall (R_{EC}), F1 score (F_{1SC}). Sentinel 2 MSI ($S2_{MSI}$) and Accuracy (A_{CC}), Precision (P_{RE}), shape, training_data.

2. Take the raw data image form (I_D) from $S2_{MSI}$ and $S2_{MSI}$) .
3. S_{hp} = ee.FeatureCollection(shape)
4. selection = S2 $_{MSI}$.filterBounds(shape).filterDate("2000-12-01","2001-01-30").filterMetadata("CLOUD_COVER", "less_than", 5) .mean().clip(shape);
5. Map.add Layer (selection, {bands:["B4","B3","B2"]})
6. Collect training points.
7. Split the C_{DT} into D_{TN} and D_{TT} in ratio of 80-20.
8. var training D_{TN} = training_data.filter(ee.Filter.lt('random', split));
9. var testing D_{TT} = training_data.filter(ee.Filter.gte('random', split));
10. Initialize the input and output parameters in the form of X and Y.
11. Train the D_{TN} using classifier = ee.Classifier.minimum Distance()
12. Apply NB algorithm (NB), MD algorithm (MD) using GEE platform
13. Evaluate the performance using confusion matrix CM $_{MAT}$.
14. Compute P_{RE}, R_{EC}, F_{1SC} and S_{UP}.
15. Stop.

14.5 Results and Discussions

In this section result and discussion are discussed. Table 14.1 shows confusion matrix for minimum distance (MD) classifier. In urban class predict 218 correct pixels, while 1 pixel mixes in to water class, 5 pixel mixes into vegetation class and 1pixel mixes into wheat class. In water class predict 190 correct pixels, 8 pixels mixes with urban, 25 mixes with vegetation, 1 pixel mixes with wheat class and 1 pixel mixes with mustard class. Vegetation class predict 162 correct pixel while 14 mixes into urban, 17 mixes into water, 19 mixes into wheat and 1 pixel into other crop class. Wheat class predict 227 correct pixel while 61 mixes with urban, 6 mixes with water, 90 mixes with vegetation, 66 mixes with mustard and 88 mixes with other crop. Mustard class predict 360 correct pixel while 5 mixes with urban, 5 mixes with vegetation, 43 mixes with wheat, 21 mixes with other crops.

Table 14.1 Sentinel 2 MSI's confusion matrix for the MD technique.

Classes	Urban	Water	Vegetation	Wheat	Mustard	Other crops	Consumer's accuracy (%)
Urban	218	1	5	1	0	0	76.93
Water	8	190	25	1	1	0	88.88
Vegetation	14	17	162	19	0	1	51.93
Wheat	61	6	90	227	66	88	70.46
Mustard	5	0	5	43	360	21	78.12
Other crops	2	0	4	12	6	25	18.33

Moreover other crops predict 25 correct pixel while 2 mixes urban, 4 mixes with vegetation, 12 mixes with wheat, 6 mixes with mustard.

Table 14.2 shows confusion matrix for NB method. In urban class predict 220 correct pixels. In water class predict 195 correct pixels, 7 pixels mixes with urban, 20 mixes with vegetation, 1 pixel mixes with wheat class and 1 pixel mixes with mustard class. Vegetation class predict 132 correct pixel while 19 mixes into urban, 22 mixes into water, 29 mixes into wheat and 10 pixel into other crop class. Wheat class predict 234 correct pixel while 71 mixes with urban, 7 mixes with water, 60 mixes with vegetation, 75 mixes with mustard and 88 mixes with other crop. Mustard class predict

Table 14.2 Sentinel 2 MSI's confusion matrix for the NB technique.

Classes	Urban	Water	Vegetation	Wheat	Mustard	Other crops	Consumer's accuracy (%)
Urban	220	0	5	0	0	0	77.97
Water	7	195	20	1	1	0	90.01
Vegetation	19	22	132	29	0	10	58.93
Wheat	71	7	60	234	75	88	70.46
Mustard	5	0	5	33	380	11	81.35
Other crops	3	1	5	13	7	20	15.33

Table 14.3 Overall accuracy and Kappa coefficient of Sentinel 2 MSI.

S. no	Classifiers	OA %	Kappa coefficient
1	NB	61.50	0.62
2	MD	70.07	0.70

380 correct pixel while 5 mixes with urban, 5 mixes with vegetation, 33 mixes with wheat, 11 mixes with other crops. Moreover other crops predict 20 correct pixel while 3 mixes urban, 1 mixes with water, 5 mixes with vegetation, 13 mixes with wheat, 7 mixes with mustard and 20 mixes with other crops. Table 14.3 shows overall accuracy and kappa coefficient for both classifier NB and MD classifiers. Table 14.4 shows PA, CA and F1-score for NB and MD methods.

14.5.1 Classified Crop Map

Sentinel 2 data's classified map is displayed in Figure 14.3. Red is used to represent an urban region, blue to represent water features, green to represent vegetation, orange to represent wheat, yellow to represent mustard and cyan to represent other crop areas on a categorized map.

Table 14.4 CA, PA accuracy and F1 Score of Sentinel 2 MSI dataset.

	NB		MD	
Classes	**PA % CA%**	**F1 score %**	**PA % CA%**	**F1 score %**
Urban	94.57 77.97	82.85	96.77 76.93	81.80
Water	81.63 90.01	79.42	83.33 88.88	86.56
Vegetation	60.33 38.93	44.95	74.46 51.93	62.30
Wheat	69.71 70.46	70.61	70.90 70.46	80.62
Mustard	67.56 81.35	60.94	77.51 78.12	83.04
Other crops	50 5.33	19.83	40 8.33	17.60

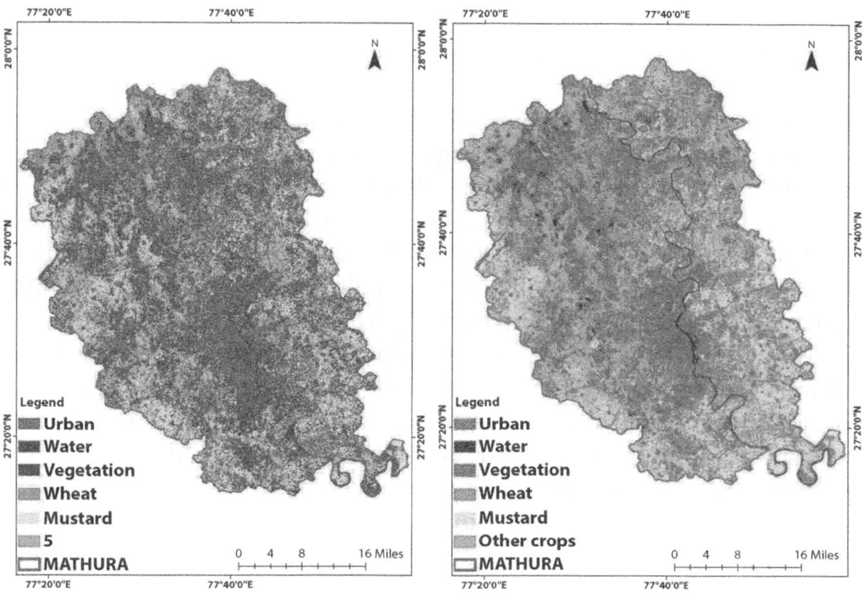

(**a**) Crop Map using Naïve Bayes (**b**) Crop map using Minimum Distance

Figure 14.3 Classified map of NB and MD classifiers.

14.6 Conclusion

The research's objective is to evaluate the GEE platform's crop categorization in Mathura. GEE offers a user-friendly and robust framework for managing vast amounts of RS imagery that are utilised for crop mapping. It simple to obtain remote sensing data and applies several categorization techniques with the least amount of effort and involvement using GEE platform. Numerous categorization techniques are available on the GEE platform. When it comes to enabling access to cloud-based RS solutions for satellite data flow, GEE performs admirably. In this comparative study find kappa coefficient of 0.70, the MD-based classification approach produced the highest accuracy, at 70.07%. Based on identical conditions, the MD classification accuracy for wheat, mustard and other crops are marginally greater than the NB classification approach. This demonstrates the MD classification approach outperforms the NB based classification method when it comes to the categorization of Sentinel-2 MSI data. However, other approaches, like NB, also produce reliable outcomes. Examine how well different classifiers, including MD and NB, perform by computing several metrics, including OA, PA, UA, and Kappa coefficients, as well as the classified map for each approach. Additionally, a comparison of Mathura's pixel-based crop mapping techniques was conducted, along with an examination of the GEE platform's efficacy for broad crop mapping. In addition, GEE demonstrated outstanding work in providing cloud platform users with access to RS pictures and strong computational capabilities that might help with extensive crop mapping. It will train our crop categorization solution through analysing different geo-location data using different deep learning techniques. It is restricted to the agricultural areas surrounding the city of Mathura. This study may be applicable if there are comparable agricultural regions with comparable hydro-meteorological conditions. A few other restrictions are the lack of field trips, particularly in the past, and dataset resolution (both temporal and geographical). It is only applicable to hazy or noisy data. Microwaves and many dates of satellite data might be used in future studies to expand on the current study. Additionally, there is chance for collaboration in the results with additional sensors and the ability to use several dates with numerous locations.

References

1. Li, X., Xu, X., Wang, J., Wu, H., Jing, X., Li, C., Bao, Y., Crop classification recognition based on time-series images from HJ satellite. *Trans. Chin. Soc. Agric. Eng.*, 29, 2, 169–176, 2013.
2. Li, H., Li, K., Shao, Y., Zhou, P., Guo, X., Liu, C., Liu, L., Retrieval of Rice Phenology Based on Time-Series Polarimetric SAR Data, in: *IGARSS 2018-2018 IEEE International Geoscience and Remote Sensing Symposium*, 2018, July, IEEE, pp. 4463–4466.
3. Abdikan, S., Sanli, F.B., Ustuner, M., Calò, F., Land cover mapping using sentinel-1 SAR data. *Int. Arch. Photogramm. Remote Sens. Spat. Inf. Sci.*, 41, 757–761, 2016.
4. Hao, P., Zhan, Y., Wang, L., Niu, Z., Shakir, M., Feature selection of time series MODIS data for early crop classification using random forest: A case study in Kansas, USA. *Remote Sens.*, 7, 5, 5347–5369, 2015.
5. Liu, Z., Liu, D., Zhu, D., Research progress and prospect of fine identification and automatic map-ping of crop remote sensing. *Trans. Chin. Soc. Agric. Mach.*, 49, 12, 1–12, 2018.
6. Thanh Noi, P. and Kappas, M., Comparison of random forest, k-nearest neighbor, and support vector machine classifiers for land cover classification using Sentinel-2 imagery. *Sensors*, 18, 1, 18, 2017.
7. Fauvel, M., Tarabalka, Y., Benediktsson, J.A., Chanussot, J., Tilton, J.C., Advances in spectral-spatial classification of hyperspectral images. *Proc. IEEE*, 101, 3, 652–675, 2012.

8. Yu, Q., Gong, P., Clinton, N., Biging, G., Kelly, M., Schirokauer, D., Object-based detailed vegetation classification with airborne high spatial resolution remote sensing imagery. *Photogramm. Eng. Remote Sens.*, 72, 7, 799–811, 2006.
9. Walter, V., Object-based classification of remote sensing data for change detection. *ISPRS J. Photogramm. Remote Sens.*, 58, 3-4, 225–238, 2004.
10. Baatz, M., Hoffmann, C., Willhauck, G., Progressing from object-based to object-oriented image analysis, in: *Object-based image analysis: Spatial concepts for knowledge-driven remote sensing applications*, pp. 29–42, 2008.
11. Geneletti, D. and Gorte, B.G.H., A method for object-oriented land cover classification combining Landsat TM data and aerial photographs. *Int. J. Remote Sens.*, 24, 6, 1273–1286, 2003.
12. Whiteside, T.G., Boggs, G.S., Maier, S.W., Comparing object-based and pixel-based classifications for mapping savannas. *Int. J. Appl. Earth Obs. Geoinf.*, 13, 6, 884–893, 2011.
13. Yan, G., Mas, J.F., Maathuis, B.H.P., Xiangmin, Z., Van Dijk, P.M., Comparison of pixel-based and object-oriented image classification approaches—a case study in a coal fire area, Wuda, Inner Mongolia, China. *Int. J. Remote Sens.*, 27, 18, 4039–4055, 2006.
14. Zhou, K., Liu, Y., Zhang, Y., Miao, R., Yang, Y., Area extraction and growth monitoring of winter wheat with GEE support in Henan Province. *Sci. Agric. Sin.*, 54, 2302–2318, 2021.
15. Phan, T.N., Kuch, V., Lehnert, L.W., Land cover classification using Google Earth Engine and random forest classifier—The role of image composition. *Remote Sens.*, 12, 15, 2411, 2020.
16. Huanxue, Z., Xin, C., Qiangzi, L., Miao, Z., Xinqi, Z., Research on crop identification using multi-temporal NDVI HJ images. *Remote Sens. Technol. Appl.*, 30, 2, 304–311, 2015.
17. Du, B., Zhang, J., Wang, Z., Mao, D., Zhang, M., Wu, B., Crop mapping based on Sentinel-2A NDVI time series using object-oriented classification and decision tree model. *J. Geo-Inf. Sci.*, 21, 740–751, 2019.
18. Luo, C., Qi, B., Liu, H., Guo, D., Lu, L., Fu, Q., Shao, Y., Using time series sentinel-1 images for object-oriented crop classification in google earth engine. *Remote Sens.*, 13, 4, 561, 2021.
19. Gorelick, N., Hancher, M., Dixon, M., Ilyushchenko, S., Thau, D., Moore, R., Google Earth Engine: Planetary-scale geospatial analysis for everyone. *Remote Sens. Environ.*, 202, 18–27, 2017.
20. Dong, J., Xiao, X., Menarguez, M.A., Zhang, G., Qin, Y., Thau, D., Moore III, B., Mapping paddy rice planting area in northeastern Asia with Landsat 8 images, phenology-based algorithm and Google Earth Engine. *Remote Sens. Environ.*, 185, 142–154, 2016.

21. Campos-Taberner, M., García-Haro, F.J., Martínez, B., Sánchez-Ruíz, S., Gilabert, M.A., A copernicus sentinel-1 and sentinel-2 classification framework for the 2020+ European common agricultural policy: A case study in València (Spain). *Agronomy*, 9, 9, 556, 2019.
22. Immitzer, M., Vuolo, F., Atzberger, C., First experience with Sentinel-2 data for crop and tree species classifications in central Europe. *Remote Sens.*, 8, 3, 166, 2016.
23. Nasrallah, A., Baghdadi, N., Mhawej, M., Faour, G., Darwish, T., Belhouchette, H., Darwich, S., A novel approach for mapping wheat areas using high resolution Sentinel-2 images. *Sensors*, 18, 7, 2089, 2018. https://doi.org/10.3390/s18072089
24. Piedelobo, L., Hernández-López, D., Ballesteros, R., Chakhar, A., Del Pozo, S., González-Aguilera, D., Moreno, M.A., Scalable pixel-based crop classification combining Sentinel-2 and Landsat-8 data time series: Case study of the Duero river basin. *Agric. Syst.*, 171, 36–50, 2019.
25. Aitkenhead, M.J., Poggio, L., Wardell-Johnson, D., Coull, M.C., Rivington, M., Black, H.I.J., Habte, M., Estimating soil properties from smartphone imagery in Ethiopia. *Comput. Electron. Agric.*, 171, 105322, 2020.
26. Felegari, S., Sharifi, A., Moravej, K., Golchin, A., Tariq, A., Investigation of the relationship between ndvi index, soil moisture, and precipitation data using satellite images, in: *Sustainable Agriculture Systems and Technologies*, pp. 314–325, 2022.
27. Majeed, M., Tariq, A., Haq, S.M., Waheed, M., Anwar, M.M., Li, Q., Jamil, A., A detailed ecological exploration of the distribution patterns of wild Poaceae from the Jhelum District (Punjab), Pakistan. *Sustainability*, 14, 7, 3786, 2022.
28. Wahla, S.S., Kazmi, J.H., Sharifi, A., Shirazi, S.A., Tariq, A., Joyell Smith, H., Assessing spatio-temporal mapping and monitoring of climatic variability using SPEI and RF machine learning models. *Geocarto Int.*, 37, 27, 14963–14982, 2022.
29. Pradhan, B., Chaudhari, A., Adinarayana, J., Buchroithner, M.F., Soil erosion assessment and its correlation with landslide events using remote sensing data and GIS: a case study at Penang Island, Malaysia. *Environ. Monit. Assess.*, 184, 715–727, 2012.
30. Hooker, J., Duveiller, G., Cescatti, A., A global dataset of air temperature derived from satellite remote sensing and weather stations. *Sci. Data*, 5, 1, 1–11, 2018.
31. Hodgson, M.E., Reducing the computational requirements of the minimum-distance classifier. *Remote Sens. Environ.*, 25, 1, 117–128, 1988.
32. Lin, H. and Venetsanopoulos, A.N., A weighted minimum distance classifier for pattern recognition, in: *Proceedings of Canadian Conference on Electrical and Computer Engineering*, pp. 904–907, IEEE, 1993, September.

33. Zhang, D., Chen, S., Zhou, Z.H., Learning the kernel parameters in kernel minimum distance classifier. *Pattern Recognit.*, 39, 1, 133–135, 2006.
34. Suwanlee, S.R., Keawsomsee, S., Pengjunsang, M., Homtong, N., Prakobya, A., Borgogno-Mondino, E., Som-ard, J., Monitoring Agricultural Land and Land Cover Change from 2001–2021 of the Chi River Basin, Thailand Using Multi-Temporal Landsat Data Based on Google Earth Engine. *Remote Sens.*, 15, 17, 4339, 2023.

15

A Lightweight Intelligent Detection Approach for Interest Flooding Attack

Naveen Kumar[1]*, Brijendra Pratap Singh[2] and Rohit[3]

[1]*DoCSE, Sardar Vallabhbhai National Institute of Technology, Surat, India*
[2]*DoCSE, Bennett University, Greater Noida, Uttar Pradesh, India*
[3]*DoCSE, IERT, Prayagraj, Uttar Pradesh, India*

Abstract

Some of the most promising options for network architecture in the future are Named Data Networking (NDN). NDN forwards, routes, and fetches content using the name of the content instead of the IP address of the host. NDN uses two types of packets, i.e., the interest packet for requesting the content and the data packet containing the actual requested content. As there is no user ID like an IP address, NDN uses a data structure called Pending Interest Table (PIT) to store the metadata of pending requests. This metadata contains the request name and the interface ID from which the interest packet is received. The router uses this entry to forward the data packet to the correct consumer by looking at the interface ID given by the PIT entry. The attacker can flood the network with malicious requests. These requests generally do not have any valid data packet; therefore, the PIT entries corresponding to these requests remain in the routers till timeout. Thus, the consumer's legitimate request has no space left in the PIT. This attack can be countered by first detecting the occurrence of the attack and then applying countermeasures like filters to block the attacker. IFA detection can be done using parameters such as incoming interest packets, outgoing data packets, PIT entries, timeout Interest packets, etc. Previous approaches use two or three parameters to detect the attack based on the statistical threshold. The accuracy of the detection can be improved by using more number of parameters for IFA detection. Finding the threshold manually for each parameter and its variations is difficult; thus, we have proposed using machine learning for IFA detection. The second problem with the router is that it has limited time to forward the packet,

**Corresponding author*: nk10121989@gmail.com

Mohit Kumar, Gautam Srivastava, Ashutosh Kumar Singh and Kalka Dubey (eds.) AI-Based Advanced Optimization Techniques for Edge Computing, (401–432) © 2025 Scrivener Publishing LLC

and storage is also limited. Therefore, it is necessary to use as few parameters as possible. In this chapter, we have simulated IFA on ndnSIM to create a dataset with traffic statistics, performed feature selection on the dataset, and applied PCA to reduce the parameters further. In the end, IFA detection has been done using several ML approaches such as SVM, KNN, MLP with BP, Decision tree, deep learning, Ada boot, etc.

***Keywords*:** NDN, IFA, ANN, interest flooding attack, named data networking

15.1 Introduction

Internet has grown from 15 nodes in Arpanet to a devastating 15.14 billions [1]. This happened due to the emergence of IoT. Now very device such as lock, washing machine, car, etc. need to be connected to the Internet. These devices consumes and emits a large volume of traffic on the Internet. The TCP/IP was initially developed (in the 1970s) for solving the problem of communication and resource sharing. But now the same TCP/IP which was earlier designed for communication in now being used for content transfer. The basic approach of TCP/IP makes it in efficient for content transfer. For example, in TCP/IP based network if Bob wants a content C. First, Bob should know the IP address of the the host having that content. This problem solved by using a search engine which gives the URL instead of IP address. Again a DNS query will be done for finding the IP address. Then a TCP connection will be created before actual content transfer. This whole process gets repeated again and again for the new request. The problem with the TCP/IP is its host-centric nature which is essential for communication between the hosts. If some how this tradition of TCP/IP could be break by focusing on the content which is to be transferred rather than the hosts the network can be optimized for the content transfer. To make network capable of handling the bulk content a set of researchers have developed network architectures that focuses on the content rather than the hosts. These types of networks are called Information Centric Network (ICN) [2]. Many networks follow the ICN philosophy that has been proposed. Out of all ICNs, the NDN is the most promising candidate for future networks. ICN philosophy makes NDN more efficient than the TCP/IP [3].

NDN uses the name of the content rather than the IP address of host for requesting the content. In this way the content can be requested directly and form anywhere. The request is done by using Interest packet and reply packet is called data packet. The data packet contains the actual content.

The router routes this request to the publisher of the content. Now the question arise how the data packet will be received by the correct receiver. To solve this problem NDN has a data structure called Pending Interest Table (PIT) which stores the metadata of each request on the router as PIT entry. This PIT entry includes the name of Interest packet and the interface list form which it is received. If multiple requests for the same content are received on a different interface of the same router then its interface ID is added to the interface list of matching PIT entry. Besides PIT NDN uses Content Store (CS) for caching the data packets in order to improve the network performance. The size of the CS is limited therefore it uses cache replacement policies like LRU, FIFO, LFU, etc. The rest of the details of NDN has been discussed in Section 15.2.

NDN secures the content by enforcing the producer to sign the data packet using its private key. The data packet can be verified by the receiver using the public key of the publisher. This public key can be retrieved by using the key locator field of the data packet. Additionally, the publisher can encrypt the content before placing it inside a data packet and the consumer can decrypt the content using the public key of publisher. In this way the confidentiality, integrity and provenance of data packet is ensured. Thus, NDN is more secure than the TCP/IP however it is vulnerable to attack on availability. These attack are cache privacy attack [4–6], cache pollution attack [7, 8], content poisoning attack [9], and Interest Flooding Attack (IFA) [9]. A complete review on the major attack on NDN is discussed in [10]. The cache privacy attack reveals the privacy of the user like its access pattern, type of content accessed, etc. These privacy related information can be further utilized by the attacker to send malware, access user credentials, etc. The cache pollution attack caches the un popular content in the CS of NDN router. Thus, the hit ratio of the CS decreases and probability the a consumer fetches a content from the cache decreases. In content poisoning attack the attacker injects the CS with fake or corrupted content. These, contents spread across the network as more and more consumers request these content. These fake or corrupted content are of no use for the requester. An attacker does IFA by sending requests for a lot of data packets that do not exist. There are malicious entries in the PIT of routers between the requester and the publisher. These entries stay in the PIT until the timeout, making PIT unavailable for the consumers. The IFA is worse than the cache privacy attack, the cache pollution attack, and the content poisoning attack because it stops all packets from moving through the network. This attack is also more straightforward to carry out than the others.

The mitigation of IFA is done in two steps. The first step is to identify whether an attack is going on or not this is called IFA detection. After the detection the second step is taken in which some action is performed for stopping the attack this is called IFA countermeasure. This chapter mainly focuses on IFA detection. Almost all the previously proposed approaches detects IFA using one or more features. Few of the features are the number of incoming Interest packets per interface (InInt), the number of PIT entries per interface (numPIT), etc. Capturing the relationship between these features and actual IFA is difficult. The statistical approaches that depends on fixed threshold can be attacked just by varying traffic. In order to make IFA detection more efficient more features are needed. Few of the authors have applied machine learning to detect the IFA but they have not focused on reducing the features by feature selection or dimensionality reduction. The router runs at line speed, it has limited time to forward the packet. Also, it has limited storage thus to process large number of features can be a burden for the router. In order to develop a lightweight detection approach and achieve accuracy, feature analysis is necessary. In our previous work [11], we compared the IFA detection result in simulation and implementation. Also, we have applied information gain for feature selection, where we have chosen 9 out of 12 features [12]. There were a few limitations in our previous approach. Firstly, there were two features in our previous approach related to PIT. One was PIT size, which is computed per router. The other was PITcount, which is computed per interface. Since all the other features were computed per interface, in this article, we have removed the feature computed per router. This is done as the ultimate goal is malicious interface detection. Secondly, we have used only one feature selection in our previous paper. In this article, we have considered 17 different approaches for feature selection. Additionally, we have used PCA to reduce the dimensions of the dataset further while not affecting the detection accuracy.

The significant contributions of this article are:

- Creating dataset by simulating IFA on DFN topology.
- Applying 17 different feature selection approaches for feature deduction.
- Applying dimensionality reduction using PCA to reduce features further.
- Applying machine learning approaches to compare the detection before and after feature reduction.

The chapter's outline is as follows: The required background ideas, such as NDN architecture and IFA, are covered in Section 15.2. Preprocessing, feature selection, dimensionality reduction, IFA modeling, and classification are some of the general tasks covered in Section 15.3. The conclusion and future steps are covered in Section 15.4.

15.2 NDN Background

This section describes the necessary background for understanding NDN and IFA. NDN architecture, which describes NDN packets, NDN data structures, NDN forwarding, and NDN security, has been discussed first. Next, IFA and its types are discussed.

15.2.1 NDN Architecture

NDN Name: NDN names possess a hierarchical structure, with string components delimited by "/". As an illustration, consider the URL "/ucla/2022/btech/cse/abc." The semantic significance of the name varies depending on the specific use case.

15.2.1.1 NDN Packet

NDN employs an Interest packet to solicit content, while the data packet serves as a direct response to the Interest packet, containing the actual content. Figure 15.1 provides the description of the significant fields of Interest and Data packet.

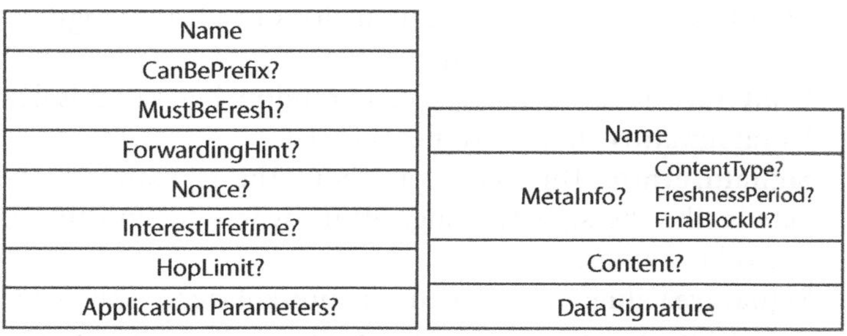

Figure 15.1 Interest and data packet.

Interest Packet Fields:

- **Name**: It is content's name that the customer wants is entered in this field.
- **CanBePrefix**: It says that the data packet name may or may not be a prefix to the interest packet name.
- **MustBeFresh**: This field is set by the consumer to say that the data packet they are receiving must be *fresh*.
- **ForwardingHint**: This field is set by the consumer to show the packet's forwarding paths.
- **Nonce**: The Name and Nonce together make it possible to identify an interest packet, which helps find looping.
- **InterestLifetime**: This field shows how long an interest packet is expected to last.
- **HopLimit**: This field tells how many times an interest packet can be sent through a network.
- **Application Parameters**: This field is used to personalize the request for the data packet and can contain any type of data.

Data Packet Fields

- **Name**: Its name is the data packet. Although it may have additional components added at the end, it is usually the same as the name of the interest package.
- **MetaInfo**: This field contains the data packet's meta data. It comprises 3 subfields:
- **ContentType**: It species data packet's type.
- **FreshnessPeriod**: The router is informed by this field of how long the data packet will remain valid.
- **FinalBlockId**: The ID of the final block in a list of fragments is provided by this subfield.
- **Content**: The real data is stored in random bytes in this field.
- **DataSignature**: It has two fields in it.
- **SignatureInfo**: This tells you about the signature. It has details like the signature algorithm, where to find the key and other things.
- **SignatureValue**: The signature is present here. This is produced by first encrypting the hash and then hashing the entire data packet.

15.2.1.2 NDN Data Structures

NDN possesses the subsequent data structures:

- CS: This part of the router is in charge of storing the data packets that it receives. The CS stores the content using a caching policy as long as its size stays the same.
- PIT retains the details of pending interest packets until the accompanying data packet is received. It records the name of the Interest packet and the list of interfaces on which a particular Interest packet is received. Every interface on the incoming list receives a data packet as it arrives.
- Forwarding Information Base (FIB), looks like a routing table in a TCP/IP network. A designated prefix is stored by FIB instead of a subnet ID.

15.2.1.3 NDN Forwarding

NDN forwarding pipeline is given in Figure 15.2. NDN forwarding process revolves around the handling of Interest and Data packets. When a new Interest packet arrives, the system first checks if the requested content is available locally in the cache. If found, a corresponding Data packet is generated and sent back to the requester. In cases where the content is not locally available, the algorithm consults the FIB to determine the appropriate next hops for the Interest packet. Subsequently, the Interest is

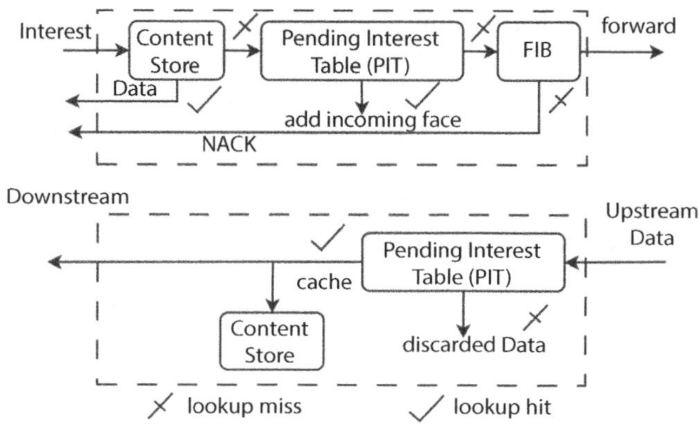

Figure 15.2 NDN forwarding pipeline.

forwarded to these identified next hops, and the Interest packet information, including the return path, is stored in the PIT.

Upon receiving a Data packet, the algorithm checks the PIT for any pending Interests associated with the received Data packet. If pending Interests are found, the Data packet is forwarded to the corresponding return paths, and the entries are removed from the PIT since the requested Data has been served. The system includes mechanisms for dropping Interest or Data packets when necessary.

15.2.2 NDN Security

Within the NDN architecture, it is a requirement for the publisher to affix their signature to every individual data packet. First, a hash value is made for the data packet. Then, the private key of the publisher is used to encrypt the hash. Upon receiving the data packet, a recipient can retrieve the public key by utilizing the key locator field within the data packet. Consumers utilize this key to decipher the signature. This ensures the provenance and integrity of every data packet. In addition, the publisher has the ability to encrypt the data packet in order to guarantee confidentiality. Therefore, NDN offers a higher level of security compared to the current TCP/IP-based network. NDN is safer than TCP/IP, but it can be attacked in new ways. IFA is one of the most severe attacks in NDN.

15.2.2.1 IFA

An NDN router's PIT is the target of an IFA cyberattack. It is similar to a DDoS attack in the TCP/IP protocol, but instead of attacking a specific service or port, IFA focuses on overwhelming the PIT. The attack inundates the PIT with malevolent entries by sending Interest packets that correspond to nonexistent content. These entries persist until they reach the timeout threshold. The attack is executed by sending a request for an Interest packet that consists of a name formed by combining a random string with an existing prefix. When the attacker sends numerous requests within a brief period of time, the PIT becomes inaccessible for the legitimate user.

15.2.2.2 IFA Type

Gasti *et al.* [9] employed several interest packet types to classify interest flooding attacks into three groups: Type-1 (static or already existing), Type-2 (made dynamically), and Type-3 (not existing). In type-1, the attacker sends interest packets over and over again for a set of content that already exists. It does not work because the PIT entries can be directly met by data packets stored in the CS of intermediate routers or sent by publishers. People who want to attack in Type 2 want content that the publisher makes up on the spot. The content probably is not in the PIT of intermediate routers, so the request goes to the publisher, who makes new content right away. In the intermediate routers, this causes PIT entries to be made. Publishers are busy making dynamic content because of the attack. This keeps PIT busy until the dynamically generated content gets to the router. When a type-3 interest flooding attack is used, requests for content that does not exist are sent. The PIT has entries that can't be met because of these interest packets. These entries stay in the PIT until the timeout, which means that the real user cannot get to the PIT. It usually takes a long time for this attack to time out, so the PIT entries it makes stay there until then. Because of this, it is now more dangerous than a type-2 attack. In the study by Dai *et al.* [13], this type of attack can be split into two groups: 1) Attacks that use a text string that does not belong and 2) Attacks that use a prefix that already exists. In the first type, attackers give the interest packet a name that is just a string of letters and numbers. It used to be that the router sent this interest packet as a broadcast, but now it sends a negative acknowledgement instead. This attack does not work in the NDN right now. In the second type, the name of the interest packet is made by adding a random string to the start of a prefix that already exists. The publisher gets these interest packets but doesn't make any data packets for them. The PIT entries will stay in the PIT until the timeout. It is easy to do this attack, which is the worst ever. Someone can also attack a certain publisher. This is the main reason why most of the work on IFA has only been on this attack.

15.3 Related Work

Afanasyev *et al.* [14] have come up with three different ways to mitigate IFA by putting a limit on Interest packets that are sent through each interface. These methods include token buckets with fairness for each interface, interest acceptance based on satisfaction, and pushback based on satisfaction. All packets on the malicious interface are stopped by these techniques, which means that legitimate interest packets may also be affected. Compagno *et al.* [15] presented the Poseidon framework for identifying and addressing IFA (Inter-Frame Alignment) issues. The detection of IFA relies on analyzing the ratio between incoming and outgoing data packets, as well as the available PIT space per interface. When both parameters are greater than a predetermined threshold, the attack is identified. The mitigation applied to an interface may also impact interest packets requested by legitimate consumers. Wang *et al.* [16] have introduced a method known as Disabling PIT Exhaustion (DPE) to address IFA mitigation. Each router utilizes a malicious list (m-list) for IFA detection. This list keeps track of the number of expired Interest packets for each namespace. If the value of this parameter surpasses a pre-established threshold, the namespace in the associated m-list is classified as malignant. No router will generate the entry for the malicious namespace. Malicious namespaces are retained in the m-list until they deteriorate. The approach relies on the expiration of a specific number of PIT entries, resulting in a slow process. Additionally, each router maintains an m-list, essential for storing consumer data on the router.

Xin *et al.* [17] have introduced an approach for detecting collusive IFA using wavelet analysis. The Power Spectral Density (PSD) is a frequency distribution utilized as a parameter for IFA identification in this approach. The presence of collusion in the IFA is identified when the value of the PSD is below a threshold. This approach is restricted to cases involving collusive IFA. Choose To Kill IFA (ChoKIFA) is a technique that was introduced by Benarfa *et al.* [18]. To identify IFA, ChoKIFA uses three parameters: name-prefix, interface-id, and satisfaction ratio. Since the satisfaction ratio is the only factor used for detection, the accuracy of the detection is poor.

Benmoussa *et al.* [19] have presented an approach to efficiently handle complicated IFA. The attack is limited and blocked by the producer's input. To spread the data of malicious Interest packets to the edge routers, specific control messages are sent. By examining the frequency of timed-out Interest packets and the satisfaction ratio of users, the edge routers identify users as malicious. ChoKIFA+ is a method that Benarfa *et al.* [20] have suggested for the identification and mitigation of IFA. This method lessens the impact of IFAs by using active queue management to distinguish between malicious and legitimate traffic. ChoKIFA+, an upgraded version, additionally adds security safeguards at edge routers for better network health and early attack detection. An Improved Collusive Flooding Attack (ICIFA) has been proposed by Wu *et al.* [21], which improves the efficacy of the current CIFA attack model. The authors have created a unique technique for transmitting attack traffic and enhanced the probe model for precise identification of downstream routing node capacity. The NDN network is more severely disrupted and the attacker's expenses are decreased by the ICIFA attack. Wu *et al.* [22] created the Bayesian Optimization Gradient Boosting Machines (BO-GBM) Fusion algorithm to counteract collusive interest flooding attacks. The technique provides a more effective detection mechanism by combining the benefits of Gradient Boosting Machines and Bayesian Optimization. Through the integration of various approaches, the algorithm enhances the accuracy and efficacy of identifying and countering these attacks, hence strengthening the security of NDN systems.

Zhang *et al.* [23] have introduced the ADMBIFA to identify and reduce the impact of blended interest flooding attacks (BIFAs). In BIFA, the attacker generates a blend of legitimate and malicious packets. They have used fuzzy logic to detect IFAs and BIFAs. Next, malicious interest prefixes were identified using K-means. Finally, a filter has been applied to block the attackers.

Most approaches discussed above use statistical thresholds to detect IFA based on one, two, or three parameters. The accuracy of detection can be further improved by using more than three parameters. When we have more than three parameters, computing the threshold for each parameter and its variations is impossible. Therefore, we are using machine learning approaches for IFA detection. The second problem is the limited router computation and storage. The large number of parameters means more computation and storage consumption. Thus, we propose to reduce the feature by applying feature selection and dimensionality reduction.

15.4 IFA Feature Selection and Detection

The IFA scenario is simulated with the help of the ns-3 [24] based ndnSIM [25] simulator. To prepare the data, choose the features, and use machine learning methods, Weka [hall2009weka] has been utilized. Many people use Weka [26] for practical reasons, learning, and research. It is an open-source Java app that lets you pre-process data, feature selection, and classification. To make it easier to understand, the analysis has been broken down into steps. Here are the steps:

- **IFA Modelling**: Simulation of IFA.
- **Data Collection**: Collection of traffic related statistics in a file.
- **Balancing Dataset**: Balancing the imbalanced data set using SMOTE.
- **Feature Selection**: Selecting most appropriate feature set for IFA detection

- **Dimensionality Reduction**: Further reducing the features using dimensionality reduction techniques.
- **Classification**: Using various classification approaches to detect the IFA in order to achieve maximum accuracy.

15.4.1 IFA Modelling

We employed the DFN topology to simulate the IFA, as depicted in Figure 15.3. The PIT size has been set to 120KB. The replacement policy for the Pending Interest Table (PIT) is persistence, meaning that a PIT entry is only deleted under two conditions: either when the router receives the data packet associated with the PIT entry or when the PIT entry reaches its expiration time. The default expiration time for the PIT entry is 4 seconds. The queue length and delay for each scenario are configured to be 400 and 10ms, respectively. The cache size is set to 1000, and it employs the LRU algorithm for replacement. The additional system configurations for DFN topology are given in Table 15.1.

The DFN topology is depicted in Figure 15.3; it consists of 8 consumers (C1-C8), 4 attackers (A1-A4), 6 publishers (P1-P6), and 11 routers (R1-R11). The simulations for all the scenarios corresponding to the DFN topology last for a duration of 600 seconds. Every consumer generates a

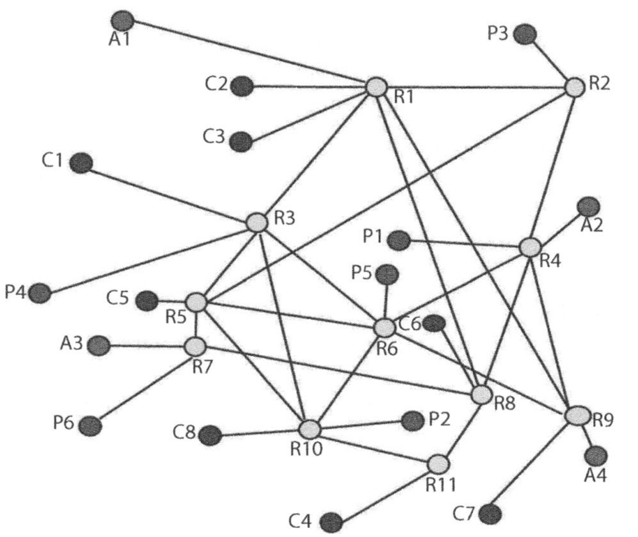

Figure 15.3 DFN topology.

Table 15.1 Simulation parameters for IFA on DFN topology.

Node	Distribution	Pattern	Frequency	Run-time	Producer	Goal
C1	Randomize	Uniform	300-500	0-600	P1	Legitimate
C2	Randomize	Exponential	300-500	30-600	P2	Legitimate
C3	Randomize	Exponential	300-500	45-600	P3	Legitimate
C4	Randomize	Uniform	300-500	60-600	P6	Legitimate
C5	Randomize	Exponential	300-500	45-600	P2,P3	Legitimate
C6	Randomize	Uniform	300-500	75-600	P3	Legitimate
C7	Randomize	Uniform	300-500	105-240, 330-465	P6,P4	Legitimate
C8	Randomize	Exponential	300-500	120-270, 375-600	P1	Legitimate
A1	Randomize	Uniform	16x(300-500)	105-240	P1	IFA
A2	Randomize	Uniform	16x(300-500)	330-465	P2	IFA
A3	Randomize	Uniform	16x(300-500)	105-240	P5	IFA
A4	Randomize	Exponential	16x(300-500)	330-465	P6	IFA

demand for 300 interest packets per second. Table 15.2 provides specific information about individual consumers in the DFN topology, including their request pattern, the publishers they request content from, and the duration of their activity. Table 15.1 provides information on various aspects of the attackers, such as their type, the publishers they request content from, and the duration of their activity.

15.4.2 Data Collection

The traffic statistics has been collected in a .csv file as shown in Figure 15.4. Dataset contains eleven features, i.e., InInterests (II), OutInterests (OI), DropInterests (DI), InSatisfiedInterests (ISI), OutSatisfiedInterests (OSI), InData (ID), OutData (OD), DropData (DD), InTimedOutInterests (ITOI), OutTimedOutInterests (OTOI), and PITsize (PS). The last column represents the class, i.e., attack and no attack. Here "0" means no attack

Time	Router	Interface	InInt	OutInt	InData	OutData	DropInt	DropData	InSatisfied Interests	OutSatisfiedInterests	InTimedOutInterests	OutTimedOut Interests	PITSize	out
477	R8	1	0	0	0	0	0	0	0	0	0	0	0	0
477	R8	2	0	374	376	0	0	0	0	376	0	0	0	0
477	R8	3	374	0	0	376	0	0	376	0	0	0	14	0
477	R8	4	376	0	0	378	0	0	378	0	0	0	29	0
477	R9	0	0	0	0	0	0	0	0	0	0	0	0	0
477	R9	1	0	0	0	0	0	0	0	0	0	0	0	0
477	R9	2	0	0	0	0	0	0	0	0	0	0	0	0
477	R9	3	0	0	0	0	0	0	0	0	0	0	0	0
477	R9	4	0	0	0	0	0	0	0	0	0	0	0	0
477	R10	0	407	0	0	404	0	0	404	0	0	0	10	0
477	R10	1	413	0	0	412	0	0	412	0	0	0	14	0
477	R10	2	0	434	430	0	0	0	0	430	0	0	0	0
477	R10	3	0	0	0	0	0	0	0	0	0	0	0	0
477	R10	4	434	0	0	430	0	0	430	0	0	0	22	0
477	R10	5	0	820	816	0	0	0	0	816	0	0	0	0
477	R11	0	0	374	377	0	0	0	0	377	0	0	0	0
477	R11	1	0	0	0	0	0	0	0	0	0	0	0	0
477	R11	2	374	0	0	377	0	0	377	0	0	0	20	0
478	R1	0	0	750	764	0	0	0	0	764	0	0	0	0
478	R1	1	0	0	0	0	0	0	0	0	0	0	0	0

Figure 15.4 Snapshot of the dataset.

and "1" means attacks. Description of these features per interface is given below:

1. **II**: Amount of arrival interest packets.
2. **OI**: Amount of sent interest packets from an interface.
3. **DI**: Amount of dropped interest packets.
4. **ISI**:Amount of arrival interest packets that are satisfied.
5. **OSI**: Amount of sent interest packets that are satisfied.
6. **ID**: Amount of arrival data packets.
7. **OD**: Amount of sent data packets.
8. **DD**: Amount of dropped data packets.
9. **ITOI**: Amount of arrival interest packets that are timeout.
10. **OTOI**: Amount of sent interest packets that are timeout.
11. **PS**: Amount of PIT entries per interface.

The dataset contains total 36000 instances out of which 31104 belongs to no attack label and 4896 belongs to attack label. It can be seen that the data is highly imbalanced. Therefore in the next step balancing algorithm have been applied.

15.4.3 Balancing the Dataset

Because the dataset is not balanced, we used the Synthetic Minority Oversampling Technique (SMOTE) [27]. SMOTE is a popular method for generating balanced data by synthetically generating instances of minor class. The process involves selecting individual instances from the minority class and creating synthetic samples by interpolating between them and their k-nearest neighbours. For each feature in a selected instance, the algorithm calculates the difference between that instance and its neighbors, randomly selects a value between 0 and 1, and combines these to generate a new synthetic instance. This process is repeated for a user-defined number of instances, effectively introducing diversity to the minority class. The resulting dataset, composed of original and synthetic instances, is then used to train machine learning models, helping mitigate biases caused by imbalanced class distributions and improving the model's ability to generalize to the minority class. After applying SMOTE the next step is to select the most appropriate feature set.

15.4.4 Feature Selection

The objective of the feature selection approach is to search for the optimal feature set for IFA detection. The router running at line speed has limited memory and computation. For the IFA detection to be effective, the feature set must be as small as feasible. We have used two types of feature selection techniques—filter methods and wrapper methods to accomplish this aim.

15.4.4.1 Filter Methods

A statistical measure is used by filter methods to give each feature a score. The score ranks the features and decides which ones to keep and which ones to get rid of from the dataset. Most of the time, the methods only look at one variable, and they either look at the feature on its own or in relation to the dependent variable. We have used Correlation based Filter Method (CFM), Clustering Variation based Filter Method (CVFM), Gain Ratio based Filter Method (GRFM), Information Gain based Filter Method (IGFM), Pairwise Correlation based Filter Method (PCFM), ReliefF based Filter Method (RFM), Significance based Filter Method (SFM), and Symmetrical Uncert based Filter Method (SUFM).

Following filter methods have been used in the article.

1. **CFM** [28] can determine how valuable an attribute is by looking at Pearson's correlation between it and the class. The value of Pearson's correlation ranging from -1 to 1. Its significance lies in providing a numerical measure for relationships, aiding in hypothesis testing, model building, and data exploration in various fields, including finance, psychology,

and quality control. However, it specifically measures linear associations and doesn't imply causation.

2. **CVFM** [29] is used to find and rank features in data that vary a lot from one another. To find the Coefficient of Variation for a given feature, divide its standard deviation by its mean. COV is given by Equation (15.1).

$$CV = \frac{StandardDeviaton}{Mean} * 100 \tag{15.1}$$

CVFM leverages clustering variation to identify informative features for machine learning models. By measuring the divergence in clusters formed by different feature subsets, it selects relevant features, enhancing model performance. This method efficiently reduces dimensionality and improves computational efficiency in various applications.

3. **GRFM** [30] determines the value of an attribute by checking the gain ratio compared to the class. The gain ratio can be given by Equation (15.2).

$$GainR(C,A) = \frac{H(C) - H(C|A)}{H(A)} \tag{15.2}$$

Here, $H(C)$, $H(C|A)$, and $H(A)$ represent the class's entropy, the class's conditional entropy given the values of the specific attribute, attribute's entropy, respectively. GRFM identifies features that provide the most discriminatory information while accounting for potential bias towards features with more categories. This method is particularly useful in enhancing the efficiency of machine learning models by selecting informative and diverse features.

4. **IGFM** [31] determines the importance of an attribute by measuring the information gain for the class. The information gain is given by Equation (15.3).

$$InfoGain(C, A) = H(Class) - H(C|A) \tag{15.3}$$

Here, $H(C)$ and $H(C|A)$ represents the class's entropy and the class's conditional entropy given the values of the specific attribute respectively. IGFM calculates the information gain of each feature and selects those with the highest information gain, thus improving model performance by focusing on the most informative attributes. This method is commonly used in machine learning to enhance efficiency and interpretability by selecting relevant features.

5. **PCFM** [32] is a technique used to identify and retain the most relevant features in a dataset by considering the pair-wise correlations between features. The idea is to eliminate redundant or highly correlated features, keeping only those that contribute unique information to the model.
6. **RFM** [33] involves a systematic process to identify and retain the most relevant features for a classification task. Initially, instance weights are assigned within the dataset. For each instance, ReliefF locates the nearest neighbors belonging to the same and different classes. Feature weights are then updated based on the differences between the feature values of the current instance and its nearest neighbors. By iteratively refining these weights, ReliefF captures the importance of features in distinguishing between classes. Finally, the algorithm computes the average feature weights and selects the top-k features with the highest weights as the final subset. The ReliefF weight for a feature X_i is calculated using Equation (15.4).

$$W(X_i) = \mathrm{L}_{j=1}^{k} \frac{-\Delta(X_i, X_{\text{near-hit}}^{(j)})}{k} + \mathrm{L}_{j=1}^{k} \frac{\Delta(X_i, X_{\text{near-miss}}^{(j)})}{k} \tag{15.4}$$

Here, k is the number of nearest neighbors considered, $\Delta(X_i, X_{\text{near-hit}}^{(j)})$ represents the absolute difference in the feature X_i value between the instance under consideration and its j-th nearest neighbor with the same class label, $\Delta(X_i, X_{\text{near-miss}}^{(j)})$ represents the absolute difference in the feature X_i value between the instance under consideration and its j-th nearest neighbor with a different class label.

7. **SFM** [34] involves a systematic process to identify and retain the most meaningful features in a dataset. Initially, statistical tests or measures are employed to assess the significance of each feature with respect to the target variable. Common statistical tests include t-tests, ANOVA, or correlation

Table 15.2 Ranking of features in ascending order based of various feature learning approaches.

Rank	CFM	CVFM	GRFM	IGFM	PCFM	RFM	SFM	SUFM
1	PS(0.34974)	OSI(4.3318)	OTOI(0.1091)	PS(0.2351)	PS(1.0917)	PS(0.01401)	PS(0.523)	PS(0.1118)
2	OTOI(0.20314)	ID(4.3316)	ITOI(0.0996)	II(0.1537)	OTOI(1.0726)	OTOI(0.0096)	II(0.41)	OTOI(0.101)
3	ITOI(0.18709)	ISI(4.2201)	PS(0.0733)	OI(0.1021)	ITOI(0.979)	ITOI(0.00784)	ITOI(0.402)	II(0.09)
4	OD(0.14992)	OD(4.2195)	DI(0.0672)	OTOI(0.0937)	II(0.9438)	II(0.00521)	OTOI(0.394)	ITOI(0.087)
5	ISI(0.14987)	OI(4.1553)	II(0.0635)	ITOI(0.077)	DI(0.8558)	OD(0.00496)	OI(0.392)	DI(0.0673)
6	II(0.12684)	II(3.8315)	OI(0.0458)	ID(0.0712)	OI(0.8092)	ISI(0.00489)	ISI(0.388)	OI(0.0633)
7	OI(0.02228)	PS(3.5417)	ID(0.0355)	OSI(0.071)	ID(0.7264)	DI(0.00429)	DI(0.379)	ID(0.0475)
8	DI(0.02002)	DD(0.02)	OSI(0.0349)	DI(0.0671)	OSI(0.723)	OI(0.00305)	OD(0.374)	OSI(0.0469)
9	ID(0.00987)	OTOI(0)	ISI(0.0311)	ISI(0.0576)	ISI(0.6723)	ID(0.00169)	ID(0.35)	ISI(0.0405)
10	OSI(0.00986)	DI(0)	OD(0.0309)	OD(0.0568)	OD(0.6698)	OSI(0.00168)	OSI(0.327)	OD(0.04)
11	DD(0)	ITOI(0)	DD(0)	DD(0)	DD(0.3476)	DD(0)	DD(0)	DD(0)

Table 15.3 Average ranking of features based on Table 15.2.

Features	CFM	CVFM	GRFM	IGFM	PCFM	RFM	SFM	SUAE	Average rank
PS	1	7	3	1	1	1	1	1	2
OTOI	2	9	1	4	2	2	4	2	3.25
II	6	6	5	2	4	4	2	3	4
ITOI	3	9	2	5	3	3	3	4	4
OI	7	5	6	3	6	8	5	6	5.75
DI	8	9	4	8	5	7	7	5	5.625
ID	9	2	7	6	7	9	9	7	7
ISI	5	3	9	9	9	6	6	9	7
OD	4	4	10	10	10	5	8	10	7.625
OSI	10	1	8	7	8	10	10	8	7.75
DD	11	8	11	11	11	11	11	11	10.625

coefficients. Features demonstrating high statistical significance, indicating a strong relationship with the target variable, are retained. This process helps eliminate irrelevant or redundant features, thereby enhancing the model's efficiency and interpretability.

8. **SUFM** [35] assess feature relevance by computing entropies, mutual information, and Symmetrical Uncertainty between the target and features. Features are ranked by Uncertainty values, aiding the selection of the most relevant ones for improved machine learning model performance through principled feature selection.

Table 15.2 shows the ranking of the features based on CFM,CVFM, GRFM,IGFM,PCFM,RFM,SFM, and SUFM filter methods. Based on Table 15.2 the average ranking of the features have been calculated which is given in Table 15.3.

15.4.4.2 Wrapper Methods

Wrapper methods evaluates different feature subsets by training and testing a model on each subset. The performance of the predictive model on each subset is used as a criterion to select the best features. The selection of features can be done based on best-first search, random hill-climbing algorithm, or any heuristics algorithm. Recently the meta-heuristics approaches have been used in solving many real life problems [36–39].

In the chapter we have used three meta-heuristics approaches as search methods, i.e., Particle Swarm Optimization (PSO) [40], Evolutionary Algorithm (EA) [41], and NSGA-II [42]. The predictive model used are Mulit Layer Perception (MLP), Naïve Bayes (NB), and Random Forest (RF). The details of the predictive models used is given in Section 15.4.6. The details of the search methods used is given below:

- **PSO** is meta heuristics algorithm that is based on the collective behaviour of the birds in folk. PSO was created by James Kennedy and Russell Eberhart in 1995. It uses a swarm of particles to represent possible solutions in a search space. The best-known position for each particle and the best-known position for the whole system are used to change its position and speed. The algorithm improves solutions repeatedly by checking how well they fit an objective function. This lets particles efficiently explore and use the search space.
- **EA** is a set of metaheuristics approaches based on biological evolution. Genetic Algorithms, Genetic Programming, and Evolutionary Strategies are some of the algorithms that use the idea of natural selection to find better ways to solve complex problems. EAs keep a population of possible solutions stored as individuals and use genetic operators such as crossover, mutation, and selection to make new generations. An objective function tells us how fit each individual is, which affects its chances of being chosen for reproduction. After each iteration, the population changes to find better solutions, keeping the balance between exploring and using the solution space. EAs are flexible and can be used to solve many different optimization problems in fields like engineering, logistics, AI, and machine learning.
- **NSGA-II** is a widely used multi-objective optimization algorithm designed to find a set of Pareto-optimal solutions in a given search space. Developed by Kalyanmoy Deb, it extends traditional genetic algorithms to handle multiple conflicting objectives. NSGA-II introduces a novel non-dominated sorting approach, ranking individuals based on their dominance relationships, enabling the preservation of diverse and

non-dominated solutions. The algorithm employs elitism, crowding distance, and a fast nondominated sort to encourage convergence and maintain a well-distributed Pareto front. NSGA-II balances exploration and exploitation by choosing individuals to reproduce based on their non-dominated rank and crowding distance. This makes it very good at solving real-world problems with many competing goals, like engineering design, finance, and allocating resources.

Wrapper methods gives a subset of features which is shown in Table 15.4. Whereas filter methods ranks the feature. In order to select the relevant features based on the two different types of feature selection approach. We created a table containing the features count which denotes how many times the feature is selected by a wrapper method. Table 15.5 shows the feature count in decreasing order (i.e., most relevant features are on top of the list). The last column of Table 15.5 that shows ranking of the features.

Now both the Table 15.2 and Table 15.5 contains features ranked from high relevant to low relevant. Comparing Table 15.2 and Table 15.5 PS, II, OTOI, OI, and ITOI chosen as most relevant feature for IFA detection.

15.4.5 Dimensionality Reduction

Dimensionality reduction methods can further reduce the number of features after feature selection. The Principal Component Analysis (PCA) method has been used to reduce the number of features. PCA tries to turn high-dimensional data into a lower-dimensional representation while

Table 15.4 Feature subset selected after applying wrapper methods.

	Search method		
Predictive model	**PSO**	**EA**	**NSGA-II**
MLP	II, OD, DI, ITOI, OTOI, PS	II, OI, ID, DD, ISI, ITOI, OTOI, PS	II, OD, DI, ITOI, OTOI, PS
NB	II, OI, ID, OD, ISI, OSI, OTOI, PS	II, OI, ID, OD, ISI, OSI, OTOI, PS	II, OI, ID, OD, DD, ISI, OSI, OTOI, PS
RF	II, OI, OD, DI, OSI, ITOI, OTOI, PS	II, OI, DI, ISI, OSI, ITOI, OTOI, PS	II, OI, ID, DI, ISI, ITOI, OTOI, PS

Table 15.5 Ranking of features based on Table 15.4.

Features	**Count**	**Ranking out of 11**
PS	9	2
II	9	2
OTOI	9	2
OI	7	4
ISI	6	6
OD	6	6
ITOI	6	6
DI	5	9
ID	5	9
OSI	5	9
DD	2	11

keeping as much of the original variance as possible. The steps to perform PCA are:

1. **Covariance Matrix**: The first thing that PCA does is figure out the covariance matrix from the given dataset. It uses the covariance matrix to show how different parts of the data are related to each other.
2. **Eigen Decomposition**: The covariance matrix must be eigen-decomposed as the next step. This leads to eigenvalues and eigenvectors. Eigenvectors show the directions of the data's most significant variance, and eigenvalues show the magnitude of that variance.
3. **Choosing the Principal Components**: The eigenvectors are ranked in decreasing order by the eigenvalues. The

eigenvector with the highest eigenvalue shows the principal component with the most variance.

4. **Projecting**: The chosen principal components are used to put the original data in a different subspace. There are fewer dimensions in this new subspace than in the original data. The number of chosen principal components sets the number of dimensions of the reduced space.
5. **Variance Retention**: The amount of variance they keep is an important thing to think about when choosing the number of principal components. The ratio of selected eigenvalues to the total sum of eigenvalues can be used to assess the proportion of variance retained.

The input for PCA is PS, II, OTOI, OI, and ITOI. The Covariance Matrix is given below.

1	–0.25	0.1	–0.12	0.24
–0.25	1	–0.11	0.1	–0.28
0.1	–0.11	1	–0.04	0.45
–0.12	0.1	–0.04	1	-0.09
0.24	–0.28	0.45	–0.09	1

The eigenvectors are given below.

Features	V1	V2	V3	V4	V5
InInt	0.4206	0.4093	0.3613	0.7142	–0.1221
OutInt	–0.4479	–0.3147	–0.4108	0.6915	0.2314
In Timed Out Interests	0.472	–0.5675	–0.2795	0.0848	–0.6081
Out Timed Out Interests	–0.2186	–0.5733	0.7872	0.0611	0.0121
PITSize	0.5933	–0.2875	–0.0538	–0.0293	0.7494

The eigenvectors ranked based on eigenvalues are given below.

Eigenvalue	*Ranked*	*Eigenvectors*
0.646	1	0.593PS + 0.472ITOI – 0.448OI + 0.421II – 0.219OTOI
0.435	2	−0.573OTOI – 0.568ITOI + 0.409II – 0.315OI – 0.287PS
0.252	3	0.787OTOI – 0.411OI + 0.361II – 0.28ITOI – 0.054PS
0.102	4	0.714II + 0.691OI + 0.085ITOI + 0.061OTOI – 0.029PS
0	5	0.749PS – 0.608ITOI + 0.231OI – 0.122II + 0.012OTOI

The first four eigenvectors have been chosen as features for applying ML in the next phase as there eigenvalues are much higher then the fifth eigenvector.

15.4.6 Classification

After applying feature selection and dimensionality reduction we have four features. These features are input to the ML approaches. The ML approaches used for IFA detection are Random Forest Classifier, Random Tree Classifier, K-Nearest Neighbour Classifier, J48 Classifier, Support Vector Machine Classifier, AdaBoost Classifier, Multilayer Perceptron with Back Propagation (MLP with BP) Classifier, and Naïve Bayes Classifier. The classification metrics used for the comparison are Accuracy, Recall, F1-Score, and Precision. The details of the ML approaches are given below:

- **Random Forest Classifier** [43] is a type of ensemble machine learning that builds a group of decision trees while being trained. Each tree is trained on a different set of data, and for classification, the predictions are put together by voting for the most accurate ones and averaging for regression. This ensemble approach makes predictions more accurate, reduces overfitting, and makes the model more robust.
- **Random Tree Classifier** [44] is one of the classifiers in the decision tree family. It adds randomness by picking a feature set at each node for building the tree, which differs from traditional decision trees. This randomness keeps the model from fitting too well and makes it more stable. The final classification is found by adding up the predictions of several random trees. Besides being similar to a Random Forest, a Random Tree Classifier usually uses fewer trees and less

computing power. It is used for various classification tasks and balances between being easy to use and making good decisions in machine learning settings.

- **K-Nearest Neighbors (KNN)** Classifier [45] works on the idea of proximity, which means that a data point is put into a category based on the majority class. The number of neighbours that are looked at is set by the user-defined parameter *k*. KNN remembers the training data and calculates only when the prediction is made.
- **J48 classifier** [46], sometimes called C4.5, is a well-known decision tree algorithm used in machine learning for classification tasks. J48 makes a decision tree by repeatedly dividing the dataset based on each node's most valuable attribute. The algorithm uses a top-down, greedy approach to maximize information gain or minimize impurity, leading to a tree structure representing decision rules. J48 works with both categorical and numerical features.
- **Support Vector Machine (SVM)** [47]: The foundation of SVM is identifying the ideal hyperplane for classifying the data into distinct groups. SVMs work best in spaces with many dimensions, and they can easily handle both linear and nonlinear decision boundaries. It finds the hyperplane that best divides the data into groups to make the algorithm work.
- **AdaBoost** [48] is an ensemble learning algorithm for sorting things into groups. Yoav Freund and Robert Schapire created AdaBoost. It turns weak learners into strong learners by giving weights and changing data points based on how well the model does. It trains a set of weak classifiers one at a time, each giving more weight to wrongly classified cases. The final classification is found by adding up the scores from the weak classifiers. AdaBoost is especially good at improving accuracy on large, complicated datasets, and it is less likely to overfit.
- **MLP with BP** [49] is a method that uses an artificial neural network with several layers: an input layer, one or more hidden layers, and an output layer. Each layer contains nodes (or neurons), and connections between nodes have associated weights. Backpropagation [50] (BP) is a supervised learning method for training neural networks. It works by changing the weights of the network's connections repeatedly

to get the error between the predicted output and the actual target values as small as possible. In this step, the error is sent backwards through the network, and the weights are changed based on how the error changes for each weight.

- **Naivë Bayes Classifier** [51] uses Bayes' theorem for classification. The algorithm finds the chance of each class for a given set of features and then chooses the most likely class to be the predicted class. Naivë Bayes classifiers are computationally efficient and easy to implement, making them suitable for large datasets.

Table 15.6 and Table 15.7 show the results after applying various classification approaches on full dataset (all 11 features) and reduced dataset (only 4 features). We have used accuracy, precision, recall, and F1-score as classification metrics. Additionally, 10-fold cross-validation has been done for fair evaluation. The results are sorted based on accuracy. It can be seen that the performance of the Random Forest Classifier is better than all the classifiers in terms of all the metrics for both full and reduced datasets.

Table 15.6 Classification result on full dataset.

	Classification metric before feature reduction			
ML approaches	**Accuracy**	**Precision**	**Recall**	**F1-score**
Random Forest Classifier	86.45	80.71	93.1	86.46
Random Tree Classifier	85.68	79.94	92.33	85.69
K-Nearest Neighbour Classifier	84.87	79.99	90.72	85.02
J48 Classifier	84.81	80.89	89.78	85.1
Support Vector Machine Classifier	83.53	78.82	89.21	83.69
AdaBoost Classifier	74.62	59.73	89.44	71.63
MLP with BP Classifier	74.2	63.97	84.13	72.68
Naïve Bayes Classifier	67.18	41.64	93.65	57.65

Table 15.7 Classification result on reduced dataset.

	Classification metric before after feature reduction			
ML approaches	**Accuracy**	**Precision**	**Recall**	**F1 score**
Random Forest Classifier	83.8	75.39	93.1	83.31
Random Tree Classifier	83.5	75.19	92.67	83.02
J48 Classifier	82.3	75.84	89.57	82.14
K-Nearest Neighbour Classifier	81.67	73.38	90.67	81.11
Support Vector Machine Classifier	80.86	74.53	87.95	80.69
AdaBoost Classifier	72.58	75.26	74.05	74.65
MLP with BP Classifier	70.92	53.96	86.83	66.56
Naïve Bayes Classifier	57.85	54.76	62.16	58.23

If we look at top-performing classifiers, then it can be generalised that the tree-based classifier performed better than other types of classifiers.

If we compare the classification metrics related to the full and reduced datasets, there is little degradation in most of the classification metrics. The reduction in the classification metrics can be seen in Table 15.8. We have used Equation (15.5) to generate the Table 15.8.

$$\%change = \frac{MetricValue_{FullDataset} - MetricValue_{ReducedDataset}}{MetricValue_{FullDataset}} * 100 \tag{15.5}$$

If we compare the performance of the Random Forest Classifier in full and reduced dataset, then approximately 3.07%, 6.59%, 0%, and 3.64% reduction in accuracy, precision, recall, and f1-score, respectively, can be seen. The percentage reduction in feature-set is ((11 – 4) * 100)/11 = 63.64%. Thus the proposed detection approach gived almost same accuracy with a reduced dataset of approximately 63 percentage.

Table 15.8 Percentage reduction in classification metrics after feature reduction.

	Percentage reduction in classification metrics after feature reduction			
ML approaches	**Accuracy**	**Precision**	**Recall**	**F1 score**
RandomForest	3.07	6.59	0	3.64
RandomTree	2.54	5.94	-0.37	3.12
J48	3.77	8.26	0.06	3.39
KNN	2.96	6.24	0.23	4.69
SVM	3.2	5.44	1.41	3.58
AdaBoostM1	2.73	-26	17.21	-4.22
MLP	4.42	15.65	-3.21	8.42
NaiveBayes	13.89	-31.51	33.63	-1.01

15.5 Conclusion

IFA is one of the most damaging attacks in NDN since it may halt the network. Thus, efficient detection of IFA is necessary. Previous statistical approaches use two or three parameters for IFA detection. They employ a fixed threshold for detection. The accuracy of these approaches is low compared to those with higher features. The approaches that use more features use ML approaches for IFA detection. The problem with these approaches is that as they use more features, the router running at line speed must spend more time aggregating these features and performing detection. Higher accuracy and low overhead can be simultaneously achieved through feature reduction. In this chapter, we have reduced 11 features to 4 features by employing feature selection first and then dimensionality reduction. We have used 20 feature selection approaches and taken the most optimal features based on their average ranking. After feature selection, 5 features are left. Then, we further reduced the feature set to 4 using the dimensionality reduction technique called PCA. After feature reduction, the classification was compared based on the full and reduced datasets. The Random forest classifier is the most efficient based on all the comparison metrics for both the cases of full and reduced datasets. The proposed detection approach gave almost the same accuracy with a reduced dataset of approximately 63%. In the future, the detection approach can be deployed on ndnSIM or NFD-based testbeds to check its performance in simulated or emulated environments.

References

1. IOT Connected Devices Worldwide 2019-2030, https://www.statista.com/statistics/1183457/iot-connected-devices-worldwide/.
2. Ghodsi, A., Shenker, S., Koponen, T., Singla, A., Raghavan, B., Wilcox, J., Information-centric networking: seeing the forest for the trees, in: *Proceedings of the 10th ACM Workshop on Hot Topics in Networks,* pp. 1–6, 2011.
3. Kumar, N. and Gupta, N.K., Comparing the performance of tcp/ip with named data networking using ns-3, in: *Proceedings of the 2022 Fourteenth International Conference on Contemporary Computing,* pp. 560–563, 2022.
4. Acs, G., Conti, M., Gasti, P., Ghali, C., Tsudik, G., Cache privacy in named-data networking, in: *2013 IEEE 33rd International Conference on Distributed Computing Systems*, pp. 41–51, 2013.
5. Kumar, N. and Srivastava, S., A triggered delay-based approach against cache privacy attack in NDN, in: *International Journal of Networked and Distributed Computing,* pp. 22–27, 2018.
6. Kumar, N., Aleem, A., Singh, A.K., Srivastava, S., NBP: Namespace-based privacy to counter timing-based attack in named data networking. *J. Netw. Comput. Appl.*, 144, 155–170, 2019.
7. Conti, M., Gasti, P., Teoli, M., A lightweight mechanism for detection of cache pollution attacks in named data networking. *Comput. Netw.*, 57, 16, 3178–3191, 2013.
8. Kumar, N. and Srivastava, S., IBPC: An Approach for Mitigation of Cache Pollution Attack in NDN using Interface-Based Popularity. *Arabian J. Sci. Eng.*, 49, 1–11, 2023.
9. Gasti, P., Tsudik, G., Uzun, E., Zhang, L., DoS and DDoS in named data networking, in: *2013 22nd International Conference on Computer Communication and Networks (ICCCN), IEEE,* pp. 1–7, 2013.
10. Kumar, N., Singh, A.K., Aleem, A., Srivastava, S., Security attacks in named data networking: A review and research directions. *J. Comput. Sci. Technol.*, 34, 1319–1350, 2019.
11. Kumar, N., Singh, A.K., Srivastava, S., Evaluating machine learning algorithms for detection of interest flooding attack in named data networking, in: *Proceedings of the 10th International Conference on Security of Information and Networks*, pp. 299–302, 2017.
12. Kumar, N., Singh, A.K., Srivastava, S., Feature selection for interest flooding attack in named data networking. *Int. J. Comput. Appl.*, 43, 6, 537–546, 2021.

13. Dai, H., Wang, Y., Fan, J., Liu, B., Mitigate ddos attacks in ndn by interest traceback, in: *2013 IEEE Conference on Computer Communications Workshops (INFOCOM WKSHPS), IEEE*, pp. 381–386, 2013.
14. Afanasyev, A., Mahadevan, P., Moiseenko, I., Uzun, E., Zhang, L., Interest flooding attack and countermeasures in named data networking, in: *2013 IFIP Networking Conference, IEEE*, pp. 1–9, 2013.
15. Compagno, A., Conti, M., Gasti, P., Tsudik, G., Poseidon: Mitigating interest flooding DDoS attacks in named data networking, in: *38th Annual IEEE Conference on Local Computer Networks, IEEE*, pp. 630–638, 2013.
16. Wang, K., Zhou, H., Qin, Y., Chen, J., Zhang, H., Decoupling malicious interests from pending interest table to mitigate interest flooding attacks, in: *2013 IEEE Globecom Workshops (GC Wkshps), IEEE*, pp. 963–968, 2013.
17. Xin, Y., Li, Y., Wang, W., Li, W., Chen, X., Detection of collusive interest flooding attacks in named data networking using wavelet analysis, in: *MILCOM 2017-2017 IEEE Military Communications Conference (MILCOM), IEEE*, pp. 557–562, 2017.
18. Benarfa, A., Hassan, M., Compagno, A., Losiouk, E., Yagoubi, M.B., Conti, M., Chokifa: A new detection and mitigation approach against interest flooding attacks in ndn, in: *Wired/Wireless Internet Communications: 17th IFIP WG 6.2 International Conference (WWIC)*, Springer, pp. 53–65, 2019.
19. Benmoussa, A., el Karim Tahari, A., Kerrache, C.A. *et al.*, MSIDN: Mitigation of sophisticated interest flooding-based DDoS attacks in named data networking. *Future Gener. Comput. Syst.*, 107, 293–306, 2020.
20. Benarfa, A., Hassan, M., Losiouk, E., Compagno, A., Yagoubi, M.B., Conti, M., ChoKIFA+: an early detection and mitigation approach against interest flooding attacks in NDN. *Int. J. Inf. Secur.*, 20, 269–285, 2021.
21. Wu, Z., Feng, W., Lei, J., Yue, M., I-CIFA: An improved collusive interest flooding attack in named data networking. *J. Inf. Secur. Appl.*, 61, 102912, 2021.
22. Wu, Z., Peng, S., Liu, L., Yue, M., Detection of Improved Collusive Interest Flooding Attacks Using BO-GBM Fusion Algorithm in NDN. *IEEE Trans. Netw. Sci. Eng.*, 10, 1, 239–252, 2022.
23. Zhang, Y., Guo, X.X., Ma, M., ADMBIFA: Accurate Detection and Mitigation of Blended Interest Flooding Attacks in NDNs, in: *2023 IEEE 24th International Conference on High Performance Switching and Routing (HPSR), IEEE*, pp. 56–61, 2023.
24. Henderson, T.R., Lacage, M., Riley, G.F., Dowell, C., Kopena, J., Network simulations with the ns-3 simulator. *SIGCOMM demonstration*, vol. 14(14), p. 527, 2008.
25. Afanasyev, A., Moiseenko, I., Zhang, L., others, ndnSIM: NDN simulator for NS-3. Tech. Rep., vol. 4, pp. 1–7, University of California, Los Angeles, 2012.
26. Hall, M., Frank, E., Holmes, G., Pfahringer, B., Reutemann, P., Witten, I.H., The WEKA data mining software: an update. *ACM SIGKDD Explor. Newsl.*, 11, 1, 10–18, 2009.

27. Chawla, N.V., Bowyer, K.W., Hall, L.O., Kegelmeyer, W.P., SMOTE: synthetic minority over-sampling technique. *J. Artif. Intell. Res.*, 16, 321–357, 2002.
28. Hall, M.A., Correlation-based feature selection for machine learning, PhD thesis. The University of Waikato, 1998.
29. Bindu, K.H., Morusupalli, R., Dey, N., Rao, C.R., *Coefficient of variation and machine learning applications*, CRC Press, 2019.
30. Priyadarsini, R.P., Valarmathi, M., Sivakumari, S., Gain ratio based feature selection method for privacy preservation. *ICTACT J. Soft Comput.*, 1, 4, 201–205, 2011.
31. Azhagusundari, B., Thanamani, A.S., others, Feature selection based on information gain. *Int. J. Innov. Technol. Explor. Eng. (IJITEE)*, 2, 2, 18–21, 2013.
32. Jiménez, F., Sánchez, G., Palma, J., Miralles-Pechuán, L., Botía, J., Multivariate feature ranking of gene expression data. arXiv preprint arXiv:2111.02357, abs/2111.02357, 2021, https://arxiv.org/abs/2111.02357
33. Kira, K. and Rendell, L.A., A practical approach to feature selection, in: *Machine Learning Proceedings 1992,* Elsevier, pp. 249–256, 1992.
34. Ahmad, A. and Dey, L., A feature selection technique for classificatory analysis. *Pattern Recognit. Lett.*, 26, 1, 43–56, 2005.
35. Singh, B., Kushwaha, N., Vyas, O.P., others, A feature subset selection technique for high dimensional data using symmetric uncertainty. *J. Data Anal. Inform. Process.*, 2, 04, 95, 2014.
36. Singh, A.K., Maurya, S., Kumar, N., Srivastava, S., Heuristic approaches for the reliable SDN controller placement problem. *Trans. Emerging Telecommun. Technol.*, 31, 2, e3761, 2020.
37. Chaudhuri, A. and Sahu, T.P., A case study on disease diagnosis using gene expression data classification with feature selection: Application of data science techniques in health care, in: *Data Science and Its Applications*, pp. 239–254, Chapman and Hall/CRC, 2021.
38. Chaudhuri, A., Binary Jaya Algorithm based on Dice Similarity for Cancer Classification using Microarray Dataset, in: *2022 IEEE World Conference on Applied Intelligence and Computing (AIC)*, IEEE, pp. 231–236, 2022.
39. Chaudhuri, A. and Sahu, T.P., Feature Selection Technique for Microarray Data Using Multi-objective Jaya Algorithm Based on Chaos Theory, in: *Machine Learning and Autonomous Systems: Proceedings of ICMLAS 2021*, Springer, pp. 399–410, 2022.
40. Couceiro, M. and Ghamisi, P., Particle swarm optimization, in: *Fractional Order Darwinian Particle Swarm Optimization: Applications and Evaluation of an Evolutionary Algorithm*, Springer International Publishing, 2016.
41. Eiben, A.E., Smith, J.E., Eiben, A., Smith, J., What is an evolutionary algorithm?, in: *Introduction to evolutionary computing*, pp. 25–48, 2015.
42. Deb, K., Pratap, A., Agarwal, S., Meyarivan, T., A fast and elitist multiobjective genetic algorithm: NSGA-II. *IEEE Trans. Evol. Comput.*, 6, 2, 182–197, 2002.

43. Pal, M., Random forest classifier for remote sensing classification. *Int. J. Remote Sens.*, 26, 1, 217–222, 2005.
44. Kalmegh, S., Analysis of weka data mining algorithm reptree, simple cart and randomtree for classification of indian news. *Int. J. Innov. Sci. Eng. Technol.*, 2, 2, 438–446, 2015.
45. Peterson, L.E., K-nearest neighbor. *Scholarpedia*, 4, 2, 1883, 2009.
46. Kaur, G. and Chhabra, A., Improved J48 classification algorithm for the prediction of diabetes. *Int. J. Comput. Appl.*, 98, 22, 13–17, 2014.
47. Noble, W.S., What is a support vector machine? *Nat. Biotechnol.*, 24, 12, 1565–1567, 2006.
48. Hastie, T., Rosset, S., Zhu, J., Zou, H., Multi-class adaboost. *Stat. Interface*, 2, 3, 349–360, 2009.
49. Gardner, M.W. and Dorling, S., Artificial neural networks (the multilayer perceptron)—a review of applications in the atmospheric sciences. *Atmos. Environ.*, 32, 14–15, 2627–2636, 1998.
50. Rojas, R. and Rojas, R., The backpropagation algorithm, in: *Neural networks: a systematic introduction*, pp. 149–182, 1996.
51. Rish, I. and others, An empirical study of the naive Bayes classifier, in: *IJCAI 2001 Workshop on Empirical Methods in Artificial Intelligence*, vol. 3, pp. 41–46, 2001.

16

An Internet of Vehicles Model Architecture with Seven Layers

Sujata Negi Thakur[1]*, Manisha Koranga[1], Sandeep Abhishek[2], Richa Pandey[1] and Mayurika Joshi[1]

[1]*Department of Computer Science and Engineering, Graphic Era Hill University, Haldwani, Uttarakhand, India*
[2]*Department of Media and Mass Communication, Graphic Era Hill University, Haldwani, Uttarakhand, India*

Abstract

Over the past ten years, a growing number of cars have been introduced that are equipped with sensors to keep an eye on several parameters, including position, speed, acceleration, tyre pressure, driver monitoring, and oil pressure. The Internet of Things, or IoT, makes it possible to gather many kinds of data from a particular area. The idea of the Internet of Vehicles (IoV) emerged as a result of the combination of findings from both movements. Devices (such as sensors, actuators, and personal devices) must use various technologies to connect with each other and the infrastructure in order to establish the Internet of Vehicles. Many design issues with these device interactions include device incompatibilities, varying characteristics and reaction time of the connection of Internet, and restricted processing and storage capacity. In order to tackle these obstacles, we put forth a thorough platform that facilitates a tiered design framework that may offer smooth inter-device communication integration inside the Internet of Vehicles ecosystem. In addition, we analyze several recently put forth IoV designs and highlight the key distinctions between them and our suggested design.

***Keywords*:** Internet of Vehicles, model, layer, security, protocol and architecture

**Corresponding author*: Sujatathakur1987@gmail.com

Mohit Kumar, Gautam Srivastava, Ashutosh Kumar Singh and Kalka Dubey (eds.) AI-Based Advanced Optimization Techniques for Edge Computing, (433–456) © 2025 Scrivener Publishing LLC

16.1 Introduction

In today's times, the Internet of Things (IoT) has been playing an important role in forming the foundation for technical breakthroughs in the vehicular ad hoc network, and it provides significant stimulation for different innovations on the Internet of Vehicles (IoV) [20]. The interaction of the vehicle with the other Road Side Units (RSU) is represented by the IoV. These units can be automobiles, roadside infrastructure, people, servers, and so forth. An Intelligent Transportation System (ITS) is a collection of technology and applications that attempt to improve transportation safety and mobility while minimising accidents. One of the most detrimental outcomes of increased road traffic is a rise in road accidents. According to WHO data, road accidents claim the lives of millions of people and injure millions more; hence, it is a worldwide issue that must be addressed. The Internet of Things (IoT) is becoming increasingly important in communication in the modern day; everything is becoming connected to the Internet [5]. The vehicle ad hoc network is gradually transforming into the Internet of Vehicles (IoV) as vehicular technology advances [2]. VANET allows every car [18] to communicate wirelessly with other vehicles. However, it has the drawback of only covering a narrow network, limiting flexibility and the number of linked cars. Furthermore, a few factors such as driver behaviour, difficult routes, and traffic congestion are impediments to VANET connection [12]. As a result, it is appropriate to state that the involvement of objects in VANET is unstable and unpredictable. As a result, the VANET was insufficient to supply services or applications to its clients [4], prompting the creation of IoV. The IoV is primarily comprised of two technologies: vehicle cognition and vehicle networking.

Over the past decade, the worldwide vehicle population has grown from nearly ninety million in 2006, to more than one billion vehicles in 2014 and is expected to surpass a total of two billion, by 2035. Plenty of these automobiles will be connected that can wirelessly communicate with different kinds of equipment (indicators, cell phones, surveillance cameras) attached to the the World Wide Web, equipment in the vehicle or equipment on the outside the vehicle, using a broad range of communications rules and mediums for transmissions (Statista, 2012). Furthermore, analysts predict that by the years 2020, twenty-five billions device will be linked to the Internet connection, creating new challenges such as emissions, roadway security [15], and infrastructure efficiency [11, 19].

Communication between the vehicles and devices are critical elements of the IoV idea referred to as a wireless network that enables exchanges of data that involve vehicle and roadside (V&R), Vehicle and Person (V to P), Vehicles and The device (V&D). The Internet of Vehicles (IoV) promotes close relationships between humans and vehicles with the aim of enhancing human capacities (including hearing, visual empathy, or geographic consciousness), circumstances, security, vitality, as well as automobile cognitive ability, (APEC, 2014, and McKinsey & Company, 2013) that will consequently contribute to various industries, especially the lifestyle of consumers, the customer automobile marketplace, as well as purchasing methods. The introduction of the Internet of Vehicles (IoV) requires devices to interact and communicate with other equipment, facilitated by various techniques depending on the type of devices (such as tested actuators, personal messaging devices, and tablets) and the type of network (like wireless sensor networks or Personal Area Networks (PAN), as mentioned by Guerrero-Ibanez, Zeadally, & Contreras-Castillo in 2015). Each device and network type has unique features, contributing to a complex communication scenario with several challenges. These challenges encompass issues such as device incompatibility, variability in web connection quality and response speed, and limited access to information extraction and storage services. Achieving efficient communication in the Internet of Vehicles environment necessitates the seamless integration of IoV with pre-existing networks and transportation infrastructure.

16.2 Literature Review

Table 16.1's literature review indicates an unexplored area in the recent advancements and comprehensive examination of the Internet of Vehicles (IoV) communication frameworks, protocols, and application-related challenges. The analysis presents a detailed comparison of cutting-edge IoV communication systems, routing, and MAC protocols. It also addresses the research issues within this field, highlighting the latest developments in specific IoV sectors [10].

This segment builds upon the current research in the field of Internet of Vehicles (IoV). Numerous studies have been conducted to delve into IoV, its standards, and practical applications:

[8], provided a comprehensive analysis of IoV and its deployment in Intelligent Transportation Systems (ITS). They have thoroughly discussed various facets of ITS, including Incident and Emergency Management Systems, Information Management systems, and Transit Management Systems. The paper explores a range of ITS applications such as Electronic Toll Collection, Traffic Management Systems, Transit Signal Priority,

Table 16.1 Current state of the art in IoV review and research needs.

References	Year	Focus area	Research gaps found
[8]	2011	Intelligent transport system (ITS) and Internet of Vehicles.	Further research on methods of communication for data-driven ITS environments is required.
[1]	2014	VANET and its associated applications.	There is no protocol at any level of the architecture.
[13]	2014	VANET architecture and protocols, including advantages and disadvantages.	The importance of particular to the application approaches for IoV communication must be emphasized.
[17]	2014	IoV cutting-edge connection and problems.	Application-specific protocols must be prioritised.
[7]	2015	VANET routing and simulation.	Protocols that are not delay tolerant are not considered.
[6]	2018	Networking and its applications serve as the foundation for VANET transmission techniques.	Application-specific procedures must be investigated.
[16]	2019	Routing and VANET in city situations.	Roadways situations must be explored.
[14]	2019	VANET protocols for routing and communication difficulties.	VANET hybrid protocols are an unexplored area.

(*Continued*)

Table 16.1 Current state of the art in IoV review and research needs. (*Continued*)

References	Year	Focus area	Research gaps found
[3]	2020	VANET routing protocols and optimisation approaches.	It is necessary to investigate IoV protocol matching on five-layer and seven-layer IoV architectures.
[22]	2021	New integrated models and key technologies related to network maintenance.	The Internet of Vehicles (IoV) aims to evolve vehicular networks by implementing new integrated models, key technologies, and security measures, while addressing challenges and future directions.
[21]	2022	IoT technologies relation to smart energy grids.	The seven-layered IoT architecture, including physical, fog computing, network, cloud computing, service, session, and application, effectively manages and processes massive data in future smart homes for energy efficiency.

Vehicle Data Collection, and Highway Data Collection. Additionally, it highlights the need for further exploration of communication mechanisms within a data-centric ITS framework.

[1], investigated the classification of routing protocols, detailing their advantages and limitations. The study delved into VANET analysis and its architectural elements. It introduced topology, clustering, hybrid, spatial, and data fusion routing techniques. The development of application-specific protocols tailored for IoV communication is an ongoing area of research.

[13], conducted a review on IoV, outlining the latest advancements in connectivity and the challenges faced. They underscored the necessity of creating multiple radio interfaces to facilitate wireless communication, which could be costly. They also noted that Vehicle-to-Structure (V2S) communication might introduce latency, rendering it inefficient for time-sensitive applications.

[17], presented a summary of VANET and its applications. They expanded on applications related to comfort and safety. Safety applications were further categorized into public safety, vehicle diagnostics, and inter-vehicle information exchange. The study also compared different simulation tools used in VANET communication but noted that protocol-level details at each design layer remain uncharted.

[7], discussed routing protocols within VANETs, particularly those effective in urban environments, considering factors such as obstacles, vehicle density, and node count. They compared position-based, topology-based, and cluster-based protocols, highlighting their pros and cons. The study suggested that further investigation is needed on protocols optimized for highway scenarios.

[6], analyzed routing strategies centered on location, topology, and clustering. Their research included a comparative study of various routing protocols, examining performance metrics, speed, simulation tools, and topology dimensions. The study proposed that hybrid VANET protocols could be further researched in the context of diverse ITS applications.

[16], described position-based routing procedures, introducing transmission strategies like unicast, geocast, and broadcast. They categorized routing information into topology, location, map, and path-based. The study differentiated between delay-tolerant applications and those sensitive to delays across one-dimensional, two-dimensional, and three-dimensional spaces. However, the area of non-delay tolerant (NDT) applications remains to be explored.

[14], reviewed IoV routing protocols and their applications, classifying them into unicast, multicast, and broadcast. They examined IoV applications in terms of safety, commerce, convenience, and efficiency. Identifying the most suitable routing protocols for specific applications is an area that requires further discovery.

[3], provided insights into geographical routing protocols and paradigms in IoV routing. The article focused on optimization methods involving computational intelligence, cloud computing, and fog computing, alongside multi-optimization-based routing protocols. The discussion

revolved around the three-tier IoV architecture, encompassing marine, aerial, and terrestrial domains. However, the consideration of five-layer and seven-layer IoV structures was not included in the study.

[22], offered an extensive review and motivation for the evolution of heterogeneous vehicular networks. They proposed integrated models and key technologies for network maintenance, including a six-layered architecture model based on the protocol stack and network elements, a network model reliant on cloud services, a big data analytical model for data acquisition and analytics, and a security model focused on detection and prevention systems.

[21], provided a synopsis of various Internet of Things (IoT) architectures, emphasizing a new seven-layered model designed for future big data-driven smart homes aimed at achieving energy efficiency. The article will concentrate on standards for different IoT technologies, such as sensing, communication, and computing, and their integration with smart energy grids.

16.3 Proposed Architecture of Internet of Vehicles

One of the most challenging aspects of the Internet of Vehicles lies in seamlessly integrating all its components, including vehicles, actuators and sensors, connectivity infrastructure, roadside systems, personal gadgets, and human users. This integration requires the development of a comprehensive layered framework for the Internet of Vehicles, encompassing a set of needs and features that can be organized as a distinct layer within this framework. A crucial aspect of this task involves determining the optimal number of layers and specifying the performance of each layer, taking into account network properties. Various challenges must be addressed during the construction of a layered architecture for the Internet of Vehicles, as highlighted by [9]. These challenges include (a) connecting devices to different types of networks, (b) adapting to evolving technologies, and (c) integrating the internet with inflexible interfaces.

In our proposed architecture, we present a framework consisting of interactions and models used for network communication. The platform is built upon a layered structure designed to facilitate seamless communication between devices. While this research does not extensively delve into the management, control, and data processing layers, some key characteristics of these levels are briefly outlined.

a. **Internet of Vehicles Interaction Model.**
In the context of the Internet of Vehicles (IoV), an interaction model refers to the framework or set of rules that govern how different entities within the IoV ecosystem communicate and interact with each other. IoV involves the integration of vehicles with information and communication technologies to improve safety, efficiency, and overall transportation experience. The Interaction model of Internet of Vehicles is shown is Figure 16.1.

Here are key components of an interaction model in IoV:

1. Vehicle Communication Protocols
    - V2V (Vehicle-to-Vehicle): Enables direct communication between vehicles. This is crucial for exchanging information about speed, position, and other relevant data to enhance safety and prevent accidents.
    - V2I (Vehicle-to-Infrastructure): Involves communication between vehicles and roadside infrastructure such as traffic lights, road signs, and smart intersections. This helps in optimizing traffic flow and providing real-time information to drivers.

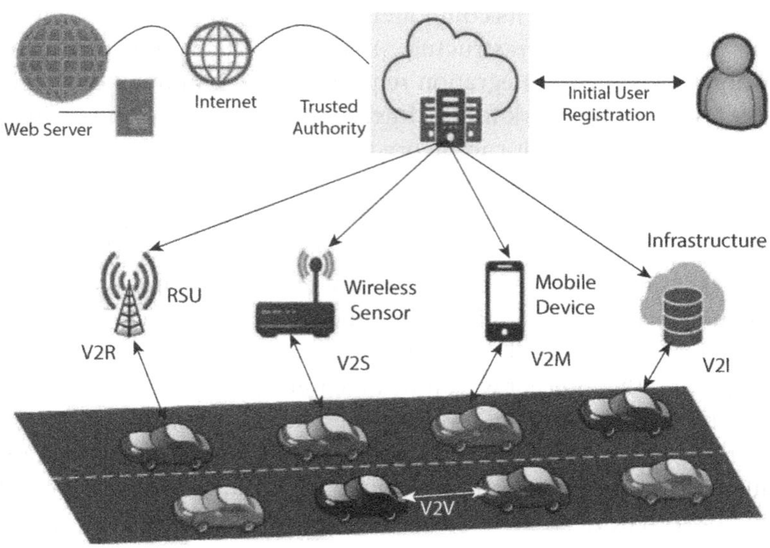

Figure 16.1 Internet of Vehicles interaction model.

2. Vehicular Ad-Hoc Networks (VANETs):
   - VANETs play a key role in enabling communication between vehicles and infrastructure. They are typically formed on-the-fly as vehicles come within communication range. The interaction model should define how these ad-hoc networks are established and maintained.
3. Data Exchange Standards:
   - Standardizing the format and structure of the data exchanged between vehicles and infrastructure is crucial. This includes the use of standardized communication protocols and data formats to ensure interoperability and seamless communication between diverse devices and systems.
4. Security and Privacy Measures:
   - Given the sensitive nature of the information exchanged in IoV, a robust security model is essential. This involves encryption, authentication, and integrity verification to protect against cyber threats. Additionally, privacy-preserving measures should be implemented to safeguard user information.
5. Traffic Management and Control:
   - The interaction model should include mechanisms for traffic management and control based on real-time data. This could involve dynamic route optimization, congestion management, and coordination between vehicles and infrastructure to improve overall traffic efficiency.
6. Edge and Cloud Computing Integration:
   - The interaction model should define how data is processed, stored, and managed. Edge computing can be utilized for real-time processing of critical data, while cloud computing can handle more extensive analytics and storage requirements.
7. Human-Vehicle Interaction:
   - Considering the role of human drivers, the interaction model should address how information from the IoV is presented to drivers. This involves user interfaces, alerts, and other means of communication to ensure that drivers are aware of relevant information without causing distractions.

8. Standardization and Governance:
    - To ensure widespread adoption and interoperability, standards and governance frameworks need to be established. These can be developed by industry bodies, governments, or international organizations to provide a common foundation for IoV interactions.

b. **Network Model of Internet of Vehicles**

A Network model refers to the structure and arrangement of communication networks that enable vehicles, infrastructure, and other components to exchange information. Here's a simplified description of the network model in IoV. The Internet of Vehicles Network model is shown in Figure 16.2:

1. **Vehicular Ad-Hoc Networks (VANETs):**
    - VANETs play a crucial role in IoV by forming ad-hoc networks among vehicles. These networks enable direct communication between nearby vehicles, sharing information about speed, position, and other relevant data.

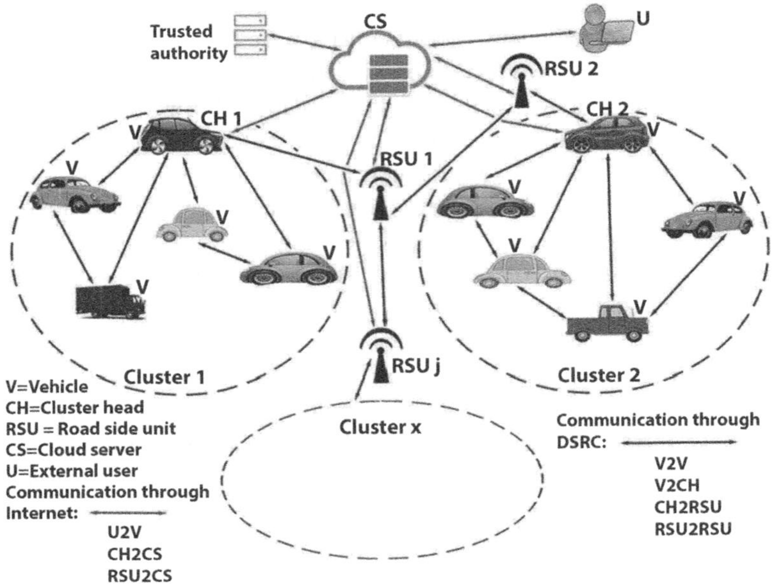

Figure 16.2 Internet of Vehicles network model.

2. **Cellular Networks (3G, 4G, 5G):**
   - Cellular networks provide a backbone for IoV connectivity, especially for long-range communication and access to the internet. Vehicles can leverage cellular networks for data exchange, software updates, and accessing cloud services.
3. **Vehicle-to-Everything (V2X) Communication:**
   - V2X encompasses various communication types, including V2V (Vehicle-to-Vehicle), V2I (Vehicle-to-Infrastructure), V2P (Vehicle-to-Pedestrian), and V2N (Vehicle-to-Network). These communication channels facilitate comprehensive connectivity and information exchange within the IoV ecosystem.
4. **Satellite Communication:**
   - Satellite communication can be used for IoV applications, especially in areas with limited terrestrial network coverage. It ensures continuous communication in remote locations and can support features like global positioning and navigation.
5. **Local Area Networks (LANs):**
   - LANs within vehicles or specific locations (e.g., parking lots, charging stations) facilitate internal communication between components such as sensors, control units, and entertainment systems.
6. **Edge Computing Nodes:**
   - Edge computing nodes are distributed throughout the IoV network to perform real-time processing of data. These nodes enhance responsiveness and reduce latency by handling computations closer to the data source.
7. **Cloud Infrastructure:**
   - Cloud services provide scalable storage, processing power, and analytics capabilities for IoV applications. Cloud infrastructure is used for data analysis, predictive modeling, and storing historical information.
8. **IoT (Internet of Things) Devices:**
   - Various IoT devices, such as sensors and actuators, are integrated into vehicles and infrastructure. These devices contribute to the generation and collection of data, which is crucial for IoV functionalities.

9. **Security and Authentication Layers:**
    - Security measures, including encryption, authentication, and intrusion detection, are embedded in the IoV network model to protect against cyber threats and ensure the integrity of communication.
10. **Standardized Protocols:**
    - Standardized communication protocols (e.g., DSRC, C-V2X) ensure interoperability between different components of the IoV network, allowing seamless communication across diverse devices and systems.
11. **Network Management and Orchestration:**
    - Network management systems orchestrate the IoV network, optimizing resource allocation, managing traffic, and ensuring efficient communication. This includes features like Quality of Service (QoS) management.

Understanding and optimizing this network model is crucial for the successful deployment and operation of IoV systems, ensuring reliable and secure communication among all elements within the ecosystem.

c. Internet of Vehicles Environmental Model

Internet of Vehicles (IoV), an environmental model refers to the representation of the external factors and conditions that impact the operation and performance of vehicles within the IoV ecosystem, as shown in Figure 16.3. The environmental model takes into account various elements such as the physical environment, weather conditions, road infrastructure, and more. Here's an overview of the key components of an environmental model in IoV:

1. **Physical Environment:**
    - **Terrain:** The topography of the area, including hills, slopes, and curves, can affect vehicle performance and energy consumption.
    - **Geography:** Consideration of the geographical characteristics, such as urban, suburban, or rural environments, can impact traffic patterns and navigation strategies.
2. **Weather Conditions:**
    - **Temperature:** Extreme temperatures can affect the performance of vehicle components, battery efficiency, and the operation of sensors.

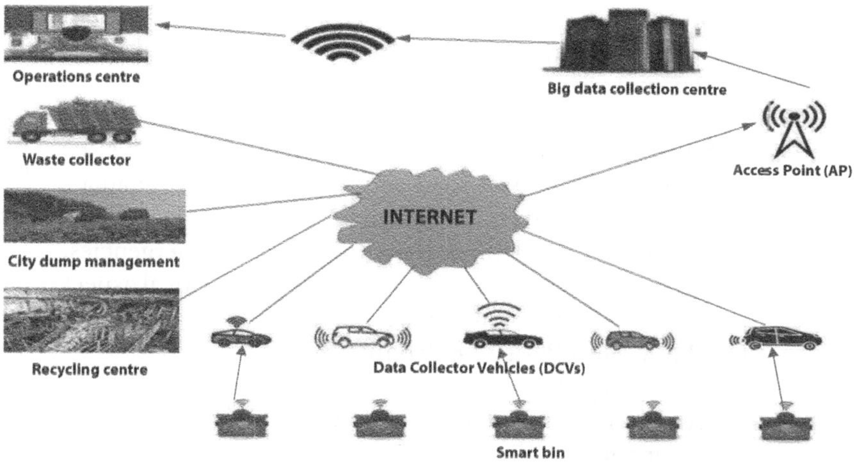

Figure 16.3 Internet of Vehicles environmental model.

- **Precipitation:** Rain, snow, or other forms of precipitation can impact visibility, road conditions, and the effectiveness of sensors.
- **Wind:** Strong winds can affect vehicle stability, especially for high-profile vehicles.

3. **Road Infrastructure:**
   - **Road Type:** Different road types (highways, local roads, etc.) have varying speed limits, traffic conditions, and safety considerations.
   - **Road Quality:** The condition of the road surface, including potholes and road markings, can influence vehicle comfort and safety.
4. **Traffic Conditions:**
   - **Traffic Density:** The density of vehicles on the road affects navigation decisions, traffic flow, and congestion levels.
   - **Traffic Signals and Signs:** The state of traffic signals and road signs influences vehicle behavior and decision-making.
5. **Pedestrians and Other Road Users:**
   - **Pedestrian Density:** The presence of pedestrians and cyclists affects vehicle speed and requires attention to safety.

- **Interactions with Non-Motorized Vehicles:** Consideration of interactions with bicycles, scooters, and other non-motorized vehicles is crucial for safety.

6. **Natural Events and Disasters:**
   - **Natural Disasters:** Events like earthquakes, floods, or wildfires can impact road conditions and require adaptive responses from IoV systems.
   - **Emergency Situations:** Rapid response to emergencies, such as accidents or medical incidents, is a critical aspect of the environmental model.
7. **Regulatory and Policy Environment:**
   - **Traffic Regulations:** Compliance with traffic rules and regulations is essential for safe and legal operation.
   - **Government Policies:** Government regulations and policies related to emissions, fuel efficiency, and safety standards shape the IoV landscape.
8. **Infrastructure Support:**
   - **Charging Stations:** Availability and distribution of electric vehicle charging stations influence the practicality of electric vehicles in the IoV.
   - **Connectivity Infrastructure:** The presence of 5G or other high-speed communication networks enhances real-time data exchange within the IoV.
9. **Economic Factors:**
   - **Fuel Prices:** Fluctuations in fuel prices can impact the usage patterns of different types of vehicles.
   - **Cost of Maintenance:** The economic feasibility of vehicle ownership and operation is influenced by maintenance costs and repair services.

An environmental model in IoV integrates information from these diverse elements to enhance the adaptability, safety, and efficiency of connected vehicles within their surroundings. Advanced sensors, data analytics, and machine learning algorithms can be employed to process real-time data and make informed decisions based on the environmental context.

d. Layered Architecture of Internet of Vehicles

The architecture of the Internet of Vehicles (IoV) is typically organized into layers, each serving a specific purpose and contributing to the overall functionality of the system. Here's a common representation of a layered IoV architecture:

1. **Device Layer:**
    - **Sensors and Actuators:** This layer includes the physical devices installed in vehicles, such as GPS sensors, cameras, LiDAR, radar, and actuators for control. These devices capture and generate data related to the vehicle's surroundings and enable control actions.
2. **Communication Layer:**
    - **V2V (Vehicle-to-Vehicle):** Enables direct communication between vehicles on the road, allowing them to share real-time information such as speed, position, and other relevant data.
    - **V2I (Vehicle-to-Infrastructure):** Facilitates communication between vehicles and roadside infrastructure such as traffic lights, road signs, and smart intersections.
    - **V2N (Vehicle-to-Network):** Involves connectivity to external networks, including cellular networks, to access cloud services, receive updates, and exchange data beyond the immediate vehicular environment.
3. **Edge Computing Layer:**
    - **Edge Nodes:** Distributed computing nodes placed at the edge of the network to process data locally. Edge computing reduces latency and enhances real-time processing capabilities, supporting time-sensitive applications.
    - **Edge Analytics:** Involves analyzing data at the edge to derive insights and make quick decisions without relying on centralized cloud resources.
4. **Cloud Computing Layer:**
    - **Cloud Infrastructure:** Provides scalable and centralized computing resources for storage, data analytics, machine learning, and long-term data storage. Cloud services are used for tasks that are not time-sensitive and require extensive computing power.
5. **Service Layer:**
    - **IoV Applications:** Hosts various applications and services that leverage the data collected from the lower layers. Examples include traffic management, predictive maintenance, autonomous driving algorithms, and location-based services.
    - **APIs (Application Programming Interfaces):** Facilitates communication and data exchange between different IoV applications and services.

6. **Security and Privacy Layer:**
   - **Security Protocols:** Implements encryption, authentication, and other security measures to protect data transmitted between vehicles, infrastructure, and the cloud.
   - **Privacy Measures:** Ensures that sensitive information is handled responsibly, protecting the privacy of individuals using the IoV.
7. **Business and Management Layer:**
   - **Fleet Management:** Manages and monitors the status of vehicle fleets, including maintenance schedules, fuel consumption, and overall operational efficiency.
   - **Monetization and Billing:** Handles payment systems and monetization models related to IoV services, such as tolls, parking fees, and subscription-based services.
8. **Regulatory and Standardization Layer:**
   - **Compliance:** Ensures that IoV systems comply with industry standards and regulatory requirements.
   - **Policy Management:** Handles adherence to traffic regulations, safety standards, and other legal aspects relevant to IoV.

This layered architecture enables a modular and scalable approach to IoV development, allowing for the integration of new technologies and services without significant disruption to the entire system. Figure 16.4 shows a diagram of the IoV layers and their main functions. It also facilitates the development of specialized applications and services at different layers to address specific needs within the IoV ecosystem.

e. User Interaction Layer

Internet of Vehicles (IoV) refers to the interface through which users, typically drivers and passengers, interact with the IoV system. This layer encompasses various elements that facilitate communication, control, and feedback between users and the IoV environment. Here are key components and considerations within the User Interaction Layer:

1. **In-Vehicle Displays:**
   - **Instrument Cluster:** Provides essential information to the driver, such as speed, fuel level, and warning indicators.

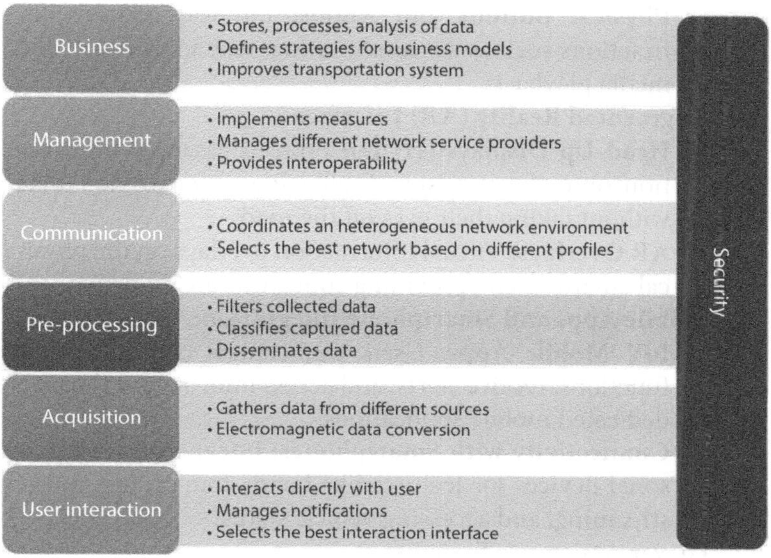

Figure 16.4 Architecture of Internet of Vehicles.

- **Infotainment Display:** Offers multimedia and navigation features, allowing users to access maps, entertainment, and other applications.

2. **Touchscreen Interfaces:**
   - **Center Console Screens:** Touchscreens enable users to interact with various vehicle functions, including climate control, navigation, and entertainment.
   - **Gesture Controls:** Some systems allow users to control functions through gestures, reducing the need for physical touch.
3. **Voice Recognition and Control:**
   - **Voice Commands:** Users can control certain vehicle functions, make calls, send messages, and navigate using voice commands.
   - **Virtual Assistants:** Integration with virtual assistants that respond to natural language queries and commands.
4. **Physical Controls:**
   - **Steering Wheel Controls:** Buttons and controls on the steering wheel for accessing features like audio volume, voice control, and cruise control.

   - **Physical Buttons and Knobs:** Physical controls for functions such as air conditioning, seat adjustment, and media playback.
5. **Augmented Reality (AR) Interfaces:**
   - **Head-Up Displays (HUD):** Projects essential information onto the windshield, allowing users to view data without taking their eyes off the road.
   - **AR Overlays:** Virtual information overlays on the physical environment, providing context-aware guidance.
6. **Mobile Apps and Smartphone Integration:**
   - **IoV Mobile Apps:** Users can control certain vehicle functions, receive alerts, and access information through dedicated mobile applications.
   - **Connectivity with Smartphones:** Integration with personal devices for features like hands-free calling, music streaming, and accessing vehicle status.
7. **Driver Assistance Systems:**
   - **Visual and Auditory Alerts:** Alerts and warnings for lane departure, collision avoidance, and other safety features.
   - **Adaptive Cruise Control Interfaces:** User interfaces for adjusting settings related to adaptive cruise control and other driver assistance features.
8. **Personalization and User Profiles:**
   - **Driver Profiles:** Customizable profiles for individual drivers, storing preferences for seating position, climate control, and entertainment settings.
   - **User Authentication:** Secure access to personalized settings through user authentication mechanisms.
9. **Notification Systems:**
   - **Alerts and Notifications:** Inform users about important events, traffic conditions, maintenance reminders, and safety alerts.
   - **Emergency Notifications:** Critical alerts related to emergencies, accidents, or system failures.
10. **Entertainment and Infotainment Systems:**
    - **Media Controls:** Interfaces for controlling music, radio, podcasts, and other entertainment options.

- **Information Services:** Real-time news, weather updates, and other relevant information.

11. **Feedback Mechanisms:**
    - **Haptic Feedback:** Tactile feedback to confirm user inputs or provide alerts.
    - **User Feedback Systems:** Mechanisms for users to provide feedback on their experience with the IoV system.

Creating an intuitive, user-friendly, and distraction-free interaction layer is crucial for ensuring the safe and enjoyable use of IoV technologies. As vehicles become more connected and automated, careful design considerations within the User Interaction Layer are essential for meeting user expectations and promoting acceptance of IoV systems.

16.4 Applications, Characteristics, and Challenges of the Internet of Vehicles (IoV)

Applications of IoV:

1. **Connected Navigation:**
    - Real-Time Traffic Updates: Vehicles access and share live traffic data to navigate the most efficient paths.
    - Adaptive Routing: Navigation tools recalibrate routes in response to evolving traffic scenarios, such as accidents or roadworks.
2. **Vehicle-to-Vehicle (V2V) Communication:**
    - Collision Prevention: Vehicles exchange dynamic data like speed and position to preemptively avoid accidents.
    - Convoys: Vehicles travel in closely-knit groups, enhancing aerodynamics and fuel economy.
3. **Vehicle-to-Infrastructure (V2I) Communication:**
    - Traffic Light Synchronization: Vehicles interact with traffic signals to streamline traffic movement.
    - Intelligent Parking Solutions: Parking sensors guide drivers to open spots, minimizing search time.
4. **Autonomous Driving and Assistance:**
    - Self-Parking: Sensor-equipped vehicles park themselves autonomously.

   - Lane Assistance: Systems ensure vehicles remain within lane markings.
5. **Predictive Maintenance:**
   - Remote Vehicle Health Monitoring: Vehicles report their status for proactive servicing.
   - Component Surveillance: Ongoing monitoring of vehicle parts to foresee and forestall malfunctions.
6. **Fleet Optimization:**
   - Route Refinement: Utilizing IoV insights to enhance route efficiency for fleets.
   - Asset Surveillance: Real-time monitoring of fleet assets for improved security and logistics.
7. **Emergency Response:**
   - Automated Distress Signals: Vehicles automatically alert emergency services post-collision.
   - Priority for Emergency Vehicles: Manipulating traffic signals to expedite emergency response.
8. **Environmental Oversight:**
   - Eco-Driving Feedback: Drivers receive input to promote eco-conscious driving habits.
   - Air Quality Sensing: Vehicles contribute to monitoring air quality metrics.
9. **Smart Grid Synergy:**
   - Optimized EV Charging: Aligning electric vehicle charging with grid demands and energy pricing.
   - Grid Stability Contributions: Vehicles aid in monitoring and sustaining electrical grid equilibrium.
10. **In-Vehicle Entertainment and Services:**
    - Customized Content Delivery: Tailored entertainment and news for passengers.
    - E-commerce Conveniences: Facilitating in-transit purchases and deliveries.

Characteristics of IoV:

1. **Connectivity:**
   - V2V Interaction: Real-time vehicular communication.
   - V2I Engagement: Dialogue with traffic infrastructure.
2. **Data Exchange:**
   - Cloud Connectivity: Vehicles interface with cloud services for data sharing.

- Sensor Data Integration: Amalgamation of diverse sensor inputs.

3. **Autonomy:**
   - Self-Driving Features: Advancement of autonomous driving capabilities.
   - Driver Assistance: Enhanced safety through automated support systems.
4. **Immediate Decision-Making:**
   - Edge Processing: Onboard data handling for swift decisions.
   - Fog Distribution: Decentralized computing for extended network reach.
5. **Anticipatory Maintenance:**
   - Health Tracking: Continuous monitoring for early issue detection.
   - Predictive Analysis: Data-driven maintenance forecasting.
6. **Traffic Intelligence:**
   - Flow Enhancement: Dynamic traffic control for congestion alleviation.
   - Route Intelligence: Real-time traffic data for optimal routing.
7. **Safety and Security:**
   - Dedicated Networks (VANETs): Specialized networks for vehicular safety.
   - Cyber Protections: Security measures against digital threats.
8. **Eco-Efficiency:**
   - Route Efficiency: Fuel and emission reductions through smart routing.
   - EV Integration: Harmonizing electric vehicles with IoV for energy management.
9. **Standardization:**
   - Unified Protocols: Compatibility across vehicles and infrastructure.
   - Global Standards: Consistent development guided by international standards.
10. **User-Centric Services:**
    - Infotainment: Personalized in-transit information and entertainment.
    - E-commerce Integration: Seamless access to online services and shopping.

IoV Challenges:

1. Security and Privacy:
   - Digital Risks: Vulnerability to cyber threats.
   - Privacy Balancing: Navigating data utility with privacy preservation.
2. Standardization:
   - Uniformity Gaps: The need for consistent communication standards.
3. Dependability:
   - Network Consistency: Ensuring reliable connectivity.
   - Service Continuity: Maintaining uninterrupted IoV services.
4. Scalability:
   - Data Management: Handling the surge in vehicular data volume.
5. Instantaneous Communication:
   - Ultra-Low Latency: Meeting the demands for real-time vehicular communication.
6. Infrastructure Adequacy:
   - Infrastructure Expansion: Upgrading facilities to support IoV needs.
7. Energy Management:
   - Power Efficiency: Balancing energy demands with connectivity needs.
8. Regulatory Landscape:
   - Data Governance: Clarifying data ownership and responsibility.
   - Regulatory Clarity: Establishing comprehensive IoV regulations.
9. Public Acceptance:
   - Trust Building: Cultivating confidence in IoV technologies.
10. Financial Considerations:
    - Investment in Infrastructure: Funding the rollout of IoV systems.
    - Vehicle Upgrades: The cost implications of integrating IoV in vehicles.

Conclusion

The IoV is reshaping transportation into a globally interconnected network, offering benefits like interactive services, adaptive controls, and potential cost savings. Initial research delineated the IoV ecosystem's components, their roles, and their interplay. Subsequently, a dual-layer network model encompassing both vehicle-internal and external elements was proposed. The fusion of automotive and information technologies within the IoV is anticipated to spur advancements in energy conservation, security, and safety. Ultimately, this integration seeks to elevate vehicular coordination, communication, and the overall user experience.

References

1. Dua, A., Kumar, N., Bawa, S., A systematic review on routing protocols for vehicular ad hoc networks. *Veh. Commun.*, 1, 1, 33–52, 2014.
2. APEC, White paper of Internet of Vehicles. *50th Telecommunications and information working group meeting*, Brisbane, Australia, 2014.
3. Ksouri, C., Jemili, I., Mosbah, M., Belghith, A., Towards general Internet of Vehicles networking: routing protocols survey. *Concurrency Comput. Pract. Exper.*, 34, 7, e5994, 2022.
4. Guerrero-Ibañez, A., Contreras-Castillo, J., Barba, A., Reyes, A., A QoS-based dynamic pricing approach for services provisioning in heterogeneous wireless access networks. *Pervasive Mob. Comput.*, 7, 5, 569–583, 2011.
5. Seth, I., Panda, S.N., Guleria, K., The essence of smart computing : Internet of Things, in: *2021 9th International Conference on Reliability, Infocom Technologies and Optimization (Trends and Future Directions) (ICRITO)*, Noida, India, pp. 1–6, 2021.
6. Wahid, I., Ikram, A.A., Ahmad, M., Ali, S., Ali, A., State of the art routing protocols in VANETs: a review. *Procedia Comput. Sci.*, 130, 689–694, 2018.
7. Cheng, J., Cheng, J., Zhou, M., Liu, F., Gao, S., Liu, C., Routing in internet of vehicles: a review. *IEEE Trans. Intell. Transp. Syst.*, 16, 5, 2339–2352, 2015.
8. Zhang, J., Wang, F.-Y., Wang, K., Lin, W.-H., Xu, X., Chen, C., Data-driven intelligent transportation systems: a survey. *IEEE Trans. Intell. Transp. Syst.*, 12, 4, 1624–1639, 2011.
9. Kaiwartya, O., Abdullah, A., Cao, Y., Altameem, A., Prasad, M., Lin, C., Liu, X., Internet of Vehicles: Motivation, layered architecture, network model, challenges, and future aspects. *IEEE Access*, 4, 5356–5373, 2016.
10. Tuyisenge, L., Ayaida, M., Tohme, S., Afilal, L.E., Network Architectures in Internet of Vehicles (IoV): Review, Protocols Analysis, Challenges and Issues. In *Internet of Vehicles. Technologies and Services Towards Smart City.*

IOV 2018. Lecture Notes in Computer Science, A. Skulimowski, Z. Sheng, S. Khemiri-Kallel, C. Cérin, C.H. Hsu (eds.), vol. 11253, Springer, Cham, 2018, https://doi.org/10.1007/978-3-030-05081-8_1.

11. McKinsey & Company, The road to 2020 and beyond – What's driving the global automotive industry, McKinsey&Company, 2013, Retrieved from http://www.mckinsey.com/client_service/automotive_and_assembly/latest_thinking.
12. Nanjie, L., Internet of Vehicles your next connection. *WinWin Magazine*, Issue 11, HUAWEI. OAA, 2011, (2016). Open automotive alliance (OAA). Retrieved December 16, 2016, from http://www.openautoalliance.net/#about/.
13. Lu, N., Cheng, N., Zhang, N., Shen, X., Mark, J.W., Connected vehicles: solutions and challenges. *IEEE Internet Things J.*, 1, 4, 289–299, 2014.
14. Senouci, O., Aliouat, Z., Harous, S., A review of routing protocols in internet of vehicles and their challenges. *Sens. Rev.*, 39, 1, 58–70, 2019.
15. Datta, P. and Sharma, B., A survey on IoT architectures, protocols, security and smart city based applications, in: *2017 8th International Conference on Computing, Communication and Networking Technologies (ICCCNT)*, Delhi, India, pp. 1–5, 2017.
16. Pandey, P.K., Swaroop, A., Kansal, V., A concise survey on recent routing protocols for vehicular ad hoc networks (VANETs), in: *2019 International Conference on Computing, Communication, and Intelligent Systems (ICCCIS)*, Greater Noida, India, pp. 188–193, 2019.
17. Al-Sultan, S., Al-Doori, M.M., Al-Bayatti, A.H., Zedan, H., A comprehensive survey on vehicular ad hoc network. *J. Netw. Comput. Appl.*, 37, 1, 380–392, 2014.
18. Statista, Connected car system shipments worldwide 2012–2016. Statista web, 2012, Retrieved November 30, 2016, from https://www.statista.com/statistics/252370/connected-car-systemshipments-worldwide/.
19. Yang, F., Wang, S., Li, J., Liu, Z., Sun, Q., An overview of Internet of Vehicles. *China Commun.*, 11, 10, 1–15, 2014.
20. Datta, P. and Sharma, B., A survey on IoT architectures, protocols, security and smart city based applications, in: *2017 8th International Conference on Computing, Communication and Networking Technologies (ICCCNT)*, Delhi, India, pp. 1–5, 2017.
21. Kutseva, M., Adaptation of Seven-Layered IoT Architecture for Energy Efficiency Management in Smart House. *2022 10th International Scientific Conference on Computer Science (COMSCI)*, pp. 1–5, 2022, https://doi.org/10.1109/COMSCI55378.2022.9912604.
22. Qureshi, K., Din, S., Jeon, G., Piccialli, F., Internet of Vehicles: Key Technologies, Network Model, Solutions and Challenges With Future Aspects. *IEEE Trans. Intell. Transp. Syst.*, 22, 1777–1786, 2021, https://doi.org/10.1109/TITS.2020.2994972.

Index

5G wireless technology, 232

Accuracy, 181, 183, 184, 185, 194, 195–199
Activation function, 187
Adaptability, 35, 38–39, 45, 48–49, 59–63
Adaptive learning modules, 47
AI for soybean (glycine max) crop, 275–281
  soybean disease image acquisition and pretreatment, 276
AI-based advanced optimization techniques, 231
AI-driven analytics, 232
Application layer, 6
Artificial intelligence, 130
Attack detection, 410
Audio analysis, 144

Bayesian neural networks, 93–95, 97, 99, 101, 107, 110, 112, 114, 122–124
Belief model, 329
Bi-LSTM, 189–192
Blockchain, 233, 236, 239, 241, 244, 247

Cache pollution attack, 403
Cache privacy attack, 403
Case study, 334
Central brain controller, 48, 50
Central intelligence hub, 47, 48
Centralized, 1, 2, 5, 6, 7, 10, 13, 14, 15, 16
Challenges and solutions smart agriculture, 270
  (AI) approach in agriculture and needs, 271–272
  needs of AI farm, 273
  role of AI in agriculture, 273–274
Cloud computing, 232, 243
Cloud computing in agriculture, 259
Communication protocols, 435
Comparison, 185, 197
Confidentiality, 403, 408
Connected vehicles, 440–441, 444
Content poisoning attack, 403
Content store (CS), 403, 407
Contextual understanding, 190
Control layer, 7
Control plane, 1, 2, 6, 7, 14
Convolution neural network (CNN), 130–131, 133, 135, 137, 149, 153, 155, 167, 168, 175, 185
Cost function, 332
C-plane, 12
CRMS (customer relationship management systems), 357
Cross-validation, 426
Cryptography, 355, 356, 364, 378
Customer churn prediction, 208

DAPP (decentralized applications), 356
Data analytics and decision support, 267
  remote monitoring, 269
Data mining, 290
Data packet, 401–414

Data plane, 2, 6, 7
Data processing, 231, 233, 234, 236, 243, 244
DBRNN, 186
Decentralized, 5, 6
Decision trees, 402, 425, 428
Deep canonical correlation analysis (DCCA), 93–94, 97–98, 107–108, 110–111, 113, 120, 122, 124
Deep learning (DL), 93–96, 98–100, 103, 107, 119–120, 124–125, 153, 155, 156, 167, 170, 181–184, 186, 198
Dense layer, 192, 193
Device compatibility
Dimensionality reduction, 404–405, 411–412, 421, 424, 428
DLIPS, 293
DMS (document data management systems), 355, 357

East west APIs, 8
Edge computing, 35–36, 232, 234, 384
Edge nodes, 47
Efficiency, 317, 339
E-health systems, 242, 244
ELSTM, 186
eMBB, 12, 13
Embedding layer, 187, 193
End-to-end security, 317, 318, 319, 324, 334
ET (Ethereum platform's), 368, 370, 371, 372

Feature based ranking, 419–422, 428
Feature engineering, 191–192
Feature selection, 404–405, 411, 415, 419, 421, 424, 428
Federated learning, 184, 186
Filter method, 415, 419, 421
Firefly algorithm, 297
Fog computing, 232, 233, 234, 235, 236, 238, 239, 243
Forget gate, 187–188
Forwarding information base (FIB), 407–408
Functional components, 53

Game theory, 321–339
GEE, 383
Genetic algorithms, 420
Gradient boosting, 82–84
Greedy, 300
Greedy particle swarm optimization using leaky relu (LRGPSO), 300
Ground dataset, 389

Healthcare, 231, 232, 234, 235, 237, 239, 240
Hidden layer, 189
Hurdles, 37, 40, 43–45

Infrastructure efficiency, 434
Infrastructure layer, 7
Input gate, 187
Input layer, 187, 190, 191, 193, 197
Input sequences, 190
Intelligent transportation system (ITS), 434, 440
Interest flooding attack (IFA), 401–405, 408–412, 428
Interest packet, 401–414
Internet of Things (IoT), 35–36, 41, 50, 231, 232, 233, 234, 237, 239, 241, 243, 244, 246, 317–339, 434, 436–438, 441–442, 453, 455
Internet of vehicles (IoV), 434–438
Intrusion detection systems, 71–82
IoT in agriculture, 257
  precision agriculture, 258
  sensor technology, 258

Keras, 192
K-nearest neighbors (KNN), 402, 425, 428
Kruskal's algorithm, 299

Latency, 35–40, 43–46, 49, 52, 59
Leaky ReLU activation function, 298, 300, 304
Linear discriminate analysis (LDA), 153, 161, 163, 166
Load balancing, 37, 52–53, 55–57, 64
Long short-term memory networks (LSTM), 93–94, 97, 99–102, 105–108, 110–112, 117, 124 , 130–132, 137, 140, 141, 144, 181–184, 187–188
LSA, 184

Machine learning (ML), 71–80, 153, 155, 156, 157, 159, 160, 161, 164, 165, 167–171, 173, 176, 383, 402, 424, 428
MANO, 10, 24
MES (manufacturing execution systems), 356
Meta-heuristics, 420
Methods and dataset, 386–391
  classifiers, 390–391
    minimum distance classifier, 390
    Naïve bayes classifier, 390
  pre-processing and image dataset, 387–390
  research area and dataset, 386–387
MFCC, 131, 133, 135–136, 140–141, 143–144, 149
Minimum spanning tree, 294
MLP with BP, 402, 420–421, 424–425
mMTC, 12, 13
Modified BiLSTM-CNN, 221–225
MSP (member service providers), 367
Multimodal data, 93–98, 100–101, 107, 112, 118–122, 124–125

Naïve Bayes (NB), 153
Named data networking (NDN), 401–411
Nature-inspired, 35–36
NETCONF, 8
Next word prediction, 181–185
Next-gen, 2, 3, 15
Next-generation network architecture, 1
NFV, 4, 9, 10, 13, 17
NFV management and orchestration, 10
NFVI, 9, 10
NLG, 182
North bound, 7, 8
NS, 4, 11
NSL-KDD dataset, 75–78

OctoBrain, 53–55
OctoEdge, 35, 40, 46
OctoEdge architecture, 47–48, 53
OctoEdge working principles, 48
Off-chain, 353, 354, 355, 356, 357, 358, 359, 367
On-chain, 353, 354, 357, 358, 359, 362, 364, 367
Open flow, 8
Output layer, 187, 189–190

Parameters, 183, 185, 193, 194
Particle swarm optimization (PSO), 296, 420–421
Payoff model, 331
pBFT (practical byzantine fault tolerance), 345, 367, 372, 373
Pending interest table (PIT), 401–410, 412–414
Performance measure, 89–91
Personal area networks (PAN), 434
Pickle library, 192
Precision agriculture, 382
Precision farming, 263
Predictive analysis, 204, 210
  content recommendation, 207
  customer behavior, 206
  sentiment analysis, 206
Predictive insights, 232
Privacy, 233, 239, 241

Proposed algorithm, 391–392
Provenance, 407

QoS parameters, 59–60

RAN, 11
Random forest, 226–228, 424
Real-time, 35–39, 45, 48–52, 60, 62–63, 68
Real-time decision-making, 232
Recommender system, 182
Recurrent neural network (RNN), 129, 132, 140, 183, 185–187
Reinforcement learning, 16, 18–21
Resource manager, 36–37
Result and discussions, 392–395
  classified crop map, 394–953
Road side units (RSU), 440, 442–443, 447, 451, 452

Scientific merits, 60–63
SCM (supply chain management system), 355, 357, 361
SDN, 4, 6–8, 317–339
Security, 231, 232, 233, 237, 239, 241, 242, 243, 245
Sensor nodes, 47
Sentiment analysis, 129–135, 137–138, 140–143, 149
Sentinel 2, 385
Sentinel 2 MSI, 387–388
Slice, 1, 3, 11, 13
Slicing, 1, 2, 11
South bound, 7, 8
Stock market prediction, 93–101, 103–104, 107, 110, 112–114, 116, 118–125
Supervised learning, 16–18
Support vector machine (SVM), 402, 425, 428
Sustainable agricultural and remote sensing, 265

Temporal attention, 93–94, 97–100, 107
Tentacle, 48
Text analysis, 130, 141, 143
Thyroid cancer, 153–157, 159, 160, 165, 166, 169, 170
Traffic congestion, 446
Training data, 182, 191
Transformer based model, 183
Transportation safety, 434
Trust management, 237, 252

UML (uniform modelling language), 358
Unsupervised learning, 18, 19
U-plane, 12
uRLLC, 12, 13
Use cases, 64–67
  cybersecurity adaptation, 67
  energy-efficient, 65
  fault detection & recovery, 66
  self-healing, 66

Vehicle cognition, 433
Vehicle networking, 434
Vehicle-to-infrastructure communication (V2I), 443
Vehicle-to-person communication (V2P), 434
Vehicle-to-vehicle communication (V2V), 440, 443, 447, 451–452
Vehicular ad hoc network (VANET), 433–435, 437, 440, 444, 446, 448, 451, 455
Video analysis, 146
VNFS, 9, 10, 13, 17, 22
VXLAN, 8

Wearable devices, 237
Web connectivity issues
Wireless sensor networks (WSN), 435
Word embedding, 129, 132, 135, 137
Wrapper method, 415, 419, 421

Printed and bound by CPI Group (UK) Ltd, Croydon, CR0 4YY
17/09/2026
14964262-0006